M.T. Publishing Company, Inc.
P.O. Box 6802
Evansville, Indiana 47719-6802
www.mtpublishing.com

Copyright © 2008
Ron Eaton
All rights reserved.

No part of this publication may be translated, reproduced, or transmitted in any form or by any means, electronic or mechanical, including photocopying and recording, or by any information storage and retrieval system, without expressed written permission of the copyright owner and M.T. Publishing Company, Inc.

The materials were compiled and produced using available information. M.T. Publishing Company, Inc., and Ron Eaton regret they cannot assume liability for errors or omissions.

Library of Congress Control Number:
2008939098

ISBN: 978-1-934729-10-6

Graphic Design by: Alena L. Kiefer

Printed in the
United States of America

SPECIAL THANKS...

...to the *Evansville Courier/Press/ Sunday Courier and Press*. Many of the un-credited photos in the pages of this book were likely taken from the Evansville newspapers, and the *Courier* was gracious enough to grant their permission for the photos to be used.

Special recognition should also be given to the following people for their contributions above and beyond the call of duty:

Ron Brand
Bill Bussing
Jon Carl
Dr. Susan Dellinger
Suzy Eaton
Robert E. Padgett Jr.
Bill Richardson
Jon Siau
Dr. Bill Stedman

The magnificent cover photo was photographed by Erik Hassler and was made possible through the efforts and generous contributions of the following:

Ron and Barb Brand
Jon Carl
The Hamilton family
Dave Johnson
Alena Kiefer
Louise Owen
Joyce Rhoades
Jon Siau
Bill Vieth Jr.
The Reitz High School archives
Willow Bowling Center

Author photo (on dust jacket) by Bruce Campagna.

Front Cover Items
- (top, left) – Bob Griese's 1978 Pro Bowl trophy
- License plate celebrating Bosse's 1962 State championship
- A bowling pin from Willow Bowling Center signed by Tom Hanks, Penny Marshall, Madonna, Geena Davis and others after a night of recreation during the filming of *A League of Their Own*
- (yellow & red) – Mater Dei wrestling singlet
- (upper right) – Don Mattingly's bat and his Memorial baseball cap
- (right) – A poster from the first event held at Roberts Stadium, a Globetrotters game on March 5th, 1956. The poster was retrieved from a pole at Weinbach and Division after Jon Siau's father, Palmer, climbed up to get it.
- (dark bat, center) – Edd Roush's 48-ounce bat, the heaviest in the major leagues.
- (large trophy) – The traveling trophy for the City football champion presented each year from 1950 to 1964 by the VFW.
- (brown) – Central High School letter sweater
- Ring from the North High School basketball State championship in 1967
- #32 – USI jersey of three-time All-American LeAnn Freeland
- The Southwestern Indiana Dope Bag
- (center) – Louise Owen's vintage tennis racket with wood press
- (behind bag) – Gil Hodges model baseball glove
- (medals on brown sweater) – Medals won by Reitz's John Alexander when he finished fifth in the mile and half-mile at a national inter-scholastic meet at the University of Chicago in 1924 (At the same meet, Jesse Owens broke three world records.)
- (right front – next to Dope Bag) – Shelly Brand's lucky shoes that she taped up so that they would last through the Lady Panthers' run to the 1981 basektball State championship.
- (middle, above tennis racket) – 1935 Reitz High School football program with team photo.

Back Cover Items
- Bob Hamilton's golf bag from the 1949 Ryder Cup
- (bottom right) – One of the five national championship trophies won by the Evansville College/University of Evansville Purple Aces
- (red) – Tom Kron's Tell City warm-up jacket
- (dark bat – left) – Jamey Carroll's bat
- (bat next to above) – Gil Hodges' bat
- Rex Mundi letter sweater
- (#52) – Jerry Memering's Vincennes jersey
- (yellow book) – a program from the first game between Reitz and Mater Dei in 1952
- (red book) – a program from a Reitz-Bosse game in 1933
- The soccer ball, signed by the team, used in the State championship game won by Memorial in 2007.
- Jockey's goggles from Ellis Park
- (tennis racket) – The tennis racket used by North's Elissa Kim when she won the 1992 State championship
- (additional items) –football shoes, pads & helmet; softball; tennis ball; Reitz letter jacket)

INTRODUCTION & DEDICATION

Let me begin with an apology. Although this book was intended to recognize some of the greatest athletes and teams in southwestern Indiana history, it was not meant to imply that those who were included were 'THE BEST' in our history. When I accepted the self-imposed challenge to write *Local Legends*, I was well aware of the inherent problems that would arise as the project developed, and the dilemma of who should be included was a constant topic of discussion. As my work on the book neared its conclusion, even I could have made compelling arguments in favor of some who were omitted. So if you feel that you or someone you love was overlooked, I sincerely apologize.

The idea for the book was a by-product of countless conversations I have had with friends and acquaintances over the years. I feel very fortunate to have grown up in Evansville and to have had the opportunity to play high school sports in this area. I played four sports at North under some great coaches and competed with and against some fantastic athletes. Although I played only a minor role, I was even lucky enough to experience the ultimate thrill of being part of a State championship team, a story you'll find later in the book.

My love of sports even inspired me to pursue coaching as a profession, enabling me to become a head football coach at age 22 after my graduation from IU. After seven years as a coach, I entered the 'real world' and spent fourteen years in the Bloomington and Indianapolis areas. While I was away, I stayed in touch with old friends, and anytime we would get together, our conversation would nearly always take a nostalgic turn as we reminisced about athletes and teams from our area's storied past. These discussions led me to the realization that many of these stories needed to be documented so that younger generations can appreciate the rich sports history of southwestern Indiana.

To begin the process, I assembled a small group of local men whom I felt were as in tune with area sports as anyone. These men, dubbed 'the River City Round Table', served as a springboard to what became a two-year labor of love. After working with the Round Table to compile a preliminary list of athletes, teams and contacts, I set out on what became an exciting adventure. As time went on, the list of subjects was fine-tuned with the help of many wonderful people from all over the area and the country. The result was a compilation of sports stories about some of our greatest and most interesting people and places.

The subjects in this book cover the years from the early twentieth century up to the present, and any athlete or team whose primary feats occurred after 1997, I deemed too young to qualify as a 'legend'. The subjects also fall within a geographical perimeter roughly from Mt. Vernon, north to Vincennes, east to Jasper and then south to Tell City.

I am very aware of how lucky I was to have grown up when and where I did, and I have often wished that my own children could have experienced athletics the way I lived them. There is no question that the world of sports has changed, but in many ways the spirit of an athlete remains the same. Some of the subjects in this book ended their athletic endeavors after high school, while others went on to outstanding college or professional careers, but the common thread is not the destination, but the journey. Hopefully, their stories will illustrate that anything can be accomplished with dedication and hard work. The athletes on the following pages may not be the definitive list of 'the best', but they are a good cross-section of the illustrious sports history of our area.

I dedicate this book to my children, Kelly, Chase and Casey, in hopes that they can appreciate the environment that has meant so much to me. More than anyone, I dedicate the book to my beautiful wife Suzy, who, although she hails from New Jersey, has listened patiently to the same old stories told over and over again.

I also dedicate *Local Legends* to generations of people who remember the days when we would wear our black canvas little league cleats until the bottoms were slick and when we would hammer nails into our wooden bats to get a few more swings out of them. To those who remember when school bands played the opponent's fight song before a game and when people actually stayed quiet until the 'National Anthem' was completely finished and the colors had left the floor. And to those who remember when cheerleaders' skirts were long and the basketball team's trunks were short.

My most sincere wish is that this book will help to bridge the generations and give youngsters the opportunity to learn just a little about days long gone by. If just one father or mother or grandfather or grandmother uses *Local Legends* to share their memories and their passion for sports, then all the work will have been worthwhile.

Those in this book, and many others who aren't, are valuable pieces of our local sports tapestry. Although those days may be gone, the memories will be with us forever.

~ Ron Eaton

TEST YOUR LOCAL SPORTS IQ

Before you get started, how about a challenge to test your knowledge of local sports history? Below is a quiz that you can use as a basis for bragging rights with your friends and loved ones. There are 50 questions with a maximum score of 200 points.

Remember, all questions refer to people and places roughly inside a perimeter from Mt. Vernon north to Vincennes then east to Jasper and south to Tell City. Get out a sheet of paper and then give yourself 15 minutes.

(1-point questions)

1. What basketball star played on the 1965-'66 University of Kentucky team known as 'Rupp's Runts'?
2. What school won the 1982 State football championship?
3. Who is the only area player to win a professional golf major championship?
4. What school holds the state record with 68 sectional basketball titles?
5. Harrison High School alum Kevin Hardy played his college ball at what school?
6. What was the name of the Trester Award before it was called the Trester Award?
7. What area woman has won over 40 national tennis titles?
8. What area school has won the most basketball State championships?
9. What local pitcher threw the first pitch in Arizona Diamondbacks history?
10. Calbert Cheaney and Walter McCarty played briefly together on what NBA team?
11. The 'Lions' was the nickname of what Evansville high school that closed in the '60s?
12-15. **(1 point each)** Name the four Evansville College/University of Evansville players who have had their numbers retired.

(3-point questions)

16. Who was the first Vincennes University basketball player to make it big in the NBA?
17. Buster Briley was a star for Evansville College in the early '60s. What was Buster's real first name?
18. What school's boys soccer team finished the 2007 season ranked #1 in the country?
19. What Central High School basketball star of the late '40s has spent over forty years as a U.S. Congressman?
20-21. **(3 points each)** Only two Evansville College/U of E players have scored over 2,000 career points. Name them.
22. What area town is home to a historic gym that opened in 1951 and was the first to have a sunken floor with no vertical beams?
23. The winningest softball coach in Indiana history coaches at what area school?
24. What football coach succeeded the legendary Herman Byers at Reitz?
25-26. **(3 points each)** Name the two Rex Mundi basketball players who were named to the Indiana All-Star team.
27. What man ran the popular Tri-State Agoga basketball tournament for over fifty years?
28. North High School's Dave Schellhase played two seasons for what NBA team?
29. What Evansville native played in three World Series with the Detroit Tigers?
30. What female became the first USI player to score 600 points in a season?

(5 point questions)

31. Heritage Hills football star Ken Dilger played his final NFL season for what team?
32. The area has never had a State champ in which of these boys track events: **A.)** 200-meter dash **B.)** high jump **C.)** discus **D.)** 800-meter run?
33. Who are the only sisters from the area to make the Indiana All-Stars?
34. What area coach retired as the winningest football coach in Indiana history?
35. What is the last area school to win two consecutive State basketball titles during the single-class era?
36. Before becoming Mater Dei's wrestling coach in 1978, Mike Goebel held the same position at what other area school?
37. In early 1978, what pro football team conducted a charity exhibition basketball game to benefit the University of Evansville after the tragic plane crash?
38. Sam Alford, the successful coach at New Castle and father of IU star Steve Alford, was a 1960 graduate of what area school?
39. In 1966, Bob Griese finished second in the Heisman voting. Who won the trophy?
40. In the movie *A League of Their Own*, what was the name of the team that called Bosse Field home?
41. Which of these athletes went to a high school and college that share the same fight song: **A.)** Michael Lewis **B.)** Walter McCarty **C.)** Wayne Boultinghouse **D.)** Bob Ford?
42. Who was the only area player to appear on the weekly TV series *Home Run Derby*?

(10 point questions)

43. What Castle tennis player was the first in Indiana history to win four State singles championships?
44. What area father-daughter basketball players hold the top two spots on their high school's career scoring list?
45. What was Don Mattingly's professional jersey number before he changed it to '23'?
46. As of 2007, what was the only area school to capture two State softball championships?
47. Who was the first Evansville native to compete in the Olympic Games?
48. What Evansville team was the last to win a basketball State championship in the one-class system?
49. Neil Reed, the IU guard who was instrumental in Bob Knight's dismissal, played his freshman year at what area high school?
50. As of 2008, what is the total number of national basketball championships won by Vincennes University, USI, and Evansville College/U of E?

Now turn to page 6 to find out how well you know your local sports.

TABLE OF CONTENTS

Introduction and Dedication 3
Local Sports IQ Quiz 4
Chapter 1 (1907-1949)
   Reitz Football: A Tradition of Excellence 7
   The Byers Family: West Side Royalty...............................9
   The 1923 Alices in Wonderland......................................13
   Edd Roush: The "$10,000 Man"......................................15
   Pete Fox: Evansville's First World Series Champion 19
   Bob Hamilton: "It's a great world!"................................20
   The Dope Bag: A 34-Year Tradition 22
   The Ping Era: When the Tigers Reigned Supreme 24
   Billy Hillenbrand: The Evansville Express 26
   100 Years of Washington Basketball 29
   Bosse Goes Back-to-Back in '44 & '45 34
   Cyril Birge: A Piece of Hoosier Hoops History...............39
   The Wildcat Wonders, Jasper's 1949 State Champs........41

Chapter 2 (1945-1965)
   Local Girls Had a League of Their Own 45
   Lee Hamilton: From the Court to the Capitol.................46
   Lincoln High School: The End of an Era 47
   Marty Amsler: Persistence and Patience Pay Off 50
   Roger Kaiser and Bob Reinhart:
      Dale High School's Pair of Aces 51
   Carson Jones: The Nebo Flash......................................54
   1950– '51: A Season to Remember 57
   Gil Hodges: An American Hero.....................................58
   Larry Stallings: He Tackled the Best 66
   Quentin Merkel: Memorial's Mr. Baseball 67

Chapter 3 (1957-1962)
   The Perfect Panthers of 1961...70
   Don Hansen: Big Man in the Middle..............................73
   Mike Madriaga: Fear Factor Made Him a Winner 75
   Princeton's Jerry Scott: 'The Snake' Could Do It All......76
   The Volkmans: Ed, Eileen and the Boys........................78
   Once in a Lifetime Journey..81
   Bosse's 1962 State Champs: A Touch of Class................84
   Dave Schellhase: A Game for the Ages 88
   Our Fields of Battle 91

Chapter 4 (1950-1975)
   Aces Basketball: An Incredible Journey......................103
   The Golden Age of Aces Basketball............................105
   Arad McCutchan: The Man with the Plan...................113
   Gus Doerner: The Mackey Marvel 115
   Hugh Ahlering: 'The Old Man' Was a Winner 116
   Ed Smallwood: The Big Smoke....................................117
   Buster Briley: Sweet Guy with a Sweet Shot 118
   Larry Humes: Still #1 120
   Jerry Sloan: Simply the Best..122
   Don Buse: From Poverty to the Pros 125
   Steve Welmer: A 'Whale' of a Career 127
   Gone But Not Forgotten 130

Chapter 5 (1958-1975)
   Bob Griese: From Sandlot to Super Bowl 133
   Senior Moments...137
   Vaughn Wedeking: A Winner On and Off the Court....140
   Jerry Brewer: 44 Years of Winning..............................142
   Larry and Haley Harris: Like Father – Like Daughter ...145

Paul Gries: A Lifetime of Sports....................................147
Vincennes University: A Stepping Stone for Talent 148
The Owen Family: Three Generations and Counting....150
The Lochmuellers: Father and Son Hall of Famers.......153
Basketball and Strawberry Shortcake 155
Vincennes Basketball: The Memering Era 158
Gunner Wyman: He Did It His Way 161
Tom Kron: UK Blue Through and Through 163

Chapter 6 (1960-1990)
   The '67 North Huskies: How Sweet it Was!................165
   Bob Ford: Mr. Clutch..170
   The Mattingly Brothers: Talent and Class 172
   Don Mattingly: Donnie Baseball..................................176
   Woodie Sublett Walker: At the Top of Her Game........180
   Bob Winchell: Brains and Brawn 182
   Scott Studwell: 'Little' Man Made It Big 186
   Andy Benes: From #3 to #1 189
   Area Bowling Centers Are Steeped in Tradition 192
   Bosse's Bulldogs: Back-to-Back Perfection.................197
   Castle's Rise to Football Prominence 200
   Cheryl Dowell: The Queen of Mean............................204
   Fútbol: The New Kid in Town 206
   Vincennes Lincoln: #1 in '81..211

Chapter 7 (1960-1990)
   Richard Lankford: The Voice of Gibson County 214
   The Lander Family: Daddy's Little Girls Made It Big...216
   The '81 Lady Panthers: Super Team – Super-stitious 219
   Kevin Hardy: As Tough as They Come 224
   Lanae Renschler: A Perfect 4 for 4 227
   Lights, Camera, Action 229
   Mike Blake: A 35-Year Stopover..................................231
   Chris Lowery: A Coach on the Floor 232
   Mark Buse: Flying High 233
   Calbert Cheaney: Mom Showed Him the Way............234
   Elissa Kim: "Off the Record".......................................237
   Walter McCarty: You Gotta Dream..............................240
   Mt. Vernon Swimming: "There is no secret."..............243
   Pat Shoulders Brought the World to Evansville 245

Chapter 8 (1985-2007)
   1994 Castle Football: From Outhouse to Penthouse 247
   Memorial Girls Tennis: A Legacy of Love 251
   USI: From Ugly Duckling to Swan 253
   'Big John' Hollinden: A Giant of a Man.......................260
   LeAnn Freeland: A Small Town Girl with Big Dreams..262
   Mike Pegram: The Man with the Golden Touch 265
   Boonville Softball: He Built It, and They Came 267
   Heritage Hills Football: Pipeline to the Pros 270
   Jay Cutler: God-Given Talent......................................273
   Ken Dilger: Super Bowl Champion.............................275
   Matt Mauck: Natural Talent, Natural Leader.............277
   Stephanie Hazlett: A Competitor at Every Level...........281
   Mater Dei Wrestling: Decades of Dominance 283
   Jamey Carroll: Little Man with a Big Heart 289

Legends in the Making 294
Acknowledgements 299
Index 301

LOCAL SPORTS IQ QUIZ ANSWERS

(1 point each)
1. Tom Kron (Tell City)
2. Castle
3. Bob Hamilton (Reitz grad) – 1944 PGA Championship
4. Vincennes (Lincoln)
5. University of Illinois
6. If you said 'Gimbel Award', we'll give you credit, but for one year (1944), it was called the IHSAA Medal before being named the Trester Award.
7. Louise Owen
8. Washington – 5 (1930, '41, '42, 2005, '08)
9. Andy Benes
10. The Celtics
11. Lincoln
12 – 15. Gus Doerner, Jerry Sloan, Larry Humes, Don Buse

(3-points each)
16. Bob McAdoo
17. Harold
18. Memorial
19. Lee Hamilton
20.- 21. Larry Humes and Marcus Wilson
22. Huntingburg (Memorial Gym)
23. Boonville (Mike Wilson)
24. Bob Padgett (1969)
25.- 26. Tom Niemeier and Earl Schneider
27. Carson Jones
28. Chicago Bulls
29. Pete Fox
30. LeAnn Freeland

(5 points each)
31. Tampa Bay Buccaneers (2004)
32. C. (discus) [200 meters – Mark Jacobs, Bosse, 1994] [high jump – Leon Martin, Vincennes Lincoln '70; Ron Jones, Mt. Vernon '80; and Chris Walker, Gibson Southern '84] [800-meters – Tyrone Browning, Reitz '97]
33. Vicki ('87) and Cassandra ('79) Lander (Bosse)
34. Jerry Brewer (Jasper)
35. Bosse (1944 & '45)
36. Castle
37. Pittsburgh Steelers
38. Washington
39. Steve Spurrier
40. Racine Belles
41. A. (Michael Lewis) [Jasper and IU, "Indiana"]
42. Gil Hodges

(10-points each)
43. Lanae Renschler
44. Larry and Haley Harris (Oakland City/Wood Memorial)
45. 46
46. Gibson Southern (2003 and 2005)
47. Charles Hornbostel (Central) – 1936 Games in Berlin
48. Reitz girls (1981)
49. South Spencer (his father, Terry Reed, was the head coach)
50. 9 (VU – 3 ['65,'70, '72], USI – 1 ['95], E.C/U of E – 5 ['59, '60, '64, '65, '71])

For every Indiana high school athlete and coach, a State championship is the Holy Grail. There have been many outstanding athletes and teams from the area who have come close over the years, but those listed throughout the pages of this book, through their dedication and hard work, have proven themselves worthy of the title of…

IHSAA STATE CHAMPIONS.

FOOTBALL

Team	Year	Record	Coach
Castle (3A)	1982	14-0	John Lidy
Castle (3A)	1994	12-2	John Lidy
Heritage Hills (3A)	2000	15-0	Bob Clayton
Mater Dei (2A)	2000	15-0	Mike Goebel
Jasper (4A)	2001	13-1	Jerry Brewer
Reitz (4A)	2007	15-0	John Hart

CHAPTER ONE
1907-1949

REITZ FOOTBALL: A TRADITION OF EXCELLENCE

Sports aficionados are very reluctant to use the word 'dynasty', primarily because of its abstract definition. Whether the word is appropriate or not, one can't argue that the Reitz High School football program has withstood the test of time.

Herman Byers is the name most readily associated with Panthers football, and rightly so when you consider his success and his longevity, but the program's history is also impressive on both sides of the Byers era.

The school's overall varsity record, from 1919 through the 2007 season, is 601-245-29 (71%), and in the last 85 years, Reitz has had only eleven losing seasons. Eighteen times the Panthers finished the regular season undefeated, eight of them under Herman Byers followed by three with Bob Padgett at the helm and the 2007 team under John Hart. There have also been several other amazing stretches of seasons strung together by Reitz coaches. Byers had three such runs: 1960-'62 when Reitz was 26-0-1; 1955-'57 (28-1-1); and 1946-'48 (25-1-2). Padgett's final four years ('74-'77) were quite a streak as well, as the Panthers lost only one game each year, two of them in the State playoffs. However, since Reitz began playing a full schedule in 1923, only two coaches have completed their tenures at the school without suffering at least one losing season: Padgett ('70-'77), and more recently, John Hart ('01-'07).

The contingent of coaches at Reitz has amassed 27 conference championships and 38 City titles, including eight straight from 1971 to 1978 under Coach Padgett. The Panthers have claimed eleven sectionals and four regionals since the State format began in 1976, and according to the Website ReitzFootball.com, the Panthers were named mythical state champions ten times. Seven of those belonged to Herman Byers ('46, '48, '52, '53, '57, '60 and '61) and two were claimed by Coach Elmer Weber ('33 and '40).

As a long-time Evansville-area resident and as a player who competed against the Panthers on the football field, I am well aware of the mystique that is Reitz football. As I wrote this story in November of 2007, I kept waiting for the Panthers to lose so that I could plug in the final numbers. I was prepared to finish on November 9th, but Reitz pulled off a miracle over Columbus East in the regional with a 61-60 win. (Yes, it was still football season.) A week later, my pen was poised again, but Reitz came back from the dead by overcoming double-digit deficits twice to defeat defending champion Indianapolis Cathedral 35-34 in another thriller.

Herman Byers is carried off the field after an undefeated season in 1960. (Photo courtesy of the Reitz High School archives)

It was only fitting that the second-winningest program in the state would demonstrate once again why this story was being written in the first place. As the 2007 season came to a close, the latest group of Panther players finished with another perfect season. Their 15-0 mark set a school record for victories in a season and gave the school its twelfth undefeated campaign. With their 33-14 win over Lowell, the Cardiac Kids delivered Coach John Hart's first and the school's eleventh football State championship, reassuring everyone that the legacy of Reitz football excellence is alive and well yet today.

Even forty years after Herman Byers coached his last game, the tradition he fostered has continued. Eleven men have led the troops at Reitz, and since 1921, not one of them has left with a losing record. Of all the schools in Indiana, only Indianapolis Cathedral (623) has more wins on the gridiron than the Panthers. If Reitz football does not fit the definition of a dynasty, it should certainly be recognized as a model of consistency over time that few schools in the nation have been able to produce.

Reitz's original school colors were orange and purple, but those colors were given to Lincoln High School. Some believe that because Reitz was located on the Mason-Dixon Line, blue and gray were chosen to represent the colors of the opposing sides in the Civil War, but according to Reitz historian Jon Carl, this is not true. Apparently, navy blue socks were ordered for the football team shortly after the school's colors were issued to Lincoln, so the school officials decided to adopt blue and gray as the school's official colors.

Reitz Successful Succession

Coach	Term	Record	Winning %
John Hart	2001-'07	73-17	81.1
Bob Gaddis	1991-'00	64-42	60.4
Bill Hape	1983-'90	46-38	54.8
Bob Ashworth	1978-'82	29-15	65.9
Bob Padgett	1969-'77	79-14	84.9
Herman Byers	1942-'68	188-49-15	79.3
Ralph Becker	1941	6-3	66.0
Elmer Weber	1926-'40	82-40-13	67.2
W.V. Slyker	1922-'24	13-13-1	50.0
C.V. Maples	1921	2-5	28.6
George Murphy	1919-'20	4-6	40.0
TOTALS	1919-2007	599-243-29	71.0

'07 PANTHERS MADE HISTORY

The 2007 Panthers also made history by being one of the last five teams to win a State title in the RCA Dome before it was razed to be replaced by Lucas Oil Stadium in 2008. In addition, Reitz quarterback Paul McIntosh became the first Evansville player to be named Mr. Football after scoring a remarkable 56 touchdowns in his final season.

After nearly 90 years of football, the Reitz Rowdies are as loyal as ever. Fans here are celebrating another State championship in 2007 at the RCA Dome. (Photo by John Wells and courtesy of the Reitz High School Journalism Department.)

In 1940, Evansville had three undefeated football teams: Reitz (8-0-1), Central (6-0-3) and Lincoln (7-0-1).

THE BYERS FAMILY: WEST SIDE ROYALTY

At 3:00 p.m. on Saturday, October 4th, 1919, Reitz High School played its first football game. The school's first touchdown was scored by Ralph Wood on a ten-yard end run. How many in attendance do you think even gave it a thought that the thirteen young men who suited up for Reitz on that brisk fall afternoon would be the first of what would become thousands to go to battle defending the Kingdom on the Hill?

George Weber was the team's coach in 1919, and he served one more year before relinquishing the position to C.V. Maples for a year. Then, W.V. Slyker took over in 1922 for two years before Elmer Weber began a 16-year reign. Weber was the school's first highly successful coach, and during part of his tenure, the school played in a conference called the Tiny Ten. Under Weber's guidance, the kingdom grew, and the Reitz faithful began to enjoy the thrill of consistent success, including the school's first undefeated season in 1933 that brought Reitz its first State championship

When Weber left after the 1940 season, Ralph Becker assumed the position for one year, and then the following year, a man stepped in who would seize the throne and take the program to heights that may never be seen again in Evansville. With his no-nonsense style and brazen self-confidence, Herman Byers would rule the local football landscape for 27 seasons spanning three decades.

George Herman Byers was born in Gentryville and attended Chestnut-Walnut Grade School in Evansville before entering Central High School, where he lettered in baseball, basketball, track and football. As a football player, he was an All-State halfback and was rewarded with a scholarship to IU after graduating from Central in 1923.

At IU, he continued to display his all-around athletic ability by earning four numerals his freshman year. He played basketball for two years before focusing his energy entirely on football. Byers had gone to college with the intention of becoming a doctor, but the more involved he got in football the more he realized that coaching was his true calling.

After graduating in 1928, Byers came back to the Evansville area and coached at Boonville High School for one year, and In 1929, he was offered a job as the head coach in both football and basketball in Goshen, Indiana. His early success was as a basketball coach, as his team advanced to the Sweet 16 in his very first year before losing by two points to the eventual State champions.

While they lived in Goshen, Herman and his wife, Isabel, had three boys, George, Phil and Jim, but after eleven years up north, they decided to head back home. For a year, Herman was out of teaching and coaching as he attempted to sell insurance, but while he was supposed to be out selling, he found himself watching a football practice at Bosse or Reitz or wherever he could find one.

The call of the gridiron was too strong for the man to take, so he accepted a job as an assistant at Bosse in 1941 under then-Bosse coach Phil Beverly. When Reitz coach Ralph Becker was called into the military, Herman got the call. And the rest, as they say, is history.

In Herman's early years at Reitz, the city schools saw a lot of each other because of the war going on overseas, and in 1943, Byers made his first real impact on the local football scene. Because of the war and the cost of travel, the city schools played each other twice. Memorial, who was ranked #1 in the state, thrashed Reitz in their first meeting, but in the second contest, Byers got his revenge. In the rematch, Reitz's Jess Standish returned a kickoff on a fake reverse (Herman loved the razzle dazzle) to tie Memorial and knock them off their perch as the state's top-ranked team.

Herman during his playing days at IU. (Photo from The Arbutus.)

Every account of Herman Byers as a coach speaks of his strict disciplinary policies and his relentless pursuit of perfection. Although most of his methods would be frowned upon today, those who played for him look back and smile at the 'torture' because of the deep respect they had for the man. "He was strict, buddy!" said Rich 'Porky' Nau, the center for the Panthers' legendary 1961 team. "He never believed in water breaks. We'd practice from 7:00 until 9:30 in the mornings and from 1:00 until 3:45 in the afternoons with no water breaks. Our teeth would be black from being caked with mud. He would say, 'Water is for sissies!'"

"He was a person that didn't take alibis," said former Reitz player Don Henry to the *Courier*. "There was always a job to get done, and there was one way to do it. That was his way, the correct way."

Herman knew what needed to be done, and he followed his detailed regimen to the letter. If he pre-planned a 15-minute period to work on a skill or a play, it was 15 minutes then on to the next. He also prepared a series of cards with situations on them to drill his play-callers on the best plays to call under certain scenarios.

Byers also did not believe in situational football, as many coaches do today, where certain plays are designed for certain circumstances, such as short yardage or third and long. He believed that if every one did his job, every play should be a touchdown. "If you didn't make a touchdown, somebody screwed up," Rich Nau recalled. "And, boy, he would show you in the game film which player screwed up."

Nau also remembered the famous conditioning traditions at Reitz. "There used to be a big path about two miles wide (exaggeration), and we'd have to run to the top and back," Porky said. "And then, if he really got mad, you ran across the football field, up through the woods and up to the parking lot to a flag pole. You went around it and then came back."

Another common thread amongst ex-players was their feeling that, although Byers was tough, he was always fair and civil. "I swear, I never heard him curse directly at a player," said Gary Barnett, an ex-player and the son of then-Reitz coach Jim Barnett. "I never saw a helmet slap, face mask grab or a kick in the butt, but I did see a few jerseys grabbed."

Herman was a creative coach, and many felt he was ahead of his time in terms of the intelligent schemes he devised. His multiple offenses (mostly out of the old Single Wing) featured buck laterals that required precise ballhandling, the deceptive Spin Series that often fooled defenders, and the Power Series with a direct snap and carry. Although Reitz was primarily a running team, every running play had a pass designed from it.

In the early years at Reitz, Herman designed a formation called the A Formation with an unbalanced line. The quarterback would either give to the fullback or fake the fullback and hand to the halfback off-tackle. Byers' A Formation would be recognized by fans today as the Wishbone, and he ran it long before Bud Wilkinson made it famous at Oklahoma.

Herman wasn't the only Byers who built a reputation at Reitz. Isabel, Herman's wife, was loved by all who knew her. "She was special," said Phil Byers, the youngest of the three Byers boys. "She was a very mild, loving person who rarely got mad. But when she did, watch out!"

Apparently, Isabel would sometimes get upset in the stands if someone would criticize her husband or son, and on at least one occasion, according to Phil, was known to take an umbrella to the perpetrator.

The oldest of the three boys, George, was the first to play for his father, but clinching a starting position was anything but a cinch. "We lived on the east side, and his freshman year he played for Bosse," explained brother Jim. "Then we moved to the west side. He came in out there as the coach's son, and they had some great athletes, like Charlie Fisher (one of the better players in Evansville). George wasn't going to play until he earned it, and everybody on the team knew that he should play. So Dad put him under a lot of pressure."

George persevered and played a lot as a sophomore and then started his junior year, as a wingback on offense and a halfback on defense, on a team that boasted Fisher at tailback, Jerry David at fullback and big Ed Wessel at outside tackle (on the unbalanced line). George was also a good basketball player and once held Central's Frank Schwitz, the city's leading scorer, to zero points.

After his senior year in 1947, George accepted a scholarship to IU to follow in his father's footsteps. Although he was frustrated at not getting the chance to run the ball, he was a three-year starter at defensive back for the Hoosiers. Following graduation, George served in the Air Force for two years and then tried out for the Pittsburgh Steelers, making it to the final cut.

With that dream behind him, he headed to California to coach football. After a successful career, George wrote two books on the sport that were sold nationwide in the early '70s. Both emphasized defense, which was George's specialty as a player at IU and as a coach when his teams led the conference in defensive stats for several years. One book discusses the Pinching 53 defense that he learned from his father. The proof of the Pinching 53's success could be seen in 1961 when Herman's Panthers, led by middle linebacker Don Hansen, completed the entire season undefeated and unscored on.

Second son Phil Byers played tailback for his father at Reitz but was also an exceptional basketball player. While playing football for his dad, pre-game planning became a ritual in the Byers household. It seems that on Friday afternoons before ballgames, Herman would lie on the couch, rest his eyes and quiz his sons on play-calling situations to make sure they were on the same page. Before every game, the first few plays would be pre-determined, and Phil believes that if someone checked the records, they would see that Reitz often scored on the first drive.

Phil went on to a great career on The Hill, earning All-State honors in both basketball and football. The 1951 basketball team had a phenomenal season, but Phil signed with IU (with a little pressure from Dad) for a scholarship in football. Later, Phil and basketball teammate Jerry Whitsell were offered a chance to go to Kansas to play for Coach Phog Allen, but Herman felt strongly that Phil should honor his commitment to Indiana.

After one year of football, Phil joined Branch McCracken's basketball squad just in time to be a part of the Hoosiers' national championship. As a sophomore, Phil was a backup point guard who averaged about ten minutes per game. The bulk of the scoring was handled by center Don Schlundt and guard Bobby Leonard, and in a dramatic one-point win over Kansas (the school Byers almost attended), Phil experienced the thrill of a lifetime.

Youngest son Jim lettered in four sports at Reitz: football, basketball, baseball and tennis. In basketball, he battled the Clayton brothers from Central as an inside player even though he was just shy of six-feet-tall. As an All-American in football, he could have gone to virtually any college of his choice because of his skills as a linebacker on defense and as a fullback who could also pass. His choice of schools, however, was a bit of a surprise, even to himself.

Phil Byers in his Heisman pose as an Indiana Hoosier. (Photo courtesy of the Byers family.)

"I always thought I was going to IU," Jim said, "because my uncles and aunts, both parents and my brothers all went there." But after considering IU and a few others, Jim found a program that fit him like a glove, the Michigan Wolverines.

Michigan had just won the Rose Bowl in 1951 and was one of the top five programs in the country, but what made the choice so perfect for Jim was the system. Michigan coach Bennie Oosterbaan, who had played against Herman in college, ran a multiple offense with spins and buck laterals, and the offense couldn't have been more ideal for Jim, who had learned all the same skills while playing for his father at Reitz.

During his career with the Wolverines, Jim played with such greats as tight end Ron Kramer, who went on to play with the Super Bowl champion Green Bay Packers, and Terry Barr, a Wolverine tailback who played defensive back with the Detroit Lions.

After graduating with a degree in Education, Jim also followed his dad into the coaching ranks, returning to the area to coach at Princeton and Boonville before becoming an assistant under Paul Beck at Evansville College.

A year later, Jim was promoted to head football coach at E.C., and ten years after that, he took over the entire sports program as the athletic director. As the AD, he was involved in several historic events, including the school's move to Division I and the tragic plane crash that took the lives of the school's basketball team, coaches and several supporters.

With their pedigree, it was no wonder that all three Byers boys were successful. Their father had prepared them well and taught them the values that would ensure success, including the importance of hard work and tireless preparation.

As Herman Byers piled up victories during his years at Reitz, he earned a reputation as a man who would settle for nothing but the best. With no playoff system in place, he knew the only way to be voted #1 was to play and defeat the best teams in the land. By scheduling teams from Muncie, Columbus, Indianapolis, Hammond and East Chicago, it made it hard to deny that Reitz was #1 if they finished a season undefeated.

Evidence of Byers' statewide reputation could also be found at coaching clinics. It was not uncommon for Herman to attract a crowd, even when he wasn't a scheduled speaker. Rich Nau enjoys passing on a story he has heard several times over the years. "Jack Schaefer was saying that he went to a clinic and most of the big coaches were in Herman's room," Nau explained. "He said Herman would give him $100 to buy beer and they'd put it in a tub and fill it with ice and Coach Byers would have a chalk talk. All the younger coaches would stay down in the clinic, but the big school guys would sit in Herman's room asking, 'How do you run this play?' or 'How would you defend this play?'"

From his throne above the local landscape, Herman Byers' status grew to legendary proportions during his 26-year reign, and his numbers speak for themselves. During his tenure, he compiled a record of 188-49-15 (79.3%), winning 14 City and 13 conference championships. Byers also led the Panthers to seven mythical State titles and eight undefeated seasons ('46, '48, '53, '56, '57, '60, '61, '62).

Another remarkable Byers legacy is the number of ex-players who became coaches. Among the 50+ that son Jim could name at one time were Archie Owen (Bosse), Ed Wessel, Morris Riley and George Alvey (North), and Charlie Ogg (Central). Amazingly, one entire Reitz backfield became coaches: Herman's son George (wingback), Charlie Fisher (tailback) and Jerry David (fullback).

When Coach Byers decided to call it quits after the 1968 season, the general consensus was that he was reluctant to change with the times. "He demanded respect. You either did it or you were gone. He was fair in my opinion," said Jerry Canterbury, a Reitz alum. "He told me one time how he'd have his boys run the flagpole and back and Herman said, 'You know what, in my last years up there, I told them to take the flagpole. They all took off, and I looked up and the last two guys stopped and turned around and stared at me (in defiance). Then I said to myself, 'It's time to get out.' Before, they didn't ask questions; they just did it."

So in 1968, the iconic coach stepped down and passed his scepter to the next in line. The man had set the standard for all who followed him, and coaches knew that at Reitz, any effort less than your best just wouldn't do. Because of Byers' success, the Reitz Nation had developed a very low tolerance for mediocrity. Some loved him and some hated him, but nearly everyone agreed that, for 27 seasons, Herman Byers was the King of the Hill.

Herman Byers (seated) and his three boys (L-R) Jim, George and Phil. (Photo courtesy of the Byers family)

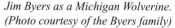

Jim Byers as a Michigan Wolverine. (Photo courtesy of the Byers family)

REITZ NOTABLES

PETE FISHER

"Pound-for-pound, the best around," is a way many characterize Reitz High School's Pete Fisher. At 5'4 and 145 pounds, Fisher stood tall among his contemporaries as a natural athlete who excelled regardless of the season. He was a play-making guard for Clarence Riggs' basketball team, an excellent shortstop and center fielder for the baseball team and a sprinter on Norm Lewellen's track team. As an example of his versatility, he also joined the school's golf team and was the medalist in the City High School Golf Tournament.

Pete's best sport, however, was football. After earning All-State honors in 1949 as a senior, he became a three-year starter at IU for Coach Clyde Smith and was the leading pass receiver in the Big Ten. Midway through his senior season, his career ended when he suffered a broken collarbone.

"If you mention athletes at Reitz, he's one of the top two or three," said Reitz alum, Jerry Canterbury. "He was shifty. He'd side-step you and he was gone."

Pete's brother, Charlie, was also an outstanding athlete at Reitz and went on to become one of the best football coaches in the state. Upon Charlie's retirement from Mississinewa, the school's football stadium was named for him.

The Fisher brothers would have to rank among the best to pass through the portals of Reitz High School, and Pete, particularly, embodied the label 'all-around athlete'. In fact, he is one of a select few, and perhaps the only athlete, who can lay claim to earning five varsity letters (basketball, baseball, football, track and golf) in a single year.

MALCOLM COOK

Considered by many to be the one of the greatest all-around athletes to come out of Evansville, Malcolm Cook was as versatile as he was talented. Cook was a starter for the Reitz basketball team and was an All-State end in football, earning a scholarship to Vanderbilt. The photo shows Cook (left) breaking the tape as he won the 1924 State championship in the quarter mile.

JOHN ALEXANDER

John Alexander was the first State champion in the history of Reitz High School and was a tremendous multi-sport athlete. In addition to competing for Reitz in football, wrestling, basketball and track, he was also a competitive swimmer, winning a medal at the Vincennes-Wabash River Swim during his freshman year in college.

John was best known for his running abilities. As a junior, he broke the previous State record but finished fourth when three other runners broke it also. As a senior in 1922, Alexander won both the mile and 880-yard run at the State meet and went on to finish fifth in both events at the National High School Track Meet in Chicago.

John was as creative as he was talented. When he was bothered by trying to wear eyeglasses on the basketball court, he designed and constructed goggles (see photo) to protect his glasses from contact. His invention proved to be 'visionary', as he went on to run track and captain the cross country team at IU while studying Optometry. After graduating, he returned to Evansville and began a successful optometry practice on the west side.

JOHN ALEXANDER
GUARD

A special thank you is due Dr. Bill Stedman. Much of the information provided concerning Vincennes (Lincoln) basketball was chronicled in his book, 90 Years of Alices.

THE 1923 ALICES IN WONDERLAND

When Vincennes High School opened in 1904, it was one of 71 member schools of the IHSAA. The school played its first and only basketball game of the year and lost 38-10 to the Freelandville Dutchmen. Vincennes won its first game three years later, defeating Princeton 17-11. By the time the school hired John L. Adams away from tiny Smithville in 1920, the program had a 16-year record of 97-60, but the arrival of the new coach was an event that would springboard Vincennes from the depths of mediocrity to the mountaintop of Indiana basketball.

John L. Adams was an innovator who wasn't afraid to think outside the box. He would occasionally send his team's reserve players to play other schools' varsity teams, "just for the experience." According to Dr. Bill Stedman's book, *90 Years of Alices...*, Adams was also "credited with perfecting the five-man defense, the forerunner of today's zone." The coach also developed his *Adams Official Score Book*, which was used by virtually every high school and college for years. In addition, Adams was an astute businessman, because when he was approached about his score book by companies like Rawlings, Wilson and Spalding, he opted to market the book himself.

Adams' greatest products, however, were the teams he put on the court. His very first team (1920-'21) won 35 of 41 games and averaged nearly 20 points more than their opponents. The '20-'21 team qualified for the 16-team State Finals at the Indianapolis Coliseum and lost in the second round.

Adams' second year at the helm was even better. The Alices of 1921-'22 plowed through their competition for a perfect 32-0 record and the state's #1 ranking. The ranking didn't hold up, though, as Vincennes lost again in the second round of the State Tourney to a Bloomington team they had beaten twice during the season. They did, however, finish with a 38-1 record, the best in the school's history.

After two great seasons, John L. Adams was just getting warmed up. The 1922-'23 team featured three returning starters from the previous year: Reese Jones (the previous year's Gimbel Award winner), Harold Mayo and Johnny Wolfe. Coach Adams had prepared a vicious schedule to toughen the boys for the State Tournament. He scheduled home-and-home games with Anderson High and single games against Lafayette Jeff, Lebanon, Columbus and Martinsville, all formidable opponents. Just before the new year, the Alices would play back-to-back games against the defending State champions from both Indiana and Illinois, Franklin and Centralia. The idea was, they had to play the best to be the best, and the Alices began the season ranked #1.

The atmosphere was electric in Vincennes in the days before television, and even radio, and the basketball team was the center of the community's social life. On game nights, the town would be out in force as the team and fans traveled, mostly by passenger train, with a pep band in tow to add a festive air.

An early-season game at Anderson caused quite a stir because of its implications. The #1 and #2 teams were to meet in Anderson, and an Anderson newspaper stated that 1,500 seats were sold and another 5,000 were turned away. Back home in Vincennes, rabid fans would be itching for info about the game, and ,fortunately, school officials worked with the opponents to arrange a telephone hookup. The plan was approved by the IHSAA, and throughout the evening, the crowd at Clark Junior High in Vincennes received reports over the gymnasium loudspeaker about the Alices' eventual 38-26 win.

Coach Adams and his crew tore through the first twenty games undefeated, and only one team (Lebanon, twice) came within ten points of the Alices. Vincennes had strung together 55 consecutive regular season wins, including the previous year, but their streak was about to end.

In February of 1923, the town was buzzing about their team's incredible run, and they were excited as they piled into the Clark Junior High gym to host a Central team they had already beaten 37-26. The Bears stunned Vincennes that evening with a 31-29 upset when Herman Byers (the future legendary football coach at Reitz) tossed in a long field goal to silence the standing-room-only crowd. Vincennes starter Ed Prullage was guarding Byers at the time and was so devastated that he refused to face his teammates in the locker room. As told in Bill Stedman's book, Prullage's teammates came out to the floor and told the dejected teammate, "That's okay, Ed, we'll win the State."

The 1923 State champion Alices. (Photo from 90 Years of Alices.)

Following the game, a story in the *Vincennes Commercial* newspaper expressed that the loss was a blessing, because "the boys were really cocky." With their minds back on track, the Alices rattled off six more wins to finish their regular season 25-1. They had begun the year as the state's #1-ranked team and had held the top spot the entire season. Now it was time to prove that their ranking was justified.

Closing his practice to the public, Coach Adams went to work preparing the boys for their 'second season'. Adams was able to rest his starters for much of the sectional opener as the Alices thumped the Oaktown Oaks 63-6. They followed that with a 28-5 shellacking of the Fritchton Eagles. After another rout, a 58-9 victory over Edwardsport, the stage was set for a sectional final with arch-rival Washington. The game was anti-climactic, though, as Vincennes pulled away to win 38-17, giving Vincennes its eighth straight sectional title.

Only the one-game regional in Bloomington separated Vincennes from its third straight trip to the State Finals. Adams opted for a light practice schedule, and the strategy paid off with a 61-8 cakewalk over Hanover. A well-rested bunch of Alices were ready for their 'Finals' exam.

At the Indiana State Fairgrounds Coliseum, Vincennes quickly dispatched the tiny Lyons Lions 38-10. The easy victories and light practice schedule gave Coach Adams' crew confidence as they headed into the grueling Saturday schedule that would require a team to win three games in one day to emerge with the crown.

Next on the agenda were the dangerous Franklin Grizzly Cubs, who were attempting to win an unprecedented four State titles in a row. Vincennes got behind early in the 11:00 a.m. opener, but Harold Mayo's hot shooting led to a 22-18 victory. The 3:00 p.m. semi-final matchup pitted the Alices against a team they had already beaten twice during the season, the Anderson Indians. Vincennes again rallied from behind for a 29-27 victory, and Coach Adams and his boys were three hours away from history.

The final game with powerful Muncie tipped off at 8:00 p.m., and Vincennes quickly took a 10-1 lead. The Alices led wire-to-wire and won the championship 27-18. To cap things off, Reese Jones was presented with the Gimbel Award and made the All-State Finals team along with Harold Mayo.

The victors returned home to a hero's welcome, and the story of the '23 team became so widespread that Fox Film News sent a crew in to do a feature-length movie about the coach and his troops. Three public showings were offered daily at the Pantheon Theater on March 9th and 10th.

It was rumored that after the '23 season, John L. Adams was being courted by several high-profile college programs, including IU, but the popular coach decided to stay put. He coached at Vincennes for 19 total seasons and won the sectional every year. He also won eight regionals to go with his State title. He finished with a record of 438-158 (73%) at Vincennes and served as the school's athletic director for 39 years before retiring in 1959. John L. Adams was inducted into the Indiana Basketball Hall of Fame in 1990, and the gym where the Alices now play bears his name.

The 1923 Vincennes team made history that year and set a mark that can never be duplicated. They not only became the school's first State champion, but they were the first State champion south of Bloomington. As the newspapers proclaimed over eighty years ago, for one glorious season, Coach Adams and his boys created a fairy tale of their own called "Alices in Wonderland".

John L. Adams was an innovator who led the Vincennes Alices to their first State championship in 1923. (Photo from Dr. Bill Stedman's book 90 Years of Alices.)

In 1915, 27 teams participated in the three-day Evansville Sectional. Evansville High School defeated Princeton 71-24 in the final.

In 1922, Vincennes fans crammed into the Clark Junior High gym to listen to reports over the telephone of a game being played over 200 miles away in Anderson. (Photo from 90 Years of Alices by Dr. Bill Stedman.)

Much of the information in this story was found in a wonderful book, Red Legs and Black Sox: Edd Roush and the Untold Story of the 1919 World Series, *written by Susan Dellinger, PhD, the granddaughter of baseball great Edd Roush.*

EDD ROUSH: THE "$10,000 MAN"

In the early twentieth century, baseball was king, and its roots were deeply entrenched in small town America. Rural Indiana was no exception, and one of our area's greatest baseball stars began his career on the dusty fields of Gibson County. With an Oakland City gal serving as his inspiration, Edd Roush fashioned an amazing career and was a key player in the most famous World Series in baseball history. In the process, he distinguished himself among all others who followed him from southern Indiana and set some precedents along the way.

The community around Oakland City was made up primarily of farmers and coal miners in the early twentieth century, and the Roush family was among them. Edd Roush and his fraternal twin, Fred, would work long hours milking cows and then riding on the milk wagon to help their father, Will Roush, deliver to families in town. When the weekends rolled around, Edd was free to pursue his passion on baseball fields across the area, and it was obvious early on that he was a special player.

At age sixteen, Edd was literally tall, dark and handsome, but the muscular farm boy was also very shy. He spent many an evening waiting at the movie theater for a pretty girl named Essie Mae Swallow, who accompanied the silent films of the time by playing the piano. Essie was shy herself, but the two loners grew close as they walked the quiet streets of Oakland City.

In the days long before video games and TiVo, fans would gather each weekend to watch their favorite teams battle on the baseball diamond, and 'semi-pro' teams were common in area towns such as Washington, Petersburg, New Harmony and Oakland City's biggest rival Princeton.

Edd's first paying baseball gig was with the Oakland City WalkOvers, sponsored by the WalkOver Shoe Company. Edd earned a dollar a game and quickly established himself as an outstanding player. As Edd and Essie grew closer, he often shared his dream with her of becoming a big league player. During one conversation, Essie told him that she had heard that Ty Cobb was earning $10,000 just for playing ball. As the two shared the dream, she began to refer to Edd as her "$10,000 man," and together the couple began a journey that would take Edd all the way to Cooperstown.

In 1911, Edd made the decision to defect and join the enemy when the Princeton Rexalls offered him $5 a game, which was *big money* in those days. Edd played second base and left field and hit .455 with a slugging percentage of 1.074, numbers that attracted some serious looks from other teams.

The next season, he joined the Evansville Yankees in the Class D League and impressed folks in the 'big city' by hitting over .400 and playing right field. With his steady play, Edd began to draw interest from 'the Bigs' when folks like Connie Mack (Philadelphia Athletics), John McGraw (New York Giants) and Charles Comiskey (Chicago White Sox) saw his batting average posted in the local newspaper. When they learned that he was out-hitting such stars as Ty Cobb and Tris Speaker, all three came to Evansville to have a look for themselves.

On August 15th, 1913, Roush was sold to the White Sox for $3,000, and when he arrived in Chicago, he was somewhat of a curiosity. Not only was he a loner, but he carried two gloves. More than a few people were perplexed when they learned that Roush would play left-handed when he played right field and right-handed when he played left. It was also odd that he didn't use his ambidexterity at the plate as a switch-hitter, preferring to hit only from the left side.

For whatever reason, Roush was not given much of a chance in Chicago and was demoted to Lincoln in the Western League. At Lincoln, he made the decision to ditch his right-handed glove and play strictly as a lefty, and when things didn't work out in Lincoln, Edd made the trip back to Oakland City to work for his father.

Hall of Famer Edd Roush swings his bat, the heaviest in the majors at the time. (Photo from the Roush family collection.)

After a short time on the farm, Edd realized how much he missed baseball, and he began to write letters to teams. After sending inquiries to Joe Tinker in Chicago, Mordecai 'Three Fingers' Brown in St. Louis and 'Whoa' Bill Phillips in Indianapolis, he received a response from Indy. Edd's mother, Laura, was totally against the idea of anyone making a living "playing a game," but against her wishes, Roush headed north.

Because Edd was underage, his father accompanied him on the trip. As the two chatted and watched the cold January landscape pass by, Edd learned a valuable lesson from his father. Although Edd loved baseball and would probably have played for nothing, his father convinced him that baseball was also a business.

"Decide how much you're worth," Will instructed his son. As the two discussed the situation, references to Cobb and his $10,000 salary became a point of reference. When all was said and done, they decided to settle for $2,000.

At the meeting, they were handed a contract that had been pre-set at $1,500. As Edd sat and pondered, he watched as his father

Edd Roush's 48-once bat, the heaviest in major league history.

taught him a lesson that he would use again and again throughout his career. "We been thinking that my son here should have a salary of $2,000," said the elder Roush. "If you can't pay it, we need him back on the farm."

With the skill of a seasoned agent, Will did not flinch, and Phillips decided to relent rather than run the risk of losing Edd. With his father's guidance, Edd had become one of the first players to truly negotiate a contract, and he had learned that if you want to be paid what you're worth, you should always be willing to pick up your hat and walk away.

In 1914, a new organization called the Federal League began to raid the American and National Leagues of players, offering lucrative long-term contracts and new stadiums with shorter fences. The more established leagues fought legal battles to thwart the advances of the marauders, but instead had to double players' salaries to keep them in the fold.

As the 'outlaw league' began its first season, Edd saw some action, but only as a sub at first base because the team's outfield was set. On July 28th, World War I began, and fifteen days later, Edd earned a permanent spot in left field. Edd's Indianapolis 'Hoosiers' won the league crown and brought Indianapolis its first and only major league championship. Edd had completed his first full major league season.

During the 1914 season, Edd also fulfilled another goal when he married Essie seven days before his 21st birthday. After the season, the newlyweds learned that the Hoosiers were in financial trouble and that the team would be moving to Newark, New Jersey. With Edd attracting attention from other clubs, he lobbied his new team for a $4,000 salary and won once again.

Roush finished the 1915 season with a .302 average, and he and Essie enjoyed their time in Newark, but the fledgling Federal League crumbled after the season. As the league dissipated, the better players were bid out to teams while the rest were 'free agents'. Roush's contract was purchased by the New York Giants for the same $4,000, but Edd was able to negotiate a $500 raise.

Early in the 1916 season, Edd shared the outfield with a young athlete named Jim Thorpe, a native American who four years earlier had set a decathlon record at the 1912 Stockholm Olympics that would stand for twenty years. Although Thorpe would have some problems later and be sent back down to the minors, the fleet-footed Roush would often marvel aloud about how he could not match the speed of Thorpe.

New York was exciting for the Roushes, and Essie got a thrill from rubbing elbows with celebrities like George M. Cohan and Eddie Foy. Meanwhile, Edd had developed a reputation for being the ideal player for his generation. Roush played during the last years of the 'dead ball era', which necessitated what was known then as the 'inside game'. With his skills at bunting, sacrificing to advance runners and aggressive base running, Edd was considered the perfect player.

In July of 1916, Roush was traded to Cincinnati and was placed in the #2 spot in the batting order. He didn't disappoint, going three for four with a triple in his debut. Edd's new roommate was Heinie Groh, a little man with a big personality who was known as "the heart of the Reds." Christy Mathewson, known as 'Matty', was Edd's manager, and he spent a lot of individual time with Roush. He corrected Edd's tendency to pull away from the first pitch and encouraged him to move up in the box. Edd also developed a technique of moving around in the box while with the Reds, which was disconcerting to pitchers who weren't sure if he was going to bunt, slap the ball or hit away.

Roush finished the season with a .267 average for the last place Reds, and he was offered a reduced contract of $4,000 to return. Edd countered with $6,000 and became one of the first holdouts when he didn't show for training camp. The Reds came back with $4,500, saying that only three players in the National League were getting more, but Edd had other ideas. When he finally gave in on the salary, he requested a no-trade clause, which was unheard of in those days. With his contract secured, Edd joined the club as the Reds began to build a championship team.

Prior to the 1917 season, Mathewson invited Ty Cobb to camp to offer some pointers, and Roush would say many times later in life that "Cobb was the best of them all. Hands down!" When commenting about baserunning, the cantankerous Cobb proclaimed, "Infielders better get out of my way. When I'm on the run, that baseline is mine."

Cobb took a liking to Roush and watched him as the 1917 season began. Early in the season, Edd injured his foot while sliding, and Jim Thorpe was called up. Roush was hitting a torrid .451 at the time and was still battling for the hitting title after his return. In August, he was hitting .347 when a youngster named Rogers Hornsby joined the race. Roush won the batting crown in 1917 with a .341 average, but Hornsby would eventually win seven titles on his way to the hall of fame.

In 1918, Roush began to notice that something wasn't right, and he began to suspect that good friend and teammate Hal Chase was possibly throwing games. Edd explained after his retirement that, "He'd be just a couple seconds too late to the ball, or the ball would deflect off his mitt, or the sun would get in his eyes on a pop-up."

Edd felt uneasy and asked Essie to stay away from Chase and his wife. He also suspected teammate Lee Magee, a native of Cincinnati who knew all the right people. Roush could never understand how a player could give in to those temptations, and his suspicions were validated when Chase and Magee were exposed and given their walking papers later in the season. Little did Edd know that the unthinkable transgression he had witnessed would rear its ugly head again very soon and that he was only a year away from witnessing one of the most notorious scandals in baseball history.

With World War I raging, the government issued a 'Work or Fight' order, requiring that any man

This is the pin given to each member of the 1919 world champion Cincinnati Reds. (Photo from the Roush family collection.)

16

not engaged in "essential" work to join the fight. Baseball was not considered "essential," and Edd headed back to Indiana to work the farm. His manager, Christy Mathewson, left to fight and served in a unit in France with baseball greats Branch Rickey, George Sisler, Grover Cleveland Alexander and Ty Cobb.

Mathewson returned from the war, left the Reds for the New York Giants and then became president of the Boston Braves. He died in 1925 of tuberculosis believed to be caused by exposure to mustard gas he and the others had inhaled while in France.

Heinie Groh took over for Matty as player/manager and was leading the league in hitting with his short 'bubble bat' well into the season. Edd made a frantic run at the batting title when he went 53 for 124 (.427) in 32 games and trailed by only eight points. His run ended on August 30th when he received some devastating news, a telegram that read:

"Will in coma (stop) Fell off telephone pole (stop) Come home (stop) Mother"

Trailing the Cardinals Zack Wheat by only three points, Edd headed home and found his father's head wrapped in layers of gauze. Less than a week later, his father was gone at the age of 50.

Edd lost the batting title by two points, and controversy followed. A rule at the time stated that if a game is protested and the protest is upheld, statistics from that game are expunged, as if the game never happened. This occurred twice in 1918. Both games involved the Cardinals, and one involved the Reds. As a result, a good game by Roush and a bad one by Wheat were erased. The rule was changed in 1920 because it was deemed unfair to players, and if it hadn't existed in 1918, Roush would have bested Wheat .336 to .335 and would have joined Wade Boggs, Ty Cobb, Rod Carew, Tony Gwynn, Rogers Hornsby, Stan Musial and Honus Wagner as the only men in major league history to win three batting titles in a row.

Prior to the 1919 season, Cincy owner Garry Hermann offered Roush a mere $4,500 for the coming season, a $500 cut in pay, citing the low attendance during the war and Roush's average dropping eight points (to .333) from the previous season. Edd was livid and demanded $10,000. Standing firm once again, Roush returned home to Indiana, prepared to holdout, just as his father had taught him.

The Reds' director sent Jimmy Widmeyer, an old friend of Edd's from Cincinnati, to visit Edd in Oakland City and negotiate his return. Jimmy told Edd that he was authorized to offer $8,000, but Edd didn't waver. Finally, Widmeyer convinced Roush that if he came back, he guaranteed that the Reds would give in to Edd's demands. At his mother's urging, Roush headed east, making Widmeyer a hero to fans and finally making Edd a "$10,000 man."

In 1919, Pat Moran, a pitching coach for John McGraw's New York Giants, came to Cincinnati as Christy Mathewson's permanent replacement. 'Matty's boys' were determined not to like Moran, but he won them over as a great leader and a man of principles. (Edd

Edd Roush (left) and Pete Lowe as teammates on the Oakland City WalkOvers in 1909. (Photo from the Roush family collection.)

Roush would say later that Moran was the "best manager" of his career.)

The Reds wrapped up the National League race on September 16th with eight games still to play, giving Cincinnati its first pennant in thirty years. They finished the season 96-44 and led the league in fewest errors (151) and fielding average (.974). Roush won the batting title .321 to Hornsby's .318 and was one of the Reds' leaders heading into the 1919 World Series.

The Reds were an unusual group because exactly half of them batted from the left side, including six of the starters. Roush and Heinie Groh were the team's star hitters, but they were team-oriented with little ego and would lay down a bunt when needed to help the team.

Prior to the 1919 season, gamblers were spreading the word to bet on the Reds to win the Series, and Jimmy Widmeyer had overheard many such conversations. Widmeyer had a shady past and had worked his way up into Cincy society after moving across the river from Newport, Kentucky. Newport was known for its gambling casinos and the questionable clientele that frequented 'Sin City'. Widmeyer had established a popular newsstand and had lots of contacts. He would also play a key role in the notorious Series that was about to begin.

As Essie busied herself by evaluating her wardrobe for the upcoming event, the Roushes enjoyed the excitement, talked often to supporters from back in Indiana and prepared for Edd's mother, Laura, to arrive for the Series opener.

While Edd and Essie basked in the limelight, a consortium of shadowy figures converged on Cincinnati. Based on later reports, it was determined that a group of gamblers and thugs, led by 'the King of Gentleman Gamblers' Arnold Rothstein, had been nosing around to see which players could be bought to sway the outcome of the Series. They quickly concluded that Cincinnati was out because of their closeness as a team. They did, however, see potential in the White Sox, who were divided into cliques and whose stars, left fielder 'Shoeless' Joe Jackson and pitcher Eddie 'Knuckles' Cicotte, were loners.

Game One in the best of nine Series began as managers Pat Moran and William 'Kid' Gleason of the White Sox shook hands and the ump hollered "Play Ball!" at 2:00 p.m. In the bottom of the first, Sox pitcher Cicotte threw his first pitch for a called strike. His second pitch was perhaps (in retrospect) the most discussed pitch in major league history, as he plunked Reds second baseman Morrie Rath on the back. The speculation, looking back, was that the pitch signaled to those involved that "the fix is on."

After a single, a sacrifice fly, a walk to Roush and a ground out, Cincinnati led 1-0. Later in the game, the Reds broke the game open and fans noticed that Cicotte's play looked suspicious. At one point, he hesitated on a throw that should have started an easy double play, and rumors about game fixing that had circulated earlier began to gain credibility.

As for Roush, his Game One produced no hits, but he did have eight putouts.

In Game Two, Edd made a leaping catch that a writer described as "one of the greatest catches ever seen in a World Series." After the 4-2 Reds win, his friend Jimmy Widmeyer pulled Edd aside and shocked him with the news of the alleged conspiracy. Because his hotel room was next to Cicotte's, Widmeyer had overheard that some Sox players had thrown the first games but had not gotten their money and were now going to play to win.

Edd thought back on curious events of the early games and concluded that something might be going on. The competitor in him, however, didn't want to believe it, as he thought, "They know they can't beat us, so they're starting a rumor." Edd didn't know how to react, so he chose to keep his mouth shut and his eyes open.

As the Series shifted to Chicago, the rumors persisted in the press. Apparently, Charley Comiskey, the White Sox owner, had received tips prior to the Series and Joe Jackson had approached Comiskey before the first game to ask to be taken out of action because of the guilt he felt from dealing with gamblers.

In Game Three, Edd got his first hit of the Series, but the Sox made quick work of the Reds with a ninety-minute, 3-0 win.

In Game Four, Cicotte pitched and was determined to win this time after tanking Game One and not getting paid for it. Whether intentionally or not, he still fumbled a ball and made a bad throw in the fifth inning that again aroused the suspicions of the press.

Roush tripled to deep center in Game Five to lead the Reds to a 5-1 win, giving Cincinnati a 4-1 Series lead. When the Sox came back against the Reds in Game Six, Roush's mind reeled as he began to wonder if gamblers had gotten to Cincinnati pitcher Dutch Ruether, who had pitched poorly in a 5-4 Reds loss.

Eddie Cicotte returned for the Sox in Game 7 and was desperate to get a win. Thanks to a weak performance by Reds hurler Slim Sallee, Chicago prevailed 4-1. Cicotte would later say under oath, "I didn't care whether or not I got shot out there the next minute. I was going to win the ballgame and the Series. I didn't care for the money after that."

With the Sox hurlers pitching around Roush and Heinie Groh, Edd was having a bad Series at the plate, hitting only .123, fueling more rumors about Cincy being in the gamblers' pockets. To add fuel to the fire, Jimmy also had told Edd that gamblers had gotten to some Reds to throw Game Seven.

With Game Eight approaching, the only thing Edd knew for sure was that he wanted to win the Series. Before the game, Roush confronted his teammates and looked straight at pitchers Slim Allee and Dutch Ruether, who was scheduled to pitch.

"I'll be out in center field watching every move, and nobody better do anything funny," Roush warned. "No damn crook is going to rob *me* of my winning share of the Series!"

Moran asked young pitcher Hod Eller if gamblers had approached him, and Eller responded: "Yup. A guy on the elevator with me...followed me to my room. He said, 'Wait a minute.' He held up five thousand-dollar bills and said, 'These are yours if you throw the game tomorrow. And there'll be five more just like them for you after the game.'"

The hurler sent the man packing, and Moran took a chance and decided to start Eller for Game Eight. Sox manager 'Kid' Gleason knew who his traitors were and didn't need confessions. His starting pitcher, Lefty Williams, turned out to be on the take, and it was said that Williams' wife's safety had been threatened. His first six pitches resulted in five hits, including a double by Roush, and four runs.

Edd finally hit the ball like Edd, going 3 for 5 with two runs scored and four RBIs. He also made an amazing sliding catch in the ninth inning as the Reds clinched the Series with a 10-4 victory. For his efforts, Roush was named the fielding star of the Series after racking up thirty putouts.

A check for $5,207.01 was the full share for each Reds player who contributed to Cincinnati's first World Series title. In addition, owner Garry Hermann gave each player an unexpected gift, a diamond stickpin engraved with the words "World Champions – 1919." An anonymous Cincy businessman offered a $500 gold pocket watch to the Reds player who "contributed the most to the final game victory." Edd Roush was selected and was presented the gift on the way home.

When the last out was recorded in the 1919 World Series, Roush became only the third player in baseball history to win a batting title and play in the World Series in the same year, joining Honus Wagner (1903 & '07) and Ty Cobb ('07-'09).

After spending seven more seasons with Cincinnati, he moved to the rival New York Giants for three years before finishing his career back with the Reds for the 1931 season. He was well known throughout his career for his 48-ounce bat, the heaviest in major league history, and for his magnificent glovework, finishing with a .972 fielding percentage.

In his ten full seasons with the Reds, from 1917 to 1926, he never batted below .321. He struck out only 260 times in 7,363 at bats (once in every 28 at bats), and never struck out more than 25 times in a season.

Roush was also known as a savvy businessman who was a pioneer of the holdout tactic, actually sitting out an entire season in 1930. In 1969, Roush was voted by Reds fans as 'The Greatest Red Who Ever Lived', and Joe Morgan once called Roush "the best of us all."

Roush died six weeks short of his 95th birthday on March 21st, 1988, one month after his twin brother Fred. Fittingly, he passed away at McKechnie Baseball Field in Bradenton, Florida while watching a spring training game.

With his beloved Essie by his side, Edd Roush had ascended to the very top of his profession and was recognized as one of the sport's elite when he received its highest honor with his induction into the Baseball Hall of Fame in Cooperstown in 1962.

The story of the notorious 'Black Sox Scandal' has been told and re-told over the years and even immortalized in the 1988 movie *Eight Men Out*. The truly regrettable part of the 1919 Series, however, is that, lost in all the mystery and intrigue was the inspirational story of Edd Roush and his Cincinnati Reds, who played with honor and resolve to bring the championship home. The quiet young Gibson County boy who once roamed the fields of southwestern Indiana had made a living doing what he loved to do most and, in the process, had become one of the absolute greatest to ever play the game.

(The following information was taken from articles in the Maturity Journal by Peggy K. Newton.)

PETE FOX: EVANSVILLE'S FIRST WORLD SERIES CHAMPION

Ervin 'Pete' Fox was one of the best players of his day and the first Evansville native to play in a World Series. Fox was born on March 8th, 1909 and began his ascent into the big leagues twenty years later.

In 1929, while playing amateur baseball locally, Fox was discovered by Bob Coleman, who signed him with the Detroit Tigers organization. After a season in the Mid-Atlantic League, the 5'10", 165-pound Fox played for the Evansville Hubs, where he hit .302 with eight home runs and was a teammate of future hall of famer Hank Greenburg. By 1933, Pete had worked his way up to the Detroit Tigers, where he quickly became a fan favorite because of his speed and gutsy play. Except for a sub-par season in 1936, when he was hampered by a bout with lumbago, Fox enjoyed a fabulous career in the Motor City and became an important contributor to the team's success.

Fox spent eight seasons with the Tigers, where he earned the title of 'most popular right-fielder in baseball' in a 1938 nationwide poll and played in three World Series. In the 1934 Series, Pete averaged .286 with six doubles. Two of the doubles came in the seventh game in an 11-0 loss to hall of fame pitcher Dizzy Dean, giving the Cardinals the championship.

In 1935, the Tigers returned to the Series, and Fox was the only player from either team to hit safely in every game. He was 10 for 26 (a .385 average), and his Tigers defeated the Chicago Cubs in six games, giving Detroit its first World Series title. Fox's Evansville teammate Hank Greenburg also completed a remarkable season with Detroit with 36 home runs and 170 RBIs.

Detroit made it to the World Series one more time before Fox's departure, and Pete could see his relationship with the Tigers ending as he played sparingly when Cincinnati took the 1940 Series in seven games.

Fox was traded to the Boston Red Sox after the Series and retired from baseball after the 1945 season. A career .298 hitter and an American League All-Star (1944), he distinguished himself against the best his sport could offer, and he never forgot his roots. He and his first wife Elizabeth (Betty) returned to Evansville and raised their two children, Beverly and Jimmy. Jimmy was named after the legendary Jimmie Foxx, a contemporary of Pete's but not a relative. Young Jimmy graduated from Bosse in 1954 and was a member of the Bulldogs' SIAC championship football team.

With his second wife, Helen, Fox had another son, Don, who played for the Boston Red Sox. Pete managed a White Sox farm team in Iowa and later scouted for Detroit before settling there in his declining years. He died of cancer in 1966 at the age of 57. Evansville's first World Series champion was still listening to Tigers games while he was on his deathbed. His life and death reflected his loyalty to the two places that mattered most to him – his second home of Detroit and Evansville, his hometown.

EVANSVILLE WAS AN NFL CITY

Few people know that Evansville was once the home of an NFL football team. At a meeting of team managers in Chicago on August 27th, 1921, the Evansville Crimson Giants were admitted to the American Professional Football Association (to be re-named the National Football League a year later). Others admitted at the same time were the Minneapolis Marines, the Tonawando (NY) Kardex and the Green Bay Packers.

The season lasted from the first of October until the last week of November, with the locals winning three out of five games. The Crimson Giants were owned by Franklin Fausch and coached by Herb Henderson, who was a player/coach along with others such as Earl 'Curly' Lambeau of the Packers and George Halas of the Chicago Staleys (to be renamed the Bears in 1922).

Travel was not easy during the early '20s, and some trips took as long as three days, which kept some regular players at home because of job responsibilities. These circumstances often resulted in teams picking up players along the way to fill the voids.

Out of the 21 teams in the APFA in 1921, Evansville 'unofficially' ranked seventh. They had no official ranking because they hadn't played the required number of games, which is why they haven't been listed in official NFL history books.

In 1922, the Giants played only three games and lost them all. The average team payroll was about $1,800 per week, with most of the players earning $50. Herb Henderson was paid $100 because of his coaching duties and because, as he put it, he had more to do, such as kicking, forward passing and playing linebacker on defense.

All three losses in '22 were played on the road because the owner had trouble securing fields for home games since he would not pay the asking price of $250 for either Bosse or Reitz field. Had he opted to pay, Evansville fans would have had the thrill of watching the Oorang Indians come to town with their star, Jim Thorpe.

The Evansville Crimson Giants played their last game on November 12th, 1922, a 13-6 loss to the Louisville Brecks. As has often been the case in professional sports, it proved to be a difficult task for a small-market city to sustain an NFL team. Of the 12 teams that were in the league in 1921, only the Chicago Bears, the Chicago (later St. Louis and Arizona) Cardinals and, against all odds, the small-market Green Bay Packers were able to stand the test of time.

Franklin Fausch and his team couldn't afford the cost of fielding an NFL team for the long haul, but for two short years, Evansville played with the big boys as an NFL city.

BOB HAMILTON: "IT'S A GREAT WORLD!"

Southwestern Indiana has not been a hotbed for developing professional golfers, but Evansville's Bob Hamilton has been called the best golfer in Indiana history and, in his day, was one of the best in the world. Hamilton was born in Virginia on January 10th, 1916. After his father died, his mother, June (Schuetz), decided to move back to her home in Evansville, where the family settled in a west side community called Avondale.

Although young Robert was a four-year starter on the basketball team at Reitz and was offered a scholarship to Purdue, his first love was golf, and his talent was obvious very early on. As a 16-year-old, he captured the 1932 City golf title by defeating the second place finisher, Harold Bootz, by eighteen strokes in front of 500 fans at the Evansville Country Club. He would not only repeat as the City champion for the next four years but would also capture the 1933-'34 IHSAA State title with a record score of 72 that would stand for eighteen years.

After his fifth City championship in 1936, the young Hamilton took his talents to the next level by turning pro, and it wouldn't take long for the young man with the soft hands and winning smile to get noticed. In just a few years, he was traveling the world and hobnobbing with some of the biggest stars in the sports and entertainment worlds.

As was the norm during Hamilton's era, Bob took a job as the club pro at Helfrich Golf Course while he played in various tournaments. He won his first Indiana Open in 1938, a feat he repeated in 1942 and 1966. The professional circuit was much less organized back then compared to today's tour that posts a schedule for the entire year so that players can plan their schedules. In Hamilton's day, players would find out about a tournament by whatever means they could and then hit the road.

Hamilton's oldest son, John, was born fifteen years before his younger brother Jim and was around during his father's barnstorming days. "The biggest tourney in the world in those days was the Tam-o-Shanter in Chicago," John explained. "One year, the U.S. Open had to switch dates because it conflicted with the Tam-o-Shanter. It's the only time the Open ever switched dates. I went up there (to Chicago) as a kid, and the first tee was, like, 100 yards long, and on both sides of the tee people were playing slot machines."

As the pros traversed the country looking for tournaments, it was also common for them to find 'action' by hustling other pros and amateurs anytime they could find a game. As Jim Hamilton points out, the practice is still common today, but matches during the 1930s and '40s were legendary. The itch for the ordinary

Bob Hamilton (second from right) receives the PGA Championship trophy as Byron Nelson (far left) looks on. (Photo courtesy of the Hamilton family.)

player to enjoy the company of pro golfers was strong, and Hamilton's popularity resulted in friendships with some of the biggest names in pop culture.

"Joe Louis (the heavyweight boxing champion) stayed at our house a lot," recalled John Hamilton. "He used to train for fights at French Lick. It was a nice out-of-the-way place where no one would bother him. My dad used to play there, so I assume that's how they met.

"Dad was the kind of guy that if you came into town, he'd say, 'Where you stayin'?' Then he'd say, 'No. You're staying with me.' And he'd call Mom and bring them home. I remember when I was eight or nine, I came home and there was a strange car in front, and Joe Louis was in our living room. Dad said, 'Come in, I want you to meet someone.'"

Bob also formed close bonds with other celebrities, like hall of fame jockey Eddie Arcaro and perhaps the world's greatest female athlete Babe Didrickson Zaharias and her husband George. He was also close with entertainers like Bob Hope, Bing Crosby, and Dean Martin. Bob's son John was even on the course with Bob when Yankee great Mickey Mantle walked up to talk to Bob's playing partner, Yankees owner Dan Topping. Bob and John watched as Mickey told Topping that the Yankees' general manager was refusing to pay Mantle the $100,000 salary he was asking for. According to John Hamilton, Mr. Topping looked at Mickey and said, "I think you're worth a lot more than that. Go tell him I said to give you whatever you want." In addition to his moments on the course with celebrities, Bob Hamilton also matched shots with some of the greatest pro golfers in the history of the game. With contemporaries like Ben Hogan, Sam Snead, Jimmy Demaret and Byron Nelson, Hamilton wasn't the best player in the game, but he definitely showed he belonged.

Bob's greatest accomplishment took place at the 1944 PGA Championship. After serving a five-year apprenticeship as a club pro (a requirement at the time), Hamilton entered the event in the first year he was eligible. In dramatic style, Bob defeated future hall of famer Byron Nelson 1-up in the match play event at Manito Golf and Country Club in Spokane, Washington. Although the current format for the Grand Slam tournament is medal play to accommodate television, match play always had the potential for drama, and John Hamilton is always willing to re-tell the story of the '44 PGA that he had heard his father discuss many times.

"Dad was 1-up going to the last hole, and he had it on the green two feet from the hole," John described. "Nelson was forty feet away, and Dad thought, 'Well, I finally got him right where I want him.' Then Nelson made his putt and Dad thought, 'Man, is he ever going to quit?' Then Dad made his two-footer to win."

The relative unknown from Evansville, Indiana had shocked the golfing world by knocking off one of the all-time greats. Although Hamilton never won another Major, he did prove that he wasn't a one-hit wonder by continuing to play well. Over the course of his pro career, he captured four more titles: The 1944 North/South Open at Pinehurst; the 1946 Charlotte Open; the 1948 New Orleans Open; and the 1949 Inverness Four-Ball with partner Chick Harbert.

In addition to his wins, Hamilton had some impressive finishes in other Major tournaments, finishing third in the '46 Masters, fourth in the '53 Masters and tied for third in the '52 PGA. Hamilton also received golf's greatest honor when he was chosen to represent his country in the 1949 Ryder Cup. Along with team captain Ben Hogan and others, like Demaret and Snead, Hamilton helped the team bring the Cup home with a 7-5 win in Scarborough, North Yorkshire, England.

In 1974, Bob's sons helped him realize another dream when the family opened Hamilton's Golf Course on Evansville's north side. For years, Bob poured himself into the project, and the boys continued the effort after Bob's passing in 1990. Due to the changing golf climate in the area, the Hamiltons announced the end to their involvement with the course in 2008.

Both Hamilton sons have been active in the game since they were young. Oldest son John was a player at Bosse, and Jim won two City championships by the time he was 19 and also won the Indiana Junior Open as a senior at Bosse. Jim played as a collegian at ISUE (now USI) and led his team to the NAIA national tournament as a sophomore. If his father were around today, he surely would enjoy watching Jim's current involvement in the game as the head men's and women's coach at the University of Evansville.

In many ways, Bob Hamilton was larger than life, and he lived his life to the fullest. His talent and cocky attitude carried him a long way and endeared him to many who knew him. Few people can match the lifestyle Hamilton enjoyed, and he was well aware of how blessed he was. This was probably never more evident than on a sunny afternoon in Florida when John was following his dad during a round of golf.

"He was playing a round of golf with Dutch Harrison and the ex-King of England (King Edward VII, who abdicated the throne to marry Wallis Simpson, an American divorcée)," John explained. "Dad was getting ready to chip a ball on the green and he says, 'Hey, Ed (King Edward), get the pin for me, would you?' Then he turns to me and says, 'Son, is this a great country or what? Here I am, a poor caddie from Avondale, and I've got the King of England holding the pin for me. It's a great world, isn't it?!'"

Bob Hamilton (far right) poses with a group that includes his good friend and frequent house guest world heavyweight champ Joe Louis (center) and Evansville sportswriter Dan Scism (left of Louis). (Photo courtesy of the Hamilton family.)

THE DOPE BAG: A 34-YEAR TRADITION

Traveling trophies have been a part of the sports world for over a hundred years, from those symbolizing the competitions of fierce rivalries to those recognizing a conference's dominant school in 'all-sports' competition. One traveling trophy that was a part of the local landscape for 34 years is virtually unknown by today's 'youngsters', those 55 or younger, but it represented a nostalgic era when Hoosier Hysteria was at its very best.

The idea was conceived in the 1920s by Franklin Hunt, the sports editor of the *Evansville Journal*, which later became the *Courier*. Designed at first to be a marketing tool for the newspaper, the trophy evolved into folklore status as it traveled eight counties in southwestern Indiana.

The object itself was given the name 'Dope Bag', a curious name to the modern generation. In those days, the term "dope" referred to "information," as in "the inside dope." The concept was designed to keep the *Journal*'s name in front of the public, and for years, it did just that. A black doctor's satchel would become the envy of more than sixty area schools as it traveled myriad miles from November 1st of 1929 to January 15th of 1963.

The process went as follows: The bag contained a metal box and, eventually, two leather-bound ledger books. When a school held the bag, it would display it in any game that involved another eligible school. The bag was sometimes placed on the floor in the center circle prior to the game to remind the fans that it was a 'Dope Bag game'. If the team that held the bag won, it would continue to hold it. If the other team won, it would take possession and continue the process. In either case, the winning school was instructed to record the following: the date of the game; location; score; the names of the officials; and the coaches and captains of each team. They were also asked to remark on attendance and sportsmanship. And, as designed, the winning school got its name in the biggest paper in the land.

As the concept developed, the process was intensified as the schools took the liberty of adding their own embellishments by affixing ribbons in their school colors to the dreary bag. In its day, the bag was an exciting enhancement to an already basketball-crazed society, but to local sports aficionados, it would become much more as the years passed.

As one can imagine, the list of names contained in the bag would be a virtual Who's Who of local basketball history.

The first Dope Bag game was played at almost the exact moment that the stock market crashed to begin the Great Depression, at a game in 1929 between Union and Mt. Olympus. Mt. Olympus became the first stop on a long journey for the trophy, and three games went by before Huntingburg gave the bag a long rest for 13 straight games.

One of the most interesting stories occurred after a game on New Year's Eve, 1931. Upon winning the Bag, Bosse coach Harry King suggested that the *Journal* give it to someone else. His reasoning was that his Bulldogs were very good, so the bag would not get to circulate as it was meant to. Whether Coach King was being philanthropic or just cocky, his analysis proved to be true, as Bosse reached the State Finals that year. The Tennyson Tigers were the recipients of King's gift, and they held the bag for 14 games.

In 1936, Huntingburg, led by standout Bill Menke, wrested the bag from Mt. Vernon and held it for the rest of the season. The following year, the Hunters held the bag the entire year with a great team that featured Don Blemker and Menke's younger brother Bob, who led the Hunters all the way to the State Finals. Huntingburg did not relinquish the bag until November 3rd, 1939,

(Photo courtesy of the Indiana Basketball Hall of Fame.)

a stretch of 35 Dope Bag games that would stand up as the longest streak in the bag's 34-year history.

Over the years, hundreds of names were recorded thanks to Franklin Hunt's creation. The 1941 Bag made a stopover in Petersburg, allowing the team's captain to enter his name in the ledger. The young man's name was Gil Hodges.

In one quirky situation, tiny Winslow completed an entire season undefeated, but because they didn't play anyone who had possession of the Bag, future hall of famer Dick Farley's name is absent from the ledgers. Others who were around during the Dope Bag era but never crossed paths with the Bag were Rex Mundi's Bob Griese and North's Dave Schellhase.

Although the Dope Bag was designed as a marketing ploy, it also served to chronicle an exciting period in area basketball history. Many of our greatest players, coaches and officials had their names inscribed for all eternity on the ledgers of the little black bag. The names of the men to the right can be found in the ledgers and can also be found on the walls of the Indiana Basketball Hall of Fame.

Nearly 100 schools, large and small, battled to be a part of this unique tradition, and the Bag changed hands exactly 100 times. On January 15th, 1963, the 411th and last Dope Bag game was played between Reitz and Central. After the game, the Bag mysteriously disappeared.

For years, this curious bit of local legend was nowhere to be found. At one point, a local coach suggested that "Someone probably stuck it in a closet somewhere." The remark turned out to be prophetic when the bag was found in 1973 buried in the back of a storage closet at Bosse High School.

With the mystery solved, the precious Dope Bag found a safe home at the Indiana Basketball Hall of Fame, where it is displayed proudly as a piece of southern Indiana basketball lore.

Jim Rausch (Reitz)
Dee Williams (referee)
Kern McGothlin (Winslow coach)
Chet Francis (Vincennes coach)
Paul 'Bear' Hoffman (Jasper)
Clarence Riggs (Central coach)
Arad McCutchan (Bosse player & coach)
Walter Riggs (Central coach)
Leo 'Cabby' O'Neill (Jasper coach)
Bob Lochmueller (Ft. Branch coach)
Bill Menke (Huntingburg)
Ed Siegel (Boonville coach)
Bob Menke (Huntingburg)
Herb Schwomeyer (referee)
Bryan 'Broc' Jerrel (Bosse)
Bob Hoffman (Jasper referee)
Lee Hamilton (Central)
Cyril Birge (Jasper referee)
Gene Cato (Oakland City)
Orlando 'Gunner' Wyman (Tell City coach)

Before school gyms were built by Reitz (1925) and Central (1927), Evansville high school games were played at the old YMCA (Fourth & Sycamore), the Jewish Synagogue (Sixth & Vine), the present YMCA (Fifth & Vine), Central's girls' gym, the Bosse and Memorial auditorium stages, and the Agoga Tabernacle.

CHARLES HORNBOSTEL: THE LITTLE-KNOWN LEGEND

Charles Hornbostel might very well be the most accomplished track athlete to call Evansville home, and yet very few people have ever heard of him. The Central High School grad not only had a record-setting career at Indiana University but he held a world record and represented his country in two Olympic Games.

After a solid but unspectacular four years at Central, Hornbostel headed for Bloomington to begin what would become a remarkable running career. The lanky middle distance runner earned three letters at IU in cross country (1931, '32, '33) and three in track (1932, '33, '34) and was a cornerstone on two Big Ten cross country championship teams. In 1931, he finished 11th as an individual and led the Hoosiers to the cross country national title.

In track, Hornbostel won three consecutive Big Ten titles in the indoor and outdoor 880-yard run ('32, '33, '34) and made it a double in 1934 when he also won the indoor and outdoor mile run. He also contributed to two more Big Ten championships on relay teams, giving him ten conference titles in all, setting a record that stood for over half a century.

During his years at IU, Charles also captured the NCAA outdoor 880-yard title three years running ('32, '33, '34) in times that ranged from 1:50.9 to 1:52.7. In addition, Hornbostel set an NCAA 880-meter record and represented America in the 1932 Olympic Games in Los Angeles, finishing sixth in the 800 meters.

Following his college graduation, Hornbostel continued to run, winning the AAU 1000-yard championship in 1934 and 1936. At the 1936 Millrose Games at Madison Square Garden, the Evansville native did himself one better when he set a new world record at the unusual distance of 600 yards with a time of 1:11.3. To cap off an amazing career, Hornbostel again represented his country and finished fifth in the 800 meters in Berlin while the great Jesse Owens won four gold medals with an embarrassed Adolf Hitler looking on at the 1936 Olympic Games.

Charles Hornbostel

From the cinder tracks of southwestern Indiana, Charles Hornbostel developed himself into one of the best runners of his generation. Along the way, his talent and determination enabled him to break records as a collegian, to set a world record, and to travel the globe and witness a memorable piece of American sports history.

THE PING ERA: WHEN THE TIGERS REIGNED SUPREME

Memorial coach Don Ping. (Photo courtesy of the Evansville Courier.)

When debates arise over which football team was the best in Evansville history, two teams quickly separate themselves from the rest: the 1961 Reitz team and the 1937 Memorial Tigers. Obviously, a dispute such as this one will never be settled because the teams couldn't meet on the field and it is impossible to compare teams from different generations.

Ironically, if fans were to attempt to build cases for the most powerful football dynasty, the same schools would rise to the top again. Was it the powerful presence of the Reitz Panthers during the Herman Byers era or the Don Ping regime during the 1930s and '40s at Memorial? Although Coach Byers is considered the godfather of Evansville football, and deservedly so, the resumé compiled by Coach Ping was just as impressive, and the seasons he put together from 1934 to 1939 may be the best the city will ever see.

Donald Wilson Ping was born in Illinois and was a graduate of James Milliken University, where he played baseball and football. He accepted his first coaching position at Carrollton, Kentucky in 1922 and stayed there until 1927. During his time there, Ping received a leave of absence to play professional baseball for two seasons in the Cardinals organization.

From Carrollton, Coach Ping moved to Marshall, Illinois to become the school's athletic director, and two years later, he was hired at Evansville Memorial to assume control of the school's football program. From his very first season as the Tigers' coach, he was on his way to dominating the local football scene and building his program into one of the most respected in the state.

Ping accepted the head football coaching position at Memorial in 1930. In the initial years, the coach was blessed with the highly-talented Tommy McGannon, but after McGannon's senior season in 1933, prospects did not look good for the Tigers. Little did Coach Ping know that his 1934 team would exceed all expectations and that the next few years would feature two of the best teams in Evansville's history and a four-year run that has yet to be equaled in the history of Indiana football.

The 1934 season began with four shutouts over Henderson (21-0) Clay (KY) (32-0), Terre Haute Garfield (6-0) and New Albany (7-0). During the nine-game season, only two opponents scored against Memorial, Owensboro in a 14-6 loss and Nashville, (TN) in a 13-6 loss, and Memorial finished with a perfect 7-0-2 record. The two ties were against Evansville teams (Central and Bosse, both 0-0), and for the season, the Tigers outscored their opponents 117-12.

The 1935 season was even more impressive, as the Tigers began with blowouts over Henderson (95-0) and Nashville (51-0). Once again, Coach Ping's crew went undefeated, with only Garfield managing a tie (0-0). Only one opponent scored against the Tigers (Reitz in a 12-7 loss), and Memorial outscored their opposition 317-7. Recognized as a State contender, a title game was arranged with Ft. Wayne Central, and Memorial thumped the northern Indiana team 13-0.

The following year featured more of the same, as the 1936 Memorial squad dominated their schedule again. With only two ties (Reitz 6-6 and Garfield 0-0), a third straight undefeated season was recorded, and players and fans alike were probably wondering how it could possibly get any better. But it did.

In 1937, surrounded by a veteran lineup, a young sophomore named Billy Hillenbrand dazzled the Memorial faithful and led his team to a season that will forever be touted as one of the best in the history of Evansville high school football. In addition to Hillenbrand, the team was led by All-State quarterback/safety Bob Hargrave and team co-captains Bob Will (right end) and James 'Bud' Hinkle (fullback). The rest of the starting lineup included center Ed Haller, guards Bob Pirnat and Walter Hess, tackles Oscar Harte and Joe Hillenbrand, end Leo Scheu and halfback Earl 'Chief' Schoenbachler.

Other letter winners on the '37 team were Bill Toon, John Delker, George Ahlering, Paul Splittorf, Bill Wimsatt, John Hauck, Francis Stock and Charlie Hudson.

The '37 Tigers steamrolled their competition on their way to a perfect 10-0 regular season, including dominating victories over city foes Bosse (45-0), Reitz (45-0) and Central (40-0). Late in the fall of 1937, the Associated Press had Memorial virtually tied with Hammond High for the mythical State championship. On Thanksgiving Day, Memorial completed their regular schedule with a 21-7 victory over a tough Clinton team, while Hammond easily handled South Bend Riley. As a result, the AP gave the nod to Hammond in a "photo finish."

The general consensus was that, if Memorial had beaten Clinton by five touchdowns or more, as they had done to eight of their nine previous opponents that year, the title would have been theirs. Bob Hargrave, the Tigers' talented quarterback, believed that two factors contributed to the closer-than-expected score against Clinton. "One of the things that made the '37 team good," Hargrave explained, "was that a lot of our players were backfield men converted to linemen, and they were quick. We were kind of a razzle-dazzle team and did a lot of spontaneous lateraling. I think everybody on the team had scored a touchdown except Joe Hillenbrand (Billy's older brother). He didn't have the finesse that Bill did. He was just a tough old Dutchman and a great competitor.

"Against Clinton, Billy was out in the open and could have walked across from the ten-yard line," Bob speculated. "He looked around for his brother Joe and lateraled to him, but the Dutchman fumbled!"

As a result of Memorial's amazing season, the *entire starting eleven* were named to the All-City team. But the snub they had received from the press up north still didn't sit well with the team, its fans or the Evansville city officials. Although Mayor William Dress was not much of a football fan, he was a man who would seize an opportunity when it presented itself. During a friendly game of Clabber one evening, he was listening to a radio broadcast of a high school game between teams from Austin, Texas and Chicago. From that broadcast was born an idea that would not only bring the Tigers the credit they deserved but would unite the city of Evansville in the process.

Mayor Dress began a search for an intersectional opponent for Coach Ping and his Tigers, but most schools wanted to travel farther south to Florida to escape the cold. By Saturday, December 4th, the mayor had completed arrangements to host the McKeesport Tigers from Pennsylvania at Reitz Bowl. The catfight between the two groups of Tigers was scheduled for Saturday, December 11th, and both teams would have chips on their shoulders and something to prove.

McKeesport is a city located in Western Pennsylvania, a football mecca near Pittsburgh known for producing outstanding players. The McKeesport football program was on a 26-game undefeated streak, during which it had outscored opponents 562-51. The '37 McKeesport team had won nine straight before tying their final game against their bitter rival, Clairton, in ankle-deep mud. The scoreless tie kept them from winning the Western Pennsylvania League title and a possible bid to play in Miami on Christmas Day.

When Coach 'Hack' Tinson and his team pulled in at the Evansville train station, they would find that they had much more than just the Memorial Tigers to deal with. Reitz Bowl would be overflowing, and an entire city would stand united in support of Coach Ping's Tigers.

One can only imagine what Memorial's players must have felt as their cleats hit the field and they looked around the mammoth arena. Bob Hargrave remembered the camaraderie he felt with the schools his team had trounced on the football field only weeks earlier. "It was an outstanding game," he recalled, "in that the coaches from the other three Evansville schools were on our sideline, the cheerleaders from the schools joined our cheerleaders, and the bands joined each other. It was more of a City of Evansville game than a Memorial game."

The game itself didn't live up to its billing and wasn't nearly as exciting as the hooplah that preceded it. In front of thousands of loyal fans, the Memorial Tigers dominated the action in a 21-0 win and confirmed what many had believed before: that Memorial deserved to be declared State champions. The game was so lopsided, in fact, that McKeesport only made two first downs the entire game, and one of those was the result of an unnecessary roughness penalty against the 'tough old Dutchman' himself, Joe Hillenbrand.

Coach Ping's Tigers were declared 'mythical national champions' by the Evansville faithful after putting the finishing touches on a remarkable four-year run. The 1937 team had finished a perfect 11-0 and had outscored their opponents a remarkable 450-13.

Were they the greatest team in Evansville history? That question will continue to create great debates for years to come. But at the very least, we can probably all agree with Bob Hargrave when he said that the '37 Memorial team may or may not have been the best of *all* time, but it was unquestionably "the best of *its* time."

Although the '37 team was the jewel in Coach Ping's crown during his tenure at Memorial, it was his consistency that was most impressive. His four-year run from the 1934 through 1937 seasons stands alone in Indiana history. No other school has completed four straight seasons undefeated. Those Memorial teams were a combined 32-0-5 and outscored their opponents 1,090-34.

Following the '37 season, Coach Ping added powerhouses South Bend Central and Gary Emerson to the schedule to avoid the 'weak schedule' stigma that prevented the '37 team from winning the mythical State championship. Although they lost to Paducah Tilghman (12-7), the '38 team, led by junior sensation Bill Hillenbrand, was dubbed the State champion by the Associated Press.

The following year, the Memorial schedule was made even tougher with the addition of Chattanooga (TN) Central and Gary Wallace. With only Hillenbrand, Norb Stone and Hermie Will returning from the '38 State champs, the Tigers lost only their first game of the season (26-13 to Gary Emerson) on their way to a #3 state ranking. Coach Ping had completed an astounding six-year run with only two losses.

The popular coach would continue at Memorial until 1945, and his 16-season record was 118-22-9, an 84% winning percentage. In 1946, he moved a few blocks east to take over the football program at Evansville College, where he coached for nine years before becoming the school's athletic director.

It has been over sixty years since Don Ping coached his last high school game, and although the game has changed dramatically, the ultimate goal of any team, regardless of the era, is to win football games. So as Monday morning quarterbacks consider the merits of the greatest local football teams and programs in our history, Don Ping's name should be one of the first mentioned, because when it comes to winning football games, no one has done it better than Don Ping.

Coach Don Ping was well known as a prankster. Hugh Ahlering, who played baseball at Evansville College, recalls grabbing his glove to take the field only to find a big wad of tobacco juice cleverly deposited there by Coach Ping.

BILLY HILLENBRAND: THE EVANSVILLE EXPRESS

Even after seventy years, when local sports fans debate over who should be recognized as the greatest football player to come out of Evansville, Billy Hillenbrand's name is still one of the first mentioned. As a high school sophomore, Billy played on the 1937 Memorial squad that is also included in discussions regarding "the greatest..." Hillenbrand's feats made a lasting impression locally, but he also made a name for himself at the college and professional levels as well.

Billy was born on a farm in Armstrong, Indiana, just west of Darmstadt, the youngest of ten children. After his father died when Billy was very young, Billy's mother moved the family into Evansville. Out of necessity, Billy worked his first job when he was eight years old, and shortly thereafter, consistently held down two or three jobs to help his mother pay the bills.

With natural athletic ability, the youngster made the seventh and eighth grade team at St. Benedict's as a fourth grader, and when he was a seventh grader, he was the team's player/coach.

At Memorial, Billy was much more than an athlete. He played the lead role in two school plays, was president of his class the first three years, and was the class vice-president as a senior. But it was on the football field that he felt most at home, playing for the school's renowned coach Don Ping.

The famous 1937 team was built around Hillenbrand's talents, and the Memorial teams during his last three years posted a record of 35-2-2. Billy scored 485 points during his high school days, averaging nearly three touchdowns per game, and there were many games where he, himself, would outscore the opponent. He also excelled as a defender, and he was so skilled that Coach Ping made him the hub of his special 6-2-1-2 defense.

For three seasons, Billy was named All-City and All-State, and by his senior season, he was being eyed by college coaches coast to coast. Billy's bow-legged gait and deceptive speed made the 6-foot, 185-pounder a recruiting target of every college in the Big Ten college plus schools from the southeast, the PAC-10 and especially Notre Dame.

In the early '40s, the football powers were the service academies, and Billy had his heart set on going to West Point. A discovery of calcified lesions on his lungs during a physical prevented him from passing, and his West Point dream came to an end. Had Billy passed the physical, he would have joined the famous Army backfield of Glen Davis and Doc Blanchard. It's interesting to speculate if Billy Hillenbrand might have been forever remembered as 'Mr. Inside' or 'Mr. Outside' if not for the medical malady.

Indiana University was the winner of the Hillenbrand lottery, and after watching from the sideline as a freshman, Billy began his storied college career in 1941. In his first year, he called the offensive and defensive plays and inspired Coach Bo McMillin to change his philosophy. Because of Hillenbrand, McMillin abandoned his pass-happy style and switched to a ground-oriented attack to accommodate Billy's talents.

Hillenbrand's coming-out party was a game in which the sophomore passed for two touchdowns and ran for one in a 21-13 upset over heavily-favored Nebraska. He also was the only player to crack the end zone in a 7-0 season-ending victory over Purdue. Billy led the team in scoring, amassing 1,641 yards of offense, was responsible for 14 of the team's 15 TDs and averaged 36.4 yards as the team's punter.

At season's end, Hillenbrand was the only sophomore to make the All-Big Ten team and was the first sophomore in Indiana history to receive serious consideration for the Heisman Trophy (finishing fifth). Perhaps his greatest achievements, however, resulted from his skills as a kick returner, as he led the entire nation in punt return yardage.

Billy's junior season was also incredible, as he continued to show his versatility. He scored three touchdowns in a memorable win over Pittsburgh and led his team to a 7-3 season. Once again, he led the nation with 481 yards on 23 punt returns in a season that was to be his last at Indiana. Hillenbrand led the team in passing both years and returned a two-year total of 65 punts for 1,042 yards for an amazing 16-yard average. Those numbers are still IU records and still rank 13th nationally some 65 years later.

Billy was an All-Big Ten player for the second year in a row, and he scored 31 TDs and gained 3,683 yards during his two seasons at Indiana. The 1942 season ended with Hillenbrand becoming the first back in school history to become a consensus All-American.

With World War II gearing up, Billy decided to leave school and enlist in the Army. He graduated #1 from Officer Candidate School out of a class of 240 and

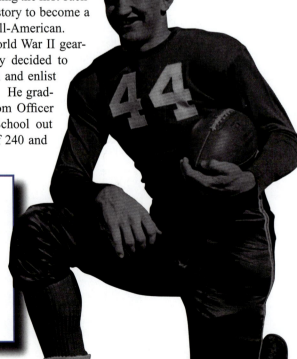

THE HAND OF FATE

Memorial's Billy Hillenbrand is given credit for starting the career of Otto Graham, the NFL hall of famer with the Cleveland Browns. In 1942, Northwestern quarterback Bill DeCorrevont threw a pass that Indiana's Hillenbrand intercepted and returned 70 yards for a touchdown. As a result, the disgruntled Northwestern coach replaced DeCorrevont with a young Otto Graham, who led the team to a 20-14 victory. And the rest, as they say, is history.

was stationed at Ft. Benning in Georgia. While there, he again got to demonstrate his skills as he competed in three sports. Out of 100,000 troops, Billy was named the base's Athlete of the Year.

In 1944, Hillenbrand was chosen to play in an all-star game against the Chicago Bears. Three of the 33 players on the team were Evansville boys: Hillenbrand, Lt. Roy Grele (Central) and J.C. Coffee (Lincoln).

Hillenbrand couldn't play in 1945 because he was in Calcutta, India, but he was chosen for the game again in 1946. The all-stars defeated the L.A. Rams 16-0, and Billy's backup was University of Wisconsin and future NFL star Elroy 'Crazy Legs' Hirsch.

After leaving the army, Hillenbrand was drafted in the first round by the NFL's New York Giants. When the Giants didn't offer the money he felt he deserved, he signed a three-year contract to play in the new All-American Conference. He spent a year with the Chicago Rockets, where he was teammates once again with Elroy Hirsch, and two years with the Baltimore Colts. While in Baltimore, Billy scored 13 touchdowns, with seven coming on receptions from a rookie quarterback named Y.A. Tittle.

When his three-year contract ended, Hillenbrand left football for the business world. He and his wife, Inge, a 1939 Central graduate, eventually settled in Indianapolis, where they lived until Billy's death in 1994.

Although Billy never came back home, his feats are legendary in southwestern Indiana. It may be impossible to compare athletes of different generations, but those who saw him play have no doubt about his status. In the words of Phil Byers, a pretty decent player himself, "Billy Hillenbrand was in a class by himself."

BOB HARGRAVE: THE LAST OF A GENERATION

Bob Hargrave is one of the few players from the famous 1937 Memorial Tigers still around to tell the stories firsthand. Although he played in Billy Hillenbrand's shadow at Memorial, Hargrave was an exceptional player himself and played collegiately at the greatest football school in the land.

Born in 1920, Bob moved on to Memorial after graduating from St. Benedict's Elementary School. While at Memorial, he lettered in baseball, basketball and football, and as a result of his success with the undefeated Tigers team of '37, he had high hopes of playing in college. His opportunity came as a result of the much-publicized "national championship" matchup with undefeated McKeesport (PA).

"Chet Grant, the Notre Dame backfield coach, had come down for the McKeesport game to see Billy Hillenbrand, but he found out Billy was just a sophomore. So he had to justify his expenses somehow and he took me instead," Hargrave stated, with a wry smile.

Whether Grant came to see Billy or not, Bob left for South Bend and entered Notre Dame as a quarterback under Coach Elmer Layden for his first three years and then under iconic Irish coach Frank Leahy. He was told that if he maintained a 77% (grade) average and stayed out for football, his education would be paid for. Although Bob didn't start until his last two years, he was a member of the team his freshman year that had a national championship in their grasp before losing the last game to USC.

His accomplishments on the field in both high school and college earned Bob a place in the Indiana Hall of Fame. From his north side home, Bob recalled a time when football was a game in sharp contrast to the one that is played today. What a rare treat it was to hear him talk about the rules and equipment and to have him draw out the formations used in a bygone era.

Players in the late '30s wore leather helmets with no face masks and webbing inside to absorb some of the shock. Not long before that, helmets could be folded up and put into a pocket.

In those days, the rules dictated that players had to play both ways, offense and defense, and also had to participate during kickoffs and kick returns, so the eleven players rarely left the field. If a player came out, he could not return in the same quarter, eliminating what is known today as the two-platoon system. When a substitute came into the game, the only player who could talk in the huddle was the quarterback. The substitute could not call the play or give any information (from the bench). In fact, the referee would stand beside him in the huddle to make sure the player stayed silent. Any coaching from the sideline resulted in a 15-yard penalty.

Offensive formations were also very different than those used today. Memorial coach, Don Ping, was known as an innovator who liked to use several sets, and Bob Hargrave recalled a game against Reitz when a new weapon was revealed. "The Reitz game (1937) was a tough one for three quarters," he recalled. "We were only leading 13-0, and we had been working on a Spread Formation that we had gotten from a pro coach, 'Gloomy' Gus Harrison. He coached the L.A. pro team."

According to Bob, 'Gloomy' Gus stayed up with Memorial's players until 1:00 a.m. on the night before a game explaining his offense. Gus named his plays descriptively instead of numerically, as most coaches did, and the only play Bob could recall in 2008 was a play called "A bottle of milk for Mrs. O'Reilly."

"At the end of the third quarter (of the Reitz game), Ping sent in the Spread," Bob continued, "which was unseen in Evansville before. It was kind of like a Pro Set now. The ends were split to the sidelines, and there was a two- or three-foot gap between the linemen instead of being foot-to-foot. We scored 32 points in the second half and beat Reitz 45-0."

Memorial's teams of the Ping era ran from several formations, and Bob Hargrave diagrammed them with precision as if he were preparing for a Saturday afternoon game at Reitz Bowl. Even today, he shows the enthusiasm for the game that made him a hall of famer and a star on perhaps the greatest team in Evansville football history.

SHORT PUNT
RIGHT

X X X Ⓧ X X X
      QB   RH
         FB
        LH

SINGLE WING
UNBALANCED RIGHT

X X Ⓧ X X X X
    QB   RH
   LH FB

TIGHT T

X X X Ⓧ X X X
     QB
   LH FB RH

SHIFTED INTO NOTRE BOX
RIGHT

X X X Ⓧ X X X
      QB RH
    LH FB

DOUBLE WING
UNBALANCED RIGHT

    X X Ⓧ X X X X
QB   RH
     LH FB

GLOOMY GUS HENDERSON SPREAD

LE   X X Ⓧ X X   RE
                   QB
            FB   RH
      LH

Bob Hargrave (#3) looks for someone to block as a quarterback at Notre Dame.

Much of the following information was found on the excellent Website, "hatchets.net", which was compiled through the exhaustive research of Bob Padgett and Bill Richardson.

100 YEARS OF WASHINGTON BASKETBALL

When Luke Zeller launched a 37-foot desperation heave in the finals of the 2005 State tournament, he fashioned a storybook ending to yet another chapter in the annals of Washington High School basketball. But his heroics were but a small part of a lengthy legacy that traces back to the early twentieth century.

Washington High School's first basketball team took the floor in a rented 'home gym' on December 16th, 1905 and came away with the school's first victory, an 18-12 win over Vincennes. Who could have foreseen back then that over a century later Washington would accomplish feats that no other area school could and that they would be playing in a 7,090-seat arena that is one of the largest in the state.

In the early 1900s, the State Finals consisted of a team from each of the thirteen congressional districts. For whatever reason, the city of Indianapolis (one of the districts) decided not to participate, resulting in a twelve-team field. The Finals field was formed either by invitations from the Indiana University Booster Club or by holding a tournament to determine a district champion. In 1915, the IHSAA required a district (sectional) tournament, and it wouldn't take long for Washington to separate itself from the crowd.

After the school's first three seasons, school officials opted to drop the basketball program due to a lack of money and fan support, but in 1912, basketball was re-instated and a newly-built school included a basement gym that held 150 spectators. Four years later, Washington was chosen to host one of the twenty sectionals statewide and emerged victorious, making the 1916-'17 team the school's first to advance to the State Finals in Bloomington.

The 1921 team was considered the school's first powerhouse. Led by Roy Burris and Claude Itskin, the team finished the regular season at 22-2. The team's average margin of victory of 25.8 points is still a school record, and they even recorded a shutout with a 53-0 whitewash of Odon.

A great season ended in controversy when Sullivan upset Washington in the sectional finals. Amazingly, WHS coach A.O. Fulkerson had to pay to get into the game and was not allowed to sit on the team's bench. The refereess were members of the Sullivan Booster Club, and there was still 1:30 left in the game when the officials called the game with Sullivan leading 15-14. In the local newspaper, Herbert Harris stated that the Sullivan players were allowed to "pile on the Washington players at will" and that the situation "should be fully investigated by the officers of the state high school association."

The 1925 team, under new coach Harry Hunter, also lost only twice during the season, both to Vincennes. Behind junior Virgil Beadles and Hollis Holland, the team won the Bedford Sectional and Bloomington Regional. The tournament drawing placed Washington and Vincennes in opposite brackets for a possible rematch in the State Finals, but Washington was beaten in one semi-final by eventual champion Frankfort and Vincennes lost in the other.

The following season, the WHS hoopsters had another good year but were ousted by their arch-nemesis Vincennes in the tournament. Though the team didn't make it out of the regional, the 1925-'26 season was a significant one in several ways. First, a young coach named Burl Friddle was hired out of college and sent to a six-week training school at the University of Illinois with the specific goal of winning a State title.

The team would also be decked out in new uniforms for the season, and to complement the new look, Friddle met with the team to vote on a new nickname. In years past, the school had used the unofficial nickname the 'Old Gold and Black', the school colors. The name 'Hatchets' was taken from a term used often by Edward G. Brouillette, a local sportswriter.

In addition to the new duds and a new nickname, the school also opened a new 4,300-seat gymnasium for the '25-'26 season, and the first game played there, on November 6th, 1925, showcased a young player from Martinsville named John Wooden.

In 1926, the Hatchets fell to Vincennes in the regional, and the following three years WHS made it to the 16-team State Finals before being eliminated. In 1927, Coach Friddle's boys fell to Ft. Wayne Central in the first round, and in '28, John Wooden's Martinsville squad took out the Hatchets 19-13 in the quarterfinals. The 1928-'29 team, led by sophomore Dave DeJernett and junior Ed 'Jingles' Engelhart, became the first Washington team to reach the Final Four before bowing to Indianapolis Tech 31-18. Coach Friddle was the first WHS coach to stay longer than three years, and with his stability as the leader and a strong returning group, the Hatchets were ready to make some history.

The 1941 Washington State champs. Front Row (L-R): Pete Wininger, Calvin Thomas, Jim Riffey, Art Grove, Bob 'Jug' Donaldson, Charlie Harmon. Back Row (L-R): Head coach Marion Crawley, Leroy 'Hook' Mangin, Forrest Crane, John 'Deacon' DeJernett, Bill Harmon, Garland Raney, Carl Boger (mgr.). This team featured five future Indiana Basketball Hall of Famers: Grove, Riffey, Mangin, Charlie Harmon and Marion Crawley. (Photo courtesy of hatchets.net.)

Marion Crawley 1942. (Photo courtesy of hatchets.net.)

Led by Engelhart and DeJernett, the 1929-'30 Hatchets completed a sparkling 21-1 regular season. With five more wins in the sectional and regional, Coach Friddle's boys were representing Washington in the State Finals for the ninth time in fourteen years.

A crucial game in the Finals came against Friddle's alma mater, Franklin, in the quarterfinals. Friddle was a member of Franklin's 'Wonder Five' that captured State titles in 1920 and '21. After a tight defensive battle, DeJernett hit two pressure-packed free throws with thirty seconds remaining to give the Hatchets a 12-11 victory.

After a 35-17 shellacking of Connersville in the semis, WHS was ready to face powerful Muncie Central for the championship. Since the game was still played with a jump ball after each basket, the Bearcats were considered favorites because of their 6'6 center, Jack Mann. Trailing 14-12 at the half, Friddle challenged the 6'3 DeJernett by stating that, if Big Dave could beat Mann on the tips, the Hatchets would win the game. DeJernett delivered, and the Hatchets came away with a 32-21 win.

The 1929-'30 Washington team had captured the school's first State championship and had recorded the best record in school history, 31-1. Englehart, DeJernett and Eugene Gilmore represented WHS on the All-State team, and Coach Burl Friddle had become the first person to play for and coach an Indiana State champion.

'BIG DAVE' DEJERNETT

A 1931 WHS graduate, Big Dave DeJernett led the Hatchets to the 1930 State title and was named All-State three times. According to "Hatchets.net", when Washington won the State title, it made DeJernett "the first black basketball player to win an undisputed state title in Indiana (and probably the nation)."

DeJernett went on to earn nine letters at Indiana Central College (now the University of Indianapolis) in basketball, track and football. After graduating in 1935, he played semi-pro basketball for the Muncie Monarchs and later played pro ball for the New York Renaissance, Chicago Crusaders and Harlem Globetrotters.

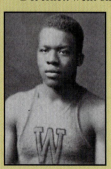

(Photo courtesy of hatchets.net.)

DeJernett was inducted into the Indiana Basketball Hall of Fame in 1976.

ROY BURRIS

Roy Burris was a member of the 1920-'21 Hatchets team that finished 22-3. In December of 2007, Burris was recognized as the new record holder of the State Tournament single-game scoring record, with a 58-point performance against Paxton. (Steve Alford of New Castle was thought to have held the scoring record with 57 points.)

Burris was Washington's all-time scoring leader for 44 years, with at least 1,124 points (some scoring stats are missing), and he was the second player in Indiana history to crack the 1,000-point mark. He was also the first WHS player to score more than 500 points in a season.

After graduation, Burris moved on to Indiana State, where he was a three-sport star and a member of the school's hall of fame. After college, he played four seasons of minor league baseball as a speedy centerfielder. After his stint in baseball, he became a starting guard for the Firestone Non-Skids, a semi-pro team from Akron, Ohio that won the 1933 National Industrial Championship.

The following year, the school was pumped up after its championship season, and a game was scheduled with the mythical national champs from Athena, Texas. Washington's Wesley Gorsage sealed the 28-26 victory for the Hatchets by scoring the last three points in the game. With DeJernett still leading the way, Washington knocked off Vincennes in the regional finals and again were headed north for the State Finals. Their dream of a repeat was derailed, however, when they fell to the Muncie Central Bearcats in the quarterfinals. The Hatchets finished the '30-'31 season with an impressive 24-6 record, and Big Dave DeJernett was named first team All-State for the third year in a row.

The next four seasons were disappointing for the Hatchets, as their teams did not survive the sectionals and Coach Friddle decided to leave after the 1934-'35 season. The 1935-'36 season opened under a new coach, Tom Rea, who had compiled an impressive record at nearby Jasper High School. There were also several changes in the basketball landscape over the next two seasons. In '34-'45, Washington became a member of the prestigious SIAC, and the State Tournament was reduced from sixteen teams to four, with regionals and semi-states much the same as they are today. In 1935-'36, the game itself was changed when the center jump was eliminated.

Tom Rea coached only one season at Washington, and his replacement, Wendel Walker, had little success for the next two years. After a 6-20 season in 1937-'38, spirits were low in Hatchet Land, but it wouldn't be long before WHS would get back to their winning ways.

The first step was taken when Washington was able to lure Coach Marion Crawley away from Greencastle for the 1938-'39 season. With a starting lineup of four juniors and super soph. Leroy 'Hook' Mangin, Washington put together a respectable 12-11 record and came within one point of making another trip to the State Finals.

In Crawley's second season, 1939-'40, the Hatchets rattled off eighteen straight wins at one point and won the SIAC with an 8-0 record. After winning the Washington Sectional and Jasper Regional, WHS came back from a 20-7 deficit in the Vincennes semifinals (semistate) to pull out a 31-30 win over Bloomington in the afternoon. That evening, sophomore guard Art Grove was sidelined for most of the game and the Hatchets lost a 20-19 heartbreaker to Mitchell to finish the season at 25-5. With Crawley calling the shots and a strong crew returning, the Hatchets were poised for another run.

After a workmanlike regular season in 1940-'41, hopes were high going into the tournament. Behind the scoring barrage of 'Hook' Mangin, the Hatchets finished off Ray Eddy's Madison Cubs 39-33 in the State Finals to finish their season at 27-5 with the school's second State title. Mangin and Charles Harmon were selected to the All-State team, and, amazingly, four of the WHS starters were later elected to the Indiana Basketball Hall of Fame: Mangin, Harmon, Grove and Jim Riffey. After the school's first championship in 1930, they couldn't repeat, but with Grove, Harmon and Riffey returning, anything short of another title would not do.

Washington opened the '41-'42 season ranked #1 in the state, and they justified that status by knocking off their first fifteen foes. After a one-point loss to Evansville Central, the Hatchets ran the table in the regular season to finish atop the SIAC at 11-1. WHS breezed through the sectional and then nipped Jasper 27-24 to take the regional behind Harmon and Riffey, who had ten points each.

COACH BURL FRIDDLE

Burl Friddle was a member of Franklin High School's 'Wonder Five' that won the 1920 and 1921 State Championships. From there, he went on to lead Franklin College to an undefeated season and a national title in 1923.

Friddle continued his winning ways when he was hired by A.O. Fulkerson to take over the Washington High School basketball program for the 1925-'26 season. In eleven seasons, he led WHS to 192 wins and the school's first State championship in 1930.

After moving to Ft. Wayne South, Friddle captured another State title in 1938. In 1943 and '44, he coached two Washington alumni, Charles Harmon and Art Grove, who were part of the 1943 Toledo team who finished second in the NIT, the most prestigious post-season tournament in the nation during that era.

Friddle was inducted into the Indiana Basketball Hall of Fame in 1969.

JAMES RIFFEY

James Riffey led the Hatchets to the 1942 State title and was a member of the 1942 All-State team. After serving three years in the Army Airborne in World War II, he headed for Tulane University, where he was a four-year starter at center from 1946-'50. He scored 1,179 points during his career with the Green Wave and was an All-SEC selection three times.

Jim spent one year with the NBA's Ft. Wayne Pistons before coaching for fifteen years in Louisville and Battle Creek, Michigan.

(Photo courtesy of hatchets.net.)

Riffey was inducted into the Tulane Hall of Fame in 1986 and the Indiana Basketball Hall of Fame in 1994.

LEO 'CRYSTAL' KLIER

Leo Klier graduated from Washington High School in 1940 at the age of sixteen. After graduation, Klier worked on the railroad so that he could follow his brother Gene to Notre Dame. Young Leo set single-season records for the Irish in both 1943-'44 and 1945-'46 by averaging 5.4 and 7.9 points per game respectively.

Kentucky coach Adolph Rupp gave Klier the nickname 'Crystal' when he stated that if Klier was in the game, the outcome was "crystal clear."

Klier was named a first team All-American in '44 and '46 while at Notre Dame, the years being separated because of a year spent in the Navy during World War II.

After graduating in 1946, Leo joined another former Hatchet, Woody Norris, playing for the Indianapolis Kautskys. In 1948, he became the first former Hatchet to play in the NBA when he played with the Ft. Wayne Zollner Pistons.

CHARLES 'CHUCK' HARMON

Charles Harmon was a star on Washington High School's back-to-back basketball State championship teams in 1941 and 1942. Harmon played baseball and basketball at Toledo and then, in the summer of 1947, he played for the Indianapolis Clowns of the old Negro League under the alias 'Charley Fine'. A month later, he signed a minor league contract with the St. Louis Browns. Although he hit over .300 for five seasons, he couldn't break through the major league color barrier. In April of 1954, Harmon got the call and became the first black player in Cincinnati Reds history.

For years, Washington little leaguers played their games on Harmon Field. When new fields were built, the city named the street leading the fields Harmon Drive.

(Photo courtesy of hatchets.net.)

Charles Harmon was inducted into the Indiana Basketball Hall of Fame in 1989 and the Indiana Baseball Hall of Fame in 1995.

JULIE HELM

Julie Helm was a 1995 Indiana All-Star and won the IHSAA Mental Attitude Award at the State Finals. She ranks #1 in most of the Washington Hatchets' offensive categories, including career points (2,236), career average (23.8) and career assists (643), to name a few. Her 2,236 career points ranks #8 on Indiana's all-time list.

After graduation in 1995, Julie left for the University of Missouri. She finished her career as the #3 scorer in Lady Tigers history with 1,925 points, a 16.3 four-year average. She also ranked in the top five in Missouri history in field goals (687), 3-pointers (123), 3-point percentage (.367) and free throw percentage (.798).

(Photo courtesy of hatchets.net.)

STEVE BOUCHIE

The lone returning starter from the 1978-'79 Washington Hatchets, Steve Bouchie, led his team to an 18-9 record and to the finals of the Evansville Semi-state. He finished his career with 1,311 points (still third in school history) and 842 rebounds, still a school record. The 6'8 Bouchie scored 31 points and had a school record 23 rebounds in a 53-52 win in the afternoon round of the semi-state.

For his efforts, Bouchie was named Indiana's Mr. Basketball, the first ever from southwestern Indiana, and was named a *Parade* All-American. After graduating, Steve played for Bob Knight and was a member of the 1981 NCAA champion Indiana Hoosiers.

Bouchie's son, Bryan, was a member of the 2005 State championship team from Washington and transferred to the University of Evansville from Valparaiso in 2008.

(Photo courtesy of hatchets.net.)

In the Vincennes Semifinal, Washington avenged their only loss of the season with a win over Central and then bombed Bedford 37-20 for the title. At the State Finals, the Hatchets knocked off Frankfort 42-32 in the afternoon and then finished off Muncie Burris 24-8 to win the school's third State championship. The repeat was complete.

Three Hatchet players, DeJernett, Riffey and Grove, were named to the *Indianapolis Star*'s All-State team, and Riffey and Harmon were named Indiana All-Stars. The Hatchets as a team were ranked #1 the whole season and were a mere one point from a perfect season. Marion Crawley's 1941-'42 Washington team finished the season 30-1 and were only the third team in Indiana history to win back-to-back State titles. (The others were Lebanon in 1917 and 1918 and Franklin in 1920, '21 and '22).

The Washington Hatchets ended a remarkable run in 1942, winning three State titles in thirteen years. Following the '42 championship, Marion Crawley would head north to coach at Lafayette Jeff, after a $300 salary dispute with WHS officials. Crawley would win two more titles during his 25 years at Jeff, but it would be 62 years before the Hatchets would reach the mountaintop again.

Several coaches assumed control of the program over the years, but with relatively little success, and for many years, the Hatchets had trouble getting past the sectional. In 1944, history was made when WHS defeated Washington Catholic in an all-Washington sectional final. Three years later, Washington Catholic made history again when they became the first parochial school to win a sectional.

Though many of the Washington teams struggled, there were some excellent players who wore the gold and black during the 62-year drought, however. In the late '50s, John Combs, Bill McCoy and Bud Garland led an upset of powerful Plainville in the sectional. In 1960, Sam Alford and Bob Miles took Washington to the regional championship game. Alford earned fourteen letters at WHS and then played at Franklin College, where he led the nation in free throw accuracy his senior year. He later won 452 games as a high school coach and coached his son Steve when he was named Mr. Basketball in 1983.

In the early '60s John Helm and Jerry Flake, 'the Dynamic Duo', set a school record as a tandem by averaging 40.9 points per game (Flake averaged 21.5 and Helm averaged 19.4). The record would stand until Craig Neal and Tom Bouchie broke it in 1983, when they averaged 43.3.

In 1966, the magnificent Hatchet House was opened and Jeff Chambers scored the first points in a 75-68 win over Springs Valley in the 7,090-seat arena.

1978 was a strange year for Indiana Basketball and the Hatchets, as the IHSAA regionals were postponed for two weeks due to a coal strike. As a result, the IHSAA permitted its 64 sectional champions to schedule two games among themselves in the meantime to keep them game-ready. Washington defeated Ben Davis at Hinkle Fieldhouse and Scottsburg at home.

In the '78 regional, the Hatchets disposed of Bloomington 53-46 at the Hatchet House and then demolished Paoli 82-44 behind Steve Bouchie and John Brown, who each tallied 24 points.

In the Evansville Semi-state, WHS defeated Scottsburg for the second time in a few days, setting up a final against Terre Haute South that would go down in Hatchets history as one of its most infamous disasters. With only one minute to play and Washington leading 53-46, anything that could've gone wrong did, and Terre Haute South scored the final nine points to eliminate the Hatchets. The '77-'78 team still ranks as one of the school's best and still holds the record for consecutive wins with 25. It is also the only Hatchet team to produce three single-season 400-point scorers. (Brown-575, Bouchie-476 and Steve Miller-404).

1979 was another historic year for WHS basketball. With Bouchie as the only returning starter, the Hatchets finished the regular season with a lukewarm 12-8 record. Six of the losses, however, took place while Bouchie was injured, and when tourney time rolled around, the 6'8 star would make his name known far and wide.

After leading WHS to the sectional title with 29 points and 10 rebounds in a 52-49 win over the Loogootee Lions, Bouchie led his team to easy wins over Bedford North-Lawrence and Southridge to win the Washington Regional.

At the Evansville Semi-state, Bouchie was spectacular as he scored the winning bucket with eight seconds left to defeat Scottsburg 53-52 in the afternoon. The senior was dominant inside throughout the game, scoring 31 points and hauling in a school record 23 rebounds.

Although the Hatchets lost in the semi-state final to Terre Haute South, with Steve Bouchie having foul problems, Bouchie finished the season with a scoring average of 27 points, and averaged 15 rebounds per game. His efforts would earn him the title of Indiana's Mr. Basketball, and he became not only the first Hatchet, but the first player from southwestern Indiana to wear the #1 jersey.

The early 1980s were a showcase for Hatchets star Craig Neal. Nicknamed 'the Noodle' for his slender build, Neal and running mate Tom Bouchie led Washington to a 25-2 record in 1982-'83 and another semi-state finals appearance. Neal was named to the All-State team and set several records that still stand today: single season points (745); single season scoring average (27.6); and career scoring average (20.0). His 1,440 career points were a record until Luke Zeller surpassed him in 2005.

Although Zeller is too recent to be called a 'Local Legend', he certainly is a legend-in-the-making. Under the leadership of Coach Dave Omer, Zeller played the lead role in a drama that is all too familiar to Hoosier basketball fans. In the championship game of the 2005 3A State Finals, Plymouth clawed their way from a twelve point deficit in the fourth quarter to force overtime. When a timeout was called by Washington with 1.8 seconds left, Washington trailed the Pilgrims by a single point and the Hatchets were inbounding the ball from under their own basket. According to reports, the 7'0 Zeller looked at Omer and said, "Get me the ball and I'll score." The words, eerily similar to those spoken by Jimmy Chitwood in the classic sports movie *Hoosiers*, set the stage for a Hollywood ending. After receiving a pass at midcourt from Justin Smith, Zeller let fly with a 37-foot prayer. As if taken from a script, the ball sailed true and split the twine as the buzzer sounded. Zeller finished the fairy tale season with a game in which he scored 27 points, grabbed nine rebounds and passed out a finals record eleven assists. As a result of his heroics, 'Cool Hand Luke' was named the state's Mr. Basketball. Ironically, Zeller's co-star during the 2005 drama was 6'0 teammate Bryan Bouchie, whose father, Steve Bouchie, was the only other southwestern Indiana player to have been named Mr. Basketball. To add to the saga, Luke's younger brother, Tyler, also earned the title of Mr. Basketball in 2008, giving Washington High School the only three Mr. Basketballs in southwestern Indiana history.

Washington High School has been a formidable basketball presence on both the local and state levels, and the school has distinguished itself as one of the elite programs in the area. The Hatchets have produced seven Indiana All-Stars, three NBA players and eleven members of the Indiana Basketball Hall of Fame. In addition, Washington has won 42 sectional titles (#1 in the area and #14 statewide) and made thirteen trips to the State Finals.

If championships are the ultimate criterion of success, then Washington's fans should be proud, because no southwestern Indiana school, and only two teams in the entire state (Muncie Central-8 and Marion-7), can match the four State titles won by the Washington Hatchets. From the early days in a rented gym at Zinkan's Hall to the Hatchet House to the miracle shot at Conseco Fieldhouse, Washington High School has forged a basketball tradition that has spanned more than a century.

BOSSE GOES BACK-TO-BACK IN '44 & '45

While war was raging across the pond in the early 1940s, a group of local teenagers were preparing to pursue a dream that had begun when they were barely old enough to bounce a ball.

In the fall of 1941, seven apprehensive freshmen first walked the halls of Bosse High School looking forward to the winter when they could don the scarlet and gray as members of the Bulldog basketball program. Most of them had worked on their games under the tutelage of a persistent father who had recognized their potential long before they would. The group, complemented by players in the classes ahead and behind them, would help Bosse accomplish a feat only four Indiana schools had achieved previously and would perform well enough to place four members of the team in the Indiana Basketball Hall of Fame.

When the season rolled around in the winter of 1941, the Bosse coaching staff consisted of head coach Harry King, assistant Arad McCutchan and freshman coach Herman Keller. Most of the boys played freshman ball under Keller, but two of them, Julius 'Bud' Ritter and Bryan 'Broc' Jerrel, were moved to the upper levels. Bosse's last really successful team was the '38-'39 team that featured such players as Jim Myers and Charlie Rayburn, but that team lost in the State semi-finals to eventual champion Frankfort in the afternoon game. Bosse fans had gotten a taste of success, and the freshman class of '41-'42 had them salivating over the prospects for the future.

In 1942, Coach King was called into the service and Coach McCutchan inherited the head coaching position. In '43, Arad McCutchan also answered the call of his country by joining the Navy, leaving Herman Keller as the heir to Bosse's basketball program. When Keller had left Boonville to join the Bulldogs' staff, he thought his head coaching days were over, and as he made plans for the '43-'44 season, the reluctant coach had no idea that he and his boys were on a collision course with destiny.

As the '43-'44 season progressed, the Bulldogs looked like anything but potential State champs. Besieged by sickness and injuries, Bosse finished the regular season with a meager 9-7 record, but the underdog Bulldogs entered the tournament at full strength and clinched the sectional with a 49-31 win over Lincoln.

As was his style, Coach Keller seldom played more than six or seven players, and each team member accepted the strategy and played his role. The usual starting lineup consisted of guards Jerrel and 5'10" Jack Matthews, forwards Norris Caudell and Gene

---

Bosse's 1944 State champion Bulldogs hold their individual trophies in celebration. Front Row (L-R): Gene Schmidt, Norris Caudell, Bud Ritter, Bill Holman. Second Row (kneeling L-R): Erwin Scholz, Don Tilley. Back Row (L-R): Broc Jerrel, Gene Whitehead, Orvel Kilpatrick (asst. coach), Jack Mathews, Herman Keller (head coach) and Norm McCool. (Photo courtesy of Broc Jerrel.)

Schmidt (both 6'3), and the 6'4 Ritter at center. Norm McCool (5'11) was the first sub on the frontline, and Gene Whitehead (6'0) filled in for Jerrel and Matthews.

After the under-rated Bulldogs captured the regional with wins over Dale (38-22) and Boonville (43-35) and the semi-finals ('semi-state') with wins over Mooresville (46-33) and Washington (40-34), the boys prepared to head to Indy, a trip that was only a pipedream a few years earlier.

One might say that a few of the '43-'44 Bosse players had been programmed for success through the influences of a father with a vision. From the time he was young, Broc Jerrel had listened carefully as his father, Rush, spent long hours talking and teaching sports. The young Jerrel, though small in stature, would evolve into a sleight-of-hand artist on the court with skills honed from dribbling blindfolded under his father's watchful eye.

Rush Jerrel also helped develop future Bosse teammates Bud Ritter, Norm McCool and Erwin 'Podjo' Scholz in their early years. On his days off from his job as a railway postal carrier, Rush would oversee the boys' progress in both basketball and baseball. The elder Jerrel, a former player at Franklin College, believed in athletics, and he believed sincerely that these boys could win a State title. "He lived for us to win the State championship," Broc recalled, "and he worked at it every day."

Ten-year-olds Bryan 'Broc' Jerrel (left), Julius 'Bud' Ritter (center) and Erwin 'Podjo' Scholz look to the future. (Photo courtesy of Broc Jerrel.)

Broc also remembers trips to the State Finals with his father and best friend Bud Ritter. They saw Washington win a State championship in 1942 and made other trips when they were younger. On one trip to Indy in 1938, Broc remembers when his father ushered Broc and Bud into Butler Fieldhouse on the Sunday after the Finals. Though "there were no magic words said," the boys got the message as they took in the ambience of the cavernous structure and shot at netless rims left over from the celebration the night before. Though Rush was a man of few words, his actions spoke volumes, and the boys understood that it was their mission to return to Indy someday and bring home a championship.

On March 18th, 1944, Rush's vision was realized, although not in the confines of Butler Fieldhouse. With World War II heating up, the fieldhouse was being used by the military, so the 1944 State Finals were moved to the Fairgrounds Coliseum. Once again the underdogs, Bosse came from ten points down in the afternoon game to knock off LaPorte 41-38. Jerrel, the team's top scorer during the season, led the way with 17, followed by Ritter's 13.

In the finals, the Bulldogs faced Kokomo, who had knocked off favored Anderson earlier. Behind a combined 21 points by Jerrel and Norris Caudell, the Bulldogs fulfilled expectations with a 39-35 victory, giving the school its first State title. In the book *Hoosier Hysteria*, author Bob Williams eloquently summed up the victory and the Bulldogs' season saying, "Bosse used a precision passing game the likes of which had never been seen before in any State Tournament."

Bosse's players re-acted to the win in the same mature manner in which they had conducted themselves from the beginning. There were no showy celebrations or index fingers raised to proclaim their #1 status, for that was not their style. "We weren't that type of players," said Broc Jerrel matter-of-factly. "We just won the State championship. That's all we did."

Although the Bulldogs were not big on tooting their own horn, they had gained the respect of fans around the state, both as individuals and as a team. The supporting cast were praised for their contributions: Schmidt as a rebounder, Matthews and Whitehead for their ballhandling and defensive skills, and Caudell and McCool for their rebounding and scoring. The team's two stars, Jerrel and Ritter, drew even more accolades and were highly respected at home also.

Bryan Jerrel was a slight 5'8, 140-pound fireball who could drive opposing teams crazy. His nickname 'Broc' began as 'Brick' because of his red hair, then morphed into 'Broc' and stuck. Broc's ballhandling skills both amazed and infuriated the crowds as he pounded the ball through his legs, each adorned with a leather knee pad. "Broc Jerrel, in the State Tournament, just wowed everybody," said Bruce Lomax, an Evansville legend himself. "I never saw anybody bounce the ball between their legs or behind their back before. He'd dribble so low and they'd try to guard him, and he'd come up and take off on you. He put on a show! They'd try to put two guys on him, and that was a mistake because right then and there, the ball was out of his hands and somebody was wide open."

Though Broc learned the fundamentals from his father, his flashy style was influenced by a player he had watched a few years earlier. "There was one guy who played before Bob Cousy and everybody,"

'Broc' 'The Flash' Jerrel. (Photo courtesy of the Indiana Basketball Hall of Fame.)

Broc explained. "I was down at Central Gym one night watching Washington play. Gene Latham (from Central) was guarding Art Grove (of Washington), and Latham was trying to steal the ball. Grove put it behind his back, and I thought, 'I'm going to do that!'" Jerrel worked hard after that to perfect the move, and his behind-the-back dribble and beautiful two-handed set-shot would serve him well at Bosse.

Over the years, Jerrel was dubbed 'The Flash' for his style and 'The Brain' for his leadership on the floor. During that era, teams were not allowed to leave the floor for timeouts, so players were responsible for strategy and motivation as each team met in the free throw circle. Jerrel and Ritter often assumed leadership roles during those moments, although teammate Norm McCool admits that occasionally they would lighten things up by pointing out attractive ladies in the crowd.

McCool also witnessed the wrath often bestowed on Jerrel because of his flamboyant style. He was known to fraternize with the crowd during warm-ups, and he would goad opponents during games. "Everybody (opponents) hated him," McCool explained. "He was one of those kinds of kids, a little-bitty, red-headed kid. Opponents just hated him, and he took advantage of that. He was the best ballhandler I ever saw. You just couldn't take the ball away from him. A lot of people thought he was a showoff, but he certainly wasn't. He was using it for a reason."

McCool also had tremendous respect for Bulldog center Bud Ritter. "Bud and Broc were as good of passers as I've ever seen," McCool said. "If you got open, they would get you the ball. Those two were the stars, no question. The rest of us just did our jobs or whatever was needed. I thought Bud Ritter was the best high school center I ever saw, including up to today."

With the praise flowing, the 1944 Bulldogs had impressed the entire state, and the scary thing was that nearly the entire team would be returning for the following season. But this time they wouldn't be underdogs.

Heading into the '44-'45 season, the only regular lost to graduation was Gene Schmidt. His spot in the starting lineup would be filled by Norm McCool, and Matthews would again back up the guards while 6'6 junior Bill Butterfield would sub on the frontline. With a State title on their resumé, the Bulldogs entered the new year with a newly-found swagger.

"We had so much more confidence our senior year," recalled Broc Jerrel. When I see Tom Brady (the New England Patriots Super Bowl quarterback) take the field, we had a similar attitude."

The confident crew completed their season ranked #1 in the state after battling Jasper for the top spot throughout the year. The Bulldogs lost only two games during the season, finishing 35-2. One loss was to Jeffersonville (27-23) after Bosse had opened the game with a 16-2 lead and inexplicably scored only seven points in the last three quarters. The second loss was a nip-and-tuck affair with Central, a team they had trounced earlier in the year. With Ritter out with the flu and Jerrel only playing the second half because of illness, the Bears hung around and won on a late shot by Bob Kohlmeyer.

In the tournament, the Bulldogs' date with history was almost derailed before it started, as Memorial battled Bosse before falling in the second game of the sectional 38-37. After avenging their earlier loss to Central with a 50-35 win in the finals, the Bulldogs were back on track to make another run. They breezed through the regional with wins over Boonville (49-37) and Tell City (77-44). A win over Bedford (44-34) in the afternoon game of the semi-finals set up a game with #2-ranked Jasper at IU's old fieldhouse. The game proved anticlimactic, however, as Bosse jumped out to a 15-0 lead and cruised 55-32. With seven seniors leading the way, Bosse would play the favorite's role for its encore appearance in the Fairgrounds Coliseum.

The Bulldogs' toughest challenge in the Finals was the afternoon game against Indianapolis Broad Ripple. Bosse trailed 20-14 at halftime, even after a half-court miracle shot by Jerrel at the buzzer. Late in the third, Butterfield scored on a tip-in followed by scores from Ritter and McCool, and a bucket by Jerrel with little time left knotted the score at 21-21 going into the final period.

In the fourth, McCool scored on a third effort to give Bosse its first lead, and two key out-of-bounds plays were the difference. Leading 36-31, Bosse put the ball in the deep freeze using Jerrel's dribbling and the team's precise passing to put the Rockets away 37-35.

In the championship game, the Bulldogs had an easier time, as they carved out a routine 46-36 victory over South Bend Riley. Ritter led Bosse with 14, followed closely by McCool's 13. Jerrel produced his typical steady effort controlling the floor and contributing 8 points. The confident Bulldogs had managed to complete a challenge that only four other schools had done before, winning back-to-back State titles, joining Wingate (1913 & '14), Lebanon ('17 & '18), Franklin ('20, '21 & '22) and Washington ('41 & '42) as the only programs to accomplish the feat.

When the conquering heroes returned home, Evansville had experienced severe flooding, but the team was still greeted by a huge throng of well-wishers, including Evansville mayor Manson Reichert, who even left his sickbed to attend the festivities.

Looking back, Broc Jerrel realizes that he was fortunate just to be a part of Bosse's history-making season. Jerrel, who was older than his teammates, had been called in January of 1945 to serve in the military. Fortunately for Broc, he had yet to complete a class called 'American Problems' that was required for graduation. As a result, he was granted a deferment and allowed to finish the season.

Broc also suffered serious back problems in January of the '44-'45 season and had to rely on a local chiropractor to save the day. "Doc Byrne adjusted me, and I walked out like new," Jerrel recalled. "He would adjust me between games during the tourney, and he worked on me in Bloomington (for the semi-finals) and at Indianapolis. If it hadn't been for him, I wouldn't have been able to play."

Since the war was winding down, Jerrel was not called into the service right away and was able to graduate with his classmates.

'Bud' Ritter (Photo courtesy of the Indiana Basketball Hall of Fame.)

The same seven young men who had entered Bosse four years earlier were leaving school as the most successful basketball class in school history. The seven seniors: Jerrel, Ritter, Schmidt, Caudell, Matthews, McCool and Erwin 'Podjo' Scholz would soon part ways, but the bond between them will last forever.

The reluctant coach Herman Keller stepped down to the reserve coach position when Harry King returned to Bosse, but his players give him credit for getting the job done. "He was one of the nicest gentlemen I ever knew," said Norm McCool. "He and Arnold Kilpatrick (Keller's assistant) put together a system, and we made it work." Keller, a four-year letterman during his years as a student at Oakland City College, served on the IHSAA Board of Control in his later years and was inducted into the IHSAA Hall of Fame in 1992.

Five members of the '45 champions, Ritter, Caudell, McCool, Matthews and Whitehead, were enticed by Purdue coach Ward 'Piggy' Lambert to join the Boilermakers' program. When asked how it came about that five players from Bosse all chose Purdue, Norm McCool had a simple explanation: "Bud Ritter was our leader, our John Wayne. We all looked up to Bud, and he talked everybody into going up there." Matthews and Whitehead never played varsity ball regularly, but Matthews helped make a little history at Purdue when he started a varsity game along with Ritter, Caudell, McCool and senior Charlie Haag, meaning that the entire Purdue starting lineup consisted of Bosse grads.

Norm McCool lettered as a freshman at Purdue but finished his education at Evansville College before joining the workforce. He and his wife Maxey (McGowan), who was a Bosse cheerleader and football queen, settled in Evansville, where Norm served as the president of the Coca Cola Company of Evansville until his retirement.

Gene Schmidt, Bosse's lone senior on the '44 team, fashioned a fine career at Texas Christian University. Gene captained the Horned Frogs for three seasons and was voted the team's MVP three times. Because his career was interrupted by the service, he became the only five-year letter winner in the history of the Southwest Conference. He was also the only TCU player in history to score in 100 straight games.

Norris Caudell was named to the 1945 Indiana All-Star team and was a two-time All-State honoree. At Purdue, Caudell was a four-year varsity player and was a team captain as a senior. He led the Boilermakers twice in rebounding and was the team's #3 scorer. He also played four successful seasons for the Caterpillars of the national AAU league.

Broc Jerrel left for the service after graduation but received furlows to return as the #2 man on the Indiana All-Stars. In 1947, he attended Texas Christian and played for two years as the team's top assist man and #3 scorer. When a new coach came in who didn't appreciate his style, Broc left and played a season with Peoria Caterpillar before returning home to finish his education at Evansville College. After earning a Masters degree from Evansville, he taught school for four years in Henderson before settling into a career working with the Indiana Superintendent of Public Instruction.

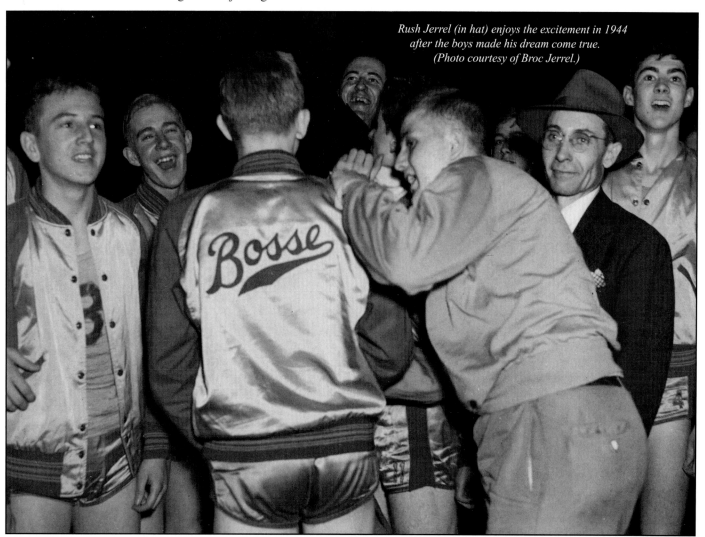

Rush Jerrel (in hat) enjoys the excitement in 1944 after the boys made his dream come true. (Photo courtesy of Broc Jerrel.)

The 1944 Bosse cheerleaders (L-R): Delores Wingfield, Maxey McGowan, Earl Harp, Joyce Gardner, Norma Ledgerwood. (Photo courtesy of Broc Jerrel.)

Bud Ritter was a three-year letterman and two-year starter at Purdue but never experienced the success he had in high school because of his lack of size for the position he played. His greatest accomplishments after high school came as a coach. He began his career in Peru, Indiana before heading to Madison in 1954. While at Madison, Ritter compiled a 227-90 record (72%) and won 13 sectionals, four regionals and one semi-state. During one stretch, Madison didn't lose a regular season game for three complete years, winning 61 straight regular season games. His closest attempt at a State title was his 1961-'62 team, led by future Evansville Aces star Larry Humes. In a strange twist of fate, the team that knocked out Ritter's Cubs was the Bosse Bulldogs, led by Jim Myers, who would go on to lead Bosse to another State championship in 1962.

The '44 and '45 Bosse teams left their mark on the local basketball landscape, and four of the players, Ritter, Jerrel, Caudell and Schmidt eventually joined Coach Keller in the Indiana Basketball Hall of Fame. The team's inspirational leader, Rush Jerrel, died unexpectedly of pancreatic cancer only seven years after the team cut down the nets in 1945. Although his death was sudden and tragic, he did live to see his vision come true. A dream that had been planted in the minds of several young boys in a backyard in Evansville had played itself out for all the world to see.

IHSAA State Champions: BOYS BASKETBALL			
Team	Year	Record	Coach
Vincennes	1922-1923	34-1	John Adams
Washington	1929-1930	31-1	Burl Friddle
Washington	1940-1941	27-5	Marion Crawley
Washington	1941-1942	30-1	Marion Crawley
Bosse	1943-1944	19-7	Herman Keller
Bosse	1944-1945	25-2	Herman Keller
Jasper	1948-1949	21-9	Leo O'Neill
Bosse	1961-1962	26-2	Jim Myers
North	1966-1967	27-2	Jim Rausch
Vincennes Lincoln	1980-1981	26-2	'Gunner' Wyman
Tecumseh (A)	1998-1999	23-4	Kevin Oxley
Mater Dei (3A)	2003-2004	21-6	John Goebel
Washington (3A)	2004-2005	27-2	Dave Omer
Forest Park (2A)	2005-2006	25-3	Tom Beach
Washington (3A)	2007-2008	23-2	Gene Miiller

CYRIL BIRGE: A PIECE OF HOOSIER HOOPS HISTORY

When Bobby Plump held the ball and then fired the shot heard 'round the Hoosier basketball world in 1954, Jasper native Cyril Birge was only a few feet away. Although he wasn't aware of it at the time, Birge had just officiated a game that symbolized what Indiana high school basketball was all about and would later be memorialized in the blockbuster sports movie *Hoosiers*.

Nearly sixty years later, 'Cy', as he was known in the basketball community, still enjoyed reminiscing about that historic March evening when tiny Milan slew mighty Muncie Central as Plump's final fling found the bottom of the net. When asked if he realized the significance of what he had witnessed, Cy quickly answered, "No, not at the time. We just knew a small school beat a big school, then it (the legend) started growing."

At age 92 (In 2007), Cy's mind was still sharp and his memory was flawless as he recalled the game and the details that some fans may not realize. He was quick to point out that, with exception of the setting, Hinkle Fieldhouse, the real game and the movie version were quite different. As a referee during the '50s, he pointed out that he never saw wooden backboards like the ones shown in the small gyms in the movie, and the final score of the final game in the movie was much higher than the 32-30 score in the real version. He also pointed out that Milan wasn't quite the David to Muncie Central's Goliath as most people think. In fact, Milan had been to the State Finals the previous year and had lost in the semi-finals to South Bend Central.

Although Cy Birge will forever be linked to the Milan Miracle, his thirty-year career, from the late '30s to the late '60s, also made him a veritable fountain of information about the golden age of Hoosier Hysteria. In fact, he was part of a little history himself before he ever put on a striped shirt and a whistle.

Cy was born on June 20th, 1915, and he developed into a fine ballplayer during his years at Jasper High School. Although his senior class consisted of only 35 students, Coach Tom Rea was able to construct a team that was one of the best in the school's history and one that almost pulled off a 'Milan Miracle' of its own.

Jasper's 1934 team is still the only team in the town's history to win all of its scheduled games in a season. At 29-2, the team lost only in the Holiday Tourney and in the State Tournament. Coach Rea, who complied an 83% winning percentage, relied heavily on his 'Big Three', Cy, Johnny Steffen and Eddie Rottet (pronounced ROH-dee).

In '34, Jasper advanced all the way to the sixteen-team State Finals and won its first two games, defeating North Vernon 30-15 and Richmond 29-27. In the semi-finals, Jasper was leading Logansport by eight points going into the final quarter, but Logansport mounted a comeback and beat jasper 31-28 and then defeated Indianapolis Arsenal Tech 26-19 for the title.

Eddie Rottet, Cy's best friend and roommate when the team traveled, was a unanimous All-State selection, and the two were looking forward to playing college ball. But a tragic twist of fate would derail their plans and change Cy's life forever.

Cy had accepted a basketball scholarship to Purdue, and Eddie had also been offered a full ride with the Boilermakers but had opted to head to Northwestern. Although Rottet was outstanding on the court, he was also a top prospect on the baseball diamond as well, and many, including Cy, felt that Eddie would become Jasper's first major league player.

As the two looked forward to college, they both secured summer jobs working with surveyors on a highway crew. On June 30th, 1934, the boys rode on a truck back to town and felt nauseous as they headed home. The next morning, they reported to work but were sent home because of their apparent illness. Cy told Eddie good-bye, and both boys departed for their respective beds to recuperate. As the days passed, it was determined that the boys' bodies had been contaminated by drinking rancid water from a livery well while on the job.

Since there was no hospital nearby, Cy suffered at home. He lost his hair and was laid up until September. According to the doctor, he was lucky to have survived. It wasn't until he was finally up and around that he discovered the news that his friends and family were afraid to tell him. When he had said good-bye to Eddie on the morning of July 1st, it was the last time he would speak to his close friend. Eddie had not been so lucky and had passed away on August 18th.

Because of Cy's illness, he had lost his scholarship at Purdue, and the confused teenager spent some time in Louisville, then back home, and then in Detroit at different jobs. He returned to Jasper in 1938 and worked as a janitor at the school. It was at this time that he also began to referee basketball games in the area.

As his reputation allowed him to expand his scope as an official, he spent years working with an insulation company, as a tire salesman, and, finally, as a sales rep for Gus Doerner's Sporting Goods store in Jasper for twenty years before his retirement in 1985.

Cyril Birge in the old Jasper gym.
(Photo courtesy of the Evansville Courier.)

Cyril's 1934 Jasper team that lost in the State Tournament's Final Four. Seated on floor (L-R): Edwin Popp, Marty Gosman. Seated (L-R): Urban Schutz, John Steffen, Ed Rottet, Anthony Berger, Clarence Fleck. Standing (L-R): Tom Rea (head coach), Cyrinus Singer, Cyril Birge, William Carnes, Claude Miller (principal). (Photo courtesy of Cyril Birge.)

In 1934, when Cy Birge's Jasper team advanced all the way to the final four at the State Tournament, the jump ball was still used after each basket. It was only two or three years later that the rule was changed.

As Cy moved up the officiating ranks, he began working small college games (Evansville College, Butler, etc.) in 1947. He also worked his first high school regional the same year.

In those days, it was customary for officials to work only two State Final Fours before stepping aside for other referees. Cy worked semi-final games in both 1951 and '52 and assumed that his Finals experience was over. He was surprised when he got the call in 1954. He is still not sure what circumstances facilitated the situation, but he and Marvin Todd became the first two men to work more than two Final Four games when they presided over the famous battle between Milan and Muncie Central.

As Cy's reputation grew, he eventually became a Big Ten official and was fortunate enough to witness some of the all-time greats. When asked to mention a few, Cy thought for a moment and then revealed some of his fondest memories. "As many games as you do, there are just a few who stick out," he said from his home in Jasper. "Someone asked me the best player I ever saw and I said, 'If there's any better ballplayer than Oscar Robertson, it would have to be Jesus Christ himself.'"

Another memorable event for Cy occurred in 1967. Cy was summoned to Chicago to officiate a Friday night game between Illinois and UCLA. He decided to take along his wife, Antoinette, and four of his children, and he opted to drive to Vincennes to catch a passenger train to the Windy City. In the midst of a horrendous blizzard, the train slowly made its way north. During the trek, the train lost its brakes, and as the conductor coasted to a stop in Chicago, there was less than an hour before tipoff.

Having dressed on the train, Cy headed for a phone to check in. As it turned out, the game had been cancelled, so Birge and his family rode in the back of a newspaper truck to their hotel. As the effects of the snowstorm cleared, it was decided that the game would be played on Monday. The trip to Chicago had been an adventure, but the Monday night game would also be a scrapbook moment for Cy, as well.

Although Birge had worked some games for John Wooden when Wooden was a young coach at Indiana State, this was Cy's first since Wooden had begun a streak of dominance that will probably never be seen again. With UCLA destroying Illinois, Lew Alcindor (later to be called Kareem Abdul Jabbar) was taking a seat after shattering the Chicago Stadium scoring record. As Cy witnessed the ovation, he heard someone shout, "Give him (Alcindor) the game ball!"

Cy wasn't sure what the proper protocol was, but he strolled over to the big man and handed him the ball. "Nobody told me to," Cy recalled, "but I was just cocky enough to give it to him."

Through his thirty years as an official, Birge has shared the floor with many of the sport's superstars. He recalled the flamboyant Al McGuire sending him a letter every year saying, "Thanks for putting up with me," and he smiled as if he was expecting it when I asked, "Did you ever get to ref for Bobby Knight?"

"I'm glad you asked that," he replied. "Bobby and I got along real good. I was up and down the floor, and he was always sitting there on the bench just as calm as he could be. But (here's the catch!) he was the sixth man at Ohio State."

Cy went on to add that Knight was a good player and could have started for most other Big Ten schools instead of riding the bench behind Buckeye starters John Havlicek and Jerry Lucas. Cy knew the reputation Knight has with officials as a coach and explained that Knight started his career the year after Cy retired. So, he lamented never having the experience by saying, "Schucks, I never got to work with him."

As a high school referee, Cy worked during the days before consolidation and before the tiny gyms were razed under the guise of progress. He recalled the cracker box gymnasium at Dubois where the gym was upstairs and the ceiling was only five or six feet above the rim. And he fondly remembered the gym of the Winslow Eskimos that had four pot-bellied stoves in the corners, which could prove to be a hazard for a back-peddling official who forgot where he was.

Cy Birge appreciated the good fortune he had as an official, and especially his association with arguably the most memorable game in Indiana hoops history. He had become good friends with Bobby Plump through the years, as they saw each other often at shindigs to commemorate the game. Plump's standard shtick was to jokingly insinuate that Birge was bribed to throw the game in

Milan's favor by saying, "Cy, I just want to let you know that this month's check is in the mail."

A year after our interview, Cyril Birge passed away at the age of 93. He left behind nine children, 24 grandchildren, and 22 great-grandchildren. He also left behind a remarkable legacy.

Though fate thrust Cy into the spotlight in 1954, his successful career as an official was the result of his own talents. He was well-known as a referee who took the 'let em play' approach and who only called them close when the action became intentional and dangerous. Though many fans can name the teams and players that played in March of 1954, very few can name the officials, and from a referee's perspective, Cy totally understood. He cited as an example a compliment he received from a coach after an ordinary night at an ordinary Indiana high school game: "We wouldn't have known you were on the floor." And, as Cy said, "That's the way it's supposed to be."

After the historic Milan game in 1954, the next time Cy Birge saw Bobby Plump was the following year as he walked onto the Hinkle Fieldhouse floor to officiate a game. He looked up and there was the high school superstar fulfilling his duties as a lowly freshman at Butler - mopping the floor.

Bobby Plump owns a restaurant in Indianapolis called Plump's Last Shot.

THE WILDCAT WONDERS: JASPER'S 1949 STATE CHAMPS

Basketball aficionados far and wide are familiar with the tale of Bobby Plump and Milan's improbable run to the 1954 State championship, but there is a lesser-known story right here in our own backyard that rivaled even 'The Milan Miracle' in the annals of Hoosier Hysteria.

When the basketball season started in 1938, no one believed that a State title was in the cards for the Jasper Wildcats, although stories persist that there were many prayers being launched in the predominantly Catholic community. Whether those requests were answered or there were other cosmic forces in play, Jasper produced a tournament run like none other in Indiana history.

Jasper had knocked on the door once before only to have the door slammed in their faces by Logansport in the semi-finals of the 1934 tournament. The 1948-'49 Wildcats were solid but not spectacular, and they lacked a superstar like Dick Farley from nearby Winslow. What the Wildcats did have, however, was an outstanding coach who ran practices like a drill sergeant and demanded precision from his troops.

Leo Cavanaugh 'Cabby' O'Neill, a Washington, Indiana native, suffered a shoulder injury while playing football at Franklin College and then transferred to the University of Alabama, where he became a three-year star for the Crimson Tide basketball team. He began his coaching career in 1930 at tiny Epsom High School in Daviess County before heading to Montgomery in 1934 and finally to Jasper in 1939, where he and his long-time assistant Louis 'Nip' Wiechner turned the program into a perennial contender.

The '48-'49 Wildcats were a balanced group who had played together since grade school. As the season began, O'Neill searched for the right player combinations, and as the story played out, the unlikely fairy tale that would eventually be written would feature a very unlikely hero.

The Jasper 1949 State champs. Front row (L-R): Student manager Bohwert, Bill Byrd, Sam Allen, John Berg, Paul Rumbach, Ed Stenftenagel, Tom Schutz. Back row (L-R): Cabby O'Neill (head coach), Assistant Coach Wuchner, Bob White, Bill Litchfield, Dave Krodel, Jerome Stenftenagel and Principal Miller. (Photo courtesy of the Indiana Basketball Hall of Fame.)

A little man named Bobby White was somewhat of a misfit on Jasper's team. The 5'6, 135-pounder had moved to Jasper late and was not one of the 'in crowd' at school. In fact, he was somewhat of a loner and a bookworm. Although he was a savvy player and could shoot the ball, O'Neill had cut him as a freshman and sophomore, but White nagged Cabby to let him hang around and scrimmage. As a junior, White made the team but played sparingly.

As a senior in 1948, White continued to work hard but had no delusions of seeing significant playing time. But everything changed for White – and the Wildcats – after the first game of the season. Following the opening game, O'Neill made the decision to dismiss a player for disciplinary reasons, and he shocked everyone by placing White into the starting lineup for the second game. Although the 'outsider' was booed in his debut, he would eventually win the Jasper fans over and provide the missing piece Coach O'Neill was searching for.

After the Wildcats finished the regular season at 11-9, the locals laughed at their chances of advancing past the sectional, especially with powerful 17-3 Huntingburg and the 24-4 Winslow Eskimos and their superstar Dick Farley standing in the way. In the opener, Jasper made quick work of the Dubois Jeeps 56-26 and then got by the deliberate style of Holland coach Lowell McGlothin to down the Dutchmen 36-28.

In the semis, Jasper faced the conference champ and their arch-rival, Huntingburg. After trailing early in the fourth period, Jasper ended the Hunters' season with a 44-35 win to put the Wildcats in the finals against powerful Winslow.

Winslow was a heavy favorite to capture the sectional, and they looked the part when they went to the locker room with a 24-14 halftime lead. Following the break, Cabby O'Neill decided to use some psychological warfare as he was walking up the ramp to the floor. He looked at the diminutive Bobby White and proclaimed, "I want you to take it over and make it happen." As if plucked from a Hollywood script, the Wildcats roared back for the victory "on the sensational hard driving of little Bobby White," as stated in the *Daily Herald*.

In the regional, Jasper staged comebacks to pull out wins over two small schools, Shelburn (61-52) and Monroe City (57-55), and after six tournament wins, Jasper was heading to the semi-state.

At the Bloomington Semi-state, played at the old IU Fieldhouse, the Wildcats clawed their way to another victory as they topped Bedford 41-33 in the afternoon game. Against the home team Bloomington Panthers, Jasper's Bill Litchfield scored with fifteen seconds left to seal a 50-49 win, sending Jasper to the Final Four for the first time since 1934.

As Jasper prepped for the Finals, the entire state was wondering what the Dubois County school with a paltry 19-9 record was doing at the Big Dance. In the afternoon game, the familiar pattern continued, as highly favored, 26-2 Auburn led 42-36 early in the fourth quarter. But as if on cue, the Wildcats responded once again and prevailed 53-48 behind Bob White's 17 points. It was hard to imagine, but after starting the tournament three weeks earlier as one of 769 teams, there were now only two still standing, and one of them was the Jasper Wildcats. Jasper had made it to the final game of the State Tournament for the first time in school history.

As the Wildcats followed their police escort to Butler Fieldhouse, Jasper's Bill Litchfield found himself stranded at the Indianapolis Athletic Club, where the team was staying. Realizing that he had missed the team bus, Litchfield hailed a cab and arrived just in time for the opening tip. The challenge for the Wildcats in the final against powerful Madison was stopping the Cubs' talented Dee Monroe. Jasper would start in their standard 2-3 zone defense but would later switch to a box-and-one, putting Tom Schutz man-to-man on Monroe. Jasper would also try to counter Madison with a balanced offense, led by top scorer Jerome 'Dimp' Stenftenagel.

Jasper's legendary coach Cabby O'Neill.

As the game progressed, Dee Monroe was a living highlight reel, popping for 21 points against Jasper's 2-3 zone and scoring 18 points in the second quarter alone. Jasper went in at halftime leading 31-28, but O'Neill knew they had to slow Monroe down. As the second half started, Schutz shadowed Monroe while his teammates played zone, and the strategy worked. For thirteen minutes, Monroe was held to nine points until Schutz finally fouled out at the three-minute mark.

The two teams continued to trade punches, and White, Stenftenagel and Johnny Berg all hit key buckets late before Jasper held the ball to secure a 62-61 win. Dee Monroe finished the game with 36 points, a new State record, and Jasper was led by White (20 points), Stenftenagel (15) and Schutz (10).

On March 19th, 1949, the Jasper Wildcats had completed one of the craziest State championship runs in history, becoming only the second team to win State with nine losses (Anderson was the other in 1935). Following the tournament, little Bobby White, the one-time outcast who barely played until his senior year, was selected as an Indiana All-Star.

When the Wildcats returned home, they were greeted by an estimated 25,000 delirious fans at the Public Square in Jasper. Their beloved coach, Cabby O'Neill, would stay in Jasper for more than forty years. He would retire from coaching with a record of 247-76 (76.5%) and then serve as the school's athletic director for many years. In 1969, he was inducted into the Indiana Basketball Hall of Fame.

The Jasper Wildcats of 1949 defied all the odds as they battled their way into the history books, and perhaps fate did play a role. Along with the prayers and hopes from the German faithful, maybe Cabby O'Neill contributed a little Irish luck along the way also. Jasper's 1949 champions won an incredible eight straight tournament games by rising from the ashes late in the game, proving that, as Dan Scism once said in the *Evansville Courier*, "You can't beat a team that won't be beaten." Like The Little Engine that Could, Jasper had shocked the world, and if Cinderella stories are your cup of tea, then the Milan Miracle had nothing on the Wildcat Wonders of 1949.

PAUL HOFFMAN

Paul Hoffman was a 1977 inductee into the Indiana Basketball Hall of Fame for his amazing career at Jasper, Purdue and in the NBA. 'The Bear' or 'Paul the Pulverizer', as he was known to fans, set a Wildcats scoring record with 780 points between 1940 and 1943 under legendary Jasper coach Leo 'Cabby' O'Neill. In an article for the *Baltimore Sun*, O'Neill once said, "Until Oscar Robertson came along, I always thought that Paul Hoffman was the best high school player that I saw. He was a modern-type player, a good shooter and a great driver. And he had as much desire as it was humanly possible to have."

In 1943, the Indiana-Kentucky All-Star game was postponed due to World War II, preventing the two-time All-State player from becoming Jasper's first representative in the game. After high school, Hoffman took his game to Purdue, where he was selected to at least one All-American team in each of his four years there. He led the Boilermakers in scoring all four years and left as the school's all-time leading scorer. He also was named to the All-Conference team all four years, becoming the first Boilermaker to do so, and was named the MVP of the All-American All-Star game at Madison Square Garden after his senior year.

In 1947, Hoffman was the first draft pick of the Toronto Huskies of the Basketball Association of America, the forerunner of the NBA. When the Huskies folded before the season, the 6'2 Hoffman was claimed by the Baltimore Bullets. As a rookie, he helped the Bullets win the NBA championship, and after averaging 10.5 points, Hoffman became the NBA's very first Rookie of the Year. He spent three years in the NBA with the Bullets, the New York Knicks and the Philadelphia Warriors.

Paul Hoffman

DICK FARLEY

Dick Farley led Winslow High School to a four-year record of 83-8, including an undefeated season during his junior year when Winslow was upset by a Jasper team that advanced to the final game of the State Tourney. Farley, an Indiana Basketball Hall of Famer, was an Indiana All-Star in 1950 and played for Branch McCracken's 1953 national champs at IU. The 6'4" guard also played three seasons in the NBA with the Syracuse Nationals and Detroit Pistons.

Dick Farley. (Photo courtesy of Roberts Stadium.)

Gym class was the only place for girls to show off their skills in the early days. (Photo courtesy of the University of Southern Indiana archives.)

Lincoln High School cheerleaders. (Photo courtesy of the University of Southern Indiana archives.)

Decked out and ready to play.
(Photo courtesy of the University of Southern Indiana archives.)

CHAPTER TWO
1945-1965

LOCAL GIRLS HAD A LEAGUE OF THEIR OWN

In the 1940s and early 1950s, the All-American Professional Girls Baseball League made history by keeping America's pastime alive while the men were overseas fighting WWII. Seen at first as a novelty act, the women of the AAPGBL quickly proved that, given the opportunity, the girls could actually play ball. The players were memorialized in the 1992 movie *A League of Their Own*, and their contributions to the game were recognized in an exhibit at the National Baseball Hall of Fame in Cooperstown.

On a smaller scale, a similar drama played out closer to home when a handful of local women thumbed their noses at baseball purists by ignoring the skepticism and finding a place to do what they loved to do. During the war years, there were few places for athletic women to 'scratch the itch' they had for sports. Mary Lou Taylor and Virginia Mattingly were two of the women who were able to find an outlet for their desire to compete.

It all began with a gentleman named Don Wilder, a fire chief in Boonville who had two daughters, Lois and Betty, who wanted to play. Mary Lou remembers the first time she met Mr. Wilder. "He discovered me on a playground," she said from her home near Rockport. "At the time, each playground (school) had a team. He was making the rounds looking for players, and he liked what he saw. I was in the eighth grade."

Wilder found out who she was and talked to Mary Lou's father, Bill Taylor. Don was the second coach who had expressed interest in Mary Lou, and Bill Taylor chose Wilder because of his sincerity. Although Wilder's daughters didn't play, he remained loyal to the group as its coach and financial backer.

Joining Virginia and other area women, such as local sports icon Louise Owen, the girls spent their summers traveling thousands of miles to tournaments and games. "We traveled in cars," said Virginia, a left-handed-hitting third baseman, "and we always had four in the backseat. I remember one trip in a Model A Ford."

Although the ladies practiced once a week, usually at Washington Grade School, most of their games were road games because of the lack of local support. Mary Lou, the team's primary pitcher, recalled an example of how the girls were perceived by the general public. During her senior year of high school, she was going to ask permission to miss the last few days of the school year because her studies had been completed. When she told the dean of women that she wanted to leave for a softball tournament, the dean asked, "Why don't you play something that's not so strenuous, like tennis?" To Mary Lou, the question could have been translated into, "Why don't you play something more feminine?"

One of the team's first sponsors was Midwest Federal, because one of the team's players, Ruth McMillan, was a secretary there. But local support in general was lukewarm at best. "No one wanted to see us play down here," Virginia explained. "They just didn't approve of it."

In May of 1950, Mary Lou, Virginia and Louise Owen even attended open tryouts for the All-American Professional Girls

This Liberty Cab girls team captured the 1949 state championship. Front Row (L-R): Mary Lou 'Tommie' Taylor, Jeannie McCutchan, Anita Dawson, Mildred Goodman, Louise Keily (Owen). Back Row (L-R): Don Wilder (mgr.), Virginia Mattingly, Rovella Hinton, Donna Peerman, Ruth McMillan, Mary Edith 'Soup' Tharp. (Photo courtesy of Mary Lou Taylor..)

Baseball League. Shortly after the tryout, Virginia received a letter from Mr. John Rawlings of the Grand Rapid Chicks. Although Mr. Rawlings expressed interest in the girls, Louise was more devoted to her tennis and Virginia and Mary Lou were happy as teachers.

Not to be denied, the team's nucleus stayed together for several years, making regular trips to Chicago, Louisville, Indianapolis and other U.S. cities, as well as Canada. There were times when they would play against men's teams, and at one point they even played in a men's league, using men as their pitcher and catcher.

The local girls captured a remarkable nine state titles and might have made noise nationally had it not been for perennial powerhouse Peoria, who always ended the girls' run at the regional level.

Mary Lou and Virginia realize that Penny Marshall won't be making a movie about the years they spent on the ball fields as young women, but the scrapbooks and mementos they treasure tell the story just the same. For a few wonderful years, they hit the road with their friends to do what they loved the most. They didn't do it for accolades or attention; they just wanted to play ball.

LEE HAMILTON: FROM THE COURT TO THE CAPITOL

Most people know Congressman Lee Hamilton as a man who has served his Ninth District constituents for over forty years. But what they may not know is that he made quite a name for himself on the hardwood before launching a career as a public servant.

Hamilton was born in Daytona Beach, Florida on April 20th, 1931. His family first relocated to Tennessee before settling in Evansville, where Lee's father became the minister at Trinity United Methodist Church while Lee attended Wheeler School as an eighth grader.

In high school, Hamilton was a three-sport athlete, lettering in tennis, cross country and basketball. As Congressman Hamilton reflects on his high school days, he realizes that he was part of an era when high school basketball was king and when Central fans in particular had high hopes for Hamilton and his teammates.

(Photo courtesy of the Indiana Basketball Hall of Fame.)

"This was right after World War I," Hamilton explained from his office in Washington. "The NCAA and NBA were just getting underway, so all the attention was focused on the high school teams in an enormous way. The whole town of Evansville came out in droves for the games. I grew up in the atmosphere of *Hoosiers*, the movie. The focus was all on basketball, and so I lived basketball for my entire high school career.

"I had very good teammates," Hamilton continued. "We were identified early on while we were still in grade school as being a potentially good team."

Under the tutelage of coaches Glen Bretz (Hamilton's junior year) and Walter Riggs (senior year), the Bears prided themselves on great defense and a balanced attack. Joe Schwitz was the team's primary ballhandler, and Gene Southwood, who went on to star at Vanderbilt, was a remarkable shooter. With the 6'3 Hamilton in the middle and strong support from others, the Bears made two runs deep into the State Tournament.

In 1947, Central advanced to the Bloomington Semi-state before falling to Terre Haute Garfield, led by Clyde Lovelette. The following year, Central was poised to bring the State title home when fate stepped in to shatter their dreams.

In the afternoon game of the '48 State Finals, Central advanced with a 48-40 win over Muncie Central, but Hamilton, who had led the team with 16 points, was injured late in the fourth quarter. Between games, doctors worked frantically to prepare his knee to withstand just one more game. "They got the cartilage back into place," Hamilton recalled, "and it was kind of a painful experience. Then they wrapped it heavily."

Despite the efforts, a Central State title was not to be. Hamilton played only a few minutes before blowing out the knee again, and the Bears fell 54-52 to Lafayette Jeff, a team they had beaten easily during the season. Hamilton was awarded the Trester Award after the game, but because his injury was so severe, the presentation was made in the locker room.

After being named All-State, Hamilton underwent surgery and rehab and then headed to DePauw to resume his career and get an education. He became a four-year starter for the Tigers and led the team in scoring as a junior and in rebounding as a senior. He was named the team's Outstanding Senior in 1952 and was later inducted into DePauw's Athletic Hall of Fame.

After graduating cum laude from DePauw in 1952, Hamilton earned a Law degree at IU. He was first elected to Congress in 1964 and has fashioned an exemplary political career that has spanned five decades. Among his accomplishments were his appointment to co-chair the committee that investigated Iran-Contra and his position as the ranking member on the Committee on International Relations.

Though his 1982 induction into the Indiana Basketball Hall of Fame may not compare to his accomplishments on Capitol Hill, one can only assume that his experiences on the court helped prepare him to serve in Washington. For those who saw him compete, it is gratifying to realize that his career as a leader was grounded in the roots of Indiana basketball.

LINCOLN HIGH SCHOOL: THE END OF AN ERA

When the announcement was made to re-designate Lincoln High School as an elementary school in 1962, it marked the end of an era that had reflected the same struggles with racial biases as those across our country. When the school opened in 1928, it was the first new school built in Evansville for the black community, and even though it was constructed while the city was in the throes of segregation, it would stand through 40 years of a slow but tumultuous progression to an integrated society.

In April of 1924, the Evansville School Board decided to consolidate the old Douglass High School with the Governor, Oakdale, and Third Avenue Elementary Schools. The board adopted a five-year plan to purchase 5.8 acres of land on Lincoln Avenue for $60,000. The Ku Klux Klan, the Taxpayers' League and other critics protested the project, but to no avail, and the school was completed and opened in September of 1928.

Irene Saucer, an Evansville teacher and wife of Lincoln High School and Evansville College athlete Willie Saucer, recently spoke of the segregated lifestyle and how today's generation are amazed when reminded of those days. "That's the way it was," she said. "Our oldest daughter is 27, and she said, 'Do you really mean that we could go down on Main Street and if I wanted something to drink, I couldn't go in a 10-cent store?'

"She'd see people sitting at the counter," Irene continued, "and she'd want to go in too, but I'd say, 'Well, honey, you can't go in there because our skin's black and all those people are white. We'd go uptown to the Loewes Theatre, and we still had to go upstairs to see the movie. You couldn't sit on the main floor."

Although true integration would eventually come to pass, Lincoln's athletes also had to withstand the challenges. Willie Saucer, a speedy running back from Lincoln who once scored three touchdowns the first three times he touched the ball in a game as a prep star, was recruited to play ball at Evansville College. Dubbed 'The Flying Saucer' by Evansville sportswriter Dan Scism, Willie recalled his days at E.C. and the problems he faced as a black athlete. "We went to a place (restaurant) and I saw the kitchen door open and the blacks were setting up a place in the kitchen. I said, 'Coach, I'm not eating back there.' The coach gave me some money, and I went somewhere else." Lodging was also an issue in those days. While the rest of the team stayed in hotels, the coaches would have to find accommodations for Willie with families in various towns.

Although Willie faced discrimination on the road, he was quick to point out that he was treated well by his Evansville College family. "My teammates were real nice. Don Watson, Gene Logel, Morris Riley (all future high school coaches), I had no problem at all with the players," he explained.

After graduating, Willie returned to his roots as a teacher and coach at Lincoln, and although times were slowly changing, the all-black school still wasn't accepted as an equal in the community. "During those days," Willie recalled, "nobody in town would play us (because of segregation), so we went to places like Dayton (Ohio), Lexington, Bowling Green, Louisville and Nashville."

Lincoln's Roy Gold guards a Boonville player as teammate Carl Gardner (#12) looks on. (Photo courtesy of Talmadge Vick.)

Willie Saucer as a teacher at Lincoln in 1959. Willie was a star running back for the school and was the first black football player at Evansville College. (Photo courtesy of Willie and Irene Saucer.)

Dan Howard was the dean of Evansville coaches with 32 ½ years as Central's coach before his retirement in 1966. Ned Niles coached for 46 years (but at different schools) for Douglas and Lincoln High Schools.

Talmadge Vick, #32 (back row), was one of only three black players on the 1957 Aces football team. (Photo courtesy of Talmadge Vick.)

Another notable Lincoln athlete who experienced the racial tribulations as both a player and coach was Talmadge Vick. As a student at Lincoln from 1946 to 1950, Vick was president of the Student Council and starred in football, basketball and baseball. He also remembers nights spent in strangers' homes because the team was not welcome in hotels.

As a senior, Talmadge threw 25 touchdown passes during his senior season but was not named to any All-City teams because only one city team would play them and he didn't have the required number of City games. Mater Dei was Lincoln's only city opponent that year, and the Lions defeated the Wildcats 27-13. In fact, of the 32 city games Lincoln played between that first game in 1949 and the last in 1962, 26 were against the Catholic schools.

After graduating with honors in 1950, Talmadge Vick left for Tennessee State University on a basketball scholarship. He lettered in basketball and football but was drafted into the Army in 1952. After his discharge in 1955, he chose to return home and resume his career and became the first and only black quarterback in the history of Aces football. In 1958, he was fifth in the nation in passing and once completed 41 of 51 passes against Murray State. When he graduated, he held school records for passing yardage, passes completed, completion percentage and the longest touchdown pass (81 yards).

Pro football's Chicago Cardinals expressed interest in Vick after his great senior season, but a teaching/coaching position opened up at Lincoln and he decided to accept it.

As the head basketball coach at Lincoln, Vick had a four-year record of 61-25, won the City title in 1959 and led the Lions to a sectional championship and regional runner-up finish in 1960. His '59 team featured the talented Walter Miles, whose son Brian became a superstar at North in the early '80s.

During his years as the Lions' coach, Talmadge's teams never played a home game because teams refused to schedule games at Lincoln . The atmosphere was not always cordial, and Coach Vick tried to teach his players the right way to handle negative situations. "At that time, all we could do was go and play and keep our mouths shut and do the best we could," Vick explained.

SMALL WORLD

Talmadge Vick's wife, Inez, has a sister, Lazel Prim, who taught Oprah Winfrey in Sunday School class in Nashville.

"I told my kids, 'You play ball, I'll do the talking and we'll see what happens.'"

Vick also had to deal with a few officials whom he perceived as being less than impartial. "The referees were going to do what they were going to do," he said. "We had some refs who were very honest and who would try to see that the best team won. But then there were some who were not going to do that."

After the school's re-designation in 1962, Talmadge Vick was re-assigned to North High School where he taught and coached before moving on to other areas in the education system later in his career. As a leader and an athlete, Vick is only one of the success stories that were produced by Lincoln High School.

One athletic distinction that Lincoln holds is being the only Evansville high school to win a national basketball tournament. Coached by Tom Cheeks, the 1940 Lions played in an all-black tournament in Tuskegee, Alabama to determine a national champion. From the 32 teams participating, Lincoln emerged to defeat Savannah, Georgia for the title 32-23. Upon their return, the hometown heroes were chauffeured around the neighborhood on a fire truck from Hose House #9, a station that served the black community faithfully for many years. Members of the national championship team were: George Barnett, Tom Bronson, Carl Butler, Nathaniel Coates, Clifton Collins, George Culver, Charles Jackson, James Keep, Leslie Kirby, James Thompkins (Thompkins Middle School is named for him) and Charles Woolridge.

Coach Tom Cheeks

In its short lifetime, Lincoln High School produced more than its share of noteworthy teams, athletes and coaches, with some distinguishing themselves locally while others went on to reach their sport's highest level. One of the school's greatest teams was its 1954-'55 team that was the first Evansville school to finish its regular season undefeated. The team was 20-0 going into the sectional before losing its second game 61-51 to Reitz.

Ted Lander and Charlie Vance were both great athletes who played on Lincoln's '57 team that lost to Jasper in the basketball semi-state. Willie Decker was the City high jump champion and a 25-foot long jumper who went to the University of Arizona to play basketball for Rick Barry's father-in-law, Bruce Lawson. Decker graduated and became a civil engineer in Minneapolis.

Freddie Bolen began his high school years at Memorial, but his lack of size prevented him from getting much playing time. After he grew five inches, his coaches wanted him to stay, but Freddie had already decided to move to Lincoln. While sitting out a year because of the transfer, Freddie grew another five inches and played his senior year as a 6'4 ½" center. He made the All-City team along with North's Dave Schellhase and Mike Volkman, Mater Dei's Paul Gries and Mark Clark of Reitz. Freddie averaged 26.8 points and once had 27 rebounds in one game. He scored 33 or more points seven times and had a remarkable field goal percentage of .678.

Calvin Martin was another talented multi-sport athlete for the Lions. Martin was known as 'Count Fleet' (for the great thoroughbred race horse that won the 1943 Triple Crown), and he used his blazing speed to become a two-time State champion in the 440-yard dash in 1943 (50.6 seconds) and 1944 (50.2). As a basketball player, Martin scored 38 points against New Harmony in the afternoon game of the sectional and 18 against Bosse in the final. Calvin was also an outstanding quarterback at Lincoln, and when he left to attend school at IU, he had hoped to play football and run track. When IU told him they wanted him to concentrate only on track, he transferred to Maryland State, where the school won 58 straight football games with him under center. After college, he played in the NFL as a backup with the Detroit Lions. At the time, the NFL was still reluctant to use black quarterbacks, so Calvin finished his career in the Canadian Football League.

James Smallins was a 1953 Lincoln grad who set the city single-game scoring record in basketball with 49 points. After graduating, Smallins became the first black basketball player at Evansville College and was the team's leading rebounder while playing with teammates Bob Walker and Boonville's Keith Combs, among others. After college, he moved to Wisconsin to coach at Milwaukee Lincoln High School, known as the melting pot of the city's schools. During a five-year span, Smallins' teams won five State titles, and from 1960 to 1963, his teams won 60 straight games, a record that stood for seventeen years. He was inducted into the Wisconsin Basketball Hall of Fame in 2000.

John 'Rabbit' Barnhill played on the '54-'55 undefeated Lincoln basketball team under beloved coach Art Taylor. After graduating in 1955, he played for legendary coach John McLendon who had studied at the University of Kansas under the creator of the game of basketball, James Naismith. Barnhill was drafted in the 11th round of the 1959 NBA draft by the St. Louis Hawks and spent ten seasons in the league with St. Louis, Detroit and Baltimore. He scored 5,085 career points (an 8.6 average) and averaged 4.2 assists per game. After his playing days were over, he spent seven seasons as the Director of Player Personnel with the L.A. Lakers before retiring in 1978.

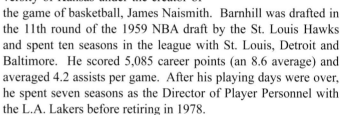
John Barnhill

Porter Merriweather, a 1957 Lincoln grad, followed John Barnhill to Tennessee State to play for Coach McLendon and became an All-American during his collegiate years. After his graduation, he starred with the Chicago Bombers of the North American Basketball League from 1964 to 1968. He was a first-team all-star twice ('64-'65 and '66-'67) and led the league in scoring for three straight seasons from 1964 to 1967, averaging between 28 and 30 points per game. After his pro career, he practiced law in Chicago.

Lincoln High School graduated its last class in 1962. As a high school, the stately building at Lincoln Avenue and Governor Street served its teenagers well for 24 years. It was a source of pride for its students, and it was a haven during an era when they were not accepted as equals by everyone. Sports were a rallying point for athletes and fans alike, and for the short time the school existed, Lincoln High School produced more than its share of thrills.

Porter Merriweather

CREDIT WHERE CREDIT IS DUE

John McLendon, who coached Lincoln grads John Barnhill and Porter Merriweather, coached professionally when George Steinbrenner hired him to coach the Cleveland Pipers of the American Basketball League. Although many pundits credit hall of fame coach Dean Smith for developing the 4-corner offense, the concept was originally created by Coach McLendon during his years as a college coach.

MARTY AMSLER: PERSISTENCE AND PATIENCE PAY OFF

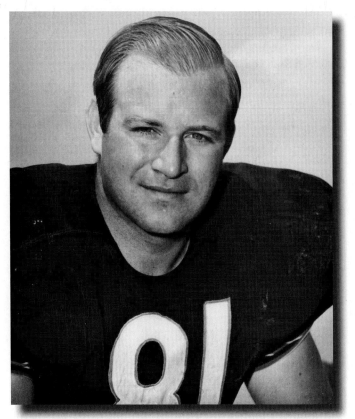

In 1965, Dick Butkus, Gayle Sayers and Joe Namath were selected in the first round of the NFL draft. They and many others taken early that year were destined for fame and fortune after stellar high school and college careers as media darlings and fan favorites. Other players, like Marty Amsler of Evansville, were merely a footnote on draft day. While the superstars were fast-tracked toward success, late-round picks like Amsler were embarking on a much more challenging journey that would test their resolve and fortitude. The odds were against Marty, but although he had taken a different path than Butkus and Sayers, he would not only play in the same league with them but he would play alongside them as teammates on the Chicago Bears.

To say Marty Amsler's athletic career was unconventional would be an understatement. In fact, if you would have attended a Bosse High School football game in 1957 to watch Marty, you would have had to wait until halftime to see the sophomore in action as a cornet player in the school band.

When the 6'1", 190-pound teenager decided to try out for the football team as a junior, it was his first attempt ever at playing a sport. After playing on the reserve team as a junior, he checked in for his senior season at a solid 6'4, 220 pounds and started both ways for the Bulldogs.

After his graduation in 1960, Marty attempted to walk on at Evansville College but didn't make the team. He then worked the graveyard shift at Kent Plastics for a year and went to night school at Evansville College and got his grades up. It would have been easy for Amsler to abandon his football aspirations and shift his attention elsewhere, but that wasn't his style.

Again, Marty tried to walk on at Evansville, and as a sophomore, he made the team and impressed Coach Paul Beck enough that he earned a scholarship for his last two seasons. Playing offensive and defensive tackle, Marty stood out to both opponents and teammates because of his exceptional speed. "Marty Amsler was the fastest big man I ever played with," said Mike Madriaga, who was the Aces' speedy halfback at the time. "He played left offensive tackle, and we would actually pull him (outside) on a quick pitch play. I had a hard time keeping up with this guy. Marty could probably have outrun me."

Marty's size and blazing speed must have also caught the eye of pro scouts, because after an All-Conference (ICC) season, he became the first Evansville College player drafted into the NFL. Tom Landry and the Dallas Cowboys selected Marty as a projected offensive guard in the 18th round of the 1965 draft.

After tearing muscle tissue from both bones in his right leg, Marty was released, and he was presented with another opportunity to call it quits. He returned home to assist Coach Beck as an offensive and defensive line coach for the Aces, but it wasn't long before the NFL came calling again.

In 1966, Marty was picked up as a free agent by the Denver Broncos, who intended to utilize his speed as a defensive end. The Broncos sent Amsler to play in the Continental Football League with a team in Wheeling, West Virginia, where he played for $200 a week. At Wheeling, Marty's size and speed attracted the attention of fourteen NFL teams, and his prospects were looking up.

The Wheeling coach, Bob Snyder, had played for the Chicago Bears and was good friends with their legendary coach George 'Papa Bear' Halas. At Wheeler's urging, the Bears agreed to sign Marty, and Amsler became a 25-year-old rookie on one of the league's most storied franchises.

As the season approached, Marty was 6'5, 260 pounds and could run a 4.7 forty-yard dash. He started the first exhibition game at defensive end and then started every game his rookie season. He was in on 773 out of a possible 880 defensive plays during the year and was credited with 31 tackles, 30 assists, 21 sacks, one interception and one fumble recovery. He also made the league's All-Rookie team and narrowly lost the Defensive Rookie-of-the-Year award to future hall of famer Alan Page of the Vikings.

Amsler is proud of the two game balls that are displayed prominently on shelves at his home, symbolizing that he was twice voted the honor by his teammates his rookie season. One of the balls was given solely to Marty after a 14-3 win over Detroit, and the other was awarded to each defensive lineman who had the daunting task of chasing Fran Tarkenton around all day in a 34-7 win over the Giants.

Motivated by his success as a rookie, Marty worked out like a maniac at a YMCA in Chicago and came into his sophomore training camp in the best shape of his life. He had only been in camp five days when a routine play resulted in an injury that would spell the beginning of the end of Marty's career. While trailing Sayers on a sweep, Marty was ready to tackle him when a rookie tight end clipped him from behind. The contact ruptured Marty's right Achilles tendon, which required surgery and ended his season.

After spending his third season with the Bears, Marty then played the 1970-'71 season with the Bengals (4 weeks) and

Packers (10 weeks). He returned to the Packers and new coach Dan Devine the next year but could never regain the speed he once had before the ankle injury. With his speed diminished, Amsler knew his career was over.

In 2008, Marty received his first NFL pension check, and with each one that comes, he can look back at a short but impressive career with pride and a sense of accomplishment. When asked to name some of the greats he chased during his era, he was quick to rattle off such names as Bart Starr, Milt Plum, John Brodie and Roman Gabriel. And when asked about the one he wanted the most, Marty didn't hesitate. "I wanted Johnny Unitas so bad," he said, "and at the last minute, three times he stepped up (to pass)."

"The same thing with Bob Griese," Marty continued, "You know, with him being a hometown boy. That's who you took your shots at, the quarterback. That was my job, and I got my licks in."

From a local standpoint, Marty played during a period that may never be seen again. At one point, there were four Evansville players in the NFL at the same time: Amsler (Bosse), Don Hansen (Reitz), Larry Stallings (Memorial) and Bob Griese (Rex Mundi).

After finishing his career and living in Chicago and working in the environmental industry for twenty years, Marty moved back home in 1995 to care for his parents and to marry his second wife, Jeannie, whom he had seen at their 35-year Bosse reunion.

As he looks back on his NFL days, Marty knows a twist of fate here and there might have enabled him to have had a longer and more productive career. In today's market, his rookie year alone would have meant a multi-year, multi-million dollar contract. But even though his largest NFL annual salary was $24,000, he knows that what he did was rare indeed. Through hard work, patience and a lot of perseverance, the cornet player from Bosse High School took his shots against some of the best players the NFL has ever produced.

> Marty Amsler played for the Chicago Bears during the period that was immortalized in the poignant movie *Brian's Song*. He was in the locker room during the famous locker room scene when Gayle Sayers made his emotional speech saying, "Brian Piccolo is sick – very sick."

ROGER KAISER & BOB REINHART: DALE HIGH SCHOOL'S PAIR OF ACES

Roger Kaiser (Photo courtesy of the Indiana Basketball Hall of Fame.)

Bob Reinhart

In the heyday of Indiana basketball, schools as small as Dale High School were considered second-class citizens. Every once in a while, however, a couple of special players come along to make a tiny hamlet buzz with excitement. Such was the case in the late '50s when Dale's Golden Aces made everyone sit up and take notice under the leadership of Roger Kaiser and Bob Reinhart.

The pair led Dale to two sectional titles, and both left the tiny school and made names for themselves in the basketball world. And even today, fifty years after their graduation in 1957, they are both still active and they are still the best of friends.

Kaiser and Reinhart started kindergarten together, and as they became teenagers, they delivered some of the best basketball in Dale High School history. Reinhart was a 5'11 playmaker, and Kaiser a 6'2 scoring machine. Both were four-year starters, and during their tenure at Dale,

Roger Kaiser at the Georgia Institute of Technology. (Photo courtesy of Georgia Tech University.)

they teamed with several other talented players to put the Golden Aces on the map in the mid- to late-'50s.

Among their teammates were the Knott brothers, Bob, David and Larry, who were neighbors of Roger's. Others to contribute were Bill Bocksthaler, Mark Weller, Harold Huffman, Leroy Spurlock and Danny Grundhoefer. Although the supporting cast was strong, by the time Reinhart and Kaiser reached their junior season, there was little doubt that the team would only go as far as their two stars could take them.

The twosome led Dale to two consecutive sectional titles (1956 and '57), a rare feat for a school with only 51 students in the senior class. Although the Golden Aces lost to Princeton in the 1956 regional and to Evansville Lincoln in the '57 regional, the talents of Kaiser and Reinhart had caught the eye of several college coaches. Reinhart had averaged around 15 points per game his senior year, and Kaiser had set a school record with 1,549 career points. Both made the All-Regional team, and Kaiser was named All-State.

During their school days, the dynamic duo were practically inseparable as they displayed their athleticism playing three sports in high school before heading off to college. They each also found their future wives while at Dale. Roger started dating future wife Beverly (Hevron) when he and Bob agreed to drive two young ladies home after a basketball banquet. The pretty cheerleader just happened to sit in the front seat next to Roger, and she's been by his side ever since. Bob would also marry his high school sweetheart, Jane (Miller) of Holland High School, during the summer after his high school graduation. Although Kaiser and Reinhart would go their separate ways, it would not take long before the two would be re-united.

Bob headed off to Kentucky Weslyan but then transferred to IU, where he would play baseball for Coach Ernie Andres and basketball for Branch McCracken. In basketball, Bob was not a star but came off the bench and helped the Hoosiers record a memorable 122-92 victory over a powerful Ohio State team that featured the likes of John Havlicek, Jerry Lucas, Larry Siegfried and a sub named Bobby Knight. Reinhart jokes about his days playing for Coach McCracken saying, "The older I get, the better I got."

In baseball at IU, Bob played third base and captained the 1961 team that posted a 21-5 record, a mark that still stands today as the best winning percentage for a season in IU baseball history.

After graduation, Reinhart came back to southern Indiana as the head coach at Oakland City High School for three years before leaving as a result of political differences. But as one door closed for Bob, his good friend, Roger Kaiser, would soon open another.

When Bob left Dale to head for college, Roger headed south to play basketball at the Georgia Institute of Technology (which would later become Georgia Tech) under coach John 'Whack' Hyder. By the time he left the school four years later, Kaiser had re-written the record books and had become one of the most revered athletes in the school's history.

Roger was a three-year letterman in both baseball and basketball and was a team captain in both sports at Tech. Although he was known best for his skills on the hardwood, he was good enough as a hitter and outfielder that the Cleveland Indians offered to sign him after his sophomore season, when he hit nearly .400. Kaiser turned them down, and although he was an All-SEC performer and made the All-Regional team as a senior, the major leagues weren't as interested in Roger as a 22-year-old as they were when he was younger.

On the basketball floor, Kaiser was even more outstanding, scoring 1,628 points during his three-year career. After his junior season, he was invited to try out for the 1960 U.S. Olympic team. The competition was fierce as the best players in the land converged on Denver to show their stuff. Major competition came from the Midwest, as the entire roster from national champion Ohio State was invited and Roger found himself battling for a spot against the same super players Reinhart had played against while at IU.

Perhaps the best of the entire group was a young Oscar Robertson from the University of Cincinnati. Kaiser got to know 'The Big O' well because of a situation that arose when Roger first arrived in the Mile High City. While checking in at the hotel, an official approached Kaiser and said, "Roger, we've got a little problem. You were supposed to room with (Jerry) West, but do you mind staying with Oscar Robertson?"

Apparently, people were concerned that white players would not be comfortable staying with black players, but Kaiser quickly put them at ease when he said, "It would be a pleasure. That doesn't matter to me; I'm from Indiana." Although his time with Robertson was short, Kaiser thinks the world of Oscar and says, "He was a perfect gentleman, and still is to this day."

With the competition so stiff, Kaiser learned that he would not be going to Rome for the Olympics, but he did return to Georgia Tech to complete a remarkable college career. In 1960 and 1961, he was named the SEC's Player of the Year and was a consensus All-American. At the time of his graduation, Kaiser owned 18 of 25 Georgia Tech offensive records, and his free throw percentage record (85.8%) still stands after 48 years.

Kaiser's talents inspired praise and honors few players get to enjoy. February 27th, 1961 was declared Roger Kaiser Day in the state of Georgia, and he was called "my best player ever" by Coach Hyder and "the finest all-around athlete in Georgia Tech history" by athletic director Bobby Dodd. Kaiser was also named one of the top 100 Georgia athletes in the twentieth century and one of the top 100 NCAA basketball players of the century.

After college, Roger signed for $14,000 to play professionally with the Washington Cats of the American Basketball League (ABL), the precursor to the ABA. For a year and a half, Roger played in three different cities as his teams kept folding, signaling the end of the ABL. When the ABA started up, Pittsburgh owned Roger's rights but offered him less money than he had made in the ABL, so Kaiser made the decision to hang up his sneakers.

As he discussed his options with his wife, Beverly recalls vividly the words Roger spoke as he pondered how he would use his Industrial Management degree. "When he graduated from college," Beverly revealed, "he said, 'Beverly, I don't know what I'm going to do, but I can tell you one thing, I will never coach basketball.'"

As is often the case, what a man says isn't always what he means. Roger would not only distinguish himself as a coach, but he would be instrumental in launching the successful career of his good friend and teammate from Dale, Bob Reinhart.

After dabbling in the business world for a year or two as a salesman in Atlanta for a company called Technical Tape, Roger called Bob Reinhart with the idea of fulfilling a dream they had talked about for years. In the summer of '63, the two started an all-sports camp for boys in the Georgia mountains, a labor of love that lasted twenty years.

In 1965, Bob contacted Kaiser to see if Roger could find him a permanent job in the Atlanta area, and Roger contacted nearby Decatur High School about a coaching position. His contact, Dr. Carl Renfro, responded by saying, "We know who we want; we want you!" Roger made it clear, however, that he was not lobbying for himself but for his best friend, and Dr. Renfro came up with a solution – he hired them both. Neither Bob nor Roger realized it at the time, but they were each about to embark on an incredible journey in the world of coaching.

For four years, the two pals teamed up to coach their two favorite sports. Roger headed up the basketball team with Bob as his assistant, and the two reversed roles in baseball. In 1970, Reinhart and Kaiser parted ways again, as Roger was offered a job as the head coach at West Georgia College. The separation would prove beneficial to both, as Reinhart would take over the basketball reins at Decatur and begin a stellar career and Kaiser would lead West Georgia into uncharted waters.

In his first year as the head coach at Decatur (1970), Reinhart guided the school to a State title, and he would repeat the feat

Beverly (Hevron) Kaiser as a Dale Golden Aces cheerleader. (Photo courtesy of the Kaiser family.)

twice more ('80 and '82). He led the Bulldogs to the State playoffs 12 out of 14 seasons and to the final game six times. During his 14-year tenure as the head coach at Decatur, Reinhart's teams won 83% of their games and the program produced numerous Division I players.

In 1983, Reinhart left high school coaching to serve as Mike Fratello's assistant with the Atlanta Hawks. After two years there, Bob accepted the head coaching job at Georgia State University in Atlanta. He headed up that program for nine years and led the school to the 1990 NCAA Tournament, a first for the school.

In 1993, he returned to pro ball as a scout for the Miami Heat under head coach Kevin Laughery. Following his two years there, he served in the same capacity for Jerry Sloan and the Utah Jazz. Bob followed his stint with the Jazz with a seven-year term scouting for the Golden State Warriors and is currently (2007) a college scout for the Milwaukee Bucks and an advanced scout for the Boston Celtics.

While Reinhart was entrenched in the pro game, Kaiser was building a career as a college coach that would place him among the greatest of all time. He left Decatur High School in 1969 and took over the program at West Georgia College in Carrollton, Georgia, where he amassed a record of 381-186 in his twenty seasons at the NAIA school. His teams produced three All-Americans: Foots Walker, Charles Hamilton and Tom Turner, a Vincennes native who played for the Alices during the Jerry Memering era. Kaiser also led West Georgia to the NAIA national championship in 1974.

In 1990, Kaiser moved down the road to Life University in Marietta, Georgia, where he was asked to start an athletic program for the small chiropractic school. As the basketball coach there, he led the team to the NAIA tournament eight times and won the title three times ('97, '99 and 2000). During the 2000 championship season, Kaiser won his 700th game as a coach, and his four national championships (one at West Georgia and three at Life) tied him with Adolph Rupp for second on the all-time list behind John Wooden's ten.

Roger's career as both a player and a coach has earned him inductions into five halls of fame: the Georgia Sports Hall of Fame; the Indiana Basketball Hall of Fame; and those from the NAIA, West Georgia and Georgia Tech. Today, he is having more fun than ever running the athletic program and coaching middle schoolers at the Mt. Bethel Christian Academy.

Roger and Beverly are fortunate to be near their children and grandchildren and to also be able to socialize with their good friend Bob Reinhart. Roger and Bob treasure the days when they ran the courts in the small gyms of southern Indiana, and although they joke about their roles as players at Dale, their respect for each other is obvious.

"I tell Roger all the time that my arm's still tired from feeding him," Reinhart joked.

Kaiser supported Bob's assessment of their high school roles, with Reinhart as the assist man and Kaiser as the shooter, and also landed a good-natured jab at his old friend in the process. "He was a very good ballplayer," Kaiser said of Reinhart. "He always told me that he wore out his arm passing me the ball so that I could wear mine out shooting.

"But if I was going to war," Kaiser continued, "I'd want to take Bob along, because if we couldn't whip 'em, he'd out-talk 'em. He would convince 'em they were wrong."

It is rare that two men who were so close even before high school would remain best of friends for nearly seven decades. Their paths have parted and re-connected several times over the years, but the strength of their bond seems to go back to their roots when they proudly wore the uniform of the Dale Golden Aces.

"That's why I love the movie *Hoosiers*," Kaiser reflected, "because when you watch it and see those gyms, we actually played in those gyms." Both Kaiser and Reinhart made names for themselves and have settled in Georgia, but when it comes to basketball, they'll be the first to tell you, they'll always be Hoosiers.

CARSON JONES: THE NEBO FLASH

Carson Jones was not a native of southwestern Indiana, but his contributions to the local sports landscape were monumental by anyone's standards. Before putting down roots in Evansville, Jones earned the nickname 'The Nebo Flash' with his heroics at tiny Nebo High School, just ten miles north of Madisonville, Kentucky. Word of his prowess on the court first started to spread when he made his high school varsity team as a fifth grader, and it culminated with an outstanding senior season in 1936.

Carson made Kentucky basketball history when he tallied an incredible 53 points in a 91-10 victory over Cinton in the semi-finals of the 7th District playoffs of the State Tournament. In that game, he connected on 23 of 30 field goals and hit seven free throws. His 53 was the highest point total scored by a player in U.S. high school basketball history, and what makes it so incredible is that the game was played during an era when the clock only stopped for timeouts and at the end of each quarter.

(Photo courtesy of Jerry Jones.)

His Nebo Golden Aces advanced to the final game of the tourney before losing to Corbin 24-18. Nebo was at a huge disadvantage at the time because in those days, a jump ball took place after each score and Corbin had a 6'9" center. Nebo finished the season 42-3, and Jones, who was named to the All-State team, opted to forgo college and head to Indianapolis to play semi-pro basketball. During the year he spent in Indy, he had the opportunity to face future coaching legend John Wooden in a game played at Butler Fieldhouse.

In 1937, Carson Jones moved to Evansville to accept a job at Sunbeam, known today as Whirlpool. Little did he know that the move would bring him to a place where he would be known by anyone and everyone in the local basketball community.

Jones was not the type to sit back and watch sports, so he immersed himself in every way he could find. He became licensed to referee in Kentucky while he played and coached in various softball and basketball leagues in the area. For ten years, his love of sports and the people who played them consumed his life. Over the years, he was a groundskeeper at the West Side Nut Club (Lamasco) Field and at Bosse Field while also umpiring little league and pony league games with his son Jerry. In 1947, Carson's love of basketball and his enthusiastic spirit would result in an event that would become, very possibly, the biggest and best of its kind in the country.

Carson's vision was a basketball tournament that would attract the absolute best talent from the Tri-state area and far beyond. From a seed in the mind of one man, the annual Tri-State Agoga tournament became a reality and after garnering the support of Dr. J. Frederick Rake, a pastor at the Agoga Tabernacle, Carson set out to explain his idea to anyone who would listen.

Not only did Jones have to find teams to play, but there were countless details to be tended to. The venue was quickly determined when Rake offered the Agoga gym, whose name would be associated with the event for many years to come. In addition, there were dates to set, officials to find, sponsors to secure and many other logistical items such as concessions, parking, and scorekeepers, to name a few. Jones was unwavering in his resolve and was willing to do much of the grunt work himself to make the tournament a success.

With the enthusiasm of a carnival barker and the tenacity of a pit bull, Jones called on every small business and large company he could find, and over the years, he would often land over 300 annual sponsors whose ads would be displayed in the tournament program. Local merchants, such as the Whirlpool Credit Union, Browning Funeral Home, Kenny Kent Chevrolet, and WFIE Channel 14, were proud to have their names associated with the month-long extravaganza.

In the early years, Jones had to dip into his own pocket to buy the trophies and/or jackets to present to the winning teams and other winners, like the best-dressed team, most valuable player, coach of the year, and best sportsmanship awards for a team and individual. Driven by his popular mantra "You've gotta promote," Jones was eventually able to cover the $10,000 cost of the event and pass on the profits to Agoga.

The tournament's most common format was 64 teams, although it occasionally hosted as many as 80 in a single-elimination format. The teams played by high school rules, with one exception. Carson added his own twist when he decided to permit a player who had fouled out to re-enter and be allowed one more foul if the game went into overtime.

It was not unusual for tournament games to draw 1,000 or more spectators, and as the tournament progressed toward its conclusion, crowds would exceed 1,500 and fans would be turned away at the door. What attracted such numbers was the incredible talent Jones was able to draw, and, looking back, the rosters are a virtual encyclopedia of area basketball history.

Several NBA stars made appearances over the years, such as Indiana Pacer greats Mel Daniels, Bob Netolicky, Darnell Hillman, and Roger Brown. Larry Bird came down after his senior year in high school, as did Indiana Mr. Basketball Billy Shepherd. The University of Evansville was always well-represented over the years, as well. In 1961, a team featuring stars Dale Wise, Mel Lurker, Russ Grieger, Hugh Ahlering and P.M. Sanders won the event under the name Cooke Chevrolet and repeated in 1965 as Lloyd's. Other former Aces to appear were Steve 'The Whale' Welmer, Rick Coffey, Brad Leaf, Andy Elkins, Don Buse, and Jerry Sloan, to name a few.

Several generations of area stars also competed over the years, many of whom are members of various basketball halls of fame. Among them were: Gus Doerner, Jerry Clayton, Bob Lochmueller, 'King' Kelly Coleman, Bob Sakel, Bob Kohlmeyer, Jerry Whitsell, John Harrawood, Larry 'Dude' Holder, Ray Roesner, Freddie Bolen, Ted Lander, Jerry Mattingly, Larry Cutsinger, Larry Harris and Junior Gee. Lochmueller, who starred at Elberfeld and the University of Louisville, holds the record for playing on six Agoga champions.

Eventually, a woman's tournament was added, and players such as Lisa Krieg and Leah Mercer from North, Leigh Ann Latshaw from Vincennes, and Lisa Bruin, Susan Thompson, Denic Black, Barb Dykstra and Shelly Brand from Reitz competed as well. In 1997, two ex-stars from USI won the MVP awards: 3-time All-American LeAnn Freeland and Dirk Surles, who led George Washington to the Sweet Sixteen in 1993 and played pro ball in the Continental Basketball Association.

Even when the event changed venues, players and fans still flocked to the tournament year after year. When the Agoga was razed in 1967, the tournament moved to Madisonville for two years before returning to Evansville in its new permanent home, the National Guard Armory.

Though the venues and the players changed over the years, the one constant was the presence of Carson Jones. His vision and his tireless dedication to the Tri-State Agoga Tournament made it a source of fun and excitement for 51 years, and it is highly unlikely that southwestern Indiana will ever see anything like it again. When Carson Jones turned out the lights at the Armory for the last time in 1998, it truly was the end of an era.

The 1951 Reitz Panthers. Front row: Don Henry (#12), Bob Gilham (asst. coach), Earl Yestingsmeyer (student mgr. – on one knee). Seated (L-R): Jerry Whitsell, Clarence Riggs (head coach), Jerry Marvel. Standing (from left clockwise): Ron Hicks (student mgr.), Merle Reed, Phil Byers, Jim Scott, Jerry Madden, Kenny Herrenbruck, Bob Imel, Dan Franzman.

Jerry Marvel's memories of home gave him hope during his darkest hour. (Photo courtesy of the *Evansville Courier*.)

1950-'51: A SEASON TO REMEMBER

The 1951 Reitz basketball team shown in the photo was one of the better teams in the school's history, and after an excellent regular season, these Panthers navigated through the State Tournament and nearly captured the championship. The special season meant a lot to the team and the fans at Reitz, but to one player in particular, the season would literally become the difference between life and death.

The '50-'51 Panthers' regular starting lineup consisted of Phil Byers and Bob Imel at guards, Don Henry and Jerry Marvel at forwards and 6'5" Jerry Whitsell in the middle, supported by Jim Scott and Merle Reed as the first subs off the bench. The Panthers were heavy underdogs heading into the Final Four, and they shocked everyone when they upset a strong Crispus Attucks team in the afternoon thanks to an excellent scouting report by assistant coach Jim Barnett. Attucks started a lineup that included: Willie Gardner and Hallie Bryant, who would both later play for the Harlem Globetrotters; Bailey Robertson, Oscar Robertson's older brother; and Ray Crowe, who would return to the school to lead Attucks to two State championships as a coach.

The seven Reitz regulars were all seniors and had made a pact early on that they would make it to Butler Fieldhouse in 1951. In the final game, the Panthers played Muncie Central to the wire. Down by a bucket with time running out, Jerry Marvel inadvertently dribbled the ball off his leg, creating pandemonium for the Reitz crowd when the official whistled Marvel for traveling, ending the Panthers' run for the title.

The '51 Panthers stayed in touch as they each went their separate ways after high school, and they've remained close to this day. It was not unusual when reminiscing at a reunion for Jerry Marvel to hang his head and say, "Man! If I hadn't dribbled off my foot and had better control, we would have won."

The agonizing memory of his blunder on the Butler Fieldhouse floor is similar to those of many athletes who have had the courage to risk failure in the quest for victory, but in Marvel's case, it paled in comparison to memories he would have later in life. In fact, recollections of his youth, both good and bad, would serve as an oasis during his darkest hour and keep him sane when faced with unimaginable circumstances.

While serving his third tour of duty as a marine in Vietnam in the late '60s, Marvel's plane was shot down and he was taken by the enemy. His captors escorted him to the infamous Hanoi Hilton, the same camp that held Senator John McCain. For five long years, Marvel withstood horrendous treatment and battles with despair, wondering if he would ever see home again.

Jerry would later tell friends about his days in the camp and the unthinkable conditions the prisoners had to endure. "He told us all about the tortures he went through," said Bernice Canterbury, who, along with her husband Jerry, remained close friends of Marvel's. "He said that during one torture, they would put you on your hands and knees and pull your head back by the hair and take a bar, kind of like a rolling pin, and twist it to grind your teeth down."

Marvel spoke often when he was home about how the American soldiers would have to tap on the walls to communicate and how loneliness would set in and the mind would begin to weaken under the strain. At a banquet at Reitz, with folks of all ages in attendance, Jerry left the audience mesmerized by his graphic descriptions. The crux of his message was that, you never know when memories will get you through, so enjoy your experiences while you can.

The memories of which he spoke were thoughts of home when he was in a faraway land and hopelessness had taken over as the days, months and years came and went. To maintain his sanity, he imagined his mother's kitchen and the familiar aromas. He could see his mom's face and see the dresses she wore. But the most vivid recollections, and the ones that consumed him daily, were those of his days as a Reitz Panther.

Marvel told many people over the years that he challenged himself to remember every detail of every game of the 1950-'51 season. A driving force that consumed him for many years was the task of remembering every player's name from every opposing team during the entire season. He also revealed that one thing that kept him going while in the camp was that he had recalled every player except one, and that the challenge to remember that ONE PLAYER gave him a purpose. As it turned out, at the moment the name came to him, he jumped up and screamed it over and over and was placed in solitary confinement as a result.

Marvel was released in 1972 and later retired after thirty years of service with the Marines. In 1995, he died suddenly from a heart attack in Pensacola, Florida. What he endured as a POW is impossible for the ordinary citizen to comprehend, but perhaps we can relate to the impact sports can have on one's life. In the grand scheme of things, high school athletics are not terribly important, but for a desperately lonely GI a world away, his memories of home and a season he spent with his high school teammates had given him the will to survive.

GIL HODGES: AN AMERICAN HERO

This sketch of the great Gil Hodges was drawn by Linda Harris, a Petersburg native and huge Hodges fan.

In all of American sports, there are very few men who were as beloved by his fans as Gil Hodges. To those who knew him as an unassuming natural athlete from a small town in southern Indiana and to the demanding fans of New York City, Gil Hodges represented all that was good about America and the sport of baseball.

Gilbert Raymond Hodges was born on April 24th, 1924 in Princeton, Indiana, the second child of Charlie and Irene Hodges. Charlie supported his family as a coal miner, and when the mine closed in Princeton, he loaded up Irene, Gil and older brother Bobby and moved to a house on Main Street in Petersburg, near the northern edge of Pike County. With the Depression making things tough on everyone, Charlie worked tirelessly in the dark tunnels that sprawled endlessly a thousand feet below sunlight.

Charlie had grown up loving sports and was an accomplished athlete himself, once considering a tryout for big league baseball, and as he watched his boys grow, he was determined that they would never have to work the mines. Over the years, the job had mutilated his body, causing the loss of an eye, two broken legs, a broken back (twice) and the loss of toes and fingers. But through it all, Charlie never complained

On weekends, Charlie, Irene, Bob, Gil and younger sister Marjorie, would pack up food and drinks and then pile into Charlie's truck to travel and watch Bob and Gil play their ball games. Bob was a year older than Gil but was in the same class at school. Like Gil, Bob was an excellent athlete in all sports and was considered by many, including his father, as the real 'prospect' for big league baseball.

Gil, known as 'Bud' to locals, was tall and lanky and possessed tremendous skills in anything he tried. "He was just a natural athlete," recalled Bob King, a local barber who was interviewed for an article by Wendall Trogden. "At pool, he could beat any of us. It was the same for ping pong, and he was as smooth on the dance floor as he was on the basketball court."

In the same article, Bob King talked about Gil's performance during the 1940 basketball sectional, when Hodges literally stole the game from the Ireland Spuds. In the waning moments, Gil made two key steals to secure a 20-19 win. The Petersburg Indians went on to defeat Otwell and Cuzco before falling to the Huntingburg Happy Hunters in the final game.

Gil also excelled on the school's six-man football team and was an excellent shot putter and broad jumper (long jumper) for the track team as well. During the early 1940s, Petersburg hosted one of the largest track meets in the state, the Southern Indiana Invitational, and the meet drew teams from Evansville and from as far away as Bloomington and New Albany. John Drof, a Petersburg native who was three years behind Gil in school, remembers 'Bud' doing very well at the meet against strong competition.

The school wasn't big enough to field a baseball team, so Bob and Gil played on local teams during the summer. Morris Klipsch, another contemporary of the Hodges boys, remembers days when Gil would use his huge hands to catch the younger boys in town bare-handed. Klipsch also recalled how Gil would pick up a basketball and make a full throwing motion, as he would a baseball, without losing his grip.

Gil's massive hands, when combined with his good size (6'2", 200 pounds) and natural timing, enabled him to wallop tape measure home runs, and his feats didn't go unnoticed. While his brother was attracting interest from the Boston Braves as a flame-throwing pitcher, Gil was approached in 1941 by the Detroit Tigers. Although he was flattered by the offer, he opted instead to attend St. Joseph's College in Rensselaer, Indiana, along with his brother, and pursue a career in coaching.

While at St. Joseph's, Gil continued to display his diverse skills as an athlete. On the football field, he was the team's hard-running fullback, and he was also the track team's best shot putter. In basketball, he was solid in all phases of the game, and on the baseball diamond, he used his large hands to make plays at shortstop and his erect batting stance to launch 400-foot home runs.

At age 19, Gil was approached by Stanley Feeble, a part-time scout for the Brooklyn Dodgers, who invited Hodges to a tryout in Olean, New York. With World War II raging overseas, Gil had enlisted in the Marines, but he headed for New York anyway to examine the possibility of playing pro ball. In New York, Gil impressed Branch Rickey, the boss's son, with his skills and his power. After the workout, Rickey took young Hodges to Ebbets Field to work out for Dodgers manager Leo Durocher, and for the first time, Gil slipped on the Dodger Blue.

Durocher worked Gil out at shortstop, third base and in the outfield and then invited him back the next day. At the second session, Hodges worked behind the plate, then at first and second before taking some swings in the batter's box. When the session was over, Leo invited Gil back for yet a third day, leaving the youngster excited but yet intimidated by the New York City atmosphere.

When Hodges returned the next day, he was surprised to learn that the Dodgers wanted to make him an offer. After calling his father to ask for advice, Gil chose to forgo his education to take his shot at pro baseball. Hodges signed for $1,500 ($750 at the time and $750 upon his return from the service).

The Dodgers had decided to develop Gil as a catcher, and with his new mitt at his side, he watched his first major league game from the dugout dressed in a Dodger uniform. In the final game of the 1943 season, Hodges saw his first action, with less than stellar results. As a starter at third base, he booted the first ground ball hit his way, and in his first at bat, he bailed out on a wicked curveball by Johnny Vander Meer before watching it break over the pate for strike three. Although he walked and stole second his second time

Hodges' freshman basketball team. Gil is on the front row, second from right, and his brother Bob is on the front row on the far left. (Photo from the Randy Harris collection.)

Gil's football team during his senior year. Notice his gigantic hands (4th row, 4th from left) on the shoulders of teammate Charlie Anderson. (Photo from the Randy Harris Collection)

at the plate, he struck out again in his third at bat on another curveball. That first taste of big league pitching revealed a weakness that would haunt Hodges for years – the ability to hit the dreaded breaking ball.

Gil headed back to Petersburg as a major league player and enjoyed his time with friends and family before leaving for a 2 ½-year tour with the U.S. Marines, where he served with the 16th Anti-aircraft Battalion as a gunner. During his term of service, Hodges saw more than his share of death as he fired at Japanese Zeros in Okinawa and Tinian, and he served his country honorably, receiving the Bronze Star and a commendation for courage under fire. When the Japanese surrendered in 1945, he returned home to a warm welcome and resumed his quest to make it in the major leagues.

In preparation for spring training in 1947, Gil worked on his new position by catching his brother Bob, who was preparing for his trip to the Braves training camp. Gil also spent time talking to his father, revealing his doubts and fears about his ability to hit major league curveballs. Gil's trip to training camp would turn out to be the beginning of a long successful career, but his brother's would not, as he would eventually blow out his arm with his overpowering pitching style.

After flying to Havana, Cuba, where the Dodgers were holding camp, Hodges found himself among some of the game's greats. Pee Wee Reese, his father's favorite player, was Brooklyn's shortstop, and a youngster named Jackie Robinson manned the first base position. The team's top catcher was veteran Bruce Edwards, who was backed up by Bobby Bragan, making Gil the team's bullpen catcher.

During the '47 season, Gil played sparingly, appearing in only 28 games. In his 77 at bats, he managed only 12 hits (a .156 average) and only one home run, but he did enjoy the team's success as he sat in the dugout during the World Series. His only appearance in the Series was in the seventh game with the Dodgers trailing the mighty New York Yankees, led by Joe DiMaggio and Yogi Berra, 4-2. In his first World Series at bat, Gil struck out with an anemic swing at yet another curveball.

Following the series, Leo Durocher asked Hodges if he'd like to play first base, a position Gil had not played much. The Dodgers had a hot young catcher coming up named Roy Campanella, and the plan was for Robinson to move to second, his natural position, with Campanella behind the plate and Bruce Edwards at third base.

The move to first base put Hodges in a very interesting position. During the historic emergence of Jackie Robinson as the player who would break baseball's color barrier, Hodges would play next to Robinson and witness close-up the challenges Jackie would face. In fact, there are some, including Randy Harris, a Petersburg native and huge Hodges fan, who feel that Gil's presence was a major contributor to Jackie Robinson's success story. In an era when blacks were considered interlopers in white society, Robinson faced scrutiny, and even disdain, from players and fans almost daily. The theory is that Robinson benefited from his defensive placement in the Dodger lineup, with captain and big brother figure Pee Wee Reese watching over Jackie from his shortstop position and Gil flanking from the first base side, using his physical strength to squelch potential incidents before they developed.

Gil's presence added stability to the Dodgers, and he quickly gained the respect of his teammates with a reputation for defending them when confrontations developed. Many have commented on and written about his

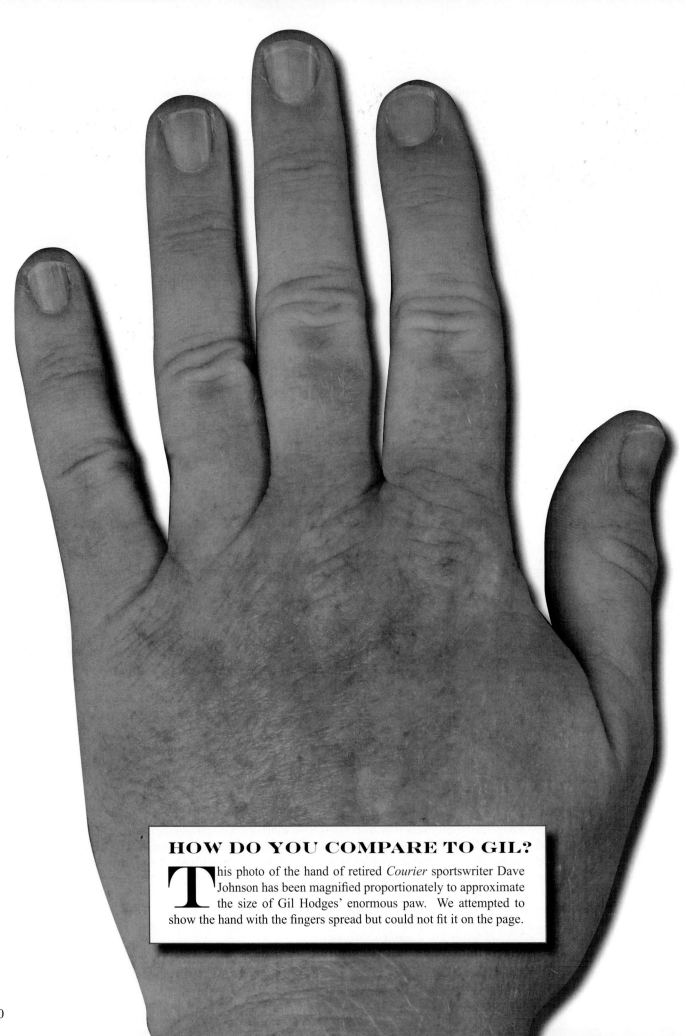

HOW DO YOU COMPARE TO GIL?

This photo of the hand of retired *Courier* sportswriter Dave Johnson has been magnified proportionately to approximate the size of Gil Hodges' enormous paw. We attempted to show the hand with the fingers spread but could not fit it on the page.

physical strength and size, and by today's standards, his 6'2, 200-pound physique would easily get lost in the crowd. One attribute that would stand out even today, however, was the enormous size of his hands. It has been said that he wore a size 13 ring. Others also claim that during his playing days, when he laid his hand down flat, the distance from the tip of his pinky to the tip of his thumb was just shy of twelve inches, a measurement that would compare to the hand of Shaquille O'Neal or Kareem Abdul Jabbar.

In 1948, Hodges played in 134 games for the Dodgers and quickly became a crowd favorite as his name was introduced with the song "Back Home Again in Indiana" emanating from the stadium organ as he strode to the plate. Although the fans still adored him, Gil finished the season with a meager .249 average and only 11 home runs. His weakness against curveballs was common knowledge, and there were rumors that he would be traded so that the team could secure a more productive first baseman.

For whatever reason, the trade never happened and Hodges remained in New York. During the winter of '48, Hodges attended a party and met a stunning brunette named Joan Lombardi. Gil didn't know that Joan was engaged at the time, but the attraction between the two could not be denied. The couple talked for hours away from the crowd, and Joan quickly became a Dodgers fan. After a whirlwind romance, the two married on December 26th, 1948 in a Brooklyn church.

Whether it was Joan's influence or having a season of experience, Gil had a solid season in 1949, hitting .285 with 28 homers. On June 25th, he hit for the cycle (single, double, triple, and home run), a rare feat in the majors, and he made the National League All-Star team for the first time. He also played his first World Series as a regular, hitting .235 while the Dodgers lost to the Yankees in five games.

In 1950, Gil continued his dependable play as he gained a reputation as an excellent-fielding first baseman while hitting .283 and having the first of five straight 30+ home run seasons, hitting 32 round-trippers. On August 31st, Hodges joined Lou Gehrig as the only players to go deep four times in a nine-inning game since 1900. In the record-tying game, he homered against four different Braves pitchers, including hall of famer Warren Spahn, one of the few left-handers the predominantly right-handed-hitting Dodgers would face all year. After his homer off of Spahn in the second inning, Gil went deep against Jumbo Roy (3rd inning), Bob Hall (6th) and Johnny Antonelli (8th) in a 19-3 Dodgers win. Gil's 17 total bases also tied a big league record at the time.

With his production improving and his selfless style of play, Hodges was becoming a darling of the New York fans. One fact that endeared him to the Dodgers faithful was that he was one of the few team members who stayed in Brooklyn year-round. When word got out that Gil and his wife were living in cramped quarters with Joan's parents and that Joan was expecting their first son, Gil Jr., there was an overwhelming outpouring from fans offering to give them a home. The effort paid off with a two-story home in the Flatbush section of Brooklyn, though Hodges insisted on paying for it.

Hodges followed his breakout season with more outstanding play in 1951, banging out 40 home runs while hitting .268. The Dodgers ended the season, however, with a heartbreaking loss that featured one of the most famous plays in baseball history. On the last day of the season, Gil and his teammates lost their chance at the World Series when the New York Giants' Bobby Thomson hit "the shot heard 'round the world." As Thomson rounded the bases after a home run, the fans at home experienced one of the greatest calls ever when announcer Russ Hodges (no relation) screamed over and over, "The Giants win the pennant. The Giants win the pennant!"

After the '51 season, 'the Boys of Summer', as the Dodgers had become known, were determined to make the '52 World Series, and they did. Although Gil had hit a respectable .254 with 102 RBIs and 32 homers, the Series against the Yankees would be one of the low points of his career. The Dodgers and Yankees alternated wins through the first six games, and Hodges was hitless in 17 at bats. Batting against left-handed Yankee starter Eddie Lopat, Gil flew out to 20-year-old Mickey Mantle in center in his first at bat. In the 4th inning, he lined out to left fielder Gene Woodling with the bases loaded and the Yankees up 1-0. The Yankees won the game 4-2, giving the Dodgers their fifth World Series loss since 1916, and Gil had finished the Series 0 for 21. To make matters worse, a reporter informed Gil that he was the first player ever to play in seven World Series games without a hit.

Following the '52 season, Gil was dejected after his Series performance, but he was buoyed by the overwhelming support received by the normally intolerant New York fans. Although he still had mental struggles with curveballs, his numbers were good and he hadn't missed a game in four seasons due to injury, reminding fans of 'the Iron Horse' himself, Lou Gehrig. In addition, he had hit more home runs in six seasons of play than any Dodger in history.

Hodges injured his hand during spring training for the 1953 season and was still in a horrible slump after the first 18 games. Once again, the fans remained loyal. By mid-May, Gil was barely over .200 and was benched by manager Charlie Dressen. With his mind open to any advice available, he was called into a meeting that would give him the tools to solve the curse of the curveball.

Apparently, the Dodgers had been secretly filming Gil's at bats and had noticed a fatal flaw in his approach to hitting a right-handed curveball. He had been striding toward third base (bailing out), causing a 'blind spot' to anything thrown from the middle of the plate out. The coaches convinced Hodges to close his stance, moving his front foot closer to the plate before the swing. After years of frustration, Gil was game for anything, and the results of the session were amazing.

With the new set-up, Gil found himself striding toward the pitcher, which kept his head in position to follow the ball better. In his next 95 at bats, he connected for 37 hits, a .398 average, and by mid-June, he had raised his average to .300. By season's end, he had connected for 31 home runs and had hit .302, his first season ever as a .300+ hitter.

Although Brooklyn once again lost to their old nemesis, the Yankees, in the '53 Series, Gil did his part with a .364 Series average. The Yankees had won their fifth straight Series, setting a big league record, but the Dodgers were two years away from exacting their revenge.

The 1955 World Series started in familiar fashion, with New York winning the first two games, but Brooklyn, under new manager Walter Alston, came back with an 8-3 win behind left-handed pitcher Johnny Podres. Hodges was off to another slow start, only one for thirteen, but that would soon change.

In Game 4, Gil walked slowly to the plate to face Don Larsen with the Yankees leading 3-2 and a runner on. With the Ebbets Field crowd watching, Larsen delivered a curve and Hodges, from his new 'Dressen Stance', made contact and parked the pitch in the upper deck, giving Brooklyn a 4-3 lead. He followed the homer with two more hits in an 8-3 Dodgers win.

In Game 5, Gil drove in the first run of the game and later laid down a crucial bunt that contributed to a 5-3 Brooklyn victory. The Dodgers were only a win away from dismissing the powerful Yankees.

The Bronx Bombers weren't going to go down easily, however. Despite their young star, Mickey Mantle, being benched because of a leg injury, New York still had plenty of firepower with the likes of Berra, Billy Martin and Phil Rizzuto. Behind southpaw Ace Whitey Ford, the Yankees won 5-1, forcing a seventh game.

On Tuesday, October 4th, Brooklyn was poised to make history as lefties Johnny Podres and New York's Tommy Byrne warmed up. Gil drove in the game's first run, and in the top of the sixth, the Dodgers held a 1-0 lead over the cocky Yankees. With Pee Wee Reese on first, Walter Alston implemented some unorthodox strategy when he signaled for power hitters Duke Snider and Roy Campanella to lay down bunts. The ploy worked perfectly, and Gil Hodges came to the plate with the bases full. After the Yankee manager brought in reliever Bob Green, Hodges launched a deep fly to center, scoring Reese. When Yankee catcher Elston Howard grounded out to Reese in New York's final at bat, pandemonium ensued. The Dodgers had finally broken the Yankee jinx and had become the first team in history to win the Series after trailing two games to none. Even more special was the fact that both runs in the 2-0 Dodgers win were driven in by southern Indiana's own Gil Hodges.

The Dodgers repeated as National League champs in 1956, but fell again to the Yankees in the Series. Gil finished the season with a .265 average and 32 homers and was superb in the Series, hitting .304 with eight RBIs.

In 1957, rumors began to surface that the Dodgers were bolting for the west coast, and the rumors proved to be true. Hodges made the best of his last season in the Big Apple by breaking the major league record for career grand slams, surpassing the record of twelve held by Rogers Hornsby and Ralph Kiner. In late September, to the fans' delight, Gil drove in the Dodgers' final run at Ebbets Field and the final run in Brooklyn history. He also won his first Gold Glove at first base, the first time the award was given, and was named to the National League all-star team for the eighth and final time in his career. After eleven happy years in New York, Gil and Joan and their four children, Gil Jr., Cynthia, Irene (named for Gil's mother) and Barbara, said goodbye to the beloved Brooklyn fans and headed for the City of Angels.

When the Dodgers arrived in L.A, they were stunned when they saw their new ballpark. The L.A. Coliseum was built as a football arena, and it looked every bit the part. The odd configuration featured a very short left field, approximately 250 feet, and even with a tall screen attached, Gil and the other right-handed hitters were salivating at the prospects. What looked like a blessing to the powerful first sacker proved to be anything but and would become one of several factors that would contribute to one of the least productive years of Gil's career.

Throughout the '58 season, Gil had problems both on and off the field that made it tough to focus on the business at hand. With the short left-field porch, Hodges' approach at the plate was altered, as he worked on pulling balls that he ordinarily wouldn't have, a tactic that seemed to take him out of his comfort zone.

On a personal level, he had to deal with being in a new city away from the mutual admiration relationship he enjoyed with the New York fans. He also had to deal with the death of his beloved father following Charlie's death in late 1957. In addition, Gil was troubled because his wife seemed miserable. Gil had seen a sampling of Joan's affinity for New York City when he had brought her to Indiana years before. Early in his career, when he decided to continue his education at Oakland City College (and play basketball) during the winter term, Joan had not adapted well to being away from the excitement of the big city. Although Los Angeles was also a huge city, the same feelings emerged again in 1958 when she found herself 3,000 miles away from her family and friends.

The result of all the changes was an unhappy man and an unproductive player, and the 34-year-old Hodges was benched for much of the season by manager Walter Alston. With many of his old pals gone, like Jackie Robinson, who had retired, and Roy Campanella, who had been paralyzed in a horrible auto accident, Gil struggled. The Dodgers, behind the young arms of Sandy Koufax and Don Drysdale finished the season in seventh place, and Hodges' new hitting approach resulted in a .259 average with only 22 home runs.

To try to right the ship, Gil made some important decisions following the '58 season. First, he realized that for Joan to be happy, she had to be in New York, so she headed east with the kids while Gil spent the season out west. Second, Gil went back to basics and worked on hitting the ball where it was pitched, ignoring the tantalizingly short left field fence. The result was dramatic, as both Gil and the Dodgers re-gained the form that had brought them success in the past.

Gil improved his production with a .276 average and 25 home runs and won his third consecutive Gold Glove, making him the only first baseman to win the National League award since its inception in 1957. The Dodgers fought their way to the pennant late in the season with Gil providing a key 12th-inning home run to beat the Cubs 5-4 with two days left in the season to put the Dodgers in a playoff with the Braves.

In the playoff series, the Dodgers faced the likes of Warren Spahn, Lew Burdette, Henry Aaron, and Eddie Matthews, and Gil was once again a major force in the outcome. When Dodgers shortstop Felix Mantilla stabbed a grounder behind second base and fired to Gil at first to end the series, the Dodgers were on their way to Gil's seventh World Series. But for the first time, the opponent would not be the New York Yankees.

The Dodgers took care of business in the '59 Series, finishing off the Chicago White Sox in six games, with Gil and Duke Snider the only remaining remnants of 'the Boys of Summer'. In his final Series as a player, Hodges finished with the highest average for either team, going 9 for 23 (.391) with a home run and a slugging percentage of .609. At age 35, as he reached the twilight years of his career as a player, Gil would soon learn that his reputation as a leader would enable him to remain in baseball and to define himself in a whole new way.

Throughout the '61 and '62 seasons, Gil's playing time was gradually reduced as new blood was pumped into the league, and his numbers dropped drastically. In 1962, he was made available in the expansion draft and picked up by the New York Mets, coached by ex-Yankee Casey Stengel. Although he only played in 54 games, it was commonly believed that he was brought in not for his skills on the field, but as a potential replacement for the 72-year-old Stengel.

Eleven games into the '63 season, Hodges was stunned when the Washington Senators called to inquire about his interest in managing in the nation's capitol. Knowing that his days as a player were over, Hodges relented and decided to give his aching knees a break and challenge himself as a manager. The Senators traded ill-fated, mentally unstable outfielder Jimmy Piersall to the Mets so that they could groom Hodges to take over for their current manager, Mickey Vernon. With a whole new world to conquer, Gil barely had time to reflect on his tremendous career.

When he retired as a player, Hodges had hit .273 for his career with 370 home runs, second only to the great Jimmie Foxx among major league right-handed hitters. He also owned the National League record for career grand slams (14) and was second only to Duke Snider (a left-hander) in career home runs and second to Snider in RBIs on the Dodgers' all-time list. He had overcome demons as a player, and now it was time to see the game of baseball from a different perspective.

Many believed that Hodges was simply too nice to be an effective manager, since he rarely questioned an umpire and he was never known to curse or raise his voice. In fact, a Dodger teammate had once told the press, "I'll tell you what kind of guy Gil is. If he came home at night and found rats in the house, he'd feed them."

As a manager, Gil's results were not immediate, finishing no better than 8th in four seasons. In 1967, Hodges' frustration got the best of him and he argued a call and was ejected for the first time in 25 seasons. The Senators finished sixth that season while the Mets struggled to a last place finish in the National League under manager Wes Westrum, who had replaced the retired Casey Stengel. Longing to go back 'home' for the second time, Gil let it be known that he wanted the Mets job.

Being the man he was, Hodges would not renege on his contract with Washington (a sharp contrast to today, with contracts hardly being worth the paper they're written on), but the Mets convinced the Senators to accept $10,000 for Gil's release. His move back to the friendly confines of New York were just what the doctor ordered for Gil, and it wouldn't take long for him to generate a historic season for the fans who still loved him.

Under Gil's leadership, the '68 Mets moved into the brand new Shea Stadium, and with Gil's physical presence, New York fans were optimistic. The theme for spring training was 'back to basics', and Gil placed a strong emphasis on fundamentals.

To open the season, the Mets blew an early lead, making it seven straight years of opening day futility. They followed that game by playing Houston to a scoreless tie for 23 innings before losing in the 24th in a game that set the all-time major league record when the game lasted six hours and six minutes.

During the season, Gil stayed loyal to his players during slumps and backed them when they refused to play a game against the San Francisco Giants out of respect for Senator Robert Kennedy, who had just been assassinated. The team flirted with the .500 mark for much of the season but finished ninth at 73-89. Late in the year, Gil suffered a minor heart attack, but, like his father, he never complained, even when he felt pains in his chest, turned pale and was perspiring profusely. Doctors ordered Hodges to rest and to stop smoking, a bad habit he had fought for years. Gil followed orders and began to exercise and drop some excess pounds, and with his body in shape, he was ready to deliver his beloved Mets fans to the Promised Land.

In 1969, Hodges did a masterful job of piloting a team with a light-hitting lineup that featured Ed Kranepool (.238) at first, Ken Boswell (.279) at second, the willowy Ken Harrelson (.248) at short and Wayne Garrett (.218) at third. In the outfield were Ron Swoboda (.235), Jerry Grote (.252), and the team's only heavy hitter, Cleon Jones (.340). The strength of the team was its pitching staff, which featured Jerry Koosman and a couple of youngsters named Tom Seaver and Nolan Ryan. Their ace out of the bullpen was the cocky and rambunctious Tug McGraw (the father of country singer Tim McGraw). The goal for the team was a .500 season, but what the scrappy bunch of lightweights would deliver would give them immortality in the annals of major league baseball.

The Mets opened the year as usual, with an 11-10 loss to the upstart Montreal Expos, but Gil's boys hung tough for the first half of the season. Before midseason, the Mets management added some pop to the lineup when they obtained Donn Clendenon, who would play a pivotal role as the drama played out. In a key game against first place Chicago, the Mets trailed 3-1 in the bottom of the ninth before a rally, sparked by Boswell, Clendenon, Jones, and Kranepool, produced a 4-3 comeback win over Cubs ace Ferguson Jenkins.

THE ORIGINAL REALITY TV

Gil Hodges was one of the sluggers who competed on a nine-episode run of the television show *Home Run Derby*. In the late 1950s, Hodges appeared with Hank Aaron, Ernie Banks, Harmon Killebrew, Mickey Mantle, and Willie Mays, among others. The winner each week pocketed $2,000, and the loser won $1,000. The players also received $500 for three dingers in a row plus $500 for each successive homer over three. Aaron was the show's big winner with $13,500.

The following night, Seaver took a perfect game into the ninth before Cubs rookie Jimmy Qualls looped a single to win the game. Though the loss was hard to take, the Mets finished the series only four games out of first. A week later, New York took on the Cubs again at Wrigley Field and captured two games out of three, and when they left Chicago, they found themselves in a pennant race, a new and glorious experience for Mets fans.

The season wasn't all peaches and cream for Hodges, however, as indicated by an incident late in the season. In a game against the Astros, star outfielder Cleon Jones jogged toward a fly ball and then lobbed a throw into the infield. Hodges, who was known for bottling up his emotions and then releasing his anger when he'd had enough, strode onto the field, past the pitcher and shortstop and into left field to remove Jones from the game. Regretting the display later, Hodges protected Jones' dignity by telling the press that Jones was running on a bad ankle and needed to be taken out.

Although their best hitter was on the bench, the Mets continued to battle and found themselves actually playing games in September that meant something. With eleven games remaining, New York moved into first place, and on September 25th, after the Cardinals' Joe Torre grounded into a double play at Shea Stadium, the Mets exploded from the bench and hysteria erupted from the stands in celebration of the Eastern Division championship. Immediately after the game, the Mets management called Gil in, tore up his contract before his eyes, and handed him a new one with a raise from $57,000 to $70,000 and a bonus for his efforts.

Hodges had taken the Mets from ninth place to first in only two seasons, and the love affair with New York City hit an all-time high.

As the Mets prepared for the playoffs, Gil was faced with a difficult decision. As dictated by the rules, he would be forced to pare his roster to 25 players. With Cleon Jones back in action, he was considering releasing pitcher Cal Koonce, who had injured his arm and was virtually useless, but that was not Gil's style. Because of Koonce's past contributions and because he was a veteran who may never have another shot to dress for a World Series, Hodges opted to keep the pitcher, a gesture that Koonce would later say he would never forget.

The Mets went to work preparing for the best-of-five series with Atlanta, which featured the blistering bats of 'Hammerin' Hank Aaron, Orlando Cepeda, and Rico Carty. As the first game began, Gil gave specific instructions to pitch carefully to Aaron. Against Braves knuckleballer Phil Nickro, New York Trailed 5-4 in the eighth before rallying for a 9-5 win behind the solid pitching of Tom Seaver.

In Game Two, Koosman and McGraw teamed up for an 11-6 win, and in Game Three, Nolan Ryan came in to relieve Gary Gentry and held the Braves in check. When Tony Gonzalez grounded out in the ninth, the Mets had achieved the unthinkable – they were heading to the World Series.

Up next for the Mets were the powerful Baltimore Orioles, who boasted sluggers Boog Powell and the Robinson boys, Brooks and Frank. In the first game, Orioles pitcher Mike Cuellar bested Seaver 4-1, but Koosman retaliated in Game Two with a 2-1 gem over Dave McNally. In Game Three at Shea Stadium, Tommy Agee led off the game with a homer off of Baltimore's ace Jim Palmer, his fifth leadoff homer of the season, and Gary Gentry kept the Orioles under control for another 2-1 win.

Baltimore was stunned in the fourth game when they fell 2-1 again, in ten innings this time, to a team they had taken lightly when the Series began. The Mets, who had wallowed at the bottom of the standings since the team's inception, were on the verge of making history.

In Game Five, the Mets trailed Baltimore 3-0 in the sixth when one of the oddest plays in World Series history occurred. Orioles pitcher Dave McNally threw a pitch in the dirt that Cleon Jones claimed had hit him. Gil took a slow stroll to the plate to discuss the matter and suggested that umpire Lou DiMuro check the ball. Upon inspection, DiMuro found a smudge on the ball and concluded that it was shoe polish, sending Jones to first

Following the incident, Donn Clendenon homered, making the score 3-2. When little Al Weis then went deep to tie the game, it was not far-fetched for Mets fans to feel that destiny was on their side. In the bottom of the eighth, Jones doubled and was driven in by Ron Swoboda's bloop single to left, giving New York a 4-3 lead. The Mets scored another run on two Baltimore errors to set the stage for the climax, and when Baltimore's Dave Johnson flied out to Cleon Jones for the third out in the ninth, the celebration began. News of the Mets' 5-3 victory was splashed across banner headlines around the country, and New York Mets were christened 'The Miracle Mets' for all eternity.

Gil Hodges had proven the doubters wrong and had become the first manager to lead an expansion team to a World Series title. He followed the '69 season with third place finishes in '70 and '71 and was preparing for the '72 season when New York fans and the baseball world were shaken by his sudden death. Just two days before his 48th birthday, Hodges collapsed and died from a heart attack while returning to his hotel room after playing golf with friends.

Gil's body was laid to rest in Holy Cross Cemetery in Brooklyn, and in 1972, with Joan and his children looking on, Gil's number 14 was retired by the New York Mets. The outpouring of sympathy was staggering, and the memories of fans across America came flooding back.

Among those who remember is John Drof, a long-time friend of Gil's from Petersburg who recalls excursions that were organized by locals to visit Hodges when he played nearby. "Back then, a passenger train went through Washington (Indiana)," Drof said, "and we'd have a whole train load of people (maybe 500) who would leave for St. Louis at 5:00 a.m. We'd put 'Gil Hodges' signs in the windows, and we'd watch the game and get back at maybe 10:00 at night."

Drof also remembers how Gil would acknowledge anyone at the game who would holler, "Hey, Bud!" because he knew they were from Petersburg.

Even 36 years after his death, there are still movements to convince the powers that be that Hodges should be in the Baseball Hall of Fame, and those who are lobbying on his behalf have some very valid points. Though naysayers would point to his .273 career average as ordinary, it is still higher than others who made it to Cooperstown, like Reggie Jackson and Mike Schmidt. It should also be noted that Hodges won three straight Gold Gloves in the first three years of the award, and that he probably would have won several more had the award been presented when he was in his prime. He also hit 370 home runs, which would translate to maybe 500 today, due to larger fields back then and better pitching before talent became diluted by expansion. When he retired, he was one of only two right-handers on the top ten list for career home runs (the other was Rogers Hornsby), and every other player on the list is in the Hall. Hodges was also an eight-time all-star and played in eight World Series, very high on the list for those who were non-Yankees. He also played on two World Series champions and managed another, a feat few can match.

Though many feel that Gil's induction is a longshot at best, because his premature death took him out of the public eye, his legacy is undeniable. It would not be a stretch to say that very few athletes were as beloved as Gil Hodges. After his death, the mayor of Washington D.C., where Hodges managed for four seasons, said, "It's not like losing a celebrity, it's like losing a member of the family."

Petersburg native Randy Harris said simply, "People looked at Gil as what a man should be. He was a gentleman, and people respected that."

As exalted as Hodges was by fans, his most endearing quality was his every-man appeal. "He was a human being with weaknesses and frailties, just like everybody else," said Mort Zachter, a Brooklyn native who is writing a biography of his childhood hero. "He had an occasional drink, and he smoked, unfortunately too much, but he had a reputation of being a guy with great integrity."

Hodges was amazing in that his character was so appreciated by the folks from his small hometown and yet the same qualities made him an icon in one of the world's largest cities. His appeal was universal, and no one described it better than Pee Wee Reese when he stated: "If you had a son, wouldn't it be a great thing if he turned out to be like Gil Hodges."

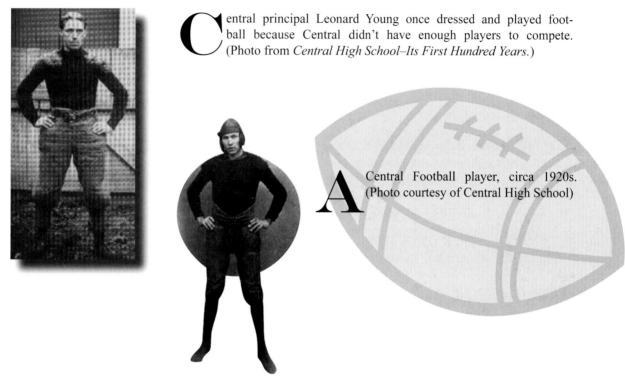

Central principal Leonard Young once dressed and played football because Central didn't have enough players to compete. (Photo from *Central High School–Its First Hundred Years.*)

A Central Football player, circa 1920s. (Photo courtesy of Central High School)

John Alexander's track shoes and the four medals he won at the state meet and the national meet in Chicago. (Courtesy of the Reitz High School archives.)

LARRY STALLINGS: HE TACKLED THE BEST

The name Larry Stallings is not one of the most recognizable by local sports fans, but his football talents took him from the gridiron arenas of southern Indiana to NFL stadiums across the country.

At Memorial, Larry Stallings played basketball and golf, but it was as an offensive tackle and, especially, as a linebacker that he made a name for himself. Competing against players like Larry Coleman and Gary West of Reitz and Mater Dei's Jerry Browning, he gained a reputation as a fierce hitter. "Larry Stallings was a tremendous ballplayer," said Morris Riley, who was North High School's head coach for many years. "I remember a game at Enlow Field when he completely dominated the game when he was at Memorial."

As a senior, Stallings captained the Tigers to an undefeated season and was honored as an All-State linebacker. He chose Georgia Tech over four or five other schools, and Tech head coach Bobby Dodd decided to play Larry as a down lineman (tackle) on both sides of the ball. In the early '60s, the Yellow Jackets played in the old Southeastern Conference, battling the likes of Alabama, Georgia, Tennessee and LSU every year.

When asked about some of the great players he faced while at Tech, Larry cited: Andy Russell, the great Steelers linebacker ('62 Blue Bonnet Bowl against Missouri); former Green Bay linebacker Dave Robinson ('61 Gator Bowl against Penn State); and a young Joe Namath at Alabama.

Larry was a small lineman by today's standards, but at 6'2 and 220 pounds, he fit the mold perfectly for the time. "Back in those days," he recalled, "our offensive line at Georgia Tech averaged 225 pounds, and we were the biggest line in the SEC." But it wasn't his size that would make him attractive to NFL scouts; it was his speed.

(Photo courtesy of Larry Stallings.)

After graduating as an Academic All-American in 1962, Larry was drafted by the Buffalo Bills (AFL) in the 8th round and by the St. Louis Cardinals (NFL) in the 17th. He decided to sign with St. Louis because, as he put it, "At that time, the NFL was considered the stronger league, and I wanted to try to play at the highest level."

As a raw-boned college graduate with an Engineering degree, a somewhat naïve Larry Stallings was about to begin a solid career in the NFL, but before he could play, he needed to sign on the dotted line. "Back in those days," he said, "there weren't any agents, so it was just me as a 22-year-old sitting down with the owner." Larry quickly settled for an $11,000 salary with a $2,000 signing bonus. (In his second year, he received a 'raise' to $12,000, which meant that, without his signing bonus, he actually played for less money.)

Before his rookie season, head coach Wally Lemm and his staff informed Larry that, because of his outstanding speed, they wanted him to move to linebacker, a position he hadn't played since high school. While he was learning to be an NFL linebacker, another rookie was also adjusting to NFL life and a new position. Jackie Smith, who had been a wide receiver in college, was being asked to play tight end for the Cardinals. He and Larry would become great friends, and Jackie would eventually become an NFL Hall-of Fame tight end. Larry's roommate for ten years was quarterback Jim Hart, who played college ball at Southern Illinois University.

During his NFL career, Larry Stallings played with and against some of the all-time greats. Among his teammates were hall of famers Larry Wilson (free safety), Roger Wehrli (cornerback) and Dan Dierdorf (offensive tackle). He also chased and tackled stars like Paul Hornung, Gayle Sayers and, in the early years, hall of fame quarterback Bobby Layne.

When asked to name the best player he faced, Stallings was quick with an answer. "I believe Jimmy Brown was the best," he stated. "Our starting center at St. Louis was 240 pounds, and big lineman weighed 270. Jim Brown was 235 pounds and could run a 4.5 (40-yard dash). You just didn't see that kind of size and speed. In my era, he was the best I played against."

As an NFL player, Larry Stallings did his job against the best players in the world, including two seasons when he was pulling double duty. In 1967 and '68, Larry had to fulfill an obligation from his college days. After finishing school as an ROTC (Reserve Officers Training Corps) graduate, he owed the Army two years. As an active duty soldier, he was stationed at the Atomic Energy Commission near Washington D.C. He would perform his job during the week and then, on Friday night, he would fly into St. Louis to join his Cardinal teammates. With no weekly practices, he never missed a beat as the team's starting linebacker.

In 1970, Larry Stallings was voted his team's Most Valuable Player and was selected to play in the Pro Bowl. He started for the Cardinals for fourteen seasons, and he did it the way he has always done it; He showed up and did his job. For fourteen seasons, the Memorial High School grad laced up his cleats and played with and against the best football players in the world.

QUENTIN MERKEL: MEMORIAL'S MR. BASEBALL

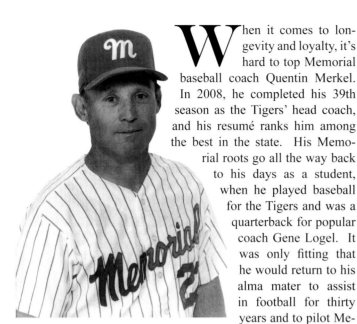

When it comes to longevity and loyalty, it's hard to top Memorial baseball coach Quentin Merkel. In 2008, he completed his 39th season as the Tigers' head coach, and his resumé ranks him among the best in the state. His Memorial roots go all the way back to his days as a student, when he played baseball for the Tigers and was a quarterback for popular coach Gene Logel. It was only fitting that he would return to his alma mater to assist in football for thirty years and to pilot Memorial's baseball program.

In his very first year at the helm, Merkel's baseball team finished 25-3 and won City, sectional and regional titles before falling 3-2 to South Bend Clay in the 1970 State semi-finals. He followed up that season with a 16-1 record and another run deep into the State tournament.

After finishing the 1974 season at only 8-4 in the City, Memorial captured the sectional after ace Andy Rice tossed a 4-0 no-hitter against Bosse and the Tigers avenged two regular season losses to North with a 2-1 win in the final.

In the regional, Rice was brilliant once again in a one-hit, 1-0 win over South Spencer, and Dan Henning fashioned an easy two-hitter over Mt. Vernon for a 15-0 rout in the final game. The two star pitchers continued their magic in the Jasper Semi-state as Rice dominated Loogootee 13-2 and Henning dismissed Seymour 6-3. But the Tigers' run ended with a 6-4 loss to Terre Haute North in the State semi-finals.

No one would argue that the late '70s were the program's glory years, as the Tigers captured the fancy of baseball fans statewide. The 1978 team, led by Evansville's pride and joy Don Mattingly, swept through the season and captured the State championship, finishing a perfect 30-0. Memorial boasted a stable of strong pitchers, led by their aces Mike Henning (12-0) and Jeff King (11-0). In addition, Ken Killebrew chipped in with three wins, followed by Greg Merkel (2), Mattingly (1), and Steve Mason (1).

With a strong nucleus returning, the 1979 Memorial team continued their dominance behind returners Mattingly, Henning, Merkel, Killebrew, Larry Bitter, Jeff Schulz, Shawn Musgrave and Larry Jochem. With solid pitching and timely hitting, the Tigers bulldozed through another regular season unbeaten, as Henning again flexed his muscle on the mound with two no-hitters (9-0 over South Spencer and 8-0 over Mt. Vernon) and a 10-0 one-hitter over North. Killebrew provided the team's third no-hitter on the season with a 10-0 win over Bosse.

Memorial waltzed through the State Tournament once again and entered the final game at State 29-0 before losing 6-5 to Logansport in ten innings. Don Mattingly, arguably the greatest high school player in area history, finished the season a perfect 10-0 on the mound and hit nearly .600 to lead the Tigers. Other big sticks for the season were Schulz (.414), Merkel (.373), Rick Frank (.341), Dave Papariella (.339), and Musgrave (.314). Though Memorial fell just a whisker short of back-to-back State titles, the school's 59 straight wins was a state record and a remarkable achievement.

Quentin Merkel's consistency over the years is second to none in the area, and his three State championships in the one-class format trailed only LaPorte (7) and Logansport (4) in the state's history (Jasper is tied with Memorial at 3). Merkel's second State championship team in 1989 was loaded with solid hitting up and down the lineup and finished fourth on the state's all-time list for hits in a season (392) and tenth all-time in extra base hits (133), led by players such as Brad Rubsam, Tim Brownlee, Brian Holt, and Aaron Gries.

The team's ace on the mound was Matt Stieler, who achieved a rare feat at the State Tournament Final Four. In the semi-finals, he came in to relieve starter Brad Mueller late in the game and recorded the win after a Tigers comeback. In the finals, Stieler started and pitched a solid game, but in the final inning, with left-handed hitters coming up for Logansport, Merkel decided to bring Mueller in to pitch and moved Stieler to second base. After Mueller showed some control problems, Merkel called timeout and decided to bring Stieler back to finish. Stieler was up to the task and closed out the game to give Memorial its second State title. The significance of the scenario is that, the way things played out, Stieler was credited with two wins on the day plus a save when he came back in the finals to save a win for himself.

Merkel admits that the '89 Tigers were not blessed with great pitching, but when it came to swinging the bat, Merkel proclaimed, "That's probably the best hitting team I've ever had." Coach Merkel continued by explaining that a study was done on the first 25 years of the IHSAA State Tournament and that the study concluded that Merkel's '89 club was the best-hitting team in the tournament's 25-year history.

One can only imagine what it must have been like for opposing pitchers to face a nine-man Murderer's Row that featured Gries (.362), Holt (.370), Rubsam (.357), Stieler (.352), Pat Schulz (.513), Adam Unfried (.464), Grady Murphy (.385), Duane Hirsch (.375) and sophomore Todd Miller (.305). The team's batting average was an astounding .382 during their 33-3 season as they pounded 24 home runs, despite playing many games at cavernous Bosse Field, and recorded 311 RBIs. Most remarkable was the fact that the '89 Tigers tallied 385 runs, a mind-boggling 10.7 per game.

Four years later, Merkel guided the Tigers to a third State championship when he orchestrated a 36-2 season with a team that he described as "not the most talented, but scrappy and competitive." Behind the strong arms of John Ambrose and John Sartore and the play of such stars as Ryan Brownlee at second base and

Shawn Merkel (Greg's son), the '93 Tigers downed Richmond 7-0 in the State semi-finals before capturing the title with a 1-0 win over Huntington. When the tournament was over, the consensus was that the Final Four was one of the best-played in State Tournament history, with not a single walk given up by any of the four teams until the sixth inning of the final game.

After nearly forty years of coaching, Quentin Merkel has earned the right to be listed among the state's elite baseball coaches, and he is showing no signs of slowing down. Over the years, he has seen countless Memorial players earn college scholarships, and a few have played beyond their college years. Those with minor league experience include Pat Schulz, Ryan Miller, Jeff Tenbarge, and fire-balling pitcher John Ambrose. The '78 State championship team produced Memorial's only two major leaguers, superstar Don Mattingly and outfielder Jeff Schulz, who spent some time with the Kansas City Royals before Bo Jackson entered the picture, making Jeff the odd man out.

Mattingly, who became one of the most beloved New York Yankees of all time, credits much of his success to the time he spent under Merkel's guidance. "Coach Merkel is my first thought when I think about Memorial," Mattingly confided, "because I really think he had a huge impact on me. He was one of the biggest influences on me because he opened my eyes that I could be really good. He was always 'get better; get better – fundamentals, fundamentals,' and that foundation of knowing how to do things properly and his belief in hard work made him successful."

Mattingly recalled vividly a speech Merkel made that motivated him to work even harder to fulfill a life-long dream. "He said, 'If you think you're the best player on this team, then you need to be the best player in the area or in the state, then the country, then the world,'" Mattingly explained. "That really influenced me. I believed that I needed to get better all the time. I was never satisfied with where I was."

Don also appreciated the success he enjoyed while at Memorial and the camaraderie that developed among the players and coaches, saying "Those are memories you never forget. You would think you might, but you don't. I've played in a lot of big games, but you don't forget that style of team. Going undefeated and winning a State championship was just a great feeling. It was a special time."

Over the years, Coach Merkel has enjoyed and helped create many special memories for the players he's mentored, and his career has been impressive by any standard. His overall record (as of 2007) was 865-311 (72%), and he led his teams to 18 City, 21 sectional, 12 regional, and 10 semi-state titles to go with his three State runner-up finishes and three State championships. In 1990, the three-time IHSBCA Coach of the Year was inducted into the Indiana Baseball Hall of Fame and is currently the winningest active coach in the state. With a proven philosophy and a dedication to excellence, Quentin Merkel has earned his place among the greatest coaches in the history of Indiana high school baseball.

Don Mattingly (#21) celebrates with Kenny Killebrew (left) and Greg Merkel (#30) after the 1978 State championship to finish the season a perfect 30–0. (Photo courtesy of Quentin Merkel.)

CHAPTER THREE
1957-1962
WHAT A YEAR!

Steve Schroer as a pitcher for the Washington Senators organization. (Photo courtesy of Steve Schroer.)

It is very possible that the 1961-'62 school year was the best year athletically in Evansville high school history. To support this claim, one only needs to consider that in 1961-'62, Evansville could lay claim to the state's top team in three different sports. The year began with Herman Byers' Reitz Panthers being named the mythical State champs when they finished the football season not only undefeated, but unscored on as well.

In the winter, the Bosse Bulldogs navigated the entire one-class field to claim the State title in basketball, and to finish out the year, the North High baseball team (shown in the photo) were declared the mythical State champs by Indiana sportswriters.

The '61-'62 North Huskies finished the season undefeated with such players as Dean Volkman, who would later star at quarterback for the University of Illinois, and Dave Schellhase, who was offered a contract by the Cincinnati Reds before heading to Lafayette and leading the nation in scoring for the Purdue basketball team.

The Huskies baseball team also featured one of the best one-two pitching combinations in local high school history. Mickey Martin finished the season 8-0 with a remarkable 0.00 ERA. Steve Schroer also finished 8-0 and would complete his career the following year with a four-year record of 28-1 and an ERA of .093.

Mickey Martin played ball at Murray State and then came home to lead the Huskies as their baseball coach for parts of three decades. In 1996, Mickey was taken from us much too soon when he lost his battle with multiple sclerosis at the age of 53.

Schroer became what was known at the time as a 'Bonus Baby', signing a lucrative contract with the L.A. Dodgers the week after his graduation. After three weeks at Salisbury, North Carolina, the 18-year-old Schroer advanced through Double A, then Triple A, then all the way to the parent club in less than three months.

By mid-August of 1963, he was wearing Dodger Blue alongside such greats as Sandy Koufax, Don Drysdale and Johnny Roseboro. Although he never appeared in a major league game, he was on the Dodgers' roster when they won the '63 World Series.

After the Series, Schroer was selected by the old Washington Senators in the winter draft and began spring training with the Senators, who were managed by local baseball legend Gil Hodges. Schroer's career was interrupted when he was drafted into the Army. During his first year in the service, he played for the All-Army baseball and basketball teams, but the following year he was shipped to Vietnam.

After his return, Steve resumed his career but confesses that "it was never the same after I came back." The year he spent in Vietnam without touching a ball had affected his velocity. Steve managed to make it back to the Triple A level but never reached the majors again. In 1970, Steve retired from baseball to enter the business world.

Although Schroer's baseball career never developed the the way he had hoped, no one can take away the hardware he picked up 45 years ago. Because of his meteoric ascension through the Dodgers' system in 1963, he joined Pete Fox as the only Evansville natives to own a World Series ring.

The 1962 State champion North High School baseball team. Front row (L-R): Jerry Stavely, Gerald Gustafson, Jim Bryant, Roger Tindle, Ron Smith. Second row (L-R): Roger Griffin (equip. mgr.), Wayne McDaniel, Mickey Martin, Steve Schroer, Bob Mason, Scott Riley, Bill Thompson (student mgr.), Paul McDaniel (coach). Third row (L-R): Ed Wessel (manager), Dean Volkman, Jim Son, Jim Brown, Ron Schlimmer, Steve Myers, Dave Schellhase, Ed Housman. (Photo courtesy of Steve Schroer.)

THE PERFECT PANTHERS OF 1961

The Evansville area has had many great football teams over the years, and several have recorded undefeated seasons. But the 1961 Reitz team placed itself on the short list of the greatest teams ever when they accomplished what only four other schools in Indiana history had done. They became the first Indiana team since 1945 to complete The Perfect Season, undefeated and unscored on.

Under their taskmaster and perfectionist coach, Herman Byers, the '61 Panthers methodically dominated every foe and made history in the process. Many Panther loyalists believe that much of the team's success can be attributed to the Panther team from the year before. In fact, there are those who will argue that the 1960 group was even better than the '61 Panthers. One who holds this view is Ken Hansen, older brother of Don Hansen, who started in both '60 and '61 and earned All-American honors for his '61 season.

"I think our team was the catalyst for the '61 team," said Ken Hansen, who graduated after the '60 season. "A lot of young kids (on the '61 team) played a lot and got a lot of experience (because of the lopsided scores). It would be interesting if the '60 and '61 teams could have played. It probably would have been a 0-0 game."

As the elder Hansen and others have said in the past, there is a valid case to be made for the '60 group. The team finished a perfect 9-0 and was ranked #1 in the state, just like the '61 team. And although the '60 team was scored on (they outscored their opponents 313-15), their defense didn't give up any of the points, making their defense unscored on as well.

Although the comparison of the two teams will continue, the fact remains that the '61 Panthers were special. Led by the three team captains, Hansen, Charlie Orth and Tom Reasor, the team was an offensive machine and a brick wall on defense. In an *Evansville Courier* article many years ago, the late Herman Byers cited the talents of several players.

Byers called 6'1, 200-pound fullback/middle linebacker Don Hansen simply the best at everything. He called Charlie Orth "the finest defensive halfback in the state," and declared that tackle/noseguard Tom Reasor was "one of the best linemen in the state." Byers also praised Doug Harp ("hard-nosed") and the Fendrich twins, Jerry and Gary, saying, "They're fast and get the job done."

The coach also complimented defensive back/tailback Danny Jones, saying, "He's got sure hands and he goes after the ball," and recognized the desire and aggressiveness of linemen Mike

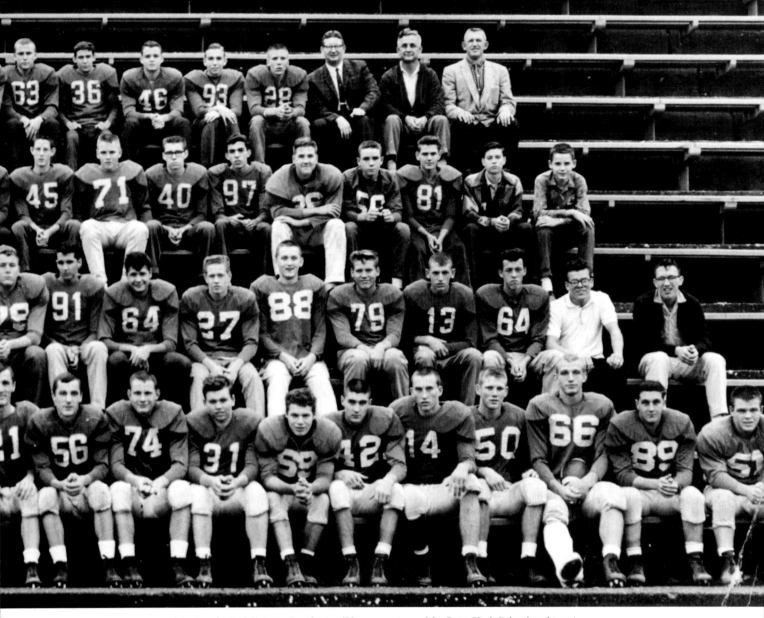

The 'perfect' 1961 Reitz Panthers. (Photo courtesy of the Reitz High School archives.)

Stucke and Bob Johann and the hard running of leading scorer Karl Klusmeier.

The '61 Panthers were like most Reitz teams in that they seemed to have an advantage before they ever took the field. Herman Byers himself had created a persona of invincibility, having already won five mythical State championships, and his football style and coaching tactics also set Reitz apart from their competition. "We were the only team to use the Single Wing, and that was an advantage over everybody else," stated Ken Hansen, who starred as a center and linebacker. "We only had to defend against T-Formation quarterbacks, while (opposing teams) had to figure out how to stop the Single Wing."

Byers' offense was basic football at its best. Every opponent knew Reitz would grind it out on the ground, but precision execution made the Panthers difficult to stop. "We didn't throw much," recalled Rich 'Porky' Nau, a center for the '61 team. "Byers' philosophy was, only three things can happen when you pass, and two of them were bad (an incompletion or an interception)."

Reitz linemen were also unique because they had to learn how to sustain blocks longer while the backs spun and faked in the Single Wing offense. The system made it virtually impossible for opponents to simulate in practice, and Byers took full advantage of the situation.

Players who suited up against Reitz during the Byers regime can also recall the intimidation factor when the boys in blue and gray would take the field. Although there were 62 players on the Reitz varsity roster in '61, Byers would often dress nearly 100 (including the reserve team, freshman team and what appeared to be the entire student body), and the stream of players seemed endless as the Panthers emerged from the fieldhouse.

To open the '61 season, Reitz pounded their opposition like speed bags with four dominating wins where the opposition never even got a sniff of the goal line. After wins over Crawfordsville (53-0), Muncie Central (66-0), Mater Dei (42-0) and New Albany (26-0), the Panthers faced their first defensive challenge. The Central Bears, under veteran coach Dan Howard, hosted Reitz and were primed and ready. Led by quarterback Carl Heldt, the Bears drove to the Panthers' nine-yard line late in the opening quarter, and on first down, missed a pass in the flat that could have gone for a touchdown. The Bears stayed on the ground for three more plays but were held to zero yardage, and Reitz passed its first true test and won the game 21-0.

As the season progressed, the silence relating to being unscored on became deafening. One problem Coach Byers faced was trying to maintain the streak and still show respect to opposing coaches. "The hardest part was that he was beating some teams pretty badly and needed to play some reserve players rather than be accused of running up the score," said Jim Byers, Herman Byers' son, in an interview for a local magazine article by writer Ed Cole. "And with reserves playing, there was always the more likely chance of someone scoring."

The players themselves didn't start feeling the pressure until later in the season. "It was about three-quarters of the way through the season," recalled Rich Nau. "Alan Horn, the line coach, made a comment during practice one day. He said, 'Hey, if you guys keep your head out of your butt and play good ball, we could go through a season unscored on.' We didn't really talk about it amongst ourselves much until the last two games."

After the Central game, Reitz disposed of Bloomington (46-0), North (26-0) and Memorial (33-0) to set the stage for the final game of the season. In front of a packed Reitz Bowl crowd, first-year coach Archie Owen and his Bosse team would get the last chance to spoil the Panthers' season. Although the Bulldogs were vastly over-matched, they did pack enough punch to throw a huge scare into the sellout crowd who had come to witness history being made.

With less than a minute to play in the half and trailing 34-0, Bosse picked up a first down to the Reitz 23 on a fake punt. Bulldog quarterback Steve Bosse then fired a perfect pass to Rickie Biggs on the 14-yard line with 15 seconds left. With time running out, Bosse again hit Biggs who turned toward the goal line before being stopped at the three. Bosse had penetrated deeper into Reitz territory than any team all season, but Reitz had again protected their end zone.

Rich Nau was on the sideline during the Bosse drive, and he has a humorous and vivid memory of what transpired in the Reitz locker room at halftime. "Coach Byers had taken some of the defensive personnel out," Nau explained. "We were beating them bad, and they hadn't gotten past the fifty-yard line. It was the last game of the year, and he was putting some younger kids in. When Bosse got down close, Coach Byers called timeout and put the starters back in.

"Coach Byers would always chew Maalox capsules," Nau continued, "and at halftime, he was foaming at the mouth. He looked like one of those commercials like 'Got Milk?'. He was furious. He was kicking the boards and he took his coat off and threw it, and his hat. He said, 'That'll be the last damn time I'm going to put you guys in!' You would have thought we were losing the football game. But you could see the pressure was on."

The pressure was finally gone when the final seconds ticked off in a 55-0 Reitz win. Coach Byers and his boys had attained perfection. After the season, many speculated how things may have been different had Reitz played Rex Mundi, the new Catholic school in town. The Monarchs finished the '61 season 9-1, led by a young quarterback named Bob Griese and a scatback named Mike Minton. Due to a scheduling conflict, the two teams didn't meet in '61, but Rex Mundi coach Ken Coudret was quoted as saying, "If we had played Reitz, I think we would have scored on them." Though we'll never know how Rex Mundi would have fared, when the next season rolled around, the Monarchs returned nearly their entire squad and were shutout 7-0 by a Reitz team that had lost 21 seniors from the previous year.

Following the 1961 season, the Panthers were rewarded with another mythical State title. It was also reported that Reitz was ranked #1 in the nation defensively and #2 offensively. Many Reitz players were recognized, as well. Five Panthers, Hansen, Reasor, Orth, Jerry Fendrich and Doug Harp, were named to the Associated Press All-State team, and Don Hansen was honored as an All-American.

Though he never liked to compare teams, Coach Byers finally relented years later when he publicly declared the 1961 Panthers his best team ever. The '61 team had finished 9-0, scoring 368 points (an average of 41 points per game) while allowing their nine opponents exactly zero. Though the debate will continue over Evansville's best team ever, in the fall of 1961, Coach Byers and his Panthers accomplished what no Indiana team had done since 1945. They had completed The Perfect Season.

Coach Byers is carried off the field by members of his 1961 team. (Photo courtesy of the Reitz High School archives.)

DON HANSEN:
BIG MAN IN THE MIDDLE

Many exceptional football players have graced the gridiron venues of southwestern Indiana over the last ninety years, and some have gone on to high-profile careers in the NFL. Although Don Hansen's name is not as recognizable as those of Bob Griese, Kevin Hardy or Jay Cutler, if one evaluates Hansen's career from high school, college and the NFL, he would rank near the top of any list of the area's all-time greats.

Born on August 20th, 1944, 22 months after his older brother Ken, Hansen was blessed with exceptional skills, but it was his great size that separated him from his peers, even at an early age. As a player for the Perry Heights freshman league (little league), Don's feats of power and strength were mythological, and his brother was often there to watch. "At Cynthia Heights (German Township at the time), the ball field faced the school and home plate was near the road," Ken recalled. "Don hit the ball over the building. He was *The Man* in the rural league."

And Ken wasn't the only one taking notice. As Don competed as an 11-year-old, parents of opposing players became concerned about the damage the brawny Hansen could inflict, especially when he was on the mound. "He threw the ball so hard that the other team's kids were scared," Ken explained. "He was as accurate a thrower as anybody, but at eleven years old, you're going to have some control problems. Whenever that happened, kids got hurt."

Fearing for their sons' safety, several parents lobbied the league to ban Don from the freshman group and suggested that the 12-year-old be placed in the junior league to compete against 13- and 14-year-olds. For the sake of peace and safety, the request was granted, and the youngster moved up to star in a league more physically suited for his talents.

Hansen entered Reitz High School at a time when the football program, under celebrated coach Herman Byers, was reaching legendary status, and the contributions made by the Hansens and many others did nothing but enhance the program's aura. At Reitz, Don focused on the two sports he knew best, football and baseball, and he was a standout in both.

As a baseball player, Don pitched and manned the hot corner at third, often blocking a ground ball with his massive body and then firing to first for the out. As a high schooler, he was a two-time All-City player, along with Bob Griese and others, and he hit .450 as a senior. Another epic tale of Hansen's power was recalled by Ron Volkman, a star from Bosse who played American Legion ball with Hansen. "He had huge hands," Volkman noted, "and I remember playing at Mt. Carmel and Donnie hit one over the cemetery. I've never seen another ball hit like that."

(Photo courtesy of the Reitz High School archives.)

Don Hansen totes the pigskin during his junior season. (Photo from Reflections, the Reitz High School yearbook.)

Under Coach Byers' guidance, Hansen became the team's brightest football star amidst a galaxy of stars who surrounded him. As he entered Reitz as a freshman, Hansen was aware that west siders demandeded a lot of their football team and that the players would be expected to contribute to the Reitz football 'mystique' that Coach Byers had fostered. "Our neighbor across the street was Tom Trainer. He was four years older and played football, and he was kind of a hero," Hansen said from his home near Atlanta. "I think it was through him that we had that kind of knowledge about Reitz."

It wouldn't take long for Hansen to learn firsthand about Reitz football, and it also wouldn't take long for the fans to learn about Hansen. Don started as a sophomore on a 4-9 Reitz team and then became a leader on two of the best teams in the school's storied history. Teammate Rich Nau, who played center, recalls very clearly the impact Don had both offensively, as a fullback, and defensively as a middle linebacker.

"Don was a perfectionist," Nau revealed. "He did everything right. He was a natural. He was a man amongst boys. He would hit that line and lower his shoulder and run you over; he was

73

a true fullback. But he was even more of a true linebacker. He was actually a coach on the field. He knew his job and everybody else's too. He led by example, and he never complained about anything. He was always, 'Yes, sir' and 'No, sir,' just a true gentleman. But as a tackler, he'd separate you from the ball."

Hansen himself downplays his abilities and opts for humor when asked about his running technique. "It was a lumbering style, let's put it that way," he joked. "It wasn't pretty, and it wasn't graceful."

Perhaps the greatest compliment concerning Don came from his coach, Herman Byers, who once told a reporter, "If you'd ask me who was the best runner on the team, I'd have to say Hansen. If you'd ask me who was the best tackler on the team, I'd have to say Hansen. No matter what you'd ask, I'd have to say Hansen. Hansen can do everything. You only have to tell him once and he's got it."

As Hansen's reputation grew, Reitz experienced possibly the best two seasons in the school's history with the 6'1, 200-pounder toting the ball and anchoring the defense. In his junior season, with Don flanked by his brother Ken and Houston Rolley on defense, Reitz dominated, outscoring their opposition 313-15 while finishing 9-0 and ranked #1 in the state.

In Don's senior year, the 1961 Panthers completed possibly the greatest season in local history as they finished undefeated (9-0) and unscored on. In Hansen's final two seasons, his teams outscored their opponents a combined 681-15, and Don was recognized with honors that reflected his success.

In addition to being named to the All-City and All-State teams, Hansen was honored as an All-American and received college offers from across the country. He made visits to Vanderbilt, Indiana, Purdue and Illinois, eventually choosing to head to Champagne to join Dick Butkus and the Fighting Illini.

With Butkus manning the middle of the Illini defense, Don was moved to outside linebacker, and he accepted the change without question. When asked what he thought of the opportunity to play beside Butkus, Hansen seemed very aware that he was in the company of possibly the greatest linebacker to ever play the game. "I've always said that Dick wasted four years of professional ball playing college," Hansen said. "He probably could have played professionally out of high school. His instincts for finding the ball were uncanny."

Don's sophomore year was successful, both athletically and personally, as he married his high school sweetheart, Sandy (Slifer), who was a Reitz cheerleader, and as the Illini finished the year with a 17-7 win over Washington in the 1964 Rose Bowl.

When Dick Butkus graduated, Don was moved back to his familiar spot at middle linebacker and earned All-Conference honors as a senior. As a result of his steady play, he was selected by the Minnesota Vikings in the third round of the 1966 NFL draft and was also drafted by the AFL's Miami Dolphins. Interestingly, if he had chosen to join the Dolphins, Evansville possibly could have had two representatives on the perfect Dolphins team of 1972, Hansen and Bob Griese. In his usual self-effacing manner, however, Hansen doubts that it would have happened, saying, "I probably would have gotten traded someplace else."

Opting instead to join the Vikings, Don found himself playing behind perhaps the greatest defensive line in NFL history, The Purple People Eaters: Alan Page, Carl Eller, Jim Marshall and Gary Larson. Although Don was named the team's Rookie of the Year in 1966, an injury and some self-evaluation almost cut his NFL career short. In the last game of his rookie year, Hansen sustained a knee injury, and late in the rehab process, he also decided to join the Army National Guard in lieu of possibly being drafted. With the rigors of basic training and active duty and his NFL responsibilities, Don made a surprising decision. He chose to walk away from football.

After two seasons with the Vikings, Don and Sandy returned home and Don joined his brother Ken in the real estate business. Although Ken stayed with it and built a successful career in real estate, Don had caught the industry in a downswing and was disillusioned. Fortunately, the respect he had earned as a player had left doors open to the NFL.

Swallowing his pride, Hansen got on the phone to Norm Van Brocklin, who had been the Vikings' coach during Don's rookie season and had since taken over in Atlanta. "I called Norm and told him I was out of money and needed a job," Don confessed, "and Norm said, 'Come on down.'"

Hansen spent seven seasons with Atlanta and was the team's MVP in 1972. In 1976, he was chosen by the Seattle Seahawks in the expansion draft and spent ten weeks there before being traded to the Green Bay Packers. After two years with Green Bay, his career ended when, in Don's words, "They fired me in 1978."

During his pro career, Hansen played against some of the all-time greats and chased down such running backs as Larry Csonka, Paul Hornung, Gayle Sayers and O.J. Simpson. He played eleven seasons with 10 interceptions and 13 fumble recoveries in 142 games.

The pro game that Hansen played was far different from the one we know in the 21st century, and because of his values and beliefs, he always kept his profession in perspective. "It really is a lot different now than it was then. We didn't have the resources. We didn't make anywhere near the money they make today. We were struggling to make a living.

"Maybe I look at it differently than a lot of people. I looked at it as more of a job and just going to work and coming home in the evening. It was nothing special; it was just work."

Today, Don works as a virology specialist selling pharmaceuticals for HIV treatment. With his family and faith at the forefront, he and Sandy and their children, Wendy, Melody and Chad, have built a great life together. Although he still feels some after-effects from his 15 knee injuries, several broken fingers, and numerous concussions, he appreciates the role football played in his life.

Even at age 64, Don Hansen still looks like he could cover a back out of the backfield on third and long, and it's hard to believe that it has been nearly fifty years since he rumbled down the field in front of thousands of local crazies. Hansen's credentials are solid, and his resumé, from his days on arguably the greatest high school team in local history to his retirement from the NFL in 1977, is second to none. But what makes Don Hansen a true standout is that, despite the honors and recognition, he endeared himself to fans and teammates by the way he always conducted himself with dignity, grace and humility.

Don (left) and older brother Ken when Don was asked to move up to an older league for the safety of the younger boys. (Photo courtesy of Ken Hansen.)

MIKE MADRIAGA:
FEAR FACTOR MADE HIM A WINNER

When Michael Edward Madriaga came into this world on October 29th, 1943, his gene pool wasn't ideal for producing a multi-sport athlete who would hold his own against others much larger than he. In fact, Mike was much more likely to do his shaking and baking in a kitchen than on the athletic field.

Mike's father came to America from the Philippines and studied the culinary arts. He eventually married Edith (King) and settled in Evansville, where he served as the chef at Smitty's and the Trocadero while Edith was a chef at F's Steakhouse. The Madriaga children also worked the restaurant business from an early age, and Mike bussed tables at Smitty's and almost followed in his father's footsteps before "athletics got in the way."

Mike attended grade school at St. Theresa before moving to Stringtown in the fifth grade and then on to North High School. Although he was always small, Mike took advantage of other assets as he honed his skills in the neighborhood where he grew up. His speed and explosive quickness came naturally and served him well as he played baseball and ran track and cross country during his first two years of high school.

He built his strength by working with Jerry Hoover, who was not only an outstanding choral music director, but also a pioneer of weight training for high school athletes. "There's not enough known about this guy," Mike said of Mr. Hoover. "He was an innovator. We didn't have fancy stuff, just cans from the cafeteria with concrete poured in them and steel rods through them. We had the Mr. North contest (a body building competition), and I think what came out of that were things like City championships and State championships."

Although Mike had made a name for himself, especially in baseball, the sport where he would attract the most attention was football, a sport he almost didn't play.

"I didn't play football until my junior year," Mike explained. "My parents thought I was too little. I was about 5'3 and 135 pounds. I was recruited out of gym class. We were playing touch football, and Mr. (Frank) Schwitz went to (football coach) Morris Riley and said, 'We've got this little Filipino kid that no one can touch out there. You'd better recruit him.'"

Coach Riley talked to Mike after his sophomore year, and Mike explained his situation. In the fall of his junior year, Mike went out for football but didn't tell his parents, who thought he was running cross country. After finding this out, assistant coaches Archie Owen and Don Watson decided to talk to the parents. "They went over to Smitty's and talked to Dad," Mike recalled. "No one would talk to Mom because she was pretty serious. They told Dad I wouldn't get hurt, and they touched a nerve when they said, 'If he's good, there are possibilities of him getting a scholarship to college!'"

Mike's mother didn't see many of his football games at North because she didn't like the violence of the sport, and Mike understands her view well. He had to avoid collisions with some very physical players and teams, like Don and Ken Hansen at Reitz and Mater Dei's defense, which Mike described as "the hardest-hitting team I ever played against."

When asked to name his strengths as a runner, Mike answered, "Well, I had the fear factor, as most backs do. I wasn't fond of being hit. I would cut and was deceptively quick. I had good vision, and I understood the game because I had good coaches."

One quirk that made Madriaga easy to spot at any athletic event was his habit of sprinting at times when other players would jog or walk. In baseball, he would sprint to first base after being walked by the pitcher, and when he would run to his defensive position or return to the dugout, he would run at full speed.

"That comes from my dad," Mike noted. "Everything was in a hurry in our family. That was just my nature. When I was young, when we went to play ball, we didn't walk. It was who could get there first. Also when I got tackled (in football), I always sprinted back to the huddle. And I don't know why I did that. Today it seems kind of goofy, but it was one of those 'ha-ha, you didn't hurt me' kind of things."

As a high school athlete, Mike was the City champion in the low hurdles and was on some excellent baseball teams at North and in Colt League, where his team reached the final four nationally with such players as Mickey Martin, Steve Schroer and Bob Griese. As a running back and safety, he made some All-American teams and was selected to the AP and UPI All-State teams as a senior, playing on a phenomenal team featuring quarterback Mike Volkman and two other great runners, John Mominee and Larry Lindenschmidt.

After earning a football/baseball scholarship to Evansville College, Mike went on to achieve an unusual distinction, earning a letter in four college sports. His second letter earned at Evansville was the most surprising. After the football season, Paul Beck (E.C.'s head football and assistant basketball coach)

Mike Madriaga as a hurdler at North.

wanted Mike to stay in shape. The basketball team didn't have enough junior varsity players, so Mike played for the 'Deuces' and earned a letter.

After his sophomore year of college, Mike was drafted by the Kansas City organization to play baseball, but his father would not let him go. Being from the old school, his father felt that his son had made a commitment to Evansville College and should honor it. Mike admits that it was probably a good thing because as his schooling progressed, it led him into teaching and coaching.

Madriaga finished his senior year as an All-ICC performer in both football and baseball, and he was ready to graduate. But there would be one more athletic opportunity. The school was starting a track program, and athletic director Bob Hudson told Mike that if he stayed, they would pay for his post-graduate courses. This situation led to the speedster earning a letter in his fourth sport, making him a rarity in college athletics.

After college, Mike taught physical education at Delaware for two years and then moved to Bosse to assist his old high school coach, Archie Owen. At Bosse, Mike coached five sports (football, baseball, track, basketball, and wrestling) before moving into administration and becoming the city's Superintendent of Athletics in 1990.

Mike Madriaga attributes much of his passion for sports to the many coaches he had over the years. "Those are my idols," he said of the men who touched his life as a young man.

Even today, when the older generation speaks of a scatback who darts and weaves through a defense, they use Mike Madriaga as a point of reference. The mighty mite with legs like pistons may have been running out of fear, but no matter how hard he was hit, he always bounced back up.

PRINCETON'S JERRY SCOTT: 'THE SNAKE' COULD DO IT ALL

Though the name Jerry Don Scott doesn't trip off the tongues of local sports fans like those of other better-known athletes, to fans of Princeton High School and Gibson County, he is still recognized as one of the finest all-around athletes from their part of the state.

Jerry was born on July 26th, 1942, and his father, Roy, brought Jerry and his older brother Larry to Princeton when Jerry was only a year old. Much of Jerry's early exposure to sports can be attributed to his uncle, 'Sugar' (Shug) Hickrod, who began working with Jerry when he was seven years old. Shug was also responsible for tagging the youngster with the nickname that would follow him throughout his life. "My uncle just started calling me 'Snake Hogan' when I was little," Jerry said, his words dripping with a southern Indiana drawl. "For some reason, it just stuck. Some people don't even know my real name."

As 'Snake' grew, his natural skills blossomed on the sandlots around Princeton, and when he reached high school age, the 5'10", 165-pound fireplug wasted no time making an impact. In 1957, Jerry became one of only two Princeton freshmen in the school's history to start on the varsity football team (the other was Dick McGowan), and he also started a few months later for Coach Otis Sparks' baseball team in the spring. As a sophomore, Jerry became a starter for Coach Bill Richardson's basketball team, which enabled him to eventually earn eleven varsity letters in only three sports during his four years at Princeton.

On the basketball court, Snake took pride in being a tenacious defender and effective passer, but he also found ways to average around 15 points per game. Jerry first learned the game when his Uncle Shug knocked the bottom out of a washtub and taught his nephew how to shoot at it using tin cans as basketballs. Shug's lessons seemed to work, as Jerry made the Tigers a contender with teammates like Joe Decker, Jerry Cooper, 'Deadeye' George Gilbert, Jackie Woods, Donnie Adler, Byrle Akers and Joe Cochrane.

Though he wasn't a prolific scorer, like North's Dave Schellhase or Oakland City's Larry Harris, Scott did find ways to score. One of his biggest fans, hall of fame Princeton radio announcer Richard Lankford, watched Jerry play numerous times and puts a humorous slant on the Snake's reputation on the hardwood. "They always told the story," Lankford revealed, "that when the dressing room door opened, Jerry was ready to shoot."

Jerry proved to be more of a natural on the baseball diamond, as he played virtually any position where he was needed. As a right-handed thrower and hitter, the Snake possessed a rocket arm and explosive bat and developed into a tremendous catcher, although he was not fond of the position. At the plate, he never hit below .400 in high school or Legion ball, while playing during the same era as Don Hansen (Reitz) and Rex Mundi's Bob Griese and Jerry Mattingly, whom the Snake considered a good friend.

Some of Jerry Scott's greatest accolades were earned on the gridiron, where he juked and darted his way through enemy defenses as a halfback and battered opposing running backs as an outside linebacker. As a sophomore, he led the SIAC 'B' Division in scoring under Coach Jim Meyers and once out-gained the entire Bosse team, led by quarterback Ron Volkman, during a 6-0 Princeton win. As a junior, Jerry scored 150 points out of the Double Wing offense of new coach Jim Byers, and as a senior, Coach Byers used every way possible to get Jerry the ball, even having him throw it occasionally.

When his senior football season was over, the Snake received honorable mention All State honors, along with Griese, and his Tigers won the SIAC 'B' Division. The conference title also created a unique scenario, because Coach Byers' father, Reitz coach Herman Byers, won the SIAC 'A' Division, making them the only father-son tandem to win conference crowns in the same year.

Scott is certain that he averaged over seven yards per carry during his high school career, but his exact numbers are not known because stats were not documented like they are today. What is certain, however, is that the Snake rang up a lot of yards while running plays like the '15-Dive' for Coach Byers and that he was exciting to watch while he did it. Jerry admits that football was his purest sport and that he wasn't a big fan of practice. But he lived for game day, and fans loved to watch his unique style that often left potential tacklers grasping at air. "For some reason or other, I just had a knack for side-stepping," Scott explained from his home on the outskirts of Princeton. "There were times I'd hit the line and just stop and the two (defenders) would hit each other."

When told that the Snake was going to be included in this book, Jim Byers agreed that Jerry was worthy and chuckled at the memory of Scott as a player and the talent he showed on the football field. "He is definitely one of the best, if not *the* best, that I coached," Byers disclosed. "I was at Princeton three years and Boonville three years and had some pretty good athletes, like Joe Loge, who played at Evansville College. Jerry was an unusual athlete. He definitely would've gotten a scholarship (for football). Indiana State was going to offer one, and, of course, Evansville College would have loved to have him at tailback because he had great hands and was a very elusive runner. He was definitely a Division I prospect. They didn't keep stats like they do today, and it's a shame because he would definitely have been over a thousand yards (for a season)."

As his senior year wound down, Coach Byers asked Jerry where he wanted to go to school to play football, and the Snake surprised him when he responded by saying, "I'm tired of school; I'm going to try and play baseball." Fortunately, his skills made that possible, and Jerry signed with the Baltimore Orioles and headed for the rookie league in Bluefield, West Virginia.

While in the minors, Scott was careful not to let anyone know that he was a catcher, and he enjoyed his first season playing the outfield and hitting a solid .298. In his second year, he started at AAA Rochester before being sent down to Thomasville, Georgia, where he played with Davey Johnson, who would go on to a brilliant career as a player and manager.

While at Thomasville, Jerry's roommate, a pitcher, let the cat out of the bag about Jerry's prowess as a catcher and the manager gave him a try when the team's top two catchers got injured. In his first game behind the plate, Scott threw out three runners, hit a home run and went three for four at the plate, prompting his manager to say, "You're catching from now on."

Two weeks into training camp in his third season, Jerry and a buddy decided to use a day off to try some horseback riding, and what was intended to be a pleasant afternoon turned out to be the beginning of the end for Jerry's baseball career. After taking a fall and dislocating his throwing shoulder, Jerry's powerful arm was never the same again and his playing days were over.

With his sports career behind him, Scott headed back to Princeton and worked at Whirlpool for five years before catching on with the North Fork Southern Railroad. As he raised his three children, daughter Debbie and sons David and J.D. Jr. (who was also a great baseball player and earned All-Big South honors at Armstrong State before signing with the Cardinals), Jerry dabbled in the horse training business. Though it was just a hobby, he loved being around Ellis Park and Churchill Downs and says that some of his best friends were the horses he worked with.

Nearly fifty years after he finished his high school career, Gibson County fans still remember the thrills Jerry Scott produced as an athlete. "What made Jerry so good," said Richard Lankford, "is that he was good in all three sports. He was a driven athlete. In football, nobody ran harder or tackled harder than Jerry. I believe, right today, that Jerry Scott, a little older and a little heavier, could go to Lafayette Park (the town's baseball field) and hit them out of the park."

Little did Lankford know that his prediction was prophetic. When Jerry was told of Richard's statement, he revealed that he had recently taken his grandson to Lafayette Park to practice and had, indeed, hit one over the fence. Even today, at the age of 66, as he shoots in the 70s on the golf course with his friends and contemplates returning to the horse training business, the Snake still has his competitive fire.

When looking at a high school career, it is easy to see why many rank Scott among Princeton's all-time greats, and no one could explain it better than sports announcer Richard Lankford. "He was the best overall athlete I ever saw," Lankford stated. "There probably have been better basketball players (at Princeton), like Bob Pritchett or Larry Kidwell or Vaughn Chavis, and maybe better football players, like Justin Lynch, but when you put all three sports together, nobody was any better than Jerry 'the Snake' Scott."

School	Year	Record	Coach
\multicolumn{4}{|c|}{**IHSAA State Champions: BASEBALL**}			
Memorial	1978	30-0	Quentin Merkel
Memorial	1989	33-3	Quentin Merkel
Memorial	1993	36-2	Quentin Merkel
Jasper	1997	29-7	Terry Gobert
Jasper (3A)	1998	30-6	Terry Gobert
Mater Dei (2A)	1999	26-8	Darin Knight
Jasper (3A)	2000	30-6	Terry Gobert
Vincennes Lincoln (3A)	2002	25-8	Brandon Pfoff
Tecumseh (A)	2003	16-12	Ron Kahle
Jasper (3A)	2006	34-1	Terry Gobert

THE VOLKMANS: ED, EILEEN AND THE BOYS

Ron, Mike and Dean Volkman were all talented athletes, but what makes their story unique is the special bond they still share as brothers in their 60s and the love and devotion they exhibit for their parents, Ed and Eileen.

The boys grew up playing sandlot ball near their home across from Vogel Grade School. "It was absolutely wonderful," said Ron Volkman, the oldest of the brothers. "Kids don't do that anymore. One time, we wrote down 35 names of guys we saw almost every day in the summer. We had a side lot, and we would have ten or twelve on a side while another ten or twelve would be watching. We would start early and play until dark. That's when Mom would feed us in the summertime.

"We had a basketball goal against the old garage," Ron continued, "and we'd just beat the heck out of each other. If somebody went in for a layup, you didn't try to block it; you just rammed them into the garage. Dad had to replace I don't know how many garage doors. We played on gravel, and we always had nicks and cuts."

Toughened up by the brutal neighborhood skirmishes, each of the three grew up to earn college scholarships for athletics, and much of their success can be attributed to good genes and a solid support system from their parents.

"Dad was a great guy, the salt of the earth," Ron said. "He and Mom were so supportive of us. None of us ever played a game, from little league through high school, that either Mom or Dad wasn't there.

"Dad was a great baseball player, too. Of course, we thought he was the greatest. He was a catcher. He played for Ingle Coal Company. They had doubleheaders every Sunday at all the little towns around here.

"He bought a rural milk route and hauled American Dairy milk to farmers in Warrick and Vanderburgh counties. He worked seven days a week for seven years one time. That's the kind of guy he was."

Although Ed passed away in 1988, the boys vowed long ago that they would all get together with their mother as a group at least two or three times a month. While joining them for one of these visits, it was easy to see the admiration the three share for this pistol of a lady.

Eileen, herself, showed tremendous athletic talent as a youngster, a trait not always appreciated by folks of her generation. "I wanted to be a boy so bad," she admitted. "Boys would come by (when she was young) and say, 'Come on, Eileen, let's go play ball.'"

Eileen played football with the boys and even pitched for the school's baseball team. She was well known for being a power hitter, and she even displayed her long ball talents in her adulthood when the two younger boys were in little league. On one occasion, a 12-year-old Mickey Martin (who would go on to become an outstanding pitcher and later the head baseball coach at North) challenged Eileen, saying she couldn't hit him. She whacked his first pitch over the right field wall to the amazement of everyone. "I was just cocky enough," she recalled, "that I said, 'That's nothing. I'll hit the next one over center field.'"

And she did – followed by a sprint around first and a hook slide into second. With the crowd roaring, an embarrassed Mickey Martin declared, "That's enough!"

The Volkman boys are also quick to point out the sacrifices their mother made as they grew up playing sports year-round with the likes of Paul Gries, Jerry Mattingly, Dave Schellhase and many others. For several years, Eileen wore the same gray suit to ballgames because when she would tell Ed that she needed a new one, he would insist that the limited money they had be used to purchase new ball gloves or bats or basketball nets. Being the good sport she was, Eileen did what she could by changing from a white to a pink to a yellow blouse. While Eileen told the story about "that damned suit," son Mike was quick to chime in, saying, "She really did look great in it."

For Ed and Eileen, it was all about the boys, and as each of their sons developed, they were always there as proud parents. Ron was the only one of the three to play ball at Bosse, as re-districting would later result in Mike and Dean playing at the brand new North High School. Ron quarterbacked Bosse's Cub football team as a 7th and 8th grader and was taken under the wing of the Bulldogs' senior quarterback Bob Padgett. Although Ron looked up to him, he does recall that Padgett was a little weak in the footspeed department. "They clocked him in the hundred yard dash with a sundial," Ron wisecracked.

Ed and Eileen Volkman with their sons (L-R) Dean, Mike and Ron.
(Photo courtesy of the Volkman family.)

As a sophomore, Ron started at quarterback and middle linebacker surrounded by ten seniors on a team coached by Bill Russler, an ex Evansville College player who had succeeded Jim Graham as Bosse's head coach. At one point, the team was ranked fifth in the state. The team's arch-rivals were the Panthers at Reitz, whom the Bulldogs would play "every Thanksgiving Day, come hell or high water," as Ron recalled. "When I played," he added, "Reitz and Bosse were like water and oil. Reitz had a cheer that said, 'Bosse, Bosse, where the girls are girls and the boys are too!'"

After a 4-0 start his junior season, Ron and his teammates lost the last six games and then all ten games his senior year. He had finished his football career with sixteen straight losses as a result of the team's decimation by graduation and injuries and playing against some great teams, like the 1958 Memorial Tigers, led by future NFL star Larry Stallings.

Ron also played baseball for two years at Bosse before giving it up to play in the very popular industrial fast pitch softball leagues in the area. As a 16-year-old catcher (just like Dad), Ron was lucky enough to catch such local stars as Bob Garrett, Gene Knapp and Joe Celania.

While his football experiences were 'character builders' and his baseball talents were being used instead on a softball diamond, Ron's greatest sports memories at Bosse were on the basketball court. From his freshman year on, Ron shared the floor with four classmates who played well together as juniors and seniors: Jim Newcomb, Paul Utley, David Crosley and Cliff Ford. The group played under the legendary Herman Keller during a time when some of the area's greatest stars were roaming the hardwood.

During their senior season, Ron and his teammates lost in the final game of the regional to a Tell City team that featured Ed Rolen (Scott's father) and a young freshman named Tom Kron. Against Madison, they watched Buster Briley score forty points while a freshman named Larry Humes was just coming onto the scene. One of Ron's claims to fame was holding Lincoln star Walter Miles to eleven points, seventeen below his average.

After graduating in 1959, Ron had the opportunity to play quarterback for Coach Jack Mollenkopf at Purdue, but it required his parents to pay for his freshman year (about $2,000). With two sons coming behind Ron, Ed and Eileen felt that Ron should instead accept a full ride basketball scholarship to Arkansas State. After five years, Ron graduated and then spent five years in the military, including one year in Vietnam, with training as a paratrooper, pilot and working with air defense missiles.

As Ron finished his high school career and moved on to compete in college, his two younger brothers were molding their own careers at North High School as three-sport athletes. As Mike competed alongside such North greats as Schellhase, Mickey Martin, Steve Schroer, Mike Madriaga and John Mominee, younger brother Dean was watching and learning.

As a little league pitcher, Mike Volkman was talented enough that his father was certain he was destined for the major leagues. During the season, Ed was so protective of Mike that he wouldn't let his son mow the lawn because he was afraid he'd get blisters and couldn't pitch. As one can imagine, the pampering didn't sit too well with Ron and Dean. "We'd say, 'That's not right, Dad,'" Ron remembered, "but Dad would say, 'Oh, no, Mike might make it to 'the bigs.'"

Mike didn't play football during his early years in high school, but his reputation as an athlete prompted coach Morris Riley to

Bosse's Jim Fitzgerald takes a tumble while Ron Volkman (#14) tries to guard his brother Mike (#32) during an unusual game at Roberts Stadium. The footing that night became treacherous when condensation appeared, the result of the floor being laid over a surface left over from an ice show the night before. (Photo courtesy of the Volkman family.)

recruit him to play quarterback his senior year. With Mike under center, the Huskies fielded one of its best teams ever as Volkman passed and handed off to speedsters Madriaga and Mominee.

North's baseball teams during Mike's tenure there were also among the best in the school's history. With fellow pitchers Martin and Schroer supported by great players like Schellhase, Madriaga, Joe Mullan, Mike Fritz and a freshman named Dean Volkman, the Huskies lost only one regular season game in 1961. In fact, the only school to defeat North in both baseball and football that year was Reitz.

Although he was a great all-around athlete, Mike's best sport was basketball. One of the most memorable games of Mike's career was played in 1959 when he was a sophomore starter. As his team prepared for the February game at Roberts Stadium, the local media hyped the story of young Mike competing against his brother Ron, who was a senior starter at Bosse. The sibling rivalry was overshadowed, however, when the Stadium became the real story. It seems the floor was placed on top of a sheet of ice that had been used the previous night for an ice show. As condensation worked its way to the surface, play became treacherous. Thanks to some quick thinking, North gained an edge when Coach Jim Rausch covered the soles of his players' shoes with tape, enabling them to win a close game. (Ron is quick to point out, however, that the Bulldogs redeemed themselves with a 20-point win in the sectional.)

In 1960-'61, Mike's senior year, the Huskies were projected to go a long way in the State Tournament but suffered a disappointing loss in the sectional. Despite the unexpected end to their season, the team was still one of the school's best ever and was exciting to watch. With a supporting cast of Joe Mullan, Gary Pfender and sophomore Ted Mattingly, Mike and future Indiana Basketball Hall of Famer Dave Schellhase piled up points by the truckload. The standard joke was for Mike to tell the hot-shooting Schellhase, "Dave, you work yourself in the clear, and then I'll shoot it," and, according to Mike, their shared philosophy was, "Never make a good pass when you can take a bad shot."

Mike strongly considered heading south to play college ball for Coach Bruce 'Slick' Hale at the University of Miami, but he opted to stay home and join Arad McCutchan's Purple Aces. As a member of a strong class led by future NBA player and coach Jerry Sloan, Mike rode the pine for two years. Unhappy with his prospects, he contacted Coach Hale at Miami, who welcomed him with open arms. (Had Mike chosen to stay at Evansville College, he would have been a member of the Aces' 1964 and 1965 national champions.)

After sharing a high school court with superstar Dave Schellhase and a college court with future hall of famer Jerry Sloan, Mike finished his college career playing beside another basketball phenom, the hot-shooting but eccentric Rick Barry, at the University of Miami.

While Mike was playing college ball, the youngest of the Volkman brothers was turning the heads of college recruiters across the country. Dean was a true multi-sport athlete, earning nine varsity letters at North. He lettered two years for Coach Rausch on the hardwood and was a four-year letterman as a catcher and third baseman on the Huskies' baseball team. But, unlike his two brothers, it was football that would be his ticket to a college education.

Described by others and himself as confident to the point of being cocky, Dean was a natural leader and a fierce competitor. No story better exemplifies both his cockiness and his leadership than that of a Friday night during Dean's senior season.

In preparation for a contest with Bosse, North coach Morris Riley had pre-planned the first four plays he wanted the offense to run. He specifically instructed that, by no means should the ball be thrown toward a certain defender. On the third play of the series, Dean lofted a pass in the flat toward (you guessed it) the aforementioned player, and the defender intercepted for a touchdown.

Most quarterbacks would make every effort to avoid the coach after such a debacle, but not Dean. He loped toward the sideline expecting a good old-fashioned butt chewing and took his medicine like a man. "Here comes Coach Riley off the sideline," Dean recalled, "and he's red, man! I just kept going, and when I passed him, I said, 'We got 'em, Coach.'"

With his backside and confidence intact, Dean led the Huskies to a comfortable 50-7 win.

During Dean's senior year, he led a very talented North team to a 9-1 season, losing only to Richmond 6-0. That year, Dean had the luxury of throwing to Lane Fenner, a 6'6" tight end who later played at Florida State and in the NFL, or handing off to a bevy of talented backs. Fullback Phil Boyd was a "physical specimen" and a bruising runner, and Jim and Kenny Thomas were lightning out of the backfield. A young fullback named Ken Bargo (who later followed Dean to college at Illinois) was also starting to make a name for himself.

Defensively, Dean manned the middle linebacker spot and was second on the team in tackles to another tremendous athlete, Charlie Broyles.

After graduating in 1964, Dean joined another very talented class at the University of Illinois. As a result of Illinois' Rose Bowl win the previous year, 27 All-Americans, including Dean, were part of Coach Pete Elliott's 33-man recruiting class. As a freshman, Dean got valuable experience against some strong upperclassmen. Evansville's Don Hansen was only two years away from beginning an impressive NFL career, and his running mate at linebacker was one of the greatest to ever play the game, Dick Butkus.

Butkus struck fear in the hearts of those who lined up against him, and stories, whether true or exaggerated, are hilarious and mythical in their nature. Dean Volkman has experienced the fear of Butkus first-hand and has witnessed and heard many stories.

"Back then, freshmen couldn't play varsity ball," Dean pointed out. "Everybody (in the country) hated to play Butkus, but we had to practice against him two or three times a week! He was intelligent and a good guy, but when he strapped on his helmet, he was an animal, even in practice."

During Dean Volkman's years at Illinois, he endured a slush fund scandal that led to Pete Elliott's dismissal, along with several of the team's best players. Despite the controversy and subsequent coaching change, Dean finished his career ranked in the top ten of several of the school's offensive categories.

Like his brothers, he had used the skills he had honed on the sandlots and fields of Evansville to better himself with a college education.

The Volkmans are also appreciative of the sacrifices made by their loving parents, from father Ed's grueling work schedule to the limited shopping budget for Eileen, all done to give their boys the best equipment money could buy.

Dean was reminded of his parents' devotion years ago when he was talking with beloved Evansville coach Don Watson less than a week before Don passed away. "I've been around sports all my life," Watson told him, "and the best athletic family I've ever been involved with are the Volkmans. But don't get too cocky, Dean. I'm not talking about you and Mike and Ron; I'm talking about your mom and your dad."

The boys have all settled in Evansville to stay near Eileen. She and Ed were always there for them, and now the boys are here for Eileen. And I'll bet that when she needs one, the boys will make sure she gets a brand new suit.

Dean Volkman signs with the University of Illinois as his father Ed (left) and brother Mike look on. (Photo courtesy of the Volkman family.)

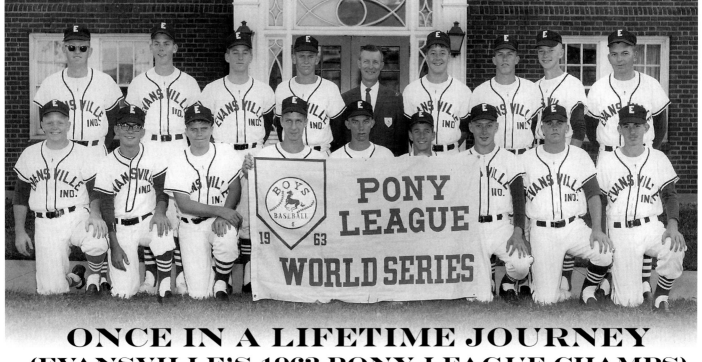

ONCE IN A LIFETIME JOURNEY
(EVANSVILLE'S 1963 PONY LEAGUE CHAMPS)

In the summer of 1963, a talented group of teenagers and a dedicated group of coaches and parents took a journey no Indiana team had taken before. And even today, more than 35 years later, they can still say they're the only Indiana team in history to win the Pony League World Series.

"I still remember it like it was yesterday", said Bill Altmeyer, who coached the team. "We had an exceptional group of talented players, and the thing about those kids is that their parents worked with them when they were young. The kids had good skills and were smart ballplayers."

Altmeyer was a 29-year-old office clerk in 1963, and he and his wife, Mary, had no children at the time. Bill was in his fourth year as a pony league coach, and he had managed the East All-Stars the previous season when they lost in the early stages of the tournament. "We lost two great players from that ('62) team in Connie Garnett and Pete Rupp," he stated to Ed Cole in an article for a local magazine. "But we had almost everybody else back."

Bill and his assistant coach, Jim Morris, had high expectations for the group because all the ingredients for success were in place, not the least of which was solid pitching. "Pitching is 75% of the game," Bill stated, "and I had four of the best." His fourth pitcher, Johnny Miller, was excellent but rarely got to pitch because of the three outstanding hurlers ahead of him, so his contributions were made as a hitter and strong-throwing left-fielder.

When it came time to hand the ball to his pitcher on any given day, Mr. Altmeyer had three reliable options. "You could probably flip a coin as to which one was the best," he said of his tremendous trio. "Gordon Slade had the best control of any pony leaguer I ever saw. He had super control and was deceptively fast

The 1963 Pony League World Champs. Front Row (L-R): Steve Lambert, David Rice, Steve Parrish, Steve Winternheimer, Barry Schaefer, Vaughn Wedeking, Barry Rollman, Terry Wedgewood, Ray Morgan. Back Row (L-R): Bill Altmeyer (manager), Don Collins, Gordon Slade, Jim Giannini, unidentified, Abe Krause, Jim Campbell, John Miller, Jim Morris (assistant coach). (Photo courtesy of Bill Altmeyer.)

because he was real smooth. He had a good curveball, and he was an even-tempered kid; He never lost his cool."

Bill chuckled as he remembered his second ace on the team, Steve 'Punkin' Lambert. "He was another tremendous ballplayer. He was very effective because he was left-handed. He didn't look like a pitcher; He was short and squatty," Bill described. Another factor that made Lambert so effective was his control – or lack of it. "I always started him first because I didn't know if he was going to last one inning or seven, because he was pretty wild," the coach explained. "He might throw three in a row over the backstop and then pitch the next four or five innings perfectly. He could walk three or four, then strike out ten or twelve. He could throw very hard. Actually, I never had to take him out because of wildness, but I was always nervous."

The team's third pitcher was Jim Giannini, who also played third base (when Slade pitched) and first (when Lambert pitched). "My team won the regular season league championship with Jim Giannini, not Lambert or Slade (who played on opposing teams)," Bill pointed out, "so that tells you something about Jim. He had great style, a high leg kick and a good curveball."

Pitching wasn't the team's only strength, however. The lineup was loaded with powerful bats that could drive in runs once the speed was on base, and that speed came primarily in the form of one of the greatest all-around athletes to ever come out of Evansville, Vaughn Wedeking.

The quintessential leadoff man, Wedeking could hit for average and turn a single into a double in the blink of an eye. It was not unusual for the speedster to steal second and third after a single or a walk. "We could even tell our opponents that he was going to steal, and he would still do it," Coach Altmeyer recalled. "He was also our center fielder, and we could play the left and right fielders close to the foul lines because Vaughn could catch everything in between them.

"Vaughn was a great kid, and he was so fast that, after three steps, he was at full speed. Teams would pitch out trying to throw him out stealing and still not be able to get him. He was a wonderful, wonderful athlete."

Like any good baseball team, the East team was solid up the middle. Besides Wedeking in center, the middle infield consisted of Donnie Collins at second base and Terry Wedgewood at shortstop. Behind the plate was Abe Krause, who was described by Coach Altmeyer as "a tremendous catcher, a great kid with a great arm."

Filling out the starting lineup in left field was either Ray Morgan or Steve Winternheimer. The rest of the roster who played their roles and contributed to the team's success were Jim Campbell, Barry Schaefer, Barry Rollman, Steve Parrish, and David Rice, who was one of only two 13-year-olds on the team (Winternheimer was the other.)

As the all-star season approached, the small contingent of parents and fans of the East Pony League were eager to watch Coach Altmeyer's 'dream team' take their first step into Evansville sports history. From their local ball field, which sat near where U of E's Braun Stadium now sits, they were headed on a journey that would take them all the way to Washington, Pennsylvania.

Ironically, this adventure was nearly over shortly after it began. First, they had to get by a tough West Side team, led by Steve Sursa, Gary Marx and others. Then the local regional was another stiff challenge. "Some of our toughest games were the early ones we played locally," recalled Mr. Altmeyer. "We were tied with Princeton after seven innings. They had a big strong pitcher, and he had to leave the game (because of innings pitched restrictions), and our second pitcher was better than theirs and we won 9-8."

The team also won close games against Joliet, Illinois (5-4) and Mt. Carmel (2-1) in the regional. As the word spread about the team's upcoming trip to 'the big dance' in Washington, PA, the community was excited, and popular local radio celebrity Marv Bates was sent east to tell the story as it unfolded.

The first game at the Series was a cakewalk, as Lambert threw a one-hitter and struck out 13 in a 7-0 win. Jim Giannini hit consecutive home runs, and Terry Wedgewood homered, as well.

After falling behind 3-0 in the first inning of the second game, the East Pony stars responded and pulled away for a 10-4 win behind Gordon Slade's four-hitter. Wedeking scored the team's first run in the bottom of the first in typical fashion. After reaching first on an error, he stole second, moved to third on an infield out and scored on a Wedgewood single. They took the lead in the third on a Don Collins walk followed by back-to-back-to-back doubles by Giannini, Wedgewood, and Slade, and Abe Krause homered in a 5-run fifth inning.

The final hurdle for the Evansville contingent was the highly-touted, heavily-flavored team from Canoga Park-Woodland Hills, California. The California team had received a telegram wishing them well from hall of fame pitcher Don Drysdale and from other members of the L.A. Dodgers, as well. The Canoga Park team was also undefeated and had outscored their tourney opponents 64-15.

Bill Altmeyer decided to start Steve Lambert in the World Series final, and the flame-throwing southpaw put on quite a show for the 4,000 spectators. By game's end, he had struck out twelve, walked three, and given up three hits in a 3-1 Evansville victory.

Once again, the crafty Wedeking ignited the team with some typical heroics in the first inning. After leading off with a walk, he broke for second on the next pitch. When the catcher's throw sailed into the outfield and the center fielder misplayed it, Vaughn rounded second and third for Evansville's first run.

With the score tied 1-1 in the sixth, it was Wedeking's speed again that proved to be the difference in the game. After another walk, he again stole second to put himself in scoring position. After the next two hitters struck out, Gordon Slade looped a soft single to center to send Wedeking scampering home. On the play, Slade advanced to second and eventually scored on a single by Lambert.

This group of fifteen teenagers had lived up to the potential that many saw in them as little leaguers. With the leadership of fine coaches and the support of loving families, they had achieved the ultimate prize their sport had to offer. To determine just how good this team was, one need only look at what some of the individuals did with their athletic talents during that season and for many years after.

- Catcher Abe Krause won the Norman R. Moser Award as the batting champion of the World Series with his .556 average.
- Reserve Barry Rollman was a member of Evansville North's 1967 State championship basketball team.
- Reserve player Steve Parrish went on to set records as a receiver with the University of Kentucky football program.
- Steve 'Punkin' Lambert pitched at Murray State for four years.
- Jim Giannini went on to pitch at the University of Miami.
- Terry Wedgewood was the Big Ten batting champion at Purdue and broke some of the records of future major league star Harvey Kuehn.
- Gordon Slade played baseball and football at Davidson College, where he led the school to its only bowl game (Tangerine Bowl). He was an All-Conference quarterback for two years and an All-Conference baseball player for three. He was drafted by the Baltimore Colts in the 7th round of the 1970 NFL draft and was also taken in the major league baseball draft by the Washington Senators (who became the Texas Rangers shortly thereafter). Choosing to play football, he played professionally in the Canadian League and the Old Atlantic Football League.
- Vaughn Wedeking became the Indiana State high school champion in the 440-yard dash and won a scholarship to play basketball at Jacksonville. There, he teamed with fellow Harrison Warrior teammate Greg Nelson and 7-footers Artis Gilmore and Pembrook Burrows as they reached the Final Four of the NCAA Tourney.

For a few short weeks, the talents of each of the East Pony League All-Stars meshed to form a history-making baseball team. The three pitchers were perfect (Slade 6-0, Lambert 6-0, and Giannini 3-0), and every member of the starting lineup hit at least one home run during the tournament. The result was a once-in-a-lifetime journey for the Evansville East All-Stars during that special summer in 1963.

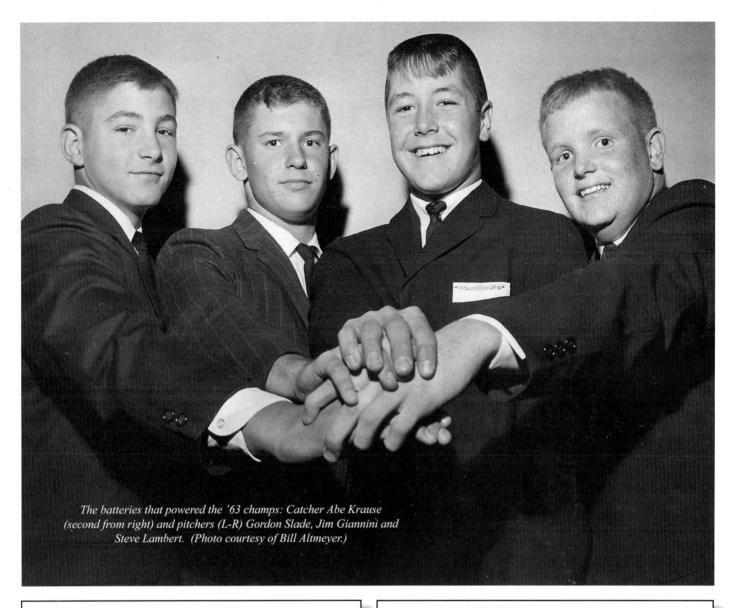

The batteries that powered the '63 champs: Catcher Abe Krause (second from right) and pitchers (L-R) Gordon Slade, Jim Giannini and Steve Lambert. (Photo courtesy of Bill Altmeyer.)

DID YOU KNOW?

The son of East Pony League assistant coach Jim Morris went on to become one of the country's top college baseball coaches. Jim Jr. coached his 29th year in 2007 and his 14th at the University of Miami. He was named the national Coach of the Year in 1994 by *Baseball America,* and in 1999 and 2001, he was named Coach of the Year by the American Baseball Coaches Association.

His teams have made it to the College World Series in Omaha in 10 of his 13 seasons at Miami, and his 2001 team were national champions.

OUTSIDE THE LINES

During the East Pony League team's stay at the World Series, the Evansville players and those from California set up a ping pong match between Evansville's manager Bill Altmeyer and the manager of the California team. The results of the match are inconsequential.

What's interesting is that, during the summer, there had been a series of robberies in the L.A. area. A two-man team, dubbed 'Mutt and Jeff' by the media, were knocking over savings and loans during the daytime, with the tall robber jumping over the counter to get the loot.

After the World Series, the duo was captured. Why is this significant? The tall thief, 'Jeff', was the ping pong-playing manager of the California pony league team!

The 1962 State champion Bulldogs. Front row (L-R): Jerry Polley, Dave Riggs, Bob Guenther, Charlie Given, Bob Adams, Chuck Wey. Back row (L-R): Jim Myers (head coach), John Wilson, Gary Grieger, Ken Rakow, Gene Lockyear, Jerry Southwood, Eric Sullivan, Al Buck (asst. coach), Jerry Canterbury (asst. coach).

BOSSE'S 1962 STATE CHAMPS: A TOUCH OF CLASS

Winning the State basketball championship has been the Holy Grail of Indiana high school sports, and the accomplishment is an experience that players, coaches and even fans cherish for a lifetime. When the Bosse Bulldogs launched their season in 1961, not many could have prognosticated what would transpire over the next four months. Local competition was probably as formidable as any in history, and the Bulldogs were led by a rookie coach and had little experience returning from the previous year. But Bosse defied the odds and, with incredible poise and confidence, took the Tri-state on an unbelievable journey in March of 1962.

In November of 1961, Bosse's basketball program was in a state of transition, coming off a respectable 12-5 regular season the year before that ended with a 56-53 loss to Tell City in the regional final. When popular coach Herman Keller left to join the IHSAA, the program was placed in the hands of Keller's top assistant, Jim Myers. The only returning regular was 6'3 senior forward Gary Grieger. At one guard would be the only other senior starter, 6'2 John Wilson, and to round out the starting lineup, Myers went with three juniors: 6'2 guard Jerry Southwood, 6'4 forward Gene Lockyear and 6'5 center Ken Rakow. The team's top reserves would be seniors Charlie Given (6'2) on the front line and Eric Sullivan (6'1) in the backcourt.

In addition to the fresh faces on the varsity, Coach Myers also decided that Bosse would sport a new look. Taking a page from Evansville College coach Arad McCutchan, the Bulldogs' uniforms would feature long sleeves with stripes around the shoulders. The fashion statement set the Bulldogs apart from their competition, but before long, the boys in red and gray would make a statement on the court, as well.

Bosse opened the season at Huntingburg and clamped down on the Hunters with a suffocating full court press from the starting whistle. Huntingburg could barely get the ball past midcourt, prompting center Ken Rakow to speak up during the first timeout. Rakow, the safety man on the press, implored Coach Myers to change tactics, saying, "Let's call off the press. I haven't even touched the ball yet!" Myers eased up as the game progressed in a dominating 72-47 win behind John Wilson's 24-point effort.

Next, Bosse's man-to-man defense and full court pressure prevailed again for a 61-57 win over a tough Tell City team featuring two Indiana Basketball Hall of Famers, Tom Kron and Coach 'Gunner' Wyman. In the third game, Grieger lit up Boonville with

29 points, and the Bulldogs were on a roll. As Bosse's size and discipline produced six more relatively easy wins over Princeton (73-55), Central (73-60), New Albany (82-69), Memorial (73-64), Jasper (77-57) and Columbus (61-52), the stage was set for the highly-anticipated matchup against powerful Rex Mundi, led by 'Big Tom' Niemeier and Bob Griese.

With Grieger scoring and Rakow pounding the boards, Bosse squandered two 11-point leads and then came from behind in a frantic closing minute to prevail 78-74 in front of 10,300 fans at Robert Stadium.

Bosse was 10-0 and getting recognition statewide when they faced scoring sensation Dave Schellhase and his North Huskies. Playing to another packed house at Roberts Stadium, Schellhase lived up to his reputation, bombing Bosse for 45 points, including a 30-footer in the closing seconds, to hand the Bulldogs their first loss 84-83.

With the pressure of an undefeated season off their shoulders, Coach Myers' crew made quick work of their next five opponents with wins over Evansville Lincoln (78-64), Mt. Vernon (83-37), Reitz (73-59), Vincennes (95-52), and Mater Dei (84-60). At 15-1, Bosse was heading down the Ohio River to face a coach who had helped bring Bosse its first State title nearly twenty years earlier.

Six bus loads of Bosse fans made the trip to Madison to watch the Bulldogs face a program that was on a 57-game regular season winning streak. The gym was filled to the rafters with 5,100 screaming fans, and the game was carried on television from Evansville to Indianapolis. Madison featured future Evansville College All-American Larry Humes and were coached by Julius 'Bud' Ritter, who had starred on the Bosse State championship teams of 1944 and 1945. Although the game was expected to be a high-scoring shootout, Bosse finished with an uncharacteristic 29 errors and shot only .265 from the floor. Madison was only slightly better and kept their winning streak intact with a 59-51 victory.

With only one regular season game left, the Bulldogs had little time to reflect on their loss. Instead, they used their maturity and intelligence to prepare for the tournament. Coach Myers and his assistants, Jerry Canterbury and Al Buck, were fortunate to have a group whose emotions weren't overly affected by their performance. Wilson, Lockyear and Rakow were straight-A students, and Grieger and Southwood were B+ students, so they were all smart enough to know that dwelling on a big win or a disappointing loss would be counterproductive.

After a ho-hum 88-51 win over Bloomington, the Bulldogs finished the regular season at 16-2, winning the SIAC and sharing the City crown with North and Rex Mundi. With the regular season over, the quietly confident Bulldogs and their soft-spoken coach were prepared to make some noise as tournament time rolled around.

In the Evansville Sectional, Bosse had little trouble in the first two games, with easy wins over North Posey (92-56) and Reitz (68-47), but things would get tougher as the tournament field narrowed. Facing their stiffest city competition, Bosse sneaked by Rex Mundi and then stymied North 88-71 to avenge one of their losses during the season and claim the sectional crown.

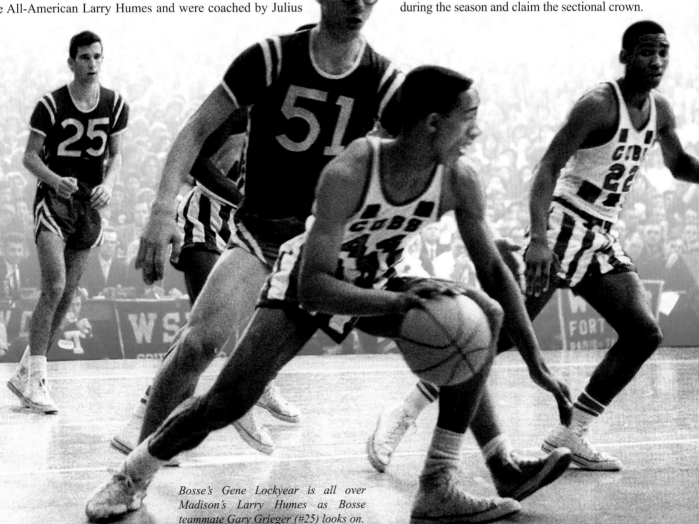

Bosse's Gene Lockyear is all over Madison's Larry Humes as Bosse teammate Gary Grieger (#25) looks on.

In the regional, fans and media alike were hyping the potential re-match between the Bulldogs and the Tell City Marksmen, but the game was not to be. Tell City, who had eliminated Bosse in three previous regionals, was upset in the afternoon by the Castle Knights. After breezing past Ft. Branch, 76-61, in the first game, Bosse made easy work of the Knights with an 84-53 victory to secure the regional title. The friendly confines of Roberts Stadium felt good to Bosse, and they looked forward to 'hosting' the Evansville Semi-state the following Saturday.

When Jasper rolled into town on March 10th, 1962, they came prepared and battled Bosse to the wire before falling 70-68, and the evening final was anti-climatic as Bosse methodically eliminated Seymour 77-57. For the first time in the tournament, the Bulldogs would hit the road, and fans from across the state would converge on Butler Fieldhouse to see another page written in the history of Hoosier high school basketball.

Bosse's Bulldogs entered the State Finals with the worst record (24-2) of the Final Four teams. As Bosse made final preparations during their Friday afternoon workout at the Fieldhouse, local fans anxiously awaited the Saturday festivities that typically surround the Indiana State Finals. Before the team's evening meal, Coach Myers even got a spiritual blessing as a show of support, as he was told that Gary Grieger, the team's only Catholic player, had been given permission by his bishop to eat meat on the Friday before the Finals. It seems the team physician, Dr. Gil Wilhelmus, had made the request to ensure that Grieger was properly nourished. So after a hearty meal and a good night's sleep, the Bosse Bulldogs were ready to face a familiar foe on Saturday afternoon.

The first team standing between Bosse and the title were Bud Ritter's 25-0 Madison Cubs. In what was reported to be one of the most poorly officiated games in State Tournament history, the Bulldogs led at every stop on their way to a 79-75 win. A total of 54 fouls, 28 on Madison and 26 on Bosse, were called, and each team had three players foul out. One player to leave because of fouls was Madison star Larry Humes, who was enticed to foul by Charlie Given's constant shot fakes. Once again, by playing smart and controlling their emotions, the Bulldogs had found another way to win.

In the evening final, Bosse was a 12-point underdog to the 27-1 East Chicago Washington Senators, who were coached by the colorful Johnny Barrato. Although East Chicago was worn down after a grueling one-point win over Kokomo, the Senators led the Bulldogs 63-57 late in the game and looked poised to celebrate. But the boys in the sleeved jerseys were not about to roll over. To a man, the Bulldogs calmly went about their business as they battled the boys from up north. Big Gene Lockyear, who wore black-rimmed glasses, as did his running mate Ken Rakow, shattered one of his lenses early in the game but never came out. Even with the outcome looking grim, Lockyear and his teammates kept their eye on the prize.

As reported in the *Evansville Courier*, a timeout late in the final game was a prime example of the approach Bosse used all season to conquer their competition. With the game on the line, Coach Myers didn't rant and rave or draw up an elaborate plan. Instead, in his typical low-key manner, he simply told his team, "Go out and make your shots." And that's just what they did.

As the Bulldogs took the floor with their backs against the wall, they staged a shooting exhibition like none other ever seen at a State Final. With 7:47 remaining, Gary Grieger connected on a 25-footer to pull Bosse within four at 63-59. Wilson then hit a one-handed set shot to pull Bosse closer. After a bucket by East Chicago, Wilson connected again and Lockyear hit one of two from the line. Seconds later, Jerry Southwood nailed two free throws to give Bosse its first lead at 68-67.

With Greiger on the bench with a charley horse, Lockyear hit from the corner and Rakow hit a spinning two-hander from the circle. After another bucket from the corner by Lockyear, Bosse took the air out of the ball and held on for the win. Lockyear finished the game with 24, and he was supported well by Grieger (22) and Southwood (18). After hitting nine of ten shots from the floor and nine of ten from the foul line to close out the game, Bosse finished their incredible season with an 84-81 victory over the Senators and secured their school's third State championship.

With the title in hand, recognition was showered on the Bulldogs like sprinkles on an ice cream cone. Four of Bosse's players, Rakow, Lockyear, Grieger and Southwood, were named to most of the All-Tourney teams picked that year, and John Wilson was awarded the coveted Trester Award. Coach Jim Myers was voted Coach of the Year by Indiana sportswriters and broadcasters and also made Indiana history by becoming the first man to win the Trester Award (it was called the Gimbel Award when he won it in 1939) and also coach a player (Wilson) who won the award.

Following the tournament, Grieger and Southwood were named to the *Indianapolis News* All-State team, and Grieger was the #2 selection for the Indiana All-Stars behind Madison's Larry Humes. Grieger would later go on to become a captain for the Indiana Hoosiers, and in 2007, he would join Coach Myers in the Indiana Basketball Hall of Fame.

Although the 1961-'62 Bosse Bulldogs were well-known as a precision unit with a totally unselfish style, those who were close to them recognized that they were quality people as well as players, and the tone was set by their coach. Jim Myers always looked back with great affection on his championship team, and in an article for a local magazine, he declared in his usual humble, yet comical, manner, "Those boys were so outstanding and talented and were such great scholars that my wife could have coached them. In fact, she told everyone she did."

Assistant coach Jerry Canterbury and his wife Bernice were also aware of how unique the group was in comparison to typical high schoolers. "They never wore casual clothes (on the road); It was always a suit and tie," said Bernice.

"They were just smart," added Jerry. "You'd just tell them something once and they'd have it. They were the greatest group of gentlemen I'd ever been around. That's always stuck with us."

Along with the seven regulars, the other Bulldogs of 1961-'62, Jerry Polley, Bob Guenther, David Riggs, Charlie Wey, and Bob Adams, represented their school and their city admirably, and each of them moved on to successful careers. Although many area schools have brought home State championships through the years, it is doubtful that any team has done it with more class than the 1962 Bosse Bulldogs.

DAVE SCHELLHASE: A GAME FOR THE AGES

Hundreds of exceptional basketball players have roamed the hardwood of southwestern Indiana courts over the years, and many were known for their offensive talents. But when it came to the innate ability to score, few were in the class of North High School's Dave Schellhase.

Schellhase (pronounced SHELL-house), was raised on Keck Avenue near Vogel Grade School by his parents, Dave Sr. and Marge. The oldest of three children (his brother Mike graduated from North in 1964 and sister Marge in '72), Dave honed his skills on the playgrounds of Evansville's east side battling the likes of Charlie Lawrence and the Volkman brothers, Ron, Mike and Dean. He played little league baseball at Garvin Park and got his first experiences at organized basketball as a student at St. Theresa, where he was a contemporary of Jerry Mattingly, the oldest of the Mattingly boys.

Coming from a Catholic upbringing, Dave wanted to attend Memorial, but when the zoning was released for the new Catholic school in town, Rex Mundi, Dave's house fell just north of the Memorial boundary. Schellhase admits that he was not keen on the idea of attending Rex Mundi, but it is interesting to ponder how local sports history may have changed had he decided to take the court with the likes of Mattingly, Bob Griese and 'Big Tom' Niemeier.

Instead, Schellhase finished at St. Theresa and headed across the street to play for Jim Rausch at North. Rausch had literally had his eyes on the six-foot phenom for months after he heard that Schellhase might become a North Husky. "We used to watch him out the second floor windows," Rausch revealed. "And we also watched Don Mattingly (years later) throw a football with both hands. We said some prayers about him coming to North, too."

Between his freshman and sophomore years, Dave grew from 6'1 to 6'4, and it was obvious to everyone that he was a remarkable all-around talent. Although he never grew taller than 6'4, his size made him an excellent receiving target in football and a formidable presence as a catcher and hitter in baseball. After an injury in football kept him from playing basketball and baseball his sophomore year, he gave up the gridiron for good.

During his last two years at North, Dave teamed up with two strong classes of athletes who produced the greatest baseball run in the school's history. With position players like Mike Volkman, Gerard Buente, Joe Mullan and Mike Madriaga and flame-throwing pitchers Mickey Martin and Steve Schroer, North compiled a 31-1 record during the 1961 and 1962 baseball seasons. The only loss occurred in the final game of the '61 season when Coach Ed Wessel let everyone play because the game had no bearing on the standings.

Schellhase, who hit .483 for his high school career, was so attractive to major league scouts as a rifle-armed catcher and powerful left-handed hitter that he was offered a contract with the Cincinnati Reds out of high school. Dave admits that he didn't have the same confidence in his baseball abilities as he did on the basketball court and, in retrospect, realizes his decision not to sign was probably a wise one, since a young catching prospect named Johnny Bench joined the Reds organization a year later.

If his confidence was a little shaky on the diamond, the same could not be said about him on the basketball court. His reputation as a prolific scorer became evident to everyone during his two full varsity seasons at North and steadily grew as he played on an even bigger stage throughout his college career.

Playing alongside North teammates Volkman, Mullan, Martin, Schroer, Lawrence, Mel Brewer and Ted Mattingly, Dave scorched the nets for a city record 1,325 career points, averaging over 30 his senior year. His knack for manufacturing points made him a treat to watch for spectators and for teammates and coaches, as well.

"Dave was a tremendous shooter," said Coach Jim Rausch as he wondered aloud how Schellhase would have done had the three-point shot been in play in the early '60s. "He had the most beautiful shot, and he was a guy who'd give you everything he had all the time. He loved the game."

Teammate Mike Volkman, who was an outstanding scorer himself, made a lofty comparison when he spoke of his running mate at North. "He was a tremendous ballplayer," Volkman said. "He was so aggressive, I'd say he was like Larry Bird in that he couldn't jump high and he wasn't the fastest guy around, but when he'd get the ball underneath, when he grabbed the ball, it was like a vice. He was 6'4 and he went up hard! It was a joy to play with him."

North's Dave Schellhase drives past Bosse's Gene Lockyear as North teammate Ted Mattingly (#31) watches. Schellhase scored 45 points in an 84-82 win. (Photo from the Jim Rausch collection.)

Schellhase, himself, appreciates the art of scoring, and he credits his father for being an early influence on him. His father had played at Central and was a referee when Dave was young, and Dave recalls how Dave Sr. would use his avocation as a training ground for his son.

"If Dad saw a good player, the next time he reffed them, he'd take me and he'd say 'Watch this guy,'" Dave explained. "He'd take me to see guys like Roger Kaiser and Terry Dischinger. I was always trying to improve my scoring. I liked to score, and I found out a good way was to follow my shot and get rebounds and loose balls and get fouled. There are lots of ways to score other than just shooting (from outside)."

Schellhase found enough ways to score to earn a spot on the Indiana All-Stars, along with Tell City's Tommy Kron, Bosse's Gary Grieger and Mr. Basketball and future Evansville College star Larry Humes. Dave's prowess as a scorer also attracted the attention of college basketball programs across the country, but a personality quirk caused some problems during the recruiting process.

After fielding offers from schools far and wide, Dave quickly narrowed his choices to three: Purdue, Illinois and West Virginia, where George King was the head coach and Tell City's Bob Lochmueller was an assistant. The problem was, Dave's definition of "narrowing down" his choices was different from the norm. "I couldn't say no to anybody back then, and I loved all the attention," he admitted, "so I told all three of them that I was coming to their school."

Realizing the dilemma, Dave Sr. sat his son down and insisted that he make a choice and notify the two 'losers', who were understandably upset upon hearing the news. Dave knew himself well enough to choose a school where he could earn a starting spot quickly. "I wasn't going to sit on the bench," he confessed. "If I went somewhere and didn't get to play, I would have left." So when Schellhase joined Coach Ray Eddy at Purdue, he knew he had found a home.

Playing a league schedule against the likes of Cazzie Russell and Bill Buntin of Michigan and Indiana's Van Arsdale twins, to name a few, Schellhase was named the Boilermakers' MVP three times and was a three-time All-Big Ten player. While at Purdue, Dave averaged 24 points as a sophomore, 29 as a junior and 32.5 to lead the nation as a senior. In 1966, he was a consensus first team All-American with Russell, Dave Bing (Syracuse), Clyde Lee (Vanderbilt) and Jimmy Walker (Providence).

Schellhase also earned kudos as a student while at Purdue, earning Academic All-American honors twice and receiving the school's Big Ten Conference Medal of Honor, which recognizes one senior from each school for accomplishments in athletics and in the classroom. Others to win the award at Purdue were John Wooden (1932), Hank Stram ('48), Rex Mundi's Bob Griese ('67) and Evansville North's Bob Ford ('72).

Following his 1966 graduation, Schellhase was chosen tenth overall in the NBA draft by the Chicago Bulls, but unlike today, the lofty status of being a high draft pick did not result in a financial windfall. In 2007, the tenth NBA pick signed for over $2 million, but in '66, Dave signed for only $72,000. As a 6'4 forward, Dave knew his chances of succeeding in the pros were slim and that re-inventing himself as a guard was a longshot at best. In addition, Chicago had two all-star guards in Jerry Sloan and Guy Rogers, making playing time scarce for Schellhase. Although he didn't see much action, Dave did appreciate the fact that he played in the NBA with some of the game's true legends. "The NBA in those days was truly great," Schellhase said. "You're talking all of them, Wilt Chamberlain, Bill Russell, Jerry West, Oscar Robertson, Rick Barry, Jerry Lucas. I saw those guys play every night, and those guys could flat out play!"

Not being one to enjoy the role of a bench player, Schellhase walked away from the NBA after two seasons to pursue another passion, coaching. After returning to Purdue for his Masters, he served as a graduate assistant there for three years before a one-year stint as the head coach at Clinton Prairie High School in Frankfort, Indiana. He then landed an assistant's job at North Dakota State. From there, he became a head coach at Morehead State University in Morehead, Minnesota, where he served for seven years before taking over the program at Indiana State in 1983. In 1987, he returned to Morehead State for eight years.

Dave believes that his days as a player were the foundation of making him a successful coach. "Everything I did in basketball prepared me to coach," he explained. "I knew how it felt to sit on the bench (in the NBA), and I knew how it felt to score a lot of points and be a star."

Schellhase had some issues during his coaching career, and with the same type of grit that enabled him to become the nation's top scorer, he made some lifestyle changes that enabled him to build a career. With his three children, Julie, Elizabeth and Doug, all grown up and gone, Dave moved back to Indiana as the Dean of Students at Logansport High School. He returns to Evansville to visit Charlie Lawrence and other friends several times a year and wishes he could get back more.

In 1992, Dave Schellhase was inducted into the Indiana Basketball Hall of Fame. Although it has been over forty years since his career ended, those who saw him play basketball would probably agree that a player like Schellhase could still dominate even in today's game. With his ferocious inside game and his smooth shooting stroke, it is very likely that Schellhase could make a run for the national scoring title even today, just as he did as an All-American in 1966.

AN EVANSVILLE FIRST

Dave Schellhase's great-grandfather was Evansville's first major league ballplayer. Al 'Shelley' Schellhase made his professional debut on May 7th, 1890 with the Boston Beaneaters. Shelley had 49 at bats in 16 games during his two-year career.

The Harlem Globetrotters were regular guests at Roberts Stadium. (Photo courtesy of the University of Southern Indiana archives.)

OUR FIELDS OF BATTLE

There are many sports venues around southern Indiana that have welcomed fans over the years, and every community can no doubt recall memorable moments in gyms and on fields that deserve mention. The following are but a few of our 'Fields of Battle' that have provided some of the greatest thrills, disappointments and even tragedies for local sports fans.

HOLLYWOOD WORKED ITS MAGIC ON HUNTINGBURG'S LEAGUE STADIUM

When Penny Marshall was searching for two baseball fields that would depict the World War II era, she found what she was looking for in southwestern Indiana. The two arenas needed would serve as backdrops for the depiction of two teams from the All-American Girls Professional Baseball League. Evansville's Bosse Field was chosen as the home field of the Racine Belles, and Huntingburg City Park Field (known today as League Stadium) was chosen as the home of the Rockford Peaches.

League Stadium's roots go all the way back to the late 1800s, when the Huntingburg Rustics blazed the base paths at the park. In 1926, fans swarmed the park to watch Oakland City native Edd Roush take the field for the Cincinnati Redlegs in an exhibition game.

The historic field had the nostalgic appearance necessary for the World War II-era film, but to make the stadium look authentic, construction crews were brought in for the finishing touches. Using the field's original grandstand, original light towers and large trees framing the outfield as a skeleton, renovation began in 1991.

The grandstand was expanded to accommodate 3,000 spectators, and a forty-foot-long, hand-operated scoreboard was built. The wire fence surrounding the stadium was removed and replaced with a solid cedar fence. To assure a realistic feel, close attention was paid to every detail. As an example, circular saws could not be used for the construction, since wood was cut straight in the 1940s. In addition, every piece of lumber was painted to appear weathered, and period advertising was painted on the fences.

The beautiful 'old' field now serves as the home of the Dubois County Bombers.

Huntingburg's League Stadium.
(Photo courtesy of the Dubois County Bombers.)

The old paddock circa 1920s. (Photo courtesy of Ellis Park.)

ELLIS PARK: AND THEY'RE OFF!

Although we don't actually do battle at Ellis Park, we do challenge ourselves at the betting windows and get to watch some great athletes at work. And although the track isn't technically in Indiana, it has helped to diversify our sports environment by offering the excitement of thoroughbred racing. Through the best of times and worst of times, James C. Ellis Park has been a fixture in the area sports landscape for decades.

In 1922, the idea was met with skepticism by many when plans were announced to build the track on a 204-acre tract on what was then known as Green River Island. The Green River Jockey Club built the facility, and the track opened on October 19th, 1922 for a five-day harness meeting. Trotters and pacers were all the rage at the time, but they gave way to thoroughbreds less than a month later.

Looking at the state-of-the-art track today, it is hard to envision the old carousel paddock, a starting gate that was pulled by mules, and fans arriving by train and ferryboat. Horses also arrived by rail at a loading platform near the grounds, and calculations for the betting odds were done by hand.

Ads in the newspapers promoted the social appeal of the track more than the sporting aspect, informing locals of proper fashion as well as what to drink and what cigars to smoke. The papers also promoted the various social clubs near the track. On Labor Day of 1940, Duke Ellington wowed the crowds at the Trocadero Club across the street.

When the Green River Jockey Club went belly-up, the track was bought by confirmed bachelor James C. Ellis, who purchased the track at auction for $35,100. The Rockport native took over the facility, then known as Dade Park, during the winter of 1924.

The track, affectionately known as 'the pea patch', was modeled after Saratoga Race Course, and its 1 1/8-mile dirt course is still the largest in Kentucky. The 1-mile grass course wasn't added until 1993.

Ellis Park has survived attacks by Mother Nature, ownership changes and the constant evolution of the thoroughbred industry itself. Through it all, it has also seen its share of notable visitors from the sports world, such as racer A.J. Foyt, Rick Pitino, NFL coach Buddy Ryan, and Edd Roush, a baseball hall of famer who grew up in Oakland City. Some of racing's finest trainers have also saddled horses at Ellis, including D. Wayne Lukas, Bob Baffert, Bill Mott and Todd Pletcher. The track's mom-and-pop approach and grassroots appeal have made Ellis Park a pleasant way to spend a summer afternoon for over 85 years.

Below are some of Ellis' memorable milestones, as seen in the track's media guide.

- September 28th, 1938 – Officials from Indiana and Kentucky agree to build a bridge near the track.
- 1932 – A wager known as the Daily Double makes its appearance.
- 1937 – A huge flood invades the Track's mezzanine.
- 1939 – The web barrier replaces the walk-up start.
- August 26th, 1939 – Mr. Ambassador sets a world record for a mile and 40 yards with a time of 1:39 2/5.
- 1941 – Leading riders earn $85 to $95 per week (compared to the average worker's $30).
- August 27th, 1941 – Track stewards disqualify Always Glad, a horse owned by James C. Ellis himself. It was the first disqualification in nine years.
- 1951 – An Evansville kid named Charles D. Anderson gets a part-time job in the mutuel department. He would later be known as 'Chic' and would become one of the greatest racing announcers of all time. Anderson called Triple Crown races for years, providing memorable moments provided by such stars as Seattle Slew, Affirmed and Alydar, and many others. His most famous call was his accounting of Secretariat's run in the 1973 Belmont to win the Triple Crown with the words, "He is moving like a TREMENDOUS machine!"
- 1952 – A 2 1/4-mile marathon known as 'the Twice Around' makes its debut
- 1955 – The name Dade Park was changed to James C. Ellis Park
- July 23rd, 1966 – Jockey R.A. 'Cowboy' Jones wins the meet opener aboard Busy Gold. He would ride Busy Gold to more than sixty wins at various tracks.
- 1969 – Evansville's WEHT broadcasts the feature race daily.
- August 4th, 1970 – Paula Herber becomes the first female to ride at

A horse approaches the finish line in front of the judges stand in the 1930s. (Photo courtesy of Ellis Park.)

Jockey Mary Bacon was a popular rider at Ellis and was the first female jockey to be a leading apprentice (1969). Mary was rebellious by nature and, according to reports, wore flowered bikini panties under her jockey silks and once posed for *Playboy*. When asked why she wore the panties, she once replied, "It gives the jockeys behind me something to look at." After winning 286 races and nearly $1 million, her career was cut short by an injury. While dying of cancer, she committed suicide in 1991. (Photo courtesy of Ellis Park.)

Ellis. On August 24th, she rode her first winner, and on Sept.1st, she won three times, including both halves of the Daily Double.

- September 1st, 1977 – Mutuel clerks handle $1 million for the first time.
- August 23rd, 1978 – A tragic fire claims the lives of 31 horses.
- July 14th, 1978 – Leroy Tauzin rides eight straight winners spanning two days.
- 1981 – Sunday racing is introduced at Ellis.
- July 31st, 1983 – Free general admission is offered for the first time in state history.
- July 8th, 1984 – Patricia Cooksey rides four winners.
- September 1st, 1987 – The Daily Double (12-8) returns $8,412.80, an Ellis Park record.
- 1994 – Princeton native Mike Pegram's Arches of Gold wins the Dahlia Stakes.
- July 1st, 1995 – Looney Lady, owned by Holland and U of E basketball star Don Busc, wins the last race.
- July 25th, 1996 – A national record trifecta payout of $126,349 (for a $2 bet) results when 73-1 Ask Mesach leads a parade of longshots home in the seventh race.
- September 1st, 1996 – Overbrook Farm's Boston Harbor wins the Juvenile Stakes with Donna Barton aboard. The D. Wayne Lukas trainee would go on to win the Breeder's Cup Juvenile and the Eclipse Award as the nation's top juvenile.
- July 19th, 2000 – The worst spill in eleven years claims the lives of three horses, and jockeys Calvin Borel, Willie Martinez and Rodney Trader are hospitalized.
- 2002 – Jon Court sets an Ellis record when he captures his fifth straight riding title.
- 2003 – Kim Hammond, of Salem, Illinois, becomes the first woman to win an Ellis Park training title.
- November 6th, 2006 – A tornado ravishes Ellis Park.
- August 4th, 2007 – Ellis Park hosts the National Claiming Crown, often referred to as 'the poor man's Breeder's Cup', and is the first Kentucky track to do so.

HUNTINGBURG'S MEMORIAL GYM

When the new Huntingburg Memorial Gymnasium was dedicated in the fall of 1951, critics scoffed at the notion that a gym of that magnitude would be viable in such a small town. But the believers proved the naysayers wrong as the glorious edifice welcomed overflow crowds to watch some of the most exciting games in the history of Hoosier basketball.

The opening of the new gym marked the beginning of an era for fans in the area. From the early days of outdoor courts and playing games in unused business buildings, livery stables and the 'old gym', the town would now become a center of activity during basketball season. The gym itself was distinctive in that there were only a few structures like it. The bowl-type design allowed for maximum seating with no interior vertical supports to obstruct the vision of spectators. This allowed for the 200- by 186-foot cream-colored brick building to provide space for 5,020 permanent seats without a single bad view in the house. The floor of the gym sits 16 feet below ground level and was the first in the area to feature the sunken floor concept that was later used at Evansville North and Roberts Stadium.

Almost sixty years of nostalgia ooze from every crevice of the old gym, and a large board on the south side of the structure highlights some of the most memorable moments in the building's history. To commemorate the gym's 50th anniversary, a poll of fans was taken in 2002 to recognize the ten greatest games ever played in Memorial Gym. Among those listed was the game on March 2nd, 1963 when tiny Ireland won its first sectional ever with a 20-19 victory over Springs Valley, with Ireland coach Pete Gill using a slow-down strategy to perfection to pull off the upset.

On March 5th, 1977, Mike Archer returned after recovering from a broken hand to score 25 points for Northeast Dubois to give the school its first sectional title with a 55-50 overtime win over Jasper. Archer went on to lead the Jeeps to the semistate.

The 1953 Central team, featuring John Harrawood and the Clayton brothers, also made the board when the 16-0 Bears squared off with a 15-0 Huntingburg team in front of 6,700 rowdy Hunter fans.

The #1 game on the list is one that locals haven't stopped talking about since the overflow crowd shook the rafters during an old-fashioned barnburner in 1993. In a first round sectional battle, Forest Park and Jasper slugged it out while two players produced the game of their young lives. Jasper's Scott Rolen, better known for his major league baseball career, put on a shooting exhibition unlike any the local basketball fanatics had ever seen, and he nearly pulled off one of the greatest comebacks in the history of sectional play.

Down by 18, Jasper coach Ed Schulteis gave instructions for his players to feed the hot-handed Rolen whenever possible. Despite a tender ankle, Rolen responded by nailing seven three-pointers in the game's final five minutes, a state record for a quarter, to finish the game with 47 points (including ten three-pointers), another sectional record.

With the help of Michael Lewis, the future IU star who had five three-pointers himself, Jasper climbed back from an 18-point deficit to pull within one on Rolen's last three-pointer with twelve seconds remaining. Jasper's comeback was thwarted, however, when Forest Park's Bob Boehman put a cap on another sparkling performance when he hit four free throws to seal the win for the underdog Rangers. Boehman's last two were the result of a controversial intentional foul called by referee Steve Meyer. To offset Rolen's big night, Boehman finished with 31 points, making an incredible 19 of 20 free throws, most of them under pressure, to seal the 85-80 win for Forest Park.

Gene Morgan, an avid supporter from the area who has attended every sectional game in the gym since 1946, remembers very well the atmosphere of Indiana basketball during the days of the one-class system. "Before consolidation," he said, "we had Jasper, Huntingburg, Holland, Spurgeon, Otwell, Stendal, Birdseye and Winslow. We had ten or twelve teams in our sectional, and it was an all-week event. This gym was filled to capacity with screaming fans."

Morgan also recalled some of the great players who entertained fans over the years, like Jerry Conrad from Milltown, who went on to play for Evansville College. Other players of note include: Al Nass and Mike Gooch of Huntingburg; Buddy Graham and Mo Beasley of Odin; Ray Roesner, who scored 26 points in leading Holland to a big win over Huntingburg in 1953; and more recently, Larry Bird from Springs Valley, Don Buse from Holland, and Mike Ballenger from Jasper.

The town of Huntingburg has worked hard to preserve their basketball treasure that is so heavily steeped in tradition. It would be difficult for the youth of today to understand what Gene Morgan and his contemporaries feel when they speak of those days only a few decades ago. "People who participate in this gym are basketball crazy," Morgan stated. "We live and die with it. It's Mardi Gras time when the sectional comes around. Years ago, when we had twelve to fourteen teams in the sectional, school was out on Wednesday, Thursday and Friday. We had games in the morning, in the afternoon and at night, and the gym was packed. This gym seated almost 7,000 people, and you had to fight for tickets. We had lotteries where they picked names to get tickets. We have fans here who will come back until the day they die."

The Huntingburg Memorial Gym is still functioning today thanks to the support of loyal fans like Gene Morgan, and with the help of private funding, renovations like the new floor and sound system have enabled Memorial Gym to remain a sectional host. The relatively new Southridge High School, located on Highway 231 just south of downtown Huntingburg, is one of the few Indiana schools whose home gym is not located on campus. Rather than conforming to the trend by building a modern arena, school officials chose instead to allow today's players the privilege of experiencing what players elsewhere can only hear or read about. Memorial Gym is like a time capsule that was never buried.

Gene Morgan says that people laughed in 1950 when the town announced that it was building such a large gym for a town with less than 4,000

people, but they aren't laughing now. There are much larger gyms, and there are gyms that can boast the latest technological advances, but none can offer the atmosphere of Huntingburg's pride and joy. Simply put, in the words of Gene Morgan, "There's not a court in the state of Indiana that compares to this gym."

In 1951, Huntingburg and Evansville Central played in front of a full house in Huntingburg's Memorial Gym. (Photo by Irving Chase.)

REITZ BOWL: A WEST SIDE CATHEDRAL

It would be hard to find a greater natural stadium in the country than Evansville's Reitz Bowl, which sits adjacent to F.J. Reitz High School at the top of Reitz Hill.

Before there was a Reitz Bowl, football was still played on the land where the Bowl now sits. "From the beginning of Reitz football, they always played in the spot that we now know as the Bowl," said Jon Carl in a documentary produced for WNIN by his class at Reitz. "It was described as 'that flat spot behind the school,' and there weren't seats; people would just sit on the hill on blankets."

Originally, a retaining wall was planned to secure the school's foundation, but, before the project got started, a brilliant piece of happenstance occurred. It seems that an insightful observer realized that, with a few modifications, a stadium could be built.

Construction began in 1921, and by the time the first game was played, there was seating for only 3,600 directly in front of the school building. After the season, construction continued, and the following year, at a cost of $52,964, it was completed as we know it today.

For the first several years, games were played in the afternoon, usually on Saturdays. In 1931, lights were added. Also in 1931, during the Great Depression, Reitz and Bosse played an extra game on December 4th to benefit charity. Reitz and Bosse also made history in 1959 when the schools played the last Thanksgiving Day game in the state of Indiana.

For a few years, the Bowl was home to the Refrigerator Bowl, named such because Evansville was considered the refrigerator capital of the world because it was home to Servel, International Harvester and Seeger-Sunbeam. The game was held in December in the late '40s and early '50s and was as significant as most other bowls in the country before television took over and snuffed out the excitement of the smaller bowl games.

The Evansville College football program was in its heyday during the Refrigerator Bowl era and appeared in the big game three times. In addition to the football game and other related events, a young lady was crowned each year and christened 'Miss Refriger-adorable'.

The aura of the Bowl has affected many an athlete who has taken the field against the blue and gray Panthers (or the red and gold Mater Dei Wildcats). The field has been the setting for countless memorable contests over the last nine decades, and area sports fans are fortunate to have a stadium like the Bowl that reflects the architecture and majesty of older arenas. Perhaps Bob Gaddis, a former head football coach at Reitz, said it best in an interview aired on a special for WNIN: "There may be bigger or more expensive stadiums in the country, but the tradition of Reitz Bowl sets it apart from the rest. The unmistakable feeling that players and fans receive upon entering the Bowl is overwhelming."

Reitz Bowl in the 1940s. (Photo courtesy of the Reitz High School archives.)

STRANGE, BUT TRUE

As unbelievable as it may sound, Reitz Bowl served as the home baseball field for the Panthers in the early 1940s. Before Lamasco Field was built, the dusty Bowl was transformed into a diamond in the spring, with home plate located in the corner at the closed end and nearest the school. If you can envision it, the left field line would be the football sideline closest to the school and the right field line would be the back of the end zone.

Ed Wessel, the long-time baseball and football coach at North High School, recalls the days vividly when he would sit in the stands as a youngster and watch ballgames in the Bowl. "I remember Red Basham, who played at Reitz, hit some all the way to the fieldhouse (in the monstrous left field)," Wessel said. "Pinky Lear was the pitcher, and Jack Schaefer (who later coached football and baseball at Reitz) played at the time."

As monstrous as left field was, right field was a different story. From home plate to the light poles was probably close to 200 feet, and just beyond the poles was a severe drop off, making the right field position quite treacherous. Because of the odd shape of the layout, special rules were used. A ball passing between the first and second poles was declared a 'ground rule single', and one between the second and third resulted in a double. Any ball hit to the left of the third pole was "all you could get."

(By the way, similar rules were used for the short right field at Lincoln High School when the Lions used their football field to play baseball also.)

IN THE PRESENCE OF GREATNESS

On September 16th, 1950, Reitz hosted a game against Louisville Flaget, and little did anyone know that the fans at Reitz Bowl were in the presence of a future superstar. Listed in the program was a 155-pound quarterback named Paul 'Harnung'. Although his name was misspelled then, it isn't misspelled today in the NFL Hall of Fame. Paul Hornung would go on to win the Heisman Trophy while at Notre Dame and team up with Bart Starr and others to become Super Bowl champions under legendary Green Bay Packers coach Vince Lombardi.

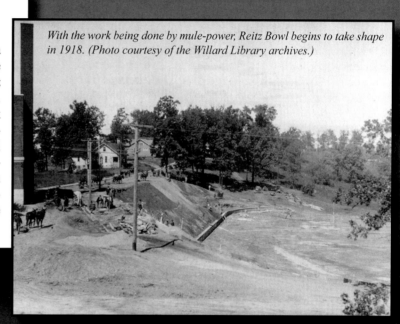

With the work being done by mule-power, Reitz Bowl begins to take shape in 1918. (Photo courtesy of the Willard Library archives.)

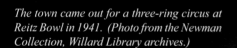

The town came out for a three-ring circus at Reitz Bowl in 1941. (Photo from the Newman Collection, Willard Library archives.)

Much of the information included in the following piece about Bosse Field was gathered from the following sources: the Evansville-Vanderburgh School Corporation, the Evansville Otters, articles found in the Evansville Courier, and articles written in the Maturity Journal by Peggy K. Newton and the late Jim Myers.

BOSSE FIELD

Bosse Field is one of the area's most treasured landmarks, and many of the greatest stars and most memorable events in our sports history have been observed in the confines of the grand old stadium.

The idea for the arena was born out of a tragedy that took place in 1914. On Friday, May 22nd of that year, more than 8,000 people gathered for a Field Day extravaganza hosted by the Evansville public schools. The venue was the old Louisiana Street baseball field, which sat between Baker and Read Streets near the stockyards. The all-wooden structure with poultry netting across the grandstand had been built in 1889 and had served as the home of Evansville professional baseball for 26 years. During the 1914 festivities, some temporary bleachers collapsed at the site and injured an estimated fifty spectators.

The event sparked a public outcry for better facilities, and popular local cartoonist Karl Kae Knecht sketched a drawing that was remarkably close to what would eventually be built. Mayor Benjamin Bosse, who had helped pull victims from the rubble after the Field Day accident, was the ramrod for the new facility. The school board purchased ten acres at Garvin Park from the city and then set the wheels in motion.

With amazing efficiency, a construction contract was awarded on January 12th, 1915 to the Hoffman Construction Company for $39,955, and only five months later, the field was opened to the public. City officials declared a holiday to honor "the best such facility in the world." The *Evansville Journal-News* declared the stadium the "building achievement of an age" and stated that it was a structure meant to outlast the generation of those who constructed it.

The entire Evansville area was buzzing on Thursday afternoon June 17th as factories and stores closed and a mile-long parade wound its way from Sunset Park to the new stadium. Every minute, a streetcar was unloading passengers from its Main Street route.

To honor the man who led the push for the construction, the stadium was named Bosse Field and Mayor Bosse was chosen to throw out the first pitch, proclaiming that this was "the biggest

Bosse Field's Professional Baseball History

YEARS	TEAM	LEAGUE
1916–'23	Evas	Central & Three I
1924	Little Evas	Three-I
1925	Rocketeers	Three-I
1926–'31	Hubs	Three-I
1938–'42	Bees	Three-I
1948–'57	Braves	Three-I
1966–'68	White Sox (E-Sox)	Southern
1970–'84	Triplets	American Assoc.
1995	Otters	Frontier

The older generation may have seen Hank Greenberg or others hit a ball on top of the building across Heidelbach beyond the right field fence. When Bosse Field first opened in 1915, the building's walls displayed the company's name: The Never-Split Toilet Seat Company.

When it opened in 1915, Bosse Field looked different than it does today. The stucco façade seen here was later replaced by brick. (Photo courtesy of the Willard Library archives.)

and best minor league ballpark in the world." As a movie camera whirred, the first game of a 'double-header' began with a Central League matchup between the Evansville Evas and Erie, Ohio. The first pitch was thrown by Jake Fromholz, and the hometown Evas defended their turf with a 4-0 victory.

After the game, the crowd enjoyed some Chero-Cola, the provider of beverages for the stadium, while preparations were made for the second part of the 'double-header'. The second event was not a ballgame at all, but rather wrestling matches contested on a makeshift mat in the middle of the field. The main event featured Yussif Hussane, the alleged heavyweight champion, and Jess Westergaarde, 'The Des Moines Giant'.

The original stadium was not brick as we know it today, but was white stucco. The bricks were added in the 1930s, and other major renovations were made during the 1940s and '50s. August 12th, 1931 was a banner day for Bosse Field, when the lights, all 285,000 watts of them, shone down on the first night game between the hometown Hubs and Decatur. Although Evansville was the last of the eight cities in the Three-I (Indiana, Illinois and Iowa) League to install lights, it was said to be "the best-lighted on the circuit."

Though the scenic arena was built for baseball, it also served as a football stadium for many years. The first night football game was played at Bosse Field on October 18th, 1929 between Central and Bicknell, and although it is probably the worst football venue ever built, the facility served as the home field for Evansville College and local high schools for many years.

Over the years, city high schools have also used Bosse Field as a centerpiece for cross country meets on occasion and extensively as the site for high school baseball games. High school players from all over the area should feel blessed that they got to experience baseball the way it was meant to be. Every city team has used Bosse Field as a home field at some time, and the high school sectionals held there every year have been perennial statewide leaders in attendance.

When the stadium was built in 1915, its main purpose was to provide the area with a home for minor league baseball, and it has done that consistently since it opened. Although Evansville has had 14 professional teams dating back to 1884, only nine have called Bosse Field home. The stadium's classic look and feel have continued to attract teams, enabling it to remain the third-oldest professional field still in use in the U.S. (the oldest are Fenway Park in Boston [1912] and Wrigley Field in Chicago [1914]).

Evansville has fielded several independent league teams over the years and has been a minor league city for six major league teams: the Boston Bees, Detroit Tigers, Milwaukee Braves, Chicago White Sox, Minnesota Twins and Milwaukee Brewers.

In 1918, 'The Great War' put a stop to baseball for a season, and there was no league play for three years during World War II. Bosse Field did not sit idle, however, as teams from local plants and shipbuilding crews used the stadium and kept baseball alive.

Some of the best years in the field's history were those when Evansville's parent team, the Detroit Tigers, made it to the World Series in 1934 and '35. In '34, local fans watched the Series closely as the Dean brothers, Dizzy and Paul, pitched the Cardinals to victory in seven games while Evansville native Pete Fox led the Series in hitting at .385. The following year, the Tigers took the title when they downed the Chicago Cubs in six games.

As late as 1941, area fans could watch up-and-coming superstars by paying 65 cents for grandstand seats (plus 35 cents for their lady), or 28 to 44 cents would get them a seat in the bleachers. For the less fortunate, there was a Knothole Gang membership available that allowed admission if you showed your card to an attendant at the north end of the stadium.

Whether it be from private boxes or the cheap seats, locals were very fortunate to watch some of the best players to ever step on a field. Among those to walk through the portals at Bosse Field were hall of famers Sam Thompson, Hank Greenberg, Warren Spahn and Oakland City's own Edd Roush. Other greats who have played there are: Don Mattingly, Andy Benes, Jack Morris, Lance Parrish, Darrell Porter, Jim Nettles, Cotton Nash, Kirk Gibson, Mark 'the Bird' Fidrich and Del Crandall, to name a few. Cincinnati's Big Red Machine once appeared for an exhibition game, giving fans a glimpse of Johnny Bench, Joe Morgan, Tony Perez and Pete Rose. Evansville has had its share of great managers as well, like Jim Leland and Bob Coleman. Even the popular Bob Uecker came to town, and he probably sat "in the FRONT ROW", to steal a line from his classic TV commercial.

With its presence seen in movies like the 1995 HBO release *Baseball in Black and White,* about the old Negro Leagues, and the 1991 hit film *A League of Their Own,* Bosse Field will be forever memorialized. From the vision and initiative of the man for whom it was named, the grand old stadium stands as a proud reminder of a magical era in local sports history, and, hopefully, with continued nurturing, Bosse Field will continue to serve local sports fans for generations to come.

Mayor Benjamin Bosse (at left with his hand in his pocket) leads the parade on opening day. Notice the crowd watching from the top row of the stadium. (Photo courtesy of the Willard Library archives.)

ROBERTS STADIUM: 50 YEARS OF MEMORIES

As this story is being written in 2008, meetings are taking place to discuss the razing of Roberts Municipal Stadium and the construction of a new state-of-the-art arena somewhere in Evansville. The proponents of change are citing the Stadium's shortcomings as a venue for non-basketball-related events as sufficient reason to put her down and rebuild. They say the 146-foot floor at Roberts is too small for professional hockey or skating events and that the roof at the stadium is insufficient to support the massive equipment used by today's musicians for a concert.

I'm sure these people have nothing but the best of intentions, and perhaps their assessments are correct. But before we lay her to rest, we need to realize that we are sounding the death knoll for a very important piece in the tapestry of our local sports history.

The grand old gal, now at the ripe old age of 52, was more than just a gym. She was a world unto herself where people were whisked away from the ordinary to the extraordinary. The atmosphere was electric, and the sectionals, regionals and semi-states were *events* for local and out-of-town teams. Those of us who were lucky enough to run through the tunnel and onto the floor at the Stadium were sparked with a special thrill that no other environment could create, and the memories of the Stadium for players and fans alike will last a lifetime.

The Stadium was the brainchild of Mayor Henry O. 'Hank' Roberts, whose vision was to provide a facility that would put Evansville sports on the map. Despite great skepticism and opposition, Roberts persevered, and the stadium that would bear his name was opened in 1956. The original facility offered a seating capacity of 7,400, but later renovations increased its capacity to its current 11,600.

On December 1st, 1956, Evansville College (U of E) played its first game there in front of an overflow crowd of 10,000, and 42 years later, U of E celebrated its five millionth fan at Roberts. For decades, the Stadium was the annual site of the Ice Capades, the Harlem Globetrotters' exhibitions and the Shrine Circus.

Through the years, spectators also enjoyed visits from political figures and musical royalty in the confines of the Stadium. John Kennedy, Gerald Ford and Ronald Reagan all appeared there, and some of the greatest musicians of all time passed through her doors. Among them were bands like Blood, Sweat and Tears, the Beach Boys and Three Dog Night, as well as soloists Frank Sinatra, Willie Nelson and Elvis Presley, to name a few.

The basketball floor has felt the sneakers of Wilt Chamberlain, when he was with the Globetrotters before his professional career took off, and the Pittsburgh Steelers, when they played a benefit game for the families of the victims of the U of E plane crash. The Lions Club hosted several NBA exhibition games that brought such stars as Oscar Robertson, Jerry West, Bill Russell and others, and college games featured such stars as Larry Bird, Walt Frazier, Artis Gilmore and Earl 'the Pearl' Monroe.

The Stadium also served as the backdrop for some of the greatest moments in the amazing history of Evansville Aces basketball, including their journeys to five national championships. But for southwestern Indiana basketball fans, nothing could match the atmosphere at Roberts during the high school season.

The Stadium was used often during the high school season when a large crowd was expected for a highly-anticipated game, but the true personality of the arena came to life when tournament time rolled around. With huge crowds resplendent in their school colors and the rich baritone voice of PA announcer Jerry Hoover serving as a backdrop, hundreds of thousands of fans got to witness our own version of 'March Madness'.

"As a coach, there was nothing like it," said Ron Wannemueller, who coached the Memorial Tigers for 21 years. "It was the epitome of high school basketball, playing a sectional at Roberts Stadium. It's hard to describe the feeling. The seating was by sections and was allocated based on school enrollment, and the sections rotated every year so that no school was always in the center."

Jim Hummel, a Memorial grad also, appreciated the exhilarating environment during tournament time. "As a fan, it was kind of like the aura of the NCAA Tournament," he described. "I mean, it was a big deal! All the schools were there, and in the beginning, it even had the Posey County schools."

Dave Johnson, long time sports columnist for the *Evansville Courier*, has a unique perspective because he witnessed the excitement at Roberts for many years but did not experience it as a player, having grown up in Illinois. "It was a big event for the schools, especially the small schools," Johnson noted. "Small schools would walk into Roberts and react like the Hickory Huskers reacted to Butler Fieldhouse (in the movie *Hoosiers*).

"I don't think people realize how lucky they were if they grew up in this area, and if they're my age and grew up in Evansville, you had the Aces, Jerry Sloan, the Evansville Braves (baseball team). You take it for granted that you grew up in this town."

Certainly there are other gyms in other towns that offered great environments to play and watch basketball, but it's hard to imagine what the last 52 years would have been like without Roberts Stadium. As the discussions continue about the old girl's fate, we can only pray that those responsible for the decision will consider the powerful memories that she helped create over the years. If the decision is made to demolish the arena, we can only hope that whatever structure takes her place can even come close to creating the kind of atmosphere the Stadium provided.

A building is constructed to serve, and Roberts Municipal Stadium delivered. Without a doubt, the Stadium has provided some of the greatest moments and most intense emotions that local fans and players have ever experienced. If we have to say good-bye to her, we should all feel very fortunate that we had the opportunity to know the old girl personally.

THE GOOD OLD DAYS?

Younger folks may not be aware that, in the old days, smoking was allowed at Roberts Stadium, but those who were around in the '50s and '60s can certainly remember. Local fans, like Rick Pittman and Jon Siau, said that they can vividly recall occasions when fans on the opposite side of the floor appeared only as ghostly images because of the blanket of smoke that lingered in the air.

The land on which Roberts Stadium was built was an apple orchard at the time and was sold to the city for one dollar.

CHAPTER FOUR
1950-1975 ACES BASKETBALL

Much of the information concerning Aces basketball was taken from a beautifully written but unpublished book by Bill Bussing, an avid Aces fan who grew up during the golden age of Aces basketball.

AN INCREDIBLE JOURNEY

When the Evansville College basketball program started in 1919, the original Aces played just four games, two against church teams and two against local independent squads. Their coach for the season was G.B. Schnurr. Starting in 1920, Evansville began playing other college teams, with an occasional contest against representatives from the YMCA.

Five different coaches presided over the Aces' first five seasons (after Schnurr were Clem McGinness, Harlan Miller and Charles Holton). The program gained some stability starting the 1923-'24 season when John Harmon took over for seven seasons before leaving to coach at Boston College. Bill Slyker, who as a football player, played in the 1921 Rose Bowl for Ohio State, took over the Evansville program after Harmon and won 56 percent of his

The 1920-'21 Evansville Aces, the school's first basketball team. Front Row (L-R) Edward Wilke, Price Thompson, John K. Jones, Lawrence McMinnis. Back Row (L-R) Charlie Evans, Lawson Marcy, Lyman Davis, Howard Lytle, Earl Hooker. (Photo courtesy of the University of Evansville, Sports Information.)

An early Aces game. Notice the formal dress of the crowd. (Photo from the Evansville Aces Media Guide.)

games during his 13 seasons. After Slyker, ex-Aces player Emerson Henke started a three-year term and posted a 29-22 record (57%). When Henke was replaced in 1946, the dawn of a new age began, as a young coach named Arad McCutchan launched his quest to guide Evansville College from the plains of mediocrity to the pinnacle of college division basketball.

As the coaches changed over those early years, so did the venues. Before Evansville College found a permanent home at Roberts Stadium in 1956, the teams played first in a small campus gym, then at the Coliseum downtown, followed by the Agoga Tabernacle and the Armory.

The urge to take the program big time as a Division I school finally materialized in 1977. Coach McCutchan, who had led the Aces to unparalleled success for thirty years, decided to coordinate his retirement with the university's move to Division I. For a brief period, Jerry Sloan was in position to replace his mentor, but circumstances developed that resulted in his decision to walk away. As a result, U of E officials brought in a fiery young coach named Bobby Watson to usher in the new era.

Tragically, the school's first Division I season was only four games old when the team plane crashed on December 13th, 1977, taking the lives of everyone on board. The excitement of the young season quickly gave way to mourning, and after the community said good-bye to their fallen warriors, the U of E administration began to slowly rebuild.

The '78-'79 season was destined to be a difficult one for whomever was brought in to resurrect the program. With only a handful of returning underclassmen and a few new recruits, Coach Dick Walters fashioned a respectable 13-16 record in his first season, and he finished his seven-year tenure with a record of 114-87 (57%). His finest year was the '81-'82 season when the Aces won the MCC with a 23-6 record and qualified for the NCAA Tournament. For his efforts, Walters was named the conference Coach of the Year.

Former IU star Jim Crews succeeded Walters and elevated the program to a new level. Although his 16-year run resulted in only a slightly better winning percentage (294-209, 58%), four of the five best Division I seasons in Aces history occurred with Crews at the helm: '88-'89 (25-6, 81%); '81-'82 (23-6, 79%); '92-'93 (23-7, 77%); and '87-'88 (21-8, 72%). Crews was the conference Coach of the Year each of those seasons, and he led Evansville to the NCAA Tournament twice ('89 and '92).

After Jim Crews left to coach at Army, Steve Merfeld was brought in, and despite his best efforts, the program wallowed in mediocrity for five seasons. Upon his dismissal, U of E officials decided to place the program in the hands of one of its favorite sons, former Aces star Marty Simmons. The popular coach who had played for Coach Crews and was later named to the 15-man All-Time U of E Team took over the reigns for the '07-'08 season with hopes of resurrecting the Aces basketball tradition.

Over the years, the Evansville College/University of Evansville program has sent thirty players to the pros, either in the U.S. or abroad, and its five NCAA small college titles is second only to the eight of Kentucky Weslyan. One of U of E's proudest achievements is that every senior in its program (56) since 1989 has earned a degree.

With talk of razing Roberts Stadium and possibly building a new facility, the memories of the glory days seem to be fading fast. For those of us who felt the thrill of standing-room-only crowds cheering or moaning in unison as a game hung in the balance, we can only hope that a new generation of Aces fans will one day see the program back where it once was – at the top of the college basketball world.

THE GOLDEN AGE OF ACES BASKETBALL

Without question, the heyday of Evansville Aces basketball was a 15-year span near the end of Arad McCutchan's coaching career. During the period from 1957-'58 until the end of the '71-'72 season, Evansville compiled a record of 284-126 (69%), had nine 20-win seasons, made twelve NCAA Tourney appearances and won five national titles.

The '57-'58 Aces featured an all-sophomore front line, the first ever for the school, with Larry Erwin, Dale Wise, and Mel Lurker. The season included arguably the biggest game in Aces history when powerful UCLA was enticed to town by Aces athletic director Bob Hudson offering them half the gate to make the trip.

A coach named John Wooden was just starting to build a reputation and had four returning starters from a 22-4 team the previous year. UCLA's roster included Rafer Johnson, who would later win the Olympic decathlon in world record fashion, and a substitute guard named Denny Crum, who would coach the Louisville Cardinals to NCAA titles in '80 and '86.

The Aces dispatched the mighty Bruins 83-76.

The season also included a matchup between the Aces, ranked #1 among 720 small college teams at the time, and the Butler Bulldogs, led by senior Bobby Plump, known for his game-winning shot in the 'Milan Miracle' State championship game. The Pierceville native put on the greatest scoring display ever against Evansville College, ringing up 41 points on 12 of 17 shooting from the floor and a perfect 17 of 17 from the line in a 101-76 demolition of the Aces.

Another hot ticket during the season was the game with archrival Kentucky Weslyan, featuring 6'3 'King' Kelly Coleman. Coleman had averaged 46.8 points a game as a high school senior in Wayland, Kentucky, including a State Tournament single game record of 68. The Aces-Weslyan matchup proved to be well worth the price of admission when Larry Erwin took a pass from Ed Smallwood and let loose with a 40-foot buzzer-beater in a 77-71 Aces win. The last-second heroics placed his heave in a class with Gus Doerner's hook shot as a freshman in 1938-'39 and John Harrawood's desperation two-hander in '56-'57.

The Aces were favorites to meet #1 Wheaton in the NCAA Finals, but they overlooked semi-final opponent St. Michael's and were upset. Although the Aces finished 23-4 and Arad McCutchan won his fourth ICC Coach of the Year award in five years, Evansville College blew a golden opportunity and would have to wait another year for a shot at the title.

As the '58-'59 season approached, hopes were high for Aces fans. Coach McCutchan was returning nine lettermen and an impressive group of sophomores. The lettermen were: Ed Smallwood, Hugh Ahlering, Mel Lurker, Harold Cox, Harold Malicoat, Jim Nossett, Bob Reisinger, Tommy Mulherin and Hal Halbrook. The sophomores were P.M. Sanders, Walt Deal and Dale Wise.

Evansville opened with an eight-game homestand, and a record number of fans bought season tickets at $20 for 14 games. The season got off to a dreadful start when New Mexico A&M took the opener in double overtime over the heavily-favored Aces. After winning the second game, the largest crowd in Evansville College history (11,088) watched Purdue maul E.C. 83-82 in a very physical game.

After that, the Aces beat Valparaiso (98-82), Ray Meyer's Depaul team (86-77) and then scored two victories to win the Holiday Tournament.

In the next seven games, the Aces squared off twice with 'King' Kelly and his Weslyan teammates. Weslyan won the first 85-72, and Evansville won the rematch 92-82. The second matchup was played in front of a Stadium crowd of 12,833 (1,079 over capacity). Kelly Coleman tallied 36 points, but seven Evansville players scored in double figures in the Aces victory.

Going into the NCAA Tourney, the Aces were 14-6 and had finished third in the ICC. Their first game in the regional was against Belmont Abbey (20-1) with a starting lineup that averaged 6'6. Belmont Abbey was led by a flamboyant young coach named Al McGuire, who would soon carve out his own place in Aces history with his antics and his affinity for the media and fans.

A snowstorm blanketed Evansville, resulting in a smallish crowd of only 4,296 to watch McCutchan's crew battle McGuire's team that started four sophomores and a freshman, all from McGuire's hometown, New York City. When the Aces broke the game open with less than six minutes left, McGuire sent his starters to the locker room.

McGuire showed his flair for the dramatic during the consolation game against Southern Illinois. Frustrated by the officiating, he slammed his coat to the floor and approached a soft drink vendor. "Give me a Coke, son," McGuire requested, loudly enough for fans to hear. "These bums (the refs) are giving me nothing!"

Later, the Section M patrons sent him an ice cream bar to cool him off, and the gesture would lead to a moment in Aces history that people still talk about today.

After McGuire's display, the finals were almost anti-climactic. In a close game, Evansville defeated Wittenburg (Ohio) 56-50 for the regional title, and E.C.'s Ed Smallwood and Hugh Ahlering were named to the All-Regional team.

In the semi-final game, Evansville faced 27-4 North Carolina A&T, an all-black team led by future Golden State Warriors star Al Attles. The Aces ran into trouble when the team's leading scorer, Smallwood, fouled out with 11:35 remaining and the Aces clinging to a 76-72 lead. Coach McCutchan immediately ordered the slow-down game, and the Aces spread the floor. From then on, Hugh Ahlering took charge, continually driving and getting fouled. The senior guard hit 17 of 18 free throws on the way to the best game of his career. He ended the game with 31 points, 8 assists and 8 rebounds in a 110-92 Aces victory.

On Friday, March 13th, the Aces took the Roberts Stadium floor in their orange road uniforms against 23-2 Southwest Missouri State. Once again, Smallwood would find himself in foul trouble, and McCutchan was again forced to spread the floor when Smallwood picked up foul number four early in the second half. The Aces slowly built an 18-point lead, and Mac was able to empty his

Jerry Clayton was one of the best players in Evansville history during his days at Central and Evansville College.

bench. Despite his foul situation, Smallwood still led the team with 24 points, supported by Mel Lurker's 19.

After the game, McCutchan praised his guards, Ahlering and Harold Cox, by saying, "With them in there, I didn't have to worry too much." The tandem, that many consider the best in Aces history, both started 56 straight games in which Evansville posted a 45-11 record (80%). Cox was a first-team All-Conference selection who had averaged 11 points in 86 games. Ahlering was an All-Tourney selection, MVP of the Finals and was an Associated Press first team All-American.

During the '58-'59 campaign, the regular season home attendance was 99,641, which ranked Evansville tenth among all 770 colleges (behind only Kentucky, North Carolina State, NYU, Butler, Kansas State, Cincinnati, Michigan State, Washington and Ohio State). After the disappointment of losing in the semi-finals the previous year, Coach Mac and his Aces had delivered the first national championship in the school's history.

Following the memorable '58-'59 season, local media and fans began to talk of taking the Aces program big-time (Division I), and Coach McCutchan saw the potential for another big year with a solid nucleus returning from the past season. Mac also agreed to host a weekly TV show, and WEHT-TV announced they would re-broadcast games on Sunday afternoons.

The defending national champs looked like anything but world beaters, however, when they struggled against the freshmen in the annual season-opening scrimmage. Coach McCutchan was predicting a 12-12 season or worse as he lamented the loss of Ahlering and Cox, his terrific tandem of guards. He decided to move Larry Erwin to guard, which left a spot for Dale Wise to move into a starting forward spot with Smallwood. Lurker was back at center, leaving the other guard position open for either of two juniors, Jim Nossett or the be-spectacled P.M. Sanders.

In the season opener against Iowa, Sanders drew the nod at guard as Ed Smallwood launched his assault on the school's scoring record held by John Harrawood. E.C. jumped out to an early 11-1 lead, but Iowa roared back. At 14:39 in the second half, Smallwood fouled out with 28 points. Wise joined him on the bench ten minutes later, and guard Ken Reising followed nine seconds after that. Iowa prevailed 86-84, continuing Evansville's exercise in futility against the Big Ten.

In the second game, Texas Weslyan brought some local flavor to the contest. The team was coached by Elmer Hanebutt, who was a member of Huntingburg's 1937 State runner-up team. Three of Hanebutt's players were locals also: Don 'Butch' Rees and David 'Jody' Giesler of Jasper and John Yager of Spurgeon. Despite 21 points by Rees, the Aces secured their first win 89-73.

The fifth game of the year was a coming out party for Evansville's Walt Deal, who had played high school ball for the Owensville Kickapoos. Deal had admitted in the *Courier* that he had given less than a stellar effort the year before. "I goofed off last year," he confessed. "I was something of a clown." Deal's emergence would give the Aces one of the best front lines in the country, and he made a statement with 24 points against Los Angeles State in a 109-99 Evansville win.

"PASS IT TO BARNETT"

While playing at Evansville College, Bob Kohlmeyer was part of a starting lineup that included three players named Barnett. Jim and Bob Barnett were brothers from Boonville, and another Jim Barnett later became a teacher and coach at Reitz.

BOB KOHLMEYER

Central's Bob Kohlmeyer was the premiere player on a 1946 Central team that was perhaps overshadowed by the great Bosse teams of 1944 and 1945 and the Central team of 1948. Bosse won back-to-back State championships, and the '48 Central team went to the final game before losing 54-42 to Lafayette Jeff.

The '46 'Big Bad Bruins', as they were called, featured Kohlmeyer, Joe Keener, Frank Schwitz (who later coached basketball and baseball at Harrison), Bob Northerner, Chuck Lamar, 'Rip' Ary and a young Lee Hamilton. Hamilton would later star for the excellent '48 Central team and go on to serve as a United States Congressman.

The Bears lost 39-36 to Anderson in the afternoon of the State Finals. Anderson was led by 'Jumpin' Johnny' Wilson with 7 points. That night, Wilson became the first player in Indiana history to score 30 points in a State Final game. He would later become a member of the Harlem Globetrotters.

Bob Kohlmeyer was a jumper himself. It was said that he could jump and put his arm across the rim. He wore #2 as an Indiana All-Star (Johnny Wilson wore #1) and went on to play for Arad McCutchan at Evansville College. Although Bob started at guard for the Aces, Arad McCutchan took advantage of his leaping ability by having him jump center.

Evansville followed with a 71-50 win over Butler, the Aces' first victory at Hinkle Fieldhouse in four years. They then headed to Owensboro to battle Kentucky Weslyan, which was coached by T.L. Plain, the former coach at Vincennes Lincoln. In a 95-91 loss, Smallwood continued to have a propensity for foul trouble, leaving the game with 16:56 remaining. On the plus side, Dale Wise tied a school record, held by former Evansville Lincoln and Aces Star Jim Smallins, when he corralled 31 rebounds against Weslyan.

The Aces' schedule was about to get interesting, as a familiar visitor from the past was scheduled to return to town. Earlier in the year, Al McGuire had spoken to a group at 'Acclaim the Aces Night'. During his talk, the king of sound bytes proclaimed, "If the Aces beat Belmont Abbey (McGuire's team) next season, I'll buy everyone in the stadium an ice cream cone." The statement was relayed by every local media source, making Belmont Abbey's visit one of the most anticipated in years.

Coach McGuire's arrival didn't disappoint, as he began his barrage of one-liners. "I feel uneasy," he said to the *Courier*. "Everybody is being too nice to us."

McGuire also asked Coach McCutchan to have the Aces wear their orange jerseys. "The only way those refs can tell the home team is by the color of their shirts," McGuire wisecracked. "I want my boys to wear (the home) white Saturday night." McGuire also added a humorous assessment of the team's record. "I won nine games, and my boys have lost one."

Always the showman, McGuire's team's excellent record and his carnival barker style prompted school officials to move in bleacher seats to expand the Stadium's capacity to 11,754. The additions were not enough, however, as 300 to 400 fans were still turned away and 12,191 (significantly over the limit) packed the bleachers, seats and aisles of Roberts Stadium.

The game itself did not live up to the hype, as Mac emptied his bench early on the way to a 74-57 Aces win while Ed Smallwood broke the school's career scoring record. Thanks to the generosity of the local American Dairy, Coach McGuire's promise was honored and everyone in attendance received a free ice cream.

A few games later, Smallwood scored 47 points against Butler to break his own record and tied John Harrawood's school record of 18 field goals in a game. Following the Butler game, the 10-1 Aces had a date with one of their biggest rivals, and Smallwood would be matched up once again with 'King' Kelly Coleman.

Even A.D. Bob Hudson was shocked when the Stadium attendance for the Kentucky Weslyan game was announced at 13,913 (2,159 over capacity). Fire marshals were not pleased, but Aces fans were, as Evansville came away with a 93-87 win. The Smallwood-Coleman battle was a virtual tossup, as Smallwood finished with 30 and Coleman 26. The game's biggest night belonged, once again, to Dale Wise, who bulled his way to 26 points and 30 rebounds.

At the end of the regular season, Evansville's record stood at 20-4 and they were ranked first in the UPI poll, as they had been for 13 consecutive weeks. Evansville was not a gracious host for the Mideast Regional, however, as the area was pelted by six inches of fresh snow. The Aces' first opponent was Arkansas State, a team that included freshman Ron Volkman, who had played his high school ball at Bosse. The snow delayed the Indians' arrival by seven hours, and the team missed its chance to practice. Evansville won the game easily, 91-74.

After thrashing the Wabash College Little Giants 89-68, the Aces were set to face American University in the first round of the NCAA Finals. With the city at a near standstill after the worst snowfall since 1918, Evansville pulled out a 101-91 win behind Smallwood's 41 points and four key free throws by Evansville Memorial grad Tommy Mulherin.

In the NCAA semi-finals, the Aces would match up yet again with Kentucky Weslyan. Wearing their visiting team orange jerseys, Evansville once again got the best of Kelly Coleman. Throughout his entire Weslyan career, he had never been able to win at Roberts Stadium, as Evansville topped his Panthers 76-69.

In the 1960 NCAA Finals against Chapman College (Cal.), Ed Smallwood drilled a jumper to put E.C. up 2-0 and the Aces were off to the races. Up by 22 with 7:24 to play, Mac cleared the bench. At 1:34, he inserted his seniors, Ken Reising, Dale Wise, Mel Lurker, Larry Erwin and Ed Smallwood, so they could finish their careers on the court in the 90-69 victory. The 1960 seniors had won 69 of 83 games (83%), including

DID YOU KNOW?

Hal Halbrook, a Reitz High School graduate and member of the 1960 national champion Evansville Aces, became one of the first heart surgeons in Indiana. In fact, he performed a transplant on Edie Bates, the wife of beloved radio announcer Marv Bates.

JOHN HARRAWOOD

John Harrawood was a star at Central in the 1950s and became a record-setter at Evansville College, scoring 1,479 points.

Harrawood was the ICC Player of the Year in both 1956 and '57 and set several school scoring records. He was also selected as a member of the 15-man All-Time Aces team voted on in 2005.

a school record 25 in 1959-'60. They were 14-1 in the NCAA Tourney with two consecutive NCAA titles, and had they not overlooked St. Michaels when they were sophomores, they might very well have won three straight.

For a team that barely beat their own freshman a few months earlier, the 1959-'60 Evansville Aces shocked everyone with the school's second national championship.

The 1960-'61 version of the Evansville Aces was a mere shadow of teams from the previous years, as only Dale Wise returned from the starting lineup from the year prior. For the first time, the Aces schedule included Big Ten powers Iowa, Purdue and Ohio State. E.C. finished the season 10-15 and was invited again to the NCAA Tourney, but the rebuilding year was a painful one. Utah and 6'9" future NBA star Bill McGill humiliated Coach McCutchan's crew 132-77, as did Purdue and their star Terry Dischinger, who lit up the gym for 43 points.

Ohio State also waxed the Aces 86-59 behind Jerry Lucas, future Celtics players Larry Siegfried and John Havlicek, future NBA player Mel Nowell and reserve guard Bob Knight.

One good sign of things to come was a 39-point performance by new recruit Buster Briley in the first freshman game of the year against Southern Illinois. McCutchan had not been able to sign such recruits as Russ Grieger (Bosse), Marty Niehaus (Ferdinand), Bub Luegers (Jasper) and his #1 target Jerry Sloan (McLeansboro, Illinois).

Following the '60-'61 campaign, the re-building process was taking shape as key recruit Jerry Sloan became disillusioned with the University of Illinois and decided to play for Coach McCutchan after sitting out a year. In the meantime, Madison's Larry Humes chose E.C. over Louisville and Purdue, Louisville Central's Sam Watkins came on board and Russ Grieger left St. Louis University to come into Coach Mac's fold.

The 1962-'63 season signaled the return of the Aces to national prominence. While Larry Humes was leading the freshmen, Jerry Sloan made his varsity debut in front of a Stadium crowd that included three busloads of fans from McLeansboro. Evansville lost its opener 62-57 to Iowa as Sloan led the team with 14 points and 10 rebounds, his first official stats since 1960.

After four games, the praise for Sloan's abilities were already flowing. "I don't think I've ever had a player that tries as hard to simply lift a team off the floor and make it win," said Coach McCutchan. Teammate Marv Pruett said, "He's out there giving you 125%, even when he's hurt," and Buster Briley simply concluded, "He's the best I ever saw!"

After losing to a strong Michigan team, led by a huge front line featuring 6'7" Bull Buntin, Evansville won the Holiday Tournament as radio team Jerry Birge and Gus Doerner called the action.

After the Michigan loss, E.C. started what would become a 17-game winning streak, and the team began to show excellent depth with a second unit consisting of Paul Bullard, Wayne Boultinghouse,

P.M. SANDERS: ATHLETICS WERE IN HIS GENES

Most loyal Evansville Aces fans know that P.M. Sanders was a steady performer for Coach Arad McCutchan and that he was a sub on Evansville's 1959 national champs and a starter for the Aces 1960 NCAA national champions. But it is unlikely that most of those fans know that he was also an outstanding track athlete.

P.M. was named for his grandfather, Prentice Martin, who was also called P.M. by his family and friends. It was no surprise when the young P.M. grew into an athlete, as both parents were accomplished at their chosen sports as youngsters. Both played basketball, and Arbutus Sanders, P.M.'s mother, was a member of the Petersburg Maidens, who were named mythical state champions. P.M.'s father, Bruce, finished second in the State meet in the pole vault with a height of 12 feet in the 1930s and held the school record at Petersburg for seventeen years.

P.M. also competed for Petersburg and excelled as a jumper. At only 6'1, he high jumped 6'4" and, like his father, was a 12-foot vaulter. After considering basketball offers from Vanderbilt and IU, among others, Sanders opted to join Coach McCutchan's program.

While at Evansville, P.M. was literally a one-man team as the only athlete representing the school in track. One obvious obstacle was the lack of facilities, so the high jumper had to use initiative to find a location to work out. After several futile efforts to find the funding to build a facility, Evansville College business manager Bob Hudson agreed to pay P.M. if he would dig his own landing pit. So Sanders hauled in sand and constructed the pit where Carson Center sits today.

Track meets for Sanders were lonely affairs, as often it was only he and his father making the long drives to meets. With no coaching and little support, Sanders still managed to pole vault 13 feet and high jump 6'5", a school record.

Nearly fifty years later, P.M. Sanders keeps his body lean as he continues to compete in the high jump in senior meets around the country. In the 60-64 age group, P.M. jumped five-feet and was recognized as an All-American for the effort.

P.M.'s son, Steve, continued the family tradition by excelling at Rockport High School. Steve earned 13 varsity letters for the Zebras before accepting a scholarship to play basketball for the Aces under Coach Dick Walters.

The athletic family tree developed another strong branch after P.M. introduced his sister Linda to Ed Rolen, a teammate of P.M.'s at Evansville. Ed and Linda married and became the parents of another pretty fair local athlete, Jasper star and major league standout Scott Rolen.

Between the Sanders and the Rolens, it's a good bet that the family tree will continue to sprout athletes for years to come.

Using the old western roll style, P.M. Sanders high jumps during his days at Rockport High School. Notice the size of the crowd and that P.M. only wore a shoe on his take-off foot because the shoes were so heavy. (Photo courtesy of P.M. Sanders.)

Lynn Mautz, Paul Utley and Walt Henry. Bullard showed his selfless attitude when he was asked to step down as a starter to make room for Jerry Sloan. "He didn't complain," Coach McCutchan told the *Courier*. "All he said was, 'Coach, don't forget me down there (on the bench).'"

The Aces entered the NCAA Tournament 19-5 as they traveled to St. Louis for the Great Lakes Regional. After beating Concordia 66-56, Evansville won a close game over Washington University (Missouri) behind Bullard's 20 points and 14 rebounds. Briley hit a 25-footer to put the game into overtime, and the Aces prevailed 85-76.

Although the Aces lost in the first game of the NCAA Finals, the future looked bright. Only one senior, Marv Pruett, would be leaving, and Larry Humes, Sam Watkins and Russ Grieger were waiting in the wings to earn their positions among a solid cast of returning players.

In the months between the '62-'63 and '63-'64 seasons, Coach McCutchan lost the recruiting battles he waged for Rex Mundi's Tom Niemeier, Loogootee's Junior Gee and Bosse's Jerry Southwood. He did, however, land Ron Johnson from Centralia, Illinois, Terry Atwater from Central, Rick Kingston of Harrison and jumping jack Herb Williams, also from Centralia.

Although the Aces typically opened at home, a Stadium conflict with the Shrine Circus sent the Aces west to begin their season at New Mexico State. Humes and Watkins had impressed McCutchan enough for him to open spots for them as starters. The new lineup resulted in Sloan being moved to guard beside Watkins, with Humes and Briley at forward and 6'9 Ed Zausch at center. Wayne Boultinghouse and Jim Smith were replaced in the starting lineup but would provide valuable minutes off the bench.

On their trip to the southwest, the Aces downed New Mexico State and then won a close one against Arizona 61-58 behind Sloan's 21 first half points. Upon their return, E.C. would take their #2 national ranking into their home opener against Iowa, and in front of a home opener record crowd of 11,715, the Big Ten jinx continued as the Hawkeyes squeezed out a 75-72 win.

After home wins over San Francisco State and South Dakota State, the Aces got ready for Big Ten foe Purdue, led by Evansville North alum Dave Schellhase. Another huge crowd of 12,437 saw Sloan hold Schellhase to five points in the first half, and Purdue's big gun never found his range, as he was held to 14 in a 110-84 loss to the Aces.

After the game, Schellhase described Sloan's defense to the *Courier*. "Sloan's the best man I've ever played against," he said. "He's all over you, and you can't make a move without looking him straight in the eye."

After the Aces had suffered a rare loss in the Holiday Tournament (78-61 to Arizona in the finals), Evansville got on a roll. In a home win over Indiana State, they set a new school scoring record in a 123-86 win, and after a 101-78 thumping of St. Joe's, Pumas coach Jim Holstein told the *Courier*, "Arad played everyone but the janitor tonight and still tromped us."

McCutchan was also quoted in the press after the St. Joe's game and showed his sense of humor. Corey Smith, the two-year-old son of Aces player Jim Smith, had sat on Arad's lap during the game,

The 1964 national champs celebrate. (L-R) Dave Green, Buster Briley, Sam Watkins, Jim Smith, Russ Grieger, Jerry Sloan, Larry Humes and Wayne Boultinghouse.

prompting McCutchan to tell the *Courier*, "He (Corey) wanted to report, but I thought I'd put enough subs in by then."

As the season progressed, a team identity began to form. Aces substitutes Paul Bullard, Jim Smith, Russ Grieger and Wayne Boultinghouse had been dubbed 'the Fabulous Four' for their solid contributions. Their efforts were so impressive that, after losing 98-92 to the Aces, Ball State coach Jim Hinga declared, "You can't call Evansville a great team; you have to call it two great teams."

After fourteen straight wins, Notre Dame broke the string with a 91-75 victory in South Bend. The Aces followed the loss with a 71-70 win over Weslyan and finished the regular season undefeated in the conference and 21-3 overall, the best record in school history.

After wins over Jackson State (97-69) and Southern Illinois (64-59) in the Great Lakes Regional at Roberts Stadium, the Aces were part of the eight-team NCAA Finals for the fifth time in eight years. In a 95-73 win over Cal Poly, Humes rang up 29 points and 11 rebounds and Sloan contributed 15 and 15. In the semi-finals, E.C. disposed of State College of Iowa 82-57.

On Friday, March 13th, exactly five years from the date of the school's first national title, the Aces took the floor against 24-6 Akron for the championship. Coach McCutchan's troops were only forty minutes from history.

It didn't take long for Evansville to flex its muscle, as Buster Briley canned three 30-footers to open the game. No dramatics would be needed to secure a victory on this night because the Aces were dominant throughout. At 3:45, the starters left for good and watched through teary eyes as the bench finished off a 72-59 win.

Briley, Sloan and Humes were all named to the All-Tourney team, and the five seniors savored the victory as they said their final good-byes to the Aces fans. Briley had come up big at crunch time, and big Ed Zausch had developed into a force inside as a rebounder and shot blocker. In addition, Jim Smith, Paul Bullard and Wayne Boultinghouse had provided phenomenal depth over the long season. Briley, who led the Aces with 16 points in the championship game, summed up his thoughts after the game: "A national championship was my goal ever since I came to Evansville."

Coach McCutchan declared his feelings publicly when he said, "Yes, I believe this is the greatest club we've ever had." A total of 134,622 fans packed the Stadium during the '63-'64 season, the sixth-highest total in the country, and they were thrilled with the team's success. Little did they know that the best was yet to come.

Looking forward to the coming season, Coach McCutchan began looking for recruits who could live up to the high standards of the current crop of Aces. One prospect that got away was Mike Warren of South Bend. Warren signed with UCLA and would later star on NBC's hit show *Hill Street Blues*. Evansville did land Rex Mundi's Jerry Mattingly, who chose E.C. over Michigan, Florida State and Purdue. The Aces also signed 6'6" Howard Pratt (Shoals) who had received offers from 35 schools, including Iowa and Mississippi State. Rounding out the class were: 6'4 Clarence Hupfer, Evansville's first recruit from Indianapolis; 6'5 Roger Miller from Anderson; and Dave Riggs from Bosse, who had led the city in scoring and was the son of former Ace Walter Riggs.

Season tickets sold for $18, and the 4,000 who purchased them waited anxiously as news surfaced that Jerry Sloan had been approached again by the Baltimore Bullets after spurning their offer a year earlier. If Sloan stayed, the projected starting lineup would be Sloan, Humes, Watkins, Russ Grieger and Larry Denton. The lineup would necessitate Sloan moving to forward alongside Humes while Grieger and Watkins manned the backcourt. Everyone breathed a sigh of relief when Sloan announced his plans to stay for his senior season. Before the season opener, Herb Williams earned a spot in the lineup and replaced Denton, which allowed Sloan to move back to the guard position. With the Stadium seating expanded to hold 12,309, the players and fans were about to embark on a journey unlike any other in Aces history.

In the season's first two games, the Aces showed no signs of the Big Ten curse, downing Iowa 90-83 and Northwestern 83-75. Larry Humes was brilliant in both, with 39 and 26 points, respectively.

The Holiday Tourney featured a game with George Washington University and brought out some well-known G.W. alumni, including Jack Butterworth, Davey Osborne and Jim Myers of Bosse and Jim Rausch and Jim Barnett from Reitz. G.W. featured guard Mark Clark, a Reitz grad, but the night belonged to the Aces 105-80.

In the Tourney finals, the crowd booed when Humes was pulled with 7:28 to go in a 90-70 win against Louisiana State. Humes was only two points shy of Ed Smallwood's single game record of 47 points, but Coach McCutchan had stated in the past that the Aces only broke records when they needed points.

Against five 'major' opponents, Humes had averaged 34.4 points, and the Aces were perfect. After defeating UMass 113-82, a Minutemen assistant coach, Jack Leaman, had some kind words for Coach McCutchan's boys, saying, "They're the best I've seen since UCLA a year ago." After easy victories over South Dakota (76-63) and Vermillion (98-71), Humes got his scoring record with 48 in a 108-92 win over Butler. The win was also Coach Mac's 300th career win.

At 13-0, Evansville welcomed a crew from *Sports Illustrated* who were in town to do a story on the Aces and their battle with the SIU Salukis and their superstar, future NBA hall of famer Walt Frazier. The game did not disappoint the packed house at Roberts Stadium. With the score tied, Coach McCutchan called a timeout with nine seconds remaining. From a designed play, Larry Humes took a shot from the right side of the foul line. The ball hit the back of the rim, bounced four times and then kissed the net to secure another Aces victory.

Evansville's season continued to enrapture the national media. In a *Time Magazine* article, the journalist tried to capture the feelings opponents experience when they visit Evansville to play. "When visiting basketball teams arrive," the article stated, "they get a big hello, a tour of the Museum of Arts and Science, a hearty steak dinner in the campus dining room, then they are gently led off to the Municipal Stadium – for their execution!"

Unlike the previous season, the '64-'65 Aces did not rely on their bench players as often, preferring to stick with a 6- or 7-man rotation, and the system proved effective as the Aces continued to roll through their schedule. After cruising to a win over St. Joe's, Evansville stood at 22-0 going into a matchup with Indiana State. The game was billed as a battle for the ICC scoring title between Larry Humes and 6'4" Sycamore star Butch Wade. Humes tallied 39 and passed Ed Smallwood's career scoring mark in a 112-84 win.

Evansville College battles Michigan.
Aces (L-R) are Paul Bullard, Jerry Sloan and Ed Zausch.

The following game was the highly-anticipated rematch with SIU. The #3-ranked Salukis were determined to put a blemish on the #1-ranked Aces' spotless season, and the two teams punched and counterpunched from the opening bell. SIU led at halftime, and the score was tied at 58 with a quarter to play. With the Salukis down 68-67, SIU called a timeout with 18 seconds on the clock. When play resumed, star guard George McNeil fired up a shot that caromed high into the air. Unlike Humes' shot weeks earlier, the ball bounced away, was frantically tipped several times, and finally gathered up by Russ Grieger as time expired. The Aces' knees had buckled, but they never fell.

All five starters had played the entire forty minutes against SIU, but their exhaustion did not dampen the thrill of finishing the regular season undefeated. The 24-0 Aces were not only the first to accomplish the feat, but they also had scored 100 points eight times for another school record. They had squeezed by arch-rival SIU twice, but they knew it was likely they would meet them again.

Over the years, opposing coaches had complained about how Evansville was at and advantage by hosting all five games of the NCAA Tournament. In an effort to pacify the coaches, the committee assigned the Aces to the South Central Regional at

Bellarmine in Louisville. A quick glance at the tournament grid also showed that, if E.C. was to meet SIU one more time, it would be for the national championship.

The Aces opened the regional with 119-77 win over Bethune-Cookman. In the final, the Aces took yet another regional title by defeating Bellarmine 81-74 on their home court. For the eighth year in a row, Evansville was one of the eight finalists for the NCAA crown, and they were heading back home to defend their title.

The 24-3 Philadelphia Textile Rams were the first challenge for Coach McCutchan and his boys, but the Aces prevailed 92-76. Jerry Sloan yanked down 26 rebounds in the game, four more than the opponent's entire team.

In the next game, Sloan pulled down another 25 boards in a 93-70 romp over the St. Michael's Purple Knights. Likewise, Southern Illinois had bested Notre Dame by 13, and the matchup everyone had hoped for had played out. It was time for Round Three!

On March 12th, 1965, a sellout crowd filled every square inch of Roberts Stadium to see if the Aces could hold off the Salukis one more time. Evansville led by four at halftime, but SIU came back and built an eight point lead of their own with less than nine minutes to play. After Evansville tied the score at 74, neither team scored again in the last 1:39. Forty minutes was not enough; the two rivals were going to overtime.

Only once all year had Herb Williams not gotten the tip, and he came through again. Sam Watkins drove the baseline for a layup for a quick Aces lead. Then Humes banked in another of his patented sweeping hook shots from the side. After free throws by Watkins and Sloan, Evansville held a five-point lead with only 35 seconds left, but SIU closed to within one at the seven-second mark. Appropriately, with one second remaining, the ball was in Sloan's hands at the free throw line. As he had all year, he delivered.

The Aces had beaten a scrappy SIU team three times by a total of five points. No other team had come within seven of the Aces all season. At 17-0, they had become the first Aces team to finish a season undefeated at home, and only one other has done it since (the '88-'89 Aces, 15-0). The 1964-'65 Purple Aces had accomplished what no Evansville team before or since has done. They had vanquished every foe to record an undefeated season.

Following the Aces' record season, Jerry Sloan left to begin what would become a magnificent career as an NBA player and coach, while Humes, Watkins, Williams and company were left to continue the legacy. The '65-'66 team finished with a respectable 18-9 record, bowing out in the regional finals to their nemesis SIU. During the four years after Humes and his crew left, the Evansville program held its own, thanks to players like Howard Pratt and Dave Weeks, but by the time the '70s rolled around, the excitement of Evansville's last national title seemed like a distant memory. Fans began to wonder if Coach McCutchan would be able to pull off another dream season before he would walk off into the sunset. The fans' prayers would soon be answered when a poor boy from nearby Holland, Indiana would lead them to national prominence one more time.

It is fair to say that the start of the 1970-'71 season was not met with great enthusiasm. Although there were several experienced players returning, their experience was with a team that finished a dismal 12-14 the year before. The prospects looked even more bleak when Don Buse, the team's best player, showed up at the first practice with his leg in a cast. The legendary star, who had emerged from his humble upbringing to become a star at Holland High School, had torn ankle ligaments while attending camp for the Olympic Basketball Committee.

By the time the season opened, Buse was back on the floor. Joining him at guard was 6'5" Rick Smith of Oakland City. Big Steve Welmer returned to man the middle, and he would be flanked by senior forwards Bob Clayton and John Wellemeyer. Bench support would come from Rick Coffey, Gregg Martin, Monte Stebbins and sophomore Curt John. John, a Reitz product who had transferred from the University of Tennessee, would not be eligible until midseason because of his transfer.

After struggling to beat the Aces freshmen 102-82 in an exhibition, the team lost their opener at home 87-82 to UNLV. Nine games later, after losing the finale of the Holiday Tournament to Weber State, the University of Evansville (the school had changed its name from Evansville College to U of E in 1968) stood 4-5, and Coach McCutchan was concerned that the team would not make the NCAA Tournament. Since the Holiday Tourney, Rick Coffey had been inserted into the starting lineup at forward, with Bob Clayton moving to center and Steve Welmer coming off the bench. Coffey had averaged 13.5 points since the move, and McCutchan gave him high praise when he stated to the *Courier* that, "If I only had one shot left, I'd just as soon see Rick take it as anyone."

John Wellemeyer also distinguished himself in the coach's eyes, as his aggressive drives to the basket drew comparisons to Aces All-American Hugh Ahlering. Wellemeyer was also a smooth outside shooter and had been on a scoring binge since January, tallying 37 at Ball State and 28 against Southwest Missouri State to raise his average to over 21 points a game.

In the midst of a six-game winning streak, the Aces clinched the ICC and delivered Coach McCutchan's 400th victory, but after losing the season finale in a 101-98 heartbreaker to Southern Illinois, the Aces looked anything but invincible.

Evansville had not been to the NCAA Tourney in two years, and they were concerned that the streak might continue. After the SIU loss, in which the Aces led the entire game before imploding in the last minute, the team vowed in the locker room that if they made it to the tournament, they would not lose again.

Daryl Buente, the team's head manager (and now U of E's equipment manager), recalled the group's thought process as they waited for the news from the NCAA. "With our record of 17-8, there were many people who doubted we were good enough to receive an invitation," Buente explained. "But since we would host the Finals again, it was advantageous to the NCAA to have us in the tournament."

Buente also recalls the announcement and his analysis of the Aces' chances. "To top it off," he noted, "we not only received an invitation but also were named a regional host. We would play all five games at Roberts Stadium." That fact was crucial because it meant that the U of E team would be able to maintain their daily routines, practice on campus and use their home locker room.

In the tourney opener, Ashland College coach Bill Musselman decided to zone the Aces, but the strategy backfired as Coffey and Wellemeyer zeroed in from outside and sniped away for 47 points between them in an 82-74 win.

In the regional championship, the Aces made light work of Central Michigan, 78-60, behind a strong effort by Steve Welmer. Don Buse turned in a typical Buse effort, 13 points, 6 rebounds and 5 steals, and was named the tourney's MVP. For the eighth time in sixteen years, Evansville was headed to the NCAA Finals.

The 1971 Finals featured one of the strongest fields ever. Assumption College was 25-1 and ranked #1 and had beaten the Aces by 15 earlier in the year. The strongest of the other six teams appeared to be Southwestern Louisana. Daryl Buente recalled his amazement when he first laid eyes on the Bulldogs. "I thought the floor might have been tilted," Buente joked. "They were the biggest, strongest-looking team I had ever seen."

In the regional opener, Hartwick opened in a zone and dared Coffey and Wellemeyer to fire from outside. The two sharpshooters were happy to oblige and helped the Aces open a 49-34 halftime lead. When Hartwick switched to a man-to-man after intermission, Buse burned them with drives to the basket and ended with 18 points, 6 rebounds and 7 assists in a 105-69 yawner.

Next up for Coach Mac and the Aces were the monstrous Bulldogs from Southwestern Louisiana. Despite their size, the Bulldogs' premier player was 6'1" guard Dwight 'Bo' Lamar, who had led the nation (small college) in scoring with a 36.6 average. In the quarterfinals, he had torched #1 Assumption for 44 points in the upset.

Wellemeyer was brilliant again for the Aces as he poured in 23 points against the Bulldogs' zone defense. Bob Clayton worked inside for 15 rebounds and was 8 for 9 from the field. Rick Coffey had another great game with 20 points, and Don Buse was – well, Don Buse – as he held future Indiana Pacer Bo Lamar to 21 points while racking up 15 points, 11 rebounds and 9 assists himself in the 93-74 Aces victory.

Bedlam erupted in the Evansville locker room as the team was now within one win of the unthinkable. Only Old Dominion stood in the way.

Because of their lackluster regular season, attendance had been uncharacteristically low, but on March 19th, 1971, the crazies were back out en masse and they had checked their sanity at the gate. Like 13,124 sardines, they were primed to see if the Aces could finish the job.

Everyone was shocked when Old Dominion opened the game in a zone defense, and Evansville's shooters made them pay, just as they had everyone else. Although John Wellemeyer had sprained his ankle before halftime, Rick Coffey picked up the slack and fired early and often, racking up 20 points to give Evansville a 51-40 lead at the break.

The Aces opened up a 20-point lead with twelve minutes left, but Old Dominion kept it interesting by closing the gap to eight. All doubt was removed when reserve Gregg Martin came up big and shook the Monarchs with two quick baskets. As U of E pulled away, 200 Old Dominion fans showed some class when they expressed their appreciation for the Aces' efforts by chanting, "You're #1! We're #2!"

The 97-82 victory placed the 1970-'71 Aces into the record books as the last college division (Division II) team to win a national championship. The '70-'71 Aces were 17-8 and unranked when tournament play began, and they had struggled to even beat their own freshman team. But after a lackluster season that left their post-season prospects in doubt, they rose like the phoenix from the ashes, and on that March evening, as they received their Bulova national championship watches, they stood at the top of the small college basketball world. They had given their beloved coach, Arad McCutchan, his fifth and final NCAA title.

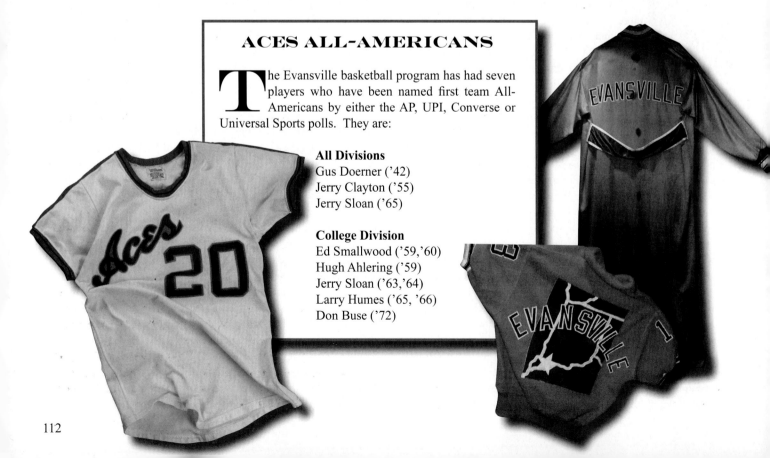

ACES ALL-AMERICANS

The Evansville basketball program has had seven players who have been named first team All-Americans by either the AP, UPI, Converse or Universal Sports polls. They are:

All Divisions
Gus Doerner ('42)
Jerry Clayton ('55)
Jerry Sloan ('65)

College Division
Ed Smallwood ('59,'60)
Hugh Ahlering ('59)
Jerry Sloan ('63,'64)
Larry Humes ('65, '66)
Don Buse ('72)

ARAD McCUTCHAN: THE MAN WITH THE PLAN

(Photo courtesy of Hugh Ahlering.)

In the ninety years that the University of Evansville has played basketball, one fact is absolute: Arad McCutchan was *The Man*. The tall, slender gentleman with black horn-rimmed glasses was the architect of one of the most successful college programs in the history of the game, and his name will forever be linked to the legacy of Evansville Aces basketball.

Arad was born in Evansville on the 4th of July in 1912, and he grew up on a farm just north of Daylight. As a youngster, he got his education in a one-room schoolhouse, and as high school loomed, he was the only eighth grader at his school. "In those days, it was an all-day thing just to come to Evansville," said Dr. Allen McCutchan, Arad's son, who played for his father at E.C. and is now in San Diego conducting AIDS research. "Going to 'huge' Bosse High School probably seemed like going to a small college."

The tall and athletic Arad wanted to play basketball for the Bulldogs, but transportation was a problem. His older sister, Bernice, taught at Bosse, but she wanted to go home after school instead of waiting around for her brother to finish every day. Fortunately, Arad's brother, Owen, was willing to help. Owen drove a bread truck and offered Arad a ride home.

McCutchan played on Bosse's varsity for two seasons and earned All-City and All-Sectional recognition before his graduation in 1930. After high school, he accepted an offer to play a few blocks away at Evansville College. Under Coach Bill Slyker, McCutchan was the team's leading scorer three consecutive seasons and captained his team to a 15-4 record his senior year.

After his graduation from E.C. in 1934, Arad took a job teaching math at Bosse and began coaching basketball in 1936. Through various math meetings, he got to know a math teacher from Central who had a daughter named Virginia Robinson. Ever the planner, the wily Arad began his pursuit. After learning that Virginia's mother enjoyed rhubarb, young Arad was picking some from the family garden one day when his father approached and asked what the lad was doing. After hearing Arad's explanation, the father wisely stated, "Ah, feeding the cow to catch the calf."

The strategy worked, as Arad and Virginia married in 1940. Virginia also became a math teacher while Arad continued to develop as a coach. In addition to his teaching and coaching, McCutchan also continued his own education, earning a Masters from Columbia University.

In 1943, Arad was called into service and became a flight instructor with the U.S. Navy, turning over the reins of Bosse's basketball program to his young assistant Herman Keller. Coach Keller then proceeded to lead the Bulldogs to two consecutive State titles in 1944 and '45. Even in his absence, Coach McCutchan's influences were still being felt in the Evansville basketball community.

McCutchan's reputation as a coach had made such a lasting impression that when he returned from the service in 1946, he was offered the top position at Evansville College. The program was still young, and all the coaches wore many hats, so Arad used the first several years to build special friendships and lay the groundwork for his basketball vision.

When he began his career at Evansville College, Arad coached virtually every sport, along with Paul Beck, Don Ping and several others. McCutchan, who also played end on E.C.'s football team when he was a student there, assisted Ping in football, and Beck served as a basketball assistant. All the coaches worked out of a small cinder block building, close to where the library is now, that also served as the football team's dressing room. In those days, coaches' salaries at small colleges were closer to those of high school coaches than to those of coaches in elite college programs, so Arad supplemented his income by refereeing and by being handy around the house to save on repair bills.

Bob Beck, Paul's son, recalled the many times that the coaches and some of the school's most avid fans would gather at postgame parties. He said it wasn't unusual to see Coach McCutchan and Coach Ping swapping stories with Bill Traylor, a strong supporter of the program, and media members like Dan Scism, Bill Fluty and Marv Bates.

The family atmosphere also existed among the coaches and team members. The basketball team would often travel in cars because, with his aviation background, Arad was not a fan of commercial flight. "Arad would take the starters," said Hugh Ahlering, an All-American from the coach's 1959 national championship team, "Paul Beck would take the second team, and Bob Hudson took the rest."

Arad as a player at Bosse.

Ahlering and others also spoke of how Arad and Virginia would often have the team over for get-togethers in the coach's basement, which he had re-modeled himself. To keep the team clean-cut, McCutchan would invite Lloyd Harper over. Harper ran a barbershop in a basement catecorner from campus and would trim all the players' hair free of charge, a practice that would no doubt draw sanctions today. Virginia, a classy lady who was loved by everyone, would feed the boys and make them feel welcome in the homey atmosphere.

Many believe the close-knit environment also aided in the recruiting process, and Arad used every source available to him. "Mac recruited within about a 75-mile radius," said Bruce Lomax, a former E.C. player and life-long Aces supporter. "He had all the doors open, and the fellas who had played for us were always bringing somebody in."

"Brilliant" was the way Aces star Buster Briley described McCutchan's recruiting style, recalling not only the way he was recruited, but others as well. "You'd bring in a boy, and when they'd get here, Coach McCutchan might walk them around," Briley explained, "but then these guys (local supporters) would come in and one might feed them and another might take them somewhere. He'd get the community involved. When we'd go on road trips, they'd go along. It was like family."

Although prospective players became sold on the community because of the family atmosphere, they also quickly gained respect for the man in charge as well. "He was such a true gentlemen," said former player Steve Welmer. "Everywhere I went after I graduated they would say, 'You played for one of the all-time great gentlemen of the game.' He was like a father figure. I still have a hand-written letter saying I was one of his all-time favorites.

"The thing I appreciated about Coach McCutchan," Welmer continued, "was that he had been so successful before we (Welmer and teammate Don Buse) got there that he wasn't concerned about his ego. He wanted all of us to be successful. It was easy to play for a guy like that."

By all accounts, McCutchan was very comfortable in his own skin and was a class act. Ed Zausch, a center on yet another of McCutchan's national champs, looks back on his former coach with deep respect. "Some of these coaches you read about," Zausch pointed out, "with a temper and profanity, he (McCutchan) wasn't like that. He was quiet and easy-going and hardly ever lost his cool. He was always a gentleman."

As his son and also a former player, Allen McCutchan had a unique perspective on the man. "He was remarkable," Allen explained, "in that as intensely competitive as he was, he didn't bring it home. Sunday morning (after a Saturday night game) was just as nice on the days we lost as on the days we won. He was a bright guy, and he kept things in perspective in a good-old-boy kind of way."

Allen was also aware of the occasions when Coach McCutchan would express his consternation for a referee. The familiar routine probably brings a smile to the faces of Aces fans who can picture Arad standing perfectly erect with his arms stiffened at his side. As he huffed and puffed, his foot would hit the floor with a loud STOMP to get the official's attention.

As a coach, McCutchan was regarded as an innovative thinker and a showman, a perfect blend of Thomas Edison and P.T. Barnum. "He recognized that basketball came down to very marginal differences between teams," Allen McCutchan revealed, "so he always looked for angles."

The Aces ran the floor much more than most teams, and McCutchan used chairs in practice to force the players on the wings of the fast break to take very wide angles to make it harder to defend. Because of their fast-paced style, the Aces had to be fit, and McCutchan made sure they were.

Larry Humes, the school's career scoring leader, recalled the blistering pre-season routine administered each year. Every player had to complete a two-mile run in under twelve minutes, followed shortly by intense drills and running the Armory steps fifty times. "After pre-season, we could have played two games in a night," said Humes. "We were in that good of shape. We won a lot of ballgames because we were in better shape than the other guys."

McCutchan also used creative ways to gain an edge in the most mundane phases of the game. His son Allen recalls an out-of-bounds play underneath where two teammates facing the ball would raise their hands lazily, looking bored so the defenders would relax. With the defenders off-guard, the ball would be tossed high for an easy basket.

Ed Zausch revealed how Arad would use a set play to score on the tip-off. While most teams were just happy to gain control, McCutchan designed a play where the 6'9" Zausch would tip it straight to a teammate at the top of the center circle who would then hit Humes who was streaking for the basket, giving the Aces a two-point lead to start the game.

Coach McCutchan was also known for his flare for the unconventional. Even the uniforms were a combination of practicality and fashion sense. Although orange was not one of the school's colors, Arad wanted his team in orange because he had heard it was the most visible color and would make teammates easier to spot against the dark clothing of a winter crowd. Although many believe he chose sleeved shirts to keep the players warm, his son Allen recalls Arad commenting that people staring at arm pits for two hours wasn't a very appealing thought. The famous (or possibly infamous, depending on your point of view) multi-colored robes worn by the players also had some practicality because of the ease with which they could

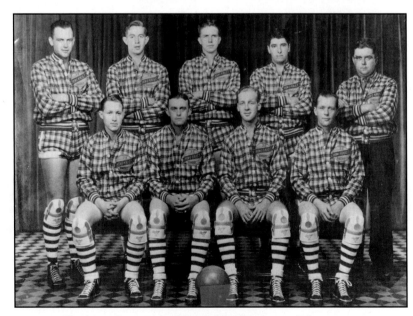

Check out the snazzy uniforms of this Honeycrust Bakery team. Arad McCutchan is far left in the back row.

be removed, but Allen believes they were actually just a case of showmanship by his father.

One of his greatest fashion statements were his red socks. Once again, there was no ulterior motive involved; it was just Arad adding a splash of color to his immaculate dark suits. What resulted from the dapper red socks was just one of the quirky traditions that made Roberts Stadium unique amongst the bland backdrops of some other venues. As fans began to notice McCutchan's red ankles, they proceeded to don all things red, and for no apparent reason that visiting teams could see, the Stadium's stands were a blanket of red instead of the school's colors of purple and white.

As the traditions and curiosities grew, Roberts Stadium became a carnival with the enthusiasm of a religious revival. Led by their quiet but dapper ringmaster, record crowds basked in the glory that was Aces basketball. Long-time fan Jim Hummel recalls those days fondly. "I can remember in the '60s, every year there was the Final Eight of the NCAA Tourney, and they played two games in the afternoon on Wednesday and two at night. Then they played the semi-finals on Thursday and the finals on Friday night," Hummel described. "On Wednesdays, we would always take a day's vacation and go to the Stadium and spend the whole day. In 1960, it snowed like 13 inches on Wednesday. All the factories were closed, but it was the biggest afternoon crowd they ever had."

From his early years at Evansville College, when he developed his talents in the confines of the Old Armory, and through the glory years at Roberts Stadium, Arad's coaching career was a success by anyone's standards. In his 31 years, he had only seven losing seasons and had an overall record of 515-313, including nine 20-win seasons and five national championships.

Arad McCutchan will always be synonymous with Aces basketball to the same degree that John Wooden and Adolph Rupp are to their schools. When Coach McCutchan retired in 1977, he was one of only two coaches in collegiate basketball history (Wooden was the other) to win five NCAA championships. And in 1981, he became the first college division coach enshrined in the Naismith Memorial Basketball Hall of Fame. But Arad McCutchan did so much more for the Evansville area than provide winning basketball. With his enthusiasm and imagination, he helped create an entire culture, and he encouraged everyone to be a part of it.

GUS DOERNER: THE MACKEY MARVEL

Among the many great players to don the uniform of the Evansville Purple Aces over the last 90 years, the very first to gain superstar status was Gus Doerner, the Mackey Marvel. Doerner graduated from Mackey High School at the age of sixteen, and he had to grow up quickly as a boy playing among men under Aces coach Bill Slyker.

Doerner was a four-year player at E.C. and was a captain his senior year, 1942. During his final season, he averaged 24.4 points a game, shattering the Aces record and ranking him third in the nation.

Doerner was always reluctant to take credit for his achievements, however, always alluding to the contributions of his teammates. One particular player who always drew praise was Lowell Galloway, who often provided the passes that resulted in Doerner scores.

Although only 6'4", Doerner was a physical presence inside and had a nose for the basket. "Gus had a unique way of playing," said Bruce Lomax, who had preceded Doerner as a player for the Aces. "A lot of his game was inside. He was left-handed, and he had a great hook shot. He'd work around in there and get his (right) shoulder into you where you couldn't get around him. It took an act of Congress to keep him from scoring."

After his graduation in '42, Gus and Lowell Galloway both played professionally with the Ft. Wayne Zollner Pistons (later to become the Detroit Pistons) and won a world championship. After spending two years in the Air Force, Doerner returned to pro ball, earning $7,800 a year with the Indianapolis Kautskys, which was big money in those days.

When his pro career was over, Gus returned home to coach the Ft. Branch Twigs for three years before entering the business world. In 1954, he formed a partnership with Bruce Lomax and entered the sporting goods business. After the partnership dissolved in 1963, Gus Doerner Sports was established and is still thriving today.

Today, the Mackey Marvel's career is chronicled in the hallowed halls of the Indiana Basketball Hall of Fame and the Corridor of Champions at Roberts Stadium. The Doerner name has been synonymous with area sports for years, and it all started when a lanky kid from Mackey arrived on the Evansville College campus. In the long line of stars who have come and gone, Gus Doerner started it all by becoming Evansville's first All-American and, along with Jerry Sloan, became the first Evansville College player to have his Aces jersey retired.

HUGH AHLERING: 'THE OLD MAN' WAS A WINNER

Aces basketball has had its share of luminaries over the years, but none took a more unusual path to stardom than Hugh Ahlering. One would be hard-pressed finding many players who never played high school ball, started their college career at the age of 23 and then finished college as an All-American on a national championship team.

After graduating from Stanley Hall Grade School, Ahlering entered Bosse in 1946 as a 5'5" freshman. At his height, basketball was out of the question, so he used his athletic skills to play baseball and tennis for the school.

After graduating in 1950, Hugh went to work at National City Bank before being drafted into the service. During his two-year tour of duty in Korea, he finally hit a growth spurt, shooting up nearly six inches to 6'0.

Upon his return from Korea, Ahlering once again took a job at the bank and began playing ball in several church leagues and independent leagues around town. Bob Hodges, a local sports figure and brother of baseball star Gil Hodges, suggested that Hugh walk on at Evansville College, because Coach Arad McCutchan had a policy of never cutting a player who chose to try out.

Because of the GI Bill, Ahlering did not need a scholarship, so he joined the team as a 23-year-old freshman to see where he might fit in. Since freshmen could not play in those days, Ahlering and his classmates practiced, played their freshman games and watched as the varsity played in the old Armory across the street from the school.

When the brand new Roberts Stadium opened in 1956, 'the old man', as he was called, was a member of the first team to call the Stadium home. Five games into his sophomore year, Hugh was moved into the starting lineup for a team that finished the season 18-8 and Ahlering was rewarded with a scholarship.

During Hugh's junior season, the Aces established themselves as a force by carving out a 23-4 record, the best in Aces history to that point. The season ended in disappointment, however, when Coach McCutchan's crew overlooked St. Michael's College in the NCAA Tournament.

As the 1958-'59 season arrived, Aces fans were geared up and ready. All five starters were returning, and many of them are still remembered fondly by fans even today. In addition to Ahlering, the Aces starters were: scoring sensation Ed Smallwood; Ahlering's running mate at guard Harold Cox; center Mel Lurker; and 6'6" Larry Erwin. With a bench led by supersub Dale Wise, the Aces finished 21-6 and played in front of nearly 100,000 red-clad fans at Roberts Stadium during the season. The magnificent season culminated with a win over Southwest Missouri in the NCAA Championship game.

At nearly thirty years old, Ahlering had completed a storybook career, and local fans appreciated what he did on the court. Ron Brand, a long-time Aces fan, recalls Hugh executing Coach McCutchan's style to perfection. "He played guard with Harold Cox," Brand noted, "and they'd come down and the ball would never hit the floor, just bang, bang, bang (with passes). That's how Mac coached."

Aces fan Bill Hazelip also remembers Ahlering. "He was one of those guys, he would drive and if the ball could get on the backboard, he had a basket," Hazelip said.

Ahlering graduated from Evansville College with an Engineering degree. He and his wife Carol have raised five daughters over the years, and yet they still enjoy pulling out the scrapbooks and reminiscing about their years as part of the Aces basketball program. Hugh Ahlering's story is as uplifting as it is unique. From his days as a pint-sized Bosse freshman who couldn't make the team, he persevered to become a member of the U of E Athletic Hall of Fame and was named to the 15-man All-Time U of E Basketball Team.

Ahlering used his intelligence and his good fortune to find a coach willing to give him a chance, and he used his maturity and experience to help lead the Aces to the first national championship in the program's history. With his teammate Ed Smallwood, Hugh was named a first-team small college All-American in 1959, demonstrating once again that 'the old man' was a winner.

Hugh Ahlering in action.

ED SMALLWOOD: THE BIG SMOKE

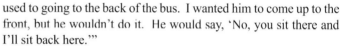

In 1956, Bruce Lomax, an avid Evansville College supporter, got a call from E.C. Coach Arad McCutchan, and even today he remembers the conversation well. "He said, 'Bruce, I've got a couple of Louisville boys I'm going to bring in. Can you set up a backyard barbecue?', Lomax recalled. "We had one and made everyone feel at home."

One of the "Louisville boys" to whom Mac referred was Ed Smallwood, a 6'4" sharpshooter with a funny-looking sideways jump shot. The Louisville Central grad was raised in one of Louisville's rougher neighborhoods by his maternal grandparents and, at the time, was the most highly-touted newcomer in Evansville College history.

When Smallwood averaged over 24 points in four freshman games, he proved that the hype was legit, and he had Aces fans itching to see him in a varsity uniform. 'The Big Smoke', as he was known to the media and fans, joined his teammates in taking the Aces program to heights never seen before, setting records along the way and establishing himself as one of Coach McCutchan's all-time greats.

Although Bruce Lomax's barbecue was designed to make Ed feel comfortable, the same can't be said for the racial climate of the times. In the mid- to late-'50s, integration had not yet been totally accepted, and there were some trying times along the way for the youngster from Louisville. Not one to make trouble, Ed seemed to accept the bias, but his teammates were not so tolerant.

P.M. Sanders, a teammate of Smallwood's, recalls an occasion when the team was exposed to the racial inequity of that generation. "We went to Indianapolis and we would always go out and eat our evening meal as a team," Sanders explained. "We went to this restaurant and we sat there and sat there. No one would wait on us, and we said, 'What's going on?'

"Ed said, 'I can tell you what's going on. They're not going to serve blacks.'

"We were naïve," Sanders continued. "As soon as Ed said that, we decided, 'Well, we're out of here!' That just wasn't right."

A similar occurrence had happened a couple years earlier during the Evansville Holiday Tournament when another black athlete, Jim Smallins, had played for the Aces. Evansville had beaten Boston College on Friday night, and Mississippi State had defeated Denver. During the pre-game meal on Saturday at the Vendome Hotel, the Mississippi State team surprised everyone by rising in unison and leaving the room to head back to Mississippi. Apparently, the school's chancellor had called them home because he found out they were about to play a team with a black player. Tournament officials quickly went to a Plan B, and the Aces beat Denver on a miracle half-court shot at the buzzer by John Harrawood.

Fortunately for Ed Smallwood, Evansville College was not Mississippi State, and he was treated well by teammates and fans alike. It was obvious to his teammates, however, that Ed was not totally comfortable being the team's lone black player. His background had taught him to "know his place," and his demeanor reflected that philosophy.

No one was troubled more by the situation than Ed's best friend, Hugh Ahlering. Ahlering and Smallwood both became All-Americans for the Aces, but they also developed a strong bond as teammates. Hugh remembers how he used to pick Ed up to take him to meetings or team outings, and even today, over forty years later, it bothers Ahlering to talk about the days when Ed would ride with him.

As Hugh began to describe how he would arrive to pick Ed up, tears filled his eyes and he hesitated. "Honest to God, I still get kind of choked up," he admitted before revealing the source of his emotion. "Ed would get in the back seat! He would not ride with me in the front seat because he was used to going to the back of the bus. I wanted him to come up to the front, but he wouldn't do it. He would say, 'No, you sit there and I'll sit back here.'"

Hugh went on to say that eventually Ed got comfortable enough to sit up front with him. Perhaps some of that comfort came from the acceptance he gained from his outstanding play. As a sophomore, he led the ICC with 113 field goals, breaking the record of 103 set a year earlier by John Harrawood. He was also named the conference's Most Outstanding Performer, making it four years in a row that an Evansville player had won the award. (Jerry Clayton had won in '54-'55 and John Harrawood had won it the next two seasons.) Evansville finished 23-4 and should have won a national title had they not overlooked St. Michael's College in the semi-finals.

Smallwood's last two years were two of the best in Evansville history, as he led the Aces to its first national title in 1959 and its second in 1960. Ed earned first team All-American honors both years, and in January of 1960, passed John Harrawood as the school's career scoring leader. His 1,898 career points are still third on Evansville's all-time list behind Larry Humes' 2,236 and Marcus Wilson's 2,053.

After his graduation in 1960, Smallwood was drafted by the St. Louis Hawks, making him the first Evansville player to be drafted since Bob Sakel in 1951. He signed a $6,500 one-year contract, but his lack of size for the position he played prevented him from making it as a pro. After leaving basketball, he worked with the Boy Scouts of America and started his own construction company.

By the time Ed Smallwood left Evansville College, he had set nearly every scoring record and had led the school to its first two national titles, and he did it with dignity and conquered some personal demons along the way. During his years at E.C., he became the standard for excellence that jump-started the glory years of Aces basketball. In the words of long-time Aces fan Bill Hazelip, "Ed Smallwood put us on the map."

BUSTER BRILEY: SWEET GUY WITH A SWEET SHOT

Harold Eugene Briley was born in his uncle's house in Kentucky while his mother was visiting, but he grew up in basketball-crazy Madison, Indiana, located between Louisville and Cincinnati. He was in this world only a few minutes when he was given the nickname that would endear him to southwestern Indiana fans forever.

"I was born premature," he said from his home at Quail Crossing. "In those days, something or someone who was big was called a 'buster'. So (as a joke) my grandmother looked at me and said, 'Boy, he sure is a 'buster!', and it just stuck."

Buster's father, William, was a steeplejack, which at that time was a person who built and worked on very tall structures, like bridges and smokestacks. (At one time, Madison had the tallest smokestack in the world.) William passed away when Buster was nine, so Buster's mother, Della, supported Buster and his younger siblings, William, Junior and Wanda, by waiting tables at the Hillside Hotel in Madison.

Because there was little to do in the small town, Buster dribbled and shot the hours away on an outdoor court near the high school. He didn't get serious about the game until he had a conversation with a professor at nearby Hanover College who also owned a feed store. "He told me that basketball could get my school paid for if I got good enough," Buster recalled. "So I decided to start looking at it."

After countless hours honing his skills, he entered Madison High School and became a starter as a freshman. By his junior season, the Madison Cubs were one of the best teams in the state, losing 82-80 in double overtime in the State semi-finals to eventual State champion Crispus Attucks, a team that averaged 6'9 across the front line.

In Briley's senior year, Madison went into the semi-state undefeated but lost to another undefeated team, the Muncie Central Bearcats, led by Ron Bonham. After the tournament, Bonham was named Indiana's Mr. Basketball and Buster was #2 on the Indiana All-Stars.

When Briley graduated from Madison, he was the school's all-time leading scorer with 1,985 points. What makes the number amazing is that, by Buster's estimates, nearly half of his field goals would have been three-pointers if he were playing today.

Buster was recruited by most of the top programs in the country and traveled to several for visits, including Purdue, Houston and UCLA. He visited Houston (long before they became Phi Slamma Jamma) at a time when they played their home games in a high school gym, and he got to meet John Wooden just before UCLA would begin a dominance that will probably never be equaled. "He had a presence about him," Buster said about the legendary 'Wizard of Westwood'. "He was laid back, but when he said something, everybody listened, even before he started winning."

Buster signed with Adolph Rupp at the University of Kentucky at the same time as Cotton Nash, but personal reasons caused him to take another look at the small college in Evansville. Briley was familiar with the area because it was a tradition for Madison to play Bosse in the final game of every season. The annual finale was started because Madison coach Bud Ritter had been a star center on Bosse's 1944 and 1945 State championship teams.

When Buster asked Coach Ritter his advice on the move to Evansville College, Ritter quickly answered, "That's the place for you," and it was all the 6'4 sharpshooter needed to hear. Joining classmates Wayne 'The Boulder' Boultinghouse, Paul Bullard and Ed Zausch, Buster wowed the fans with his deft touch and won them over with his energy and personality.

As a sophomore, the first year a player was allowed to play back then, Buster carried much of the scoring load for Coach Arad McCutchan's Purple Aces, and he was not shy about letting it fly. In fact, he'll jokingly tell anyone who'll listen that he holds the record for the most shots in a game with 43.

Buster also has a sense of humor about his prowess (or lack of) as a defensive player. "I couldn't guard a bank," he joked. "I would always guard their worst offensive player. My job, and I was good at it, was to let them shoot. In fact, my favorite word (on defense) was 'HELP!'."

One guy who provided much of the 'help' for Buster was his good friend Ed Zausch. Zausch was popular with fans for using his 6'9" frame inside. When speaking of Buster's questionable defensive

Buster Briley (left) said it wasn't unusual for him to shoot with his left hand, as he's doing here in 1962. (Photo from The LINC, the Evansville College yearbook.)

WHERE, OH WHERE CAN BUSTER BE?

Buster Briley's back door was adjacent to the Madison High School gym, which was a good thing. During his sophomore year, his team was warming up for a home game but Buster was nowhere to be found. The coach sent someone to Buster's house only to find him still taking his pre-game nap, one of Buster's rituals. After a sprint to the gym, a groggy Buster made it to the gym in time for the second quarter.

skills, Zausch is diplomatic with his tongue-in-cheek answer. "He put effort into it," Zausch said from his Evansville office, "but let's just say it wasn't his primary objective. It was my job to stay in the middle and be a backup inside. Of course that sometimes got me in foul trouble. I think I got half my fouls because of Buster."

Although Zausch kids about Buster's defensive ability, he is very adamant about Briley as an offensive threat. "Nobody in college at that time had the touch he had," Zausch said. "If they had had the 3-point shot then, I don't know what his records would have been. That was his range."

When asked what separated Buster from other shooters, Zausch recalled an example that took place during some downtime while the team was on the road. "One of the best ways to describe Buster's talent is like when we would pitch quarters to the wall (to kill time)," he explained. "One would hit the wall, the next would be short and the next would be right at the baseboard. It took one long, one short and then he was on every time. He had great motor skills and hand-eye coordination."

Buster's sophomore year also brought one of the most memorable moments in U of E basketball history. In a game at home against Notre Dame, an Irish player hit a free throw with one second on the clock. The ball was inbounded to Buster and he hurled it 86 feet and hit nothing but net. Amazingly, Buster never saw the ball go in. "I spun around (after the shot) and landed face-down on the floor," Buster recalled. "I was at the end near the tunnel, so I just ran into the locker room. I didn't know it went in until someone told me, and I didn't see it until I watched (the taped game) on TV."

Over time, the myth of 'The Shot' grew. Most people will say that the shot won the game and that the overflow crowd went crazy. The fact is, the shot only meant that U of E lost by eight points instead of ten, and half the crowd had left or were leaving when the miracle shot left Buster's hand. Nonetheless, a small disk (most people would say it was a golden spike) marking the spot of the historic heave was placed on the floor and stayed there for years.

As Briley and his classmates became seniors, they were joined by a very talented sophomore class that included Jerry Sloan, Larry Humes and Sam Watkins. The team, made up primarily of seniors and sophomores, would go on to win the school's third College Division national championship, sending Buster and his class out on top.

After studying Business and Education, Buster was contemplating a career in coaching and, in fact, was the frontrunner for a job that was open in Vincennes. Because of an intervention by Bud Ritter, Buster's high school coach, we'll never know how history might have changed had Buster taken the job and been successful, leaving no vacancy eight years later for future hall of famer Gunner Wyman. Instead, Ritter convinced Buster that his personality wasn't suited to handle the parents and politics of high school coaching.

Briley abandoned his coaching aspirations and entered the world of insurance sales. His gregarious nature and celebrity status made him an instant success, but the combination also turned out to be a double-edged sword. Potential clients welcomed the hoops hero with open arms, and the job quickly turned into long lunches and late-night gatherings over cocktails. The lifestyle engulfed Buster and sent him spinning out of control, and he is very candid about his past and admits that he feels fortunate to still be around to enjoy life.

"I think I'm blessed at my age," he said recently. "At one time, I had too much fun. It escalated, and it got to the point where it was just brutal. I went down to 120 pounds. When you start drinking like I did, you don't eat.

"I'm an alcoholic," he confessed. "I mean I'm an alcoholic who doesn't drink, but I'm still an alcoholic. I still go to AA four times a week, and I haven't had a drink since September of 1993."

As a player, Buster ended his high school career as one of the best high school scorers in Indiana history. Although he never had a 50-point game, he had 48 three times. Even today, he stands #41 on Indiana's career scoring list, and all but sixteen of those ahead of him played during the three-point era. As a collegian, he played on one of U of E's greatest teams, and even to this day, he has his Indiana All-Star jersey and his gold watch from his 1964 national title.

Buster Briley has overcome personal tragedy and adversity and is now living happily and healthily with his wife Beth. Perhaps the most telling legacy Buster left behind is evident on the faces of fans when they reminisce about the days of yore. More often than not, whenever Buster Briley's name comes up, the first response one gets is a smile.

DID YOU KNOW?

It didn't take much for Aces star Buster Briley to get used to wearing a robe while sitting on the bench with Coach Arad McCutchan's Evansville Aces. Oddly enough, he wore robes on the sideline at Madison High School as well. His coach was former Bosse star player Bud Ritter.

Buster was one of the Aces' most popular players. He is shown here signing autographs for some local boys. The dark-haired lad with his eyes fixed on Buster is none other than Evansville attorney Les Shively. (Photo courtesy of Buster Briley.)

LARRY HUMES: STILL #1

Not many college basketball programs can say that their career scoring leader launched his last shot while Lyndon Johnson was still in the White House. For a record to stand for over forty years is impressive, but what makes Larry Humes' record as the Evansville Aces' leading scorer truly special is that he did it without benefit of the three-point shot and he did it in only three years, because freshmen were not eligible when he enrolled in 1962.

Larry Humes was born on August 12th, 1943 in Madison, Indiana, the son of Frank and Louise Humes. With a sister and six brothers, Larry grew up poor, but the family got by as best they could on the income from their father's job as a mechanic and their mother's as a custodian. "We always had food on the table," Larry said, "but we had hand-me-down clothes from the Salvation Army and Goodwill. You never thought anything about it because most of the people around you were the same way. You learn to appreciate what you have."

Larry's two older brothers, Eddie and Frank Jr., and his sister Elizabeth did not play basketball, but when Larry made a name for himself in high school, the younger brothers followed in his footsteps. In fact, the Madison Cubs went from 1959 until 1975 with a Humes in the lineup. At 6'4, Larry was the tallest of the brothers, but each was good enough to turn basketball into a college education.

Following Larry, was Howard, better known as 'Bugsy', who was an Indiana All-Star and went to Idaho State. Next was Willie, who attended Vincennes before following Bugsy to Idaho State. During his senior year in college, Willie finished as the second-leading scorer in the country with a 49-point average, just one point per game behind the 50-point average of Notre Dame's Austin Carr. Younger brother Junior, or 'June Bug', also starred at Madison and then played at IUPU Ft. Wayne.

It didn't take long for Madison coach Bud Ritter and the fans to see that Larry was something special. As a freshman, the lanky Humes yanked down 19 rebounds against an Indianapolis Attucks team that averaged 6'9 across the front line.

Larry set most of the scoring records at Madison as a four-year starter, but many were broken a few years later by his siblings. Larry's single-game record of 47 points was broken by Bugsy's 48, which was then broken by Willie's 49. But they couldn't match Larry's career numbers, as his career scoring record still stands today.

Larry's career at Madison is possibly the greatest four-year stretch in Indiana history. During his freshman season, the Cubs lost one regular season game, and for the remainder of his career, his teams never lost another one.

After his first two seasons, Madison lost in the semi-state, first to eventual State champ Crispus Attucks, then to Muncie Central his sophomore year. When he was a junior, Madison was beaten in the regional, but as a senior, Larry nearly led the Cubs to the Big Dance. After beating Anderson in the semi-state finals behind Larry's 47 points, the Cubs advanced to the State Finals. Both semi-final games were upsets, with East Chicago Roosevelt knocking off Kokomo and Humes' Cubs losing to eventual State champion Evansville Bosse, a team Madison had beaten earlier in the year.

After the tournament, Humes was named Indiana's Mr. Basketball and joined Bosse's Gary Grieger, North's Dave Schellhase and Tell City's Tommy Kron as Indiana All-Stars. The Stars beat Kentucky by one point at Freedom Hall and then lost a two-point game at Hinkle Fieldhouse.

Approached by nearly 100 colleges, Larry narrowed his choices to Evansville College, Purdue and the University of Cincinnati, because of its proximity to Madison. As he analyzed his options, Larry turned to his high school coach for advice and guidance. Madison coach Bud Ritter knew Evansville well as a star on Bosse's 1944 and '45 State championship teams, and he had strong feelings about Evansville College as a good fit for his young star.

"When you're young, you think you know everything," Humes says in retrospect. "Coach Ritter kind of took me under his wing and guided me in the right direction. He thought Evansville College would be a good place for me to get a good education, and people there loved sports. I took his word for it and have never regretted it."

As a student at Evansville, Larry and his wife Cecele, his high school sweetheart, became good friends with Jerry Sloan and his wife Bobbye because the two were the only married players on the team. Together, the two friends led Coach McCutchan's Aces to the greatest two-year run in the school's history, thanks to Sloan's all-around game and Humes' natural talent for scoring.

Humes' skills were quickly embraced by teammates and fans during his four-

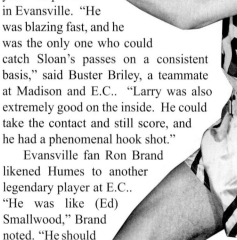

(Photo courtesy of the University of Evansville, Sports Information.)

year stopover in Evansville. "He was blazing fast, and he was the only one who could catch Sloan's passes on a consistent basis," said Buster Briley, a teammate at Madison and E.C.. "Larry was also extremely good on the inside. He could take the contact and still score, and he had a phenomenal hook shot."

Evansville fan Ron Brand likened Humes to another legendary player at E.C.. "He was like (Ed) Smallwood," Brand noted. "He should have been in the pros."

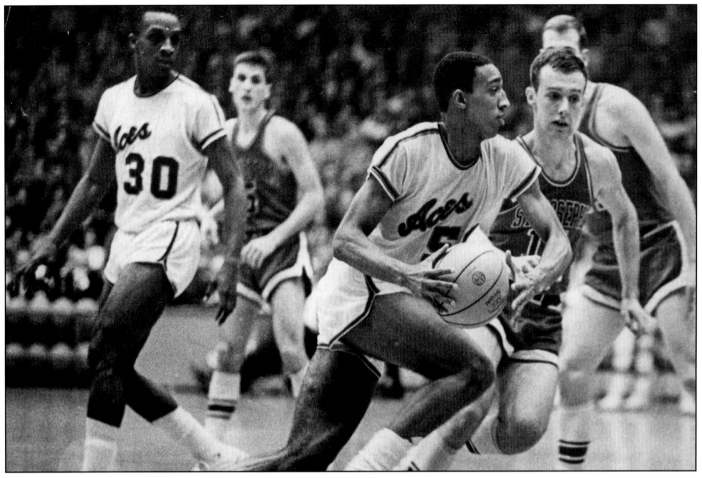
Humes drives against St. Joseph's College as teammate Herb Williams looks on.

Although Larry's all-around game was solid, he knew as well as anyone what people expected of him – to put points on the board. "You have scorers, and you have shooters," Humes explained. "I wasn't a shooter; Buster Briley was a shooter. A scorer gets a lot of steals and free throws because you go to the basket a lot. Being a scorer is nothing a person can teach you. You just have an instinct and score any way you can."

Aces fans during the Humes era remember well the smooth flowing hook shot Larry launched from various angles, and when the pressure was on, he could deliver with uncanny accuracy. "I learned it from Bud Ritter," Larry disclosed. "That hook shot to me was like a jump shot to other players because I was pretty consistent with it. And after making the hook a few times, I could fake and go around (the defender) for a layup."

For two years, Larry shared the floor with Sloan, who was a year ahead of him. The two were virtually unstoppable, leading the Aces to two national titles and an unprecedented undefeated season in 1964-'65, Larry's junior year. Coach McCutchan used an unorthodox strategy in utilizing his two stars' talents, and the roles each played had some impact on their futures after college. On defense, Sloan would guard an opposing team's forward while Humes would defend the team's guard. Offensively, Humes would use his skills in close, driving and drawing fouls, while Sloan played the guard position, handling the ball and shooting from outside.

When Larry was drafted in the third round of the 1966 NBA draft by the Chicago Bulls, his lack of experience and reputation as a guard could have cost him a pro career. At only 6'4, he was too small for the forward position and was cut on the final day.

Using his degree in Recreation and Physical Education and his Masters in Guidance Counseling, Larry set out to start a career in teaching and coaching. After five years each at Indianapolis Shortridge and Howe, Larry returned to Evansville to serve as an Aces assistant. After two and a half months, he was offered the head coaching job at Crispus Attucks and left once again for the Circle City. He later became an assistant coach under Billy Keller and Bill Green at the University of Indianapolis before spending the final years of his career as a counselor in Indianapolis middle schools.

From the time Larry arrived on the Evansville College campus in 1962, his work ethic and talent contributed to a level of success unequalled in Aces history. During his junior season, he set the school's single-season scoring record with 941 points. He was a three-time conference MVP, three-time member of the NCAA All-Tourney team and a first team small college All-American in 1966.

In only three seasons, Humes set the school's career scoring record with 2,236 points, a record that still stands over forty years later. He is the only Aces player to average over thirty points in a season, and he did it twice (32.5 in '64-'65 and 31.0 in '65-'66), and he is one of only four players in the school's history to have his jersey retired (the others are Gus Doerner, Jerry Sloan and Don Buse).

Even with the youngsters of the modern era sniping away from the three-point line, no Aces player has been able to surpass Humes' records. He played a huge role in the greatest era in Aces history, and those who got to see him play will never forget his performances. When it came to putting the ball in the hole, no one did it better than Larry Humes.

JERRY SLOAN: SIMPLY THE BEST

When Jerry Sloan arrived at the Evansville College campus in 1961, he was the biggest fish Coach Arad McCutchan had landed in his sixteen years as the Aces' head coach. But like any monster catch, the victory didn't come without a lot of patience and effort.

Gerald Eugene Sloan was born on March 28th, 1942 in McLeansboro, Illinois, the youngest of ten children. When Jerry was four, his father, Ralph, passed away and his mother, Jane, had to work the farm, which was sixteen miles from the nearest town. While Mom tended to the chickens, hogs and cattle, Jerry and his siblings got their education in a one-room schoolhouse where fifteen to twenty kids, spanning grades one through eight, learned their lessons from one teacher.

Those early years were tough, but the lessons he learned as a youngster would prove to be very valuable to Jerry as both a player and a coach. "We were always taught we had to work to survive," Sloan said from his hotel in Boise, Idaho, where the Utah Jazz were holding training camp. "It taught us that we weren't going to be given everything. We had to work for it."

Jerry started playing basketball on a dirt court because the school had no indoor gym. After practice, he had to walk or hitchhike eight miles home. When the time came for him to enroll at McLeansboro High School, he knew he wanted to play ball, but he wasn't sure what his chances would be of making the team. His biggest concern was his small stature. For those of us who watched him as Aces fans, it's hard to imagine what Jerry Sloan looked like as a 5'6" high school freshman.

Fortunately, by the time his sophomore season started, he had grown an amazing eight inches and would not only grow to an eventual 6'5 but would re-write the school's record book along the way. Many of the records that Jerry set in the late-'50s and 1960 still stand today. In fact, the biggest challenger to his records was his son Brian, who went on to star at Indiana University.

Nearly fifty years later, Jerry is still the school's leader in points scored in a season (710) and career (1,720) and is the school's all-time career leader in rebounds, as well, with 1,096. Brian is third in career rebounds and holds the school's single-season rebounding mark with 457 (in 1983-'84), while Jerry holds down the second and third positions.

As one of the top players in Illinois, many college programs had their eye on Jerry, including Arad McCutchan. After much deliberation, the gangly, shy farm boy decided to head to Champagne-Urbana to play for the fighting Illini. It didn't take long, however, for him to realize that he was a fish out of water.

"I went to the University of Illinois and couldn't get adjusted there," Sloan admitted. "It was so big, I was lost. I had never been out of the county except for basketball games. I got homesick." After two months, Jerry decided to leave Illinois and transfer to Southern Illinois University, but it only took one day as a Saluki for Sloan to convince himself that it was time to head back home.

Upon his return, Jerry did what most of the men in the area had done for years; he took a job in the oil fields. In January, Jerry's mother asked him a question that served as a catalyst for him to begin what would become an amazing basketball career.

"Are you going to do this for the rest of your life?" she asked him.

Sloan looks for a shot against Iowa with Herb Williams nearby. (Photo courtesy of the University of Evansville, Sports Information.)

That one simple question prompted Jerry to take action. On a Monday morning, he got on the phone with Arad McCutchan and the wheels were in motion. After a visit from Coach McCutchan, Aces athletic director Bob Hudson and two E.C. backers, Bruce Lomax and Dr. Harry Whetstone (a local dentist), Jerry was told that there wasn't a scholarship available because it was the winter quarter. Coach McCutchan's easy-going style prevailed anyway, as Sloan agreed to move to Evansville and wait for his opportunity.

Arrangements were made for Jerry to work at Whirlpool until the spring quarter started, and he was put up in a private home while waiting to start classes. His anxiously-awaited arrival on the court was only a few months away. The big one that nearly got away was finally landed and ready to be put on display.

From the time Jerry took the floor for the first time in 1962 until his final game in 1965, he set a standard for Aces basketball that has been nearly impossible for players who followed him to live up to. His style of play endeared him to teammates and fans alike, and he quickly became the most respected and admired player in Aces history.

"He was one of the most hard-nosed players I've ever been around," said Bruce Lomax. "He was the type that you'd better lace up your boots because he's going to get after you. He's one of the great ones."

Long-time Aces fan Bill Hazelip remembers Jerry's imposing presence and raw-boned physique. "He had huge hands,"

Hazelip said. "He could pick up a basketball like most people pick up a baseball."

Teammate Buster Briley also remembers Sloan's physical skills, as well as his qualities as a teammate. "He'd give you the shirt off his back, but when he was on the court, he was all business," Briley said of the teammate known as 'Spider'. "He had the strongest hands I've ever seen. I saw him flick a ball away with his finger from a guy who was holding it with both hands.

"It was amazing watching him stalk a man on defense. You could see it in the way he would move that he was ready to pounce. Larry Humes got half his points on fast breaks because he could read when Sloan was going to make a steal."

Briley also pointed out that, although Sloan wasn't a great scorer, he would score when he needed to. Buster also described Sloan as a phenomenal passer and recalled feeling a breeze as an unexpected pass from Jerry whizzed by his ear.

Coach McCutchan raved about Sloan's defensive skills and his ability to draw charging fouls, saying at one point, "He's number one among anybody as far as any player I've ever coached."

During his three-year career at Evansville, number 52 led the Aces to a 76-9 record (89.4%), including 35 straight at one point. In the ICC, Sloan's Aces teams finished 35-1 and won the conference title every year. Jerry was named the conference Player of the Year twice ('62-'63 and '64-'65) and was a three-time UPI small college All-American. In 85 games at E.C., Jerry averaged 15.5 points and 12.4 rebounds and led the Aces into the small college NCAA final eight all three years.

Jerry Sloan as a coach with the Utah Jazz.
(Photo courtesy of the University of Evansville, Sports Information.)

During his tenure, Evansville's NCAA Tournament record was 12-1, and he was named to the All-Regional team three times. Most importantly, Sloan led the Aces to two national championships ('64 and '65) and was named the Most Outstanding Player both years, becoming only the third player to earn the honor twice.

Sloan's final game as a collegian symbolized his entire career. In the championship game that completed the only perfect season in Aces history, Sloan scored 25 points and reeled in 25 boards, setting a new NCAA final game rebounding record. Jerry Sloan had lived up to the hype and had rewarded loyal Aces fans with the best three-year run in the school's history. Now it was time for the quiet guy from southern Illinois to ply his trade against the best players in the world.

During Jerry's junior year at Evansville College, he had been selected by the Baltimore Bullets in the third round of the 1964 NBA draft, based on a strong performance in the Olympic trials. After his senior year, he was selected again by the Bullets, but this time as a first round pick. Sloan played sparingly with the Bullets, averaging only sixteen minutes and 5.7 points per game, and the following year, he was the first player taken by the Chicago Bulls in the expansion draft, earning him the nickname 'The Original Bull'. When he joined coach Red Kerr and the Bulls, he landed in another blue-collar city that would embrace him in much the same way as he was during his college days.

In his very first year, Sloan led the Bulls to the playoffs, averaging 17.4 points and 9 rebounds per game. Over his 11-year career, he was a two-time all-star and was one of only eighteen players in history to be named to the all-defensive first team four times. In 755 career games, Jerry scored 10,233 points (a 14.0 average), had 1,815 assists (2.4), and averaged 7.4 rebounds per game, an unusually high average for a guard. On February 17th, 1978, he became the first Chicago Bull to have his jersey (#4) retired.

When asked how it felt to play against all-time greats like Oscar Robertson, Jerry West, Wilt Chamberlain and Bill Russell, Sloan responded with typical humility, saying, "I was just lucky to be able to play in the same building with those guys."

Jerry's tireless work ethic and team-oriented philosophy made him a hot prospect for the coaching ranks when his playing days were over. Arad McCutchan had actually approached Sloan during his playing days with the possibility of Jerry taking over the Aces program when McCutchan retired, and in 1975, Arad announced that he would retire in two years and that Sloan would succeed him.

The highly anticipated return of the Aces star would not come to be, however. After only five days on the job, Jerry left amidst rampant speculation. The reasons for his exodus are known only to a few, and when asked to elaborate, Jerry responded, as always, with class. He chooses to let bygones be bygones and to not dwell on the past.

In 1979, Sloan was hired to pilot the Chicago Bulls, winning thirty games his first year with players like Artis Gilmore and Reggie Theus. In his second year, he led the Bulls to the playoffs, but he was fired in midseason of the following year after a poor start.

When the Bulls cut him loose, Jerry headed back to McLeansboro, something he always seemed to do when he needed to "get his bearings." For a couple years, he kept his life simple, watching his son Brian play ball. He also found himself wanting to attend grade school and junior high games, which made him realize that coaching was still in his blood. So when Brian graduated in 1984, Jerry started looking for work.

He made plans to return to Evansville once again to coach the Evansville Thunder, a Continental Basketball Association team, but before he coached a game, he got an offer he couldn't refuse. Frank Layden of the Utah Jazz asked Jerry to join the team as an assistant.

Although Sloan was pursued by other teams as a head coach, Jerry chose to stay with Layden and the Jazz. His loyalty was rewarded when Layden stepped down in December of 1988 to become president of the franchise and Jerry was named the new head coach.

Sloan was preparing for his twentieth season with the Jazz when he was interviewed in October of 2007, and his approach today is the same as it always has been – it's time to go to work. His talents have made him the fifth-winningest coach in NBA history with 1,035 wins, trailing only Lenny Wilkins, Pat Riley, Don Nelson and Larry Brown. During his 19 seasons with the Jazz, he has had only one losing season and has taken them to the playoffs 15 times. Twice, Sloan led Utah to the NBA Finals, only to fall to Michael Jordan's Bulls. In 1998, Jerry was named the NBA Coach of the Year, and he has had ten 50-win seasons. In 2001, he became the tenth coach in NBA history to record 800 wins, and in 2007, he became only the fifth coach to reach 1,000.

Jerry Sloan is the longest-tenured coach with the same franchise in all of major professional sports, and since his hiring with the Jazz in 1988, there have been over 200 coaching changes elsewhere.

During his tenure with the Jazz, Sloan had the chance to coach one of the greatest tandems in the history of the NBA, and he feels honored to have done so. John Stockton, known as 'Old School' because of his style of play and his preference for the old-style short shorts, retired in 2003 as the NBA career leader in assists (15,806)

> In high school, Jerry Sloan was known as 'the Fabulous Fox' because the team's nickname was the Foxes.

and steals (3,265). His teammate, Karl Malone, known as 'The Mailman' because he always delivered, retired a year later as the league's second most prolific scorer, behind Kareem Abdul Jabbar.

When asked his impressions of the duo, Sloan didn't speak of their skills or their stats; he spoke of their work ethic. "The first thing they did, they got themselves in great shape," he said. "On the very first day of training camp, they could've probably played a 40-minute ballgame. Not many guys do that. They were dedicated to be as good as they could be every day."

The words Jerry spoke concerning Stockton and Malone could also be used to describe his own career as both a player and coach. As a coach, his legacy is still being written, but as a player, he showed the world how the game was meant to be played. He beat the odds by escaping the oil fields of southern Illinois to enjoy success beyond his wildest dreams.

Although he wasn't born or raised in Evansville, in a way he grew up here. During his short stay in our midst, his dogged determination and refuse-to-lose attitude carried Aces fans to the pinnacle of their basketball world. Jerry Sloan will always be our adopted native son, and he will always be respected for his talent and his humility. Of all the players who have worn the purple and orange, Jerry Sloan was simply the best.

EVANSVILLE'S #1 FAN

Marvin Gray, shown here with Don Buse, is a popular sports figure from Evansville and has been a fixture at Evansville sporting events for nearly fifty years. Marvin was known for wearing a letter sweater, jersey or jacket of each team that was playing on a given night. He was also known for his amazing ability to recall stats, players' numbers and other minutae from years past.

At Bosse Field, Marvin manned the large scoreboard during high school and minor league games, and he was often seen enthusiastically pushing the broom at Roberts Stadium before games and at halftime. Sportswriter Dave Johnson recalled a particularly slow evening at the Stadium when he took notice of young Mr. Gray for a possible story. After observing Marvin at several games, Dave concluded that Marvin Gray made exactly 22 swipes (floor lengths) every time he swept the Stadium floor. A useless piece of information from a bored sports journalist.

DON BUSE: FROM POVERTY TO THE PROS

Of all the local athletes who have thrived and experienced success, perhaps none were a product of their environment as much as U of E great Don Buse. Donald Roy Buse was born on August 10th, 1950, the second youngest of the seven children of Opal (Hagemeyer) and Andy Buse. After his father died when Don was three, he and his family struggled to make ends meet. Don's mother worked odd jobs and did her best, but the kids grew up "very poor" and spent the majority of their young lives on Welfare.

Although life was not easy for the Buses, Don accepted it for what it was and decided to make the most of the hand he was dealt. "I think when you grow up like that," he theorized, "you want to prove you're as good as the other kids. You're a little insecure. So I think that had something to do with the drive I had."

As a young boy, Don spent a lot of time playing outdoors, partly because he loved it and partly out of necessity. "There were a lot of years we didn't have a TV," he recalled, "so we'd wad up a pair of socks and shoot it into a trash can. We would play anywhere we could find a place. Basketball and baseball were my two main sports."

Don was also fortunate to have two older brothers, and each of them played a role in making him the player he became. "Rex was two years older than me," Don pointed out. "We used to compete like hell, him and me. Just having somebody who's as good as you are or maybe better was a great situation to be in."

Don's oldest brother, Junior, was his idol growing up and provided young Don with his first glimpse of organized sports. Andrew Jr. was a star for Holland High School who averaged 18 points per game while a wide-eyed Don would sit in the stands as a youngster. "As a kid, I'd get down as close to the floor as I could," Don stated in a *Huntingburg Press* special edition honoring him, "sitting there in the front row of the bleachers and watching those guys practice and play games. They were my idols, and I said back then, 'That's what I want to be.'

"I can still remember how we had to slip in through the door up there for the old Huntingburg Sectional," he continued, "because it was always sold out. How I got in without a ticket was because the Holland Dairy had a booth in the gym. There just happened to be a door right behind the Dairy booth, and I sneaked in some way through that door."

Don attended school in Holland through grade four and then moved to Stendal from his fifth grade through his sophomore year, when Stendal consolidated with Winslow. The Buses then moved back to Holland, where their father's family was from. During his last two years of high school, Don would make his mark in the annals of Indiana basketball history and begin a climb to the highest level of his sport.

In just two years at Holland, Buse was fortunate enough to find a father figure to guide him and to experience the kind of thrills that could only be felt by a small school player competing in a one-class basketball system. Buse is quick to recognize Holland coach George 'Woody' Neel as a major contributor to his ultimate success.

"Coach Neel used to have us wear rubber overshoes on top of our sneakers during practice," Don informed the *Huntingburg Press*. "He figured if we could play with boots on, we'd become more agile and should be able to keep up with anybody in the game. That was a little coaching trick he used to give us an edge."

In Don's junior and senior years, he led the Dutchmen to two consecutive sectional titles, a feat seldom accomplished by smaller schools. His senior season was truly special in that Holland not only won the sectional, but finished the regular season a perfect 23-0. As a senior, Don led the Dutchmen in scoring (22.5) and rebounding (14.0) and was named an Indiana All-Star. The small-town boy with the big-time game had proven that he belonged.

During the spring of 1968, Buse had some college options to consider, but schools more than sixty miles away had an uphill battle. "I went to Jacksonville to visit," Don explained, "when Greg Nelson and Vaughn Wedeking (two great players from Evansville Harrison) were there and they hadn't signed Artis Gilmore and Pembrook Burrows yet (two 7-footers who would lead Jacksonville to the NCAA Finals). I liked it, but I didn't want to go that far from home."

Don also visited Alabama, Western Kentucky, Kentucky Wesleyan and McNeese State (Louisiana), but he was also aware that a coach named Arad McCutchan had been keeping his eye on him for a couple years. "Arad had seen me play when I was a junior," Don explained. "We were playing Huntingburg, and he was up there to see John Wellemeyer." (Wellemeyer was a senior and signed with the Aces after the '66-'67 season.)

Buse opted for UE and joined a recruiting class that included 6'7 Steve 'The Whale' Welmer (Columbus, IN), 6'8 John Couch (Fairfield, IL) and 6'4 Rick Coffey (Center Grove, IN). As juniors, this group would join Wellemeyer, Rick Smith (Oakland City), Curt John (Evansville Reitz) and others in celebrating an NCAA Division II national championship. Don Buse was named the MVP of the tournament and was the 1971 Division II Outstanding Player of the Year.

As a senior, Buse became the fourth-leading scorer in U of E history and was named a small college All-American. In 2000, he joined Gus Doerner (a 1942 graduate), Jerry Sloan (1965) and Larry Humes (1966) as the only U of E players to have their jerseys retired.

Throughout his high school and college careers, Don Buse had gained a reputation as a steady point guard and tenacious defender with a blue collar work ethic. The question now was: Can his game match up with the best players in the world?

In 1972, Buse was drafted by the Phoenix Suns of the NBA and in the third round by the Virginia Squires of the ABA. The 6'4", 190-pound guard became an Indiana Pacer on August 15th when his draft rights were acquired from Virginia. When he joined the Pacers, he was amidst such ABA greats as George McGinnis, Roger Brown and Mel Daniels, and as a rookie, was a member of the Pacers' third ABA championship team.

Buse played with the Pacers for four seasons (three in the ABA and the team's first in the NBA) and was an all-star twice (ABA in 1976 and NBA in 1977). His best season was in 1976-'77 when he led the league with 4.21 steals and 8.2 assists per game while averaging 12.5 points (the only time in his career that he would average over 10 points).

On September 6th, 1977, Buse was dealt to the Phoenix Suns in a deal for Ricky Sobers. He spent three seasons in Phoenix, where he averaged a respectable 8.0 points and 4.4 assists per game. It was during his Phoenix years that his defensive talents were recognized. After all three seasons, he was named as a first team selection on the NBA All-Defensive Team.

In November of 1980, Don returned to the Indiana Pacers in exchange for a pair of second round draft picks and cash. Once again, he made the All-Defensive Team, making it four years in a row for that distinction.

After two seasons with the Pacers, Don finished his career with stints in Portland (one year) and with the Kansas City Kings (two years). As a Pacer, Buse had set several team records, including a record 84 games played during a season ('75-'76). He also set Pacers records for assists in a season (689) and in a single game (20 against the Denver Nuggets) and for steals in a season (346).

It is said that Don was given the nickname 'Boo' by Pacer teammate Mel Daniels because Don was like a ghost on defense, and for thirteen seasons, Boo had held his own as an NBA player. He had used his toughness and cat-like quickness to combat stars like Magic, Kareem, 'the Big O' (Oscar Robertson) and even a young Michael Jordan.

In the *Huntingburg Press*, legendary Pacers coach Bobby 'Slick' Leonard portrayed Don as the perfect player for his position. "Boo was a throwback to the old style of a guard that could do everything," Leonard said. "He really was what I would call the complete guard. He was the total package. And, if he were playing today (2000), he'd make a lotta money. In today's marketplace, I would have put Boo somewhere in the vicinity of four to six million dollars a year."

After his retirement in 1985, Don worked as an assistant for a year under Cotton Fitzsimmons and for half a season helping Jerry Reynolds in Sacramento. More than anything, he wanted to settle down back home in southern Indiana.

Although Don Buse didn't make the mega-bucks today's players receive, he is content at his home between Huntingburg and Holland. To keep busy, he is involved in a few businesses with ex-Aces teammate Curt John and dabbles in horse racing. He also has kept his hand in basketball by serving as an assistant boys basketball coach at nearby Southridge High School.

Don Buse has returned to his roots. He has gone from a small boy with something to prove to the very top of his chosen profession. He has flown first class and rubbed elbows with the rich and famous, but regardless of the rewards and accolades, he never forgot where he came from.

This Buse family photo was taken at about the time of the death of Don's father, Andrew. Kneeling (L-R): Nina and Fay. Holding ball: Andrew Jr. Top (L-R): Mary, Rex, Don (age 3), Sue and Mom (Opal Buse). (Photo courtesy of Don Buse.)

STEVE WELMER: A 'WHALE' OF A CAREER

Of all the players who have passed through the Evansville Aces basketball program, few were as popular as Steve 'The Whale' Welmer, both with fans and teammates alike.

Steven Vincent Welmer was born on June 1st, 1950 in Columbus, Indiana. Steve and his sister, Susan, and brothers, Gary and David, were all extra tall and very athletic. Susan is a three-time City golf champ, and the three boys all earned full rides to college for their athletic skills. Gary went to Indiana Central (now the University of Indianapolis) on a football/baseball scholarship, and David, at 6'9, played basketball at Ball State under coaches Jim Holstein and Steve Yoder.

Steve, just a whisper under 6'10" himself, played three sports at Columbus High School and was also a very active student. As a member of the concert choir and as a participant in school musicals, he developed a presence that would serve him well as an athlete and later as one of the top college basketball officials in the country.

In high school, Steve excelled in baseball and was a center and defensive end on the football team, but his future would be shaped by his performance on the basketball court. As an All-Conference and All-State center, Welmer was recruited by such schools as Northwestern, North Carolina and Arizona State, but his choice to play 'small college' ball at Evansville College was influenced somewhat by the opinions of his high school coach.

Coach Bill Stearman, one of the most successful coaches in Indiana history, was known for playing tough competition, and for many years, Columbus played Evansville Bosse, home-and-home. This exposure to the Evansville area and Coach Stearman's respect for the Aces' legendary coach Arad McCutchan were important factors in Steve's decision to further his education in Evansville.

Steve chose E.C. because it met two key criteria he was searching for in a college: Evansville was close enough to allow his parents to see him play, and the school would allow him to play both basketball and baseball. As he arrived at school in the fall of 1968, Steve joined a freshman basketball class that would do more than its part in maintaining the school's strong basketball tradition. With classmates such as Reitz High School's Curt John and future NBA star Don Buse, Welmer would enjoy a great career and a special season that was on par with the greatest in the school's history.

As a baseball player at Evansville, Steve was a huge target at first base for shortstop Don Buse and the other infielders. Under Coach Wayne Boultinghouse, Steve was the first sophomore to lead the ICC in hitting since Ball State's Marv Rettenmund, who went on to play and coach in the major leagues.

In the late '60s, freshmen were not allowed to play on varsity teams in the 'major' sports, so Steve and the others had to play a non-varsity basketball schedule. Steve showed his potential in his first year by being the fifth-highest scoring freshman in the country, with a 29.7 average. This was also the year when he was christened with the nickname that will forever be a part of his legacy at Evansville College.

"Bill Fluty (from the *Evansville Courier*) pinned that one on me," Steve revealed from his home in Florida. "I was 'The Bird' in high school because that was my dad's nickname. Our freshman year (at Evansville) we were pretty good, and we were consistently beating the varsity in intrasquad games. Fluty said, 'This guy looks like a whale on the floor and moves like a porpoise,' so 'the Whale' stuck with me."

(Photo courtesy of Steve Welmer.)

In the early years at Evansville, Steve admits that it was a chore to keep his weight in check, and it was at the urging of Evansville's beloved coach that Steve began to take his fitness seriously.

"Coach McCutchan told us that if we were going to win championships, I had to be a part of it," Steve recalled. "I was the only true center we had. So I knuckled down my junior and senior year. Our last two years we didn't lose a conference game, home or away. I'm really proud of that."

Not only did the Aces go undefeated in the conference, but they captured the national championship during Steve's junior year, becoming the fifth Evansville team to accomplish the feat.

During Welmer's senior year, he earned small college All-American honors in both baseball and basketball for the Aces, and as he was preparing to leave school to start a career, he was very much aware of the good fortune he had experienced as a basketball player. "I played for a high school coach (Stearman) and a college coach (McCutchan) who were hall of famers," Steve said. "And we always played in front of packed stadiums. Not a lot of people can say that."

After college graduation in 1972, Steve headed to Indianapolis, near his home, to become a field sales rep for American States Insurance. While in Indy, he played on a semi-pro team with ex-Evansville high school stars Bob Ford (North) and Larry Weatherford (Bosse) as well as Bobby Wilkerson and Scott May, who both starred for Bobby Knight at IU.

In 1974, he moved back to Columbus to help with his father's beer distributorship. While in Columbus, he was approached by a friend with an opportunity to pursue a career that would land him in the Indiana Basketball Hall of Fame – not as a player, but as an official.

Like most referees, Steve began his officiating career at the bottom. In fact, his first experience was during his days at Evansville College as an intramural referee earning $3 a game for spending money. His first 'real' officiating job came from Jerry Newsome, a buddy of Steve's who once was the all-time scoring leader at Indiana State before a guy named Larry Bird came along. Jerry was already a working official, and he arranged for Steve to work some high school junior varsity games while Jerry did the varsity games.

In his second and third seasons of officiating, Welmer was placed on a faster track than most when Newsome had to replace his partner, who had encountered some conflicts and health problems. Steve got the call. He immediately inherited a full varsity high school schedule and even some small college games, like Hanover, Depauw and Franklin.

When Newsome later ran into medical problems of his own and had to slow down, Steve continued to move up the ladder. Due to his fast start, Welmer was chosen to officiate three Indiana high school State championship games before the age of 35 (1982, '84 and '85). The State Final game in 1985 was his last high school assignment and featured the Marion Giants, led by legendary coach Bill Green.

In only eight seasons, Welmer had progressed from officiating high school JV games to the Division I level (he did his first Division I game in 1982). In 1993, he joined a small group of men ("25 or 30") who officiate full-time, meaning they have no other outside jobs. Since '93, Welmer has worked the largest Division I schedule in the country. In 2007, he worked 118 games out of only 136 calendar days available, leaving him very little down time during the 20-week season.

Steve says that Division I officials can make a good living but that college basketball is a big business, and refs are treated well but are also constantly under the microscope. "A guy who has a decent schedule can make $40,000 to $60,000 a season for one or two games a week," Steve explained. "All large conferences pay about $1,000 for the game fee with a $200 per diem for hotel, food and rental car."

When asked about the scrutiny and potential dangers of the job, Steve was candid about the expectations and precautions. "At every game, there is a person who is paid to be there and chart the calls and give the conference a game report," he revealed. "There is a lot of accountability. We have to undergo background checks every year, and they look at our bank accounts (to look for signs of gambling, payoffs, etc.)."

Steve also described how each school will make sure that the officials are met upon their arrival and escorted to the officials' room without contact with fans or media. Some conferences, like the Big Ten, require that police wait for officials after the game, escort them to their car and make sure the officials have left safely.

On the court, Steve readily admits that his size is an advantage at times and that officiating is not the place for someone with thin skin. "I'm fortunate to be tall," Steve confided, "because the coaches know that I played. I can look the center in the eye. I have an acceptance factor. There's nothing that those centers can try to do that I didn't try when I played.

"There's nothing a coach or player can say to me, either, that I haven't heard somewhere along the line," he continued. "I've heard it all. In fact, if someone gives me a line that I haven't heard, I'll stop and say, 'Hey, that's pretty good!'"

Welmer also understands that it's part of the job to endure the wrath of irate fans and that part of the problem is their lack of understanding. "I'll hear people say, 'How can you miss that? It happened right in front of you,'" Steve pointed out. "Well, you're not always looking there, especially with three-man crews. Sometimes the nearby area may not be what you're responsible for. I've always said that, before anybody should be able to yell at a referee, they ought to put on that striped shirt one time and try it. It would give them a little respect for what we're trying to do."

Although the job can be challenging at times, Welmer also admits that it has enabled him to hobnob with some of the sport's elite and to witness close-up some historical moments. "I was fortunate to do a couple of Shaquille O'Neal games when he was at LSU," Steve said. "I've had Michael Jordan and Penny Hardaway (from Memphis), who, as far as a college player, was the greatest I personally have seen.

"This year ('07), I tossed it up for the #1 against #2 when Wisconsin (#2) played at Ohio State (#1) on CBS, and that doesn't happen very often. The last time (before that) it happened for me, I had Michigan-Duke when the Fab Five was at Michigan and Hill, Hurley and Laettner and that bunch was at Duke."

As a college official, Steve has certainly distinguished himself. He has worked the NCAA Tourney every year since 1993 and is currently sanctioned by nine Division I conferences. He works hard to maintain his working weight of 255 pounds and says he'd like to retire in three or four years. Whenever that day comes, Steve will be able to look back and say that, with his size, personality and command of the floor, he became one of the best in the game.

Steve Welmer would be the first to say that he has been blessed as both an athlete and in his chosen career, and he still maintains his ties to Evansville and counts teammates Don Buse and Curt John among his closest friends. Although 'the Whale' was with us for only four years, he will always be considered part of the Aces family.

Steve Welmer is one of the top NCAA officials in the country.

SCOTT HAFFNER

Scott Haffner, who played for the Aces from 1986 to 1989, was selected in the second round of the NBA draft by the Miami Heat. Haffner holds the Aces all-time single-game scoring record with 65 points against Dayton in 1989.

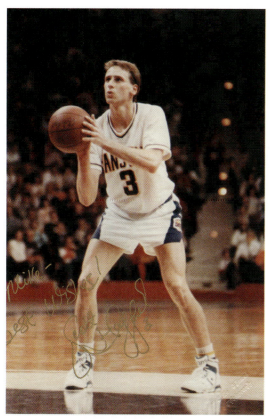

(Photo by Mike Thomas.)

GONE BUT NOT FORGOTTEN

As the yuletide season of 1977 approached, Aces basketball fans were excited as a new era was just gearing up. But the exhilaration would quickly give way to anguish on the darkest day in local sports history.

On the heels of the retirement of iconic coach Arad McCutchan, the University of Evansville was launching its first season as a Division I program. With a young group of players and a coach with youthful exuberance, the Aces had started the season 1-3 but were heading into the holidays with high hopes and big dreams. Those dreams were shattered, however, when the unthinkable occurred.

On Monday, December 13th, at 7:21 p.m., a chartered plane carrying 29 passengers and crew crashed into the muddy landscape near the Evansville airport just ninety seconds after takeoff. Everyone on board was lost, and the entire country joined friends, family and fans in dealing with the aftermath of the tragedy.

The '77 Aces were led by first-year head coach Bobby Watson, a former assistant at Oral Roberts University who understood the UE tradition. Watson's charm and enthusiasm had generated 1,000 new season ticket holders for the team's inaugural season in Division I, and he had even revived the beloved team mascot, the riverboat gambler Ace Purple. After the 1-3 start, the team was scheduled to leave for Nashville for a contest with Middle Tennessee State in nearby Murpheesboro. But the ominous events that led up to the flight would ultimately lead to disaster.

After a three-hour wait, due to inclement weather and the late arrival of the twin-engine DC-3 owned by a fledgling Indianapolis company called National Jet Service, Air Indiana 216 taxied for takeoff. The plane lifted off through a thick fog and apparently began to experience problems almost immediately. Due to what was later determined as poor weight distribution of baggage and human error, the jet veered through the murky sky into the rain-soaked land near the Melody Hills subdivision just southeast of the airport.

As rescue workers sloshed their way through the mire looking for survivors, word began to get out, and the community was forced to deal with the gravity of the situation. The *Evansville Courier* chronicled the event in a beautiful tribute, likening the

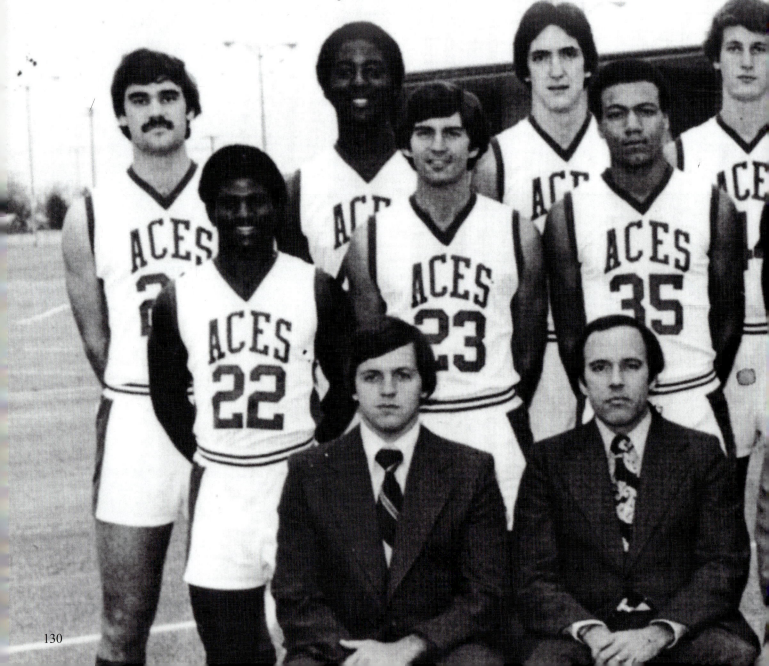

rain to tears from Heaven, and the catastrophe was conveyed nationally by Walter Cronkite and others.

Everyone was touched by the event, especially the families of those lost, and the outpouring of support was heart-warming. Five days after the crash, on Sunday, December 18th, 4,000 mourners gathered at Roberts Stadium to pay their respects, joining U.S. Senator Birch Bayh, Indiana Governor Otis Brown, and Evansville Mayor Russell Lloyd Sr.

Later in December, U of E's long-time rival Southern Illinois University hosted the Holiday Tournament in Evansville, a longstanding tradition, and the participating schools declined any proceeds beyond their costs from the money spent by the 10,000 fans who attended. In addition, the '76 Super Bowl champion Pittsburgh Steelers conducted a charity exhibition to benefit the school.

Those lost in the crash were: Coach Watson, fourteen team members; three student managers; six friends and staff, including U of E business manager Bob Hudson and popular radio personality Marv Bates; and five crew members.

As a tribute to those lost on that fateful night in '77, the university constructed the Memorial Plaza on campus to honor them. In a ceremony to begin the project, the first few bricks were laid by family members of the deceased. The memorial consists of two stone slabs bearing the names of the victims and a fountain shaped like a basketball that serves as an 'eternal flame' and is affectionately called 'the weeping basketball'.

Area fans never got to enjoy seeing the young, vibrant Bobby Watson chase his vision or watch the young team mature as players and men. Tragedies like the crash on December 13th, 1977 are events that leave everyone reaching for answers. The fact is, there are no answers. For those who are left to mourn, the memories will have to suffice, and it is only fitting that we can remember Coach Watson and his boys as the first team to win a Division I game wearing a Purple Aces uniform. Although we never got to watch the team reach its potential, they are an important part of the Aces legacy. The memorial that stands in their honor will be a constant reminder that they are…

...Gone but Not Forgotten

The 1977-'78 Evansville Aces. Front Row (L-R): Associate Coach Mark Sandy, Associate Coach Stafford Stephenson, Head Coach Bobby Watson, Associate Coach Ernie Simpson, Student Coach Scott Doerner. Second Row (L-R): Tony Winburn, Kevin Kingston, Mike Joyner, John Ed Washington, Kraig Heckendorn, Greg Smith, Mark Siegel. Third row (L-R): Bryan Taylor, Barney Lewis, Steve Miller, Ray Comandella, Keith Moon, Mike Duff, Warren Alston. (Photo courtesy of the University of Evansville, Sports Information.)

Popular radio announcer Marv Bates was on his way to broadcast his first regular season Aces game when he was lost in the 1977 crash. (Photo courtesy of the *Evansville Courier*.)

...GONE BUT NOT FORGOTTEN
AIR INDIANA 216, DECEMBER 1977 CRASH

Team:
Warren Alston
Ray Comandella
Mike Duff
Kraig Heckendorn
Michael Joiner
Kevin Kingston
Barney Lewis
Steve Miller
Keith Moon
Mark Siegel
John Ed Washington
Marion 'Tony' Winburn
Greg Smith
Bryan Taylor

Staff and Friends:
Coach Bobby Watson
Mark Kniese – Mgr.
Jeff Bohnert – Mgr.
Mark Kirkpatrick – Mgr
Bob Hudson – Bus. Mgr
Marv Bates
Charles Goad
Maury King
Charles Shike
Greg Knipping

Flight Crew:
Gaston Ruiz
Pam Smith
Bill Hartford
Ty Van Pham
James Stewart

CHAPTER FIVE
1958-1975

BOB GRIESE: FROM SANDLOT TO SUPER BOWL

Bob (right) and brother Bill in 1954 showing off the new uniforms bought by their father. (Photo courtesy of Father Ted Tempel.)

For many local athletes who grew up during the '50s and '60s, the playgrounds, alleys and sandlots were havens where young boys could spend hour after hour heaving buzzer beater jump shots to win imaginary State championships or throwing passes to score make-believe winning touchdowns. For Bob Griese, the dreams he dared to dream as a youngster came true when he led his team to victory in not one, but two Super Bowls.

Bob and his brother Bill and sister Joyce grew up on Mary Street just south of Deaconess Hospital. The working class neighborhood was a great environment for learning grass roots values and for spending afternoons and summer days playing ball with whatever equipment was available.

"We were kind of a poor family, and we didn't have a lot," Griese said from his home in North Carolina. "But it seemed like we always had everything we wanted in the way of balls and bats. I remember my dad buying us a football jersey and shoulder pads."

Bob's father, Sylverius (known as 'Slick' to his friends), owned a plumbing company, and his mother, Ida, was a secretary. When Bob was ten, his father passed away from a heart attack and the neighborhood became a respite for the Griese boys. Father Ted Tempel, a childhood friend and long-time mentor of Bob's, recalled those times long ago and how the two never miss a chance to reminisce when Bob makes it back home.

"There was a little side yard next to 305 Mary Street, and that's where we played football," Father Tempel explained. "When he comes to town, we drive around and we'll drive down the alley. We would also play baseball, and we had a basketball goal out there too."

Bob recalled the same excursions with Ted and marvels at how time changes one's perspective. "Every time we went back (to the neighborhood), the smaller it got," Bob noted.

As the boys grew, their world grew also, and they discovered larger venues for their games. "When we got older, in grade school, we'd pass notes around about having a game at Willard Library after school," Bob recalled. "That was one of our big places to play, and, again, that field got smaller as the years went by. I was always the smallest and the youngest because I was playing with Bill and Father Ted and their friends, so I was always coming in with a bloody nose and my

(Photo courtesy of Purdue University.)

133

Sylverius 'Slick' Griese holds Bob in 1945. (Photo courtesy of Father Ted Tempel.)

mother was always worried that the boys were being too rough on me."

Bob's brother Bill, who was two years older, looks back on the sandlot days as a rite of passage for his generation, and he can see how those days helped to shape his younger brother's future. "Our mother never had to worry where we were because we were always in the alley playing basketball or at Willard playing football," he recalled. "When there was an argument, you worked it out or you got in a fight. After the fight, you dusted yourselves off and you were friends again.

"Bob was the littlest of the group," Bill added. "He was the runt. We made him center the ball all the time. As he developed, we soon discovered that, hey, he could catch and he could throw. So we started blocking for him and he would throw it to us."

Father Ted also looks back now and realizes how he saw Bob's potential early on. "I really think a lot of it was innate in him," said Father Ted. "It seemed like he was a natural, from a little boy on. He was very disciplined. In those days, discipline was pretty normal. You didn't get out of line. First of all, because the neighborhood raised you."

When Bob was old enough for organized sports, he played baseball in the North Little League at Garvin Parkand started as a fifth grader on the eighth grade basketball team at Assumption School. He had always planned on following Bill to Memorial High School, but when the boundaries were set for the new Rex Mundi, the boys' paths would separate. Since Bill had started at Memorial, he had the option to stay there, but Bob had no choice.

Bob recalls how the circumstances were not easy to deal with. "The tough thing was my brother leaving the house going to one school while I was leaving to go to a different high school," he said. So Bob joined a class of freshmen who would become the first class to attend all four years at the new First Avenue Catholic school.

As a freshman, Bob's first high school athletic experience occurred on August 15th, 1959 when he attended his first football practice. "They needed bodies," Bob recalled, "because there weren't a lot of juniors and seniors. Ed Labbe was the coach, and he asked me what position I played. I had never played organized football. At Willard, my brother or (Father Ted) Tempel would be calling the plays and they would always look at me last and say, 'You hike the ball.' I didn't want to tell Coach Labbe I was a center, so I told him I liked to catch the ball.

"The first play, I lined up at wide receiver. The next play, he said, 'Why don't you take this one at quarterback?' I think he had read that I had pitched some no-hitters (in baseball), so I think he knew I could throw the ball."

And, from that moment on, young Bob was on his way to becoming a 'local legend'.

During Bob's first two years, Rex Mundi took some thrashings from the more established schools, but there was one victory that was bittersweet for the Griese family. During Bob's sophomore year, Rex Mundi was due to meet Memorial, and Bill remembers it well. "I remember Coach (Gene) Logel telling us that it would be an embarrassment if Rex Mundi would beat us," Bill recalled.

On the first play of the game, Rex Mundi ran a quarterback sneak. Bill, who played middle guard, beat a double team and tackled his brother. Later in the game, the upstart Monarchs pulled off the upset when Bob scampered around the end for a touchdown and then kicked the extra point for a 7-0 Rex Mundi win.

With teammates like Jerry Mattingly and Mike Minton, the Griese years at Rex Mundi were some of the best in the school's short existence. One of the most memorable football moments for Rex Mundi fans was a piece of trickery by new head coach Ken Coudret. Late in a game against Tell City, receiver Mike Minton and another player went toward the bench as if they were leaving the field. Meanwhile, only one sub came into the game. Before reaching the sideline, Minton stopped, still in the field of play. As the Monarchs came to the line, Minton was all alone with no defender near him. Griese dropped back and hit the wide open Minton streaking down the sideline for a touchdown. The 'Sleeper Play' had worked to perfection.

During his four years at Rex Mundi, Bob's versatility as an athlete was on display year-round. As a baseball pitcher, he was undefeated for the school team and was 11-0 for the Funkhauser Legion team that traveled to the World Series in New Hampshire and featured some incredible talent, including Rex Mundi teammate Jerry Mattingly and North's Mickey Martin, Steve Schroer and Dave Schellhase.

As a basketball player, he was a heady point guard and relentless defender, and in football, he never left the field because he quarterbacked on offense, played defensive back, returned kicks, punted and did the place-kicking. But the success he experienced and the recognition he received in all three sports were due to much more than just God-given talent.

Bob's dedication was obvious to everyone who knew him, and Rex Mundi teacher and super fan Pat Welsh recalled a standard joke around the school. "Teachers used to kid around by saying, 'You can't leave school early enough to beat Bob Griese onto the field,'" she related. "He was out there every day practicing kicking. He worked hard at it."

In spite of his obvious talents, it might surprise some that Griese was not a red-hot commodity coming out of high school in 1963. "I wasn't highly recruited," Bob admitted. "One of the (Baltimore) Orioles' scouts came up and wanted me to sign with the Orioles. I told him I had signed with Purdue and I was going to go to school, so that was the end of that. I got a call while I was at Purdue during pre-season practice, and it was Baltimore calling again. Baseball was my first love, and I think Illinois, Indiana and Purdue were the only ones interested in me as a football player."

When Bob accepted his scholarship to Purdue, he was stepping into the shadows of such great Boilermaker quarterbacks as Len Dawson and Bob DeMoss. But he quickly emerged from their shadows and into the limelight to write his own chapter in the long legacy at 'Quarterback U'.

As a freshman, he was not eligible for the varsity, so he played on the freshman team and also played basketball, which head football coach Jack Mollenkopf had promised he could do. He had planned on playing baseball also, but Mollenkopf made it clear that the QB job was wide open and if Griese played spring baseball, there was no way he was going to start in the fall.

Coach Mollenkopf had never started a sophomore quarterback during his years at Purdue, but Griese had earned his respect and drew the assignment to open the season. If there were any doubts about his abilities, Bob erased them when he scored all 19 points in a win over Miami of Ohio. Under the tutelage of Purdue quarterback coach Bob DeMoss, Griese improved his throwing style by changing his three-quarter motion, influenced by his years as a baseball pitcher, to an overhand delivery. The change would serve him well as he developed a quicker release and became a very accurate passer.

Griese also played a second year for the Boilers' basketball team as a sophomore, earning a starting spot at point guard midway through the season. But after moving directly from football into basketball and then to spring football, the young athlete decided that it was time to say good-bye to roundball and focus on his football career.

During his junior football season, Griese led Purdue to a 25-21 upset of top-ranked Notre Dame, completing 19 of 22 passes, and in his senior year, he led the school to its first Rose Bowl appearance in the school's history. After losing only two games in 1966 (to Notre Dame and Michigan State), Purdue finished second in the conference to Michigan State. Since the Spartans had played in the Rose Bowl the previous year and the rule stated that a Big Ten school could not repeat, Purdue was next in line to make the trip to Pasadena. Against the USC Trojans of legendary coach John McKay, Purdue fullback Perry Williams plunged across from the two to put the Boilermakers up 14-7, with Bob kicking the second of two extra points. USC scored late and McKay opted to go for two points and the win, but Purdue's defense held and Griese finished his college career with a 14-13 victory.

As a three-year starter for the Boilermakers, Bob was a 57 percent passer (348-609) and was a consensus All-American his last two years, finishing second to Florida's Steve Spurrier in Heisman Trophy voting as a senior. With a degree in Industrial Management in hand, Bob awaited the NFL draft to assess his options. Even with the success he had experienced at Purdue, pro football was not something he was counting on.

"I was just happy to get an education," Bob said. "I hadn't even thought about the NFL. Back then, the draft wasn't on ESPN. You didn't know if you were drafted or not. I think one of the Purdue coaches told me. I didn't even talk to anybody (from a pro team)."

Bob was drafted by the Miami Dolphins in the first round (4th overall) of the 1967 draft. The Dolphins were owned by Joe Robbie and TV star Danny Thomas and were in only their second season as a franchise. The team was coached by George Wilson, who was at the end of his coaching career and whose son George Jr. was the quarterback. Things looked bleak for Miami, but their selection of the young QB from Evansville was the cornerstone of a building process that would transform the Dolphins from a league laughing stock into a franchise that would become the gold standard of the NFL.

During Miami's first three seasons, the team's cumulative record was 12-29-1, but some wise drafts and acquisitions would soon pay huge dividends. In 1968, fullback Larry Czonka was drafted out of Syracuse with the eighth overall selection. The next year, Miami traded for undersized linebacker Nick Buoniconti (Patriots) and offensive guard Larry Little (Chargers). The Dolphins gave up a first round pick in 1970 to bring in head coach Don Shula, and he immediately led Miami to a 10-4 record.

Bob (right) and his son Brian before the 1998 Rose Bowl game. (Photo courtesy of Father Ted Tempel.)

In 1971, behind their famed 'No-Name Defense' and the running of Czonka, Jim Kiick and Mercury Morris, Miami played in its first Super Bowl, losing 24-3 to the Cowboys. The pieces were in place to make some history, and Griese and the Dolphins were a year away from a season the likes of which had not been seen before and have not been seen since.

After a 14-0 regular season, the Dolphins faced the Pittsburgh Steelers in the conference finals. Griese had been out with a back injury and was on the sideline as the Dolphins trailed 10-7 early in the second half. Bob eventually replaced Earl Morrall and brought Miami back for a 21-17 win, sending the Dolphins to their second straight Super Bowl.

The Dolphins took the field in Super Bowl VII as 1 ½-point underdogs to the Washington Redskins, with Coach George Allen and his Over the Hill Gang. The teams felt each other out and traded punches until the Dolphins drew first blood on a 28-yard pass from Griese to Howard Twilley late in the first quarter. Just before halftime, Miami struck again on a one-yard plunge by Jim Kiick for a 14-0 lead.

After a scoreless third quarter, one of the more famous plays in Super Bowl history occurred when a 42-yard field goal was attempted by Garo Yepremian and then blocked. As the ball bounced right, Yepremian picked it up with the Redskins' Bill Brundige in hot pursuit. Yepremian tried to pass to Larry Czonka, but the ball squirted into the air instead. The flustered kicker then batted the ball to Washington defender Mike Bass, who easily avoided Yepremian's feeble attempt at a tackle and sprinted 49 yards for the score. The play was christened 'Garo's Gaffe' and will forever be known as one of the biggest blunders in Super Bowl history.

Griese and his teammates held on for the win, however, and the Miami Dolphins had accomplished what no other team had ever done. They finished 17-0 to complete 'The Perfect Season'.

A year later, the Dolphins made history once more. After finishing the regular season 12-2, they again advanced to the Big Dance, making them the first team to play in three consecutive Super Bowls. Miami was so dominant that Griese only needed to throw seven passes. He competed six of them as the Dolphins defeated the Minnesota Vikings 24-7 at Rice Stadium in Houston.

Griese's Dolphins never made it to another Super Bowl, but Bob played seven more years before retiring after the 1980 season. He had quarterbacked 101 of the 135 victories in the club's history and had led them to two Super Bowl titles. He was a consensus All-Pro in 1971 and '77 and was a six-time Pro Bowler. He became the fourteenth quarterback to pass for over 25,000 yards, tallying 25,092 while completing 1,926 passes out of 3,429 attempts (56.2%). He was inducted into the College Football Hall of Fame in 1984 and the Pro Football Hall of Fame in 1990.

Following his retirement, Bob used his football knowledge and work ethic as a color man for the NFL on NBC for five years and then joined Keith Jackson on ABC covering college football. One of his highlights as a broadcaster was covering the 1998 Rose Bowl. Michigan was undefeated and playing for the national championship, and their opponent was Washington State (Keith Jackson's alma mater), quarterbacked by the highly-touted Ryan Leaf.

When the final whistle blew, the Wolverines had secured a 21-16 victory and the national title. Bob could hardly hold back the tears when Keith Jackson announced in his distinct southern accent, "Whoa, Nellie, do you want to know who the MVP is?" When Jackson revealed that Brian Griese, Bob's son, had won the award, Bob admitted that he "was one proud daddy."

All three of Bob's sons walked on and earned college scholarships, Scott at Virginia, Jeff at North Carolina, and Brian at Michigan. Brian was drafted in the third round of the 1998 NFL draft by the Denver Broncos, and the 2007-'08 season was his tenth year in the league.

Bob and Brian authored a book together titled *Undefeated: How Father and Son Triumphed Over Unbelievable Odds Both On and Off the Field,* which chronicled the struggles both men faced after losing a loved one. Bob lost his father when he was ten, and Brian lost his mother, Judi, when he was twelve, so both Bob and Brian have used their good fortune to create foundations to help others.

Bob Griese was one of those rare athletes who had a natural feel for sports, who listened and learned, and who worked hard to get better. He has represented his hometown well in every phase of his life. As we all watched the ball spiraling from Bob Griese's hand in the 1970s, it felt good to know that the skills he displayed to millions of viewers on Super Bowl Sunday were honed on a grassy field of dreams right here in southern Indiana.

GRIESE GIVES BACK

In 2006, Bob Griese appeared on the popular television game show *Wheel of Fortune.* He won the game, and his winnings went to Judi's House, a home founded by his son Brian and named for Brian's mother, to help grieving children.

Morris Riley got to hire his own coaching staff when he began coaching at North in 1956, and he did a pretty good job. Three of them joined him in the Indiana Football Hall of Fame. Shown left to right: Ed Wessel, Riley, Archie Owen and Don Watson. (Photo courtesy of Mike Madriaga.)

"SENIOR MOMENTS"

LEE WALDEN SHOOTS FOR THE STARS

Lee Walden was never tall enough to play basketball at the level of some people, but in his mid-60s, he has found a way to make a giant impression on thousands of fans who appreciate his extraordinary talent. In less than five minutes, Lee has the ability to leave observers dumbfounded as he entertains them on the court by doing what he does best – shoot the basketball.

Although Lee played some basketball while in high school in Pittsburgh, his short stature prevented him from taking his passion to the next level. After serving in the Army and playing on a team at Ft. Knox with Evansville Aces star Ed Smallwood, Lee chose to study at Logan Chiropractic College in St. Louis. While there, a classmate convinced him to consider southern Indiana as a place to set up practice

After visiting the area, he decided to settle in Huntingburg because the town did not have a chiropractor. But the difference in lifestyle between Pittsburgh and the small town created a bit of culture shock for Lee, his wife Vickie and their children, so they moved west to Evansville to set up practice. In the mid-'90s, he decided to move his practice back to Huntingburg but to keep his home in Evansville. It was at about this time that his basketball adventure began.

Lee became a regular at the YMCA basketball court, and fellow players informed him about the Senior Olympics that are held every other year at various sites around the country. He began competing in 3-on-3 basketball at the Games in 1999.

While competing at the 2005 Senior Olympics in Pittsburgh, a sports agent suggested to Lee that his talent might be very entertaining for fans at halftime of a basketball game. The words sparked Lee's imagination, and he went right to work.

Having known some athletic directors from his chiropractic practice, he made some calls. His first contact was Russ Newman from Tecumseh. After explaining that he would like to do an exhibition by shooting fifty 3-pointers at halftime of a varsity game, his proposal was met with skepticism. Newman was taking a chance on a possible embarrassment and wanted to know what number Lee would guarantee. Unprepared for the question, Lee blurted out "40." Newman agreed to the set-up and told Lee that he was going to announce the guarantee to the student body to get them fired up for the event. Not only was Lee going to shoot publicly for the first time in front of hundreds of screaming basketball fans, but he had added even more pressure with his bold guarantee.

On the night of the exhibition, Lee was apprehensive but excited. He knew he had to perform in order to entice other schools to give him the opportunity.

And perform he did. In less than five minutes, with just one basketball and one rebounder, he shot ten 3s from five spots around the arc and buried 42 of them. In shock, he trotted off the floor to a standing ovation.

As the word spread during the 2005-2006 basketball season, Lee was able to book fifteen exhibitions, all done for no compensation, just his love of the game. In addition to shooting at several high schools, he appeared at some area colleges, as well, including USI, U of E and Kentucky Wesleyan.

After his first season, Lee and his wife had to decide whether to think bigger or leave well enough alone. They decided to go for it. After searching the internet for schedules, they booked 39 events for 2006-2007, including sixteen college games.

Lee performed at the University of Pittsburgh, Tennessee State, Butler and in front of 19,000 fans at the University of Louisville. For 2007-2008, he had already booked with Bruce Pearl at Tennessee and Evansville's Chris Lowery at Southern Illinois.

The highlight of the season came when Lee was asked to shoot exhibitions for both the boys and girls games of the 2007 Indiana/Kentucky high school all-star game. At halftime of the girls game, Lee connected on 47 of 50, and at the boys game, he drained 42, an amazing total of 89 out of 100!

When Lee Walden speaks of his 'hobby', he throws around numbers like 42 out of 50 or 48 out of 50 as if anyone could do it with a little practice. But anyone who has fired at the hoop from 19 feet, 6 inches knows that it takes amazing skill and concentration to hit those percentages consistently. In over fifty exhibitions during his two seasons, his lowest score has been 32 with a high of 49 at a game between Mater Dei and Memorial.

Lee's dream is to hook up with a company (perhaps Wilson or Spalding) and be their goodwill ambassador. That way, after retirement, he could travel and represent his client at exhibitions and clinics around the world.

Perhaps that scenario would enable him to experience more thrills like the one when he worked the University of Louisville game in '07. As he was shooting his last ten from the corner, the Louisville players were standing at the tunnel ready to take the floor. When Lee hit his last shot, Cardinals coach Rick Pitino passed him and said, "Nice shooting, sir," and gave Lee the thumbs up.

All the hours spent firing a basketball at a hoop have paid off for Lee Walden in ways he never thought possible. The little man with the deadly touch has performed for basketball legends and all-stars. So if you're driving in the area and happen to see a license plate that reads "3-PT GURU", honk your horn and give Lee Walden a big thumbs up.

LOCAL TEAM WINS GOLD

For ten years, Joe Willis had been traveling to locations across the country chasing an elusive gold medal at the Senior Olympic Games. Playing with various combinations of teammates, he had come close but had never taken the crown in his favorite event, 3-on-3 basketball. In June of 2007, Joe's determination paid off as he and four teammates bent forward to receive their gold medals after claiming the national championship in the 70-74 age division at the Senior Games in Louisville.

"I thought this may be the team that could do it," Joe said, "and I was right in my thinking. We've been practicing together twice a week for about a year and a half, and we play younger guys. My son (Steve) is off on Thursdays, and he played against us a lot, and that helped us. Chris Goodman (from WFIE Channel 14) would play against us now and then. Sometimes our passes would be intercepted (by the younger, quicker players), but we figured when we played guys our age, they wouldn't be."

After retiring from Whirlpool ten years ago at age 61, Joe refused to become a relic and diligently worked out at the YMCA with the pursuit of the Olympic gold always in the back of his mind. By finding a group willing to make the same sacrifices, the pieces were in place to make a run for the title.

To qualify for the Nationals, a team must win at the state level, and for Joe and his squad, there was only one other age group team to defeat. After beating Kokomo 45-32, they were set to compete in Louisville. The Nationals were a much tougher challenge, with 34 teams competing in the age division. The rigorous schedule showed no mercy. Over a three-day period, the men played nine games and commuted each day to and from Louisville. On Saturday, they defeated a team from North Carolina and then lost to a West Virginia team. One more loss and their quest would be over.

Their hope was to keep winning and have a rematch with West Virginia to avenge the defeat, but West Virginia was eliminated along the way and the local crew gained momentum. On Sunday, Joe and his crew defeated Arizona (48-36), Colorado (45-35) and Oregon (51-34). On the drive back, they had a lot to think about as a very long and challenging day awaited them.

At the Senior Games, team basketball is played 3-on-3, in the half-court, and in two 12-minutes halves with a running clock. After a victory over Georgia, the boys needed every tick of the clock during their second game on Monday as they faced another tough North Carolina team who was determined to send them home.

With the score tied and time running down, the team set up a play designed for Joe to shoot, but the opponents' defense was ready for it. "It was designed for me to take the shot," Joe recalled, "but I was behind the backboard and they were converging on me. Bob Walker is an excellent 3-point shooter and he was wide open, so I kicked it out to Bob and he buried the three at the buzzer."

After the big win, the team went on to defeat New Jersey in the semi-finals (39-26) and Texas in the championship game 41-37. The tired crew had done what they set out to do, and the Monday and Thursday workouts ALL YEAR LONG had paid big dividends.

The consensus among the players was that the role played by each team member contributed to the success of the team as a whole. "We had good team unity," said Joe Willis, "which was the key to the whole thing." Bob Walker, who played at Evansville College with James Smallins, Clyde Cox, John Harrawood, Jerry Clayton and Bob Wessel, was the set-up man who would find the open man and pass. When the defense would sag on Bob's teammates, they would kick the ball to him so he could shoot from long range.

Bob Ewin, who played at Millersburg High School and Oakland City College, was the team's 'Chairman of the Boards' as he led the team in rebounding and played solid defense.

Despite hip problems, Jim Duffey provided valuable minutes as a sub when the starters needed a rest or got into foul trouble. Jim played at Butler with Milan legend Bobby Plump and then coached at Boonville High School before becoming the school's principal until his retirement in 1998.

Richard Koressel was a Mater Dei grad who also contributed off the bench, despite coping with sore knees.

Without question, the go-to-guy for the Evansville five was the team's organizer, Joe Willis. Joe did not play organized ball past high school, where he played for Gene Cato, who would go on to serve as the commissioner of the IHSAA. At the Senior Games, Joe averaged over thirty points as he maneuvered under the basket with his sharp elbows clearing the way for him to bank in a shot or draw a foul. Joe has also gained a reputation on the Senior circuit. In Louisville, when asked why they were entering the gym for a game their team was not playing, a spokesman for a group of 15 to 20 people replied, "We're over here to see Joe Willis!"

Described by some as a "freak of nature," the 6-foot-tall practicing minister has drawn superlatives from everyone who has seen him play, with some going so far as to compare him to the great Michael Jordan. Although the 'Jordan of Geriatrics' takes little credit for the team's success, his teammates and fans speak of him with the highest regard.

"Joe was unstoppable for a guy his age," said teammate Bob Walker. "He was like a scoring machine."

"I don't think there's a person in the world that's Joe's age who could beat him one-on-one," added Lee Walden, a local chiropractor who has competed against Joe for years. "That includes ex-NBA players, ex-Harlem Globetrotters, anyone. Joe can flat play ball."

Surrounded by a group of selfless players who didn't care who scored or got the credit, Joe Willis is humble and attributes the group's success to a wonderful "team chemistry." Although he scoffs at the comparison to Mr. Jordan, I'm sure he'd like to equal Michael Jordan's feat of winning six championships. And knowing Joe Willis, I wouldn't bet against him.

The 2007 Senior Games national champions (L-R): Richard Koressel, Bob Walker, Joe Willis, Bob Ewin, Jim Duffey.

Joe Willis, 'the Jordan of Geriatrics'.

On March 13th, 2007, 75-year-old Jack Weatherholt (left) blew away the laws of probability when he recorded two holes-in-one during a round at the Players Club in Henderson. According to *Golf Magazine*, the odds against the feat are 67 million to one.

VAUGHN WEDEKING: A WINNER ON AND OFF THE COURT

In 2007, Jon Siau, an Evansville teacher, coach and avid sports fan, compiled a folder to send to the Indiana Basketball Hall of Fame. In the folder were 48 letters of support for a 58-year-old man who, years ago, had left an indelible impression with his God-given talents and his clean-cut image. Tragically, he was stricken with a debilitating disease a few years ago and is not able to appreciate the words written on his behalf by coaches, teammates, family and friends. But whether he is inducted into the Basketball Hall or not, he will always be remembered as one of Evansville's most versatile athletes.

Vaughn Wedeking was the epitome of the term 'all-around athlete', a phrase that was common in the past but has become all too rare in the new age of specialization by high school athletes. An 'all-around athlete' played at least three sports and flowed easily from one season to the next without missing a beat. Wedeking not only played four sports for Harrison High School, but he excelled, both as a player and a leader, while he earned twelve varsity letters.

As a baseball player, Vaughn used his blazing speed and exceptional hand-eye coordination to star at Harrison, in Legion ball, and as a member of the only local team to win the Pony League World Championship. As a senior, he led the city in hitting (.488) and was named the MVP on both the *Courier* All-City and All-Conference teams.

As a runner on the cross country and track teams, his long, effortless stride and his endurance made him appear to run in slow motion. His senior year, he captured the State championship with a time of 48.4 in the 440-yard dash after rocketing past three runners in the closing stretch on a cinder track.

On the basketball court, the 5'11", 165-pound point guard led the Warriors to a three-year record of 58-7 (89%) and led the state in free throw accuracy his senior year at 91.9%. During one stretch, he made 41 straight free throws, a school record.

His Harrison teams won three consecutive City and conference titles and, at one point, won 51 consecutive regular season games. Although he was recruited by colleges for his track and baseball talents, he was pursued hardest as a basketball player and was ranked as the 12th-best guard in the country as a senior in 1967.

Vaughn chose to join Harrison teammate Greg Nelson and headed south to Jacksonville University, where, once again, he experienced phenomal success. A three-year starter, he led the Dolphins to the most successful three seasons in the school's history with a 66-13 record (83.5%). In 1970, Vaughn piloted a team that featured 7'2" future NBA star Artis Gilmore into the NCAA final game, losing to UCLA 80-69.

Throughout his years at Jacksonville, Wedeking drew high praise from such coaches as John Wooden, Adolph Rupp and Abe Lemmons, among others. He was also named to the 1970 Small-American team for players under six-feet tall. He always stayed cool under pressure and found a way to win, and his work ethic and dedication were a constant.

Although his athletic abilities were extraordinary, he was even more respected as an individual. After graduating from Jacksonville with a degree in Biology, Vaughn shunned the temptations of pro basketball to pursue his career goal by attending the Indiana University School of Dentistry. Vaughn and his wife and twin boys settled in Oregon, where he continued to set an example for the people who knew him.

Although most of us knew of Vaughn primarily as an athlete, those who knew him personally had a far deeper appreciation of the man. In her letter in the hall of fame folder, Vaughn's mother spoke of how her son donated dental services to medically-impaired adults and how he freely gave his time to the Portland Zoo, once even performing a root canal on a Siberian tiger.

High school teammate Greg Fenner wrote: "I have NEVER, nor will I EVER again see an all-around athlete as talented as Vaughn Wedeking. He shot hoops at any and every outdoor court within five miles of his home, riding his bicycle while holding his ball under one arm."

Vaughn's wife, Dayle, whom he met during their freshman year at Jacksonville, spoke of how he coached their twin sons, Drew and Graham, during their early years and how Vaughn's illness has affected the family. She described how Fronto-Temporal Dementia (FTD) is in the same family as Alzheimer's and how it manifests itself more in behavioral changes rather than memory loss.

"Vaughn is blissfully unaware and unconcerned about the extent of his illness," she stated in her letter. "His quirky sense of humor is gone, as is his zest for life. The Vaughn we all knew and loved is gone, but at least we will always have the memories we hold so dear."

Those memories are special to all of us who were lucky enough to watch the mighty mite provide so many thrills throughout his athletic career. Every letter written to encourage his induction into the Hall spoke not only of Vaughn as an athlete, but also of him as a man. Perhaps the submission that best summed up his character was one written by Frank Pace, a producer for Warner Bros. Television and a member of the Jacksonville University Board of Trustees.

"I suppose athletes aren't supposed to be role models," he wrote. "However, if every athlete, every husband, every father and every professional could be like Vaughn Wedeking, what a wonderful world this would be."

This Harrison mile relay team finished third in the State meet. (L-R): Bob Koehl, Steve Winternheimer, Mark Haight and Vaughn Wedeking. (Photo courtesy of Charlie Siesky.)

A CUT ABOVE

Harrison's Charlie Siesky is the only coach from the area to be inducted into the Indiana Association of Track and Cross Country Hall of Fame.

Female inductees include Bosse's Cassandra Lander, Castle's Alisa Raymond and Forest Park's Ann Schwoeppe.

Male athletes inducted are: Gene Lockyear (Bosse), Terry Brahm (Heritage Hills), Mark Buse (Southridge), Ron Jones (Mt. Vernon), Tom Martin (Memorial) and Don Sellers (Harrison).

JASPER'S JERRY BREWER: 44 YEARS OF WINNING

As Jerry Brewer discusses his 44 years as the head football coach at Jasper High School, he seems much more comfortable and relaxed than when he roamed the sidelines guiding the Wildcats through the mine field that is southern Indiana football. With his self-deprecating humor and humble demeanor, a stranger might wonder how this slow-talking, laid back gentleman could have been a coach at all, much less the winningest high school football coach in Indiana history.

Coach Brewer was born on March 30th, 1937 in Paducah, Kentucky, and graduated from Tilghman High School in 1955. As a running back and defensive back, he earned a scholarship to Western Kentucky, and after graduation, Brewer signed a contract to be the head track coach and assistant football coach at a school in Canton, Georgia. Shortly thereafter, he was offered the head football position at Jasper for more money and decided to travel north instead of south, and that single decision enabled him to go places he probably never could have imagined.

Jasper had resurrected its football program only six years earlier, and now the young coach was responsible for its success. When asked why he thought the administration had decided to hire someone with no experience, Brewer's answer was short and honest: "Because I was cheap," he deadpanned in his slow southern drawl. He was also honest about how unprepared he was back in his early years, saying, "I thought I had a lot of answers until those first two or three years (at Jasper). I found out quick how much I didn't know."

Although Jerry was doing his learning on the job, the fact is, he was a winner from the start. His first team (1959) finished 5-4, and that's the closest he would come to a losing season for the next three decades. His '61 team led the state in scoring with 406 points, as did his 1967 team (413). In 1966, the Wildcats won their first SIAC title with a 9-1 record, which tied the previous year's team for the best record in school history. The '66 season included a 67-0 trouncing of Castle and a lone loss to Evansville Rex Mundi. The Monarchs were also the only blemish on another 9-1 season the following year.

In 1976, Jasper traveled nearly 300 miles to face Mishawaka Marian in the school's first State championship game, and despite the efforts of such stars as Tony Ahrens and Dan Smith, fell 34-7. The Wildcats returned to the Finals the following year after a 10-0 regular season. To qualify, they had to come from behind twice in a 27-22 win over Memorial. After besting Clarksville 55-14 in the sectional and Mooresville 21-12 in the regional, #1-ranked Jasper fell to #2 Plymouth in the Finals.

Jasper's Jerry Brewer. The coach's famous hat now lives in the Indiana Football Hall of Fame. (Photo courtesy of the Evansville Courier.)

In 1987 and 1995, Coach Brewer suffered his third and fourth major disappointments. In '87, Jasper, led by Brett Wininger, the state's leading rusher, fell to Hobart 31-0 in the State Finals, and in '95, they lost again in the Finals to South Bend St. Joe. As the years passed, Jerry was beginning to wonder if the Wildcats would ever capture a title. As hard as his teams tried, it would take the dawning of a new millennium for the battle-weary Brewer to finally reach pay dirt.

"I was starting to feel like I couldn't win the big one," Brewer admitted as he watched a groundskeeper work on the high school's football field. "We were State runner-up four times and couldn't kick the door down. I'd felt like I'd almost used up my time here."

In 2000, the Cats completed their ninth undefeated regular season but were downed 31-13 by Vincennes in the sectional. After his 42nd season at Jasper, Coach Brewer pondered his situation and made a gut-wrenching decision. He informed the school board that he would coach two more seasons and would then walk away. The boys in black and gold had two more chances to win the big one for their coach, but it would only take one for them to deliver.

The 2001 Wildcats completed their regular season at 8-1, with their only blemish a 14-7 loss to Heritage Hills. After convincing sectional wins over Mt. Vernon (33-0) and Floyd Central (21-7), Jasper squeaked by Zionsville 18-17 in overtime to complete the first phase of their quest. In the semi-state, the Wildcats came from behind to upset favored Indianapolis Cathedral 27-21, and the loyal Jasper fans were once again making reservations for the all-too-familiar trip to Indy.

Since Coach Brewer had 'been there and done that' four times prior, he utilized every shred of experience to make this trip count. Since the game was to be played in the RCA Dome, he made arrangements for the team to practice at IU's indoor facility and even indoors in Evansville, which acclimated his team to the humidity and the different effects indoor play had on breathing patterns. He also planned the itinerary so well that the team's arrival at the stadium was only one minute off from the scheduled time.

Brewer's plans worked to perfection, and behind the performances of such players as Brian Lewis, Justin Mehringer and Ben and Chris Schmidt, Brewer and the Jasper Nation were finally able to celebrate. During the game, Chris Schmidt batted away two would-be touchdown passes, and teammate Cade Kneis had a late interception to seal a 35-20 State championship win.

In Brewer's final season, 2002, the Wildcats nearly returned to the Dome for the sixth time, falling in the semi-state 10-6 to eventual State champion Indianapolis Roncalli. After the season, Coach Brewer was true to his word and said good-bye to his team for the last time. He would be leaving the program in good hands, however, as he handed the reins to Tony Ahrens, a former player and an assistant coach for 17 years.

When Jerry took the job at Jasper in 1959, he had no idea that he would one day watch his grandson play for the Wildcats. As he reminisces about his 44 years at JHS, it becomes obvious why he was so successful as he imparts his wisdom and humor.

When asked the secrets of his success, there was no hesitation as he took a deep breath and, in his slow, deliberate style, carved his answer.

"One, you'd better have some horses," he declared. "It's the truth! Like the old saying goes, 'I've never seen a pony win the Kentucky Derby.' And discipline is a big ingredient. I had some run-ins with some real good athletes, but those were the rules, and if you can't follow them, then have a nice day. I had to think about the future, what the consequences were going to be down the road."

Brewer's coaching philosophy and style of football were staples of a program that sustained itself through several generations. Jasper had run the Single Wing formation before his arrival, and Brewer shook things up immediately with his T-Formation. Before his first season, he looked for the best athlete he could find, Mick Stenftenagel, and put him at quarterback, and he was fortunate in his first year to inherit Jerry Schmidt, a fullback who would go on to play at Illinois. He still jokes that one of the hardest facets of the Jasper job was learning how to spell and pronounce all the German names in the community.

Brewer was also notorious for emphasizing the running game, and he is well aware of the sometimes-not-so-subtle criticism of his grind-it-out style. "People have said, 'You don't want to eat at Brewer's house,'" the coach joked, "'and you don't ask him to pass the salt because he don't know how to pass.'"

Every Jasper player and every opponent knew exactly where Jasper's bread was buttered, the play Jasper calls 'The Toss'. For years, Jasper tailbacks like Luke Schmidt, Mike Berger and Kevin Cartwright piled up yards of real estate by catching 'the toss', reading the fullback's block on the defensive end and then cutting inside or outside.

Jerry is also quick to point out the many great assistant coaches he's had over the years, such as Tony Ahrens, Joe Rohleder, Terry Gobert, Gerald Roberts and Geoff Mauck.

Matt Mauck (Geoff's brother), a Brewer disciple who starred at LSU and as an NFL quarterback, had an insightful observation about his former coach. "A tribute to him is that he let his assistant coaches coach," Mauck said. "I think a lot of coaches are afraid to let the assistants have some control, but he was at the stage in his career, he was so proven, that he allowed them to have a big say."

Perhaps the biggest secret of all to the Jasper football program's success is the steady presence of its fiercely loyal fans. Coach Brewer summed it up best when he said: "We have great community support. We have a saying, 'When you take on Jasper, you take on the whole community.'"

Through the years, Jerry Brewer had several opportunities to take jobs with other programs, including Vincennes, Seymour and Hanover College, but he chose instead to stay in Jasper to raise his family. He smiles when he speaks of his wife, Jorene, and although she passed away in 1995, he still appreciates the enthusiasm she had as a coach's wife. "She was probably my biggest critic," Brewer reported. "She wanted to know if I was saving timeouts for Christmas presents. I'd get home and have to answer a dozen questions. 'Hindsight is great,' I would tell her. 'If I knew that play wasn't going to work, I wouldn't have called it to begin with.'"

Today, Coach Brewer helps out occasionally with the maintenance of the football field and plays golf at least twice a week. He also serves as a bailiff in the local court, although he's perplexed about one thing. "They won't let me have a gun," he revealed.

"They said, 'As long as you're a Kentuckian, you can't have one.'" As for football, he now sits in the stands with the 'experts' (fans) and confesses to being a bit of a Saturday morning quarterback. "I'll be the first one to say that I've second-guessed a couple of things," he admitted, "but I'm not down there. You gotta remember, (the coach) only has 25 seconds to make a decision, and he's going to be right sometimes and wrong sometimes."

During his 44 years as a coach, the numbers prove that Brewer was right a lot more often than he was wrong. At his retirement, he had compiled a career record of 368-105-2 (77.8%), an average of 8.4 wins per season, and nine times his team finished the regular season undefeated. Brewer's Wildcats won 21 Big 8 Conference titles, ten sectionals, ten regionals and four semi-states to go with the 2001 State championship. Twice he was named Indiana Coach of the Year ('77 and '83), and three times he was chosen to coach the Indiana South All-Star team, as an assistant in 1983 and as the head coach in '76 and '02. In 1992, Brewer was inducted into the Indiana Football Hall of Fame, becoming only the second man to be inducted while still active. But perhaps Coach Brewer's greatest honor was bestowed on him after the 2007 season when the arena where he prowled the sidelines for over four decades was officially christened Jerry Brewer Alumni Stadium.

When Brewer retired in 2002, he left his profession as the winningest football coach in Indiana history. He attributes the feat merely to the fact that he "was just around for a long time," but it was much more than that. At the age of 22, he discovered a place that suited him perfectly, and he was smart enough to stay and build a happy life. Although he may downplay it, the fact remains that, of all the men who have coached football in Indiana, no one has left the field a winner more times than Jasper's Jerry Brewer.

FOR THE RECORD

According to the Indiana Football Coaches Association, several individuals and teams from the area hold lofty positions in the Indiana record book.

- Jasper's Jerry Brewer has more wins than any coach in Indiana history with 368. (Bob Clayton of Heritage Hills is eighth with 264 (and still counting), Reitz's Herman Byers is 21st with 234, and Castle's John Lidy is 37th with 209.
- Mater Dei's Jake Schiff
    CAREER ('99-'01)
        TD passes-130
        Completions-755
        Passing yards-12,195
    SEASON ('01)
        Passing yards- 4,468
- When John Barber of Princeton ran for 99 yards in 1997, he tied 17 others for the longest run from scrimmage
- Tecumseh's Cory Julian is tied with 12 others for the longest pass reception of 99 yards (2002).
- In 2001, Mater Dei set records for a team with 556 yards passing in a game and 4,554 in a season.
- The record for points allowed in a season (ZERO) is held by ten teams, including Evansville High School in 1903 and Evansville Reitz in 1961.

IHSAA STATE CHAMPIONS:
GIRLS BASKETBALL

Team	Year	Record	Coach
Reitz	1980-1981	26-1	Louise Owen
Castle	2005-2006	25-3	Wayne Allen

GYMNASTICS

Individual	School	Year	Event
Jeanine Susott	Reitz	1972-1973	floor exercise
Jane Davies	Harrison	1975-1976	floor exercise

LARRY AND HALEY HARRIS: VERY MUCH LIKE FATHER-LIKE DAUGHTER

It is very likely that Larry and Haley Harris are the only father-daughter tandem in Indiana who have the distinction of being the #1 male and female scorers in the history of their school. Larry, who played for Oakland City High School in the '60s, leads the list of Oakland City scorers with 1,594 career points, while Haley, a 1995 Wood Memorial (an Oakland City consolidation) grad, finished #1 among females with 1,573.

With a well-proportioned 6'5" frame, Larry was a solid all-around athlete for the Mighty Oaks, earning fifteen varsity letters. In track, he finished second in both hurdle events to Mark Haight of Harrison in the regional, running in the "high 14s" in the high hurdles, an impressive time on a cinder track.

Larry was also a four-year letter winner in baseball and football. As a "hybrid quarterback" who ran a lot, he led southwestern Indiana in scoring and was selected to play in the North/South All-Star Game. Larry chose not to play in the game, however, because he had committed to play basketball for the University of Illinois and then-Illini coach Harv Schmidt didn't want Larry to risk injury.

During Larry's senior basketball season, the Oaks fashioned the finest season in school history, finishing the regular season and sectional undefeated at 23-0. The team had good size for a small school, with four starters 6'3 or taller. Two of the starters who complemented Harris were Rick Smith, who played with Don Buse on the 1971 Evansville College national championship team, and Dane Smith (no relation to Rick), who played collegiately at McNeese State.

Oakland City's '67-'68 season was halted by Bob Ford and the North Huskies in the afternoon game of the Evansville Regional. In that game, Larry and his teammates held North superstar Bob Ford to only ten points, but the Oaks couldn't stop the hot-shooting Steve Holland, who compensated with thirty points from his guard position. Oakland City and North were locked in a one-point game with 2:30 to play when a collision occurred between Harris and Ford. The call was made against Larry, fouling him out and opening the door for North to win by eleven. The Huskies went on to win Evansville's last boys State title in the one-class system, leaving the Mighty Oaks to always wonder "What if?"

After high school, some bad decisions derailed Larry's basketball career at Illinois, and he openly confesses that he should have concentrated more on his studies. "I didn't do very well," he admitted. "I messed up a really good opportunity. I was immature and didn't take my responsibility seriously."

Although he was invited to stay at Illinois, Larry decided to finish his schooling at home at Oakland City College. He majored in Education and improved his focus to the point that he won the Donald K. Jewel Award as the senior athlete with the highest grade point average.

As a player at O.C.C., Larry averaged 26.0 points as a sophomore, 21.7 as a junior and 25.6 his senior year, setting school single game records for points (50), field goals made (17), free throws made (17) and rebounds (32).

Larry began teaching the year he graduated and has coached several sports off and on since the early '70s. In 2007, he began his second stint as the head basketball coach at Wood Memorial.

Larry's daughter, Haley, was a can't-miss prospect who was blessed with great genetics and an environment that would help her develop her potential. Larry met Haley's mother, Cynthia, at Lamey's, a popular teen hangout of the '60s, and although Cynthia didn't have the opportunity to play sports in high school, she was a cheerleader and was very tall and athletic.

Besides her strong pedigree, Haley also benefited from being exposed to sports while she was young. In addition to hanging around while her father coached, she also had the benefit of watching her mother coach volleyball and tennis at Wood Memorial.

Haley Harris and proud papa Larry after Haley's Wood Memorial team won the 1995 sectional. (Photo by Frank Streber.)

As Haley moved up through the ranks in youth sports, it was easy to see that she had the makings of a special athlete. In fact, her high school career very much mirrored her father's, as she also proved to be a versatile multi-sport athlete.

In track, Haley was the top qualifier at the State meet as a high jumper in both her junior and senior years (finishing third both years). She set the Evansville Regional record at 5'8 ¼" and broke the school record at 5'9 ½".

As a hitter in volleyball, Haley was All-Conference all four years and was the conference MVP as a junior and senior.

With her skills on the basketball court and her resumé in track and volleyball, the 6'2", 155-pound Haley was a legitimate Division I prospect in all three sports. As almost an afterthought, Haley also competed at #1 singles on her mother's tennis team and was the sectional champion in 1993 and '94 with a career record of 45-4.

Haley's basketball coach at Wood Memorial was Charlie Brauser, the same man who coached Larry in high school, and his feelings about Haley were obvious in comments he made in a brochure promoting her as a potential Indiana All-Star.

"In my thirty years of coaching (boys and girls), Haley is the hardest-working player I have ever coached," Coach Brauser wrote. "She handles the basketball, rebounds, plays defense and offense, and runs the floor better than any girl I have had the privilege of watching."

During Haley's high school career, her scoring production increased every year: 9.0 as a freshman; 20.8 as a sophomore; 23.6 as a junior and 27.7 as a senior. During her senior year, she was 62.5% from the floor and was a 78.4% free throw shooter, setting school single game records for blocks (9), rebounds (25) and points (46 against a good North Posey team).

Haley capped off her season by being selected as an Indiana All-Star. After being recruited by virtually every top basketball school in the country, including Kentucky, Indiana and USC, she accepted a full ride to the University of Louisville.

At Louisville, Haley started every game her freshman year and made the Conference USA All-Freshman team. She also led her team in rebounding and was the team's third leading scorer. After her sophomore season, her photo was chosen for the front cover of the school's media guide for the upcoming campaign. After scoring 20 points against Auburn in her sophomore season finale, Haley had no idea that it would be the last game she would play for the Lady Cardinals. Just as her high school career had mirrored her father's, her college career was about to take a detour that was also eerily similar to Larry's.

After two outstanding seasons at Louisville, Bud Childers, the coach who had recruited Haley to play for him at Louisville, left the program, which caught Haley off-guard and triggered some irrational thinking on her part. For reasons that Haley still has trouble explaining, she decided to leave Louisville to transfer to the University of Southern Indiana.

"I think it was an immature decision at the time," Haley said in retrospect. "I kind of attribute it to being 19 or 20 years old at the time, and I wish I could go back and make a better decision, but once it was done, it was done. I know it was hard for my dad because he could see that I would regret it."

Haley transferred to USI and played the second semester of her junior year with only limited success. The style of play was different, and she felt that she didn't fit in. Anyone who knew her could see that the young player's heart just wasn't in it anymore.

After sitting out the next year, Haley decided to finish her schooling at (where else?) Oakland City University, just as her father had done. With her degree in hand, she returned to Louisville and became a second grade teacher.

Like her father, Haley was a versatile high school athlete, earning 16 varsity letters (to Larry's 15), and, like her father, she made some decisions in college that she now regrets. But neither Larry nor Haley wallow in the quagmire of what might have been. Instead, they would prefer to enjoy things as they are – a father and daughter who are still ranked #1 and #2 among all the Oakland City males and females who ever played the game.

Larry Harris shoots a jumper in 1970. Number 22 is Oakland City teammate Roger Benson.

Haley Harris during a 39-point game against Princeton.

PAUL GRIES: A LIFETIME OF SPORTS

It didn't take long for Paul Gries (pronounced 'Greece') to realize that he was never going to be a magnificent physical specimen, so instead of dwelling on what he didn't have, he learned to focus on his strengths. By using his quickness, his savvy and his mental toughness, Paul earned respect as a player and then as a coach.

As a youngster, he developed his skills in pickup games around town against the stiffest competition he could find, and he approached sports with a work ethic that he learned early on. "My parents were great," Paul explained. "Before we could go play ball, Dad would say, 'OK, Paul, there's two rows of green beans in the garden. You get those weeds picked and you can go play.'

"There's that priority; basketball and baseball were down the list. Even to this day, all my brothers and sisters, we really enjoy work, and I attribute that to my parents."

Paul spent many hours at playgrounds like Vogel School playing and 'working' as he competed against local players like Mike Volkman and Dave Schellhase (two future North High stars). "There were games over there every day," Paul recalled, "and Jerry Mattingly (Rex Mundi) would come over and (Evansville College greats) Jerry Sloan and Larry Humes would come down and play."

Paul also cited a game called 'corkball' that helped develop his baseball skills. "We'd play on the side of our house or we'd go over to the Mattingly's," Paul said. "We would take a ball of cork and put tape around it so we could see it. Then we'd cut off a broom handle for a bat. You should try to hit a 2-inch ball with a broomstick. You talk about eye-hand coordination!"

As he entered Mater Dei in 1957, 'Paulie', as he was known to friends and competitors, was highly respected on both the court and the diamond. Even as an upper classman, Paul grew to only 5'8 and 140 pounds, but despite his small stature, he was the focus of attention for opposing teams. When he was a senior, a quote appeared in the paper by then-Rex Mundi sophomore Bob Griese saying: "We're all looking forward to our game with Mater Dei, and I think if we can stop Paulie Gries, we'll stop Mater Dei."

Few teams had success stopping Gries during his days with the Wildcats, as the fiery sparkplug torched the nets for over 20 points a game as a junior and nearly 22 as a senior. Three times in his career Paul rang up 40 points or more, and he still holds the school's single game record with 44.

After his graduation in 1961, Paul left for Indiana State to play ball, and after his senior season in 1965, he signed with the Washington Senators and headed for rookie ball in Virginia. The next year, he was playing A-Ball in Burlington North Carolina when his career was interrupted by a call into the military. When his year-and-a-half tour ended, Paul opted to pass on an attempted comeback in baseball and set his sights on a teaching career.

After many years as a grade school teacher at Union School and Plaza Park, Paul moved to Central to assist John Wessel with the baseball program. He was considered for the Harrison job when Frank Schwitz retired, but the job went to Steve Fritz.

When John Wessel retired at Central, Ted Niemeier took over the baseball program for a year before stepping down and passing the torch to Paul in 1980. With the same work ethic he showed in his father's garden rows, Gries built Central's baseball program and left gallons of sweat on the land where a beautiful baseball facility now sits.

Unlike college or professional baseball, a high school baseball coach doesn't have the luxury of a grounds crew to maintain a field. The coach must also organize concession personnel, manage fund raisers and schedule other workers, so he must learn to wear many hats. Not one to let things slide, Paul toiled to keep the program up to his standards. "The way I did it and the way a lot of coaches do it, you're talking about 12- to 14-hour days," Paul explained. "If you want that field the way you want it, you have to work at it."

As the years wore on, the physical demands and the task of trying to keep seniors focused on baseball after they'd already graduated took their toll on Paul. In 1995, he suffered a mild heart attack and had a stent implanted, and in 2001, he stepped down as Central's coach.

During his 21-year career, his teams won 406 games and lost 196 (67%) while winning seven SIAC titles, seven sectionals, two regionals, one semi-state and making one State Tournament final (finishing as the runner-up in 1987). Gries was named the Conference Coach of the Year three times ('81, '87, and '98) and was chosen to be the North-South All-Star coach in 1987. In addition, he was named the National Regional Coach of the Year in 2000 and was inducted into the Indiana Baseball Hall of Fame in 2002. Along the way, he coached such greats as Andy Benes and the Lindauer brothers, Derek and Dirk, who dominated with their pitching in the '80s.

Not one to rest, Paul Gries has continued to stay active by spearheading the efforts of the Friends of Bosse Field and the Hot Stove

League, an organization that raises funds to support local youth sports. His relationships with sports celebrities like Don Mattingly, Andy Benes, Jamey Carroll, and many others have resulted in the annual Night of Memories extravaganza that has brought in over $500,000 in five years. In more recent years, he has also volunteered his time to the Good Sport's Build, a local arm of Habitat for Humanity.

Few people in the area are as respected, both professionally and personally, as Paul Gries, and he has earned the trust and friendship of many of our most celebrated athletes. It is hard to estimate the impact Paul has had on the community over the years, but the little man has left a huge impression on the local sports landscape. After escaping the madness of coaching, he has tempered his activity in order "to have some sanity and physical and emotional well-being," in his words. But Paul's motor is always running, and those who know him realize that, if there is a job to be done, you can always count on Paul Gries.

Paul Gries in 1965 while he was with the Washington Senators organization.

DID YOU KNOW?

Evansville Central's Dirk Lindauer holds the area record for most wins in a season by a pitcher with 16 in 1987, only one short of the state record held by four pitchers (three of the four were from LaPorte).

Mike Henning of Memorial holds the area record for shutouts in a career with 13 from 1977-'79, sixth best in state history.

(Based on stats compiled by the Indiana High School Baseball Coaches Association.)

VINCENNES UNIVERSITY BASKETBALL: A STEPPING STONE FOR TALENT

Vincennes University has been a model of excellence in the junior college community for nearly fifty years and has served as a launching pad for many future NCAA and NBA stars. The program has won three National Junior College Association of America national championships, all under head coach Allen Bradfield: 1964-'65, '69-'70 and '71-'72. The 1971-'72 team finished a perfect 33-0.

The Vincennes program started in earnest, playing full schedules, in 1952, and for the next 52 years, showed consistent success under the tutelage of two outstanding coaches. Bradfield (1952-'79) won over 77% of his games, and his successor, Dan Sparks (1970-'05), won over 78%. The two combined for a record of 1,313 wins against only 370 losses.

Coach Bradfield was named the NJCAA Coach of the Year three times during his 26 seasons at Vincennes ('65, '70 and '72), and the program produced four first-team All-Americans: Bob McAdoo ('71), Ricky Green ('75), Courtney Witte ('83) and Shawn Marion ('98). The list of players who passed through the program on their way to success at the NCAA Division I level is lengthy, but eight former Trailblazers eventually made it all the way to the NBA. They are listed below with their years at VU, their NCAA colleges and their professional teams.

'62-'64 Jerry Reynolds (asst. coach) – Sacramento Kings
'69-'71 Bob McAdoo (University of North Carolina) – (Buffalo) Braves, Knicks, Celtics, Pistons, Nets, Lakers
'70-'72 Clarence 'Foots' Walker (West Georgia College) – Cavaliers, Nets
'73-'75 Rickey Green (University of Michigan) – Warriors, Pistons, Jazz, Hornets, Bucks, Pacers, 76ers, Celtics
'76-'78 Tony Fuller (Pepperdine University) – Pistons
'78-'80 Dan Sparks (Weber State) – (Miami) Floridians (ABA), Bulls
'91-'93 Eric Williams (Providence College) – Celtics, Nuggets, Cavaliers, Nets
'96-'98 Shawn Marion (UNLV) – Suns

BOB McADOO

Bob McAdoo was the first Vincennes University player to make the Big Time, and he did it in a big way. McAdoo left VU in 1971 and is still one of the school's top ten scorers with 1,292 points. During his final season, he averaged 22 points per game, and after being named an NJCAA All-American in 1971, Bob headed for North Carolina to play for hall of fame coach Dean Smith and the Tar Heels. In his only season at N.C., he led the team to a Final Four appearance and again was named an All-American.

After being selected in the first round of the 1972 draft by the Buffalo Braves (now known as the L.A. Clippers), the 6'9", 225-pound Greensboro, North Carolina native began a professional career that would take him all the way to the hall of fame. McAdoo earned Rookie of the Year honors in 1973, averaging 18.0 points and 9.1 rebounds. In his first four seasons, he won three consecutive scoring titles ('74-'76) and an MVP award ('75).

Generally considered the best-shooting big man in NBA history, McAdoo is still the third-youngest player to reach 10,000 points (25 years and 148 days), trailing only Kobe Bryant and Tracy McGrady. After the 1974-'75 season, Bob was named the NBA's Most Valuable Player, averaging 34.5 points, 14.1 rebounds and 2.12 blocks per game while shooting 51.2% from the field and 80.5% from the stripe.

Over his 14-year NBA career, Bob had stints with six teams and was named to the all-star team five times. His next to last NBA stop was as the sixth man for Pat Riley's first championship team, the 1981-'82 Los Angeles Lakers, where he joined three other future hall of famers: Magic Johnson, Kareem Abdul Jabbar and James Worthy.

In 1986, McAdoo finished his NBA career with the Philadelphia 76ers, but his playing days were not over. Seeing an opportunity, he headed across the pond to play in Italy, where his teams won three Italian Championships and the European Championship twice. Once again, McAdoo excelled, as he won the Most Valuable Player award in both the Italian League and the European Championship.

Wherever Bob McAdoo has gone he has been a winner. In high school, he was a state champion high jumper with a record leap of 6'9", and, showing his versatility, he was named to the North Carolina High School Band Team as a saxophone player. In college, at Vincennes and North Carolina, he experienced a national championship and All-American honors, and as a professional, his accomplishments earned him a place in the Naismith Basketball Hall of Fame.

Although his career at Vincennes lasted only two years, Bob McAdoo's impact on the school's program was profound. He raised the bar for future Trailblazers' aspirations, and he became a part of southwestern Indiana sports history.

DID YOU KNOW?

Bob McAdoo was a technical advisor for the 1993 basketball movie *The Air Up There* starring Kevin Bacon.

VINCENNES UNIVERSITY

THE OWEN FAMILY: THREE GENERATIONS & COUNTING

When reminiscing about families who have impacted the Evansville sports scene, the Archie and Louise Owen clan would have to rank near the top of anyone's list. From the late 1940s and into the 21st century, the Owen family has been a constant in the local sport landscape.

Archie and Louise met while they were students at Evansville College. Archie had originally gone to IU on a football scholarship but decided to transfer to E.C. to play instead. Both he and Louise were eventually inducted into the University of Evansville Hall of Fame, he for football and she for tennis.

The couple was married in 1952, and Archie worked as an assistant coach in Morganfield, Kentucky for one year before going into the Army. Son Mike, the oldest of four children, was eighteen months old before Archie saw him for the first time after his tour in Korea. Three daughters followed Mike, and each played tennis in high school before leaving for college and settling elsewhere. Martha (Harker) set the school record for consecutive wins at Bosse and is now a school nurse living in Indianapolis. Leanne (Dennis) went to Murray State on a partial tennis scholarship and is a Physical Education teacher in Greensboro, North Carolina. The third Owen sister, Susan (Happe) won a full ride tennis scholarship to the University of Evansville and played on Bosse's girls basketball team that made it to the State Finals. She was an excellent tennis player but had the misfortune of having to play Lanae Renschler (a four-time State champion from Castle) early in the tournament every year. Susan is a second grade teacher in Brentwood, Tennessee.

Mike Owen was the only child to settle in Evansville after his college days. He played quarterback for Archie at Bosse and was also an outstanding tennis player, like his mother. Mike won numerous tennis titles over the years, including Evansville Junior and Senior Championships and the Pocket City singles title. He was also a member of the Indiana Junior Davis Cup team. After graduating from Murray State, Mike followed in his father's footsteps and entered the coaching profession. He started his career at North as the tennis coach and volunteer assistant football coach. In 1979, the late Dennis Sexton hired him at Central as an assistant football coach, and Mike worked his way up to offensive coordinator.

On his 31st birthday in 1985, Mike was hired as Central's head football coach. Like his father, he experienced some lean years, winning only a single game during one four-year stretch, but his upbringing gave him the strength to persevere. Again like his father, Mike led his teams to some high times, as well, and twice he led the Bears to undefeated seasons (1987 and 2006).

The Owen family sports contributions didn't end with Mike's retirement. Not only is Mike going to work on his tennis game so that he can add to the six state titles he's won, but he and his wife, Susan, have spawned a third generation of athletes and coaches to perpetuate the Owen family legacy. Daughter Sarah played tennis for Mike at Central and was a sectional champ her senior year. Mike's and Sarah's two sons both were multi-sport athletes at Central and played football for their father, just as Mike had for Archie.

Oldest son Andy cut the nets down four times during his high school basketball career as the Bears won four sectional titles. He also played tennis only part-time because of his full-time commitment as a quarterback for the Bear's football team. While he was at Central, he set all the school's passing records before graduating in 1996. Following high school, Andy went to the University of Indianapolis on a football scholarship. From U Indy, he returned home to become an assistant under his father at Central, and in 2007, he was named to replace his father as the new head coach, making him the third generation of Owens to be a head football coach in the Evansville school system.

Chris, the youngest son of Mike and Susan, completed a highly successful high school career in 2007. He was outstanding on the basketball court and the baseball diamond, but his greatest achievements took place as the quarterback of his father's last, and most successful, Central team. Chris led his team to a perfect 9-0 regular season and finished number nine on the state's all-time career passing list, breaking all his brother's passing records along the way. With his 3.79 grade point average, Chris chose to pursue a college career as the quarterback for Kentucky Wesleyan College.

After sixty-plus years of contributions to the local athletics, the Owen family is three generations strong and still counting.

The Owens, Evansville's First Family of Tennis. (L-R): Archie, Louise, Mike, Martha, Lee Ann, Susan. (Photo courtesy of the Owen family.)

Archie and Louise. (Photo courtesy of the Owen family).

ARCHIE OWEN: A LEGACY OF LOYALTY AND LOVE

Archie during his playing days. (Photo courtesy of the Owen family.)

Arthur 'Archie' Owen was not the winningest coach in the history of Evansville football, but few before him or since have been more respected by their peers and their players.

Archie was born on July 29th, 1929 in East Moline, Illinois, but soon after, his family moved to Evansville, where Archie played football under Herman Byers at Reitz. As a senior, Archie anchored Reitz's first undefeated team in school history (1947).

At Evansville College, Archie played under another legend, Don Ping, and was a member of two Ohio Valley Conference championship teams ('48 and '49).

After returning from the service, Owen went to law school in Cumberland for six months before returning to take a job at Cedar Hall. He then was an assistant under Morris Riley at North from 1955 to 1960. In 1961, he became Bosse's head football coach and would serve in that capacity for 23 years, compiling a record of 111-99-13. At Bosse, Archie's teams won eight City championships and two SIAC titles, and his 1967 team was undefeated. He was named the Evansville High School Football Coach of the Year seven times. It was always easy to spot Archie on the sidelines because of his quirky fashion statements. "Archie always had to have white socks," said his wife, Louise. "And he wore a white t-shirt, even if it was freezing, just like Woody Hayes (of Ohio State.)"

Through the highs and lows of his coaching career, there was one thing that Archie never lost – the respect of his players. "It wasn't about winning or losing," said Glenn Grampp, a local trial attorney who played tackle at Bosse. "Playing for Coach Owen was a great learning experience that helped me as a young man and, quite frankly, still does today."

Grampp was a 1966 graduate and played on some very successful teams at Bosse with such notables as quarterback Gordon Slade, receiver John Moon and others like Jim Heinrich and John Hoover (who are now physicians). Grampp remembered seeing Archie around town in his years after retirement and realized that his respect hadn't subsided over time. "I would see him out drinking his Pepsi and peanuts (one of Archie's quirks), and I could never call him 'Archie'," Grampp recalled. "I always called him 'Mr. Owen' or 'Coach Owen'."

Grampp's most vivid memory of his old coach was a halftime speech. "He wrote 'PRIDE' on the chalkboard, and then he said the word real softly," Glenn explained. "Then he said it louder and then a little louder and then he threw his chalk against the board (to get the team's attention). It was an eloquent speech about pride and doing your best and not quitting.

"I was a good friend of Bruce Pearl (USI's sensational basketball coach)," Grampp continued, "and I told him about Archie's speech. Pearl used it later to coax his team out of the doldrums at halftime to pull out a win."

Glenn Grampp's affection for Coach Owen was evident, and he still carries around a note in his wallet written by his mentor. He spoke of how Archie impacted his players for a lifetime. "He may not have had some of the best team records," Grampp admitted, "but I bet if you went back and looked at his roster, you'd find a lot of young men who have been successful and are good family men who would probably say that they got that training from Coach Owen. It goes deeper than sports. He set in place some of the building blocks that young men could use to build their lives."

Star quarterback Gordon Slade couldn't agree more. "I feel the same way about Archie that everybody else does," Gordon said from his office near Atlanta where he is a real estate banker. "He's one of my favorite people of all time. He just cared for his players. He treated everybody like a son and with dignity, and he always had a big smile on his face."

Archie's family adored the man for the same qualities that his players did. "What I always appreciated about Dad", son Mike reflected, "was that he lost 19 out of 20 one time (in fact Archie always joked he had to cheat to get the one win), but he turned it around and won a lot of games. They always wanted to play for him."

Archie's wife, Louise, remembers the man and what it was like being a coach's wife. "I loved it", she said, "but it was a good week if we won and a bad week if we lost. And that's a terrible philosophy."

Both grandsons, Andy and Chris, always competed in games wearing something that reminded them of their grandfather. "After my granddad passed away," Chris explained. "we were going through the closets, seeing all the neat stuff he had, and I found an old red t-shirt that said 'SIAC Champions' on it and it had a drawing of Granddad Archie on it (drawn by local teacher and artist Jon Siau). I've worn it in every game I've played from my fourth grade year through my senior year."

Archie Owen passed away in 1998, and he left behind an amazing family and hundreds of players whose lives he touched over the years. Whether it's a note in a wallet, a shirt on a young athlete's back or just fond memories that make someone smile when they think about him, Archie's great heart and spirit are still a part of our lives long after he left us.

Andy and Chris in the t-shirts they wore under their pads to honor Granddad Archie. (Photo courtesy of the Owen family.)

LOUISE OWEN: QUEEN OF THE COURTS

Southwestern Indiana has produced some incredible female athletes over the last thirty years, with hundreds of talented young ladies distinguishing themselves in a variety of school sports and many earning partial or full athletic scholarships to help them further their education and improve their chances for successful careers. But before the days of Title IX, a handful of women were bucking the odds and demanding that the world take notice, using nothing more than their love of sport to motivate them to greatness. Among those pioneers is arguably the finest female athlete in area history, Louise Owen.

Louise Keily Owen was born on September 8th, 1929, the year the Great Depression began. As a youngster, there were no organized sports for girls, so she would find games wherever she could. Across from her home at 712 SE Riverside were some tennis courts where Louise would play with her good friend Katie Kelso or anyone else she could find. Or sometimes she would spend hours hitting tennis balls against her house.

She began playing competitively at about age 14 or 15. "We didn't know what junior tournaments were," Ms. Owen said, "so most of it was against adults." At one time, her mixed doubles partner was Lee Hamilton, who had been a sensational athlete at Central and would later serve in the U.S. Congress.

When Louise was a student at Central, there were no girls athletics, and even at Evansville College, the tennis team only had one tournament a year, at Milliken University. She does boast, though, that she once beat Frank Schwitz (who later became a successful basketball coach at Harrison) in an intramural tennis match. (Louise does admit, however, that Frank had to hurry because he was due to pitch for the Aces baseball team).

From 1946 to 1948, Louise was a member of the state championship fast pitch softball team. Louise was primarily a catcher, and these were times when she would catch four games in one day (a testament to her stamina). The coach of the team was Don Wilder, the fire chief in Boonville, and all summer long, the team would travel the country and even into Canada. After one championship, Mr. Wilder gathered the team together and presented the game ball to Louise for getting the game-winning hit.

Ironically, Louise would get another game-winning hit twenty years later in another state championship game. By this time, the girls had switched to slow-pitch and won state titles three years in a row ('69, '70, and '71). The same group of girls would play basketball in the winters to stay in shape for softball season.

Besides her softball achievements, Louise began to gain a reputation as an excellent all-around athlete. Jerry Canterbury, a long-time friend of Louise and her late husband Archie, remembers witnessing Louise's athletic prowess while she was in college. "It was a Powder Puff football game," he recalled, "but they played tackle in full pads. They had to change the rules because every time Louise got the ball, she ran for a touchdown. She was so strong and fast (though not very big at only 5'3" and 120 pounds), and she'd run right through and the girls would bounce off. At halftime, they changed the rules so that Louise couldn't carry the ball."

Despite her talents on the softball and football fields, it is tennis that provided Ms. Owen with a stage on which to display her talents literally around the world. For over thirty years, Louise has competed against age group competition and emerged victorious against the best her generation has to offer.

"Her first big tournament was at Forest Hills," said good friend and fellow competitor Woodie Sublett Walker. "It was on grass, and she'd never played on grass. She wasn't seeded or anything, and no one had ever heard of her. She got to the quarterfinals in singles and the semis in doubles."

Louise is a great doubles player, and her accomplishments include high finishes in mother/daughter tournaments with daughters Susan and Leanne, a state championship with her son Mike and even a local tournament title with Archie. As a group, the Owens were named the Central Indiana Tennis Family of the Year in 1981.

In age group tennis, Louise has been highly ranked for years, both nationally and internationally, and her travels have taken her across the country and around the globe. Her talents have enabled her to see countries such as Australia, Germany, Austria, Yugoslavia, South Africa and many more.

Among her long list of tennis achievements (as of 2007) are 44 national titles, ten international titles as a member of Cup teams, three world singles championships and five world doubles titles. In 2004, she was honored by the U.S. Tennis Association for winning a Gold Slam Championship, representing wins on four surfaces: grass, clay, indoor and hard court.

What made Louise so good? "First of all," said Woodie Sublett Walker, "to play in those age groups, you have to keep your health and be able to run. She was a Physical Education teacher at Reitz, and she was running steps at the Reitz Bowl.

"She was not a power player," Ms. Walker continued. "Her serve was not that hard, but she plays the net beautifully. That's why she's such a good doubles player. And she just doesn't miss."

We'll never know what heights Louise Owen might have reached had she been born thirty or forty years later, but, when asked, the person who knew her game as well as anyone had a definite opinion. "She was one," her friend Woodie said, "who, if she had come along later, could have played on the pro circuit. She would have been competitive at that level."

How good was Louise Owen? Perhaps those words by Ms. Sublett Walker say it all.

Louise during her younger days. (Photo courtesy of the Owen family.)

Top right photo: Louise was also a star softball player. (Photo courtesy of Mary Lou Taylor.)

WHO'S THE BOSS?

Jon Siau, a good friend of the Owen family, tells a funny story that also reveals a lot of truth. Jon coached a slow pitch softball team on which Archie Owen pitched and Archie's son Mike played second base.

"One evening at Howell Park," Jon recalled, "Archie walked seven batters in a row. Mike signaled to me by slapping his glove and said, 'Hey, Jon! Get him out of there!'"

"That's your dad!" I said. "That's Archie Owen! I can't take Archie Owen out of the game!"

When Archie walked the next batter, Siau got some direction from another source. "I heard a voice from the other side yelling, 'Take him out, coach!,'" Jon said. "It was Louise, and it was time to make the move."

Jon had gotten the OK from the boss.

THE LOCHMUELLERS: FATHER AND SON HALL OF FAMERS

There have been many fine local basketball players whose sons have followed in their footsteps by becoming outstanding players as well. But in 2008, Bob and Steve Lochmueller accomplished a feat that had only been achieved once in nearly 100 years of competition in the state of Indiana.

When Bob Lochmueller was a youngster in Elberfeld, his high school did not even have a gym, so the boys gathered for pickup games at crude courts in all kinds of weather and watched the high school team play at the Bluegrass Church and Community Center just south of town. By the time Bob reached high school, Elberfeld had built a gym, and the rail thin, 6'2", 140-pounder developed into a solid player.

A three-year starter, Bob led the Hornets to the best record in school history his senior year. After graduating in 1945, he was drafted into the service near the end of World War II and served for 19 months. With the help of Uncle Sam and Mother Nature, Bob grew to 6'6 with 190 pounds on his muscular frame.

When he returned home, Lochmueller worked in a coal mine and spent evenings and weekends playing independent basketball. The local independent leagues back then often drew the attention of college coaches, and Bob was discovered by the University of Louisville and made plans to join the Cardinals. When a miscommunication occurred, he headed for Western Kentucky instead. After one week there, he found that he was unhappy, so he returned home to be near his girlfriend (and future wife) Nancy (Merten), who was from Oakland City.

In the fall of 1948, Bob enrolled at Oakland City College for two quarters (fall and winter) and played ball with local baseball legend Gil Hodges, who came home after spending the summer with the Brooklyn Dodgers. Over the Christmas break, Hodges married his girlfriend, Joan, a Brooklyn girl, and Bob, Gil, Joan, and Nancy became close friends. Bob marveled at Gil's athleticism and how the 6'4" Hodges was skillful enough to play guard.

Lochmueller re-connected with Louisville in the spring of 1949 and joined the team for the '49-'50 season. Bob had an outstanding career at Louisville and helped the program reach new heights. During his three years there, Lochmueller averaged 10.8, 19, and 17 points respectively, and the Cardinals qualified for the NCAA Tournament (1951) and the equally prestigious NIT ('52) for the first time in the school history.

Bob was named to several All-American teams, and after his graduation in 1952, he was the first round (eighth overall) selection of the Syracuse Nationals of the NBA. The Nationals' star at the time was Dolph Schayes, and although his NBA career was cut short because of a knee injury sustained in college, Bob had a chance to play with Schayes and compete against some of the all-time NBA greats.

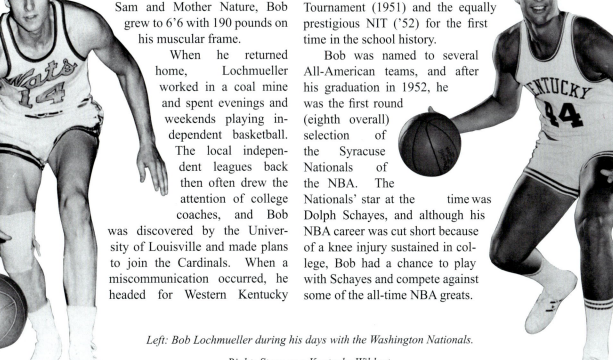

Left: Bob Lochmueller during his days with the Washington Nationals.

Right: Steve as a Kentucky Wildcat.

One instance he thoroughly enjoys joking about is his encounter with the 'Houdini of the Hardwood', Bob Cousy. Lochmueller's Nationals were down by ten points late in a playoff game, partially because a couple players had fouled out while trying to guard Cousy. "There was no shot clock then," Bob pointed out, "and he (Cousy) just dribbled and fancy-danned around. Finally, the coach sent me in and said, 'If you can't steal the ball, foul him!' I caught him five times in seven minutes. I still hold a record! Fouling out the fastest in an NBA game!"

Bob also played against the great George Mikan, the 6'10" NBA icon whose domination required several rule changes just to contain him. Lochmueller crashed into screens set by the big Minnesota Laker several times, and the encounters left lasting memories as Bob said, "When you ran into him, it was like running into a wall."

During his one year with the Nationals, Bob re-injured his knee, and it was time to evaluate his situation. Nancy, now his wife, was not fond of the arctic atmosphere of Syracuse, and the couple decided to return home and start a new life.

Before he knew it, Lochmueller found a new passion when he accepted a coaching position at Ft. Branch. With a talented bunch that included Lowell Hayhurst and 6'3" Jimmy Lee, the Twigs finished at 22-3 and may have made some real noise in the State Tournament if they hadn't run into Central's Clayton brothers in the regional.

From Ft. Branch, Bob moved to county rival Princeton, which offered more salary and a larger school. There, he had two great seasons that included a strong tournament run in 1955-'56. Behind players like Larry Hennenberger, Larry Skelton, and J.R. Bishop, Princeton advanced all the way to the semi-state before falling to Terre Haute Gerstmeyer in the finals, ending the Tigers season at 25-2.

After stops at Richmond and Seymour, Bob left for the University of West Virginia, where he assisted his old roommate with the Nationals, George King, for two years. After that, Bob and Nancy made their final stop on the coaching trail when he landed a job in Tell City, a perfect place for raising their two children, Steve and Liz.

Starting in 1965, Lochmueller coached fifteen seasons for the Marksmen and won nine sectionals and two regionals. In 1980, he laid down his clipboard for the last time, retiring with a coaching record of 399-150 (73%). One of his greatest joys as a coach was watching the development of his son Steve, who shattered records at Tell City and was highly touted by colleges in two sports.

Steve Lochmueller was born in 1952 while his parents were in Syracuse for Bob's season with the Nationals. As Steve reached his teens, Bob and Nancy were settling into their new home in Tell City, and it didn't take long for Steve to develop into an exceptional athlete. He would grow to 6'7", 210 pounds and become a dominating force as both an offensive and defensive tackle for Joe Talley's football team. On the basketball court, he started for three years for his father and led the Marksmen to three sectional titles and one regional championship.

Steve credits both his father and Coach Talley for much of his success and feels fortunate to have been at Tell City when he was. "Joe Talley and my father provided the guidance and direction that molded my upbringing," Steve said from his office in Lexington, Kentucky. "History has shown that during Dad's and Coach Talley's tenure, as well as other coaches, the program at Tell City was at its pinnacle. Joe and Dad were courted by other places, but Tell City was their home, and they stayed there."

By the time Steve graduated in 1971, he had re-written the Tell City record book, setting new standards for career points (1,355) and rebounds (948) among many others, several of which still stand. One of his strengths was his ability to draw fouls, a knack that resulted in school records for most free throws made in a game (19) and season (218).

When Steve's senior season ended, he was named to the All-State team and was notified that he had made the Indiana All-Stars. After he was asked for his shoe size and uniform size, he was told to keep the news quiet because the team hadn't yet been announced publicly. Mysteriously, when the announcement came, Steve's name was not on the list, and to this day, he's not sure what happened.

With that experience behind him, Steve began to examine his college options, and the process he went through was anything but ordinary.

As a two-sport star, he had the opportunity to play football at several schools, including Notre Dame, and from a basketball standpoint, he quickly narrowed his choices to four: Purdue, Indiana, Maryland, and Kentucky.

"Two things happened in thirty days that influenced me," Steve explained. "Number one, Dad was being considered for the head coaching job at the University of Louisville. It came down to Denny Crum and Dad. Had Dad gotten the job, I may very well have gone to U of L.

"Second, Coach Knight came down, and I liked what I saw. I could have ended up playing for him. Steve Green and I visited IU together, and Coach Knight told us that we would be his foundation, his first two recruits as a first-year coach. Then a newspaper writer came out and said that Coach Knight was having Steve Green and this other guy as his foundation.

"At age eighteen in the early '70s, I grew up to believe that what was in the newspaper was factual. I found out later that the writer had a grudge against my dad. Coach Knight and his staff tried to do damage control, and it wasn't that I didn't believe them, but the damage had been done."

Purdue was also eliminated early when Steve received a heartfelt phone call from head coach George King, his father's ex-roommate and good friend, and Steve's appreciation was obvious as he explained the conversation: "Coach King said, 'Stevie, we want you to come here, but I'm going to be honest with you. I'm A.D. and head coach now, and there is a possibility I may give up the coaching position in a couple years.' That was honesty you don't see often these days. I really appreciated that. He was a class act."

After weighing all factors, Steve decided to follow in the footsteps of another Tell City legend, Tom Kron, and play for the University of Kentucky. During his freshman year, Steve watched as Kentucky was undefeated and ranked #1 in the nation, and as a sophomore, he came off the bench to relieve Wildcat center Jim Andrews. His junior year, Steve started some and was the sixth man for Coach Joe B. Hall's crew that featured Kevin Grevey, Jimmy Dan Conner, and Mike Flynn.

As his junior season wound down, reality kicked in and Steve contemplated another path. Realizing that playing professional basketball was a longshot, he decided to join Kentucky's football team as a senior. After the football staff beefed him up to 265 pounds, Steve earned a starting spot at defensive tackle and played until he developed a hematoma in his thigh and was out for seven weeks.

As basketball approached, Steve realized that he was too far behind his teammates to contribute, so he sat out his senior season. He contemplated red-shirting and returning to both sports for a fifth year, but decided instead to graduate with his class and get on with his life.

Today, Steve is happy raising his children with his wife Christi and is the president and CEO of Sumerset Houseboats, the world's largest manufacturer of its kind. Two of his partners are fellow Wildcat alumni Jamal Mashburn and Ron Mercer.

While Steve runs his business, Bob visits often and enjoys his retirement in Tell City. A special reunion took place in 2008 when Bob sat as a proud father and witnessed his son being honored in Indianapolis. On March 19th, 2008, the Lochmuellers made history when they joined Jack and Dave Colescott as the only fathers and sons to be inducted into the Indiana Basketball Hall of Fame.

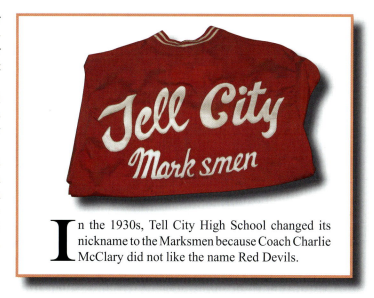

In the 1930s, Tell City High School changed its nickname to the Marksmen because Coach Charlie McClary did not like the name Red Devils.

BASKETBALL & STRAWBERRY SHORTCAKE

It isn't surprising that Kendall (Virgin) Kreinhagen followed in her grandfather's footsteps, but no one could have predicted the amazing success she would have at a very young age.

Kendall grew up on Evansville's west side, and she was the apple of her granddad's eye from the day she was born. During her early years, she learned to compete under the watchful eye of her grandfather, Jerry Canterbury, and her first observations of a basketball team were made while she was a pre-teen watching Jerry coach Bosse's Lady Bulldogs. She would eventually become a multi-sport athlete, like Jerry, and she would use him as a role model as she developed into one of the rising young stars in the Indiana high school coaching ranks.

Jerry Canterbury was "a little-bitty shaver" when he entered Reitz High School as a freshman in 1944, but despite being vertically challenged, he was still determined to make the freshman basketball team. When he didn't make it, he was asked if he would be the team's manager, and he accepted. Taking advantage of the situation, he hung around after practice to shoot baskets, and by the end of the season, he had worked his way into the starting lineup.

After a sophomore season spent on the varsity's second five, the little man prepared for two final years of high school that would showcase him as one of the city's premier all-around athletes. Jerry started at guard for the Panthers his last two years and led the city in scoring during the regular season of his senior year. Top-scoring honors for the entire year went to Central's talented Lee Hamilton, as Hamilton's Bears defeated Canterbury's Panthers in the sectional and progressed all the way to the State Finals, giving Hamilton several more games to amass points.

Jerry was also the first City cross country champion when the sport was first contested in 1947. In those days, the runners would run at Garvin Park, starting in front of Bosse Field and running past Bud Miller's tavern to finish where they had started.

Jerry Canterbury uses some body language during his days as a coach at Bosse.

As a track athlete, Jerry broke Bob Cole's City record in the mile run. Cole had broken the record of future Evansville College coach Arad McCutchan, and the record Jerry set as a senior in 1948 was later broken by long-time Harrison track coach Charlie Siesky. Canterbury also ran in the State meet all four years, finishing 5th, 4th, and 3rd, respectively, in his last three. "I never could beat that guy from Anderson, Johnny Stayton," Jerry said. "He broke the national record. He beat me by five seconds. I was 4:29, and he was 4:24."

After high school, Jerry ran track at Evansville College, a new sport at the school coached by Arad McCutchan. As a basketball player, Jerry played a supporting role on the first team in E.C. history to win twenty games, and after graduating in 1952, he wasted no time getting on with his life. "He graduated on Tuesday," said Bernice, his wife of nearly sixty years, "then we got married on Saturday, and three weeks later, he got his papers to go into the Army."

After two years in the military, serving as a 130-pound M.P., Jerry took a coaching job in Grayville, Illinois. The following year, he got a chance to come back home. In those days, prospective coaches had to start in the grade schools, so Jerry taught at Cynthia Heights and Dexter while other future head high school coaches like Jim Myers, Don Watson, Ed Wessel, Bob Walker and Frank Schwitz, also taught at the elementary school level.

In 1961, beloved Bosse coach Herman Keller left to work at the IHSAA, and Central assistant coach Jim Myers was called to take over the head position at Bosse. Jerry was recommended as an assistant by Jim Graham and served as the Bulldogs' freshman coach during the '62 State championship season.

After serving as the junior varsity coach for fifteen years, Canterbury was approached about the girls varsity position, and in 1977, he accepted the job coaching the sport that was in only its second year of existence. Other pioneer women's coaches of the era were Louise Owen at Reitz, Ron Johnson at North and, later, Ron Overton (the father of PGA golfer Jeff Overton) at Central.

For fourteen years, Jerry guided the Lady Bulldogs, and he oversaw the progress of three of the best female athletes in Bosse's history, Cheryl Dowell and the Lander sisters, Cassandra and Vicki. His 1984 team, featuring Dowell and guards Vicki Lander and Charlene Tinner, finished the season 24-2 and advanced all the way to the Final Four at State. For his career, Jerry had only two losing seasons and finished with a record of 196-72 (73%). He also won 8 City championships, 7 sectionals, 5 regionals, and a semi-state.

Canterbury was revered by his players as a great teacher of fundamentals and as a coach who made the sport fun, and his impact on his players is evident when they speak of him. Jerry enjoyed his career as a basketball coach, and his joy continues today as he watches his granddaughter, Kendall Kreinhagen, follow in his footsteps. She has taken lessons she's learned from her grandpa and forged one of the finest starts to a coaching career in Indiana history.

Kendall Virgin was born in 1978, the first daughter of Debbie and Gary Virgin. Her first exposure to organized sports was playing T-ball at West Terrace before advancing to girls slow-pitch softball at age seven. She got her start on the basketball floor in elementary school, where she played co-ed ball because very few girls wanted to play. As a fourth and fifth grader, she was a starter on the boys team.

It was during those early elementary school years that Kendall began hanging out with her grandfather at Bosse's practices, and we may never know the full impact those hours had on a precocious tomboy with big dreams. "It was one of those things that are always going to stick with me," she said from her home in Indianapolis, "and I'm so fortunate to have been able to do it. I can remember when I was five or six, every Saturday I would go with my grandfather out to Bosse. I would occasionally run through drills or I'd rebound or get water for the girls. As soon as practice was over, we would always stop by Kuester's and he'd buy me strawberry shortcake.

"When game time came around," she continued, "I got to go in the locker room, and I had a little red Bosse sweatshirt and got to interact with the girls and listen to pre-game speeches. I'd be involved in the pre-game warm-up by rebounding or getting them towels. And then, as I got older, I was able to get involved a littler more from a basketball standpoint. It was a great time in my life."

As one could imagine, Kendall became a crowd favorite as her skills improved over time. She also endeared herself to the team, and as a token of their affection, she was introduced before games and even awarded a varsity letter by her 'teammates'.

As Kendall progressed through school, Jerry thought it best that she separate herself from Bosse's program and focus on her future at Reitz. After playing for the City championship at Perry Heights Middle School, Kendall was ready to make a little history of her own on The Hill.

At Reitz, Kendall earned eleven varsity letters in four sports: basketball, softball, cross country, and golf. After establishing herself as an excellent all around athlete, she turned her focus to playing basketball in college.

Following her graduation in 1996, Kendall spent two years playing ball at Vincennes University before heading to the University of Indianapolis. At U Indy, the 5'7" guard became popular with coaches and teammates because of her knowledge of the game and her scrappy style. During her two-year stay with the Greyhounds, she tied a GLVC record for free throws in a game without a miss (10), and in the same game, she had 20 points and 10 assists. Kendall also set a record for steals in a GLVC tournament game when she swiped the ball seven times in front of family and friends at Roberts Stadium.

Little Kendall Virgin presents flowers to Zora Lander at Senior Night. (Photo courtesy of Jerry and Bernice Canterbury.)

After graduating with a degree in Elementary Education in 2000, Kendall wasn't sure if coaching was in her future or not. She felt fortunate when she landed a job teaching fifth graders at Eastbrook Elementary School in Pike Township, but then she was offered a position she wasn't sure she wanted. Through the husband of a fellow teacher, she was offered the junior varsity job at Indianapolis Brebeuf Jesuit, and after one year, the head coach decided to move to Australia. Only one year removed from being a college student, Kendall found herself in charge of a high school program.

After a reasonably normal rookie season, Kendall continued to learn on the job and sought tips wherever she could find them. Thankfully, her husband, Kevin Kreinhagen, was also an athlete and coach. She had met Kevin while he was a record-breaking quarterback at U Indy. He was good enough to be invited to try out for Mike Holmgren and the Seattle Seahawks, and he even played in a pre-season game on TV against the New York Giants. Holmgren apologized to Kevin when he informed him that he was the last one cut, and the young QB came back to Indy and accepted a job as the offensive coordinator at North Central High School. As the two young coaches talked shop during the summer of 2003, neither of them could have suspected what the next few months would bring.

Coach Kendall Kreinhagen motivates her Brebeuf team. (Photo by Dr. Tom Fischer, courtesy of Brebeuf Jesuit High School Athletic Department.)

Kendall's 2003-'04 Brebeuf team was loaded with potential, and expectations were high. She would be the first to admit that the talent was there, but, thankfully, the kids were also in some pretty capable hands. "I inherited a wonderful group of kids," said Kendall of the athletes who returned for the '03-'04 season. "When they came in as freshmen, that class was pretty much tagged to win the State championship sometime. It was just a matter of when it was going to happen."

Kendall was referring to a class that featured Indiana All-Star Amber Jackson and a strong supporting cast. After losing in the semi-state during Jackson's sophomore season and falling in the sectional the next year to Beech Grove, led by future Purdue star Katie Gearlds, Kendall's seniors-to-be were primed to fulfill their destiny in March of '04.

With a four-girl front line rotation that stood 6'6, 6'3, 6'1 and 5'11 and the leadership of Jackson and talented point guard Amanda Quattrotchi, Brebeuf swept through the tournament and then defeated Ft. Wayne Bishop Luers for the Class 3A State title. At the tender age of 25, and in only her second year as a coach, Kendall Kreinhagen had experienced what most coaches, including her grandfather, never get to experience. But after a dream season like that, what does a 25-year-old do for an encore?

Fortunately for Kendall, the Brebeuf cupboard wasn't bare after the '04 senior class graduated. While Jackson and company were making Brebeuf history, a young freshman was waiting her turn to bask in the limelight.

Although Ta'Shia Phillips was a valuable contributor as a 6'6 inside presence on the '04 championship team, she would only get better as her skills caught up with her size. During the 2006-'07 season, Phillips led a young team all the way to the State championship, and along the way, created a memorable moment for Jerry Canterbury. As the tournament played out, Kendall's Brebeuf Braves were paired against the #9-ranked Lady Bulldogs of Bosse in the semi-state, and the Evansville media hyped the matchup and grilled Canterbury about where his allegiance would lie. Like a true diplomat, Jerry tactfully evaded the queries and espoused his support for both sides. Although he never made his true feelings public, one would have to believe that the edge went to the young woman who was once the little ball of energy with whom Canterbury had shared some amazing memories during his days as a coach.

In a nip-and-tuck affair at Jeffersonville, Brebeuf ousted Bosse with a rally in the last two minutes to pull out a 55-53 win behind Phillips' 30 points and 19 rebounds. Brebeuf would continue on to capture another State title, giving Kendall her second championship after only six years on the job. Phillips would be honored as the state's Miss Basketball and would be named a McDonald's All-American before heading to Xavier to continue her career. Coach Kreinhagen, one of only two female coaches in the Finals of the State Tournament (among the four classes) in 2007, was named the Marion County Coach of the Year and the ICGSA Coach of the Year.

In her first six seasons as a head coach, Kendall had compiled a 106-43 record and had captured three sectionals, two regionals, two semi-states, and two State championships. Her State title in 2003-'04 made her the youngest (at 25 years old) coach to accomplish the feat and turned her into a hot prospect in the coaching ranks. Though she has been approached for higher-profile positions, she responded with a definitive "No" when asked if she had considered moving on, saying, "I am in a very fortunate situation being at Brebeuf. It's a wonderful school and wonderful community. I love the kids, and I like my situation."

When Kendall decides to retire from coaching, she knows that it will be a family decision, and regardless how long it lasts, she knows that much of her success came from the experience she gained while watching her grandfather. "I liked the way he talked to his players," Kendall reflected. "He was able to develop a relationship so that they knew he truly cared about them as people. You know, you can know all the X's and O's in the world, but if you can't relate to the players, you're not really doing much. That's what I got the most from him."

Jerry Canterbury taught his granddaughter about much more than just coaching; he taught her to do things the right way, and he taught her to be a winner. As Kendall's own daughter, Kaiden, grows up, maybe she'll be able to sit on the bench and watch, just as her mother did twenty years earlier. And maybe, for old time's sake, when all the basketballs are put away and the gym is locked up, Kendall and Kaiden can stop on the way home for a little strawberry shortcake.

VINCENNES BASKETBALL: THE MEMERING ERA

Jerry Memering holds records at Vincennes (Lincoln) that have held up for forty years, yet when he watches the players who have followed him and then reflects back on his playing days, he sees a startling contrast. "I was kind of a dinosaur (by today's standards)," he admitted. "I wasn't an 'athlete' the way the term is used today. Today it means you can jump over the moon and can dunk from anywhere on the court. I was just fundamentally sound. I knew how to play the game because I had good coaching."

Jerry attributes his early basketball training to his sister Carolyn, who also is the mother of another Vincennes star, Courtney Witte. "She was a jock but had no place to play," Jerry revealed, referring to the lack of high school sports available to girls in the 1960s. "She was the ladies golf champ at the Elks Country Club in her early teens. She was the one who had me out playing basketball."

Memering was blessed with good size and was always the biggest kid in his class. He was a six-footer in the seventh grade, and by the time he reached high school, he was a sturdy 6'4. Head coach T.L. Plain, who had returned to the school for a second coaching stint in 1964 (he had previously coached there for two seasons from '57 to '59), immediately moved Memering to the junior varsity and then to the varsity permanently for the seventh game. During his rookie season, Jerry scored in double figures ten times on a team that finished 10-14.

As Memering grew into his eventual 6'7" frame, he became a consistent force for the Alices. During his sophomore season, the team improved to 16-7, and Jerry scored in double figures in all 23 games, with a high of 28 in the regional against North Central.

Although Vincennes has won two State championships (1923 and 1981), many of the Alices' older fans believe that the 'Memering era' provided the best teams in the school's history. When T.L. Plain left in 1967 after Memering's sophomore year to become an assistant at the University of Louisville, a strong group of returning players fell under the guidance of a wily, proven coach who would demand that they reach their potential. 'Gunner' Wyman, who had led Tell City to new heights, walked into a situation that was tailor-made for his no-nonsense approach. Memering and the talented 'Mac' McCormick were complemented by a strong supporting cast that included Ken Brandon,

Jerry Memering (Photo from 90 Years of Alices by Dr. Bill Stedman.)

Roger Hollen, Larry Landry, Randy Bowman and Jay Peters.

As is the case with most successful seasons, the stars seemed to align just right and everything seemed to fall into place. If the 1967-'69 Alices teams were a BLT sandwich, Memering and company were the bacon and Coach Wyman was the lettuce. All that was missing to complete the delectable delight was a tomato to top things off. A minor miracle provided the missing piece when a shaggy-haired junior named Tom Turner made a decision that would change his life and provide the final ingredient for the Alices' recipe for success.

"I went out for freshman basketball, but I hated school and my grades kept me from playing," Turner confessed as we sat in his Vincennes home. "My grades got better my sophomore year, but I decided to not even try to play."

During his sophomore year, Turner went to watch some high school games as he played ball in a church league and in pickup games around town. A Vincennes player, Ken Brandon, saw Tom playing outdoors and convinced him that he should try out his junior year.

"Gunner Wyman came to town and he didn't know me from Adam," Turner recalled. "I remember seeing him walking to the gym at Adams Coliseum and I said, 'Coach, I'd like to play ball.' I didn't know they'd already started (pre-season) training. He took my name and said, 'Don't get in touch with us; We'll get in touch with you.' I thought, 'Well, that's the end of that!'"

Many coaches would have dismissed the incident and written the youngster off, but something intrigued Coach Wyman enough to check out the rag-tag wannabe. He decided to approach Roger Benson, his assistant coach, to get his take on Turner. Once again, all it would have taken was a negative word from Benson and the story would have ended before it began. But Benson suggested that the boy might be worth a shot.

During gym class one day, Wyman summoned Turner to join him at the end of the floor. He put chalk on Tom's fingertips and asked him to reach as high as he could on the wall to make a mark. He then told Tom to jump to measure his vertical leaping ability. After measuring the jump at well over thirty inches, Wyman gave the 6'4" Turner the chance he needed, and the final piece of the puzzle was in place.

Between Memering, Turner and Mac McCormick, a 6'1" play-making guard, many feared that one basketball wouldn't be enough to keep them all happy, but Wyman mixed all the players' talents like a master chef.

The Alices started the '67-'68 season with an 87-78 win over a tough Reitz team. Memering led with 22 points, followed by McCormick (17), Landry (11) and Hollen (10). After a 17-point win over South Knox, Vincennes took on the reigning State champion, Evansville North, and their All-American center Bob Ford. The Huskies prevailed 51-47, handing the Alices their first defeat.

When the dust cleared at the end of the regular season, Vincennes had finished 18-2, losing only to North and a talented East Chicago Roosevelt team in the finals of the Holiday Tourney.

Jerry Memering scores against North's Bob Ford. (Photo from 90 Years of Alices by Dr. Bill Stedman.)

Tom Turner (#22) fights for a rebound during the Washington Regional. (Photo from 90 Years of Alices by Dr. Bill Stedman.)

After a bye, the Alices thumped Petersburg 85-46 in the sectional behind Memering's 28-point effort. In the title game, the same South Knox team that had been blown out earlier in the season led at the end of the first three quarters and nearly upset the Alices.

The '68 regional was a breeze for Coach Wyman's crew as they dominated both L&M (88-63) and Cloverdale (87-57). However, the road ahead for the Alices would prove to be much tougher.

At the Evansville Semi-state, Vincennes had to come from behind to conquer Jeffersonville 77-69, setting the stage for what *Courier* sportswriter Don Bernhardt would later call the best high school game ever played at Roberts Stadium. The Reitz Panthers, featuring Curt John, Charlie Farmer, Tim Fletcher and John Walters and coached by Jim Barnett, took the Alices to the wire but fell short by a single point 71-70.

At the State Finals at Hinkle Fieldhouse, eventual State champs Gary Roosevelt ended the Alices' season 65-48. Coach Wyman's boys had completed a 24-3 season, but with three strong juniors returning, the team and their fans had high hopes for the upcoming year.

When the '68-'69 season began, everyone was aware of the firepower Coach Wyman had at his disposal, with Memering, McCormick and Turner returning. McCormick led the way in the opener with 22 points. In the season's fourth game, Vincennes avenged the loss to the North Huskies the year before with a game that proved to be a virtual highlight reel for Jerry Memering. With Bob Ford now at Purdue, Memering had his way with North's young pups, scoring 38 points in a 102-64 laugher. Memering also set a school record in the game when he made twenty consecutive free throws before missing his twenty-first.

After a year's experience, Tom Turner was blossoming as a bona fide star and a great complement to his two classmates. The three seniors led a dominating run through the regular season with an average winning margin of over 18 points per game, and only three teams came within ten points of the Alices: Terre Haute Wiley (77-69), Seymour (74-66) and Washington (62-61). When the regular season ended with a 68-37 win over Robinson (IL), Vincennes had completed the year with a perfect 20-0 record, one of only a handful of local teams to ever do so.

Entering the 1969 State Tourney, the three seniors were anxious for a second chance in the State Finals. Once again, they breezed through the sectional with easy wins over South Knox, Sullivan and North Knox.

At the Washington Regional, the Alices withstood a 24-point night by Otwell's Steve Barrett and used a balanced attack for an 87-70 win. The top scorer was Randy Bowman (22 points), followed by Turner (20), Memering (18) and McCormick (16). In the finale, Memering and Turner scored 27 and 20 points, respectively, in an 89-57 rout over L&M.

At the Evansville Semi-state, Coach Wyman notched his 50th win at Vincennes with a hard-fought 75-71 victory over a tough Scottsburg team led by the talented Bill James, who tallied 38 points. In the final game, Turner led the Alices with 21 points in a win over Evansville Rex Mundi. For the second straight year, the Alices were on their way to the State Finals, and they took a perfect 27-0 record with them.

In any other year, Vincennes would have been the prohibitive favorite to take home the title, but joining them in the final four in 1969 were two other undefeated teams, Marion and Indianapolis

Washington. The fourth team, Gary Tolleston, was the Alices' first opponent and had lost only one game all season, completing possibly the toughest Final Four in IHSAA history. After losing to Tolleston in the afternoon, the Vincennes team watched as George McGinnis and Steve Downing led Washington to the championship with a 79-76 win, becoming only the third team in Indiana history to finish the tournament undefeated.

The Memering era was over, and the 6'7 center then became the first Vincennes player chosen for the Indiana All-Star team. Memering had made a name for himself and had received letters from every major college program. One of his trips was a memorable visit to the University of Kentucky where he sat down with legendary coach Adolph Rupp, who took the soft-sell approach.

"Rupp told me, 'We'd like you to come here, but you have to do what's best for you,' Memering recalled. "Then he said, 'You need to understand that if you come to Kentucky, we'll be good. And if you go somewhere else, we're still going to be good.' And, of course, he was right."

Jerry admits that Rupp, or any other coach, didn't have much of a chance because he was mentally and emotionally committed to Indiana from the start. When he arrived at IU to play for Coach Jerry Oliver, he joined McGinnis, Downing, John Ritter and Bootsie White in a strong freshman class. Memering's college career was unspectacular, by his own estimation, and he only started a few games, but he did, however, get the opportunity to play for Bob Knight when the controversial coach arrived in Bloomington in 1971.

As a senior role player for 'the General', Memering contributed to Knight's first Big Ten championship and his first trip to the NCAA Final Four. The Hoosiers were eliminated in the semifinals by John Wooden's UCLA Bruins, featuring Keith 'Silk' Wilkes, Swen Nater, Pete Trgovich and All-American Bill Walton. Jerry is proud to tell people that he held Walton scoreless, but he will then smile and admit that it was during a one-minute span at the end of the game while UCLA was holding the ball.

Tom Turner, the second chance kid, made the most of his opportunity and moved on to a fabulous college career. The forward with pogo sticks for legs averaged over 16 points during his two-year high school career and scored in double figures in all 28 games his senior season. He also set the school's modern-day single-game scoring record with a 43-point effort against Bloomfield, a record that stood for twenty years.

Tom began his college career down the street at Vincennes University, where he was a starter on VU's NAIA national championship team that starred future-NBA great Bob McAdoo. After his two years with the Trailblazers, Turner took his talents northeast to a school in New Hampshire. As luck would have it, Jerry Reynolds, who had been an assistant at VU but was now a head coach at the University of West Georgia, contacted Tom and convinced him to warm his bones in the south.

At West Georgia, Turner got his degree and plastered his name all over the school's record books in the process. He was inducted into the school's Athletic Hall of Fame in 1988 and held twelve scoring records when he finished his career. He was also a starter on the school's first junior college national championship team, scoring 28 points against Alcorn State in the finals. At the time of his hall of fame induction, Turner was still the conference's all-time leading-career scorer with 1,696 points. He was a two-time All-American, and his 26.5 scoring average his senior year set a record that stood for thirteen years.

After college, Tom and two of his college teammates, 'Foots' Walker and Jerry Faulkner, were selected in the pro draft. Tom was chosen in the sixth round by the Washington Bullets, coached by K.C. Jones, and he tried to compete with fellow rookie 'Truck' Robinson but didn't make the team's cut. After leaving Washington, he returned home to raise a family and to attend the Indiana Police Academy.

Turner fully realizes how fortunate he was as a young sophomore at Vincennes. "If it hadn't been for them giving me a chance," he said of Gunner Wyman and Roger Benson, "I would never have finished high school, I would never have played college basketball and I would have never been a police officer. I was lucky, and I had some fine coaches."

Tom Turner was not just lucky that he got a second chance, but he was also lucky to play for a high school coach like Wyman and to play with a rare talent like Jerry Memering. During his years at Vincennes, Jerry Memering played in 100 of the school's 102 games. He scored in double figures in 51 of his last 58 games and led his teams to four regionals, three semi-states and two State Finals. Memering is still today the school's all-time career scoring leader with 1,650 points, and his final two years, when the Alices went a combined 51-4, are among the best in the school's history.

Jerry Memering and his talented teammates gave the community a very tasty two years to enjoy. Although the Vincennes faithful never got to sample the savory flavor of a State title, the Alices fans of the Memering era did get to enjoy some mighty fine cuisine.

IHSAA STATE CHAMPIONS:
BOYS CROSS COUNTRY

Individual	School	Year	Time
Jim Kaiser	Mater Dei	1986-1987	15:24.5

'GUNNER' WYMAN: HE DID IT HIS WAY

Orlando 'Gunner' Wyman has been touted as one of the area's most successful coaches since he arrived on the scene in the early '60s. The controversial coach was known as much for his testy temperament as he was for his tremendous talent, and he would be the first to admit that he was not in the business to win popularity contests. His son, Will, who played for his father and followed in his footsteps as a coach, believes his father was a product of his past.

"He grew up in a rough environment," Will explained, referring to Gunner's early days in Mayfield, Kentucky. "He also went into the Marines at an early age, and I think that had a big influence on who he was and how he was."

Will also conveyed the oft-told story about his father's nickname. "When he was growing up (in his teens), he and some guys went out bird hunting," Will said. "This guy hit Dad with a little bit of birdshot. The story is, Dad made the guy walk a distance and turn around and then Dad peppered him with birdshot. The next day at school, somebody called him 'Gunner', and the name stuck. Dad said it was a dumb thing to do but that they were young and stupid."

Gunner was born on December 28th, 1925 and was named for his father, who was a carpenter by trade. His mother, Katherine, was a homemaker who also taught piano lessons.

After high school, Gunner served as a marine in China and Guadalcanal in World War II. Upon his return, he used the GI Bill to enroll at Florida State, where he played basketball during the early days of the school's program. He also met and married his wife, Sally, during his years at FSU.

After graduating, Gunner worked at an atomic energy plant in Paducah. Even though he had to take a pay cut, he chose to leave the plant to become the first coach at Wingo High School in Nortonville, which later became the South Hopkins consolidation.

In the fall of 1958, Gunner and Sally packed up and brought one-year-old Will and his two older sisters, Ann and Molly, to Tell City, and it was during his time as the Marksmen's coach that Gunner's reputation started to take form. Tell City had won some sectionals but never a regional before Wyman's arrival, and the fiery coach wasted little time in changing all that. Gunner's troops won four straight sectionals and three straight regionals behind the play of superstar Tom Kron. During Kron's junior year, the Marksmen advanced all the way to the State Finals before losing to Indianapolis Manual and the Van Arsdale twins in the afternoon game. In Wyman's final year at Tell City, his team went 19-1 losing only to eventual State champion Bosse.

That summer, the Wymans moved north after Gunner accepted a coaching job at Hammond High School. Things were fine at first, but when the school's enrollment dropped by 800 students after two new schools were built, Gunner started looking to move back closer to home.

In 1967, Wyman's relentless preparation and work ethic meshed perfectly with a talented group in Vincennes led by All-Stater Jerry Memering, and Gunner hit the ground running again. Known for making notes in the scorebook for future reference and for his intolerance for mediocrity, Wyman immediately guided the Alices to elite status.

During Wyman's first two seasons, his teams won 51 games and lost only one while advancing to the State Finals each year. Even with all the success, his anti-social style kept the coach from being fully embraced by the school's fans. Even Jerry Memering admitted that the hard-nosed loner was hard to understand.

"I'm probably like a lot of players," Memering admitted, "in that I think a heck of a lot more of him now than I did in those days. I thought he was a son-of-a-(gun) a lot of times. I think good coaches have that characteristic. You know, they demand more of you than what you think you've got to give."

Memering also recalled how Gunner refused to be swayed by the opinions of outsiders. "He didn't have a lot to do with the community," Memering disclosed. "You'd never see him at a coffee shop talking basketball with fans. He didn't want to be influenced, and he didn't have parents' meetings saying, 'Here's why your boy's not starting.' If I were coaching, I hope that's the way I would've run things myself.

"But you'd better win if you're going to be that way," Jerry continued. "Coach Knight was that way at IU, and some of his problems started when he didn't win as much."

Will Wyman, who sat on the bench when he was small and later played for his father at Vincennes, saw first-hand how his father's temper and attitude invited criticism. "I could see how his bluntness could probably rub people the wrong way," Will confessed. "He told it the way he saw it. He had some struggles with referees from time to time. I know in one sectional, he had four or five technicals. He could be tough on officials, and he was known to drop a word or two of profanity. I know there were people who thought he was arrogant."

Despite his flaws, his record spoke for itself, and there are many who saw him as a genius at his profession. During his 14 seasons at Vincennes, Wyman's record was 234-101, and his overall record was 527-214 (71%). His teams won 21 sectionals, 9 regionals, played in 4 Finals Fours and won one State championship. Wyman was twice named the Coach of the Year by the Indiana Sportswriters and Broadcasters, and he coached the Indiana All-Stars to two wins over Kentucky in 1981.

In *Indiana Basketball History Magazine*, *Evansville Press* sportswriter Tom Tuley gave this assessment of Wyman's dedication: "In my most active years, I probably saw about 70 high school games each season. Wyman saw twice that many, and he was always there for a reason.

"In 1962, he lost only one game – to eventual State champion Bosse. My guess is that after that, Wyman saw virtually every game Bosse played. One night in Madison, where Bosse was scheduled to play against the Cubs, Bosse coach Jim Myers turned to me at dinner and said, 'I'd like to go to the bathroom, but I'm afraid I'll find Wyman in there!' That's the kind of guy Gunner was."

In the same article, longtime *Courier* sportswriter Jack Schneider said, "I believe that the best-coached teams I observed were produced by Gunner Wyman."

In Dr. Bill Stedman's book, *90 Years of Alices*, the author states, "What Wyman could do is coach his talent to the utmost and figure a way for them to win. He was also uncanny at coaching once the game started."

Supporting Stedman's point was T.L Plain, whose place Wyman took in 1967. Plain, who left to become an assistant at the University of Louisville, paid Wyman the ultimate compliment, saying, "If you've got one high school basketball game to win, I'd want Gunner Wyman coaching that team. I've never seen a more thorough coach in preparing a team to reach its potential. And once the game starts, his coaching gets even better."

When a disgruntled bunch of Vincennes fans called for Gunner's firing in 1979, the coach promised that if he were permitted to stay to see the sophomore class through their senior year, he would quit voluntarily when the season ended. In true Wyman style, Gunner guided those players through a storybook senior season and led them to the school's first State championship in 58 years. When the season was over, he made good on his word. Just as he had done throughout his 23-year career, when it was time to leave, Gunner Wyman did it his way.

GUNNER'S LAST WORDS

Gunner Wyman passed away on July 15th, 2008. As you can see in this photo, he wanted to be remembered for his ties to Indiana basketball with these words etched on his gravestone that memorialize his bitter rivalry with Jasper and his wonderful sense of humor. Kneeling (L-R): Gunner, Tom Turner, Jerry Memering, and Roger Benson. Standing: Tom Ernst.

TOM KRON: UK BLUE THROUGH AND THROUGH

(Photo courtesy of Collegiate Images.)

Few would argue that Tom Kron was the greatest all-around athlete to come out of Tell City High School, but what many may not know is that Kron had a vision for his future at a very early age.

Kron was born on February 28th, 1943 in Owensboro, Kentucky, the second son of Max and Mary Mason Kron. Much of young Tom's athletic ability came from his father, who played a year of basketball at Purdue before transferring to the University of Louisville to play football.

As young Tommy grew up in Tell City, it was easy to see that he was a natural, and his days were spent playing whatever sport was in season. His love for basketball and his admiration for the University of Kentucky Wildcats inspired him to write a letter when he was still in grade school. In his letter to legendary UK coach Adolph Rupp, he boldly expressed his interest in joining the Wildcats' program upon his high school graduation. Coach Rupp probably got a chuckle from the boy's writings, but as things turned out, the boy's gumption would eventually be backed up by incredible talent and Coach Rupp would one day come calling on Kron to grant the boy's wish.

At Tell City, Tom was a three-sport athlete. Although he only ran track part-time, he is still listed in the top five performances in a few events. In football, Kron was a quarterback who could "throw a football into a peach basket from fifty yards," according to Harrison High School's Dennis Bays. Joe Talley, the Indiana Football Hall of Fame inductee who coached the Marksmen for eighteen years, began his career in Tell City when Kron was a sophomore and declared after his retirement that Kron was the best quarterback he ever coached.

In the winter, when Tom would trade his football cleats for his Converse basketball shoes, he was fortunate to move from one hall of fame coach to another. As a three-year starter for Coach Gunner Wyman, Kron led Tell City into virgin territory, capturing three sectional and three regional titles for the first time in school history. As a sophomore, Tom was named to the All-Regional first team along with teammates Don Huff and Sonny Conner. His junior year, Kron and the Marksmen advanced all the way to the Final Four of the State Tourney but fell in the afternoon to Indianapolis Manual and the Van Arsdale twins, Tom and Dick. The State champion that year was Kokomo, led by the great Jimmy Rayl.

Expectations were high for Gunner Wyman's 1961-'62 team, with Kron at the controls and classmate John Arnold returning, but the team was dealt a devastating blow when 6'4" Dennis Kress tragically died from an injury sustained during football practice. The Marksmen still carved out a fine season before falling to

Tom Kron, seated between his parents, Mary and Max, signs his long-awaited letter of intent with the University of Kentucky while UK coach Adolph Rupp (second from right) and Tell City coach 'Gunner' Wyman (far right) look on. Standing next to Coach Rupp is Tom's older brother Dick. The gentleman standing at left is unidentified. (Photo courtesy of Collegiate Images.)

an excellent Castle team in the regional. Castle, in turn, lost to Evansville Bosse, who would go on to capture the State championship under hall of fame coach Jim Myers.

After his senior season, Kron was named to the All-State first team and played on the Indiana All-Stars with Jimmy Rayl. Although it is known that he was second on the Tell City team in scoring, behind Arnold, Kron's exact high school stats for his career have been misplaced, but regardless of his final numbers, his talent did not go unnoticed by college recruiters.

Although he had numerous options, Tom's college choice was a no-brainer when Adolph Rupp extended an invitation for the 6'5 point guard to join UK's program. Kron's childhood wish had come true, and his four years in Lexington would not only prove to be rewarding, but historic as well. As a sophomore, Kron began to show glimpses of the player he would become, and as a junior, he was firmly entrenched as the floor leader in Rupp's system

In 1965-'66, his senior season, Tom played the point for a starting lineup that consisted of Pat Riley, Larry Conley, Louie Dampier and Thad Jaracz. Since no starter was taller than the 6'5 Kron, the crew was affectionately dubbed 'Rupp's Runts'.

With Riley and Dampier emerging as the team's superstars, Tom was required to adjust his focus and sacrifice his scoring to distribute the ball more to his teammates. Although his average dropped three points a game from the previous season (from 13 to 10 points), his unselfishness contributed to an excellent season.

Entering the 1966 NCAA Tourney, the Wildcats were 24-1 and were favored to win the school's fifth national championship. After dismissing Dayton and Michigan in the early rounds of the tournament, Kentucky knocked off Duke 83-79 to set up a game that carried much more significance than just an NCAA title. Tom Kron, the kid from a small town in southern Indiana would be playing in a game with historical implications.

The Wildcats' opponent in the 1966 Finals was Texas Western, known today as the University of Texas-El Paso (UTEP). Western's rise to the pinnacle of the college basketball world had created a media frenzy, and journalists from coast to coast flocked to College Park, Maryland to watch the event. The curiosity was caused by the anticipated lineup of Texas Western coach Don Haskins. For the first time in NCAA Division I history, a school would open the game with an all-black starting lineup, and Coach Rupp's Wildcats, all white, were the opponents.

Although much was made of the racial undertones of the game, with many portraying Coach Rupp as a racist, the facts don't support the premise.

"That's one of the misconceptions of that game," Larry Conley stated in an interview a few years later. "It was as if we all of a sudden showed up and started playing against black players. We'd been playing against black players for years." Conley went on to confirm that the Michigan team that Kentucky had beaten earlier had four black starters and that Adolph Rupp had been scheduling teams with black players for years, something very few coaches from the South would do.

In the same article, Coach Haskins downplayed the significance, as well, and pointed out how Kentucky's team showed class after Texas Western defeated the #1-ranked Wildcats 72-65. "Every one of those young guys – Pat Riley and the whole bunch – after the game, came down to shake hands with our players," Haskins pointed out. "Everybody wants to talk about the black thing and the white thing. Well, there it is. It was just a basketball game."

Tom Kron averaged 34 minutes a game his senior year at Kentucky and was a steadying force during their 27-2 season. An example of his reliability as the team's floor general was his consistency at the foul line. During his three seasons, Kron averaged over 80% from the line every year, with a high of 85.1% during the team's championship run in 1965-'66.

Kron was selected with the 24th pick of the 1966 NBA draft by the St. Louis Hawks and spent three years in pro ball (with the Hawks, Seattle and the Kentucky Colonels), averaging over ten points and seven rebounds in his last two seasons. Although his pro career was not long, he will forever be linked to Kentucky basketball. Rupp assistant Joe B. Hall (who would later become the Wildcats' head coach) once described Kron as "a complete player, offensively and defensively," and a UK sports publicist once stated that, "Tom Kron was probably one of our most underrated people."

Although Tom Kron will forever be remembered as one of Rupp's Runts, who were immortalized in the movie *Glory Road*, his talents were appreciated long before 1966. On November 30th, 2007, Tom passed away from complications from bladder cancer, and, according to an obituary in the *Lexington Herald Leader*, visitors from around the country came to pay their respects.

Kron was inducted into the Indiana Basketball Hall of Fame in 2001, and in 2004, he was recognized in the city where it all began. In a ceremony honoring him as one of the members of the first class, Tom's Kron's image was placed in his high school's hall of fame to represent the lasting impressions he left as a Tell City Marksman.

CHAPTER SIX
1960-1990

I would like to offer special thanks to Daryl Buente and Ed Cole whose articles in Indiana Basketball History Magazine and Maturity Journal, respectively, were valuable sources for much of the information used in this story.

THE '67 NORTH HUSKIES: HOW SWEET IT WAS!

As a member of the 1967 North Huskies basketball team, I personally know the elation that is felt by every player, parent, student and fan when one's team stands atop the Indiana basketball world as the State champion. Although my role was minor compared to most of the players, it was still one of the highlights of my life.

In 1966, Coach Jim Rausch and his staff had high hopes going into the basketball season. For four years, they had been anticipating what this group of juniors and seniors might be able to accomplish. Bob Ford, the junior headliner of the '66-'67 Huskies, recalls vividly how the hype started with a murmur back in 1962 and gradually increased over the years.

"There was some conversation about going far in the tournament that had been mentioned back in grade school," Ford recalled, "because we'd put together some long runs (at Vogel Grade School) of being undefeated and just really crushing some teams that were pretty good. And then you're going to pick up some really terrific athletes from other schools in the district. We (Vogel) had the nucleus. It was just a matter of putting the other four or five guys together to make it work."

Ford's reference to grade school related to a team that featured eighth graders Steve Holland, Jim Hildebrandt and Ron Jesop, along with Ford as a seventh grader. This group would eventually become four of the five starters on North's championship team. Vogel had lost only one game during Ford's tenure there, to a

The 1967 State champion Huskies. First Row (L-R): Barry Rollman, Ralph Chapman, Ron Eaton, Ed Crowe. Second Row (L-R): Daryl Buente (manager), Mark Mason, Preston Smith, Jim Hildebrandt, Bob Ford, Ron Jesop, Steve Holland, Dave Senning, David Jones (manager). Third Row (L-R): Lance Sandleben (manager), Clarence Riggs (business manager), A.L. Meadows (principal), Dale Fehd, Rodney Owens, Tim Daniels, Jim Rausch (head coach), Robert Walker (assistant coach), Richard Hougland (assistant coach).

Dexter team led by future Harrison stars Terry Wedgewood, Jim Giannini and Steve Parrish and coached by future Harrison track coach Charlie Siesky.

Entering the '66-'67 season, it was safe to say that there was a cautious optimism in the air, but Coach Rausch knew that there was a minefield of talented teams in the area to negotiate along the way. Many local pundits proclaimed the race a virtual toss-up between North and three other city schools. Bosse was led by hot-shooting Larry Weatherford and James Utley, with strong support from John Hoover, Gene Ballard and the massive John Barnett. Reitz would be formidable with a lineup that included future U of E player Curt John, Mike Jeffries, Mike Derrington, Steve McCullough and Bob Parkman. And perhaps most impressive of all were the Harrison Warriors, who started five players who would all play Division I sports: Vaughn Wedeking, Terry Wedgewood, Greg Nelson, Greg Fenner and Bob Winchell.

Coach Rausch looked back and agreed with the assessment in an interview for the *Maturity Journal* in 2002. "It may have been the most outstanding year for Evansville high school basketball," he said. "Four city teams had been ranked in the state's top ten at some time during the year, and remember, there was only one class of basketball."

Behind the 6'7 Ford, the Huskies opened the season with eight straight wins, including one-point thrillers over Jerry Memering and the Vincennes Alices and Reitz. In North's next game, Weatherford lit up North for 33 points in a 68-62 Bosse win. After another five-game winning streak, Frank Schwitz's Harrison team handed North its second loss behind Wedeking's 22 points. North closed out the regular season with four more wins and began preparation for the challenge of the tough Evansville Sectional. The future State champions had completed a great regular season but had not even won the City or conference titles.

North's coaching staff of Rausch, Bob Walker and Dick Hoagland knew they had to focus on the task at hand and not look ahead. When I asked Coach Rausch recently if the thought of a State championship had crossed his mind, he responded as if he'd been asked the question a thousand times (which was probably the case). "I didn't dare think about it," he said. "We were probably the fourth best team in town. No one expected us to win. In fact, the only person who did was (local sportswriter) Larry Stephenson. He picked us to win the State."

On a personal note, the tough sectional was a factor during an interesting event that few people are aware of. According to IHSAA rules, schools could only dress twelve players for a tournament game. In 1967, there were fourteen of us who regularly dressed for varsity games, thus creating a dilemma for Coach Rausch. The coaches discussed the matter and concluded that ten players deserved to dress throughout the tournament, regardless of how long we lasted. That left four players, including yours truly, in a state of limbo.

Coach Jim Rausch relied heavily on his Big Three (L-R): Bob Ford, Jim Hildebrandt and Steve Holland. (Photo from the Jim Rausch collection.)

The four of us were summoned to the center of the floor and informed of what was to transpire. Mr. Rausch apologized for the situation and then explained that he was going to use a coin flip to determine how things would play out. The 'winners' would have the option of dressing for the sectional and semi-state, if we got that far, or we could opt for the regional and State Finals. Our fates were literally in Coach Rausch's hands. (Can you anticipate the ending?)

As the coins fell, I and another player (I won't mention names to avoid potential embarrassment) emerged victorious. Now our fates lay in our own hands. As any red-blooded skeptic would do, I (along with the other winner, I might add) decided that our sectional was so tough that we'd better dress while we had the chance. If you play out the rest of the scenario, that meant we were sitting in the stands at Butler Fieldhouse during our team's finest hour. My only consolation is that, when I recently asked Coach Rausch what he would have done, he agreed that he probably would have made the same choice.

Looking back at the '67 State Tournament, one could make a case that 'destiny' played a role in our run to the championship. Team manager Daryl Buente noticed that things seemed to fall in place as the tournament began. "When the tournament pairings were announced, many of us noticed a favorable pattern," he said in his article. "North would play the first game of every Saturday through the State Finals (allowing for maximum rest). We also would wear white as the home team for every game, and our first seven games would be played at Roberts Stadium, where we had played four regular season games."

Buente also explained that a possible advantage was gained by an observation made by North's choir director Jerry Hoover, who was also the public address announcer at the Stadium. Mr. Hoover believed that the large blue curtain at the open end of the stadium was a better background to shoot against and, therefore, we should shoot at that end in the second half. Consequently, the team managers made sure to place the warm-up balls at the free throw line at the closed end to start each game.

For added luck, the North players would also practice the ritual of rubbing the head of Coach Bob Walker's young son, Kent, as we took the floor.

North's long run to the championship almost ended before it began, as the Huskies were the underdogs against Reitz in the Evansville Sectional. In a hard-fought battle, North prevailed 58-54.

On Saturday morning, the Huskies defeated Central and then watched as Harrison and Bosse locked horns. The Harrison-Bosse game was a crucial element in the Huskies' success story for two reasons. First, Bosse upset the powerful Warriors; and second, the game was so intense that Bosse's players were exhausted and had only a few hours to rest. Coach Rausch has often said that everything might have ended differently had North met Harrison in the finals. As things turned out, a tired Bosse team was no match for North, and the Huskies won 59-44. After the game, another ritual was born when Coach Walker proclaimed, "How sweet it is!"

When Bob Ford was asked about the emotions of winning the school's first sectional, he recalled an encounter from a year earlier that had stuck with him. "We lost to Harrison the year before in the sectional," he explained, "and we were walking off the court. I can't remember if it was Vaughn Wedeking or Greg Nelson who said, 'You guys had a great season. This is our year, and next year is yours.'"

After the sectional, Daryl Buente remembers that there was some talk about some teams North might see down the road. Michigan City was ranked #1 for most of the season, and Indianapolis

North fans were out in full force during the '67 State Tourney. (Photo from the Jim Rausch collection.)

Washington was making noise with two juniors named McGinnis and Downing. "Coach Rausch told our team not to worry about the teams up north," Buente noted. "He said that they would knock each other off and that we wouldn't have to beat them all, that we only need to prepare for our next game."

The "next game" to which Coach Rausch referred would be no walk in the park for the Huskies, as the undefeated Oakland City Trojans were coming to town. The North coaching staff had little information about the Trojans, but Coach Rausch was lucky that his good friend and fellow George Washington University alum Jim Barnett stepped up to help. Although Barnett's Reitz Panthers had lost to North, he was gracious in his willingness to share scouting reports with Rausch throughout the tournament. Wood Memorial had four starters close to Ford's size, including scoring machine Larry Harris and Rick Smith, who later played at U of E. With Coach Barnett's help, the Huskies downed the Trojans and the Boonville Pioneers to take the regional title.

The Huskies were now two wins away from a trip to State and their date with destiny. In the morning game of the Evansville Semi-state, North played New Albany and came away with a 65-58 victory behind Ford's 29-point effort. Next up were the Purple Eagles of Terre Haute Garfield, led by their sensational guards Howard Williams and Mike Turner. The sellout crowd at Roberts Stadium was about to see one of the wildest finishes in the history of southern Indiana basketball.

The entire game was close as the teams traded blows throughout the evening. With little time on the clock, North trailed by one and called a timeout. North's cheerleaders and fans were in tears as the prospects looked bleak. As expected, the strategy was to put the ball, and the Huskies' fate, in Bob Ford's hands. After a pass from Preston Smith, Ford fired up a ten-footer from the left-side with six seconds remaining. The ball hit the rim and careened upward, high above the backboard. The silence was deafening as the crowd held its collective breath. After what seemed like an eternity, the crowd roared as the ball found the net.

But the game was not over. Garfield inbounded the ball, raced down the court and fired up a last-second shot. As if scripted by a Hollywood screenwriter, Bob Ford soared from out of nowhere to swat the ball out of bounds. Utter pandemonium is the only way to describe what ensued as the North faithful stormed the court. The North Huskies were on their way to Indy.

When asked recently about those historic final seconds, Bob Ford took an analytical approach to the situation. "The shot was low, and that's why it went straight up," Ford theorized. "All I was thinking was, 'Please go in! Please go in!' And the block, that was really stupid! That's a good way to commit a foul. But I was just reacting to what was going on on the court."

Call it luck or call it fate. The fact was, North was going to State!

During the middle of the next week, the North team traveled through a snowstorm to practice at Butler Fieldhouse. Coach Rausch's plan was to try to keep the team in a familiar setting and to keep the routine as normal as possible. Earlier in the season, North had traveled to the Circle City to play Indianapolis Wood. The environment had been hostile and the competition fierce. After watching every Wood player dunk the ball in pre-game warm-ups, North knew they were in for a battle. Wood, behind 6'11 Greg Northington and 6'7 Kenny Morgan, jumped out to a 20-point lead. But in the second half, Ford dominated the paint, fouled out both big men and brought the Huskies back for a huge win.

Rausch's strategy of scheduling an Indianapolis team paid off, as he arranged for the team to stay in familiar surroundings at the same hotel where they had stayed during the season.

In preparation for the afternoon game at the State Finals, Jim Barnett had provided Coach Rausch with another excellent scouting report. As a result, Bob Ford put on a clinic, scoring 35 points in a win over perennial state power New Castle.

The Huskies dressed in the dungeon-like locker rooms beneath the fieldhouse and then watched the first half of the second game. The coaches noticed that Marion Crawley, the future hall of fame coach of Lafayette Jeff, had instructed his boys to fall down to draw fouls against Ft. Wayne South's superstar center Willie Long. The tactic worked, and Long fouled out in the third quarter. The shady strategy put Ford on high alert going into the final game. The crafty Crawley was the winningest coach in Indiana and had beaten another Evansville team for a State title (Central in 1948), but Rausch and his crew would not let him win this one.

North trailed Jeff at halftime 39-36 but held the Broncos to only 19 second half points. North battled back for the lead, and when a 75-foot desperation shot missed, the Huskies celebrated a 60-58 win. At eleven years of age, North had become the youngest school ever to win the Indiana basketball State championship.

After the game, Marion Crawley had some kind words when he spoke to the press. "That's the best job of defense we've ever had on us!" Crawley said. "And Ford is as good an individual as I have ever seen in the State Tourney. The big difference, though, was Steve Holland. He went around us and got the ball to the big guy."

"The big guy" was sensational throughout the 1967 State Tournament, and he shattered records along the way. Bob Ford was arguably the best high school clutch player in Evansville basketball history, but he would be the first to admit that a lot of credit for the championship goes to his coaches and teammates.

After the season in 1967, there were some naysayers around the community who proclaimed, "Anyone could have coached that team to a championship." The fact is, "anyone" couldn't have done it. Coach Rausch handled his personnel perfectly and made good decisions throughout. The team was also blessed with great assistant coaches. Bob Walker was cool under pressure and knew the game as well as anyone, and Dick Hoagland was the perfect assistant who did whatever was asked of him. Even the team's student managers, Lance Sandleben, David Jones and Daryl Buente were extraordinary.

In fact, Ford credits Rausch with contributing a key element to the historic season. "Probably the thing that won the tournament for us was the work we did in the pre-season on the 1-3-1 offense," Ford said in a recent interview. "The decision to go with the Tennessee (1-3-1) offense perfectly fit the personnel. It made it very difficult on defenses."

The '67 North team represented two excellent athletic classes at the school. Virtually all the team members were multi-sport athletes, and six of them were starters on one of the best football teams in the school's history. During the championship season, each player was instrumental in the team's success.

Ford and Steve Holland grew up together and played one-on-one every summer on a dirt court at Holland's house. Steve played the point in the 1-3-1 and was a deft passer, often hitting Ford with what is known today as an 'alley-oop' pass. His snappy, no-look passes were ahead of the times, and he could bury shots from long range with amazing accuracy.

Jim Hildebrandt and Preston Smith played the wings in the 1-3-1. Jim was solid in all facets of the game, and 'Smitty' was a great defender with quick moves to the basket.

The fifth starter, Ron Jesop, was an All-State football player who didn't play basketball for North until his senior year. Ron was a demon on the boards and played down low in the 1-3-1 offense. As Ford said, "Ronnie put a lot of miles on his shoes running the baseline."

The two super-subs were Dave Senning and Mark Mason, both Stringtown Elementary grads. Dave was Mr. Reliable and could play both the baseline and the wing. Mark was quick and was all arms and legs, or as Bob Ford put it, "It was like being guarded by a spider."

The remainder of the cast played important roles, too, whether it was during games or simulating opponents in practice. The rest of the team were seniors Barry Rollman, Ed Crowe, Dale Fehd and Ralph Chapman; juniors Rodney Owens and yours truly; and sophomore Tim Daniels.

March of 1967 was a magical time for the North Huskies and our fans. For all those who lived it, the memories return in bursts as one image inspires another. Here are just a few:

- Pep assemblies on Fridays and victory assemblies on Mondays with teacher Jim Crawford leading the 'Husky growl' and football coach Morris Riley organizing ridiculous skits.
- Super-hot cheerleaders (Brenda Arnold, Kathy Wilhite, Kathy Williams, Jeanne Wilson and Sarah Elmendorf) in their new uniforms with dark green shorts instead of skirts and dark green knee socks.
- The new green blazers worn by the team when in public.
- Beloved principal Adrian Meadows, who was retiring at the end of the year and was carried off the floor by the players after the sectional.
- Marv Bates doing the play-by-play of all the tournament games on WGBF.
- Sportscaster Jerry Birge bringing the team White Castle hamburgers after the championship in Indianapolis.
- The firetruck ride from Garvin Park to the Stadium where 9,000 fans were waiting.
- Coach Rausch losing track of his wife, Mary Ann, at Garvin Park, forcing her to get a ride with Civil Defense Police.
- Mayor Lloyd presenting the team with a key to the city.
- Coach Rausch's quote to the press: "We drove a Ford to the State championship."

The Huskies were the last Evansville boys team to win a State title in the one-class format. It was an honor to be a part of North's dream season in 1967, and even as I enjoyed the final celebration while wearing my green blazer instead of a uniform, I will never forget the experience. Even after forty years, we can all look back and say, "How sweet it was!"

Opposite page: How sweet it was as the North Huskies celebrated their 1967 State championship. Shown are: Bob Ford (#22), Preston Smith (left of Ford), Ron Eaton (behind Ford), Mark Mason (right of Ford), Rodney Owens (leaping) and Lance Sandleben (student manager – right of Owens). (Photo from the Jim Rausch collection.)

BOB FORD: MR. CLUTCH

In 1966, a group of young men entered the high school basketball season knowing that they had a legitimate shot at being the last team standing when the State Tournament ended in March. The reason for their optimism was 6'7" Bob Ford, a player the North faithful had been watching since his elementary school days.

Robert Alan Ford was born on January 26th, 1950 and grew up just a block down Morgan Avenue from Vogel Grade School. He never knew his father, but his mother, Lucille, nurtured and supported him as he grew from a gangly youngster into a legitimate superstar.

Bob was always large for his age, and his size enabled him to earn a spot on Vogel's eighth grade team as a sixth grader. During his three years on the grade school team, Vogel lost only one game, and although Bob's size was obvious to everyone, his basketball and leadership skills were advanced also. When asked how he developed the fundamentals at such an early age, Ford cited two sources. The first was his stepbrother, Randy Wilkinson, who was several years older, and the other was his coaches. "Randy taught me the basics," Bob revealed. "He taught me how to dribble and pass. And then it was backed up by what the coaching staff did. I had Bob Walker (who would later serve as Jim Rausch's assistant at North) as a fifth grader and then Bill Harrawood came over to Vogel to coach. I thought they were really good at teaching fundamentals at that time. I think that's kind of gone by the wayside nowadays."

As a youngster, Ford honed those skills by spending countless hours on the court. Randy, his stepbrother, lived two doors down from the Southwoods, Gene and Jerry, and Bob would spend Saturdays and Sundays battling Jerry, his idol at the time, on a court near Washington Grade School.

Between his sixth and seventh grade years, Bob grew six or seven inches and began to catch the eye of the North coaching staff. Although the added size made him even more effective on the court, there was a downside to the growth spurt. As he reached his teenage years, he had to cope with Osgood-Schlatter Disease, a common malady among active teenagers that causes a tender bump just below the kneecap. The problem was not career-threatening, but Bob was forced to endure the pain it caused during exercise.

Ford entered North as a 6'4" freshman and started his high school athletic career on the freshman football team. With his size and soft hands, he made a great target as a tight end and also played a little quarterback. He loved football but quickly learned the dangers of the sport when he injured his shoulder while playing middle linebacker. As the basketball season approached, he realized that his future lay on the hardwood and not the gridiron, so he hung up his pads for good.

Although North head coach Jim Rausch was well aware of Bob's abilities, he chose to start Ford with his classmates on the freshman team, and Coach Rausch still believes it was the right decision. "I think we did that with all the players," Rausch stated recently. "We just wanted them to get a little taste of coming up the ladder a little bit. Some just moved up a little faster than others."

After a short stint with the freshmen, Bob moved up to the JV team and by mid-season, was a varsity regular. Although no one else was surprised at the rapid rise up the ladder, it caught Bob off-guard. "I didn't have any thought of playing varsity ball as a freshman," he said from his office in Lafayette. "I was just glad to be playing; it was fun. Moving up to JV and the varsity was unbelievable."

Throughout his freshman season, Bob continued to have problems with his shoulder. Several times the bone would slide out and have to be popped back in, requiring him to wear a brace during part of the season.

During his high school years, Ford took advantage of North's philosophy of developing well-rounded students and immersed himself in several school activities. As a four-year member of the track team, he was an excellent high jumper and qualified for the State meet as a junior. He also served as class vice-president and was a standout with the school's renowned vocal music program. As a vocalist, Bob performed with North's concert choir and varsity singers and sang the lead roles in the musicals *Kismet* and *South Pacific*. Although Bob downplays his abilities as a singer, his music involvement and love for the activity would play a surprising role in his college choice when his high school days were over.

Bob Ford drives during the semi-finals of the 1967 State Tournament. (Photo from the Jim Rausch collection.)

Eventually growing to 6'7", Bob's high school career was one of the best in Evansville's history. In 1967, he led the Huskies to the coveted State title, and he did it in record fashion. His 128 points in the tournament's last four games set a State record, and his 27 points against Lafayette Jeff in the final game led the team to a 60-58 victory.

Ford drew praise far and wide for his performance in the State Tournament. Vincennes star Jerry Memering, who swapped sweat and elbows with Ford several times during their playing days, remembers Ford's skills well and applauds Ford for his ability to perform when the game was on the line. "His tourney run in '67 was phenomenal," Memering recalled. "He made every big play he had to make. He was very good fundamentally, and he had good range; he could step out and shoot.

"He had that little jump hook," Memering continued. "Back in those days, coaches were still teaching the sweep hook shot. Everybody shoots the 'baby hook' now. He made it from the free throw line."

The combination of his size, his great physical skills and his intense mental approach to the game made Ford a treat to watch. He had an uncanny ability to sense where a defender was and to lean just the right way to draw a foul. Although he was cool under pressure, he was also a fierce competitor who wanted the ball when the game was on the line. His flare for the dramatic became legendary as he produced memorable moments during North's historic run through the State Tournament and during his four-year varsity career with the Huskies.

In addition to leading North to the school's only basketball State title, Bob also finished his career as Evansville's all-time leading scorer with 1,816 points, a 24.2 average over four years. During his senior season, he also averaged 19 rebounds per game and set North's single-game scoring record with a 48-point effort against Boonville.

Ford made several All-American teams and was cited in an article in *Sports Illustrated* as the #1 player in the country. Ironically, the powers-that-be in Indiana did not see fit to name Ford as the state's Mr. Basketball, however. That honor went to Billy Shepherd of Carmel. Ford was voted #2 and played on the all-star team with future University of Evansville and NBA star Don Buse.

As one could imagine, Ford was courted by every program in the country, but he quickly narrowed his choices to Indiana, Purdue, Tennessee and Kentucky. He was also offered a scholarship to UCLA and, looking back, realizes that he could have earned four national championship rings as a classmate of Curtis Rowe, Sydney Wicks and company.

Instead, Bob chose to pursue his education in West Lafayette. When asked why he chose Purdue, Ford pointed out that the Boilermakers looked solid with Rick Mount and Bosse's Larry Weatherford already there and that he had heard good things about the Purdue Glee Club, a group that would offer a setting for him to continue to express himself through his singing. In fact, Bob admitted that a visit by a Purdue coach to a North High School musical sealed the deal in his mind. "I thought that if someone would drive over 200 miles to come to Evansville to hear me sing off-key, I ought to go to school there," Ford joked.

Bob enjoyed Purdue's glee club for four years and was named to its hall of fame. As a player, he moved into Purdue's starting lineup at mid-season of his sophomore year. During his tenure at Purdue, he battled the likes of Bob 'the Big Cat' Lanier of St. Bonaventure, and he still has a scar on his eyebrow from a vicious elbow from North Carolina's 7'4" Tom Burleson.

Ford was a Boilermaker team captain and was named first team All-Big Ten and Academic All-American in 1972. He finished his career with 1,233 career points (a 17-point average) and 648 rebounds (8.9). After playing for the U.S. in the World University Games and the Pan American Games, Bob was selected in the sixth round of the NBA draft by the New York Knicks and in the fifth round by the ABA's Memphis Tams.

When asked about his attempt at a pro career, Bob recalled how a few months in Memphis made his decision relatively easy. "I was a 'tweener'. I was not big enough for the power forward position, and I was too slow to be a swing man or a guard," he said matter-of-factly. He added that, after trying to guard Dan Issel (Kentucky Colonels) and Roger Brown (Pacers), the realization hit him that it was time to move on and get a 'real job'.

Although he had planned on coaching and teaching Drama, Bob chose to enter the world of broadcasting, working in sales, production and on-air. He is best known for his role as a color commentator for Purdue and the Big Ten. Although the rights to broadcast Purdue games have changed hands several times, Ford has survived all of them over the last 25 years. He and his wife, Polly, now reside in West Lafayette. Their three children, Rob, Andrew and Kara, all played high school sports and probably are aware that their father was a star for the Boilermakers. What they probably don't realize is the exceptional player he was as a high schooler and his place in the history of his hometown.

When discussing the greatest basketball players in Evansville's history, a handful of elite players are always mentioned. Dave Schellhase led the nation in scoring at Purdue, as did Calbert Cheaney while at Indiana. Cheaney and fellow Harrison alum Walter McCarty had long NBA careers. Older fans may throw out names like Central's Jerry Clayton, Lincoln's Porter Merriweather or Bosse's Broc Jerrel, but for those of us who watched him and played with him, we submit that, as a high school player who played his best while he was on the biggest stage, no one did it like Bob Ford.

THE MATTINGLY BROTHERS: TALENT AND CLASS

In spite of all the coaching they've had and the competition they've faced on the way to becoming professional athletes, Randy and Don Mattingly both agree that the most valuable lessons they've learned took place at home long before they were making headlines. The strong foundation that allowed the two to thrive and succeed was laid by loving parents, Bill (known as 'D' to his friends who called him by his middle initial) and Mary, who provided their five children with a love of sports in an atmosphere free from pressure and criticism.

One might think that raising five children in a small three-bedroom home would result in chaos and claustrophobia, but Bill and Mary found a solution. Whether it was from thoughtful planning or divine intervention, the couple's five kids arrived into the world five years apart, which meant that all five were never living at home at the same time. After the oldest, Judy, was born in 1941, Bill and Mary welcomed four sons, Jerry (1946), Randy ('51), Mike ('56) and Donnie ('61), all of whom became exceptional athletes.

Throughout their childhoods, the boys' home on Van Dusen, just west of Stringtown Road in the shadows of North High School, was a hub of activity for anyone looking to play some ball, and more than a few future stars were regulars in the neighborhood. "Doug and Spike Bell would come over," recalled Randy Mattingly, "and Randy, Rick, Ronnie and Rusty Mason. Mike and Pat Casalena, Greg Hoffman. And (North's) Preston Smith would come to the church to play basketball."

In the fall and winter, football was the game of choice, and the boys learned both toughness and tactics as they competed without pads. "We didn't like to play tag (football)," Randy explained. "There was a sign that we used to use as an extra blocker. If you got to that sign and a guy was using a pursuit angle, you could block him off. We sometimes played on a very narrow lot at another church. There, you had to become a north-south (straight ahead) runner. You knew you were going to get tackled every time, so you would find ways to get extra yardage."

During baseball season, Over the Line was the game of choice, and, once again, skills were learned naturally before the boys were ever exposed to coaching. "We never had enough people, so we always closed off a field, and you could choose which field that was," Randy said, "so being able to hit the ball to right or left field was a factor."

Finding people was never a problem for basketball, however, and sometimes the older Mattinglys had to look out for the little ones. In Randy's case, that meant Mike and Donnie. "You'd try to get invited to your (older) brother's games," Randy pointed out, "or you'd go down and wait in line. When I was one of the older ones, I always made it a point to include my younger brothers. On Saturdays, it would be nothing to have three teams waiting to play."

Don Mattingly never got to play the role of older brother, but he does remember taking the court against the big boys. "Just playing against older competition, like Randy and Michael, made me better," he said. "Randy would always keep me in the games, and he'd say, 'You stand over there and I'll get you the ball and you shoot it,' or 'If you're on defense, just chase the ball.' So that's what I would do. You learn to compete."

As each Mattingly son progressed to play organized sports, the games became true family affairs, with the whole crew migrating from one field or gym to another to support each other. "I was dragged to every ballpark in the area, I think," said older sister Judy. "We all cheered for whoever was playing." Bill and Mary were also present at the boys' games, but unlike many parents today, they left the coaching to the coaches. "Our father played basketball in high school, and our mother was very athletic but had no place to play (because there were no sports for girls)," Randy explained. "They were real patient. You never felt pressure to play. If you didn't have an event yourself, you went to your brothers' games. Everybody went to everybody else's games. Most families only had one car, and the only babysitters I remember were my older brothers and sisters."

Both Randy and Don attribute much of their athletic success to their parents' influence and believe that parents today would be wise to follow the philosophy that Bill and Mary

The Mattingly boys (L-R) Michael, Randy and Donnie stand behind their parents, Mary and Bill ('D'). Oldest son Jerry was lost in a construction accident years earlier. (Photo courtesy of Randy and Melissa Mattingly.)

This incredible photo was put together by the Courier photography department to depict Jerry Mattingly's multiple athletic talents. (Photo courtesy of Karen Brucken and the Evansville Courier.)

practiced. "There was very little criticism," Randy revealed, "so there was no reason for me to fear failing, so that wasn't even in my thoughts. I never heard anything negative from my father unless it was an incident of bad sportsmanship."

Don Mattingly echoed his brother's comments exactly when he was asked about the way he was raised. "Looking back now, I really think my father had a huge influence on me. Since my dad passed away (in 2007), I've thought about it more and more. I look back, and my dad never, ever, ever, not once, criticized me after a game. And only once in my life, I think it was after a fifth grade basketball game, did he say I'd played well. As I look back and think about it, because of that lack of criticism, I ended up playing fearless. I was never afraid of making mistakes, and I made plenty of them, but I grew up without that fear."

With a strong foundation in place, each Mattingly son was well-prepared when they were old enough for high school sports. The oldest sons, Jerry and Randy, were both key players in the brief but remarkable life of Rex Mundi High School on First Avenue (the building is now the home of Ivy Tech). "Jerry was always big for his age, and so was Don," Randy noted. "They both had mature bodies. Jerry played varsity sports as a freshman. He started in baseball as a freshman, and in football, he was moved up to the varsity as a freshman but didn't play. In basketball, he started as a sophomore. As a sophomore, he was 6'2, 210 pounds. He weighed more in high school than he did in college."

Though older sister Judy graduated from Mater Dei, Jerry entered Rex Mundi during the era of Bob Griese (who was a year ahead of Jerry), 'Big Tom' Niemeier, and all-around athlete Mike Minton. Rex Mundi was competitive in all sports during the early '60s, and Jerry was a big contributor to that success. In 1964, Rex Mundi became the first Indiana parochial basketball team to play in the Final Four, and Jerry, despite having an ear infection, scored 19 points for Jerry Alstadt's team in a loss to eventual champion Lafayette Jeff.

Jerry earned All-City honors in all three sports and was respected by teammates and opponents alike. "He was good in all of them," said Bob Griese, a teammate in all three sports. "He was very competitive, and he was very bright."

Coach Jerry Alstadt was in total agreement with Griese's comments, saying, "Jerry Mattingly played on the team that went to the Final Four in 1964, and he was the backbone of the team. We went to him when we were in trouble. He was the glue that kept the team together."

While in high school, Jerry also played left field on the Southern Vendors American Legion team that advanced all the way to the World Series, and he led the team in hitting with a .358 average. In addition, Jerry was honored as the 1963 recipient of the Louisville Slugger Award for the highest batting average in the nation during American Legion national competition. Although he was recognized as a big stick at the plate, Jerry was also known for his aggressiveness. "Jerry was such an awesome competitor," said sister Judy. "When he ran the bases, he was like, 'Get out of my way or I'll run over you!'" Jerry's athletic versatility drew interest from professional baseball scouts, and he received college offers for all three sports. After rejecting football offers from Florida State and Purdue, basketball offers from Michigan and Murray State and a combination scholarship to IU, he chose to stay home to play baseball and basketball at Evansville College.

When Jerry started his basketball career with the Aces, Jerry Sloan was a senior, Larry Humes and Sam Watkins were juniors and Herb Williams was a sophomore. Jerry was a point guard in Arad McCutchan's two-platoon system and performed well enough to be named to the Indiana College All-Stars that played a similar group from Kentucky.

In 1969, Jerry served as a graduate assistant for a year before accepting a job at Evansville Day School coaching soccer and basketball. In the summer of '69, just as he was beginning a new career, Jerry was killed in a construction accident during the building of the new I-64. In the blink of an eye, the oldest son of Bill and Mary Mattingly was gone, and the Mattingly kids had lost a hero.

At the time of his death, Jerry left behind his wife Karen, his high school sweetheart, and two beautiful daughters, Michelle (age 3 at the time) and Jill (age 1). He certainly would be proud of how Karen worked hard and dedicated herself to raising his girls, and he would no doubt have enjoyed his four grandchildren,

> **BY THE WAY**
>
> Mike Thompson, a high school teammate of Jerry Mattingly's, launched a 65-foot shot that found the bottom of the net during the Final Four in 1964. Later, a marker was placed on the floor denoting that it was the longest shot ever made in Butler Fieldhouse.

A FITTING TRIBUTE

Jerry Mattingly's daughter, Michelle, was very involved in the welfare of children. When she passed away at the age of 38 from breast cancer, she was working to raise funds for the pre-school at St. Theresa. In her memory, St. Theresa named the school to reflect the names of Michelle's children. The school is called Little (Lauren) Cherub (Colton) Pre-school (Peyton).

Lauren, Colton and Peyton (Michelle's children) and one-year-old (in 2008) Isabella (Jill's daughter).

Before his tragic death, Jerry was the idol of all the Mattingly boys, and Randy vividly recalls watching Jerry compete and saying, "That's what I'm going to do!" Like his older brother, Randy excelled in football, basketball and baseball at Rex Mundi, and, also like Jerry, he was All-City and All-SIAC in all three sports, earning nine varsity letters. The 6'4, 185-pounder pitched and played second and shortstop for the baseball team and guard on the basketball team, but his greatest talents were showcased on the football field.

By the time he graduated in 1969, Randy had broken most of Bob Griese's passing records, and again like his older brother, he fielded college offers in all three sports. He was recruited mostly for football by schools such as Purdue, Indiana, Illinois and Minnesota, and smaller schools like Evansville College, Murray State and Indiana State were interested in his basketball talents. His final decision was to sign with Florida State as a quarterback and to play baseball for the Seminoles in the spring.

Randy left for Tallahassee in the summer of 1969 to prepare for school and was only there a short time when he received the devastating news of Jerry's accident. Before he ever attended a class, Randy was headed back home.

After dealing with the shock of the family tragedy, Randy weighed his options and decided to stay near the family and follow in Jerry's footsteps by enrolling at Evansville College. Although football was his primary sport, Randy played basketball his freshman year at E.C. and baseball during his junior year. A testament to his natural athletic ability was an incident that led to his participation in a sport he'd never even considered before. "There was a track meet during spring football practice," Randy explained, "and we had to let them finish the event before we practiced. I was watching and kidding around and I asked if it was too late for me to throw the javelin. I had my football pants on and I took my shoulder pads off. I threw it, and I didn't win the meet, but I beat our best javelin thrower."

Randy threw the javelin the rest of his sophomore season and also during his junior year, when he threw long enough to qualify for the Nationals (185 feet). In an event he'd never even tried before and only dabbled in at Evansville College, Randy amazed everyone and, in the words of then-E.C. athletic director Jim Byers, "he threw the spear like he'd been throwing for years."

The only sport Randy played all four years was football, and he paid his dues before he reached star status. For his first two seasons, he played wide receiver while Craig Blackford finished his outstanding career with the Aces. When Randy finally took over, he led the nation in passing and was named a Division II All-American, and by the time he finished, he held several school passing records. In addition to his arm, there were other traits that were appreciated while he was with the Aces. "Randy had a lot of fortitude," said Jim Byers, "because playing quarterback at Evansville back then, you got beat up pretty good. But Randy jumped up every time. He was a tough kid."

Randy's size and strong arm made him one of the few small college QBs to catch the eye of NFL scouts. He was chosen in the fourth round by the Cleveland Browns in the 1973 draft before being sold to Chicago after training camp. After that, he was traded to Buffalo and then signed by Cincinnati after being released – all in this first year.

In addition to his skills at quarterback, Randy was also a very talented punter, and he punted everywhere he went. After he was released by Cincinnati, he was picked up by St. Louis but decided not to sign and became a free agent because the World Football League was starting.

He eventually decided that the Canadian League was his best chance at playing time and headed for Saskatchewan in 1974. His position was tenuous there because a league rule restricted each team to 16 Americans on the roster at any time to allow Canadians to play. Although he punted the whole time, he did see some action at quarterback for the Rough Riders as a backup to Ron Lancaster, who held all the CFL passing records.

Following his stint in Saskatchewan, he was traded to the Hamilton Tiger Cats and became the team's starter before finishing the '76 season with the British Columbia Lions. Following the season, he became a free agent and considered his next move. When he learned that a coaching position was available at Evansville Harrison, Randy left professional football and headed home once again. After three years serving as a Warriors assistant in football, basketball and baseball, he entered private industry and put a wrap on his career in athletics.

Unlike Randy, third son Michael didn't play ball in college but was an excellent player in high school, earning All-City honors in both basketball and baseball. Known as the most reserved of the boys, Michael was caught at the tail end of the Rex Mundi era. After playing three seasons for the Monarchs, he headed to Memorial for his senior year. He attended USI for a year to play basketball but decided to enter the workforce after a year instead. When Michael left Memorial, the youngest of the Mattinglys was still in the eighth grade, but in a few short years, he would not only make a name for himself locally, but across the state and all of America as well.

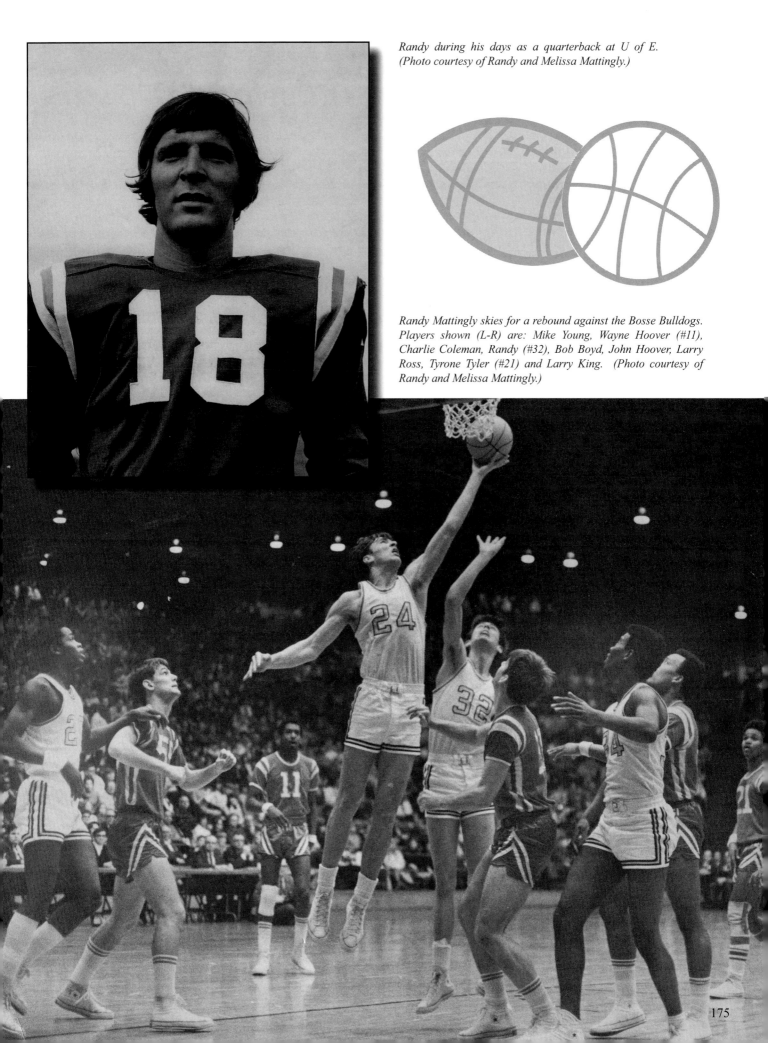

Randy during his days as a quarterback at U of E. (Photo courtesy of Randy and Melissa Mattingly.)

Randy Mattingly skies for a rebound against the Bosse Bulldogs. Players shown (L-R) are: Mike Young, Wayne Hoover (#11), Charlie Coleman, Randy (#32), Bob Boyd, John Hoover, Larry Ross, Tyrone Tyler (#21) and Larry King. (Photo courtesy of Randy and Melissa Mattingly.)

DON MATTINGLY: 'DONNIE BASEBALL'

There is no question that Don Mattingly was blessed with a wealth of God-given ability, which many local fans were privileged to witness even when Don was very young. But he also had the advantage of developing under the tutelage of three talented brothers, loving parents and an older sister who helped foster his growth as an athlete. Obviously, no one knew that little Donnie would eventually become the sweet-swinging left-handed star of the New York Yankees, the most revered franchise in sports history, but everyone could see early on that he was something special.

Donald Arthur Mattingly was born on April 20th, 1961, the fifth of 'D' and Mary Mattingly's children and the youngest of four brothers. In the early years, Donnie watched and learned as older brothers Jerry, Randy and Mike shifted effortlessly from one sport to another as the seasons changed. When Donnie became old enough, he was slowly accepted into neighborhood games, and for years he competed as a right-hander, but more out of necessity than by choice.

"We were all right-handed," said older brother Randy, "so when he played, he'd borrow our gloves. You kind of got hand-me-downs back then. We didn't find out for a long time that he was left-handed. Somewhere along the line, he got a left-handed glove and started throwing left-handed."

When Don put on his first official uniform at the North Little League field, his reputation finally expanded outside the neighborhood, and his ambidexterity was part of his mystique and even caused a bit of controversy. At one point, Don's coach, Pete Studer, tried to pitch him in two consecutive games, which was strictly forbidden to protect young arms from overuse. Studer's argument was that, since Donnie was going to pitch one game right-handed and the other left-handed, the rule shouldn't apply. Although Studer's tactic wasn't serious and was only used to point out Donnie's unusual skill, the rule was enforced. Another little league story which proves that truth is sometimes stranger than fiction also involves Coach Studer. It seems that one day, Studer, who was from the east coast and a big Yankees fan, looked at Randy Mattingly and proclaimed, "I'm going to watch this guy play in Yankee Stadium one day!" Now what are the odds that an off-the-cuff remark like that would foretell something that would actually come to pass?

Although Don's pitching was impressive, it was his hitting that caused word to spread throughout the city. "Even then, he was a consistent hitter," said brother Randy. "He was always disciplined. When he was nine years old, he had the highest batting average in the (9-to 12-year-old) league. But Dad didn't want him to know about it because he didn't want him to have that kind of success that early. Don wasn't even aware of it until later."

As word spread, crowds at the North League got a little bigger. "I was managing little league on the west side (Helfrich) when he played," recalled Ron Brand. "A guy came over and said, 'Hey, let's go over to Garvin Park and see this kid! Ron, you won't believe it when you see him!' So we went over and watched. He hit one over the fence, and after the game, do you know what he did? He stayed there to practice! When I asked a guy why, he said, 'That's all the kid wants to do is play baseball.' Even at that age people were talking about him."

It is not an exaggeration to say that Don Mattingly's success and eventual fame and wealth were directly impacted by lessons he learned while very young. In fact, he and Randy are certain that one of Don's greatest assets as a hitter was developed, literally, in his own backyard. "We played Wiffle Ball in the backyard, and we had this huge tree in right field," Randy explained. "If Don pulled the ball, he'd be making an out, so he became adept at hitting the ball into left field. Don became an opposite field hitter because that's where the opening was in our backyard.

"When you're that age, you're just subconsciously doing what works, so he had a bit of an inside-out swing and actually wasn't taught to pull the ball until he became a professional."

Don totally agrees and realizes that the little backyard on Van Dusen may have been a major contributor in his learning to excel at a facet of the game that only the great ones learn to master. "It was

Three-year-old Donnie (right) as Rex Mundi's mascot at the 1964 State Finals.
(Photo courtesy of Pat Welsh.)

Young Don Mattingly (circa 1972) accepts his trophy for the punt, pass and kick contest after winning the local, state and regional competitions before making it to the final eight in the national competition in San Francisco. (Photo courtesy of Randy and Melissa Mattingly.)

another kind of gift that formed me as a player," Don admitted. "I really believe it's what taught me to hit the ball the other way."

As Don completed his elementary schooling at St. Theresa, the high school that brothers Jerry and Randy attended, Rex Mundi, had been closed. Although it was assumed that he would attend Memorial, the issue wasn't etched in stone. "If I had had my druthers, I would have gone to Mater Dei," Don confided. "Eighty percent of the guys I went to school with were going to Mater Dei. But Mom and Dad wanted me to go to Memorial, and, looking back, it was a blessing for me."

One of the "blessings" Don alluded to was the relationship he built with Memorial baseball coach Quentin Merkel. Merkel had been following Don for a long time and boosted his confidence when he told him on the first day of school that he was going to play on the varsity as a freshman.

As were his brothers, Don was also a multi-sport athlete throughout his high school career, and he was exceptional in every sport. As a football player, he was a quarterback and defensive back who displayed toughness and leadership. Contrary to a popular myth, Don says that he did not roll to his left and throw left-handed and vice versa, although he does admit he may have used his right hand on short 'pop' passes on occasion.

On the basketball court, Don was a two-time All-City guard and averaged 15.2 points his junior year and 17.2 as a senior. His brother Randy feels strongly that, had Don not signed to play baseball, "he could have played Division I (college ball) in any of the three sports.

The Memorial baseball program experienced some of its finest moments during 'the Mattingly era', and Don left some memories that many will never forget. As a team, the Tigers won 59 straight games during Don's last two years, going undefeated and winning a State title in 1978 and remaining undefeated his senior year before falling 6-5 in ten innings to Logansport in the State championship game.

As an individual, Don's statistics were staggering, but the attribute most often mentioned has nothing to do with physical talent. "He was a dream player to coach," said Coach Merkel. "He was one of those guys, he was so talented but he worked hard. When he was in grade school, if he knew somebody was practicing on the east side, he'd ride his bike over to get swings in. He was always looking for a place to get some extra swings."

Merkel also cited another example during Don's years at Memorial. "We were getting ready to play in the '78 State championship," Merkel recalled. "We came out here (at the school) to practice in the afternoon in the heat in June. U of E had an old batting cage hung up attached to a pole and a volleyball standard, and he'd get some players together and they'd climb over the fence (at U of E) and hit for hours before practice. And he'd do that every day! It was his work ethic. He knew what he wanted was to be a major league ballplayer. Some kids you have to drill 'em and drill 'em. But you show him something one time and he had it."

In high school, Don was also an outstanding pitcher for the Tigers, finishing 10-0 with a 1.49 ERA as a senior, but it was his ability at the plate that left people in awe, especially those who watched him day after day. His eye-hand coordination was remarkable and his demeanor unflappable. At times, even Coach Merkel was amazed by what he saw as he watched the teenager in the batter's box. "He was as comfortable with two strikes as most players are with no strikes," Merkel commented. "I don't care what they threw him, he'd hit it and most times hit it hard. I have never had a player hit the ball as often or as hard as he did. He hit balls that were like missiles."

During his four-year career at Memorial, Don was ranked #1 in the country with 140 RBIs and was ranked #2 in triples (22) and third in batting average (.462). As a junior, he hit .500 and he hit safely in 27 of the team's 30 games, with only five strikeouts in 115 plate appearances.

His senior year was even more astonishing, as he finished the season at .558 with eight doubles, nine triples and six home runs. Once again, he hit safely in 27 of 30 games for the State runnerup Tigers.

Another story that has circulated about Don Mattingly over the years refers to his senior year at Memorial, but this, unlike the ambidextrous quarterback tale, is NOT a myth. In 121 plate appearances during his 1979 senior season at Memorial, Don Mattingly never struck out! In addition, to the best of anyone's recollection, he never swung and missed. This fact can't be verified, of course, but the closest I could come to finding confirmation were statements from Randy Mattingly. Randy, who got to watch a lot of Don's games in 1979, says that when he saw Don miss a ball in the sectional, his teammates laughed and razzed him mercilessly afterwards, indicating that, perhaps, it was his first swing and miss of the season. Randy also stated that he watched Don play several American Legion games and never saw him swing and miss. Either way, the thought that the feat is even a possibility is incredible.

During Don's senior season, professional scouts were a common sight at practices and games, and although he didn't have blazing speed or the strongest arm, it's not surprising that one of the top scouts told Coach Merkel that "he'll make it with his bat."

Although Don's father was the pragmatic type and felt that his son should play the percentages and go to college instead of challenging the long odds of making it in pro baseball, Don had other ideas. All he ever wanted to do was play in the major leagues. His goal was to be the #1 pick in the draft, but he quickly realized that, although he could hit, his other skills were average at best.

Don had predicted that he would probably be selected by Cincinnati or St. Louis, since those teams have a lot of scouts in this area. He had also received inquiries from the Detroit Tigers, since their Triple A team was located in Evansville. Needless to say, he was shocked when the New York Yankees selected him in the 19th round of the 1979 draft.

As he left for the minor leagues, he approached the opportunity as he always had and was just thankful that he could still play the game he loved.

"I remember going to the minor leagues and I thought that was the greatest thing ever," Don said. "You play every night and sleep during the day. It was like American Legion ball but with a lot more games. I looked at the minor leagues as a great time."

After five years in the minors, the 5'11, 185-pound Mattingly finally made it to 'the Big Show', and his work ethic and humility made him an instant favorite. Someone from the outside looking in might see Don Mattingly and New York Yankee fans as The Odd Couple, but in reality it was a match made in Heaven. "With their history, the Yankees were a perfect fit for me," Don explained. "New York's a demanding city, and it's always about performance. That was what I was all about. There's plenty of stuff to do, but there's also plenty of attention for guys like me who just want to play. If you go out and perform, that's all you have to do there.

"They're smart fans, and they are really informed. They know when you get a bunt down or move a runner over or make a good defensive play. They understood the little things I did. A lot of places wouldn't have."

The "little things" Mattingly did added up to an incredible career. In his fourteen seasons with the Yankees (from 1982-1995), he was the premier first baseman of his era. As a fielder, he won nine Gold Gloves, and in 1993, he set a record for first basemen with a .998 fielding percentage. For his career, he finished with the best fielding percentage of any first baseman in American League history (.996). In addition, he played second and third base on occasion.

As a hitter, Don compiled a lifetime average of .307 with 1,099 RBIS and 2,153 hits, fifth on the Yankees all-time list. From 1984-'89, he put together six incredible seasons, earning a spot on the American League All-Star team each year. For each of those six seasons, he hit over .300, had at least 186 hits and, except for 1988, drove in at least 100 runs. During that period, no one had more RBIs (684), and only Wade Boggs (1,269) had more hits than Don's 1,219.

In 1984, Mattingly won the American League batting title (.343), beating out teammate Dave Winfield (.340) on the last day of the season. Don's .343 average made him the first Yankee left-hander to hit over .340 since Lou Gehrig in 1937.

In 1985, Don was named the league's Most Valuable Player, ringing up a career high in home runs (35) and leading the league with 145 RBIs.

In '86, he set a Yankee record for doubles (53) and hits (238) in a season and became the first Yankee since Gehrig with three straight 200-hit seasons.

In 1987, Don homered in eight consecutive games (July 8th-18th), tying yet another AL record, and he set or tied five more major league marks, including: six grand slams (he had not hit one prior to '87); ten home runs in eight games (during his July streak); and at least one extra base hit in ten straight games (breaking Babe Ruth's 1921 record).

For his career, Don hit 131 home runs in Yankee Stadium, placing him seventh in club history. In 1991, he was named only the tenth team captain in Yankee history, and in 1992, he became just the sixth Yankee to play in at least 150 games in six different seasons. As his career wound down in the '90s, Don began to develop chronic back problems that affected his hitting, but he still led the league for three straight seasons in fielding percentage.

In 1997, two years after his retirement, the New York Yankees honored Mattingly by retiring his #23 and dedicating a plaque in his honor. The plaque reads: "A humble man of grace and dignity, a captain who led by example, proud of the pinstripe tradition and dedicated to the pursuit of excellence, a Yankee forever."

As he should be, Don is very proud to be a part of the Yankees' legacy, and throughout his years as a player, as a coach and as an alumni at old-timers games, he has rubbed shoulders with many legendary Yankees. He has become close to such stars as Mickey Mantle, Whitey Ford, Lou Piniella, Phil Rizzuto and even 'the Yankee Clipper' himself, Joe DiMaggio.

He still enjoys mystifying his old teammates the way he did us locals when he plays catch right-handed until they notice he's throwing with the 'wrong' hand, and one of his favorite memories is an annual ritual with one of the Yankees' all-time greats. "Catfish Hunter and I would have a little game every spring," Don explained. "When he wasn't playing anymore, we'd go to a back field and we'd have a five-inning game and he'd try to get me out. That was one of the things I loved doing every year."

Of all the Yankee greats, one of Don's favorites is the lovable Yogi Berra, whose attitude toward life mirrors Don's philosophy. "Yogi's the best," Don said. "He's unbelievable. He treats you the same all the time. Yogi treats everybody from the doorman to Joe DiMaggio the same. I learned early on that you learn from everybody.

"When I saw a player treat fans wrong or without respect, I thought, 'Man, you look like a jerk,' and I thought to myself, 'I don't want to look like that.' You end up forming that from your parents and the way you grew up. I don't care if it's the electrician at Yankee Stadium or whoever, I wanted to treat them all the same. I know they're hard-working and have families. I want them to look at me and say, 'Hey, that guy talks to me every day!' I just try to treat people with respect."

When Mattingly prematurely retired in 1995 due to back problems, he appreciated his past but looked forward to his future. When he was passed over in 2007 for the managing position to replace Joe Torre with the Yankees, he took a philosophical approach. Although he believes he was ready to manage and has the right temperament to succeed, he feels the snub was a blessing in disguise that allowed him to spend valuable time taking care of his family.

Don is spending the 2008 season as an assistant to Joe Torre, who switched coasts to manage the Los Angeles Dodgers. Don looks forward to increasing the workload soon and eventually managing someday, and wherever he ends up, he will take his hometown values and work ethic with him.

The man who was christened with the nickname 'Donnie Baseball' by fans and media has enjoyed his time away from the game he loves and is doing something he's always wanted to do. For the first time in a long time, he's spending quality time with his three sons, Taylor, Preston, and Jordan, and he's getting more involved with his community.

He has generously offered his time to talk to youngsters about the fundamentals of baseball and life, and he works to help others without publicity or fanfare. Three days a week, Don rises early to help his pastor, Randy Anderson, at a local soup kitchen, and he says that the gesture is as much for him as it is for others. "I'm finding out that helping somebody else makes me feel better," he explained. "I don't know if it's spiritually or biblically, but when we help others, we help ourselves. I've been involved in fundraisers and giving money here and there, but I've never really been home long enough where I could put my hands on something.

"The last time I was home for an extended period of time, my kids were young, and I really wanted them to grow up normally. I didn't want to be out in public, to be honest. Now, the boys are grown, and I want to put my hands on something, not just give money to it. I'd rather go down (to the soup kitchen) and mop the floor, just do some small part to help."

There are many who feel that Mattingly belongs in baseball's hall of fame, and his numbers compare favorably to some already inducted, but if the early voting is an indication, his odds are not good. But Don's legacy as a player and as a man goes much deeper than his image in a museum in Cooperstown. Mattingly was one of the last of a dying breed, a player who deeply loved and respected his sport. He is considered a true throwback by many, a man who could have succeeded in any era and who spent his entire career with one team.

It only takes a brief conversation with Don Mattingly to understand that he truly is a reflection of his roots. Thanks to the love and inspiration of his parents and his sister and brothers, the local boy with big dreams became one of the most respected players in the history of professional baseball.

Although Don Mattingly is best known for his baseball career, as a prep player, he was also a college prospect in basketball and football as well. (Photo courtesy of Randy and Melissa Mattingly.)

DID YOU KNOW?

When Don Mattingly changed his number from 46 to the familiar number 23, he did so in honor of his brother Jerry, who was killed tragically in a construction accident at the age of 23.

When Don Mattingly was inducted into the Indiana Baseball Hall of Fame in 2001, he became the first player to be inducted as soon as he was eligible (out of baseball for five years).

WOODIE SUBLETT WALKER: AT THE TOP OF HER GAME

On a shelf in her office stands an autographed photo of Martina Navratilova and Tracy Austin, and hanging above her desk is a plaque that reads "Tennis is my racket." These two keepsakes represent a good portion of who Woodie Sublett Walker is today.

Phyllis Woods came into this world on October 8th, 1929 in Terre Haute, Indiana. Her father was known as 'Woody', so Phyllis adopted the name and feminized it to 'Woodie'. Her involvement in tennis was almost unavoidable, as her two older brothers were both highly-ranked junior players. Her brother Jim graduated from IU in 1942 and later attended Harvard after the war. Brother Dick also graduated from IU and, like Jim, was the captain of IU's tennis team.

After graduating from Terre Haute Wiley High School, Woodie followed her brothers to IU before marrying and moving to Evansville, where she finished her schooling at Evansville College.

There were no school tennis teams when Woodie was young, so she spent her high school and college years playing local tournaments and working out with the IU men's team while she was there. She was quite an accomplished player herself and became a teammate and good friend of Evansville tennis great Louise Owen. As her involvement in teaching tennis and officiating began to consume much of her time, she slowed down as a competitor and eventually stopped competing altogether in 1980.

Woodie began officiating tennis in 1968 on the local level. At that time, no training or information was available on how to be an umpire or referee. At about the same time, she and Bill Butterfield started Evansville's first indoor tennis facility on Lynch Road. Butterfield then built the Tri-State Racquet Club (now known as the Tri-State Athletic Club), which Woodie managed for thirteen years as her officiating duties increased.

In 1970, Woodie served as a chair umpire at the U.S. Open for the first time, something she did for many more years as the Open moved from the grass at Forest Hills to the hard surface currently used at Flushing Meadow. While she was earning her stripes nationally, she was also improving the sport here at home. In the '70s, Woodie began a local officiating program even before such programs existed nationally, and her work to refine the officiating system would later be the foundation for improvements on a much larger scale.

In 1975, Woodie became the first woman president of any USTA (United States Tennis Association) district when she was named to lead the Central Indiana Tennis Association. She also served on Central Indiana's Junior Davis Cup selection committee ('77-'79) and helped organize the National Junior Tennis League in Evansville (1980). She later became the first woman certified as an international official.

In the early 1980s, Ms. Walker's outstanding work was attracting the attention of the sport's top brass, and she quickly assumed more and more responsibility on the professional level. In 1982, she served as the Assistant Chief Umpire at the U.S. Open and received a 5+ rating (out of 6) from the Grand Prix Supervisors who dubbed the Open "the best officiated Grand Slam event in the world."

The rotating crew system was a revolutionary idea that solved several problems that had existed prior to its use, and Woodie remembers how the idea came about. "It started many years ago when a friend and I were talking at La Quinta and we had to work an entire match (under the old system)," she recalled. "Your first match may have been a long five-set men's match. Then the next match (while you're off) may be a women's match where a player retires. So in 30 or 40 minutes, you're back on. You couldn't get anything to eat, and you got tired.

"And also," she continued, "if someone wasn't doing a very good job, it became an embarrassment to be taken off in the middle of the match. So we brainstormed and decided to rotate people in, which was unheard of. At the Open, one crew comes on for an hour and another crew goes off for an hour. This way, they have an hour to eat, rest their eyes and get re-hydrated in the umpires' lounge and then they go back on."

Because of Woodie's creative thinking, the improved system is now used around the world. The rotation system also enabled tourney officials to handle situations during a match. "If you're having problems on a court with a linesperson," Woodie explained, "we are in contact with the chair umpire and we can act accordingly. We can change a whole crew and no one thinks anything about it because they think it's a regular crew change."

Woodie also explained how officials on the court use signals to adjust to situations: "If a line umpire is having a bad day or a player gets on an umpire, even if the umpire is right, the good line umpires will watch the chair. Sometimes the chair will signal (spinning his or her fingers) and the baseline umpire will switch with the sideline umpire so that the player sees a different person."

In addition to developing and overseeing umpires, Woodie has been very involved in the innovations that have changed professional tennis. In 1983, she was instrumental in the introduction of computers used at the U.S. Open and in getting a program written for both the umpire's office and the referee's office. This system has now evolved into a computerized scoreboard (that we see on TV) that immediately goes out over the internet. Now that's being connected!

Woodie was also involved in the early prototypes of line-calling devices. "We knew it was coming," she said, and she was part of the group who tested and evaluated the new systems. An early system, called Accu-Call, had metal lines embedded in courts that would be used with balls laced with metal dust. It never caught on because it couldn't be used on grass and other things would set it off, like the metal tips on shoelaces.

The Cyclops was popular for many years and was reasonably reliable for calling service lines, and the new Hawk Eye was first used in 2006. Hawk Eye uses eight cameras set all over the court and doesn't read the ball itself but rather a projection of different angles that presents the image in a digital reproduction. This results in an elongated path showing where the ball landed and how it flattened out on impact. The new technology was so trusted that the officials implemented a new challenge system in 2007 to allow players to question the calls of umpires.

In 1985, Woodie Sublett Walker was the Chief Umpire at the U.S. Open and received a perfect rating of '6' from the Men's International Professional Tennis Council, and it has been that quest for perfection that has propelled her to where she is today. She has sat as the chair umpire at Wimbledon and the French Open and has chaired the finals of three U.S. Opens, overseeing such greats as John McEnroe, Ivan Lendl, Martina Navratilova, Tracy Austin, Billie Jean King and Chris Evert.

In 1995, Woodie received the McGovern Award from the USTA, the highest award given to a chair or line umpire who has given a lifetime of dedication, service and expertise to tennis officiating. Today, she assists Rich Kaufman in every facet of officiating at every U.S. Open.

In 1996, Woodie worked the Olympic Games in Atlanta as the Chief of Officials and has served her country and her sport in countless other ways. She is known and respected by tennis players and fans all over the world, and she has earned that respect by being open to new ideas and dedicated to the purity of the sport. She is a pioneer who has overseen drastic changes in tennis, and she has not shied away from decisions made under extreme scrutiny. Even today, as she nears the age of eighty, she travels 35 weeks a year to do her job. Whether she's been in the chair or behind the scenes, Woodie Sublett Walker has always been at the top of her game.

Minnesota Fats was a frequent visitor to Evansville and loved to play to a crowd. Fats bought all of his Cadillacs from George Wright and often visited George's home to play pool. Fats is shown here with Mr. Wright (left) and Hubert 'Daddy Warbucks' Cokes, a local oil man and gambler. (Photo courtesy of George A. Wright.)

BOB WINCHELL: BRAINS AND BRAWN

Bob Winchell was an athlete who used both his mind and his physique to achieve success in his chosen sports. With his extraordinary size, 6'4", 235 pounds, he was a load to handle on the basketball court and a dominant force in the shot put circle.

As a basketball player, Winchell was admittedly a supporting role player on one of the better teams in the state. The Harrison teams of the late '60s were extremely talented but always seemed to stumble at tourney time. When North won the State title in 1967, it was Harrison and Bosse that were touted as the most likely to make a long run in the tournament. Harrison won the SIAC with a starting lineup who all became Division I athletes, a very rare accomplishment in any team sport.

Winchell was an enforcer under the basket for Harrison who later took his talents to IU and became a track star. Greg Fenner, a 6'5" forward, went to Purdue and started for the football team. Harrison guard Terry Wedgewood also left for West Lafayette and led the Big Ten in hitting with the Boilermakers' baseball team. Center Greg Nelson and talented guard and all-around athlete Vaughn Wedeking played basketball for Jacksonville on teams that featured future ABA and NBA star Artis Gilmore. In 1971, Nelson and Wedeking were part of the Jacksonville team that advanced to the national championship game before losing to UCLA, ending the Dolphins' season with a 27-2 record.

Although Winchell played basketball, baseball and football at Harrison, he is best known for his ability in the shot put ring. His physicality gave him a strong foundation in the event, but it was his mental approach that enabled him to advance to the elite level. His high school coach, Charlie Siesky, remembers how Bob approached his event from an intellectual standpoint.

"Bob Winchell knew more about the shot put than anybody around," Siesky said. "And that included me as a coach. He'd come over to me and say, 'Coach, I'm not getting the distance I want. I think my angle (of the elbow) is 76 degrees, and I think it should be 78.' He would tell me what to look for, and then I'd try to help."

As a sophomore and junior, Bob didn't medal at the State meet, but his senior year, he was seeded #1 going into the final weekend. He had thrown 61 feet, 5 ¾ inches during the SIAC meet for a personal best and was psyched for the State Finals. It wouldn't be easy however, as the event came to a dramatic conclusion. Going into his final throw, Winchell was trailing a thrower from Ft. Wayne South. According to Charlie Siesky, Bob was thinking too much and was suffering from 'paralysis by analysis'.

Although Siesky couldn't help with Bob's technique, he decided to take a psychological approach. "I gave the best advice I ever gave," Siesky explained. "I said, 'Bob, forget all that stuff and just throw the thing.'" The words of wisdom worked, as Winchell launched a throw of 61' 1 ¼ inches for his first State championship.

Following his win, Bob left for Bloomington to pursue his education and his track career, and he quickly learned that it took more than precise angles to compete on the college level. The throwers he was facing were behemoths.

"In high school, you can throw it from a PT boat (a small frame)," he explained metaphorically, "but in college (with a 16-pound shot), you have to throw it from a battleship. So I got bigger and stronger; I went from 235 pounds to 290. I was benching over 300 pounds and squatting close to 600."

Although Bob knows that the added strength and size were important, he also believes that his experiences at Harrison helped prepare him for major college athletics. "I still believe to this day that the thing that helped me in the shot put was playing basketball, because you need quickness across the circle."

Whatever the reasons, Winchell excelled at IU, winning four Big Ten championships (both indoor and outdoor in 1970 and '71) and breaking conference records along the way. His IU record of 59' 3 ½ inches stood for over ten years. He also threw the discus at IU, with his best throw of 178 feet coming close to the conference record.

While in college, Bob abandoned his Pre-Dental curriculum and pursued a career as a chiropractor. Even today, he stays involved in athletics. Although he admits that he's "too fat" and can't generate speed like he used to, he still throws the shot in the national Senior Games competition and was the winner in Baton Rouge in 2001. His chiropractic practice has also sponsored several softball teams over the years in different age groups and divisions, and there have been times when Bob has coached 35+, 40+, 45+ and 50+ teams at the same time. His efforts as a player, coach and sponsor have resulted in nearly thirty state titles and four national championships.

For over forty years, whether with his brain or his brawn, Bob Winchell has proven that, one way or the other, he will always find a way to get the job done.

(Photo courtesy of Indiana University, Sports Information.)

ALL IN THE FAMILY

Bob Winchell's father finished second and third in the shot put at the State meets in 1922 and '23, and his daughter, Cara, threw the shot for Illinois State.

Winchell unleashes the shot in 1966. (Photo from The Legend, the Harrison High School yearbook.)

A RARE FEAT

Only four Evansville schools have had two different individuals win State track championships in the same year. Shown in the photo are North's Tad Grafton (left), Coach Jon Siau and David Williams. The four duos to achieve the distinction are:

- Harrison, 1967 (Bob Winchell – shot put and Vaughn Wedeking – 440-yd. dash)
- Bosse, 1977 (Lauretta Wills – long jump and Cassandra Lander – high jump)
- North, 1981 (Tad Grafton – pole vault and David Williams – 3200-meter run)
- Reitz, 1997 (Craig Schwartz – 400-meter run and Tyrone Browning – 800-meter run)

IHSAA STATE CHAMPIONS: GIRLS TRACK

Individual(s)	School	Year	Event	Time/Height/Distance
Deatris Cheaney	Bosse	1998	100m hurdles	14.45
Krista Fentress, Natasha Sutton, Lynnie Williams, Lauretta Wells	Bosse	1975	440-yd. relay	50.4
Brenda Weidenbenner	Jasper	1974	long jump	17- 6_
Lauretta Wells	Bosse	1977	long jump	19- 0
Cindy Farrand	Castle	1976	high jump	5- 7
Cassandra Lander	Bosse	1977	high jump	5- 6_
Cassandra Lander	Bosse	1978	high jump	5- 7
Amy Ward	Boonville	1986	high jump	5- 8
Elizabeth Reid	Gibson Southern	1993	high jump	5- 6
Kayla Tucker	Harrison	2004	high jump	5- 8
Kayla Tucker	Reitz	2005	high jump	5- 8
Alisa Raymond	Castle	1992	shot put	44- 1
Alisa Raymond	Castle	1993	shot put	46- 5
Alisa Raymond	Castle	1994	shot put	44- 10_
Kathryn Smith	Vincennes Rivet	1985	discus	142- 7
Alisa Raymond	Castle	1993	discus	138- 1

Grant Glackman

Steve Clutter

SCORE ONE FOR THE UNDERDOGS

Although little Tecumseh High School didn't have two track State champions in the same year, what the school accomplished in 1972 was just as impressive. From the little school with less than 250 students, two athletes broke State records in the same year.

Steve Clutter broke the long jump record with a leap of 24' 1½" but held it for only a few minutes before Harold Vaughn of Lafayette Jeff broke Steve's record with a leap of 24' 3½" to take the title of State champion away from Clutter. Steve's teammate, Grant Glackman, did even better, capturing the State pole vaulting championship with a State record vault of 15' 7¾". In addition, Grant's leap gave him the top height in the country at the time for high school vaulters. Glackman later vaulted at the University of Alabama and twice placed second in the SEC. During his college years, he improved his height to over 17 feet.

IHSAA STATE CHAMPIONS: BOYS TRACK

Team	Year		
Washington	1913-1914		
Washington	1914-1915		

* State Meet Record

Individual(s)	School	Year	Event	Time/Height/Distance
Mack Jacobs	Bosse	1994	200m dash	21.67
Victor Brown	Reitz	1983	400m dash	47.61
Tracy Smith	Bosse	1995	400m dash	47.62
Chad Schwartz	Reitz	1997	400m dash	48.5
Tyrone Browning	Reitz	1997	800m run	1:54.73
Adam Renfro	Central	1980	3200m run	9:05.29
David Williams	North	1981	3200m run	9:08.78
Jim Kaiser	Mater Dei	1987	3200m run	9:04.52
Bryce Brown	Harrison	2005	110m hurdles	13.83
Bryce Brown	Harrison	2007	110m hurdles	13.69
Bryce Brown	Harrison	2005	300m hurdles	* 36.34
Bryce Brown	Harrison	2006	300m hurdles	36.56
Bryce Brown	Harrison	2007	300m hurdles	* 36.26
Schultz	Evansville H.S.	1916	100-yd. dash	10.4
Hale	Central	1924	100-yd. dash	10.1
Curtis Smith	Lincoln	1955	220-yd. dash	21.9
Cornell Garrett	North	1976	220-yd. dash	21.3
Heuring	Petersbug	1915	440-yd. dash	53.8
Wampler	Vincennes	1923	440-yd. dash	53.3
Calvin Martin	Lincoln	1943	440-yd. dash	50.6
Calvin Martin	Lincoln	1944	440-yd. dash	50.2
Bill Rommel	Reitz	1946	440-yd. dash	50.6
Malcolm Cook	Reitz	1949	440-yd. dash	50.3
Vaughn Wedeking	Harrison	1967	440-yd. dash	48.4

IHSAA STATE CHAMPIONS: BOYS TRACK (CONT.)

*State Meet Record

Individual(s)	School	Year	Event	Time/Height/Distance
Duckwall	Vincennes	1908	880-yd. run	2:08.2
John Heffernan	Washington	1912	880-yd. run	2:10.6
Richard Ballou	Washington	1914	880-yd. run	2:12.5
Hedge	Boonville	1923	880-yd. run	2:00.3
John Alexander	Reitz	1924	880-yd. run	2:05.4
Don Sellers	Harrison	1973	880-yd. run	1:53.2
Tom Martin	Memorial	1977	880-yd. run	1:50.9
Alexander	Reitz	1924	mile run	4:41.7
Robert Eggleston	Washington	1948	mile run	4:31.5
Hoyt Ingraham	Washington	1915	120-yd. hurdles	17.6
McGuire	Central	1929	120-yd. hurdles	17.1
Ronnie Snodgrass	Bosse	1959	120-yd. hurdles	14.6
Hoyt Inraham	Washington	1915	200-yd. hurdles	27.8
Whalen King	Princeton	1943	200-yd. hurdles	23.5
Leon Martin	Vincennes Lincoln	1970	high jump	6'6"
Ron Jones	Mt. Vernon	1980	high jump	* 7-1
Chris Walker	Gibson Southern	1984	high jump	6-10
Donald Ashby	Central	1960	long jump	21-7
Otha Thomas	Central	1961	long jump	23-3
Jim Thomas	North	1964	long jump	23-2
Steve Cobb	Vincennes Lincoln	1971	long jump	22-9
Richard Carter	Petersbug	1949	pole vault	12-8
Richard Carter	Petersbug	1950	pole vault	12-3
Grant Glackman	Tecumseh	1973	pole vault	15-7
Tad Grafton	North	1981	pole vault	14-9
Mark Buse	Southridge	1989	pole vault	15-9
Mark Buse	Southridge	1990	pole vault	16-0
Mark Buse	Southridge	1991	pole vault	15-6
Ronnie Smith	Bosse	1960	shot put	55-5
Gene Lockyear	Bosse	1963	shot put	59-4
Bob Winchell	Harrison	1967	shot put	61-1
Marlon Flemming	Reitz	1975	shot put	61-9
Scott Ambrose	Mt. Vernon	1989	shot put	61-0
{ Darrell Bacon, Norman Jones, Prince Coleman, Mack Jacobs	Bosse	1994	400m relay	42.15
{ Marcus Ivy, Ronald Riffert, Anthony Thomas, Eugene Tramill	Bosse	1991	1600m relay	3:18.08
{ Anthony Thomas, George Madison, Tracy Smith, Mack Jacobs	Bosse	1993	1600m relay	3:16.06
{ Robert Downey, Robert Swords, George Mattingly, George Flick	Washington	1917	mile relay	3:38.2

In 1980, Mt. Vernon's Ron Jones soared over the high jump bar at 7'-1¼" at the State meet, a record that has not been equaled since.

SCOTT STUDWELL: 'LITTLE' MAN MADE IT BIG

When John Scott Studwell entered Harrison High School in 1968, no one could have envisioned how the scrawny 5'4", 110-pound freshman would one day punish NFL running backs as a linebacker for the Minnesota Vikings. Scott watched from the sideline for most of the freshman football season and was disappointed when he wasn't chosen for the basketball team. But it wouldn't take long for Mother Nature to step in and for the 'little' man to make a big impact on the local sports scene.

In just over a year, Scott's growth hormones kicked in and he was transformed into a 5'10", 165-pound sophomore who was determined to make the most of his new frame. His mother, Barbara, understood Scott's pain during his freshman year but was confident genetics were on his side. "When he was a little older than a newborn, our pediatrician said, 'I've never seen such muscle tone on a baby this age,'" his mother recalled.

Barbara also recalled a time when she was puzzled when Scott received an 'F' in "motor control" when he was in kindergarten at Washington Grade School. "I went to the school," Barbara explained, "because here's a kid who can do anything and everything at the age of five. His teacher told me he couldn't *skip*. So we came home and skipped up and down Brookside Drive one afternoon until we conquered it."

The kindergarten experience was an example of the determination Scott would display repeatedly as he grew up in a sports-minded family. Jim Studwell, Scott's father, was a four-sport athlete in Glen Ridge, New Jersey, and was inducted into the school's athletic hall of fame. Barbara, Jim's high school sweetheart, played basketball and field hockey and ran track.

Scott's oldest sister, Andy, fell in love with horses and rode competitively, and his youngest sister, Sally, ran track at Bosse. But Scott's biggest influence growing up was his older brother, Bill. Scott watched as Bill ran track and played basketball and football at Harrison. As an All-State player in football, Bill was recruited by Jim Byers to play at the University of Evansville, where he caught passes from U of E hall of famer Randy Mattingly.

When Scott experienced his growth spurt during his first two years of high school, he used the inspiration from his brother and decided to focus on football and work on pumping himself up in the weight room.

Looking back, Scott takes a philosophical approach to his transformation. "I was obviously the runt of the family up to that point," he said from his office in Minnesota. "It wasn't any big deal; it's just the way it was. I started lifting weights about the same time I started to grow. I had the sand plates (weights) at home, and we had access to the YMCA, so I would go down there. Then I started working out at The Pit, and I got significantly stronger. Those guys were die-hards."

As Scott filled out, his strength and physique were awe-inspiring to all who observed him. Long-time Harrison coach Mitch Marsch recalled an incident in the school's gym that amazes him to this day. "Scott was coming through the gym and we were practicing track indoors," Marsch explained. "The shot putters were practicing with the indoor shot, and Scott picked it up and literally threw it farther than anybody on the team. He threw it nearly fifty feet. We had markings on the floor."

As Scott sculpted his body into what Mitch Marsch described as "Tarzan-like," he continued to grow. Marsch believes that those early days as an under-sized bench-warmer were the key to Studwell's success. "He was the best case

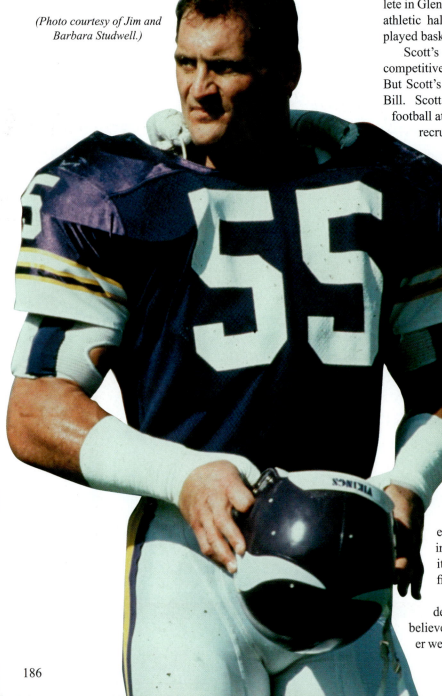

(Photo courtesy of Jim and Barbara Studwell.)

of a 'little guy grows up' that I've ever seen," said Marsch, who was an assistant at Harrison during Studwell's career, "because he never forgot that, at one time, he was little, so he took it out on people (opposing runners)."

When told of Marsch's words, Scott downplayed the theory and pointed to another motivation. "I don't know if I ever had an actual complex," he concluded, "but there was some sibling rivalry. My brother was a very good athlete and a multi-sport participant. I think that competition helped me want to work and try to get better."

By this time, Scott had been nicknamed 'Stud' by his teammates, and he had focused his thoughts on becoming the best football player he could be. He didn't see significant playing time until his junior year, but by his senior year, he was a 6'2", 205-pound physical specimen who was chosen for the North-South All-Star game and was drawing the attention of major college programs. Scott and his parents were approached by schools like Louisville, Kentucky and even some Ivy League schools, but their list was quickly narrowed down to a few from the Big Ten.

When all was said and done, Scott chose Illinois, and when he arrived on the Illinois campus, he was doing several bench press reps at 315 pounds. Although he was recruited as a linebacker, the Illinois coaching staff often experimented with the freshmen by using them at alternate positions on offense and defense. Scott worked out at linebacker and tight end and saw some minimal playing time on special teams.

During Scott's sophomore year, the coaches continued to tinker with his position. "They attempted to move me to defensive end during the spring," Scott recalled, "and I kind of 'grew' into a defensive tackle. I probably got as heavy as 270, which was too heavy. And it wasn't a 'good' 270. So I played defensive tackle just that one year."

The next season, Scott injured his knee and was red-shirted. "I sat out and lost all the weight," Scott said. "They moved me back to linebacker, and the rest is history. So the injury was definitely a blessing in disguise for me."

Studwell finished his career at Illinois with 342 tackles, second only to the legendary Dick Butkus. He was named to the All-Big Ten first team, was a second team All-American selection in 1976, and was later named to the University of Illinois All-Century team.

After graduating, Scott was selected by the Minnesota Vikings in the seventh round of the 1977 draft, signing for $22,000 and a $5,000 bonus. During a 14-year career with the Vikings, he played against some of the greatest players to ever put on pads. When asked to name a few, the first to be cited was 'The Sweet One' himself. "I played against Walter Payton for nine or ten years," Scott said. "He had his 'A' game every time he stepped on the field.

"Barry Sanders was probably the most dangerous back I ever played against, and Earl Campbell was probably the most physical. I also played against the great Steeler teams early in my career, with Franco Harris, Mike Webster and Terry Bradshaw. My rookie year, we even played against Czonka and Griese and those guys (the great Miami Dolphin teams)."

During his career, Studwell showed his durability by being one of only five Vikings to play in over 200 games. He also played in twelve playoff games and two NFC Championship games ('77 and '87), and as a 6'2", 228-pound middle linebacker, he was selected to the Pro Bowl in 1987 and '88.

Scott gives his baby daughter a ride while standing next to his wife Jenny after a Vikings training camp session. (Photo courtesy of Jim and Barbara Studwell.)

Over fourteen seasons, Scott recovered fifteen fumbles and intercepted eleven passes. He holds Viking records for career tackles with 1,981 (of which an amazing 1,308 were solo tackles), and tackles in a season (230) and game (24 against Detroit in 1985). He was named to the 25th and 40th Anniversary All-Viking teams and holds the NFL record for most tackles by a player with one organization.

Since his retirement in 1990, Scott Studwell and his wife Jenny have stayed in Minnesota to raise their son and two daughters. The Vikings thought so highly of Scott that he is still with their organization and will likely stay there until his second retirement. He is currently serving as the team's Director of College Scouting and continues to bleed Viking purple. "This has been an absolute labor of love for about thirty years," he stated. "I've been very fortunate not only to play here but to stay here in the front office. The commitment on both sides has been tremendous."

Scott Studwell is living proof of what can be accomplished through hard work and a positive attitude. He walked into Harrison High School as a 110-pound weakling and he walked out a 'Stud'.

LOVE AT FIRST SIGHT

Scott Studwell met his future wife, Jenny, while she was "slinging drinks" in a hangout called The Rusty Scupper.

On a lark, Scott Studwell entered the NFL arm wrestling competition that was held in Las Vegas and shown on ESPN. His Viking teammate, Jim Hough, was entered as a heavyweight, and Scott entered as a lightweight. Scott won the lightweight division, and when Hough injured his arm, Scott took his place and also won the heavyweight division, beating Eddie White and Joe Klecko twice. It was the first time Studwell had ever arm wrestled.

MARLON FLEMMING: A MOUNTAIN OF A MAN

Marlon Preston Flemming was born November 7th, 1956, and even then, at 13 pounds, he was bigger than the kid next to him.

The son of William Flemming and Leola Rogers McGee, Marlon would always play quarterback on the sandlot because he had the strongest arm, but as a student at Wheeler Grade School, there were no sports that were appropriate for a boy his size. His job, he said, was to rake the sand pits at track meets.

As a freshman at Reitz, Marlon was excited to play on the freshman football team, but he got frustrated when he found himself on the sidelines. He described himself as a "practice participator," and he could never understand why, with his size (5'11 and 250 pounds) and speed (he ran a 5.7 in the 40-yard sprint), he could not get playing time. Marlon decided that if he was going to watch the game, he would quit the team and do it from the stands.

Fortunately, Marlon was able to actually participate as a member of the school's track team as a freshman. Although he was an average discus thrower, he quickly showed great potential in the shot put. As a freshman, Marlon threw around 35 feet, and he improved to 45 feet as a sophomore. But it was his junior year that would propel Marlon Flemming toward his status as a 'local legend'.

After some coaxing from head coach Bob Padgett, the gentle giant decided to give football another try. Marlon was only a part-time football player for Coach Padgett his junior year, but his shot put distance improved another ten feet, qualifying him for the State meet with a throw of 55'10".

By the time his senior year arrived, Flemming had grown to a 6'1, 292-pounder and was set to stake his claim to fame in both sports. As a two-way starter and special teams player on the football team, he was named All-City, All-Conference, All-State and prep All-American. As a shot putter, Marlon threw his personal best in the Evansville Sectional with a heave of 65'8", and at the State meet, his toss of 61'9" made him a State champion.

With his size and athleticism (he had enormous hands and could dunk a basketball), Marlon was recruited to play football at Indiana University. For three years, he played middle guard and defensive tackle before being converted to a right offensive tackle, but an injury prevented him from completing his four years of football at IU.

Today, Marlon Flemming spends a lot of time as a volunteer coach helping area throwers improve their performance. With his wife, Marlene, he has raised two children and dotes on his granddaughter, Arissa. From being a youngster who didn't fit in because of his size, Marlon Flemming used his strength and tenacity to become a standout on the football field and to separate himself from the competition in the shot put circle. For track fans who attend the Evansville Sectional and check the program to look for record holders, they will see Marlon's record still there after 33 years, the longest-standing record of them all.

ANDY BENES: FROM #3 TO #1

If you're looking for a story about a high school phenom with can't-miss potential, you can stop reading right here. Andy Benes (pronounced BEH * nuss) was an extraordinary athlete as a prepster, but no one, including Andy, could have foreseen that when he graduated from Central High School in 1985, the lanky youngster would one day be the top pick in the major league draft just three short years later.

Andy entered Central as a 5'11, 130-pound freshman and started his annual sports regimen of football, basketball and baseball. Although his skills were solid, he made the normal progression in all three sports: freshman ball, then junior varsity as a sophomore, then varsity for the last two years. His potential as an exceptional all-around athlete truly blossomed after he hit a growth spurt between his sophomore and junior years and shot up to 6'4 and 190 pounds.

As a football player, Andy broke virtually every school record, and most fans still believe that Benes is one of the top three quarterbacks in the school's history.

Fans also say that Andy's best sport in high school might have been basketball, and Andy agrees. "People who don't know a lot about me assume that I was really good at baseball in high school," Benes said from his home near St. Louis. "I was probably best in basketball, and I loved playing basketball."

On the court, Andy was more of a role player his junior year, with an average of between eight and ten in all three major offensive stats, points, rebounds and assists. During his senior year, after growing to 6'5 and 200 pounds, Benes became a true scoring threat, averaging 18+ points per game. His most memorable game was in the sectional final against Bosse. Central and Bosse were the favorites in '85 and drew each other in the first round. Andy woefully recalls missing a free throw that would have won the game in regulation, although he did come back to hit the shot that sent the game into double overtime. Central ended up losing to Bosse, but Andy finished the evening with 42 points.

As a baseball player at Central, Andy was a pitcher and shortstop and says that he was a good hitter but not great. Looking back, after knowing where baseball took Andy, one would assume that he was a dominant pitcher as a prepster, but the truth is, he wasn't even #1 *on his own team*. In fact, he wasn't even #2. "In 1985, Andy was our third pitcher," said retired Central baseball coach Paul Gries. "I had three pitchers that could have gone to the major leagues if they had wanted to. John Mills was our left-handed ace. He struck out 126 batters in ten games. Chris Glaser was second, and he also played shortstop and first base."

"Andy was so sharp, and still is today," Gries continued. "His intelligence was above most others. He may not have thrown the hardest, but he was a pitcher, not a thrower. I take a lot of kidding today saying that's how smart I was – Andy Benes was my third pitcher."

During his senior year, Andy received a lot of interest from smaller schools to play all three sports, and he had a baseball offer from Georgia State. He chose, however, to stay home and play baseball for Jim Brownlee's Evansville Aces. It wasn't until later that Andy found out why Brownlee wanted him to come to U of E. "Jim Brownlee told me, 'I decided I wanted you to pitch for me after I refereed a high school football game you played in.' Andy explained. "I had gotten knocked out in the first half and I came back and played, and he (Brownlee) said he knew after watching me get knocked down several times and get back up, that he wanted me there."

Andy's scholarship at U of E was mostly football and academic, and he became the only Aces athlete of his decade to play football, baseball and basketball at the school. He was recruited by Evansville as a pitcher and quarterback, but because the Aces had Randy Hobson at QB, Andy played tight end. Benes was also asked to join the basketball team during his freshman year when injuries left first-year coach Jim Crews with less than ten players. Andy worked out with the team and played in a couple of games and then continued his busy freshman year with the baseball team.

On the mound, Benes had a mediocre freshman season, going 4-6 with a 5.92 ERA and 47 strikeouts in 73 innings. Prior to his sophomore year, he decided to forgo football to concentrate on baseball and his studies as a Pre-Med major. But when Hobson broke his ankle before the football season, Dave Moore, the Aces football coach, approached Andy about reconsidering his decision.

"That was actually my first business negotiation," Andy pointed out, "because I said, 'No Way!' And then they said, 'We'll pick up your room and board,' and I said, 'And my books?' I figured for around $4,000 that I was paying for room and board, it was a great deal for my parents."

Andy Benes represented his country as a member of the 1988 U.S. Olympic team. (Photo courtesy of the University of Evansville, Sports Information.)

Andy returned to the gridiron and quarterbacked five games until Hobson's return, resulting in Andy moving back to tight end. He finished the season as the team's fifth-leading receiver and passed for 1,400 yards.

In the spring of 1987, Benes began his baseball season and also got married in March. His wife, the former Jennie Byers, is the daughter of Jean and Phil Byers and the granddaughter of legendary Reitz coach Herman Byers. Jennie and Andy had dated while in high school, and Jennie was an excellent athlete herself, playing the #1 spot on the golf team and #2 singles and #1 doubles on the tennis team.

Andy's sophomore baseball season at U of E was respectable, as he went 7-5 with 85 strikeouts in 84.1 innings and finished with a 4.38 ERA. After the season, Benes decided to spend the summer pitching for Clarinda, Iowa in the Jayhawk League. As the summer season progressed, an amazing transformation took place. Andy Benes had left Evansville as Clark Kent, but he would return as Superman.

With his new bride as his inspiration, Andy's body filled out even more as he added muscle. By the end of his sophomore season at U of E, Andy had thrown a respectable 86-88 miles per hour, but by the time he returned from Iowa, he was at 90+ mph on the slower-reading radar gun, the equivalent of 100 mph on the guns used today.

Beaming with a new-found confidence, Benes launched a junior year that would take him from a player who wasn't even a major league prospect to the hottest commodity in the country. By the time Andy's junior season rolled around, he was attracting a lot of attention, with up to twenty major league teams attending the games he pitched. When asked how he handled the sudden attention, he confided that he was glad he wasn't a 'diaper dandy' in high school like Don Mattingly or Scott Rolen. "For me, it was a lot of fun," Benes recalled, "because it was only for a short time. I'm glad I didn't have to make that choice out of high school. I know how valuable the college experience was for me."

With the baseball world watching, the new and improved Andy Benes finished the season with a 16-3 record, recording 188 strikeouts in only 146 innings while giving up only 36 walks. In one year, his ERA dropped nearly three runs, from 4.38 to 1.42. For his efforts, Andy was chosen amateur baseball's Pitcher of the Year by *Baseball America*, and he led the Aces to a school record 44 wins. As an individual, he set U of E records with seven shutouts and three one-hitters and set strikeout records for a career (312), season (180), and game (21 against North Carolina-Wilmington). Andy also led the Aces to the NCAA Tourney, and while there, he put on a performance that elevated him from being just a top prospect to being The Man. On May 26th, in the 1988 NCAA West Regional, Andy shut out the best team in the land, the #1- ranked Arizona State Sun Devils. Paul Gries remembers the day well and the impact it had on him as an Evansville native and Benes' high school coach. "I was listening on the radio," Gries said, "and Andy pitches a great game and (Mater Dei grad) Rob Maurer hits the home run (for the Aces) and they win 1-0. That's what made Andy the #1 pick in the draft."

Before he would move on to the big leagues, however, Andy had one more incredible memory to make. He recalled a moment before his junior season when he heard guys talking about trying out for the Olympic team and thinking, "That's really cool!" After traveling to Millington, Tennessee to try out, Andy was chosen to represent his country. Joining him, among others, were: Jim Abbott, the pitcher from the University of Michigan who only had one hand but went on to a major league career; Ben McDonald, who pitched in the majors with Baltimore and Milwaukee; and future major leaguers Tino Martinez (first base), Robin Ventura (third) and Ed Sprague (catcher).

Andy won a game during the qualifying round but did not get to pitch at the Olympics in Seoul, Korea, not even in relief, because McDonald won with a complete game in the semis and Abbott beat Japan in the finals with another complete game. Although baseball was only a demonstration sport in '88 (It would become an official event in '92), Andy has a medal that is very similar to the 'official' medals. By the time he finished his fantastic spring and summer, Andy had already decided that he would forgo his senior year and take his shot at pro ball.

Knowing that the Padres had shown a lot of interest in him and that they held the #1 spot in the draft order, Andy wasn't shocked when he was chosen as the first overall pick in the 1988 major league draft. To begin the 1989 season, he was fast-tracked to the parent club because his experience in the Olympics was the equivalent of playing in the minors. After four months at AA Wichita and only one month at AAA Las Vegas, Andy joined the parent club in San Diego, where he started ten games at the end of the season.

Andy as a senior quarterback at Central. (Photo courtesy of the Central High School yearbook.)

For the next thirteen years, Benes enjoyed a fantastic major league career. After his seventh season in San Diego, Andy spent five seasons in St. Louis ('96-'97 & '00-'02), two in Arizona ('98-'99) and some time in Seattle ('95). Over his fourteen-year career, Benes appeared in 404 games and had a 155-139 record with a 3.97 ERA. In 1993, Andy represented the National League in the all-star game, and the following year he led the majors in strikeouts with 189. In 1998, he was selected by the Arizona Diamondbacks in the expansion draft and received the honor of starting the first game and throwing the first pitch in D-backs history.

Andy's greatest major league memories, however, are of people and events that relate to his family and his childhood home. Neither of Andy's younger brothers, Alan or Adam, got to play high school ball in Evansville because a job opportunity for their father took them away just before Alan was to enter high school. But both Alan and Adam did make it to the minor leagues, and Alan even spent some time with the Cubs, Cardinals and Rangers at the major league level. At one point in their careers, the three boys were all in the Cardinals organization, making them teammates.

One of Andy's fondest memories took place on September 6th, 2002 at Busch Stadium. For only the seventh time in major league history, two brothers (Andy and Alan) were to square off as opposing pitchers when Andy's Cardinals hosted Alan's Chicago Cubs. The media hyped the game, and the boys' parents, Chuck and Karen, drove from Des Moines, Iowa to witness the event. To complete the 'family affair', Andy's son Drew was the Cardinals' batboy.

Andy's emotions about the brother vs. brother matchup are mixed because of the way the drama played out. Andy, who was in the midst of a hot streak, threw a complete game, giving up a two-run homer in the ninth inning to lose the shutout. Alan, on the other hand, had a day he would rather forget. The Cubs lost to St. Louis 11-2, and all eleven of the Cardinals' runs were scored in the third inning. Andy led off the inning with a broken bat single to left, and when he came to the plate later in the inning, the Cards were up 5-0 and his thoughts were conflicted.

"I was just trying to hit a ground ball and get the inning over with, because I felt so bad for Alan," Andy revealed. "He wasn't pitching bad at all. I just kind of threw my bat at the first pitch. It just dumped over the second baseman's head and it knocked Alan out of the game." (The Cubs ended up scoring six more runs against relievers.)

"We don't talk about that," Andy continued, "but we do talk about the fact that it was the last time two brothers have started against each other in the big leagues."

Andy would pitch four more games in 2002, his last season, and he only gave up one run in all four games combined. Amazingly, he didn't receive a win for any of them due to a lack of run support. Ironically, since he retired the following season because of chronic back problems, the win against the Cubs was his last, giving it special meaning. "I think its pretty cool," Andy said, "that my last win was against my younger brother, my all-time favorite teammate."

Memories of Andy's second unforgettable experience involved another local boy, Don Mattingly, and Andy says that recounting the moment still makes the hair on his neck stand up. "I was pitching in Yankee Stadium for the Mariners in the second game of the Division Championship series," Andy recalled. "We were ahead two runs and I gave up a home run to Ruben Sierra. Donnie (Mattingly) was up next, and he hit a changeup over the right-center field fence, and I'll never forget it. It was so loud and the fans started chanting "DON-NIE BASE-BALL," and the game stopped for like ten minutes.

"It was just one of those moments," Andy continued. "Just to see the admiration and respect of fans who are really tough. I was in the middle of my career, and it was amazing to see how much they loved him. Even though I wasn't excited about the home run, it was really neat."

Andy's career is impressive by any standards, and he can be proud and satisfied as he looks back. Over the years, he played a role in some amazing twists of fate and coincidence. His last major league victory was won against his brother, a statistical longshot, for certain. When Don Mattingly hit the home run against Andy in the playoffs, it was the last home run of Mattingly's career, making Andy Benes the answer to a baseball trivia question. It is also remarkable that when Andy struck out his last batter in 2002, the crowd gave him a standing ovation as the Busch Stadium jumbotron flashed the number. His final strikeout had given him exactly 2,000 for his career.

Today, Andy Benes is working to earn his college degree at St. Louis University, saying, "I'm finishing what I started back in 1985." The Business and Communications degree he will earn is important to him for two reasons: because he wants his kids to see him finish and because he had promised his mother when he signed to play major league baseball.

In addition to his schooling, Andy stays busy with Bible study groups and working with a new start-up bank that involves a group of Christian businessmen. He does anti-drug campaigns for the Cardinals and does a Saturday morning TV show on Fox Sports Net. His co-host is Fredbird, the Cardinals' mascot, and the show, called *Cardinals Crew*, is designed to talk to kids about important things like staying fit and making good decisions. As he describes his new role, he takes a light-hearted approach to his career path. "I tell the kids all the time that I was teammates with Albert Pujols, Jim Edmonds and Scott Rolen," Andy said, "and now I hang out with Fredbird. I'm learning what humility is."

Although Andy is very busy, it is not at the expense of his children. He has coached or is helping to coach each of them as they compete as youngsters. His daughters, Brynn and Bailey, like volleyball and basketball. His oldest son, Drew, was drafted in the 47th round by the Cincinnati Reds but decided to play for Arkansas State and get an education. And his youngest son, Shane, has a lot of athletic potential, according to his proud grandpa, Phil Byers.

Andy Benes seems happy in his own skin, and he appears to have kept his career as a professional athlete in perspective. He was a great player who used his intelligence and God-given talents to build a career. Now, he is dedicating his time and efforts to raising his children, and he is using his successful career as a tool for helping others.

Andy averaged nearly 20 points a game for the Central Bears. (Photo courtesy of the Evansville Courier.)

AREA BOWLING CENTERS ARE STEEPED IN TRADITION

The sport of bowling has been waning in popularity since the early '70s, but there was a time when the bowlers who excelled in the smoky bowling houses in the area were respected almost as much as the top performers in the more mainstream sports. As the game progressed technologically, the facilities became more pristine and family-friendly, but the heart and soul of the sport still lie in the nostalgic days when life was as simple as the game itself.

The exact origin of bowling is hard to pinpoint, but its roots can be traced back to at least the reign of King Henry VIII in the 15th and 16th centuries. The sport was brought to America by English, Dutch and German settlers and became popular in New York, Ohio and Illinois in the 1800s. The American Bowling Congress (known as the United States Bowling Congress today) came along in 1895 and standardized the rules for the tenpin variety currently used, and in the 1950s and '60s, the sport burst onto the scene nationally with televised productions of *Make That Spare*, *Celebrity Bowling*, and professional tournaments on ABC.

Although the sport's history in our area is a bit sketchy, one of the local pioneers was Adele Jensen, who became the first single woman to own a bowling house when she owned the Wabash Recreation Center in Vincennes in the 1920s. She then opened Jensen's Recreation at Third and Walnut in Evansville. Jensen's was on the fourth floor of the Wright Building, which, according to George Wright, was the first air-conditioned building in Evansville. Ms. Jensen also owned West Side Lanes across from where the Gerst Haus is now in a location that later became a Jerry's Market. She then partnered with Larry Seiler and Warner Mueth to own the Rose Bowl on First Street above the Gaslight nightclub. (It is also interesting to note that the daring Ms. Jensen became the first woman to bowl in Birmingham, Alabama when she insisted on rolling a few games on a stopover during a train ride to Florida.)

According to information from a *Courier* article by Jeff Crowley, the building where Jensen's was located also housed the Auto Hotel at the time, as well as Ice Services Inc. and the office of dentist Darrell Dewey. Jensen's occupied the entire fourth floor and offered five-cent cokes and candy bars, as well as great sandwiches and soups, at their snack bar. The facility featured twelve bowling alleys and eight pool tables and charged seven cents a line to bowl, with pin boys like 'Ho-Ho' Thompson and Fred Waller risking life and limb as pins flew at them like missiles from all directions. In the early years, it was common for bowling alleys to share space with pool tables. In fact, in 1928, there were more pool halls than bowling houses in the Evansville area, offering ample opportunity for those on the hustle.

In the early '50s, Jensen sold the lanes to Edward Torstrick, who ran the business until 1956, when he sold the lanes to Charlie Rayburn, who then moved the alleys to Willow Lanes. From the late 1940s and into the '50s and '60s, bowling experienced a boom locally, and for years, bowling centers cropped up all around the area.

In Evansville, Pocket's Billiards housed ten lanes on two different floors at Third and Main at the location that later became the Farmer's Daughter restaurant. Others like Kegel Keglers, near First Avenue and Franklin, and Lawndale Lanes at Green River and Bellemeade soon followed. These were later joined by Colonial (Weinbach and Washington), Diamond (Diamond Avenue and Old 41), Meadow (near North Park Shopping Center) and Arc Lanes (near Washington Square Mall). Other bowling alleys could be found at the State Hospital, the 4-H Center and the YMCA.

Perhaps the most successful bowling house in the area over the years has been Franklin Lanes, which stayed consistently strong

Russ Neathery teaching a class on scorekeeping. (Photo courtesy of Franklin Lanes.)

Jim Vaughn walks a student through the paces during Franklin Lanes' 'Ladies Learn to Bowl' class. (Photo courtesy of Franklin Lanes.)

through the efforts of Russ Neathery (and now Dave King). The business was opened in 1942 by a couple of union men who ran the union business of shipyard workers from the offices upstairs during World War II. After the war, the building was sold to Joe O'Daniel and Kenny Kent (two prominent automobile dealers), who owned it until 1956. In '56, Russ Neathery purchased Franklin Lanes and made it his mission to introduce the sport to every man, woman and child who would listen.

Neathery, an excellent bowler himself, implemented a plan to indoctrinate as many people as possible into the world of league bowling. With help from ace bowler Jim Vaughn and others, Neathery held bowling classes that taught fundamentals, etiquette and scorekeeping to novices who were interested in giving the sport a try. One of his primary goals was to overcome the sport's seedy reputation and to de-mystify the sport so that participants could recognize it as a source of fun and socialization.

Neathery looks back on those days fondly and recalls how the atmosphere was quite different than the modernized version known today. He recalls the meager scoring tables where bowlers used score sheets with advertisements on them and had to actually keep score themselves (gasp!) with pencils. He also remembers the cigarette trays on the front of the scoring desk, the towels hanging from each side and the rocker-arm that slowed the balls as they rolled up the ramp to enter the ball racks. He also worked closely with the pin boys, a job that many youngsters today may not know even existed. Men and boys, like 'Ho-Ho' Thompson (who got his name, by the way, because he could be heard yelling "Ho-Ho!" as the pins would scatter), would earn five cents to thirty cents a game as they sat precariously on platforms between the lanes. After each shot, they would roll the ball down a ramp to return it to the bowlers, then clear pins from the deck and trough, and then scramble back to their perch to await the next onslaught.

Neathery pointed out that hand size was an important factor for pin setters, as they had to grab several pins, weighing two to three pounds each, and hoist a heavy ball hundreds of times during a session. "We had one boy, Leroy Johnson, who set lanes 13 and 14," Neathery recalled, "sometimes six or seven days a week, and he'd make $40 or $50 for a week's work. Back then, that was decent money." But Neathery also recalls the hassle of finding decent workers to do the pin setting, saying, "Sometimes we'd have to go down to the creek to hunt up pinboys."

From the early days of the sport's evolution to the modernized version today, Russ Neathery has seen it all, and his work at Franklin made it the most successful house in town for many years. One aspect that gave him a leg up on the competition was his 'Ladies Learn to Bowl' classes, which opened up a whole new market. By introducing the fairer sex to the sport, he was able to schedule leagues during the daytime to supplement the already strong evening leagues that involved mostly men. For years, Franklin hosted morning (9:30) and afternoon (12:30) leagues Monday through Thursday and a morning league on Friday in addition to three shifts of men's leagues (5:00, 7:00, and 9:00) in the evenings. Although other proprietors would eventually learn from Neathery's success and follow suit, there was a period when the Brunswick Corporation recognized Franklin Lanes as the #1 house in the country in terms of number of lines (games) per lane.

The bowling craze became strong in the 1950s and '60s as the sport began to appear on television, creating stars like Don Carter, Dick Weber, Billy Welu and many others. Television also created a bowling buzz locally as the sport was aired on local television, as well. The basement of the Carpenter Building, owned by Channel 7, was the site of several programs that were contested on alleys built strictly for TV production purposes. *Jackpot Bowling* was popular and featured host Jerry Talbert, color man Irv

Bowling was a little more formal when ladies started to bowl in the 1950s.
(Photo courtesy of Franklin Lanes.)

Senzell (also a fantastic bowler) and perky scorekeeper, Marilyn Jean Rittman (another excellent bowler).

School's Out was another popular television favorite that showcased high school students who competed at both bowling and miniature golf. Perhaps the most successful of the local bowling fare, however, was *Beat the Pro*, sponsored by the Fendrich Cigar Company. Hosted by Joe Celania, bowlers would match their skills each week against Bob Bellew, a pro from Owensboro who owned lanes in Henderson and was one of the original 33 professional bowlers.

Another catalyst to bowling's popularity was the AMF Ten Pin Classic, a women's tournament that started in Evansville in the mid-'50s and is still going strong today. The annual tournament is the second-largest women's tournament in the U.S. (and possibly the world), trailing only the Women's International Bowling Congress Tournament.

Over the years, the sport of bowling has undergone an amazing transformation, from complete automation for scoring to the equipment used. Older bowling balls were made of wood so dense that they wouldn't float, and then vulcanized rubber came into vogue in the '20s and '30s before giving way to plastic and polyester in the '60s. Today, there are even balls made of broken glass, called 'particle balls', along with the popular new 'reactive resin' balls. From the balls to the pins to the lanes to the buildings themselves, the sport is worlds away from its roots. Jeff Crowley, one of the finest local bowlers of all-time and a bowling writer for the *Courier*, believes the greatest contributor to the sport was one that we all take for granted today. "Without question, the automatic pin-setter," Crowley responded when asked what innovation changed the game the most. "It sped up the game and enabled bowling centers to be larger so that more people could participate. Prior to that, you had to have somebody set the pins. Also, once they started to become automated, there came a change. They started calling them 'alleys' instead of 'lanes', so bowling's reputation started to change into something that was more of a family game instead of something that was looked down upon."

Through its evolution, many local bowlers and owners have worked to keep the game they love alive. Among them are: Bud Turpen from Princeton; Jerry Copeland (Vincennes); and Paul Moss (Wheatland), who rolled the second 800 series at Franklin Lanes (Paul Shucker had the first). Owners like Earl and Mona Werne, who built a facility in Mt. Vernon, and Del and Jean Wilson from Princeton have also been advocates of the sport through the years. Other greats, like the ones shown on these pages, have used their love of the sport to distinguish themselves and to become ambassadors as the bowling world competes for the country's leisure dollar.

Like golf, bowling is a sport where a handicapping system enables everyone to compete, and there are as many different styles as there are participants. The sport is unique in its simplicity and yet so complex that a fraction of an inch can mean the difference between success and failure. The ambiance in a bowling house is like none other, and the sounds of the ball rotating down the lane and then crashing into wooden pins is unique in the world of sports. Whether one is drawn to the lanes by the pursuit of perfection in league competition or the simple challenge of man against the pins for a recreational outing, one thing is for certain: There is no other sport like it.

DID YOU KNOW?

According to the United States Bowling Congress, only five women nationwide have converted the 5-7-10 split in sanctioned play, and two of them are from Tell City, Indiana – Lucy Kratzer in 1996 and Clara Kress in 2005.

This bowling pin was signed by members of the cast of A League of Their Own after an excursion to Willow Bowling Center.

In the 1960s, Russ Neathery became the first Evansville bowler to average 200. He also owned and operated Franklin Lanes, making it one of the most successful bowling houses in the country. (Photo courtesy of Franklin Lanes.)

Jim Vaughn, known as 'Spider' because of his thin build and long limbs, rolled a 300 game while in high school at Reitz. Jim was one of Evansville's premier bowlers in the '50s and '60s and held the record for the highest average at Franklin Lanes (210) for many years until he later broke it with a 216. He also bowled professionally for a while, finishing second to hall of famer Dave Soutar at a tournament in Muddy, Illinois. (Photo courtesy of Franklin Lanes.)

Jeff Crowley, a 1978 Reitz grad, reached bowling perfection when he rolled a 300 game while still in high school, and he has duplicated the feat 33 times in sanctioned play, giving him the record for the most 300 games by an Evansville native. In 1978, Jeff became the youngest Evansville bowler to record an 800 series (803) and also became the second youngest when he rolled an 826 in 1980 to set the city record.

Crowley has recorded ten sanctioned 800 series and won the prestigious Peterson Classic in 1997, setting a record for the largest winning margin when he won by 156 pins. In addition to winning several other tournaments, Jeff finished 11th in singles and 19th in doubles at the 1985 ABC Championship Tournament in Tulsa, Oklahoma.

Sammie Prevo was the first Evansville woman to average 200 in a sanctioned league and the first to roll a 300 game. (Photo courtesy of the *Evansville Courier*.)

Helen Fuquay is considered by many as the best woman bowler in Evansville history. Helen started bowling in the 1940s and shot a 700 series at a time when the feat was virtually unheard of. She also averaged over 190 at a time when the figure was extremely rare. (Photo courtesy of Franklin Lanes.)

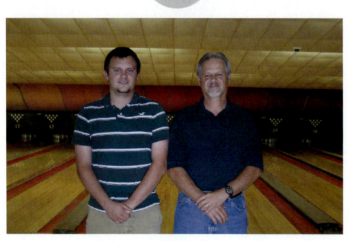

Duane Poole (right) and his son Justin.

Duane Poole became the first Tell City bowler to record a 300 game when he reached perfection on February 12th 1990. Duane has recorded thirteen sanctioned 300s and has five of the nine sanctioned 800 series at Tell City, including the house record 844 that he rolled in 2004. During the same week of Duane's 844, his son Justin broke the youth house record with a 757 series.

In the 1990s, Joyce Cummings became the second Evansville woman to bowl a perfect game. (Photo courtesy of Franklin Lanes.)

Bosse's 1981-'82 State Final Four team. Front Row (L-R): head coach Jeff Mullan, Milt Stirsman (equip. mgr.), E. Douglas (student mgr.), Ryan Gray (student mgr.), Marshall Mason (asst. coach), Harold Malicoat (asst. coach). Back Row (L-R): Doug Bell, Jeff Chestnut, Monty King, Myron Christian, Derrick Dowell, Ken Claybourne, Randy Fintress, Evie Waddell, Mark Freels, David Kendrick, Tim Lander, Mike Rogers.

BOSSE'S BULLDOGS: BACK-TO-BACK PERFECTION

In the early 1980s, Evansville Bosse produced a two-season run that put them among the elite teams in local history. Both teams suffered heartbreaking losses in tournament play that prevented them from fulfilling their potential, but their overall achievements were still impressive by any standards.

The Bulldogs of 1981-'82 featured one of the strongest two-man combinations the area had seen, and Joe Mullan and his assistants, Marshall Mason and Harold Malicoat, surrounded the team's stars with a solid crew of role players. Bosse sent a message early in the season with easy wins over their first eight opponents, winning five games by at least twenty points. In the ninth game, the Bulldogs got a taste of things to come when Heritage Hills played keep-away for much of the game before falling 44-43. The slow-down would become a common tactic against the Bulldogs as teams realized they couldn't contain Bosse's powerful front line for a full 32 minutes.

With senior Myron Christian and junior Derrick Dowell roaming the paint, few teams could match up with Bosse's inside game, and the rest of the Bulldogs were smart enough to put the ball in the big men's hands at every opportunity. The duo accounted for nearly 65% of the team's points and 55% of its rebounds, but there was much more to the Bulldogs than just their two headliners. According to the coaches, all the boys came from blue collar backgrounds with parents who fostered strong values. "All the guys had good attitudes," said Harold Malicoat, Bosse's freshman coach at the time. "That's what made them a good team. They were a family. They were a close bunch and a fun bunch to watch play."

Behind Christian and Dowell were five players who averaged between three and six points per game: 6'3 senior Monty King (5.5 points/game); senior Doug Bell (5.1); sophomore Evie Waddell (4.5); senior Ken Claybourne (3.6); and sophomore Mark Freels (3.5).

After the squeaker with Heritage Hills, the Bulldogs knocked off their next four opponents rather easily, including a 74-66 win over a Terre Haute South team that they would see later in the year. Then Bosse put its 12-0 record on the line in the much-anticipated contest with Evansville North. The entire area was buzzing to see if Bosse's streak would end against the Huskies, led by Robbie Jones, Todd Erwin and the ultra-talented Brian Miles.

Back in the early '80s, many of the high school games were carried locally on WFIE Channel 14, and U of E coach Dick Walters did the commentary for the telecast. On this night, at a packed North High gym, he saw three outstanding players who had the potential to become stars for the Aces' program, and Miles, Dowell and Christian didn't disappoint as the game played out. With 1:08 to go, it was all but over for the Bulldogs as they trailed the mighty Huskies by eleven points, but somehow, Bosse clawed their way back. Without the benefit of the three-point shot, Coach Mullan's crew trailed by only two in the waning seconds. With their perfect record on the line, the Bosse faithful watched as Myron Christian launched a missile from midcourt that tickled the twine and sent the game into overtime. Deflated from the dramatic comeback, North couldn't recover and fell 74-66, keeping the Bulldogs' perfect season intact.

The 6'5" Christian had pulled off the miracle to put his team in position to win, and it was no shock to Coach Mullan, "Myron was probably the most confident player I ever coached," Mullan revealed. "He had an air of confidence about him. He never thought anybody could beat him. A lot of people thought he was cocky, but it wasn't arrogance. He was an amazing kid to coach."

After six more wins, including another overtime win (70-64) over North, Bosse had completed a perfect 20-0 regular season, creating high tournament aspirations for the players and fans. In the sectional, everyone expected to see round three between Bosse

Derrick Dowell as a USC Trojan. (Photo courtesy of University of Southern California, Sports Information.)

Myron Christian goes airborne in a pivotal game against North to lead the Bulldogs back from a nine-point deficit with a minute remaining to defeat the Huskies.

and North, but the Huskies were upset by Harrison and the Bulldogs dominated the tournament with easy wins over Mater Dei (82-59), Memorial (73-47) and a tired bunch of Harrison Warriors (60-27).

Their performance was equally dominant in the Evansville Regional as they trounced Vincennes (53-32) and Heritage Hills (78-50), a team they had beaten by only a point earlier in the year.

In the semi-state, Bosse again faced two familiar opponents. Late in the season, the Bulldogs had won a slow-down affair over stubborn Bedford North Lawrence 52-51. In the afternoon game of the semi-state, the North Stars took the air out of the ball again but still fell 37-35. In the final, Terre Haute South took Bosse to the wire, but the Bulldogs prevailed 64-63 in overtime. At 25-0, the Bulldogs had locals dreaming of another State title, but it was not to be.

Bosse's luck ran out when they lost a 58-57 nail-biter to Gary Roosevelt in the afternoon game at the State Finals. Roosevelt eventually lost to Plymouth, who was led by a memorable performance by Scott Skiles (now a coach in the NBA). It is widely believed by many area fans that, if Bosse could have pulled off one more miracle finish against Roosevelt, they could have dominated the inside and taken Plymouth in the finals.

The 1981-'82 Bulldogs finished 27-1 and two points shy of playing for a State championship. In the spring, four members of the team would graduate: Monty King, Ken Claybourne, Doug Bell and, of course, Myron Christian. Following the season, senior-to-be Derrick Dowell's resolve was tested and the Bulldogs' immediate future was placed in jeopardy when a medical problem Dowell had dealt with for years was taken care of.

"Derrick had one leg shorter than the other," Coach Mullan revealed, "and he had major surgery between his junior and senior years. (Doctors in Indianapolis) grafted a bone from his hip and put it in his lower leg to equal the length of the leg."

Coach Mullan was with Dowell through the process and had nothing but respect for the way the young man handled it. "That was a major operation," Mullan affirmed. "His rehab was a tough four to six months. I used to take him to (U of E's) Carson Center every day to swim because the doctors said it was the best therapy for his recovery."

When November rolled around, Derrick's toughness and dedication paid off as he prepared to face the new season. Everyone knew that the success of the 1982-'83 version of the Bulldogs would rest heavily on his broad shoulders, and often he would share the floor with four guards. Although much of the starting lineup from the previous year had graduated, there were a few returning who had contributed valuable minutes. Evie Waddell and Mark Freels were back, and others, like Jeff Chestnut, Chris Johnson and sophomore Robert Calhoun, would grow into significant contributors.

With his co-star gone and a new supporting cast, Derrick Dowell showed why he was one of the best players in Evansville history. Once again, the Bulldogs did whatever was necessary to win, as they dispatched one opponent after another. When the regular season was over, they were 21-0 and had defied all the odds by completing two consecutive seasons with a spotless record. Although their season would end with another heartbreaking loss, to Princeton in the final game of the Evansville Regional in four overtimes, Bosse's place in history was secure. The two Bosse teams, 1981-'82 and '82-'83, will forever be linked because of their remarkable regular seasons and because of the two stars who led the way.

Myron Christian averaged 21.8 points and 8.2 rebounds his senior year, was named to the All-State team and was selected as a member of the Indiana All-Stars. He took his impressive talents to Indiana State, where he played for two seasons before transferring to Kentucky Weslyan. After sitting out a year, he became a two-year starter for the Panthers and averaged in double figures both years. As a senior, Myron played a key role in helping Wesleyan capture a national championship. With his degree in hand, he returned to the area to raise a family and watch his son, Myron Jr., play ball for Owensboro Senior High School.

Like Christian, Derrick Dowell was named to the Indiana All-Stars and was an All-State player, but he was also honored as a prep All-American as well. As he prepared for graduation in 1983, his impact on Bosse's program was not lost on his coach. "Derrick was probably the best player I ever coached," Joe Mullan said. "He was such a great leader. The rest of the team just looked up to him. His teammates had so much trust in him. They knew that somehow, some way, Derrick would lead us to another win."

Dowell averaged 17.1 points as a junior and 26.8 as a senior for the Bulldogs. He also hauled in 13 rebounds and passed out 2.3 assists per game, which made him a valuable commodity to college recruiters. After contemplating his options, Dowell headed for the west coast to wear the red and gold of the USC Trojans.

While at USC, Dowell started ten games as a freshman, averaging 6.4 points and 4.6 rebounds and earned a spot on the PAC 10 All-Freshman team. As a sophomore, the 6'6, 222-pounder upped his numbers to 11.6 points and 8.3 rebounds and shot an impressive 56% from the floor as a starter for the Trojans. His coming out party was a 24-point, 21-rebound effort in a 78-77 double overtime win over UCLA, and his overall play for the PAC 10 champion Trojans earned him All-Pac 10 honorable mention.

Dowell became an even greater presence his junior year, upping his scoring to 15.5 per game. In an 88-74 win over Arkansas, he had one of his greatest games as a collegian when he scorched the Razorbacks for 34 points and 15 rebounds.

Derrick's senior season at USC was called "one of the finest seasons by a Trojan" by the school's sports information department, and his play made him a unanimous All-PAC 10 selection. He led the Trojans in scoring (20.8), rebounding (8.8) and steals (2.2 with a school record 62 for the season). His 585 points placed him third on USC's all-time single season list and was the most since John Block's record 654 22 years earlier.

Dowell also topped the 20-point mark fifteen times and scored 30 or more five times, including a career-high 35 against UCLA. He registered nine double-doubles (double figures in scoring and rebounding) nine times and had 27 in his career. A tribute to Derrick's consistency was the fact that he scored in double figures in every game his senior year and was the Trojan's leading scorer 21 times and their leading rebounder 15 times. When he finished his career in 1987, Dowell was third on USC's all-time career scoring list (1,484 points) and was one of only two Trojans to be among the top five in career scoring and rebounding.

Dowell's amazing college career served as an inspiration to younger sister Cheryl, who traveled west herself two years later for a sterling career at Long Beach State. Derrick's play also caught the attention of NBA scouts, but fate would step in to send him in another direction. In the 1987 NBA draft, he was selected as the 14th pick of the second round (37th overall) by the Washington Bullets, but shortly before he was scheduled to leave, he tore his achilles tendon, ending his basketball career. Dowell's strength of character enabled him to accept his injury and re-focus on having a life after basketball. Today, he is raising a family with his wife Pam and is a practicing minister here locally.

It is interesting to speculate where Derrick Dowell's talents would have taken him, because he had all the necessary characteristics to be successful. Although we'll never know what might have been, we can state for certain what was. As a collegian, he was a remarkable player for a major university, and as a high school player, he should be placed among the very best in local history.

During Dowell's final two high school seasons, Bosse's record was 51-2, and he and his coaches and teammates should be proud of what they accomplished. They were the first, and still only, Evansville team to finish two successive regular seasons without a loss, and their 41 straight regular season wins place them sixth among all teams in the history of Indiana basketball.

North's Brian Miles was Bosse's greatest adversary during their remarkable run in the early '80s. The son of Lincoln High School great Walter Miles, Brian was a four-year letter winner in basketball and track and earned first team All-State honors in basketball as a senior.

After his graduation in 1983, Brian moved on to a great career at Oral Roberts University, where he set a school record for field goal accuracy with a .660 percentage and earned a degree in Business Administration.

CASTLE'S RISE TO FOOTBALL PROMINENCE

In December of 2000, John Lidy was inducted into the Indiana Football Hall of Fame. Most area fans are aware of the success Coach Lidy experienced during his coaching career, but before his teams became perennial powerhouses in the '80s and '90s, there were lessons to be learned by the young coach and his staff.

Mr. Lidy became Castle's head coach in 1973, and with only limited success in the early years of the program, he was constantly searching for ways to make his program competitive with other area schools. The realization hit home after two of the worst seasons in Castle football history. In 1978 and '79, the Knights were a combined 1-19, and the coaching staff agreed that the problem was crystal clear. Castle's players were physically inferior to the competition. Lidy and his coaches decided that the best solution was a year-round weight training program, so following the '79 season, Castle players hit the weight room for 60 to 75 minutes a day during the off-season and for 20 minutes daily during the season.

In three short years, Castle would transform its program from the area's local whipping boy to one of the best programs in the entire state. In 1980, the stronger Knights finished 6-3, and in '81, they improved to 10-3. Lidy had made believers of his players and fans, and their faith was soon to be rewarded with the ultimate prize.

As motivation for the 1982 Castle team, Coach Lidy reflected back on the previous year. Castle lost three games in '81, to Mater Dei (13-10), Terre Haute South (21-14) and Carmel (49-13 in the semi-state). Those scores were displayed on a sign that was hung above a locker room door. Under it, Lidy wrote "3 reasons to spill your guts." The 1982 team took the message to heart and worked hard to prepare themselves for what was to become a defining year for the Castle football program.

The '82 team was smaller than typical Castle teams of the past, but they were strong. Coach Lidy told the *Courier* that he liked the makeup of his team. He told reporters that he had 25 players who bench pressed 200+ pounds and twenty who could squat 300+. He also stated that the Knights' "quickness is better than it's ever been."

Castle had lost record-breaking quarterback Jay Burch to graduation and were replacing him with Mike Davis, who had played defensive back the previous year. The team returned 11 of 22 starters, including the hard-running tandem of brothers Dave and Chris Brosmer and their excellent place kicker Matt McDowell. Standout Joe Huff, who later went on to an outstanding career at IU, was back, but the bulk of the linemen would be first-time starters with an average weight of less than 200 pounds. Castle's historic season was about to begin.

It didn't take long to gain redemption for one of the prior season's losses. Castle's opener was against the always dangerous Mater Dei Wildcats. Mater Dei coach Frank Will had lost 81% of his starters to graduation and was also replacing his quarterback (Chris Sitzman in '81) with the highly-touted John Townsend.

The August 27th matchup attracted enough attention that it became the first local high school game to be broadcast live. WEHT, Channel 25 aired the game, with Bill Weber doing the play-by-play and retired Harrison football coach Don Watson providing the color commentary as Castle avenged the previous year's loss with an impressive 28-0 win.

Week two featured Warrick County rival Boonville. The playoff system at the time allowed a team to scratch an opponent so that the game wouldn't count against them in the playoffs. The Pioneers had blown out Washington 34-0 the prior week but were wise to scratch Castle, as the Knights out-gained Boonville 381 yards to 41 in a 52-0 shellacking capped by two TD tosses from Mike Davis to Joe Huff.

In game three, Castle gave up their first points of the season on an 88-yard kickoff return by Harrison's Lamont Williams but won easily 29-7. The Brosmer brothers romped for 210 yards.

Castle defeated Bob Ashworth's Reitz team 24-7 in the fourth game as Dave Brosmer ran for two TDs and Matt McDowell, the 5'9" kicker, booted his second field goal of the season.

The Knights' fifth win of the season, a 41-0 trouncing of Central, showcased a bit of Coach Lidy's creative side. Shortly before halftime, Mike Davis handed off to tight end Kenny Brown on a reverse and Brown then threw 30 yards to Dave Brosmer, setting up a Castle touchdown.

In game 6, Castle achieved the second step in avenging the three losses from the '81 season with a 35-0 drubbing of Terre Haute South. Quarterback Mike Davis ran for a touchdown and threw for two more (6 yards to Kenny Brown and 34 yards to Deon Chester).

The offensive line, a question mark before the season began, was dominant through the first half of the season. Coached by Johnny Evers, who would eventually become Castle's athletic director, the pint-sized powerhouses were manhandling opponents.

By the seventh week of the season, Castle was rated #4 in the state, and their next opponent, Memorial, was rated 18th in class AAA. In that week's *Courier*, Coach Lidy expressed his concern about the ball-handling and play-action passing of Tigers quarterback Bob Scheitlin. He needn't have worried, however, as Castle was dominant again in a 33-6 win in front of 7,000 fans at Enlow Field.

After Memorial put a scare into Castle, scoring first for a 6-0 lead, the Knights dusted off another trick play. They retaliated with a 79-yard flea flicker (now called the 'hook & ladder') when Davis threw to Deon Chester who then lateraled to David Brosmer. Davis also threw TD passes to Joe Huff (88 yards) and Neil Chapman (32 yards).

Going into the last three games of the season, the Castle staff began to look at the State playoff picture. In the early '80s, every team was not guaranteed a spot in the tournament, and although Castle was ranked #3 in the polls, they still needed to win two games to be guaranteed a spot and three to have home field advantage in the opener.

Following wins over Terre Haute North (30-6) and Bosse (34-7), the Knights prepared to complete their regular season against North at Central Stadium. Despite a stellar effort from North quarterback Brad Green, who was 7 for 13 passing in the first half and had intercepted two Castle passes while on defense, Castle closed out its first ever undefeated regular season with a 27-7 win.

The playoffs were about to start, and it was time for the Knights to prove that they could play with the big boys.

As the 3A playoffs began, Coach Lidy's Knights were ranked #2 in the state, and after their perfect 10-0 season, they would host the explosive Richmond Red Devils. The previous year, Castle had squeaked by Richmond 17-16 after falling behind 17-6 at halftime. Although Richmond's leading receivers were Lloyd Spicer and Randy Gibson, Coach Lidy's biggest concern was 5'3", 130-pound receiver Cory King. Responsibility for coverage would fall on Castle's defensive backs, Kenny Brown, Chris Brosmer, Deon Chester and Gary Gilles. Castle's top three tacklers, noseguard Chris Scales and linebackers Pat Lockyear and Rodney Russell, would be responsible for stopping the running game.

Richmond was certainly concerned about stopping the Knights' offense, as well. Castle had run for nearly 2,000 yards (Dave Brosmer-1,002, Chris Brosmer-555, and Neil Chapman-380), and Mike Davis had completed 72 of 131 passes (55%) for 14 touchdowns. In addition, kicker Matt McDowell was a threat, after making 37 of 41 PATs and booting three field goals on the year.

On a rainy Tuesday night in November, the Castle Knights moved one step closer to Indianapolis. After trailing 7-6 in the first quarter, Castle scored ten second quarter points on their way to a 23-7 win, and defensive end Joe Huff recorded three of the five sacks of Red Devil quarterback Stan Welsh.

Coach Lidy's troops and the faithful fans from Paradise were heading north for a game that would come to be known as 'The Miracle in Martinsville'.

In a November article by Don Bernhardt in the *Courier*, Coach Lidy predicted the upcoming showdown between his Knights and undefeated Martinsville might be "an old-fashioned brawl."

"It ought to be a physical game," Lidy stated. "We think we can get physical with anybody. It'll be a knock down and drag out. We hope to do the knocking down and they do the dragging out."

Martinsville was coached by the highly-respected Bill Siderwicz, and Coach Lidy's 1981 team had given the Artesians a 35-7 spanking a year ago. The sixth-ranked Martinsville squad had earned its way into a rematch with Castle by pounding Columbus East 35-0. They were riding a 30-game winning streak and were averaging 31.5 points to their opponents' 6.9 (very similar to Castle's 32.3 - 4.4).

John Lidy (Photo courtesy of the Evansville Courier.)

The Artesians' offense was led by 6'1", 180-lb quarterback Rob Bancroft, who had drilled Columbus East for 281 yards on 18 of 20 passes the previous week and had thrown for nearly 2,000 yards on the season.

Though everyone was projecting a physical brawl in the regional championship on Saturday November 6th, 1982, the 9,000 fans in attendance were also treated to some stunning finesse and eleventh-hour heroics. In fact, the game was only seconds old when Castle's Deon Chester made the first of several game-changing plays. From his cornerback position, Chester picked off a Bancroft pass and sprinted to the Artesian 4-yard line, resulting in a Chris Brosmer touchdown and a 7-0 Castle lead.

After the ensuing kickoff, Martinsville showed its resiliance and marched 86 yards to tie the game.

Martinsville's next score was the result of an error in judgment after a penalty. Castle had stopped Martinsville deep in Artesian territory after a third down play. A penalty had been called on Martinsville and the official approached Castle captain Rodney Russell. The Castle bench was signaling to decline the penalty and force a punting situation, but Russell's vision was blocked by players on the field. By accepting the penalty, the Knights gave Martinsville a second chance, and the Artesians capitalized with an acrobatic 30-yard completion on the next play and a subsequent drive for a touchdown. Castle completed the halftime scoring with a Matt McDowell field goal for a 17-14 lead.

With under nine minutes left in the game, Martinsville put Castle's collective backs against the wall with a 76-yard scoring drive that gave them a 21-17 advantage. The Knights may have been on life support, but they weren't dead yet, and the stage was set for 'the Miracle in Martinsville'.

With under three minutes remaining, there were 71 long yards looming between John Lidy's undefeated Knights and their date with destiny. On the sideline, Dave Brosmer made a play-call suggestion to Coach Lidy and his staff. As it turned out, based on the way Martinsville was defending them, the coaches had already considered the play. When Brosmer expressed the same idea, the coaches decided to go with it.

In athletics, handling situations like these are the difference between those who make it and those who almost make it. As a coach, you analyze the risk versus reward then you make the call and hope the stars are aligned in your favor. With the crowd's deafening roar in the background, Coach Lidy made the call. The play in question was one that had worked earlier in the season in a key game against Memorial – the flea-flicker.

According to a *Courier and Press* report, when the play was sent in to the huddle, receiver Deon Chester was in total agreement. "I just knew it was gonna work," Chester reported after the game. "I just kept thinking to myself, 'Catch the ball. Catch the ball.'"

And catch it he did. Chester hauled in the pass from Mike Davis at Martinsville's 45-yard line and saw Dave Brosmer streaking down the sideline. A perfect lateral from Chester caught Brosmer in stride, and the running back gobbled up the last 45 yards to set up a rematch with the Carmel Greyhounds for the semi-state crown.

Nearly twelve months had passed since John Lidy and his troops had felt the sting of a 49-15 lashing by Jim Belden's Carmel Greyhounds that had propelled Carmel to the State title while sending Lidy and his boys on a 200-mile trip home, pondering what went wrong. But this year, it would be Castle's turn to inflict the pain.

Coach Belden had won 27 straight games since coming to Carmel before losing to North Central 22-14 to begin the '82 season. The defending State champions had been hit hard by graduation, but like any great program, they don't re-build, they just re-load. After the North Central loss, Carmel proceeded to win the rest of their games that season, giving Coach Belden a 38-1 overall record at Carmel.

Early in the year, Carmel had used five players on both offense and defense, but as the season progressed, younger players stepped in and enabled the Greyhounds to field two separate offensive and defensive teams. In newspaper reports at the time, Coach Belden sounded supremely confident. He spoke highly of Greyhound quarterback Scott Rogers, who had thrown for 1,400 yards and 17 touchdowns with only two interceptions, and fullback Jim Caldwell, who had done major damage to the Knights the year before.

A sellout crowd was expected, and, according to the *Evansville Press*, there was discussion about moving the game to Reitz Bowl because of its 10,000-seat capacity. But even though some fans would have to stand, Coach Lidy was adamant about playing the game on the Knights' home turf.

The Castle faithful were out in force on Friday November 12th, and Mother Nature did her job by giving the 3,000 Carmel fans a cool welcome with a wind chill factor near zero.

Carmel turned the ball over five times, and after Dave Brosmer scored the game's first touchdown in the first quarter, Castle continued to frustrate the Greyhounds with timely defensive plays and the ball-handling skills of quarterback Mike Davis. Castle's misdirection plays and Davis' fakes had Carmel's defense grasping at air all night long, and the Greyhounds' only score came against Castle's prevent defense in the fourth quarter to make the final score Castle 21, Carmel 8.

In the next morning's *Evansville Courier*, it was obvious that the players and coaches were aware of a goal they had set more than three months earlier. As linebacker Pat Lockyear scribbled the word "avenged" over the locker room door, Coach Lidy explained the significance to a *Courier* reporter. "This is the last one of the three (names on the board)," he pointed out. "Mater Dei, Terre Haute South and Carmel beat us last year. Now, we've (avenged) all three."

For the Castle team and coaches, however, there was one more item to check off their 'To Do' list, just one little piece of unfinished business – the Hobart Brickies.

1982 was a record-setting season for the Castle football program and for many individuals as well. Quarterback Mike Davis passed for 1800+ yards, breaking the record set the previous year by Jay Burch, and running back Dave Brosmer set records for career receptions and yardage for a season and career. Defensively, linebacker Rodney Russell set the record for tackles in a season (180), while kicker Matt McDowell owned all of Castle's kicking records by season's end.

On Saturday, November 20th, the team was poised to reach another milestone, Castle's first team State championship in any sport. Although it was the Knights' first appearance on Indiana football's biggest stage, the same was not true for their opponent. The Hobart Brickies had come within a touchdown of a State title in 1979 and 1980.

A rainy night was forecast at North Central Stadium as two future Indiana Football Hall of Fame coaches (Castle's John Lidy and Hobart's Don Howell) prepared to go to war. As they had all season, Castle would rely on their quickness and tenacity against a much larger opponent. "Hobart was huge," recalled then-Castle assistant coach Johnny Evers. "Most of our kids were 180, 190, but Hobart was 240s and 250s. There were college and pro teams that weren't that big. I walked out and one of their lineman said, 'Where are your big people?' In fact, one coach told us, "Your team won't survive the game; you'll have kids carried off the field."

On the game's first play, Castle set the tone with a 52-yard pass that almost went for a TD. Moments later, Castle opened the scoring with a two-yard Dave Brosmer touchdown run and finished the first quarter with a 7-0 lead.

Early in the second period, Hobart tied the game with a beautiful 51-yard pass from Mike Mills to 6'6" receiver Tony Shirk.

Later in the second period, Castle took control, with Brosmer scoring twice, one on a 25-yard pass from Mike Davis and the other on the old reliable flea-flicker. After a 41-yard Hobart field goal just before halftime, the teams went to their respective locker rooms with Castle leading 20-10.

Near the end of the third quarter, Hobart gained some momentum with a 7-play drive and an 11-yard touchdown on a pass from Mills to Mark Yetsko, making the score 20-17 Castle.

In the fourth quarter, a Castle miscue while attempting to punt left Hobart with a short field, and the Brickies took their first and only lead on a 4-yard run by junior Jeff Vanderplough. Hobart's 2-point conversion failed.

The stage was set. With Castle down 23-20, their march to victory began, as they used the same balanced attack that had served them well all year. Perhaps the game's biggest play was made by wide receiver Deon Chester. When a 36-yard pass was batted into the air, Chester wrestled the ball from a defender at Hobart's 40-yard line and sprinted to the 25 before being brought down.

After a 14-yard pass to Kenny Brown and an 8-yard sweep, Chris Brosmer powered over the left side to give the Knights the lead, and Castle held on for the 27-23 win.

This group of over-achievers had done something no group before them could do, and many followers of the program also give credit to the seniors from the year before. That group had seen Castle through the lean years. They were 1-19 their freshman and sophomore seasons, followed by a 6-3 season as juniors and a 10-3 senior year that inspired Castle's players and fans to realize the possibility of what they could only dream about before. Their inspiration and the efforts of the '82 team helped Castle become a dominant force in the conference and the state for many years.

In three short years, Castle's football program had gone from the bottom of the barrel to the top of the world.

Twelve years later, Castle would win another football State title, and there may be more in the future, but only the '82 team can lay claim to being the first.

Castle's Joe Huff shown here as an Indiana Hoosier. (Photo courtesy of the Evansville Courier.)

> Castle High School's first varsity football game was a 27-6 loss to a Rex Mundi team led by a young sophomore quarterback named Bob Griese.

CHERYL DOWELL: THE QUEEN OF MEAN

Like many local youngsters, Cheryl Dowell developed her athletic ability on her backyard basketball court playing with her older brothers and neighborhood kids. Although her parents, Macon and Mamie, were concerned about little Cheryl getting injured, her father insisted that the others let her play and then stood nearby to make sure she got her fair share of court time.

Toughened up by her older brothers, Lamont (who played at Vincennes University), Dwight (Southeastern Illinois) and Derrick (Southern California), the youngster was ready when she got to Fairlawn School. Cheryl was always tall for her age, and her height and advanced skills earned her a spot on the sixth grade team as a fourth grader.

As she followed her brothers to Bosse High School, she earned a starting spot on Jerry Canterbury's varsity squad as a freshman. With her inside presence, even as a freshman, she prompted North coach Ron Johnson to turn to Jerry Canterbury and proclaim, "I'm getting out of this game!" When asked why, Johnson laughed and told Coach Canterbury, "Because you've got that girl for three more years. We don't have a chance!"

A power forward in the truest sense of the word, Cheryl was always told by her father to be aggressive on the court. "Some people thought I was mean, but I just thought of it as playing the game," Cheryl said. "It was time to get down to business." In reality, both Cheryl and Coach Canterbury agreed that meanness was not part of her nature. Canterbury described Cheryl as friendly, humble and thoughtful and believed that because she had a rugged style, she may have been perceived as mean-spirited.

During her years at Bosse, Cheryl grew to 5'11" and captured virtually every local honor available while battling outstanding players like Mater Dei's Julie Goedde and Memorial's Jill Hartman. As a senior, Cheryl joined Hartman as a 1985 Indiana All-Star and then weighed her college options. As she considered her college choices, she needed to look no farther than her own home for motivation. She looked to her older brother Derrick.

"I always admired him," Cheryl recalled. "As we got older, the colleges started coming after him and he was in the newspaper, and I thought, 'Wow! This is something big!' And then he got a scholarship and was going to California. He was leaving me, and I just cried because he was going so far away. But he told me, 'You can do it too!' That was a big motivator for me."

Cheryl's talent attracted offers from nearly every major program in the country, including USC, Long Beach State and Tennessee. Pat Summitt – the winningest Division I basketball coach of all time (man or woman) – called frequently trying to convince Dowell to play for the Volunteers.

As time passed, Cheryl began to feel the tension. "I wasn't used to all that, and I felt pressured," she admitted. "The coaches were very aggressive, and my mom was trying to leave it ultimately up to me, and it was really too much for me. It's all a game, and the coaches would push themselves on me."

It got to the point that Cheryl wouldn't even answer the phone when the coaches started calling every day because it was getting late in the process. At the eleventh hour, she finally made her choice; she, too, was headed to California.

"I went to Long Beach State because I wanted to be where Derrick was (Derrick was at Southern California)," Cheryl explained, and when asked why she didn't join him at USC, she gave an honest but humorous reply: "I didn't want to be *that* close. I didn't want him in all my business."

At Long Beach State, Cheryl was an All-Conference player and set a record for most consecutive games played, earning her the nickname 'Durable Dowell'. She never missed a game, and she was a starter from late in her freshman year through the end of her college career. As a 6'1" forward, she averaged 16 points and 13 rebounds per game.

One of Cheryl's biggest thrills was playing against one of her idols, USC's Cheryl Miller (the sister of Indiana Pacer great Reggie Miller). Southern California was strong during Miller's years there, and the rivalry between the schools was fierce. During Cheryl's sophomore season, the two schools were scheduled to play at USC, and the media hyped the story angle of whom Derrick Dowell would be rooting for. The game was televised, so everyone back home got to watch as Derrick and little sis Cheryl sang the National Anthem before tip-off. As for the game, Cheryl Miller avenged an early-season loss when she tipped in a missed shot in the closing seconds for the win.

During Dowell's years at Long Beach, the 49ers twice made it to the Final Four of the NCAA Tournament, losing to Pat Summitt's Tennessee team in 1987 and to Auburn in '88. When Cheryl graduated with a Psychology degree, it looked like her playing days were over, but that wasn't necessarily so.

Four years after leaving Long Beach, Cheryl was married with two small children, and out of the blue she received a phone call about a newly-formed basketball league, the WNBA. At first, Cheryl said no because she was settled and she realized that basketball had served as a means to an end, a college degree. But with prodding from her husband and kids, she called the coach back.

When the coach asked, "Are you in shape?" and "Are you overweight?", Cheryl's answer was honest….she wasn't and she was. Cheryl was given four weeks to get ready, so she dug out her high-topped tennis shoes and went to work. With her mind reeling, she set out to lose twenty pounds. As the time passed, Cheryl became concerned about the logistics of playing and raising a family, so she decided to turn to a familiar source for support and advice.

"She was always a big influence in my life and my world," Cheryl said of her mother, Mamie. "I just knew she would be supportive, and I said 'Ma, I'm going to the WNBA! I've got a trainer and I'm working out!'"

Mamie's response was less than enthusiastic. "What are you doing?!" she asked Cheryl. "You have small children and a good husband, and you just bought a home. Who's going to watch the children while you're gone?"

As usual, Mom made perfect sense, but curiosity had gotten the best of Cheryl and she let her agent persuade her to try anyway. When she found out, however, that after the three-month season, most of the players were expected to continue playing overseas, Cheryl realized that her mother was right and that it was just too much.

Today, Cheryl Dowell Crowell is doing something she always wanted to do. She is a practicing cosmetologist and is happy being a wife and mother to her four kids. After putting her playing days behind her, she realized that basketball had served its purpose and that it was time to get on with her life.

(Photo courtesy of Long Beach State University, Media Relations.)

FÜTBOL: THE NEW KID IN TOWN

Over the last thirty years, no sport has grown in popularity in our country more than soccer, or fütbol as it is known worldwide. Locally, the sport's emergence was spearheaded by three men, two from the same family and one who put U of E soccer on the map.

When soccer's local evolution is discussed, one name quickly comes to the forefront: Bill Vieth (pronounced veeth). Bill was an excellent soccer player himself, earning All-American honors at St. Louis University and playing in the NCAA Finals three years in a row. In the 1962 title game, St. Louis was defeated by a Westchester State (PA) team that featured a young player named Jerry Yeagley. Yeagley went on to a remarkable career as the coach at IU and has the distinction of being the only player to win the NCAA in his final year as a player and as a coach. To honor his career, IU's soccer facility bears Yeagley's name. After the '62 loss, Bill Vieth and St. Louis returned to the next two NCAA Finals and won them both.

In 1965, Bill and his wife, Mary Ellen, moved to Evansville, and Bill quickly noticed that something was missing. Coming from St. Louis, a hotbed for soccer, Vieth examined the sports landscape and realized that the only active soccer program was Evansville Day School. The situation was so bleak that Day School had to play teams like Indianapolis Country Day and Louisville Country Day just to find competition.

In 1974, Bill made a decision to get involved, and his efforts have paid huge dividends for athletes across southern Indiana. Realizing that he needed help, he turned to Kemper Lease, an executive with IBM, for support. With little more than their enthusiasm, the two men called on Stan Atkinson, the owner of the local Pepsi franchise. To inspire Atkinson, Vieth and Lease showed him a film of Brazil soccer icon Pelé and then made their proposal. Their vision was to develop a youth soccer league to teach youngsters fundamentals and then to continue expanding as the kids reached the high schools.

The presentation convinced Atkinson, and the program's first sponsor was on board. As Bill continued to organize the youth league, another opportunity arose that would increase his workload but would also be a catalyst for fulfilling his dream. Ironically, as Vieth was beginning his mission, the University of Evansville announced plans to start a soccer program as well. Bill agreed to coach and to help raise the money to support it. But as he balanced his time between the U of E program and his job at Citizens Bank, he still kept his focus on the area's youth program.

The youth league began with nine-, ten- and eleven-year-old boys for the first two years. In the first year, six teams, about 100 kids, played at the Vann Avenue field, and in the second year, the numbers doubled. When girls were added the third year, Harold Gourley, the principal at Highland Grade School, decided that a north side league should be started to help accommodate some of the 24 teams that were forming.

As the sport's popularity grew, new age-group divisions were started, and support continued to grow from sources such as Dave Remmert from Pizza Hut. With enthusiasm at an all-time high, Bill approached the EVSC's director of athletics, Jim Graham, about developing a high school program. Although the idea was met with skepticism at first because of the lack of familiarity with soccer and other inherent problems with starting a new sport, Vieth's determination prevailed.

Once again, a local merchant stepped up to make the project viable. Norm McCool, an ex-basketball star at Bosse High School and owner of the local Coca Cola franchise, agreed to sponsor the high school league. A vacant field just north of the State Hospital and just east of where the Red Cross is now was transformed into two fields where the high schoolers would play. After meeting with the Catholic Board and convincing Mater Dei and Memorial to participate, the program was up and running. Following a short season in 1977, the schools began playing 20+ games per season.

For three years, Bill Vieth piloted the U of E program before turning it over to Bob Gaudin in 1977. After leaving U of E, Vieth turned his attention elsewhere and partnered with Dick Shymanski in piloting the program at Memorial High School. For the '78 and '79 seasons, Shymanski served as the head coach, and then Bill took over for two years. One of the players he coached was his oldest son, Bill Jr., who would not only make a name for himself as a player but would later follow in his father's footsteps as a coach.

The Evansville Aces during the 1985 NCAA Tourney. (Photo courtesy of the University of Evansville, Sports Information.)

Bill Sr. coached the Tigers in 1980 and '81 and watched Bill Jr. earn *Parade* All-American honors both years as a midfielder, setting school records along the way with 104 goals and 29 assists for 237 points in his four-year career. Bill Jr.'s teams also won three State titles (1979, '80 and '81) when the sport was sanctioned by the Indiana High School Soccer Association (IHSSA). At that time, there were approximately 100 schools playing, and under Bill Sr.'s guidance, the IHSSA would oversee the sport until the participation numbers reached the level necessary for IHSAA acceptance.

After his graduation from Memorial in 1982, Bill Jr. left to play at St. Louis University, and while he was away, the Aces program was heading into new and exciting territory. After Bob Gaudin led U of E to its first winning season in 1978 (13-6-0), the school hired an experienced coach from the St. Louis area to take the program to the next level. As local high school soccer was heating up in the early '80s, Fred Schmalz would help fan the flames by masterminding a string of seasons that would place the U of E program among the nation's elite.

Schmalz was raised only three miles from where Bill Vieth Sr. was raised in north St. Louis. After playing in the Catholic Youth Leagues, Fred left for Quincy College, a school that didn't have a soccer program. By his junior year, the school had started a program and Fred played on the school's first team. The squad had a lot of good players from the St. Louis area and finished the season undefeated, but since the school had not done the proper paperwork, the team didn't qualify for the national tournament. The next season, the team lost only two games, and in the third year, Fred was part of an undefeated squad that won the NAIA national championship.

After graduating, Schmalz left to attend grad school at Western Illinois, where he served as a grad assistant in soccer. He then took the head coaching job at the University of Wyoming. In 1972, he left to coach Davis & Elkins College in West Virginia, an NAIA small college soccer power, and in his seven years there, his teams reached the Final Four six times.

When Jim Byers, U of E's A.D., interviewed and hired Schmalz in February of 1979, Fred looked at the Evansville job as a great opportunity, but although he was excited about the move, the same couldn't be said about his wife Linda. Fred and Linda had just completed the home of their dreams in West Virginia and were putting on the finishing touches when U of E called. The new job made it tough for both of them, as Fred continued to teach Exercise Physiology at Davis & Elkins and then commuted to Evansville every other weekend to tend to his duties here. From February until spring, he continued the traveling while Linda was dreading the departure from her beautiful home. As any coach should, Fred appreciated the sacrifice Linda made, but he quickly points out that, "She's never let me forget it."

In 1979, Schmalz assumed control of the U of E program and experienced modest success, posting three winning seasons as he began to bring in his own recruits. His 1982 team, featuring second team All-Americans Just Jensen and John Nunes, thrust the program into the national spotlight by qualifying for the NCAA Tournament for the first time in school history. Although they lost 1-0 to Indiana in the first round, the team had raised expectations and made everyone hungry for more.

Two years later, in 1984, the U of E program hit its stride and launched a seven-year run that would stack up with the best in the land. Schmalz began attracting some of the finest foreign and

Bill Vieth Sr. during his playing days at St. Louis University. (Photo courtesy of St. Louis University.)

domestic talent available and produced a 129-27-8 record (83%) during the run. His teams won the conference tournament three times, qualified for the national tournament every year from 1984-'91 and reached the College Cup (NCAA Final Four) twice.

The 1985 team captured everyone's fancy when it became the first U of E team to finish the regular season undefeated and play in the College Cup. After defeating Indiana (3-0) and Penn State (1-0), the '85 Aces entered the semi-finals 21-0-2 before bowing to UCLA 3-1.

In eleven years, no U of E team had scored more than 57 goals, but the '85 team passed the mark at mid-season, finishing with 93. The #1-ranked Aces featured three third team All-Americans: Dan McHugh, defender Mike Mikes and midfielder Andrew Norton. The team's strength was its depth, proven by the fact that none of the All-Americans were named the team's MVP. That honor went to junior Mick Lyon.

The next four U of E teams continued the winning tradition, compiling a combined record of 67-20-4, behind such stars as Mikes, Lyon and Rob Paterson. After three first-round exits in the tournament, however, Schmalz and his staff wanted more, and the 1990 team would come through in a big way.

The 1990 version of the Aces weren't prolific scorers like the '85 team, but their defense was unparalleled. The goalkeepers, led by All-American Trey Harrington, allowed only seven goals all season, and no opponent scored more than once against the Aces. The team also posted a school record 20 consecutive wins

Coach Fred Schmalz led the Aces to the NCAA Tournament eleven times and to the College Cup (NCAA Final Four) twice. (Photo courtesy of the University of Evansville, Sports Information.)

David Weir arrived at the University of Evansville slow and weak in 1987. During his four years here, he got stronger and faster and moved from defender to forward. In 1990, he tallied 24 goals and 11 assists for 59 points, second in school history. His 24 goals were the most in the nation as he led the Aces to the College Cup. A first-team All-American at Evansville, David went on to become the first U.S. collegian to compete for a European team (his home country of Scotland) in the World Cup. (Photo courtesy of the University of Evansville, Sports Information.)

and set NCAA Division I records for most wins in a season (24) and most shutouts (17). With three All-Americans leading the way, Harrington, defender Scott Cannon and forward David Weir, the Aces once again made the College Cup, after NCAA Tourney wins over Boston University and Indiana. Once again, U of E entered the semi-final undefeated (24-0-2) and ranked #1 but suffered defeat, this time to Rutgers 1-0.

The seven years from '84–'91 were the heyday of Aces soccer and made Evansville a perennial contender on the national level. The program would win the conference tournament two more times under Schmalz ('91 and '96) and produce one more first team All-American, Graham Merryweather ('91). When Fred Schmalz retired in 2002, he left a legacy of success that won't be forgotten. As a member of the University of Evansville Athletic Hall of Fame, Fred's image is displayed with Bill Vieth Sr. (coach) and many of his former players. When he stepped down, Schmalz retired as the eighth-winningest coach in Division I history, with 403 victories. During his 24-year tenure as coach of the Aces, he elevated the program to heights most thought impossible, and he will always be remembered as one of the greatest coaches in the history of the school.

As Schmalz was beginning his unprecedented run with the Aces in 1986, another amazing streak was beginning right down the street at Memorial High School. With soccer starting to blossom in the area, Bill Vieth Jr. stepped into the head coaching position with the aim of continuing the Tiger tradition as one of the elite soccer programs in the state. Since soccer was not yet sanctioned by the IHSAA, the Indiana High School Soccer Association continued to organize and oversee the sport. Bill Vieth Sr. was heavily involved and made sure the organization conformed with IHSAA guidelines so that when schools were ready, the transition would be seamless.

As his son took the helm at Memorial, Bill Sr. was aware of how the growth of the youth soccer program and the development of the U of E program by Fred Schmalz were intertwined with the evolution of high school soccer into an IHSAA program. "During those years, the early '80s, when Fred came, there was very little soccer on television," recalled Vieth Sr. "So the only place they could see soccer at a fairly high level was by watching U of E. As Fred developed his program into one of the top ones in the country, it gave the kids here a chance to see that, and, you know, kids began to imitate the good players they saw. It helped to build not only the enthusiasm but also the skill level throughout the community."

Many area schools were able to produce a few outstanding players and teams over the years, but it was Memorial that

Defender Scott Cannon, a Memorial High School grad, was named a 1990 first-team All-American and was selected as a member of the USA Full National Team. (Photo courtesy of the University of Evansville Sports Information.)

Bill Vieth Jr. during his days as an All-American at Memorial. (Photo courtesy of the Vieth family.)

Memorial's Tim Vieth (left) played his college soccer at Duke. (Photo courtesy of Duke University.)

consistently fielded winning teams. When Bill Vieth Jr. took over in 1986, the program had already won five IHSSA State titles ('79, '80, '81, '83 and '84), and Vieth Jr. didn't miss a beat as he led the Tigers to the school's first undefeated season (15-0-3) and a State championship in his first year there. Vieth, who was assisted for many years by Jay Frederick, added four more State titles to his resumé in the next seven years ('88, '89, '90 and '92) before the IHSAA finally received enough votes by school principals to convert soccer to a fully sanctioned IHSAA sport in 1994.

Although Memorial continued to be one of the state's premier programs, the conversion to the IHSAA appeared to put a hex on the Tigers. Time after time, they would get close, but their first IHSAA title continued to elude them. In fact, Castle, another consistently successful program, arrived on the IHSAA mountaintop first when they won the boys title in 2000. For the next seven years, no area team could match Castle's feat until Memorial finally got the gorilla off their back with a remarkable season in 2007. The '07 Memorial squad not only captured the title with a 1-0 win over Chesterton but they finished the season undefeated (23-0-2) and were ranked as the #1 team in the nation.

Over 29 seasons of playing a full schedule, the Memorial High School boys soccer program has compiled a 519-88-50 record (85%) and has never had a losing season. The Tigers have fashioned three undefeated seasons ('86, '90 and '07) and have had four seasons where they have lost only their final game in the tournament.

Memorial has produced seven high school All-Americans: Bill Vieth Jr. ('80 and '81); Jack Mitchell ('82); Mike Traylor ('84); Scott Cannon ('85 and '86); Tim Vieth, (Bill Sr.'s youngest son - '87 and '88); Paul Barton ('91); and Mitch Day ('07). Over the years, Memorial teams have won 24 City titles and 23 sectionals and have been to the state's Final Four 19 times, winning eleven State championships.

Although soccer, as a sport, is merely an infant compared to most other area sports, there is no question that it is here to stay. When the World Cup was held in the U.S. in 1994, it was far and away the biggest sporting event in the world, with ten American cities hosting games in the month-long, 60-game format. As the game has evolved into a more offense-oriented sport, television has brought the game into millions of homes, and a fact that may surprise many is that, in terms of registered youth players, America outnumbers any other country in the world. Whether the old-timers like it or not, the sport is not going away, and Bill Vieth Jr. has watched as the sport has blossomed.

"The Europeans I know watch a game of baseball and say it's the most boring game they've ever seen," Vieth pointed out, "yet somebody who grew up watching baseball understands that the intricacies are what make the game interesting. It's the same way for soccer fans.

"People are starting to understand. You can't go watch your grandkids over and over again and not start to understand and appreciate what's happening out there. I don't think soccer will ever replace baseball or football or basketball; those are American sports. But I do think soccer will become the fourth major sport."

How far the sport will go is yet to be seen, but how far it has come is truly remarkable. Thirty-plus years ago, soccer was like an orphan that no one wanted. But as people grew to know it, they grew to love it. The tournaments held here at the Goebel Complex and other venues stack up with some of the best in the nation, and several area high school programs have earned respect statewide. Though many more will surely follow, Bill Vieth, Bill Jr. and Fred Schmalz were three of the sport's local pioneers. Each of them brought vision to the tasks at hand and helped the sport of soccer find a home in southwestern Indiana.

THE BEST OF THE BEST

The following area players have been recognized as All-Americans by either *Parade* or the National Soccer Coaches Association of America.

- Bill Vieth, Memorial ('80-'81)
- Jack Mitchell, Memorial ('82)
- Mike Traylor, Memorial ('84)
- Scott Cannon, Memorial ('85)
- Tim Vieth, Memorial ('87,'88)
- Paul Barton, Memorial ('91)
- Chad Cole, Harrison ('92)
- Mitch Day, Memorial ('07)
- Sean Hoek, Castle ('07)

THE GOEBEL COMPLEX

The Goebel Complex on North Green River Road is one of the finest facilities of its kind in the country. According to retired University of Evansville soccer coach Fred Schmalz, the complex may never have been built if not for Mayor Frank McDonald Jr. While Vectren was in the process of purchasing Riverside 1, Mayor McDonald commented that the property was being sold too cheap and that they should pay another $1 million. His statement caused the price to be raised, and the city used the money to buy Goebel Farm.

The complex sits on seventy acres and features nine irrigated Olympic-sized fields and one $555,000 Olympic-sized astroturf field (only the second of its kind in Indiana). Also included at the facility are parking for over 400 vehicles, a spacious visitors center with concessions and restrooms, and a picnic area.

The $3.1 million facility, managed by Schmalz, has enabled southwestern Indiana to become a prime destination for teams from all over the Midwest to come to compete, bringing millions of dollars into the area. At the same time, the complex gives local players and fans a state-of-the-art venue to enjoy the sport as young soccer stars develop.

IHSAA STATE CHAMPIONS:
BOYS SOCCER

School	Year	Record	Coach
Castle	2000-2001	21-1-2	Doug Diedrich
Memorial	2007-2008	23-0-2	Bill Vieth

GIRLS SOCCER

School	Year	Record	Coach
Memorial	1996-1997	19-3	Joe Lattner

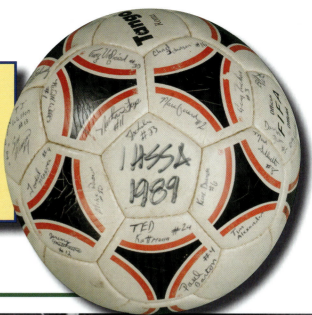

This soccer ball was used in Memrial's 1989 State Championship win and was signed by members of the team.

VINCENNES LINCOLN: #1 IN '81

The 1981 Alices. Kneeling (L-R): Cheerleaders Kris Tolbert, Angie Eck, Stacy Westfall, Jenny Watson. Front Row (L-R): John Lackey (student mgr.), Jim Martin, Brent Claycomb, Jeff Agee, Doug Crook, Randy Combs, Mike Kimmell, David Hill (student mgr.). Middle Row (L-R): Assistant coaches Kim Prout and Eonnis Query, Ron Stryzinski, Robin Talbott, Courtney Witte, cheerleader Lisa Landrey, Brian Spradling, Karl Donovan, Tim Vieke, assistant coach Roger Benson, head coach 'Gunner' Wyman. Back Row (L-R): Mickey Hert (student mgr.), George Rogers Clark (scorekeeper), Robert Hill (ath. bus. mgr.), James Pittman (principal), Robert Taylor (asst. principal), Richard Hutchison(asst. scorekeeper), Tom Ernst (time keeper). (student mgr. Roger Cannon was not present.)

As the crowd noise subsided on the floor of Market Square Arena in March of 1981, one might have expected to hear a director yell, "CUT!" as the curtain fell on a storybook ending for the Vincennes Alices. The tale behind the tumultuous journey to the championship had all the makings of a Hollywood movie, and the drama was not lost on the Alices' coaches or players.

Cast in the lead role was the team's controversial coach, Gunner Wyman. His supporting cast was a group of talented players who personified the word 'TEAM', led by seniors Doug Crook and Courtney Witte. The saga began three years earlier when Coach Wyman completed the 1978 season with the worst record in his illustrious career. Not known for his public relations skills, Wyman's abrasive style had irritated enough people over the years that a covert group of disgruntled fans decided to circulate a petition calling for his removal. Although he was supported by a loyal superintendent and school board, Gunner wanted his talented sophomores-to-be to know about the petition and to have a chance to express their thoughts.

Dave Hill, now the athletic director at Lincoln, was a sophomore player in 1978 but served as the team's manager in 1981. He recalls vividly the words spoken by coach Wyman. "He called us all in and said, 'Do you want me to quit? I'll quit right now if you guys want me to quit,'" Hill explained from his office. "Then he came out and told the newspaper, 'I'll retire when these boys (the sophomores) graduate.'"

A subplot of the movie occured that spring when the sophomores painted a mantra on the backyard court of Dr. Dan Combs, the father of sophomore Randy Combs. The message was simple: "#1 in '81." The boys had decided to dedicate themselves to winning the State title, and the stage was set for their exciting journey.

The first act of the drama took place during the winter months when the Alices destroyed their first fifteen opponents by an average winning margin of nearly twenty points. During their hot start, the boys in green defeated some stiff competition, beating Reitz, Harrison, Central, Terre Haute North and Indianapolis Washington.

Act Two began with a reality check, as Coach Wyman's crew, then ranked #2 in the state, were slapped with back-to-back losses to Terre Haute South and Barr-Reeve. It was gut check time for the team's six seniors: Crook, Witte, Combs, Ron Stryzinski, Jeff Agee and Karl Donovan. The seniors, who had never played on a losing team during their years together, would have to regroup and turn their season around. Stryzinski and Donovan contributed 18 and 10 points, respectively, in the Alices' next game, an 83-63 win over Memorial, and Vincennes ran the table to end their regular season at 18-2.

Although 'Mr. Outside', Doug Crook, and 'Mr. Inside', 6'8" Courtney Witte, got most of the attention, the other four seniors, plus junior Tim Vieke and sophomore Robin Talbott, all had games where they scored at least twelve points. It was obvious the boys could shoot, but that wasn't the key to the Alices' success.

Gunner Wyman was known for his relentless style of defense, and his '81 team ran his 2-2-1 full-court zone press to perfection. Since Wyman didn't believe in playing zone in the half-court, if the opponent advanced the ball past the center line, Wyman's boys would shift into a tenacious man-to-man. The Alices learned Wyman's system so well that only one team scored more than sixty points during the regular season (Memorial in an 83-63 Vincennes win).

To open Act Three, Vincennes easily won their sectional, something the school had done 51 times in the previous 65 years. After the final game, in which Courtney Witte scored 27 points to go with 23 rebounds, Hugh Schaefer, the coach of the South Knox Spartans, was the first to officially jump on the Alices' bandwagon. After his team lost 90-53 in the sectional final, Coach Schaefer proclaimed that Vincennes would win the State championship.

At the Evansville Regional, Derek Lindauer and the Central Bears threw a scare into the Alices before Robin Talbott helped Vincennes rally for a 57-50 win. Vincennes came from behind again to take the regional title from Mt. Vernon behind Doug Crook's 31 points.

Crook continued his hot streak in the Evansville Semi-state with 31 points in an afternoon win over Brazil. The seniors were one win away from fulfilling their dream of going to State, and only Floyd Central stood in the way. In the night game, Crook led the way again with 18 points, and Tim Vieke was right behind with 17. The Alices pulled away in the third quarter and punched their ticket to Indianapolis with a 65-53 victory.

The players on Gunner Wyman's '81 team had played their roles perfectly, and the prophecy painted on the Combs' backyard court had come true. The coach who had promised to see his players through to this day, despite public protests, had kept his word and had played his leading role well. All that was left was the Hollywood ending.

Wyman's job at this point was to put his players in position to win, and his experience and savvy helped him do just that. Dave Hill looks back and appreciates Wyman's decisions at the time. "I still try to model what we do today after what we did then," Hill admitted, "like staying in a hotel away from everybody and keeping everything as low-key as possible because the game is why you're there and not all the hoopla."

In the afternoon game at Market Square Arena, Vincennes used a workmanlike effort and a 30-point outing from Doug Crook to prevail over Shenandoah 72-53. The Alices were one game away from the school's first basketball championship in 58 years. After the game, Gunner Wyman provided another Hollywood moment that would set the tone for the Alices' grand finale.

"We were having dinner in a suite at the hotel before the game," Dave Hill recalled. "There were some people from Anderson in the hallway. (The Anderson Indians were the Alices' opponent in the Finals.) They kept yelling, 'What's an Alice?' Gunner just sensed that we were all nervous, and suddenly he slammed his hands down on the table and then stood up. Everybody looked up, and he yelled, 'I'll tell you what an Alice is. Tonight, it's an Indian ass-kicker!' The room just busted out laughing. It was like, 'OK, it's on now!'"

In the finals, Crook scored 7 of Vincennes' first 11 points, and Vincennes built a sizeable lead. The Alices' two stars shouldered the load, as Crook ended with a game-high 25 points while Courtney Witte dominated the paint with 21 rebounds, giving the school its second State championship.

Crook and Witte were named to the All-State Finals first team, and Crook became only the 14th player to score more than 100 points in the last four games of the IHSAA Tournament.

As the credits rolled at the conclusion of the '81 Vincennes Lincoln fairy tale story, one could look back and see that the real drama didn't play out on the court. The stories behind the story were those of a group of teenagers who used a paint brush to tell the world of their intentions and of a leading man who crafted perhaps the finest effort of his career in his final performance as a coach. Gunner Wyman resigned after the season, keeping the promise he had made two years earlier, and when he walked off the court after his final game as the coach at Lincoln, he was leaving under his own terms, and he was going out a winner.

CHAPTER SEVEN
1960-1990

TERRY BRAHM: U.S. OLYMPIAN

Like any red-blooded Heritage Hills athlete, Terry Brahm had visions of scoring touchdowns and making game-saving tackles for Coach Bob Clayton's Patriots, but Mother Nature had other plans. At 5'11 and 145 pounds soaking wet and after a knee injury in 1979, Brahm abandoned his dreams of football fame and set out on a path that would lead to national prominence and a spot on the United States Olympic Team.

As a sophomore on the Heritage Hills track team, Brahm was asked to fill in for the Patriots' regular miler, who was injured. In his very first race, Terry set a school record, and by the end of the season, he had lowered his time from 4:45 in his first race to 4:23. After a second place finish in the 1,600-meter run at the State meet as a junior and a fourth place finish as a senior, Brahm accepted an offer to run at Indiana University.

As a runner at IU, Brahm became a world-class athlete while training under hall of fame track coach Sam Bell. Earning letters at IU from 1982-1986, the St. Meinrad native was a six-time All-American in cross country and track while winning four Big Ten indoor championships in the mile and 2-mile and outdoor Big Ten and NCAA titles in the 5,000 meters. When he broke Jim Spivey's IU record in the mile, his time of 3:52:37 placed in the top ten fastest miles ever run by a collegian, ahead of such icons as Villanova's Marty Liquori and Oregon's Steve Prefontaine.

Brahm's singleness of purpose enabled him to set his sights on the world stage. In an interview with the *Indianapolis Star*, Brahm spoke of the grind that middle distance running entails. "I've gotten up every morning to run with the premonition I would go to the (1988) Olympics, or else I wouldn't have gotten up to run," Brahm told reporter Bill Benner. "Then I came to practice every afternoon because I believed I could do this. You make a conscious decision to pursue the Olympics, or else you're not going to get up and run in January when it's below zero and snowing outside."

In June of 1986, Brahm won the 3,000 meters to help the U.S. defeat England in the McVities Challenge, and later, he finished second in the World Indoor Championships in the same event. As a 5,000 meter runner (3.1 miles), Brahm was one of America's most consistent performers, battling fellow American Doug Padilla in meet after meet on the track circuit.

When the moment of truth finally arrived at the Olympic Trials, Brahm, Padilla and Sydney Maree easily clinched the three 5,000-meter spots on the U.S. team. Terry's years of self-discipline and perseverance had paid off, and he prepared to leave for the 24th Olympiad. The 5,000-meter race in Seoul was won by John Ngugi of Kenya in 1988, and although Terry Brahm did not qualify for the finals in Seoul, he had come a long way from his home in rural Indiana.

Terry Brahm had used his intelligence and tenacity to earn a college education and to place himself among the elite in his sport. The kid who reluctantly put away his football helmet in 1979 had earned a place in the IU Sports Hall of Fame and had become one of the few local athletes to represent our country in the Olympic Games.

(Photo courtesy of Indiana University, Media Relations.)

RICHARD LANKFORD: THE VOICE OF GIBSON COUNTY

To say that Princeton's Richard Lankford loves the radio business would be a huge understatement, and he will gladly tell you that he has cherished every minute he has spent broadcasting sports for the last 55 years. Even today, Lankford can be heard doing play-by-play whenever WRAY covers sporting events, and through his many years on the air, he was witnessed some of the greatest athletes in Indiana history.

Lankford was born in Michigan City, but the Great Depression forced his father to leave his job with the railroad when Richard was only a year old. The family moved south and settled in Mt. Carmel, Illinois, where Richard grew up and was a three-sport athlete in high school. After his graduation in 1947, the 6'2" Lankford played basketball at Illinois State before injuring his knee in 1949. In the fall of '49, he transferred to Oakland City College for two more years of school before marrying his wife, Helen, in 1951 and leaving for a two-year tour in the Army in 1952.

While Richard was serving in Korea, his father, M.R. (his given name was Major Raymond, but he was always known as M.R.), was building a reputation in the broadcasting business, eventually owning five radio stations and a small television station in Princeton. Upon his return from the service, Richard found himself drawn into the family business, earning $35 a week working for his father.

WRAY radio has been around for a long time, and the same could be said for the station's current owner, Richard Lankford. Although none of M.R. Lankford's children professes to have had a desire to get into the radio business, it seems old Dad had developed a master plan. As things played out, each of the kids, Richard and his two brothers and two sisters, eventually became involved.

Richard's career as a sports announcer can be attributed more to fate than design, as his debut was the result of unusual circumstances. It seems the station had contracted to do a game in Jasper in 1954 but the station's regular announcer had come down with laryngitis. With the advertising already sold, M.R. was forced to devise a 'Plan B'. Without notice, the Plan B was Richard and his brothers. On the way to Jasper, the three brainstormed, and it was decided that Richard would call the game while younger brother Stuart would use his great voice to do commercials and older brother Ray Jay would engineer and keep score. Somehow the brothers pulled it off, and when the regular announcer later moved on, Richard took his permanent place behind the mic and has been there ever since.

In the early years, Gibson County was home to ten high schools, and Richard's face still lights up as he conjures up the memories from a bygone era when he covered games for the Princeton Tigers, Patoka Wrens, Mt. Olympus Mountaineers, Francisco Owls, Oakland City Oaks, Mackey Aces, Haubstadt Hornets/Elites, Ft. Branch Twigs, Owensville Kickapoos and Hazelton Lions.

Some of Richard's fondest recollections are of the cracker box gyms that were always packed to the rafters on Friday nights with fans that far outnumbered the seating capacity of around 200. In some cases, school officials didn't have places for the broadcast

Richard Lankford (right) doing play-by-play alongside his son Jeff.
(Photo from the Lankford collection.)

crew to sit because it would mean sacrificing four or five seats for fans. At the old Mackey gym, Lankford and his cohorts had to set up a card table that protruded onto the playing surface. When asked how it affected the game, Richard gave the simple response, "They just dribbled around us." He also recalled another instance where the overflow crowd at the popular Mt. Olympus Holiday Tournament dictated that the WRAY crew be put at a table above the women's restroom.

At Rose Hulman, for an Oakland City College game, Lankford was asked to climb a 40-foot scaffold to broadcast. After first refusing, he and his partners carefully made the climb, equipment in tow, when they found out that the engineering students had built the contraption just for them. Richard also ran into some creative challenges at the high school football games he covered, like the game at Sullivan when he found himself sitting on the top row of the gym looking out a window at the game in the distance. Though announcers today might wince at the thought of such poor conditions, Lankford relishes the memories and philosophizes by saying, "My, how times have changed. Back then, you just did what you had to do."

As the conversation about the character of the old gyms wound down, Richard pointed out that, even today, broadcasting is not always a bed of roses. Though many of the vintage gyms of the '50s and '60s were cold during the winter basketball season, nothing can compare to the arctic setting at Mater Dei High School. "No gym was as cold as Mater Dei's gym," Richard said from his office at WRAY, almost trembling from the thought. "We broadcasted from the back row with our backs against the windows, and the wind just whistles through there. Whenever we're there, we keep our topcoats on and wear gloves."

Though Richard may have been cold and cramped, he loved doing the high school games, especially when tournament time rolled around. Young folks today would not believe the atmosphere of the sectional tournaments of the '50s and '60s, and Lankford recalls vividly when "Patoka came alive in '55" and the Wrens captured the title. He also recalls the excitement when Larry Harris led Oakland City to an undefeated season before falling to eventual State champ North in the 1967 regional.

Lankford has special memories of the mania that surrounded the ten-team sectional, featuring all the county teams, and how fans would stop at nothing to be part of the overflow crowds. One particular sectional stood out for Richard when asked about the overwhelming enthusiasm fans had for Indiana basketball. After a blizzard blanketed Gibson County with a seven-inch snowfall that covered the fence posts, Richard's car was towed three times before he made it to the gym. Other loyal fans went to even more extremes. Sanford Sanders, who served as the Superintendent of County Schools, never missed a sectional game and weathered the aforementioned storm by walking over seven miles from Mt. Olympus just to watch the tournament.

The broadcasts in the early days were far different than those of today. Until the mid-'60s, AM radio was a listener's only option. Because AM signals radiate much greater distances after sundown, WRAY was forced to operate only during daylight hours so that its signal would not interfere with other 1250-frequency stations in Illinois and Arkansas. The FCC mandate meant that if local listeners wanted to hear a ballgame, they had to wait until the next day. This required Richard and his crew to tape a Friday night game on a big-reel tape recorder and then re-play the action on Saturday afternoons.

Lankford estimates that he has broadcasted over 4,000 games during his career, and he has witnessed some great talent as he followed the action from his perch behind the microphone. Some of his favorite coaches over the years were Larry Holder, Jim Jones, Bob Lochmueller, Bill Richeson, and 'Gunner' Wyman. Among the best county players he covered were: Bob Meier and Stan Young (Francisco); Roger Emmert (Haubstadt); Al Dixon and Vep Hill (Hazelton); Bob Harmon (Mackey); Ron Jackson and Jim Thompson (Mt. Olympus); Bill Stone (Patoka); Walt Deal and Virgil Ferguson (Owensville); Sherrill Marginet and Joe Luttrell (Ft. Branch); Billy Bingham, Greg Wilkerson, and Larry Harris (Oakland City); and Roy Stoll, Bob Pritchett, Buddy Rogers, Steve Ritchie, Brad Fichter, Travis Trice and Larry Kidwell (Princeton).

When pressed to identify the absolute best he has seen statewide during his years covering the State Tournament, Lankford gave the query some serious thought before responding. After mentioning such greats as the Van Arsdale twins (Indianapolis Manual), George McGinnis (Indianapolis Washington), Rick Mount (Lebanon), Jimmy Rayl (Kokomo), Ron Bonham (Muncie Central) and Oscar Robertson (Crispus Attucks), he seemed supremely confident when he divulged his somewhat surprising top three.

"I would have to go with Larry Harris at # 3," Richard answered, "because of the great years he had in the late '60s on those great teams at Oakland City. Then I would say Tyler Zeller (the star of Washington's 2008 State champions). He had tremendous skills on a 7-foot frame. And Damon Bailey (Bedford North Lawrence) would be #1. I saw him in front of 40,000 fans for a high school game, and that will never happen again with the class system. He could do it all. He scored over 3,000 points in his career, and I don't foresee that record being broken."

In his 55 years on the job, Richard has worked with only four partners: his brothers, Stuart and Ray Jay; his son Jeff; and his nephew Steve, who was a member of the 1965 Princeton team that advanced to the State Finals. When Richard retires, he plans to turn over the reins to his son, making Steve and Jeff the third generation of Lankfords at WRAY. But according to Lankford, the transition won't happen anytime soon. For a while at least, fans will still hear his trademark "BOOM!" when a player's shot caresses the net from long range, and they'll still feel the excitement in Richard's voice as he calls the action.

Lankford has been honored by inductions into the Oakland City College and Associated Press Halls of Fame and was even named the Indiana Broadcaster of the Year, but his true legacy is his contribution to local sports. For as long as he's behind the mic, he'll continue to emulate his idol Jack Buck and strive to convey each game as an unbiased observer. His exuberance for sports is unquestionable, and his perspective as a proven veteran is invaluable. When talking with Richard, it's easy to see that he considers himself a very lucky man. "If anybody ever loved their job, it's me," he reflected from behind his desk. "I mean, I absolutely love it! When I sit down to do a broadcast, it's just unbelievable!"

Not many people are so fortunate to make a living doing something they truly love, and Richard Lankford appreciates his profession as much as his listeners appreciate him. Whether his career ends soon or many years from now, he will forever be known as The Voice of Gibson County Sports.

THE LANDER FAMILY: DADDY'S LITTLE GIRLS MADE IT BIG

Vicki and Cassandra Lander are arguably the best pair of sister athletes to come out of southwestern Indiana, and both attribute their success, in part, to backyard sessions with their father. The girls' father, Ted Lander, was an insanely-talented athlete for Evansville Lincoln High School in the 1950s. He was so good, in fact, that many from that generation place him in some very elite company.

"Ted Lander is one of the finest all-around athletes to come out of here," said Ron Volkman, a contemporary of Lander's who played at Bosse. "You've got Jerry Browning (Mater Dei) and Bob Griese, but Ted Lander has to be up at the top. He averaged maybe 30 points in basketball, and he was an amazing hitter and fielder (in baseball). He played whatever he wanted to play."

Ted was such a talented baseball player that one of his coaches at Lincoln, Willie Saucer, was prepared to drive him to Cincinnati to try out for the major leagues, but Ted didn't want to go. He chose instead to go into the Army after high school. As a basketball star, he was so renowned that fans were hoping to see him match up in the State Tournament with a young star from Indianapolis named Oscar Robertson, but Lincoln's journey was halted in the semi-state. In 1955, Ted starred with Walter Miles, John Barnhill and others as Lincoln's basketball team became the first city team to finish a regular season undefeated.

After returning from the Army, Ted and his wife, Zora, went about the business of raising their four children. It came as no surprise that all the children were athletes. Zora, herself, played the old-fashioned basketball game (where three players played offense and three played defense) and was an excellent softball player who was known for using the 'basket catch' like her favorite player Willie Mays.

The Lander sons were both fine athletes at Bosse. Alan was a center and linebacker for Coach Archie Owen in football, and Tim was a quarterback who also played on the outstanding 1981-'82 Bosse basketball team. Alan's son Matt, Ted's and Zora's grandson, was a 6'4 graduate of Bosse who played for John A. Logan College in Illinois starting in 2007.

But with all the athletic DNA coursing through the veins of the Lander family, perhaps the greatest concentration belonged to the Lander daughters, Cassandra and Vicki. Both girls are aware of their genetic blessings, and all the kids recall their father's influences during backyard basketball games.

"That's where I got all my skills," Vicki says of her father. "He played baseball, he played basketball, and he swam competitively. He was just an overall athlete."

Many hours were spent playing basketball on the goal Ted had placed on the garage behind their home. "I'll never forget this," said Alan Lander. "My dad would play '21' with us, and one day Dad hit the first two points and then stood at the free throw line and hit 19 straight and won the game, and he said 'That's why free throws are important.'"

Cassandra and Vicki also tell similar stories of working with their father. Both recall their dad's watchful eye as he insisted that the boys let the younger girls play with them and how Ted would work with them on their shooting when they were as young as four or five.

The Lander kids know how fortunate they were to have had the guidance of two great parents, and their mother realizes just how important the family unit was. "It was during a time when kids had a momma and a dad," Zora confided. "And it takes two to raise kids. My mom and dad made me study, and we made them study. They were great kids."

Cassandra Lander was a diminutive dynamo during her playing days at Bosse, and although basketball would be her ticket to a free education, she was also an amazing track athlete. She was a two-time State champion in the high jump, which was no small feat for such a petite young lady. She won the 1977 title with a leap of 5'6 ¾" and the '78 championship at 5'7". Her best jump of the season was 5'9 ¼". Not bad for a 5'5" female.

Her high school basketball coach, Jerry Canterbury, has high praise for the oldest of the Lander sisters. He recalled a game when a referee witnessed Cassandra leap over much taller girls and touch the rim. The referee walked over to Canterbury and said, "Did I just see what I think I saw?" Canterbury just smiled and shrugged. Coach Canterbury, who has played, coached and witnessed virtually every athlete to come out of the area for over fifty years, put Cassandra's talents in perspective when he declared, "Cassandra Lander and Louise Owen, in my opinion, were the best female athletes to come out of Evansville."

Vicki Lander at UNLV. (Photo courtesy of the University of Las Vegas-Nevada, Sports Information.)

In high school, Cassandra played the #2 guard for Bosse on a team that featured some outstanding players, like center Felicia Bush and guards Lisa Bruin and Carrie Hester. Women's basketball was just coming into its own when Cassandra played as a freshman in 1975-'76. During her final three seasons, the Lady Bulldogs went 35-6 and Cassandra was named to the Indiana All-Star team.

According to Cassandra, the onus of finding a college to play for during that era was left up to the athlete, not the universities. "Girls had to contact the school first before the school could recruit them," she explained.

With not much to go on, she selected ten schools she thought she might like and then followed her instincts. The University of Arizona was a possibility, but she thought their nickname was too ordinary. ("Everyone was the 'Wildcats'.") Then she saw the Arizona State 'Sun Devils' and thought, "That's Cool!" So she contacted ASU and one or two others and waited.

Coach Canterbury had some brochures left over that he had prepared to promote Cassandra as an All-Star candidate, and so he sent one to Arizona State. ASU then called Cassandra and told her that they couldn't pay for her to come out but that they were very interested. After her parents agreed to fly her west, Cassandra visited the campus and began a recruiting process that may be the only one of its kind in basketball history.

Arizona State sent a player to pick Cassandra up at the airport and had arranged for another player to work Cassandra out (at the gym). Cassandra was confused that the coach was never around, but she went along with the program and played hoops with the player anyway. "I wore her out all weekend," Cassandra recalled. "I'm not trying to brag, but I thought 'Oh, my goodness! If she's the best they have, they can't be very good!' I ran circles around her!

"We hit it off," she continued, "and the coach called her later. I was actually sitting there when he called. She said, 'Coach, sign her up.'"

And this is where the story gets interesting.

The next day, after Cassandra had returned home, the coach called her and confessed that he had gotten wind that he was going to be fired. He said that he was going to overnight a letter of intent to her and that she should sign it and return it immediately. He knew that if the new coach came in before Cassandra was signed, there would be nothing he could do to help her. But if the letter was signed in time, the school couldn't take it away from her.

Oddly enough, Cassandra was signing with a coach she would probably never play for and, amazingly, had never laid eyes on. "I never met him, never saw him, and he never saw me play," she said.

The gamble paid off for both parties, however, as Cassandra had a remarkable career at ASU playing under the new coach, Julienne Simpson, who had been a co-captain on the 1976 U.S. Olympic team. (The other co-captain of the Olympic team was Pat Head, later Pat Summitt, who would go on to become the winningest Division I coach, man or woman, in NCAA history.)

At ASU, Cassandra played alongside Kym Hampton, who later played in the WNBA with the New York Liberty. The Sun Devils were highly-ranked during her last two years but lost to the eventual national champions both years in the NCAA Tourney (Louisiana Tech in '82 and Cheryl Miller's USC team in '83).

Cassandra Lander while at Arizona State.
(Photo courtesy of Arizona State, Media Relations.)

Cassandra tried out unsuccessfully for the 1980 Olympic team, but she looks back on her college years with great satisfaction. She had gotten to compete against some great players, like USC's incredible lineup of Cheryl Miller; Rhonda Windham; the McGee twins, Pam and Paula; and Cynthia Cooper, who went on to star for the WNBA's Houston Comets. Cassandra was inducted into ASU's hall of fame in 2006 as the schools #2 all-time leading scorer with 1,670 points (a 14.1 average.) She was also the school's all-time leader in steals and had career highs of 35 points and 12 rebounds in a single game.

Cassandra says that she is a believer in fate. Today she loves her job as a flight attendant and feels blessed for the days she spent at Arizona State. With fate on her side, she owes it all to the Sun Devil nickname and a man named Paul Long, the coach she never met.

Using her older sister as a role model, Vicki Gail Lander followed in Cassandra's footsteps in more ways than one. Like her sister, Vicki played for the popular and successful Bosse coach Jerry Canterbury, and Vicki will admit that Cassandra was a tough act to follow. "She was a great basketball player and athlete," Vicki said from her home in Queen Creek, Arizona. "When I was in grade school, people were looking forward to me coming to Bosse to see the comparison."

As a freshman at Bosse, Vicki started on one of the best teams in the school's history. Led by all-everything Cheryl Dowell and Charlene Tinner, the Lady Bulldogs finished the season 24-2 and were one game shy of playing for the State championship

Like Cassandra, Vicki credits her success to seeking out the best possible competition during the off-season. Cassandra and her best friend, Lindsey Bowling from Harrison, spent many hours at the YMCA playing pickup games with the boys. Vicki did likewise by playing solely against the best boys in town to prepare for her seasons.

Wearing the same #32 as her sister and her father, Vicki became a dominant player herself as her high school career progressed. Over her four years, she scored 1,843 points and led the state in scoring as a senior with her 31.1 per game average. Like her sister, Vicki's play earned her a spot on the Indiana All-Stars, which provided another showcase for her as she looked ahead to playing college ball.

By the time Vicki was considering college, the recruiting process for women had evolved so that it was closer to what it is today. Although she was approached by several high-quality programs, such as Penn State, Indiana and Purdue, Vicki was looking for a place where she could enjoy college life far away from home. Little did she know that fate would play a role in her destination just as it had for Cassandra.

During Vicki's senior year, Cassandra suggested that Vicki join her on a road trip. Cassandra was friends with Sheila Bolla, the head coach at the University of Nevada-Las Vegas, and thought it would be fun to visit 'Sin City' for a weekend. Both girls swear that basketball was the farthest thing from their minds when they left for the desert.

"I had no idea about going there (to school)," Vicki related. "They weren't even recruiting me at the time. She (Bolla) just asked me if I played basketball, and I said, 'Yeah.' She sent one of her assistant coaches down to see me play, and after that, they offered me a scholarship. We were just going for a weekend trip in Vegas!"

During Vicki's years at UNLV, she crossed paths several times with fellow Bosse teammate Cheryl Dowell, who had a magnificent career at Long Beach State. Vicki graduated in 1991 with a degree in Criminal Justice and was named to the All-Mountain West Conference first team as a senior. She still holds the top two spots in the Lady Rebels record book for season free throw percentage, shooting .824 in 1988-'89 and .831 in '89-'90.

Like her sister, Vicki stayed near her college alma mater and now serves as a police officer for the city of Queen Church. Though they were eight years apart in age, the Lander girls had many more similarities than differences throughout their athletic careers. Their father, who died in 1985 from a neck injury sustained from a fall at the fire station where he served as a firefighter, watched the girls play whenever he could. Though he never got to see Vicki past her early high school days, her eventual successes would not have surprised him. With all the hours he spent with his kids shooting hoops in the backyard, he probably realized early on that both his girls were going to be something special.

AMAZING BUT TRUE

The only two Evansville high school basketball teams to finish a regular season undefeated included members of the Lander family. In 1955, Ted Lander starred with Walter Miles to lead Lincoln to an undefeated season. In 1982, Tim Lander was a member of Bosse's amazing team that was undefeated until the final game of the State Tournament. The team was led by two of the best players in Indiana, Derrick Dowell and Myron Christian.

THE '81 LADY PANTHERS: SUPER TEAM – SUPER-STITIOUS

Just like many teams that rise above the competition to achieve greatness, fans of the 1981 State Champion girls basketball team from Reitz could see the team's potential long before the girls reached high school. As the pre-teens grew into Lady Panthers, the group evolved into a team whose coach was not afraid to be a little unorthodox and whose players displayed quirks and superstitions that endeared them to fans and media alike.

Five years prior to Reitz's March celebration, the school decided to hire Louise Owen as its first girls basketball coach. Although she was an accomplished athlete, Louise had never coached the sport, but she did have an eye for talent. While Ms. Owen was learning the ropes, just down the road, three girls from Helfrich Park Elementary were wearing the boys' old uniforms and winning a City championship. These three, Shelly Brand, Missy Morrow and Denic (pronounced duh-NEEK) Black would become starters on Owen's championship team four years later. They would be joined by starters Brenda Sue Butler and Barb Dykstra and a strong backup group: seniors Cathy Oxley and Tricia Suggs; juniors Tammie Manchette and Valerie Guest; and sophomores Toni Ervin, Lisa Martin and Beth Drone.

When asked recently if she could have imagined a State championship before the season started, Coach Owen said, "No, but we had hoped. Shelly (Brand) was a shooter and quick, and Barb (Dykstra) was just as quick and a natural athlete. And Missy Morrow, bless her heart, she was a good rebounder. And Denic, she wasn't tall, but she was a terrific center."

After an 11-6 season the year before, Louise decided to take several of her players to watch the State Finals. She hoped that by watching Southport defeat Columbus East, the girls might dare to dream. When the team met for the first time prior to the '80-'81 season, Louise could see that the trip to Indy had sparked a fire in the bellies of her girls.

As Coach Owen asked each girl to express her goal for the season, the first team member talked about winning the City, then another added the sectional. When the first mention was made of winning the State, the girls giggled as if it were a joke. But as the season got underway, they couldn't help but wonder.

When the season started, the Lady Panthers were determined to become even better at their patented running game. Their aggressive full-court press and relentless fast break offense were orchestrated by assistant coach Joe Weber. Many feel that when Weber joined forces with Owen the prior year, the final piece to the puzzle was in place, because their two styles of coaching complemented each other perfectly.

"What Louise didn't know, Joe brought to the table," said Barb Dykstra, the team's second-leading scorer. "Louise had a little bit of knowledge about everything. She knew how to win and how to motivate people because it was instilled in her, and Joe brought the fundamentals to the game. He brought in our press offense and our press defense. Where Joe would be a little more vocal, Louise would just say, 'Come on, Barbara.' And people don't call me 'Barbara'. When she said it, it meant more than just, 'Come on, Barbara.'"

The 1981 State champions. Front Row (L-R): head coach Louise Owen, Denic Black, Barb Dykstra, Shelly Brand, Missy Morrow, Brenda Sue Butler. Second Row (L-R): Beth Drone, Tammie Manchette, Valerie Guest, Lisa Martin, Toni Ervin, Patricia Suggs, Cathy Oxley. Back Row (L-R): equip. mgr. Lonnie Albin, principal Edmund Higgs, team managers Susan Koewler and Angela Geiser, athletic bus. mgr. Jim Bratt, asst. coach Joe Weber.

Shelly Brand totally agreed with Dykstra's assessment. "Coach Owen was a very classy lady," Shelly said. "She always had an upbeat attitude. As a team, Coach Owen and Coach Weber were fantastic."

Missy Morrow took the coaching analysis one step farther when she said in a *Courier* article, "Coach Owen was the peacemaker, and Coach Weber was the playmaker."

Practices were sometimes brutal, as the girls logged countless miles to enable them to maintain the frenetic pace of their run-and-gun style. Fortunately for the girls, Coach Owen also saw the benefit of a lighter atmosphere from time to time. "She made things fun," said Shelly Brand. "She made us run a lot, but she also let us play games and laugh and giggle." With their bodies in shape and their spirits high, the girls were ready to play.

Coach Owen was also wise to schedule scrimmages with Reitz's freshman boys team. The innovative idea made it tough for the girls to defend the stronger, quicker boys, but it gave them an advantage on their competition when they squared off against other girls.

Reitz launched their historic season by running over, under, around and through their first ten opponents. Their eleventh game was the highly-anticipated matchup with the powerful North Huskies, led by Lisa Krieg, Peggy Brawn and Susan Thompson. The game was close from start to finish as the bigger Huskies battled the quicker Panthers, and Reitz led 49-48 with five seconds remaining as the thrilling finish played out.

After a missed free throw, North's Jennifer Mooney raced downcourt. Shelly Brand braced to draw a charge, and the whistle blew as the buzzer sounded. The ruling was made that the whistle beat the buzzer and that Brand had committed the blocking foul. Consequently, Mooney sank one free throw and North eventually won in two overtimes.

Shelly Brand feels that the loss to North was just what the team needed at that point in the season. "When we lost to North in overtime, we realized, 'Hey, we *can* lose,'" she said recently. "And that woke us up a little bit and got rid of our big heads. We didn't like to lose."

As things turned out, the Panthers were a fraction of a second from a perfect season, because with a new sense of urgency, they ran the table for the rest of the year. Coach Owen believes that, even though they finished the regular season 16-1, the tough local competition prepared them for their tourney run. In fact, five of the seven city teams had winning records, and Bosse tied Reitz for the City championship.

After a tough regular season, Coach Owen knew that the biggest tournament dangers lay in the early stages, the sectional and regional. After two surprisingly easy games over Bosse (76-43) and Mater Dei (69-38), the only obstacle left was their arch-nemesis, North. The Huskies led by nine at halftime (35-26), but then Reitz, behind Brand's 31 points, took the lead and then held off a frantic North rally for a 61-60 win.

Who knows how far the Huskies might have gone had they prevailed that night. North coach Ron Johnson was both philosophical and gracious in his comments in the *Courier*. "I thought whichever team won that game would have a chance to play pretty deep in the tournament," he said. "That Reitz team personified Louise Owen's spirit. When they met adversity, they faced it head-on."

At the Gibson Southern Regional, Reitz disposed of Jasper behind Brenda Sue Butler's 21 points. In the final, Reitz shot only 28% from the floor (14-50) but won a nail-biter 44-42 over Boonville behind huge efforts from Cathy Oxley and Lisa Martin. The Lady Panthers were halfway home, but they had some stiff competition ahead.

Heading into the Bedford Semi-state, Coach Owen decided to take the no-frills approach, and the players still laugh when they recall the experience. It seems that while the other schools arrived in chartered buses and stayed at the finest hotels, the Reitz team pulled in to the pink Rosemont Motel in a yellow school bus. Although the girls probably felt like the Beverly Hillbillies, the strategy paid off, as Reitz completed another leg of their historic journey.

In the afternoon game, Barb Dykstra hit all eight of her fourth quarter free throws and led the Panthers in scoring with 20 points in a 52-45 win over Seymour. In the final game, Denic Black was relentless in blocking out New Albany's 6-foot sophomore center Kelly Thomas, and Dykstra again led the Panthers in scoring with 19 points in a 62-55 victory. The team piled into their yellow bus and left for home, knowing that they were heading to Indy to continue the chase for their dream.

As plans were made for the trip north, some of the girls had developed some odd habits over the preceding weeks. Missy Morrow had been sleeping with her game shoes, and Shelly Brand had become so attached to her shoes (tan Nike running shoes) that when they began to fall apart, she used duct tape to hold them together. Barb Dykstra had begun to clip her fingernails daily. Shelly's pre-game meal had to be a peanut butter and jelly sandwich, and she had been listening to the same tape, "The Jazz-Singer", in her car's tape deck since early in the season because she thought it would break the team's lucky streak if she took it out. Looking back, each superstition seems silly, but with a previously unthinkable goal only two games away, the girls were not about to tempt fate.

The difference in atmosphere at State was obvious when the girls were driven into Market Square Arena with a police escort for their practice session, and Coach Owen's unique style stood out to the fans and media who observed as the four teams each took the court to work out. Shelly Brand remembers it well. "Everybody else went in and had hard practices," she recalled. "Coach Owen went in, rolled the balls on the floor and said, 'Have fun!' She knew we were the type of players who liked to have a good time."

The girls enjoyed themselves shooting long-range bombs and even walking up to the top levels of the cavernous arena and marveling at how small people looked at floor level. Some media were critical of Owen's methods, but it wouldn't take long for them to see the genius behind her apparent madness.

Amazingly, Reitz, at 25-1, was the only unranked team in the Final Four, showing the apparent lack of respect for teams from the area. If the Panthers wanted respect, they were going to have to earn it. Their first challenge would be the toughest they would face the entire year, the top-ranked Marion Giants.

Early in the afternoon game, starting forward Missy Morrow jumped for a block against Marion star Judy Burns and Morrow's arm smashed into Burns' mouth, requiring both to be examined by trainers. Missy's arm was quickly bandaged, but Burns suffered two broken teeth that kept her out for eight crucial minutes.

Reitz built a 27-14 lead with less than two minutes left in the half but then suffered a dry spell that Coach Owen described as "a very long six minutes" in the *Courier* the next day. The drought ended when reserve Toni Ervin hit a foul shot nearly four minutes into the third quarter. At that point, Marion, behind the courageous Burns, had taken a four-point lead. Barb Dykstra then hit three times to give Reitz a 38-36 lead at the end of the third quarter.

Reitz's high-octane system enabled them to pour it on in the final period and come away with a 55-46 victory behind Brand's 21 and Dykstra's 18 points. Morrow and Black were also impressive, with 13 and 10 rebounds, respectively. The Lady Panthers had a few hours to rest before their date with #4-ranked Rushville.

All season long, Coach Owen had used her contacts around the state for scouting reports of upcoming opponents, and the State Finals were no different. "My nephew, Geoff Gooch (an Evansville boy and U of E grad who is a sports fanatic and lives in the Indianapolis area) volunteered to stay between games and scout," Louise explained, "and he did a *good* job scouting Rushville!"

Between games, the size of the Reitz crowd grew as locals heard about the semi-final win and made the three-hour trek to be there for the grand finale. What the crowd witnessed was a masterful performance where the girls in blue and gray hit on all cylinders and made the game look easy.

Those unfamiliar with Reitz's style, like the TV announcers covering the game, were skeptical that the Panthers could maintain their break-neck pace without crashing and burning. But the girls didn't give it a second thought as they pressed from the opening tip. "We knew we were going to play two games on Saturday," said Barb Dykstra. "There wasn't any time to worry about getting tired if we wanted to play our game. We wanted to run, and we wanted to press. That's the way we were programmed to play."

Coach Owen substituted liberally from the outset to keep fresh legs in the game, and Rushville was no match for the lightning-quick Panthers. Shelly Brand dominated with a 31-point effort, 20 in the second half. Missy Morrow was her steady self with 13 points and 15 rebounds, and Denic Black did a wonderful job guarding 6'3" Rushville center Chante Stiers. The Lady Panthers had shocked the world, and even themselves, and were returning home as State champions.

The '81 Reitz team was smaller than virtually everyone they played, but they were nearly perfect that season because of their blazing quickness, their stamina and the team-first concept inspired by Coach Owen and Coach Weber. Shelly Brand was named the tourney's MVP, and Louise Owen and Brand both represented our state in the annual Indiana-Kentucky All-Star game. (Barb Dykstra would be chosen the following year.)

The girls were greeted back home by thousands of crazy fans, satisfied in the knowledge that each and every one of them had contributed to achieving a dream that they could only giggle at when they met as a team only four months earlier. They became Evansville's first girls basketball State champions, and they were the last area basketball team (male or female) to win a championship in the one-class system. And they did it all with a coach who wasn't afraid to be herself and a group of girls whose quirks and superstitions endeared them to everyone who knew them.

To the victors go the spoils. Barb Dykstra, Shelly Brand and Missy Morrow celebrate with coach Joe Weber in the background. (Photo courtesy of Ron and Barb Brand.)

Shelly Brand's "Lucky" shoes had to be taped to make it through the season.

BARB DYKSTRA: BORN TO PLAY BALL

Barb Dykstra knew early on that sports would play a major role in her life. Growing up, she lived with her parents, Stanley and Dorothy, and her older brother Alan on Reitz Hill near the school. "I got most of my experience playing in the backyard with neighborhood kids," she said. "Or we would use the school's practice field. We were always playing basketball, baseball, football or Wiffle Ball."

Often competing against boys, she used her competitive nature to hold her own. "I just didn't like to lose," she admitted, and she used that fiery nature to become one of Evansville's finest female athletes.

At Evansville Lutheran Grade School, Barb played volleyball and earned a spot on the seventh and eighth grade girls team as a sixth grader. From there, she would move on to Reitz, where she and childhood friend Shelly Brand would lead the Lady Panthers to the school's first State basketball championship.

"Shelly and I date back to when we were five years old, and later we played little league baseball," she recalled. "We were on the first team that won the City. They called it the Ponytail League, and we played at the West Side Nut Club field near Helfrich."

Shelly Brand also remembers the early friendship and attributes much of the success at Reitz to those early days spent with Barb. "Barb and I kind of grew up together," Shelly noted. "She was the closest thing I had to a sister at that time. Well, Missy Morrow, too (another future Reitz teammate.) The three of us basically hung around together constantly. Barb was my partner on the basketball court. I think I could tell you almost every move she was going to make, and Barb could tell you every move I was going to make. When we were on the court together, it was just easy."

Barb was a solid all-around athlete at Reitz. She played on the volleyball team and won the SIAC in the 100-yard dash in track. Her last two years, she played soccer and was recruited by basketball coach Louise Owen to try tennis her junior year. Owen, a legendary tennis player herself, was smart and paired Barb with another new recruit, Shelly Brand. Although neither had any formal training and their games were somewhat "ugly," their camaraderie and athleticism made them an excellent team.

Dykstra was recruited by Indiana State and looked at some places near Grand Rapids, Michigan, her parents' hometown. She decided, however, to play for Coach Linda (Wambach) Crick at the University of Evansville, where she would team up one more time with Shelly Brand, who had joined the team a year earlier.

The quiet Dykstra was never one to toot her own horn, but if she had wanted to, she could have made quite a noise. In 1981, she was one of only two juniors to make the All-State basketball team, and as a senior, she was selected as an Indiana All-Star. At U of E, she was inducted into the school's hall of fame in 2004.

During her years with the Aces, the women's game went through a major transformation when the three point shot was introduced. Now, as she reminisces from behind her desk as director at the Evansville YMCA, Barb contemplates the comparison between the girls of today and those on the '81 Reitz team: "I don't think girls today are any more athletic than the team we had. We were fast, we were good shooters and rebounders, and we had good instincts. Teams who excel now have the same kind of drive."

As an overseer of young athletes at the YMCA, Barb Dykstra is in a perfect position to guide them, because she knows what it takes to succeed. She serves as an example of what can be accomplished if one has a love for the game and the desire to do what it takes to make a dream come true.

SHELLY BRAND: A TRUE DADDY'S GIRL

If you would have driven through a certain west side neighborhood on June 23rd, 1972, the odds were good that you would have seen little Michelle Lynn Brand walking the streets in her raggedy railroad cap and bib overalls looking for a ballgame. As Shelly knocked on doors to find someone to shoot hoops or toss a baseball around, little did she know that, on that very day, legislation was being passed that would enable her to pursue the same athletic dreams that boys had enjoyed for years.

A 37-word Constitutional amendment called 'Title IX' mandated that, "No person in the United States shall, on the basis of sex, be excluded from participation in any education program or activity…" But Shelly was oblivious to the impact the legislation would have on her future, because on this day, just as on any other day, all she wanted was to play ball.

From the time she was a toddler, this self-proclaimed 'daddy's girl' spent countless hours working with her father in the backyard and driveway. Shelly's father, Ron, was an All-City and All-Conference football player for Bosse. He was a linebacker and center for the Bulldogs, and he also played basketball and tennis at Bosse. Shelly's mother, Barb, evolved into a sports fan over the years and is the first to admit that her daughter's athletic genes came from her father.

The father-daughter bond that would be the inspiration as little Shelly grew began when she would tag along while Ron was working with Shelly's older brother, Mike. Mike played sports when he was young and was a defensive end for Reitz when Bob Stephenson led the Panthers to a State runner-up finish in 1977. Barb Brand remembers the early days well when her daughter's love for sports emerged. "When Shelly was small, Ronnie (Dad) would take Mike up to the gym at St. John's United Church of Christ, and Shelly, of course, followed," Bard recalled. "Mike would get tired of playing, but Shelly always wanted to stay longer."

Shelly remembers those days fondly as well. "We had a pitcher's mound in the backyard," she said. "It was all made for Mike. We would go to parks, and Dad would pitch and Mike would hit and I would shag balls. Then they would say, 'Shelly, do you want to hit?' So at first, I was in the shadow of my brother. I think just watching my dad coach Mike, I picked up on it at a younger age than most do. Eventually, I think Dad decided, 'You might be a player, too!' I'd go to my brother's games and I'd be dressed in a uniform too, and after the games, I'd go out and run the bases and slide. I had to be dressed like my brother and do everything he did."

Ron Brand saw his daughter's potential at an early age. "Anything that involved a ball, whether you kick it, throw it or hit it, Shelly just loved it and took off with it," he explained. "I remember one day, there was a knock on the door and Bobby Scheller said, 'Can Shelly come out and play?' Barb said no because Shelly had done something wrong and we wanted her to stay in the house. Barry looked up and said, 'She's gotta come out. She's our quarterback!'"

During her developmental years, Shelly competed with the boys in football and was a star baseball player in the first girls little league in Evansville. But it became obvious early on that basketball was her passion and might be her ticket to a college education. "With basketball, we'd go to the church and Dad would set up chairs and have me dribble around them," Shelly revealed. "Some people might think it's awful, but he'd tie my right hand behind my back so I had to dribble with my left and get ball control with my weak hand. He would blindfold me and have me dribble without looking at the ball.

"In the driveway, I would shoot over a ladder with a bucket on top, just like a defender. Some people still laugh at me because I have a very high arch on my shot. Dad had some very interesting techniques, but that made it fun."

Shelly didn't just love sports; she was driven by an internal desire to excel. "You could see it as she was growing up," Ron pointed out. "We had a goal in our driveway that she used clear up through high school. We would work on shooting and ballhandling. When she would mess around with the ball behind her back and so forth, I would write 'Don' on the tip of one shoe and 'Buse' on the other so that when she would look down, it reminded her to take care of the ball. (U of E star) Don Buse was her favorite. I'd tell her, 'Your shooting will come later; just take care of the ball.' When she would shoot free throws, she would have to hit 25 in a row before she would quit. That was her plan."

It was that quest for perfection that would enable Shelly Brand to achieve success beyond her wildest dreams.

After graduating from Helfrich Park Grade School, Shelly entered Reitz and became a starter on the basketball team her freshman year. During her four years at Reitz, she set virtually every school basketball record, many of which still stand. She graduated in 1981 as the school's all-time leader in points (a position she still holds), assists and steals. She earned 14 varsity letters (4 in basketball, 3 in volleyball, 4 in track and 3 in tennis), and in tennis, she and her friend and basketball teammate Barb Dykstra were City champions.

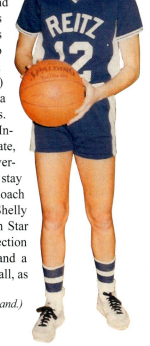

Her senior year, Shelly averaged 17.6 points, 7 rebounds, 4 assists and 2 steals per game as she led Reitz to the State championship and was named the tournament's MVP. She was also honored as an Indiana All-Star and hit two key free throws (with a swollen thumb that was injured earlier) in the last two seconds to seal a win over the Kentucky All-Stars.

After being recruited by Indiana, Ohio State, Indiana State, Western Kentucky and the University of Evansville, she decided to stay and play in her hometown for Coach Linda Wambach at U of E. Shelly was a four-year starter, a North Star Conference All-Conference selection her junior and senior season and a three-year letter winner in softball, as

(Photo courtesy of Ron and Barb Brand.)

well. When she graduated in 1985 with a 3.6 GPA and a degree in Education, she had set school records with 1,713 career points and 34 points in a single game. Her 1,713 career points stands as a school record yet today. The practices in her driveway over the years paid off, too, resulting in Shelly leading the country in free throw percentage her junior year (87%).

Shelly also met and married her husband, Steve Adlard, while she was at U of E. Steve, a highly successful soccer player from England, was in Evansville on a student visa to get his Masters. They were married at the end of Shelly's senior year. In fact, Shelly was pregnant during the last half of her senior season and had to sign waivers from the NCAA saying that she wouldn't hold them responsible if anything happened.

Steve and Shelly made several moves after her graduation to accommodate Steve's career as a soccer coach. His coaching success has taken them to West Virginia, North Carolina, fifteen years as the head coach of Marquette University in Milwaukee, and to Idaho as the Director of Coaching for the state.

Their daughter, Susie, graduated in '07 with a degree in social work, and their son, Andy, was a Club All-American in soccer in high school and has traveled all over the world with the U.S. Development Team. He was recruited by all the top 25 soccer programs in the country and began playing for Indiana University in the fall of 2007.

Shelly Brand-Adlard's impact on the local sports scene was impressive by anyone's standards. Because of Title IX, she was able to experience things that her high school coach, Louise Owen, never could. In a letter to coaches around the state to encourage their votes for the Indiana All-Stars, Ms. Owen expressed her opinion of Shelly:

To my fellow coaches,
We are blessed every so often to be able to coach a very good player. Only rarely do we have the opportunity to coach the truly great player, and Michelle Brand is this type of exceptional athlete.
Michelle Brand is the finest basketball player I have ever coached...Her desire, dedication and determination make her a winner. She has met the challenge of being a leader on the court as well as in the classroom.

The little girl with the cap and bib overalls had done what she was hoping to do as she walked her neighborhood streets. After wearing out countless basketballs in the driveway, Daddy's little girl had grown into one of the finest players in Evansville history.

KEVIN HARDY: AS TOUGH AS THEY COME

Kevin Lamont Hardy was known for his easy-going, fun-loving style while growing up on Evansville's east side, but when he took the field for the Harrison Warriors, it was no joke.

Hardy spent the first eleven years of his life in Washington D.C. before moving to Evansville with his parents, Herbert, a construction worker, and Imelda, who taught third grade at Howard Roosa. When young Kevin signed up to play football in the Lakeview Optimist league, it was his first exposure to the tackle variety of the sport. He had played flag football for three years in D.C. but had never experienced the exhilaration of the sport when the pads start popping and full contact was allowed. He would eventually discover that it was a sport that would allow him to use his natural physical gifts to earn a college education and to forge a career as a professional athlete.

In his first year of Lakeview football, Kevin was four pounds overweight to meet the 110-pound restriction for being eligible to run and catch the ball, so he went on a self-imposed diet. Through sheer will power and self-control, he reached his goal and spent his first season scoring touchdowns. A year later, genetics could not be denied and he toiled in the trenches as a 'black striped' lineman on offense and as a linebacker on defense.

Kevin also demonstrated early on that his athletic skills extended beyond the gridiron as he played LVO youth basketball and East Little League baseball as a pitcher and center fielder. He didn't know it at the time, but his involvement in the east side little league would continue past his playing days and would play an important role in his future as a football player.

When Hardy enrolled at Harrison High School in 1987, he was a slim 6'3 with a strong facial resemblance to Calbert Cheaney, a basketball star who was a junior at the time. The two looked enough alike, it seemed, that Kevin was occasionally put in some

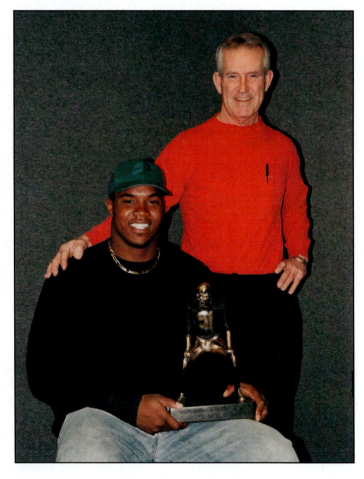

Kevin Hardy sits with his Butkus Award as the nation's best college linebacker. At his side is his high school coach at Harrison, Mitch Marsch. (Photo from the Mitch Marsch collection.)

awkward situations. Bryan Speer, a contemporary of Hardy's and Cheaney's and now the school's head basketball coach, remembers such a circumstance and the irony involved as he looks back. "Every gym we would go to, everybody would want Calbert's autograph," Speer recalled. "But Calbert and Kevin looked so much alike that people would come up to Kevin and ask him for his (Calbert's) autograph. Kevin would always sign his own name, and then they (the autograph seeker) would ultimately throw it away because it wasn't Calbert's. Little did they know what it (Kevin's autograph) was going to turn out to be."

During his four years at Harrison, Hardy used his size and athleticism to become an excellent multi-sport athlete, just like his older sister Carol (basketball and track) and, later, his younger brother Brian (football, basketball and track). As a sophomore, Kevin dressed for a strong Warriors basketball team that featured Cheaney, 6'8 Carl Heldt, 6'8 Jay Stewart and guards Kevin Tapp and Chris Lowery. Hardy's football coach, Mitch Marsch, was a fan of Kevin's no matter what sport he was playing. "He was a banger on the boards," Marsch said of Hardy as a basketball player. "He would beat you to death under the basket. I remember when he fully frustrated Parrish Casebier (a star player from South Spencer) all night. Kevin was on him like a shadow."

When basketball was over each year at Harrison, Kevin would head for the track, where he was a standout as well. His speed and explosiveness made him a star for Coach Charlie Seisky's team as he qualified for the State meet in two events. As a hurdler, he qualified in the highs with times in the high 14-second range, and he ran the lows in the 40-second range. He also qualified for State in the high jump and, at one point, set the City record by launching his 6'4, 215-pound body over the bar at 6'9".

But it was on the football field where Kevin's awesome combination of power and quickness allowed him to emerge for the world to see. Although his primary positions were tight end and middle linebacker, Coach Marsch moved him around to find ways for him to touch the football. In certain situations, Kevin would line up at running back, and his size made him a terrifying threat as a kick returner because, in Marsch's words, "He could run like a deer."

Two games stood out to Marsch when asked to comment on Hardy as a player. The first was a touchdown run Hardy made on a reverse against Memorial, and the second took place in the sectional championship game against Castle. The Knights had blasted Harrison earlier in the year, and Marsch wasn't sure how to approach the game. The only thing he knew for sure was that they had to keep the ball away, as much as possible, from Castle star Gator McBride. Unfortunately, Harrison's kicker landed the ball directly into McBride's hands on the opening kickoff and the Warriors were down 7-0 fifteen seconds into the game.

Harrison hung tough by throwing their pet pass play, an out pattern to Hardy, for much of the game. Late in the contest and down 7-3, Scott Marsch, Harrison's outstanding quarterback and Coach Marsch's son, picked up a tendency in Castle's defense: He saw that Castle's cornerback was sprinting to the outside (to stop Hardy) as soon as the ball was snapped. Coach Marsch drew up an impromptu play and Hardy faked the outside move and then exploded over the middle to haul in the game-winner, giving the Warriors the championship.

Kevin finished his senior football season as an All-State honoree and even made some All-American teams, but the interest from some colleges was only lukewarm because he had missed most of his junior season with mononucleosis. Coach Marsch was frustrated by the snubs because he felt that when IU stopped showing interest during Hardy's junior year because of the illness, other schools seemed to follow. Marsch pointed out that when Indiana finally entered the picture when Kevin was a senior, it was too little too late, prompting Marsch to take a jab at Bill Mallory's floundering program by saying, "You miss a couple of Kevin Hardys, and you're in trouble!"

The school that didn't miss was the University of Illinois. Mitch Marsch credits the Illini recruiter for having an open mind when it came to Hardy. After looking past the illness and watching some game film of Kevin, the recruiter drew a comparison to hall of fame Green Bay Packers star Leroy Jordan, saying that, "If the runner stays on the field, Kevin Hardy will get him."

Hardy also gives credit to Randy Rogers, who always had the inside track because he showed interest early on. Rogers was the head football coach at U of E during the years that Kevin spent umpiring for East Side Little League baseball after he left the league as a player. Rogers' sons had played there, and the coach had expressed interest in Hardy as he watched the young man work. Rogers later became the recruiting coordinator at the University of Illinois and made sure he stayed in touch with Hardy as the young man grew into a major college prospect.

Although Kevin received correspondence from many colleges while he was at Harrison, a letter from Rogers when Hardy was a sophomore gave the Illini a leg up on the competition. "They were always the frontrunner for me," Hardy said from his home in Florida, "and it was because of Randy Rogers."

Late in the process, Kevin had narrowed his choices to Purdue, Indiana, Illinois and Tennessee, but the Illini won him over with their persistence. He would leave Evansville in 1991 as a lanky teenager with unlimited potential, and five years later, he would leave Illinois as one of the most celebrated players in the country.

As a freshman at Illinois, Hardy redshirted his freshman season to bulk up and get acclimated to college life. As he watched the team work out, he saw that the competition was fierce at the linebacker position in his class and the class directly above his. He had seen one of the linebackers, Dana Howard, when he made a recruiting visit during the spring of his senior year at Harrison. "I remember him making a hit and it echoed (across the field)," Hardy said, "and everyone was saying that he's a freshman linebacker and he's going to be this and going to be that."

Howard proved observers right over the next few years, and Hardy made some noise, as well, as he joined a phenomenal linebacking corps at Illinois. During his sophomore season, Hardy was chosen as a second team All-Conference selection while the other three linebackers, fellow sophomore Simeon Rice and juniors Dana Howard and Jon Holocek were first team choices. The foursome drew lots of media attention, and the writers quickly christened Hardy's three running mates "The H Boys and Simeon Rice." Kevin found himself on the outside looking in but used the snub as incentive to earn the respect he deserved. "It was an inner motivation for me," he explained, "because you never want to be the weakest link. I worked hard to be at their level."

Hardy's determination paid off as he manned the outside linebacker spot opposite Rice during his junior year. At season's end, Rice and Hardy joined inside backer Dana Howard on the All-Conference first team while Holocek was demoted to the second team. As the four roamed the field in the 3-4 defense used by Illini coach Lou Tepper, Illinois was dubbed 'Linebacker U' by the national media.

Following Kevin's junior season, Dana Howard was presented with the Butkus Award, which honors the nation's top linebacker each year and is named after Dick Butkus, an Illinois alum who is considered by many to be the best linebacker in history. Howard and Holocek would soon leave for the NFL, and there were rumors that Simeon Rice might forgo his senior year and join them and that he was projected as a first round pick.

As things turned out, Rice opted to stay, and that decision turned out to be a blessing for Kevin Hardy. As bookends in the Illini defense, it was difficult for teams to corral both of the studs who manned the outside areas of the field. Consequently, Rice's phenomenal athleticism often drew double teams from the opponent and allowed Hardy to roam free and wreak havoc on opposing offenses.

When the season was over, Hardy had become the Big Ten's career leader in sacks with 44 ½ and had set a conference record with 595 career tackles. In addition, he was not only a consensus All-American but he was the recipient of the Butkus Award, making he and Dana Howard the first teammates in NCAA history to win the award back-to-back.

As the 1995 NFL draft approached, Kevin was curious what was in store when he analyzed the first five teams in the draft order: the Jets, Jacksonville, Arizona, Baltimore and the New York Giants. "If I had my pick of those five teams, I would have gone to the Giants," Hardy revealed. "Now, I didn't want to be the fifth pick, but I would have loved playing for the Giants."

Hardy went through the process by making recruiting trips, first to Baltimore, where he met with defensive coordinator Marvin Lewis and other coaches, and then with Dan Reeves and the Giants. New York said they would select Hardy if he fell to number five, so Kevin felt secure that he was at least a top five pick. He was also told that the Jets were considering him for the #1 pick and that Arizona was interested at #3. Ironically, Jacksonville was the only team that never made contact, but when their choice came up, Hardy was their choice.

In Kevin's rookie year, he was named to the NFL All-Rookie team and the Jags knocked off John Elway and the Denver Broncos, who were favored to win the Super Bowl, before losing to Drew Bledsoe and the New England Patriots in the AFC Championship game. Kevin followed up his rookie season by breaking the club record for tackles in a season, with 186, and after two years, he had established himself as one of the best young linebackers in the league.

In 1999, the Jaguars would once again have an outstanding season, with Hardy leading the defense while the offense produced big numbers thanks to quarterback Mark Brunell, running back Fred Taylor and receivers Keenan McCardell and Jimmy Smith. The Jags lost only twice in '99, both times to Tennessee, and the Titans pulled the hat trick when they eliminated Jacksonville in the playoffs behind quarterback Steve McNair and running back Eddie George. Hardy ended the year as the AFC leader in sacks with 10.5 and once again led the Jags in tackles with 153. The 1999 season was a banner year for Hardy and his teammates, as he and seven Jaguars were named to the Pro Bowl and Kevin was named to the AP All-Pro first team.

During his six years in Jacksonville, the Jags twice came within one game of playing in the Super Bowl, and Kevin's maturity and intelligence not only enabled him to be a leader on the field, but off the field as well. He spent three years as the Jaguars' player representative with the Players Union, not only dealing with policy and negotiation but also implementing programs to help the players deal with life after football, a process that would later help Kevin as his own career wound down.

After six years in Jacksonville, Hardy was signed as an unrestricted free agent by the Dallas Cowboys, and after a year there, he signed a four-year $14 million deal with the Cincinnati Bengals. When the Bengals informed Kevin that they wanted to move him to middle linebacker, he realized that his career might be nearing its end. It is a common practice in the NFL for a coach to move an outside linebacker into the middle when it is perceived that the player has lost a step in quickness, and Kevin understood.

For years, Hardy had been bothered by an abnormal condition called sacralization, causing his fifth lumbar vertebra to fuse with the sacrum, a part of the pelvis. The problem caused more and more stiffness over the years, and Kevin could feel a difference on the field. The condition finally got the best of him after his second year with the Bengals. "I would have times when I would run and feel fine," he described, "and then I would sit down on the bench and I would stiffen up so quick. As an athlete, when you're used to playing at a certain level and then not able to keep up, it's just time to shut it down. I wanted to play more, but I just couldn't do it."

In May of 2005, Hardy walked off the field for the last time. He finished his pro career with 742 tackles (563 solo), 36 sacks, 43½ tackles for loss, 11 forced fumbles, 7 fumble recoveries, 5 interceptions and one touchdown in 134 games. With his playing days behind him, it was time to practice what he preached as a six-year union representative.

He soon found out, however, that quitting football was much easier said than done. "You can prepare and prepare and prepare," Hardy lamented, "but when it's over, it's like, 'Man! It's really over!' The hardest part is when you turn on a game (on TV) on opening day and some of the guys you played with are still playing. It's the camaraderie with the guys that you miss. It's a tough deal, but it was a great experience, and I'm proud and honored that I was able to go through that."

Hardy admits that he misses the contact with the fans and being recognized in public, and he says that he'll always treasure his days in the NFL. Even thirteen years removed from his pro debut, he recalls his greatest memory as if it were yesterday. "To this day, the thing that really stands out in my mind is that very first game of my career at home (in Jacksonville) against the Pittsburgh Steelers," hardy divulged. "Just being in the tunnel and they introduced my name and I ran out. It was great because you're playing the best of the best, and the energy is so intense."

Although it wasn't easy to leave the game he loved, Kevin Hardy seems content with his life after football. He appreciates the fact that he is in a financial position where he can relax and enjoy life until another challenge comes along. In the meantime, he enjoys cruising the water in his forty-foot boat in Florida with his wife Terrie and their two sons, Langston and Camden. Though his back may ache from time to time, Kevin Hardy's enthusiasm and joy when speaking of his life as a football player make it obvious that he wouldn't have traded it for the world.

LANAE RENSCHLER: A PERFECT 4 FOR 4

In early 2007, Lanae Renschler Harden spoke into her cell phone as she drove home to Newburgh for a family outing. She would occasionally pause to tend to one of her two daughters (Madeline and Catherine Grace) and then return to the conversation to reminisce about her days as one of Indiana's finest high school tennis players. The 39-year-old lawyer from Indianapolis was doing what she had done all her life – multi-tasking.

The multi-tasking was a by-product of the way she was brought up, because academics were just as important as athletics in the Renschler household. Lanae's parents, Larry and Connie, were teachers (Larry at South Spencer and Connie at Sharon Elementary in Newburgh), and Lanae's older brother, Todd, was Castle's valedictorian and is now a urologist. It was a given that little sister would excel in the classroom as well, but the lanky blonde also found time for sports. Lanae was a standout in volleyball and soccer and even pitched in a girls baseball (not softball) league when she was young. But her true calling was tennis. She would become so skilled in her sport that she would eventually accomplish a feat that no Indiana high school player (male or female) had ever achieved before.

When Lanae was eight years old, she tagged along with her parents to watch them take a tennis lesson. When the youngster asked if she could take lessons also, her father relented, but with one provision.

"I said 'OK,'" Larry Renschler explained, 'but if you're going to do it, you're going to have to practice.' We'd take a lesson and then come home and work on just what her coach had said to work on."

At age nine, Lanae got her first taste of stiff competition, and the lesson she learned was that success would not be a walk in the park. "We put her in the Tri-State Open," Larry recalled, "and this little girl from Indianapolis, Barb Carp, did us the biggest service in the world. She beat us 6-0, 6-0. We said, 'The next time we play her we're going to beat her!' And the next time we played her it was 6-0, 6-0 Lanae."

By the age of eleven or twelve, Lanae was starting to take tennis seriously, and the sacrifices were shared by the entire family. "It takes a big financial commitment and a lot of time," Lanae admitted. "Although my parents certainly weren't poor, we weren't as wealthy as most of the tennis families. We lived in the same house all my life, and I'm sure my tennis prevented them from moving to a bigger home."

To cut down on the cost of court time, Larry or Connie would drive Lanae to and from lessons that started at 5:30 a.m. and 10:00 p.m., when the court time was free. As Lanae got older, her routine consisted of a morning practice (5:30-7:00), an afternoon practice on weekdays (4:30-6:00), and 3 ½ hours of practice plus two hours of matches on weekends.

As her junior career took off, Lanae was quick to recognize her parents' roles in not only being there during her ascent, but also for keeping her feet on the ground. "Mom and Dad were different than parents are nowadays," she said. "Back in our generation, if a coach told you to do something or if you didn't play at the position you thought you should play (in a team sport), our parents would say, 'Well, you need to improve.' Parents nowadays want to know what's wrong with the coach.

"My parents were always very supportive, but they were not indulgent. They were practical and realistic, which I think helped prepare me for life."

As a 14-year-old, Lanae won the prestigious Memorial Day Open, where she defeated both pros and amateurs. During her junior tennis career, her summers were almost 100% dedicated to the sport, and her success attracted attention from college coaches across the nation. During her teen years, she won the Western Open, the National Clay Courts and the Western Clay tournament three times. As a 17-year-old, she achieved her highest national ranking at #11.

Lanae's junior resumé was impressive, but it was her accomplishments as a high school player that would earn her a place in Indiana history.

The common refrain from people who knew the young Ms. Renschler was that "Lanae didn't know how to lose," and that assessment was proven time and time again during her high school tennis career. Lanae completed her four years at Castle undefeated, and not only did the powerful southpaw never lose a match, but she never lost a set in high school. In fact, only twice did she even have a set point against her.

During her high school days, Lanae's father rarely got to see her victories. In fact, Larry saw very little tennis throughout his daughter's entire career. Why? Anxiety would make him walk away, sometimes to relieve his nausea. "I couldn't stand it," Larry

Lanae, age 16, at the Junior Nationals.
(Photo courtesy of Larry and Connie Renschler.)

confessed. "I played basketball, I coached basketball, and the pressure didn't bother me. But I could never, ever watch Lanae. I wanted to, but I couldn't."

Whether Larry saw the matches or not, Lanae Renschler would be able to make a claim that will be hers and only hers until the end of time. She was the first Indiana tennis player to win four State championships. But that historic feat almost didn't happen.

In 1983, as a 5'8", 108-pound freshman, Lanae defeated previously unbeaten Sonya Garshnek of Crown Point, followed by three consecutive State Final wins over Brenda Hacker of Homestead. But her fourth, and record-setting, State title might never have come to pass without a motivational technique that was as old as time itself.

"After my junior year, I thought about not playing for Castle," Lanae related. "I really had nothing to gain and everything to lose. But my coach (Marc Anderson) told me I was a chicken. He said it would be a huge mistake and that I'd always regret it. And I'm very grateful that he got me to play my senior year. That's a record I'm very proud of."

Following her stellar career at Castle, the quintessential student-athlete had her choice of colleges. With her tennis accomplishments and a near-perfect high school grade point average (all A's except for two B's in four years), Lanae was courted by Harvard and other Ivy League schools as well as every top tennis school in the country, including Florida, Duke and the University of California. Looking for the perfect combination of tennis and academics, she chose the University of Texas. The Lady Longhorns tennis team was ranked #4 in the country at the time, and Lanae thought she would enjoy studying Pre-Law in Austin.

As a freshman, Lanae played #2 singles at Texas, but late in the year, she developed tendonitis in her right wrist so bad that she couldn't open a car door. Even though she was left-handed, the pain was excruciating when she hit her two-handed backhand. That season, the team was hit hard with several injuries, so much so that the coach had to recruit students from campus to fill some spots. Being a true team player, Lanae played through the season with a heavily-taped wrist.

Although she finished the year, the injury was severe enough that Lanae was sidelined for eight months. She would never return to a high spot in the lineup again. "I was never as good as I once was for sure," she admitted. "It was a combination of things. I can't just blame it on the injury. Maybe sitting out for eight months was just too much and I couldn't come back."

Not one to dwell on what might have been, Lanae was always willing to bleed orange for her Texas teammates. The Lady Longhorns won the Southwest Conference all four years she was there and were ranked #4 nationally her senior year, making it to the NCAA Final Four. Lanae was named her team's MVP during her final season, despite playing #6 singles and #3 doubles (the lowest spots in the lineup). The award was a tribute to her selfless attitude and emphasis on the team aspect of the game. "I am proud of that," she said, "because I think I adapted to a situation where other people might have just given up or been demoralized. But I won a lot of matches and was a good teammate."

It should also be mentioned that Lanae not only received an excellent undergraduate education from Texas (she attended law School at IU), but that she also met her future husband in Austin. It seems that Lanae was scheduled for a random drug test and knew that male athletes would be there too. She got up very early and put on make-up and curled her hair (always prepared!) and headed to the screening.

When she saw Curry Harden (a Longhorn baseball player), he was carrying a urine sample in his hand, and she asked her roommate about the "cute guy." After a blind date, set up by the roommate, the two hit it off and have been together ever since.

Today, Curry and Lanae live in Indianapolis, where he is the head baseball coach at Hamilton Southeastern and she is a successful attorney who juggles motherhood and law just like she balanced academics and tennis in her younger days.

In 2001, Katie Martzolf of Park Tudor High School became the second player to win four State titles in her high school career. When the final match was over, no doubt there was celebration for what Ms. Martzolf had achieved. What no one knew, however, was that the one person who could say "been there – done that" was sitting right there in their midst. Lanae Renschler Harden had learned about the situation and decided to go watch. She sat in the crowd, alone, and watched as the match unfolded. "No one probably even knew I was there," she reflected. "I just kind of hung out and watched the match and then took off after she won. It wasn't my time to take away the spotlight."

Lanae may have walked away that day unnoticed, but she will forever be listed in the annals of Indiana high school tennis because, no matter how many times someone wins four State titles, only one player can lay claim to being the FIRST. And that player is Lanae Renschler.

Lanae reminds us of a young Farrah Fawcett as she plays a match while at Castle. (Photo courtesy of the Evansville Courier.)

LIGHTS, CAMERA, ACTION!

Bosse Field will never be the site of the World Series, but it did play one in the movies.

In 1991, the call went out for extras for the production of a new sports movie by Columbia Pictures called *A League of Their Own*. With Penny Marshall in charge, the Evansville area was chosen to provide the background for the period piece that centered around a women's professional baseball league as it filled a void for fans while the men were away fighting World War II.

Ms. Marshall used over 30,000 locals as extras and a few others for slightly larger roles in the film that featured such stars as Tom Hanks, Geena Davis and Madonna. The Tri-state was buzzing as preparations were made and locations for filming were selected in Vanderburgh, Warrick and Posey Counties in Indiana and in Henderson, Kentucky.

Mike Madriaga was the Supervisor of Athletics for the EVSC at the time and called the scope of the movie project "mind-boggling." One of Madriaga's responsibilities was overseeing the modifications to Bosse Field. The stadium was chosen because of its architecture and history, and it played its role well as the home field of the Racine Belles and the site of the World Series scenes near the end of the film.

One problem that plagued Bosse Field and had to be addressed was the infestation of pigeons that had imposed squatting rights and made the stadium their home. The pesky birds were not only a problem for filming but for local sporting events as well. A bag of popcorn was like a homing device for the pigeons, and those who dared to hold a bag in their hand were subject to kamikaze attacks from above. Madriaga and his crew racked their brains to find a solution. "We tried snakes and owls and everything," he explained. "We finally pigeon-proofed it by putting up netting, and it made Bosse Field a better place."

Thousands of locals served as extras in the film, and some can be seen in brief cameo appearances. Delisa Chinn, a superb ex-athlete from North High School, was shown during a scene where she retrieves a foul ball in the stands and wings it back onto the field to the amazement of Tom Hanks and others. Because Delisa is an African-American, the display may have been used to emphasize the fact that black athletes were not admitted into the league even though they may have been more than qualified. Michelle Funk-Niemeier, another North alum, is seen in the movie when 'Marla', the homely slugger for the Racine Belles, is whacking balls in the gym during her tryout for the team. Funk-Niemeier is actually doing the hitting while padded and 'uglied up' to look like 'Marla'.

With Bosse Field and League Field in Huntingburg serving as the movie's main baseball venues, the next project for the production team was filling out the rosters for the teams in the movie. Nearly 500 girls tried out to play the opponents of the featured team, and some made the cut. One who tried out and got much more than she'd bargained for was Shelly (Brand) Adlard, an Evansville Reitz alum who starred in softball in high school and also played on the 1981 Reitz team that won the girls State basketball championship.

When Shelly showed up for auditions in mid-July of 1991, little did she know that she was about to embark on a four-month odyssey that would allow her to schmooze with some of the biggest stars in show business. Out of the hundreds trying out, it didn't take long for director Penny Marshall to notice her, and Shelly was stunned by what transpired. "Penny Marshall kind of picked me out as somebody who looked like Lori Petty (an actress who played the younger sister, Kit, of Geena Davis' character, Dottie)," Ms. Adlard explained. Shelly wasn't sure of the significance until one day during a lunch break. As Shelly was leaving to get some food, she asked Ms. Marshall, "Do you want me to get you something?" When she returned and Marshall asked what she owed, Shelly said, "You don't owe me anything," to which Ms. Marshall responded, "I'll get back with you. You're going to get a lot more than that."

Shelly soon found out what Penny Marshall had meant. Because of her resemblance to Lori Petty, Shelly was asked to serve as the actress's double. This meant that she would be around for the entire production and would spend a lot of time with the cast members as they traveled from location to location during the filming. What started out as a lark was now becoming serious work.

One of the most popular cast members with the locals was Tom Hanks. Mike Madriaga remembers him as very approachable and down to earth. "He would have someone hit fungos (fly balls) to him in the outfield, and he'd run them down and try to catch them in his golf cart," Madriaga recalled. "He genuinely loved Evansville. He brought his family here, and they went fishing."

Hanks' down-to-earth demeanor and love for baseball also allowed Shelly Adlard to form a bond during the filming. "Tom Hanks and I kind of had a thing going at lunch. One day, I was walking by and he had the pitching machine going and I said, 'Hey, would you like me to feed the machine for you?', and he said, 'Yeah, sure!'

"After he was finished, he said, 'OK, your turn,' and he fed the balls while I hit. From that point on, he'd put me at the front of the lunch line and we'd hurry to the pitching machine."

Shelly Adlard appeared in several memorable scenes in the film, although, as is the nature of a double, the viewer doesn't notice her. In one scene, Tom Hanks' character, Jimmy Dugan, throws Lori Petty's character into the shower. When the crew couldn't find his stunt double, Hanks agreed to do it. The body we see over Hanks' shoulder in the movie, however, is not Petty, but Evansville's own Shelly Adlard. In fact, she has a Polaroid photo of her draped over the actor's shoulder and the words "Get off my back" on the photo in Hanks' handwriting.

Shelly is also seen in several other scenes, but without close scrutiny, we as viewers would never know it. In a black and white scene, a girl slides into third base and Shelly tags her out and raises her glove. In another scene where 'Marla' is hitting balls in a gym, one of the pairs of legs in the background is Shelly's. In a photo at the hall of fame near the end of the movie, the doubles and extras are shown and Shelly is nearest the camera. In another scene, where the two sisters (Davis and Petty) are running in a field in the distance, Shelly is one of the girls shown.

Those scenes are all indicative of what a double, or stand-in, does during the making of a film, but before the filming was done,

Shelly found herself in a situation that would place her in the most memorable scene in the movie and change her status from 'double' to 'stunt double'.

As the film crescendos to its climax, there is a scene where Kit (Lori Petty) barrels into her sister (Geena Davis) at home plate and scores the winning run. Geena Davis, whose character receives the blow, was replaced by a male stunt double. When the crew started to ask for a replacement for Petty, Shelly Adlard spoke up and volunteered. "At first it was not supposed to be a full collision," Shelly pointed out. "We were just supposed to act like we hit and then throw our bodies, but Penny Marshall looked at the film and said, 'I want to get closer; It has to be full contact.'

"They wanted to bring in the stunt person," Shelly continued, "but I said, 'No, I'll still do it.' They put some pads under the catcher's equipment and asked me if I wanted some and I said, 'No, that's OK.' So we did it, and Penny said, 'OK, Shelly, now hit her harder this time!' After the hit, I had to make sure my face was away from the camera. That was my direction, 'Hit her as hard as you can, and turn your face away from the camera.'"

Shelly described the movie experience as both "exciting" and "boring," and she missed her husband and kids terribly during the shoot. But she also reflects on it as a once-in-a-lifetime opportunity. Because of her elevated status as a stunt double, she is listed in the credits and still receives small royalties from time to time.

For the rest of us, we can brag to anyone who will listen that one of the best sports movies of our generation was filmed right here in the Tri-state, and that for four months during the summer of 1991, Penny Marshall brought a fantasy world to the Tri-state in which we all got a chance to play.

> ### DON'T BLINK!
> If you watch *A League of Their Own* closely, you can see Carson Jones, the basketball guru who ran the very popular Tri-state Basketball Tournament for many years. Carson appears in the background as one of the groundskeepers at Bosse Field, a job he did for many years in real life.

The stuntman at left took the hit from Shelly Adlard (right) in the dramatic scene when the movie portrayed Lori Petty's character ramming into Geena Davis' character. (Photo courtesy of Ron and Barb Brand.)

These lovely ladies, decked out in their period costumes, were part of the local contingent who contributed ambience to the movie A League of Their Own. (L-R): Carol Coon, Mary Schreiber, Jan Smith, Cheryl Schellhase, Shelly Adlard, Barbara Brand, Sandy Morrell.

MIKE BLAKE'S 35-YEAR STOPOVER

WFIE Channel 14's Mike Blake has had his finger on the pulse of local sports and shared his thoughts and opinions with local sports fans for nearly forty years, and the dean of tri-state sportscasters has helped us celebrate our greatest triumphs and mourn our most tragic losses. Little did Mike know that what he thought was going to be a brief stop on the way to the big time would become a life-long love affair with southwestern Indiana sports.

As a student at Mt. Carmel High School, Mike played basketball and was a backup catcher on the baseball team, where he got the chance to catch the team's star pitcher, Denny McLain, who later became the first major league pitcher to win thirty games in a season since Dizzy Dean in 1934. Forty years later, McLain is still the last pitcher to accomplish the feat.

After graduating in 1962, Mike attended Loras College in Dubuque, Iowa, where he majored in Political Science and minored in Speech. In 1966, he moved to the University of Iowa for his Masters in Speech and Dramatic Arts, area of Radio, TV and Film.

On October 3rd, 1968, the 24-year-old Blake was inducted into the military at the height of the Vietnam era. On Christmas Eve, Mike was flying to Denver thinking he was going to be stateside working at a hospital at Camp Carson. But those plans soon changed. On May 30th, the day a young Mario Andretti won his first and only Indy 500 (Mike remembers the day well), Blake was on a tarmac getting ready to board a plane for South Vietnam.

Blake ended up with the 101st Airborne with a job on the Armed Forces Network. "I was kind of like a Robin Williams, in the movie *Good Morning, Vietnam,*" Mike explained. "I also did news and sports. It was great; you didn't have to worry about ratings."

He came back to the states in 1970 and looked for a job the entire summer. Mike remembers his father being skeptical about his efforts. "My dad thought he had an 'Irish Setter' on his hands," Mike quipped. "My dad said, 'Hey, Mike, you got a Masters. Are you going to get a job anytime soon?'"

While interviewing for a job at WGN, Chicago's superstation, the interviewer picked up the phone and dialed the '812' area code. On the other end were two men: Mike Vandeveer, who would later become Evansville's mayor, and Chet Behrman, who was WFIE's head of programming and also the man who portrayed the beloved character Uncle Dudley.

The men flew Mike in the next day for him to audition for a job doing weather and some staff announcing. On the way from the airport, Vandeveer asked Mike if he would consider doing sports, and Mike responded that sports were definitely his preference. With beloved sportscaster Jack McLean in poor health, the plan was to groom Mike as the main sports man while he honed his skills doing Saturday night sports.

At first, Mike looked at WFIE as a brief stopover while he pursued his goal of big market television. In 1971, he met his wife, Jen, and, in fact, told her, "Honey, in six months or so we're outta here!"

In 1977, Mike's aspirations were almost realized when he was offered a weekend sports job in Miami, which included being the host of *The Shula Show*, featuring hall of fame NFL coach Don Shula. Now with two children to consider, Mike and Jen packed their bags and were ready to head south. Only a persuasive argument from WFIE general manager Conrad Cagle changed Mike's mind.

Mr. Cagle explained to Mike that the Evansville Aces had just gone Division I and that Channel 14 would be broadcasting the games. Mike would get to do the play-by-play, and those words were all Blake needed to hear.

Soon after, Mike got to know a very dynamic young Aces coach named Bobby Watson, who, in Blake's words "turned this town on its ear – in a good way." His relationship with Watson and his players was a close one, and it was that familiarity that would test Mike's emotions during one of Evansville's darkest hours.

"My biggest story, of course, was the 1977 plane crash," Mike stated. "That changed everything. I had been covering a high school basketball game (at the time of the crash) and I walked in the door of our offices. We knew there had been a plane crash, but we thought it was a small plane. There was no ESPN in those days, no cable, and we were getting calls from all over the country."

Because of his closeness with the players and staff, Mike took the news harder than many. "It was very tough on all of us," he recalled. "Even though we only got to know them a short time, Bobby Watson was a very dynamic guy, and Marv Bates (who was the voice of the Aces) was a great guy. And the kids were, just like the kids today, a great group of people.

"The community should be of proud how they handled the tragedy and came back," he continued. "And there were multiple gestures – the (Pittsburgh) Steelers came to town to play a benefit basketball game. And Coach (Bob) Knight agreed to bring the Hoosiers here for an exhibition to help rebuild the program."

Over the years, Blake has also reported on some of the finest people and events in the area's history. He has interviewed the likes of Don Mattingly, Walter McCarty, and Calbert Cheaney, and was even aware of some of our local legends before he ever came to the area.

"When I came to town," he recalled, "there was still the mystique of the Reitz Bowl. I had buddies who played on the Hammond High team, which used to come down and play Reitz. In Hammond they used to say, 'Who's Evansville REETZ?' And then ten years later I was covering the Panthers. It was an era of great coaches; you had Archie Owen at Bosse, Morris Riley at North, Gene Logel and Don Watson."

When asked, Bruce Dockery, Memorial's athletic director, put some perspective on what Mike Blake has meant to the Evansville sports community. "Mike is an ambassador for high school sports," Dockery said. "I don't know that you could go any place in the country where a TV sports guy gives as much high school coverage as he does. As a matter of fact, he does it so well, we're spoiled."

With his smooth, deep voice and easy-going demeanor, Mike Blake has demonstrated a passion for what he does. Although he once yearned for greener pastures, he has endeared himself to the public and become one of us. Though Evansville was originally meant to be one short stop on the road to the Big Apple, Mike and Jen decided to make it their home. As he puts it, "Now, 37 years, four kids and three grandkids later, we're still here."

CHRIS LOWERY: A COACH ON THE FLOOR

Chris Lowery has utilized his basketball savvy and point guard mentality to become one of the top young coaches in Division I basketball, and the 1990 Harrison grad is quick to give credit to his Evansville roots. Lowery controlled the action as the Warriors' point guard at a time when the school was producing some of the best talent in the school's history.

"We had so many good players," Lowery said from his office at Southern Illinois University. "Brent Kell was on our team, and Kevin Hardy. Walter (McCarty) was there, and Calbert (Cheaney) was still there too." Kell went on to star at U of E during the Andy Elkins-Reed Jackson era, and the other three would fashion successful careers as professional athletes, McCarty and Cheaney in the NBA and Hardy in the NFL.

Chris Lowery used his abilities to fast-track himself into the elite coaching ranks, and he credits much of his success to the responsibilities he learned and the coaching he received during his tenure at Harrison. "The point guard has to be the coach on the floor," he explained. "He has to be a direct extension of the coach. Playing for Coach (Jerrill) Vandeventer (at Harrison), he was very demanding, and he expected me to be demanding, too. Sometimes that's tough when your teammates are your friends."

Lowery also credits the experience he received on the neighborhood courts and playgrounds when he was young for preparing him as a competitor. "That was huge," he said about the neighborhood battles. "We played baseball, football, everything. When you finished playing one thing, you'd go play another. Bellemeade and Wesselman Parks were the two main basketball playgrounds. If you were any good, you came there. Cal Cheaney, Dirk Surles, all the really good players from my era were there."

Lowery ran the show while on the court at Harrison, and his 16-point scoring average and five assists per game earned him a scholarship to SIU. During his tenure at Southern Illinois, his teams made it to the post-season all four years, twice to the NIT and twice to the NCAA Tourney. Following his graduation, Chris became an assistant at SIU under Bruce Weber and then followed Weber to Illinois, and after a year at Illinois, Chris found himself in the right place at the right time. When Matt Painter left SIU to become the head coach-in-waiting at Purdue, the Salukis took a chance and brought Lowery back to Carbondale to replace Painter.

(Photo courtesy of Southern Illinois University.)

Although Chris was only 31 and had no experience as a head coach, he wasted no time proving that he was up to the task. During his first three years at the controls of SIU's program, Lowery compiled a record of 78-26 (75%), culminating in a fantastic '06-'07 season where he was named the MVC Coach of the Year. His team finished the regular season in '07 with a 25-5 record that included a road win over highly-ranked Butler. The Salukis were rewarded with a #4 seed in the NCAA Tournament, the highest seed for an MVC team since Larry Bird's Indiana State Sycamores in 1979. After taking the team to the Sweet 16 for only the third time in school history, Lowery was rewarded with a 7-year contract extension.

Current Harrison coach Bryan Speer, who was a high school teammate of Chris's, is not surprised by Lowery's early success, saying that Lowery "was always a natural leader and student of the game." By working hard and absorbing knowledge from every source available, Chris Lowery has transformed himself into one of the best and brightest young coaches in America.

MARK BUSE: FLYING HIGH

Mark Buse proudly displays his State championship medal as a sophomore.

From the time he could walk, Mark Buse had a ball in his hand, and like any red-blooded Hoosier, he had hoop dreams as far back as he can remember. Fortunately, he had the talent to back up his ambition and became an outstanding basketball player, but it was his combination of strength and speed that would make him a world class athlete in a totally different sport.

Mark was the youngest of five children of Edwin and Mary Lou Buse, who raised their kids on a farm in Holland. The oldest of the Buse children, Bev, didn't have the opportunity to play sports in high school, but Mark's older brothers set an example for young Mark when they became athletes at Southridge High School. As Mark tagged along, he watched his brothers play basketball and became enthralled with pole vaulting as he watched brothers Scott and Brad catapulting themselves skyward at high school track meets. Scott Buse held the Southridge record until his younger brother Brad broke it, but those records became history when Mark came along to not only break school records but to develop his craft to the point that he would become one of the elite vaulters in the country.

At Southridge, Mark's strong 6'2" physique made him a star on the basketball court and a solid contributor to the Raiders' tennis team, where he played doubles as an underclassman and singles his junior and senior years. On the basketball court, Mark was good enough to start as a freshman and to earn All-Conference honors his last two years, averaging nearly 20 points per game.

But it was in the spring that Mark's greatest talents were put on display. As a freshman, Buse vaulted an amazing 15' 1" and finished tenth at the State meet, but as he continued to hone his craft over the next two years, he would finish his high school career with a feat that very few Indiana athletes have ever achieved. With speed that enabled him to win the sectional 100-meter dash in 10.7 seconds as a senior, he was able to attack the plant box and ride the torque from his fiberglass pole to attain amazing heights.

As a sophomore in 1989, Mark never lost, and his vault of 15'9" made him a State champion and earned him a #10 national ranking. During his next season, he improved over a foot with a vault of 16' 10¾", captured his second straight State title and reached #4 nationally. With the guidance of his older brothers and track coach Ron LaGrange, Mark was far from finished, however, as he recorded the top height in the country his senior year with a personal best of 17'1".

In addition, Mark captured a third State title, making him the first pole vaulter to do so (only one other has done it since) and only the 18th athlete in 100 years to 'three-peat' in any event.

With his #1 national ranking in 1991, Mark was a hot prospect to college coaches. He pondered going to a small D-1 school so that he could continue to vault and play basketball, but he chose instead to join Coach Sam Bell and his nationally-ranked program at IU.

During Mark's freshman season, the Hoosiers captured the Big Ten championship, and Mark continued to improve, soaring to another personal best of 18-feet and finishing fifth in the Nationals. A year later, he captured the NCAA championship when he produced his best jump of the year at 18' 4 ½". Buse's junior and senior seasons were also impressive, as he consistently cleared 18-feet, reaching 18' 6 ¾" as a junior and 18' 4 ½" as a senior and placing third both years at the NCAA meet.

After his senior year, Mark cleared 18' 4 ½" at the 1996 Olympic trials but fell just short of making the team. With his Olympic dreams dashed, he returned to IU for a few years to assist Coach Bell and then used his degree in Computer Information Systems to secure a job as a network engineer at Kimball International in Jasper.

As Mark enjoys married life and looks forward to the arrival of his first son in 2008, the Holland (Ind.) native can look back with satisfaction on a career in one of the most beautiful events in all of sport. "It's quite a rush," Buse said about vaulting. "When you leave the ground, your instincts take over and it's over almost immediately."

Mark Buse used his God-given talents, his size, strength and exceptional speed, to become a three-time State champion, an NCAA champion and nearly a U.S. Olympian. As a prep star, he became the very best among all American high school vaulters during his career and, without question, he should be listed among the elite pole vaulters in Indiana history.

Mark Buse clears the bar during his days at IU.

CALBERT CHEANEY: MOM SHOWED HIM THE WAY

(Photo courtesy of Indiana University, Media Relations.)

Cheaney was one of the best hurdlers in the state during his high school days. (Photo courtesy of the Evansville Courier.)

When Calbert Nathaniel Cheaney came into this world on July 17th, 1971, he had no idea how blessed he was to be resting in the arms of the mother God had given him. Under her watchful eye, young Calbert avoided potential pitfalls and focused his energies into his schooling, his faith and his love of sports, and under her guidance and direction, Calbert would develop into one of the greatest players in the history of college basketball.

During his early years, the Cheaney family lived on Gum Street in downtown Evansville, and Calbert and his friends would ride bikes all over town to wherever they could find a pick-up game. At the age of ten, Calbert's parents divorced and his mother, Gwen, moved the family to the Indian Woods Apartments on the east side. With Gwen being a single mother with a full-time job at Bristol-Meyers, much of young Calbert's time was spent launching shots for hours on end at a basketball goal near his new home. "I would shoot and shoot all day until Mom told me to come in," Calbert recalled. "There was a little blue light that shined on the court. I'd re-enact playing certain games or hitting the game-winning shot, and when the blue light came on, I knew it was time to go in."

Looking back on his childhood, Calbert realizes that being a well-rounded athlete helped him lay the foundation for his future success. "A lot of kids now don't realize that if you play different sports, it will help tremendously," he said, "because they help develop different skills. Kids can get burned out if they play just one sport."

As a little leaguer at the South League field near Lodge school, Cheaney played first base and center field and occasionally pitched. Though he is known as a southpaw, he batted right-handed. (He also plays golf from the right side.) In the Lakeview Optimist football league, Calbert spent time at running back, wide receiver and defensive back.

At Lodge Elementary, Calbert made the sixth grade team as a fourth grader and later played at Washington Middle School. It is hard to believe today, but Calbert says he didn't always play like a superstar. "I wasn't always good," he admitted. "I was athletic, but I hadn't learned to play the game."

Cheaney also found out in middle school that if he was going to play sports, he would have to play by Mom's rules. As basketball season approached, Gwen didn't like what she saw on Calbert's report card. Although his grades met the school's standards for participation, Gwen expected more and quickly put an end to her son's season. "I cried for a month," Calbert said, "I tried to reason with her, but she wasn't hearing it."

Young Calbert got the message loud and clear and learned what his sisters had known all along. Older sister Camille and younger sister Elizabeth were sprinters on Harrison High School's track team, and as far as academics were concerned, they knew that Mom's word was the law. "It didn't matter how good you were at sports," Camille Cheaney Douglas said in an interview for a local magazine. "If we didn't keep our grades up and behave ourselves, we didn't play."

Anyone who knew the Cheaney kids was aware that Gwen was a mother who was determined that her children stayed on the right track. In the same magazine article, long-time family friend Donita Hester summed up the family dynamic well. "She was strict with the kids," Ms. Hester explained. "When she said 'MOVE', the kids moved."

Harrison coach Dennis Bays experienced Gwen's philosophy first-hand before Calbert even enrolled at Harrison. "Mrs. Crawley (Gwen re-married after her divorce) kept athletics in perspective," Bays stated in the aforementioned article. "When Calbert was in the eighth grade, we had a summer basketball camp. The other kids showed up, but not Calbert.

"When I called to ask about it, I found that Mrs. Crawley didn't want Calbert to participate because she didn't want him running the streets. I had to call three times to convince her to let him come. She made me promise to pick Calbert up in the morning, keep him with me the whole time and return him to his door when he was through."

Gwen Cheaney (she re-assumed the Cheaney name several years ago) is not embarrassed at all by the stories told about her firm-handed parenting style and, in fact, feels that it was her duty. "I was brought up to believe that when you have responsibilities, you have to take care of them," she said from her home in Newburgh. "We were brought up in the church, and that was a big factor. It might sound harsh to a lot of people, but you can't compromise with kids. You have to do what's best for them. It was just my job."

With his priorities firmly in place, Calbert entered high school as a 6'1 freshman in 1985. Although he played all sports as a youngster and still believes in the benefits of being a well-rounded athlete, he stuck with basketball and track at Harrison. On the track, he was an exceptional hurdler, running 14-flat in the highs and holding several records when he left school. In his junior year, he was the only Harrison athlete to qualify for the State meet, and he could have continued running track in college if he had chosen to. Instead, he passed on track his senior year to focus on the sport that would serve as a vehicle to national fame and a long and successful career.

During his four years at Harrison, Calbert grew to 6'7, and although he had great size and athleticism, it was another asset that set him apart. Chris Lowery, the successful young coach of the SIU Salukis, was a teammate of Cheaney's and witnessed every day what Calbert did to better himself. "Calbert is the definition of someone who works hard to be the best possible," Lowery pointed out from his office at SIU. "We knew he'd be good, but we didn't know he'd be one of the best players ever at IU and in the Big Ten. It would have been really easy for him to just coast because he was really talented, but he worked very hard to become better."

Bryan Speer, the current head coach at Harrison, agrees, but also includes Calbert's contemporaries when discussing work ethic. "They were all the hardest workers," Speer said, referring to Cheaney, Lowery, future NFL star Kevin Hardy and Walter McCarty, who was a freshman when Calbert was a senior. "Calbert was very quiet," Speer continued. "You didn't see him out much. He just worked hard."

Cheaney is quick to give credit to then-Harrison coach Jerrill Vandeventer for helping to develop Calbert's skills and for providing motivation for the young player to believe in himself. "He called me into his office when I was a sophomore," Cheaney recalled, "and told me I had an opportunity to become a Division I player. At that time, I didn't even think about getting a scholarship. I just wanted to get my college degree and move on. I started hammering the nail harder after that."

As Calbert hammered, he molded himself into a silky-smooth scorer who could slash to the basket or pull up for his sweet left-handed jumper. As a junior, he averaged 21 points per game, and he was scoring at a 28-point clip when disaster struck during his senior year. When the #2-ranked Warriors rolled into the Hulman Center to battle #1 Terre Haute South, all of Indiana took notice as the two undefeated teams squared off. One of South's stars was Tony McGee, who would later play football at Michigan and in the NFL, and another was hot-shooting lefty Brian Evans, who would move on to IU two years later and lead the Big Ten in scoring in 1995-'96.

In front of a packed house, Calbert landed awkwardly on McGee's foot and had to leave the game. The diagnosis was a broken foot, and, as it turned out, the injury was unavoidable. "The doctor said it was inevitable that I was going to break it," Cheaney explained, "because the bone was so soft."

With his senior season cut short, Cheaney had still impressed enough people to be named to the Indiana All-Star squad (he didn't play because of his injury) and to be courted by some of the best programs in the country. Although U of E recruited Cheaney extremely hard, Calbert wanted to play farther from home, so he narrowed his options to Purdue, Kentucky and Indiana. When he chose to enlist in Bob Knight's army, he knew what he was signing up for, but he was also leery about the competition he would face.

"At that time, we had the best recruiting class in the country," said Calbert. "We had Pat and Greg Graham, Chris Reynolds, Lawrence Funderburke, Todd Leary and Chris Lawson. I was probably the lowest-rated recruit of the class. I was just hoping to play the best I could and play hard and graduate (in Criminal Justice with an eye on becoming a lawyer) and then get a job."

As Calbert prepared to start his college career, there was much speculation, as always, about how he would handle Coach Knight's style. Though the public may have been concerned, neither Cheaney nor those who knew his background gave it a second thought. In the local magazine article, family friend Jackie Pore had a simple evaluation of the situation. "Calbert was going from one stern hand to another," Ms. Pore pointed out. "If he could handle Gwen's discipline, he could handle Coach Knight."

Calbert expressed similar feelings when asked of the task of dealing with the unpredictable Knight. "You may not believe this," he responded, "but my mom was worse than he was. Seriously! People were telling me when I was in high school that 'Coach Knight is going to yell at you one time and you're gonna want to quit.' I heard a lot of that. I knew I'd be OK because I had a tough mother."

During his years at IU, Calbert and his classmates were impressive. His teams were consistently ranked in the top five nationally during Cheaney's junior and senior seasons, and his Hoosiers defended their home court relentlessly as part of a streak from February of 1991 to February of 1995 when Indiana won 54 straight home games. The Hoosiers also nearly captured the 1992 national championship before losing a foul fest to Duke in the Final Four.

With Cheaney leading the way, the Hoosiers finished his senior season ranked #1 in the AP poll. During his college career, Calbert scored 30 or more points thirteen times and averaged nearly 20 points, with a high of 22.4 as a senior. Cheaney won 105 games while at Indiana, more than any other player, and his teams were 87-16 over his last three seasons (.845), capturing back-to-back Big Ten crowns and winning nine NCAA Tournament games.

As an individual, Calbert was named All-Big Ten and All-American three times ('91, '92 and '93) and was a four-time MVP choice for the Hoosiers. He was also chosen as a member of the first team on the Indiana Hoosiers All-Century Team. He finished his years at Indiana as the all-time career scoring leader for IU and the Big Ten with 2,613 points, a mark that may stand forever if the

Calbert jumps center against Parrish Casebier of South Spencer. (Photo by Mike Thomas)

conference's best players continue to bolt for the NBA. In 1993, Cheaney was named the Big Ten MVP, won all twelve NCAA National Player of the Year awards and was a unanimous first team All-American. To cap off his great college career, Calbert was named the Naismith College Player of the Year and won the 1993 John R. Wooden Award.

The young man who was concerned about whether he could even cut it four years earlier was now in position to do something he dared not even dream about as a youngster. He was heading to the NBA.

In the 1993 draft, Calbert was picked sixth overall by the Washington Bullets (now Wizards). He proved durable and consistent, averaging 70 games and double-digit points for six seasons in Washington before signing with Boston in 1999. After one year with the Celtics, Cheaney spent two years with Denver, one with Utah and his last three with the Golden State Warriors. In nine of his thirteen NBA seasons, Calbert appeared in at least 60 games and gained a reputation as a steady, dependable scorer and leader.

The 2002-'03 season was a special one for Cheaney, as he joined the Utah Jazz. Not only did he get the opportunity to play for Evansville College legend Jerry Sloan, but he was the starting shooting guard during the final season in the careers of John Stockton and Karl Malone, both future hall of famers. "It was a tremendous experience playing with those two because they're such great guys," Calbert recalled. "And the greatest thing about Coach Sloan, that was not usual for the league, is that he doesn't care who you are. He would yell at Stockton and Malone just like the younger players. That was the attitude he had. He didn't play any favorites."

Since Calbert's last NBA game in 2006, he is enjoying time with his wife, Yvette, and their two children, Julian and Sydney. He also has devoted time to giving back to his community. "Kids are our future," he explained, "so you have to try to invest in kids to help them make the right decisions and be responsible. It's our job as adults to teach them and help them. That's all that matters to me. That's why we built the facility at St. James Missionary Baptist Church (where Calbert's family went while he was growing up), so that they could have recreation programs and day care, somewhere for the kids to go and have a good time and learn about life."

After spending some time away from basketball, he has now started to contemplate entering the coaching profession, most likely at the collegiate level. No matter what the future holds for Calbert, he knows that he will be prepared because of the loving but firm guidance he received from his mother. "She brought me up the way a child should be brought up," Calbert revealed. "She was strict with me and kept me on the right path, and I love her for that."

In the words of ex-Harrison coach Frank Schwitz, "Calbert will always remember where he came from – and he'll always remember Mom!"

Mom raised her three kids well. (L-R): Camille, Calbert and Elizabeth. (Photo courtesy of Gwen Cheaney.)

Right: Gwen Cheaney

One of Calbert Cheaney's favorite pastimes is movies, and he has accumulated over 1,000 DVDs over the years, mostly action films like his favorites, *Star Wars* and *Gladiator*.

ELISSA KIM: "OFF THE RECORD"

Anyone who knows Elissa (pronounced uh-LEE-suh) Kim speaks first of what an incredible young women she is. Almost as an afterthought do they also mention that she was one of the best tennis players Evansville has ever produced. As a youngster, Elissa grunted and perspired on courts all over the country making a name for herself on the junior tennis circuit. But the vision for her future in the sport wasn't hers; it was her father's, and as Elissa played into her teens, it is unlikely that either she or her father could have foreseen that secrecy and deception would play a huge factor in her ultimate success in one of the biggest matches of her career.

Elissa's father, Dr. Chong Kim, and her mother, Jin Kim, raised Elissa and her siblings (sisters Soo Jin and Jane and brother Eugene) to respect the values of their Korean culture. Among them were a steadfast work ethic and the responsibility to give back to their world. The work ethic propelled Elissa to prominence in the early years but also led to some doubts as she grew into a teenager.

While growing up in Korea, Elissa's father was exceptional at gymnastics and volleyball, but he didn't discover tennis until after he moved to Evansville and took lessons at the Tri-State Athletic Club. When Elissa was eight years old, her father brought her to the club, and the journey began. Her father would be her primary coach for the next ten years, while her mother provided all the other necessities.

"Her influence in the whole equation was supporting me in the sense that she's the one who took me to all my tournaments and lessons," Elissa says of her mother. "She sort of did the dirty work. In junior tennis, basically an entire summer is dedicated to traveling to tournaments, and she did that for ten years. My dad never went to a single one. It was my mom shuttling me around."

As Elissa's skills progressed, her father could see that her talents were significant and could possibly provide her with a college scholarship. As she was progressing to as high as #35 in the country, Elissa was also feeling the drudgery that comes with the grind of the tour. "It was a whole circuit, just like the pros have," she explained. "The ultimate objective for all of us was to get to Nationals, so you had to get through a series of tournaments to qualify."

Elissa began to question her dedication in her teenage years as she traveled five or six weeks in the summer and played the indoor circuit during the winter. She missed the day-to-day things. "While other kids would come home and watch TV or go to the mall with friends, my life was to go to practice, to study, and then get up and do the same thing the next day," she confessed.

Although she knew it would disappoint her father, Elissa was stubborn in her quest to lead a "normal life" and decided to put her racquet away. "I wanted to pursue social stuff," she admitted, "things that in the really big scheme of things don't matter. But as a teenager, you think it's all important at the time. I had a very short-sighted view of what I thought was good for me. But I can't say any of the pursuits I went after were meaningful."

And how did her father react to her new-found revelation?

"More or less, it was a reluctant allowing," Elissa recalled. "But there were protracted battles over this. I thought I knew more than him. I tried to quit, and I wasn't very disciplined. I wanted to pursue other things that didn't require as much work, frankly. Eventually, because I was bossy about it, he sort of gave in."

(Photo courtesy of Jon Siau.)

It didn't take long for Elissa to re-evaluate. At the start of her freshman year at North High School (1988), she established herself as a top cross country runner. She also began to feel the urge to wipe the cobwebs off her tennis racquet and re-dedicate herself. Her father had assured her that she would eventually want to take up tennis again, and the young teen soon found out that, once again, father knows best.

"Fortunately for me," she stated, " he didn't rub it in my face that he was right. We just proceeded on. I admitted to myself that I had lost so much time and that I should never have quit when I did."

Her high school cross country coach, Jon Siau, was also North's tennis coach, and he was thrilled to have his star runner return to her strongest sport. Although it had been several months since Elissa had played tennis, her freshman season didn't show it. She advanced to the 1989 State Finals with a perfect 25-0 record. Carmel freshman Holyn Lord, whose sister Courtney was a State champion from Indianapolis Brebeuf, spoiled Elissa's perfect season in the finals at Indianapolis North Central.

Elissa's sophomore season was nearly identical to the previous year, as she breezed to the State Finals not only undefeated, but having never lost a set. Once again, Holyn Lord spoiled the party, and it became obvious that since Ms. Lord was the same age, Elissa needed to solve the Holyn Lord mystery before she could win on the state's biggest stage.

After a 2-6, 3-6, thrashing by Lord in the State Finals, Elissa and her mother stayed in Indianapolis for over a week. College scouts were coming around to watch, and the Kims thought it would be wise to stay for two prestigious junior tournaments. At home in Evansville, Mr. Siau anxiously awaited the results. "The phone rang," he recalled, "and it was Elissa, and she said, 'Siau, guess what?'"

Siau could tell from Elissa's excitement that something great had happened, and when she told him that she had beaten Lord, he knew her confidence had been restored. Elissa's victory over her arch-nemesis set the stage for a memorable junior season, one that would start just like the last two but would present challenges the teenager could never have imagined.

(Note: Ironically, Elissa and Holyn Lord would never play each other again. Unusual circumstances prevented Holyn from playing high school tennis her last two years, but she did go on to a successful college career at Notre Dame.)

Elissa breezed through the regular season before an unexpected hiccup. For the first time in her high school career, she lost before the State Finals. After wins over Castle's Libby Vote (6-0, 6-3) and Chotsani Farmer of Reitz (6-0, 6-0), Elissa lost in the SIAC finals to Memorial's Sara Jane Stevenson.

"The loss was the best thing that could have happened," said Coach Siau, "because the pressure of the (undefeated) season and the on-going college recruiting was suddenly lifted off her shoulders."

Although Memorial continued to dominate the sectional as a team, as they had for several years, Elissa avenged her earlier loss to Sara Jane in the sectional final. She also went on to defeat Nan Smith of Columbus North in the regional final. She was off to State again with new-found confidence after defeating Holyn Lord, but this is where the story gets interesting.

After the regional, the Kims arrived back in Evansville around midnight on a Saturday. Elissa arrived home exhausted and went right to bed. That night, she arose to go to the bathroom, and as she made her way in the darkened room, she tripped and fell. She had forgotten that she had left her racquet bag in the middle of the floor, and the fall resulted in several strained ligaments on the top of her right foot.

The following Monday, Elissa was in her fifth period class when Mr. Siau coincidentally stopped in to speak with the teacher. The room went silent, and the teacher asked if he wanted to speak to Elissa. Jon looked in Elissa's direction and said, "No, I'll see her at practice later on."

As he looked more closely at his star player, he laughed. She was holding two crutches. Totally oblivious to the situation, he reacted to what he thought was a prank. "That's not funny," he proclaimed. The room was filled with giddy juniors, yet Coach Siau heard not a sound. When he realized what was going on, his heart fell to the floor. His thoughts? "Her dream of winning a State championship was dissolving before our eyes!"

Just four days before they were to leave for Indy, Elissa was still on crutches. She didn't practice, of course, and Coach Siau was fielding constant requests to interview her. He was starting to get questions about why Elissa wasn't practicing, and his explanation that they were trying to keep her fresh was making the media skeptical. After some persistence by one of the *Courier* reporters, John made the writer agree that what he was about to say was off the record. He made it clear that he meant OFF THE RECORD! After hearing the story, the reporter insisted that the injury was real news and needed to be reported.

Admirably, the *Courier* writer honored his promise and the secret was kept, despite efforts of editors and staffers to convince Mr. Siau to allow it to go to print. The coach knew that it was a long shot for Elissa to even compete, let alone win, but his biggest fear was of word getting out. He knew that it was common practice for coaches to scour the local papers to find any edge they can. Coach Siau, in fact, had copies of the South Bend newspaper because one of Elissa's main competitors, Sara Stanchin, was from South Bend. If Stanchin's coach got wind of the situation, Elissa's chances would be virtually gone.

Two days before her match, Elissa was still on crutches, but, amazingly, she had shown no signs of disappointment. On Friday, Elissa, her mother and Coach Siau drove to Indianapolis to meet with the leading therapists and sports medicine experts in the state, who tried heat treatments, cold treatments and even shock stimulation before taping the injured foot. Elissa and her 'entourage' then left to test the foot for the first time since the accident and agreed to return to the clinic at 5:00 a.m. on Saturday. Elissa remained calm.

They couldn't risk being seen at North Central (where the matches would take place), so they drove to Brebeuf High School. Luckily, the courts that were usually locked were open and available. John began to feed Elissa balls, trying not to make her run too much. After eight minutes, Elissa had had enough. She gently dropped her racquet on her bag and walked to the parking lot.

Instinctively, Jin, her mother, wanted to go to Elissa and console her, but Coach Siau thought it best to leave her to her own thoughts. "She's just seen her hopes of a State championship go up in smoke," he said to Jin.

Soon, Elissa hobbled back, put her racquet away and asked if they could leave.

When they arrived at their motel, Elissa was greeted by the best medicine she could have hoped for. A group of her friends had driven up from Evansville to surprise her. They all went to Red Lobster to eat (a tradition of sorts), and the subject of her injury did not come up the rest of the evening.

After a restless night, the three again returned to the therapist's office, and the doctors asked how the taping had worked the night before. After discussing several possibilities, Coach Siau suggested taping the foot to pull the arch upward to relieve some of the stress. The doctors agreed that there was "nothing to lose" and proceeded with the taping.

The moment of truth was approaching. Would Elissa be able to compete, or would she and her supporters have to make a long, disappointing trip back to Evansville?

With a level of deception one might see in a spy novel, Siau and Kim decided to take the cloak and dagger approach and hope for the best. At North Central, Elissa checked in, careful not to give away her dilemma. Coach Siau requested a private meeting with the IHSAA assistant commissioner, Mildred Bath, informing her of the possible (no, probable) withdrawal from the tournament. Ms. Bath was shocked and disappointed.

Elissa was scheduled to play Kim Walkey of Lafayette Jeff in the semi-finals. Sara Stanchin would play Margaux Pettit from Indianapolis Pike. During warm-ups, the strategy was for Elissa to act nonchalant, so as not to give away her secret.

Elissa briefly left the court for some time by herself. She then returned to give the verdict. Coach Siau got a cold chill when she looked at him and said, "Siau, I'm going to give it a try."

"At that moment," John said in a recent interview, "I knew that if anyone could pull this off, she could."

Interestingly, an IHSAA rule change at the time also contributed to how this drama would play out. In past years, coaches were not allowed to be courtside, but the new rule allowed them to sit alongside their players during changeovers.

As the match started, Elissa's strategy was to try and move her opponent around without having to chase balls herself. She won the first game and sat down on the changeover. Mr. Siau knelt in front of her and placed her foot on his knee. He pretended to be tying her shoe, but he was actually elevating the foot to relieve the pressure, and they continued the charade throughout the match.

At one point, they heard the Lafayette Jeff coach say, "Kim, do you know what foot I'm talking about?"

Elissa clutched the arms of her chair and said, "Siau, they know!"

"I don't think so," her coach replied.

Then they heard the Jeff coach say, "Are you foot-faulting with your right or left foot?"

"How can they not know?" Elissa wondered aloud.

Miraculously, Elissa won her match 6-3, 6-0, and they slowly made their way to the van to ice her foot.

As they left to go to Wendy's for lunch, Elissa remarked that, given her injury, she didn't know how she could possibly beat Sara Stanchin. But Coach Siau had a surprise for his star player.

During Elissa's match, Coach Siau had been watching Ms. Stanchin's match two courts away. At one point, he saw Stanchin look over at Elissa and react by dropping her jaw. She had realized what no one else had: Elissa Kim was injured!

As it turned out, Stanchin's realization that Elissa was hurt and that she (Stanchin) had a good chance of winning the championship caused her to lose focus and lose her match.

"It must be your day," Coach Siau said to Elissa, "you play Pettit!"

After returning to the courts, Coach Siau felt a tap on his shoulder. As he turned, Elissa said, "Let's go win a State title."

Elissa wasted little time dismissing Miss Pettit 6-3, 6-2, and the unlikely championship was hers. Reflecting back on the storybook tale, Elissa is philosophical and practical. "You know, it's funny," she said. "People look back on that and say, 'Wow! That's so great! She got hurt and managed to recover.' I sort of look at it and say, 'It wasn't that big of a deal. I mean, it was painful and totally annoying, and I shed a lot of tears at the time. I said to myself, 'What is this hand of cards I've been dealt?' And, at the time, I'm sure it seemed incredibly dramatic.

"But at the same time, I sort of got over it fairly quickly in the sense that I realized 'it is what it is.' I mean, you just go out and play. It's just the course of what happens in an athlete's life and in life in general. You either respond or you don't."

Elissa Kim responded in a big way in 1991. The following year, she was president of her senior class and homecoming queen. Oh, yeah, her tennis season wasn't too bad, either. She marched through the season undefeated and became the first Evansville tennis player (male or female) to win back-to-back IHSAA championships.

With a high school career record of 98-3 and her 3.5 grade point average, Elissa earned a full ride to Northwestern University. She graduated in 1996 with a double major in History and Religion and, although she cherished her tennis accomplishments, she realizes that those days were merely phases of her life.

She married Geoff Clapp, a jazz drummer, and now, as Elissa Kim Clapp, she is Vice-President of Recruiting and Selection for Teach America. Her job is to find people who will go where most people won't (impoverished rural communities, Indian reservations and inner cities) to help give a hand up to people in need. With her type-A personality and incredible work ethic, Elissa Kim's career choice is a reflection of her Korean heritage, and, without a doubt, has made her father very proud.

(Photo courtesy of Jon Siau.)

IHSAA STATE CHAMPIONS:
GIRLS TENNIS

Team	Year	Coach
Memorial	1990-'91	Brenda Walling
Memorial	1992-'93	Brenda Walling
Memorial	1993-'94	Brenda Walling
Memorial	1994-'95	Brenda Walling
Memorial	1995-'96	Brenda Walling

Individual	School	Year
Lanae Renschler	Castle	1982-'83
Lanae Renschler	Castle	1983-'84
Lanae Renschler	Castle	1984-'85
Lanae Renschler	Castle	1985-'86
Elissa Kim	North	1990-'91
Elissa Kim	North	1991-'92
Margo Stevenson	Memorial	1994-'95
Stephanie Hazlett	Heritage Hills	1995-'96

Doubles Team	School	Year
Angela Sabella/ Tricia Trapp	Memorial	1994-'95
Erin Geisler/ Dana Schitter	Jasper	1998-'99
Elizabeth Hedde/ Brittany Perkins	Vincennes Lincoln	1999-'00
Abby Greif/ Catherine Hofmann	Memorial	2004-'05

WALTER MCCARTY: YOU GOTTA DREAM

When Walter McCarty was off by himself shooting hoops at Plaza Middle School in the late 1980s, there was no way he could have dreamed that he would one day compete against the greatest players in the world on the courts of the NBA. But then again, there's also no way he could have known that he would grow to 6'10" or that some childhood friends would provide inspiration while his skills caught up with his body.

Walter always loved being around the basketball court, but his lack of self-confidence made him shy. "Plaza is where everybody went, and that's where I used to learn," Walter explained on a visit to a basketball camp held by Harrison coach Bryan Speer. "I remember one day I was on a side goal and the guys were three or four years older than me. I wasn't too keen on playing with the big guys. I was just working on my game on the side and Calbert (Cheaney) called me over and asked if I would play with them. Once I did that, I got more confidence."

Although Walter had good size for a seventh grader (5'10), he admits that he was anything but a prodigy. "I was totally uncoordinated because I was growing so fast," Walter said. "My body was a little bit ahead of my skills. I used to be frustrated all the time, but I just kept working at it. There were times when I didn't play in middle school. I sat the bench. I remember my mom (Joy) would drop me off and I would say, 'Mom, you can just go home; I'm not going to play.' But she would say, 'No, I'm going to come in. Just stay patient.' And she would come to every game whether I played or not.

"I was awful! I couldn't make a layup in seventh grade. I remember one day over Christmas break and we were having practice. I was on a fast break and it bounced off the backboard to half court. I got so frustrated, I stormed off the court and I was in the bathroom crying and upset. But I was determined to get better. There was a period from my eighth grade year to my freshman year where I gained a lot as far as getting to know my body. I got better and better because I always worked at it."

Walter also found some personal motivation in middle school that he says few people know about. "There was someone, I won't say his name because he's a very good friend of mine, and in middle school, he was *the guy*," Walter disclosed. "He was the guy all the girls cheered for. One thing that always motivated me at that age was that I would work out every day so that I could kick his butt one day. He doesn't even know it, but early on, he was a lot of motivation."

Walter proved that envy could be a strong incentive when, at 6'3", he gave his idol a lesson on the last day of school. After a game of one-on-one, Walter drew raves from onlookers who were amazed at the transformation Walter had gone through during his middle school years.

McCarty also believes that he was impacted greatly as a youngster by being around players who were a little older. He would eventually become an outstanding player at Harrison High School, and the players he admired when he was young would become teammates and life-long friends as each went on to outstanding sports careers. Cheaney, who became an All-American at IU, has remained a friend and was even a teammate when the two spent a year together with the Boston Celtics. Chris Lowery and Kevin Hardy were also instrumental in Walter's development as a player. "I lived right down the street from Chris (now an outstanding coach at Southern Illinois University), and I used to love watching him play," McCarty said. "When you see guys play on another level who are very talented, it's a motivation to work hard. And Kevin Hardy (who went on to become a star linebacker at Illinois and in the NFL) was always telling me, 'whatever sport you play, you have to work at it.' I think we all knew we could do something special, and we just fed off each other.

(Photo by Mike Thomas.)

"We weren't guys who were going out and getting in trouble," McCarty continued. "Whenever you saw us, we were out playing ball, trying to get better and trying to do the right thing. There were a lot of kids coming out of Evansville who, if they would have just focused, they could have done something special. We were just fortunate and blessed that we were really focused. I don't know if it was the school or our parents."

By the time Walter finished his freshman year at Harrison, he stood 6'7", and he would grow to nearly 6'10" before his high school career was over.

After a sensational high school career and recognition as an All-American, Walter examined his college options. "I got letters from a lot of schools," McCarty said, "but I never was the type to waste anybody's time. A lot of kids just take visits to take visits, but I wasn't about getting on a plane to travel. I really enjoyed being around my friends too much, like Bryan Speer and other guys I played with. I always said that there would be schools I would go to if they came around. Kentucky was one of them. I liked Purdue, and U of E really courted me hard. I wasn't going to visit U of E, but my mom wanted me to go as a courtesy.

"I told IU to stop wasting their time. Calbert was there, and people were trying to get me to follow in his footsteps, but I knew where my bread and butter was. I knew the best place for me was where they were running up and down the floor and shooting (three-pointers).

So instead of playing at Indiana, where he felt like Coach Knight would have asked him to put on weight and set a lot of picks, Walter put his talents in the hands of Rick Pitino at Kentucky. Bryan Speer felt strongly that UK was where Walter would end up, and he recalls vividly the evening when Kentucky came calling.

"Rick Pitino and C.M. Newton sat right up there," Speer indicated as he pointed to the east end of Harrison's gym. "We won. Jasper was good, and we were good. Jasper had Scott Rolen, who was an Indiana All-Star, and a guy named Andy Noblitt. They had another kid named Scotty Mills, a little bitty guy who could jump out of the gym and actually did try to dunk one.

"It was a pretty good game, and Joel Thomas (of Harrison) ended up stealing the show that night. Walter didn't play well by Walter's standards, maybe seventeen points and nine rebounds. Pitino, when he left here, there was a quote in the paper that said he thought Walter was the best high school player in the country. And Walter didn't even play very well!"

At Kentucky, Walter packed on forty pounds of muscle and had a successful career in the Wildcats' run-and-gun system. In 1994, McCarty nailed a three-pointed that completed the largest second half rally in NCAA history, a 31-point comeback over LSU. He was also a cornerstone of the 1995-'96 Kentucky team that captured the NCAA national championship, averaging 11.7 points and 4.5 rebounds per game while finishing second on the team with 206 rebounds and nailing 28 three-pointers for the season.

At the end of the '96 championship season, Walter would graduate with a degree in Communications and would say a temporary farewell to Coach Pitino as he headed for the NBA. But in a few years, his solid reputation as a person and a leader would eventually result in a reunion between McCarty and his college mentor.

As he waited for the 1996 NBA draft, Walter was well aware of the business aspect of professional sports, and he watched and waited as the process unfolded. "It was weird the way it played out because Phoenix was going to take me at #15," McCarty explained. "I remember sitting at the table and Phoenix was talking to me and my agent. They said Kevin Johnson had just retired, and now they're in need of a point guard. So they picked Steve Nash.

"If I went to the New York Knicks, I was going to get a Nike deal. This is stuff people really don't know about. New York took me, and it was a great situation. I played with a lot of veterans: Patrick Ewing, John Starks, Larry Johnson, Charles Oakley, Herb Williams, Chris Dudley."

McCarty also remembers his first exposure to NBA life and how the lessons he learned in his youth served him well during his eleven-year career. "I remember the first day of training camp. (Knick's coach) Jeff Van Gundy sat us down, the three rookies (Walter, John Wallace from Syracuse and Dontae Jones from Mississippi State) and on our lockers he put "PATIENCE." He said 'The biggest thing you need is patience. I don't care how good you are, I'm not going to play you guys. You're on a veteran team, and you need patience.'

"That really helped my career," McCarty added, "because I had a lot of time to learn. Because I learned patience, I always stayed ready to play. Scotty Brooks (a teammate) used to tell me, 'This is our game time during warm-ups.' We played one-on-one hard! If we got in the game, we were ready to play. You just do your best and try to be professional and get ready to play, because you never know when that chance will come again. It turned out to be a life lesson."

But before Walter could demonstrate what he had learned, he was exposed to another harsh reality of NBA life. "I remember being in a hotel room getting ready for a game," Walter recalled. "We were playing Boston. I got a call from Coach Van Gundy, and he said, 'You've just been traded to Boston.' He didn't want the trade, and I thought, 'Wow!', so I just stayed there until the Celtics sent somebody over to pick me up."

McCarty spent that evening sitting in the stands watching the team he was part of a couple of hours before play the team he would be joining the next day. "That's the way it works,"

(Photo by Mike Thomas.)

Walter said matter-of-factly, "and I wasn't married, so it was an easy transition. It allowed me to go from not playing to a starting role. I could really get experience and learn."

McCarty joined a Celtics starting lineup that included Antoine Walker, Ron Mercer and Chauncey Billips, and he averaged 9.6 points and 4.4 rebounds in his first season. Walter spent over seven years with Boston and was a fan favorite because of his gutsy play and his knack for making the big shot. In 2005, the Celtics initiated a youth movement and traded the 30-year-old McCarty to Phoenix, where he spent half a season before moving to the L.A. Clippers for his final NBA season.

During his pro career, Walter played every position except point guard, and because of that, he got to guard a variety of the game's greats. Among them were: Scottie Pippin, Glen Robinson, Reggie Miller, Chris Mullin, Allen Iverson, David Robinson, Shaquille O'Neal and Michael Jordan.

In 2006, Walter walked away from basketball to enter a new phase of his life. His years as a player have enabled him to explore the business world with ex-teammates Ron Mercer, Jamal Mashburn and others, and he has also been able to pursue his other passion – music. Over the years, Walter displayed his voice while singing the National Anthem before high school games and prior to All-Star Saturday Night on the eve of the 2006 NBA All-Star Game. In 2003, he released an R&B/soul album called "Moment for Love", and he has written music for other artists and for Warner Bros. and other companies.

After earning millions of dollars from his NBA career, Walter has avoided the trappings of professional sports and kept his priorities intact. In 2007, he once again joined his former college coach when he accepted an assistant coaching job under Rick Pitino at the University of Louisville. The reunion turned out to be

a sweet one, as the Cardinals made a run deep into the NCAA Tournament in 2008 before falling to #1 seed North Carolina. Perhaps McCarty's future lies in coaching or perhaps in another field, but if his past is any indication, his foundation is solid no matter what the pursuit.

"He was a great player and even a better person," said Chris Lowery. "He's a tremendous person and obviously very gifted. You knew he was going to be special."

Walter McCarty is humbled by his success and is well aware of his good fortune, both in terms of a career and in the friendships he still treasures. And surely he is amazed at how a gawky seventh grader ended up living such a life. "It's been great, the doors that have opened from basketball," McCarty reflected. "I never dreamed in a million years I'd be doing the things I've done. I don't know if it was the school or what it was, but for some reason, all the friends I have, except for the Kentucky guys, are guys I went to Plaza with. Chris, Kevin and Calbert, it's great to see those guys get their due for all their hard work. They've been with me every step of the way."

> In 1998, Walter McCarty appeared in the movie *He Got Game* as the character 'Mance'.

Walter McCarty sings The National Anthem while at Harrison with UK's Rick Pitino and C.M. Newton watching from above. Photo courtesy of the Evansville Courier.)

IHSAA STATE CHAMPIONS:
BOYS SWIMMING

Individual(s)	School	Year	Event	Time
John Schmitt	Reitz	2004-2005	200-yd. freestyle	1:39.25
John Schmitt	Reitz	2004-2005	100-yd. freestyle	45.75
Bryce Hunt	Castle	1999-2000	100-yd. backstroke	49.42
Jonathon Wainman, David Franklin, Ryan McNally, Thomas Rueger	Mt. Vernon	1997-1998	200-yd. freestyle relay	1:25.52

GIRLS SWIMMING

Individual(s)	School	Year	Event	Time
Kimberly Nicholson	Harrison	1978-1979	100-yd. backstroke	59.35
Stacy Westfall	Vincennes Lincoln	1979-1980	100-yd. breaststroke	1:09.33
Jane Coontz	Castle	1980-1981	200-yd. freestyle	1:52.21
Jane Coontz	Castle	1980-1981	500-yd. freestyle	4:55.99
Natlie Koch	Memorial	1982-1983	100-yd. breaststroke	1:08.48
Mandy Crowe	Mt. Vernon	1994-1995	100-yd. backstroke	55.50
Melissa Sugar	Day School	1996-1997	100-yd. freestyle	50.24
Melissa Sugar	Day School	1996-1997	200-yd. freestyle	1:49.6
Leslie Van Winkle	Harrison	2001-2002	100-yd. breaststroke	1:05.17
Jenae Gill	Southridge	2003-2004	100-yd. backstroke	56.52

MT. VERNON SWIMMING: "THERE IS NO SECRET."

When asked the secret to Mt. Vernon High School's swimming dominance over the last seventeen years, head coach Larry Zoller was very concise in his answer. "There is no secret," he answered. "We just try to work harder than our competition."

Zoller takes great pride in his program and his facility, but even though Mt. Vernon's swimming facility is impressive by local standards, there are several schools from central and northern Indiana that have facilities many colleges would love to have. This fact, plus the massive populations of some schools, makes it virtually impossible for area schools to compete for a State title. Although Mt. Vernon has never finished higher than seventh at State, they have consistently been a dominant swimming program in southwestern Indiana.

The timing was perfect for the program to begin its successful run when the opening of their new pool in 1991 coincided with the arrival of Larry Zoller as the team's new coach. Prior to Zoller's arrival, the swim team practiced in three lanes at USI and had been coached by a series of lay coaches (non-teachers). Then, in 1990, Rex Mundi grad Brenda (Fulton) Kramer, who had just accepted a job with the school system, took over the program. When Brenda was asked if she would step down in '91 to make room for Coach Zoller, she relented for the sake of the program. She graciously agreed to step down to an assistant position, and not only have she and Larry been partners as coaches but Brenda married Zoller, making the duo companions away from the pool as well.

Brenda and Larry Zoller have been a winning team since 1991.

Larry and Brenda knew their task would not be easy. As is the case in most schools in Indiana, it isn't easy to convince athletes to abandon their 'hoop dreams' and take the plunge into unknown waters. It also isn't easy to persuade teenagers to roll out of bed in the morning for 5:30 a.m. practices.

"I put in a lot of time, and I expect the kids to put in a lot of time and work hard," Larry said from his poolside office, adorned with newspaper clippings from the past. "They have to practice four or five hours a day during the season, an hour and a half in the morning and two or three hours after school."

When Larry stated, "There is no secret," he was referring to the self-discipline and sacrifice necessary to be successful as a swimmer and as a swimming coach. Larry says that it is not unusual for his day to begin at 5:15 a.m. and end after 8:30 p.m. because of time spent with his high schoolers and with the younger kids in his feeder program.

Swimmers are a rare breed, somewhat like cross country runners, who log mile after lonely mile strengthening muscles and conquering mental obstacles to make themselves better. The average swimmer churns out over 10,000 yards per day, which equates to over 100 miles just during the season. Because of the effort it takes, Zoller said he has never had to cut anyone from the team because they tend to "cut themselves," and keeping the swimmers motivated as they swim the miles is half the battle.

"You have to understand that's what it takes," Zoller explained. "You improve in little bits. You (the coach) have to be demanding, but in a compassionate way. You have to believe in the kids so that they can believe in themselves, because who's going to practice all those hours if they don't think it's going to be worthwhile? Who's going to do that? The kids have the self-discipline; I just nurture it."

Another aspect that makes swimming unusual is that it is very rare for a swimmer to be highly successful and also play another high school sport. Since most of the feeder kids gravitate toward basketball and football, a school the size of Mt. Vernon is at a distinct disadvantage in the one-class format used for the State swimming competition. Since depth often wins meets, Larry works with the experienced kids while Brenda has been assigned the role of working with new swimmers to give the team the needed numbers to be competitive.

"We've had kids who don't even want to put their face in the water but they want to come out for the 'swim team'," Larry admitted.

Brenda's patience is challenged when working with the newbies, but she also gets to see tremendous results. "Larry only sees gradual improvement with the kids he works with," Brenda said, "but I get to see huge improvement." One of the best examples was John McMahon, who came out as a freshman even though he played soccer and was a kicker on the football team. During his freshman season, he swam with his head above the water for part of the year, but by his senior season, he qualified on a relay team that scored points at the State meet.

Larry and Brenda are very aware of one advantage they hold over the other local schools: their state-of-the-art swimming facility. As Larry stepped out of his office to show off the pool area, his eyes lit up and his voice raised a pitch or two as he proudly led the tour. Being newer than twenty years old, the surrounding air is cool and dry, making it much more comfortable for swimmers and spectators. The facility has upper level seating and can hold 500 fans in addition to seating on the pool's deck, making it a natural for a sectional every year.

The facility consists of a diving well and a 25-yard pool with touch-sensitive pads at the end to instantly determine the winner of a race and then flash the times on a large scoreboard high on the wall.

As Larry strolled along the deck of the pool, he pointed to a bank of interconnected computers and monitors that are used to program workouts and evaluate the swimmers during practice. A security camera is programmed to follow kids on the surface of the water and to record their workout for closer review after practice. A pre-programmed clock keeps pace of the desired intervals for each distance so that the swimmers can stay on pace. Larry's favorite 'toy', however, is one that aids in the improvement of a facet of swimming that the casual observer may overlook.

"This is our other 'assistant coach'," Larry proclaimed proudly as he pointed to an underwater camera. He also gave a quick lesson on one of the nuances of his sport as he pointed out that many races are won and lost while the swimmers are beneath the surface. Apparently, some swimmers are faster underwater than on top because, although their arms aren't working, there is less resistance underwater. The technique involves proper form in the kicks and the ability to hold one's breath without getting exhausted. As a Mt. Vernon swimmer demonstrated the method by easily swimming the length of the pool without surfacing, Larry explained that rules now dictate that swimmers must come up for air before reaching a yellow float on the ropes, because exceeding the distance not only can give an unfair advantage but can be dangerous, as well. "People have actually died because they passed out underwater," he explained.

As a certified SCUBA diver, Larry often spends thirty minutes or more at the bottom of the pool using the underwater video camera to record his swimmers' techniques. As the swimmers progress, they learn exactly how many kicks they need to reach the float and they can maximize their speed before surfacing. The valuable seconds spent underwater can make all the difference during competition, and Larry has a specific example of how significant the difference can be.

Mandy Crowe is, without doubt, the school's biggest swimming success story, but she may have never reached the heights she achieved without Larry's astute coaching and his underwater 'eyes'. Although Mandy was proficient at all the strokes, her strength was in the backstroke. As a freshman, she finished eighth at the 1991-'92 State meet in the 100-yard backstroke while another freshman, Ashley La Sell from Columbus East, won the event. If Mandy was to ever win State, she would not only have to face La Sell for three more years, but also Lia Oberstar from Ft. Wayne Bishop Dwenger, who was also in the same class.

For the next two seasons, Mandy fell short, as La Sell won again in '92-'93 and Oberstar captured the title in '93-'94. Mandy had one more chance, and she went to work to shave fractions from her time. One thing that Coach Zoller noticed when watching film of the losses at State was that Mandy was far and away the best swimmer on top of the water but she was losing time when beneath the surface.

Larry worked hour after hour to help Mandy improve what swimmers call "the fifth stroke" (underwater swimming), and she

Larry at work with his favorite 'toy', his underwater camera.

improved both underwater and on her turns. Mandy could have easily resigned herself to being better than average, but she just wasn't built that way. "Mandy was special because she never gave up," Coach Zoller recalled. "She kept working at it, and she knew she could do it. She had great support from her parents (Robert and Cecilia), and we had a great team that year that was very supportive."

With all her supporters in the crowd, Mandy Crowe swam the race of her life and dominated against two girls who had won three State titles in the event. Not only did she win her school's first and only individual swimming championship, but she set a State meet record (55.5 seconds) that held up for thirteen years and was still the fourth fastest 100-yard backstroke ever recorded at State as of 2007.

The Zollers know that it is a tall order to compete year after year with the powerhouses up north that have five times the enrollment and larger facilities that allow them to train many more athletes at one time. Perennial juggernauts like Carmel and North Central still have a big edge, but Larry Zoller says smaller schools like West Lafayette and Yorktown are closing the gap.

The Zollers have set the standard in southwestern Indiana and have made a splash at the State level, as well. Larry's record as a head coach stacks up admirably with other dominant programs in other sports in the area, like Memorial soccer and Heritage Hills football.

In 23 seasons, Zoller's teams have gone 233-40 (85%) in boys dual meets and 209-42 (83%) in girls dual meets. Mt. Vernon's girls have won 14 of the last 15 sectionals while the boys have won 12 of the last 14. In addition to Mandy Crowe's State title in '94-'95, the boys program celebrated its first and only State winner when John Wainman, Thomas Rueger, Ryan McNally and David Franklin took the gold in the 200 freestyle relay in 1997-'98.

Larry Zoller knows that a team State title is all but impossible, but he takes pride in what a school of Mt. Vernon's size has accomplished in swimming. One of America's swimming organizations calculates how schools with similar enrollments would fare in a national competition (using times in each event) and then publishes its 'mythical' results. A few times, Mt. Vernon emerged as the #1 team in the country, and they are consistently ranked in the top five. Maybe someday, Indiana will switch to the class system for its State swimming competition, but until then, for the Zollers and the Mt. Vernon swim program, an occasional 'mythical' national championship will just have to do.

I DIDN'T KNOW THAT!

NCAA swimming events use yards as their distances except during Olympic years, when they switch to meters. There are three categories of records: 'long course' (swam outdoors in a 50-meter pool), 'short course – meters', and 'short course – yards'. Records set at a 'yards' distance can be converted to metric and vice versa, but they are not considered official. Each category has its own set of 'official' records.

State champion Mandy Crowe. (Photo courtesy of the Mt. Vernon High School archives)

Mandy Crowe is Mt. Vernon's only individual State swimming champion, winning the 100-yard backstroke at the 1994-'95 State meet in record time (55.50 seconds). She also medaled as a member of Mt. Vernon's medley relay team. In addition to her backstroke records at Mt. Vernon, she also still holds the school's 50-yard freestyle record and held the butterfly record before it was broken in 2006.

Mt. Vernon's most decorated swimmer continued her career with the Florida Gators, where she finished in the top eight in the country during each of her four years.

PAT SHOULDERS BROUGHT THE WORLD TO EVANSVILLE

When local attorney Pat Shoulders received a phone call back in 1986, there was no way he could have guessed the impact it would have on his life. It seems that *Courier* executive Terry Hebert was looking for an event that would complement the Arts Festival held annually in Evansville. The goal was to attract a different group of people to the downtown area.

The proposed event was a road race, and Pat Shoulders was just the man to pull it off.

"I had quit smoking in 1985, and I'd started running," Pat said from his office high above the riverfront. "I thought, 'What can we do to separate us from the everyday event?'"

Pat had run in marathons (26.2 miles) that had been run over bridges, and the idea struck him: "If New York City, a place with eight million people, can shut down three bridges and run 20,000 people in a marathon, why can't we run across this bridge?"

The structure in Pat's vision was the bridge to Henderson on Highway 41, and being "young and stupid" (his own words), he set out on a mission that would become bigger than he had ever imagined. The event that would become known as the River Run would not only outlast the Arts Fest that it was supposed to enhance, but it would become an enormous event in its own right.

The first step was to determine the distance of the race, and the most common road race distances were 5K (5,000 meters) and 10K (10,000 meters). Pat found a spot in Henderson where people would be able to gather before the race and measured the distance to a 'finish line' on the riverfront. It was roughly 7 ½ miles. After some research, it was discovered that another recognized distance for road racing was 12K, which happened to be very close to the 7 ½ miles. The route and distance had been determined, but Pat's work had only just begun.

With a fervor that only comes from being too naïve to realize the enormous challenge, Pat wheedled his way through the political mazes of not one, but two states. He quickly found that it was not easy to convince elected officials that it would be a good idea to shut down a major thoroughfare for seven hours while 2,000 people went for a jog on a Saturday afternoon. To this day, Pat

(Photo courtesy of Pat Shoulders.)

doesn't know how he did it and contributes his success primarily to "blind luck."

With both cities (Henderson and Evansville) and both states agreeing to shut down the bridge, a major obstacle was cleared, but still more challenges lay ahead. By setting up the course as a 'point-to-point' race, Pat was faced with a problem that other races didn't have. Most races are set up as either a 'loop' or an 'out and back' course, which means they start and end at the same place. By making the River Run a point-to-point race, the athletes would park near the finish line and have to be transported to the start. As the race grew, it took thirty buses two trips each to carry the mob to Audubon Raceway (where harness races used to be run) for the start of the race.

With the support of local sponsors like the *Evansville Courier*, St. Mary's Medical Center, D Patrick/Mercedes-Benz International and many others, the Arts Fest River Run not only attracted casual road racers, but some of the sport's elite as well. Every runner was awarded a medal and a nice gift bag and was treated with a huge party at the finish line. Through sponsor support, the prize money grew to $35,000 in the later years, and the money and reputation as a unique, quality event attracted some of the best runners in the world and even placed Evansville in the national spotlight when the race was broadcasted on ESPN.

Over the years, the River Run has drawn runners from nearly all fifty states and from every continent except Antarctica. To attract the great runners, Pat also had to ensure that the course met all the criteria dictated by the USA Track & Field organization. The course had to meet specifications on distance, wind, and other factors to be sanctioned, and because it did, several records were set, some of which still stand today.

Two 12K world records were broken on the River Run course. Joseph Kimani of Kenya set the record here in May of 1997 with a time of 33 minutes, 31 seconds.

Running USA maintains 12K records for every age from 5 years to age 84, and, as of August 2007, three records were set at the River Run. Rebecca Stockdale-Woodley from Chaplin, Connecticut set the female-age 44 record in 1995 (43:20), and Nancy Grayson of Northville, Michigan set the female-age 45 record in the same race (43:38). The record that brings Pat Shoulders the most pride, however, is held in the female-age 78 division. In 1998, a new record of 1:34:36 was set by Phyllis Ruthenburg, a hometown girl from Evansville, Indiana.

In 2001, Pat Shoulders said farewell to the crowd near the finish line after supervising his last River Run. He turned it over to the Evansville Parks Department, who hosted the race for one more year before abandoning the project. Without the tireless dedication of Pat and his friends and family, many of whom were with him for the entire 15-year run, the race had lost its legs – and its heart.

Pat Shoulders speaks proudly as he reminisces about the years he spent on the race. "We wanted to make this one different than where the runners can go anytime," he said, "and the difference was running across that bridge with a U.S. highway shut down, running from one state to another state.

"The greatest runners in the world came into this town and ran," he continued. "We started this when we were young, and we finished it with gray hair. It was a labor of love, but fifteen years was enough."

Pat always wanted to run across that bridge himself, but he never got the chance because he was always busy with preparations. If anyone deserved to enjoy the course, it was the man whose vision it was in the first place. It is unlikely that an event as immense as the River Run will ever take place again in the area, and Pat Shoulders and everyone involved should be very proud for hosting an event that brought the best runners on the planet to our little corner of the world.

The River Run was a labor of love for everyone involved. Pictured after the 1993 race (L-R) are Lisa Shoulders, Pat Shoulders, Bill Rodgers, Samantha Shoulders and Andy Shoulders.

CHAPTER EIGHT
1985-2007

1994 CASTLE FOOTBALL: FROM OUTHOUSE TO PENTHOUSE

It had been twelve years since Castle had sat atop the Indiana football world as a State champion, but there were high expectations from the school's faithful for the 1994 Castle Knights.

Coach John Lidy had proclaimed to the press that this team was "the biggest and strongest in Castle history," and several weightlifting records were broken during the pre-season. Quarterback/linebacker Vince Lidy broke the overall record (10 events) with 1,428 pounds, and Jeff Elmer set the inclined bench press mark with 270 pounds. Most of the team attended Bill Mallory's IU football camp in the summer, and the team was returning fifteen lettermen from a 7-3 season. The feeling was that if some sophomores and juniors could fill in the gaps, this exceptional senior class could lead the way to a memorable season.

Before the Knights could look ahead to the possible playoff scenarios, they had a very tough SIAC schedule to deal with. Many of the Evansville teams had great potential also. Mater Dei had high hopes for one of its best teams in a while, led by quarterback Chris Koester, and Central had a strong arm of its own in Andy Owen.

Harrison featured quarterback Keith Lander throwing to Jeremy Redd and A.J. Bost. Bosse could use the many talents of future IU star Levron Williams, and North could compete with future Notre Dame and NFL star Deke Cooper, as well as quarterback Andy Cuprison and speedy receiver Kareem Neighbors.

The fierce local competition would eventually cast doubt in the minds of Castle fans, but it would also toughen up the boys in blue and gold and prepare them for a wild and gut-wrenching ride when tournament time rolled around.

As expected, Castle's massive line had little trouble against an over-matched Boonville team in Castle's opener. Boonville recorded only two first downs (none after the 9-minute mark of the second quarter) in a 42-0 Castle win.

Going into the second game of the season, Castle coach John Lidy knew that he hadn't beaten Bosse in five years. (In fact, no one had a better winning percentage during the four previous seasons than Bosse coach Jeff May, at over 76%). The Bulldog defense packed the middle, and on offense, Bosse tailbacks Da Shay Johnson and Jermaine Woolfolk combined for over 100 yards. The game's crucial play was a 22-yard Bryant Elkins pass that

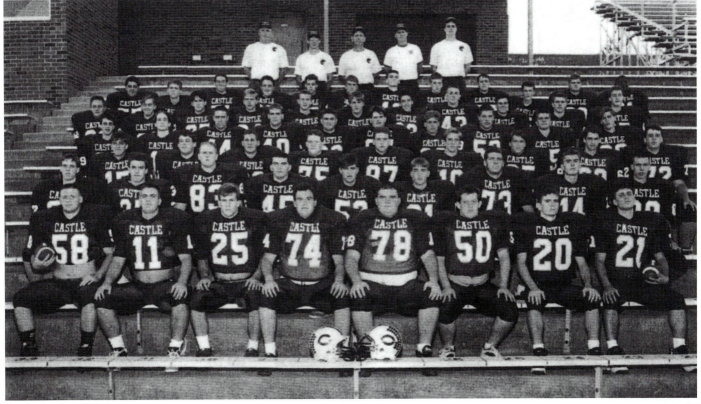

Levron Williams went high to grab at the five-yard line, setting up a touchdown by fullback Ontario Jackson with two minutes left, giving Bosse a 23-20 victory.

Week three was more of the same. Eric Tasa was Central's star, rushing 22 times for 221 yards, but after falling behind 19-7 in the third quarter, Castle smash-mouthed its way to a 22-19 lead with two drives capped by Vince Lidy touchdowns. Just like the previous week, the game would come down to late game heroics, but it was the Bears, not the Knights, who would provide them. With fifteen seconds left, Central coach Mike Owen had a decision to make: kick a 23-yard field goal to tie, or go for the win. Coach Owen decided to go for broke, and his son Andy found Jimmy Klusmeier open in the end zone and lofted the ball toward the receiver. Klusmeier lost his footing, but he kept his focus and hauled in the game winner for a 26-22 win.

Castle's bus ride home found them searching for answers after such a disastrous start. At 1-2 and 0-2 in the conference, Castle's bandwagon that was overflowing in the pre-season was leaking like a sieve. Fans who crowed like peacocks weeks earlier were quickly turning into boo-birds, and things didn't look any rosier for the next week, as the Knights had to make a return appearance at Central Stadium to face the North Huskies.

If Castle was looking for a chance to catch its breath after losing nail-biters the previous two weeks, the North Huskies were not going to cooperate. For the third week in a row, the Knights would be tested to the max.

The North-Castle showdown had the makings of an explosive night, and it didn't disappoint. Tony Salpietra and Vince Lidy provided the punch on the first drive, and defensive back Matt Holweger gave Castle a 14-0 lead with a return of a fumble for a touchdown.

Solid offense by both teams led to a 28-20 Castle lead, and with only a few seconds remaining in the fourth quarter, Andy Cuprison connected with Andy Miller to pull the Huskies within two. North's two-point conversion was successful, and one can only imagine what the Knights were thinking as they prepared for overtime.

In the extra period, Castle got the ball first and scored on second down on a Salpietra run to take a 35-28 lead. Central retaliated with a Cuprison throw to tight end Brian Bennett. Cuprison, who also place-kicked for North, missed the kick to tie, however, and Castle finally came out on top in one of the brutal SIAC battles.

With the win over North, Castle had seemingly righted its ship, as the Knights rolled to wins over Reitz (24-14), Harrison (28-24) and Mater Dei (38-15). The fickle Castle fans who had abandoned the ship earlier were now falling all over themselves to climb back on as the tournament began.

Much had been said in the media about the lack of respect that southern Indiana football had received over the years, but as sportswriter David Jackson wrote in October of 1994, "The simple fact is that since the IHSAA adopted a playoff system in 1973, the Evansville area had produced just one State champion, Castle's 1982 team. Other teams had made it to the finals (Boonville-'74, Reitz-'77, Jasper-'78 and '87, Southridge-'82, Tell City-'86, and South Spencer-'88), but we'd had only one winner in twenty years."

But Castle was about to change all that.

When the sectional pairings were released in the fall of '94, it was apparent that Castle's draw was the envy of everyone. The Knights would travel to lowly New Albany (1-6) and then would likely follow with two games on their home field. Not only was the draw appealing because of New Albany's record, but it allowed Coach Lidy the chance to fire his team up by using the revenge factor. "In '92, they waxed us pretty good at our place (49-28)", he told a *Courier* reporter. "A lot of our seniors played in that game; they remember." But before Castle could begin preparation for their date with history, they had one more SIAC opponent to deal with.

Although Memorial's Tigers put a scare into the Knights early with a quick touchdown after a Tony Salpietra fumble, Castle flexed its muscle and scored 33 unanswered points to win 33-7. Although the Knights were disappointed in losing the SIAC (to Bosse), they were now motivated to prove that their heavy lifting during the summers would pay off in a big way.

The first two games of the '94 sectional were showcases for Castle's little big man, Tony Salpietra. The 5'9", 180-pounder nearly broke the school record against New Albany with 257 rushing yards in a 38-7 victory. He followed that effort with 127 yards on 13 carries in a 42-17 win against the under-sized Floyd Central Highlanders. The Knights were on cruise control and heading for a collision with the Reitz Panthers.

On Friday, November 4th, Castle took the field for the third time that season against Bob Gaddis' Reitz Panthers (they had met in the Jamboree before the season). Although Castle had won seven straight, Coach Lidy was concerned about the passing of Reitz quarterback Duce Reeder and the running ability of Shane Ricketts. After falling behind early, as they had in their previous three games, Castle wore down the out-manned Panthers for a 23-10 win in a driving rain that turned Castle's field into a quagmire. Next stop for Castle: Martinsville and a record-breaking quarterback.

Although Martinsville was only 8-3 on the year, they were as dangerous as any team in the state. Earl Haniford, the strong-armed junior quarterback for the Artesians, was the state's passing leader (2,960 yards, 28 TDs) and needed only sixteen yards to surpass former Warren Central great Jeff George's career total of 8,126 yards. For the Knights to win the regional title, they would have to control Haniford and do something no other team had done this season, beat Martinsville on their home field.

The first half was a "track meet," as Castle athletic director Johnny Evers recalled, and it was 28-28 at halftime. Both team's stars lived up to their billing, as Haniford completed 21 of 29 for 284 yards and Salpietra ripped Martinsville's defense for 248 yards on 27 carries. Castle's Vince Lidy also had a big first half with 104 yards on 18 carries.

The second half was scoreless until Salpietra scampered for 29 yards to give Castle a 35-28 lead. The play of the game came on the next series when Haniford dropped to throw on 4th and 11 and Castle defensive lineman Shawn Humm shed his blocker and sacked Haniford to give Castle the ball with less than a minute remaining. Two kneels by Vince Lidy sealed the victory and set the stage for another miraculous night in Paradise.

The bandwagon was bursting at the seams as the Castle faithful prepared for the arrival of the Carmel Greyhounds on Saturday, November 19th, and a packed stadium was expected for the 5:00 p.m. start. After nine straight wins and finally cracking the state's top ten rankings, the Knights began the week with full intentions of beating Carmel and playing for a State title the following weekend. But their optimism dwindled when they learned that one of their leaders was done for the season. Coach Lidy announced to the team that it was believed his son, Vince Lidy, had contracted mononucleosis and was scheduled for more tests on Thursday. Mr. Lidy sounded certain when he spoke with a *Courier* reporter. "He's a good football player and a good kid," the coach said. "He didn't get to finish out a great career."

But further proof that destiny was on Castle's side this season came when the doctors explained after the tests that the mono was in a dormant stage and Vince was cleared to play. Were there more miracles on the horizon?

Just one, but it was a dandy.

For the first 46 minutes or so, the game was an unspectacular affair, with Carmel hanging on to a 14-13 lead with under two minutes to go. Castle was out of time outs and desperate. Carmel nearly scored on an end-around but was driven out of bounds on the two-yard line with about 1:30 left on the clock, giving the Greyhounds a first-and-goal situation. Coach Lidy knew that the victory was Carmel's if the quarterback would just kneel two or three times and run out the clock. But if Carmel chose to run the ball instead, the coach was ready with the only strategy that would give the Knights a chance. "Coach Lidy made the call to let 'em score," recalled Castle A.D. Johnny Evers. "A couple of our kids didn't understand what he was talking about."

As luck would have it, Carmel played right into Castle's hands and scored. Even if they made the extra point, the Knights would still be down by only eight points with a chance to tie. Castle got lucky again when Carmel kicker Jason Williams missed the point after. It was Carmel 20, Castle 13.

After the kickoff, Castle was forced to take to the air. Two long competitions from Lidy to Andy Southworth and Johnny Clark put Castle on the Carmel nine-yard line. Three plays later, Vince Lidy read that Carmel was spreading wide to cover the pass and tucked the ball and ran a quarterback sneak for a touchdown. Now, Coach Lidy had a decision to make.

Without hesitation, the decision was made to go for two points instead of kicking for the tie. The play was "Reverse 47 Pass", and after a fake, Vince Lidy found 6'7", 277-pound tight end Jeremy Johnson all alone in the end zone for his only reception of the night. It was hard to argue now that the '94 Castle Knights were not a team of destiny. Fans had just witnessed the 'Miracle in Paradise', and although the exact time and yard line are a little fuzzy, "89 yards in 89 seconds" will always be a part of Castle football lore. Castle was headed to the RCA Dome.

In his 22nd year at Castle, Coach Lidy was coaching for his second State title. Castle's opponent, the Portage Indians, were 13-0 but much smaller than the Knights. In a *Courier* article, Portage coach Craig Buzea estimated that Castle's linemen outweighed his by about 85 pounds per man. Portage was also playing for the school's second State title (they defeated Reitz 33-14 in the 1977 championship game). During the season, they had knocked off defending State champion Hobart 43-7, so most considered them a heavy favorite over Castle.

"Portage was one of the top 15 in the nation and were considered untouchable," Johnny Evers recalled. "And we were the poor schmucks from the South."

As in many games during the year, this game was a matchup between a smallish diverse team and the much larger Knights who made no secret about their plan to run, run, run. But the biggest influence on the outcome of this game may well have occurred long before the teams took the field.

"The Portage team and fans stayed at the Omni Hotel (in Indianapolis), and it was a big party," Mr. Evers revealed. "But we never stayed the night. We went up on Thanksgiving Day and practiced and came home to sleep in our own beds. Coach Lidy said, 'This isn't a party. I want them away from all this mess.'"

Teams were allowed to choose their practice dates, so Castle opted for the holiday to avoid a crowd, "No one was at the Dome," Mr. Evers added. "That was the idea. We didn't want any press. We didn't want any attention. Some of our parents were upset with us, but we said, 'Our only goal is to win the game.' Our kids will tell you, that's probably the smartest thing we did."

Tony Salpietra was a workhorse for the 1994 State champion Castle Knights.

So with their game faces on and their minds focused, the Knights ran through the RCA Dome tunnel confident and prepared. The game itself was almost anticlimactic after the dramatic weeks prior, and Tony Salpietra, who was just shy of 2,000 yards for the season, would be relied on heavily as Castle took the field for the 4:00 p.m. game on Saturday, November 26th.

After a scoreless first quarter, Castle fell behind in the second period on a screen pass from Nick Wellman to David Ortiz. At that point, the Knights had not even had a first down, and the outlook was bleak. But immediately following the touchdown, the Knights made their first big play of the game. Vince Lidy got a piece of the extra point try to limit the Indian's lead to 6-0. On the ensuing 56-yard drive, Tony Salpietra scored on a 2-yard run followed by a Jason Hall extra point, giving Castle a 7-6 halftime edge.

The second half was all Castle, as the Knights rushed for 176 yards and held Portage to minus 2. Salpietra was the workhorse with 191 yards on 31 carries and three touchdowns in the 30-12 win. Castle's monstrous line dominated Portage and wore them down as Castle did what they do best – run. "We have a sign up in our office that says, 'Hey, diddle, diddle, run up the middle,'" Coach Lidy told *The Indianapolis Star* after the game. "Our philosophy is real simple. We run left and we run right."

Most media coverage of football games focuses on the achievements of the players who handle the ball, the so-called 'skill positions', but more often than not, these successes wouldn't happen without the efforts of the unsung heroes in the trenches. Johnny Evers, who coached most of the Castle linemen, cited an example that went largely unnoticed in the Castle-Portage final. "Portage had a kid named Spurrier who was probably the best lineman in the state, and we had Patrick Mayes," Evers explained.

"I walked out after the game and that Spurrier kid looked like a piece of hamburger. Patrick had literally dragged him from one end of the field to the other."

Vince Lidy, Tony Salpietra and the other Castle runners were always quick to credit the line any time they got the chance. Along with the chiseled 6'2, 220-pound tackle Mayes were center Doug Hurt (6'3, 249), guards Jeff Elmer (6'3, 330) and Shawn Humm (5'9, 225), tackle Ben Stewart (6'3, 262) and tight ends Jeremy Johnson (6'7, 277) and Allen Lidy (6'1, 200).

1994 had been a roller coaster ride for John Lidy and his team. The journey began with a pre-season filled with high expectations for what many called one of the finest senior classes in the school's history. Then, the bubbles didn't burst but were severely deflated when Castle started 1-2 and nearly lost the fourth game of the year. After winning five straight to finish the regular season and three more in the sectional, the Knights went on to beat Earl Haniford and Martinsville on the Artesian's home field for a regional title.

During the next two weeks, it seemed that Castle had an angel sitting on their shoulder pads as they defeated Carmel with the 'Miracle in Paradise' and then suffered through the prospects of losing their quarterback and team leader to mono. But, once again, Lady Luck was on their side as Vince Lidy was cleared to play in the State Finals.

There is no question that this team's success was the product of dedication, talent, and perseverance. But, as is the case for many championship seasons, a little good fortune along the way didn't hurt, either.

LOCAL CLUB SHOWCASES LOCAL TALENT

Mike Thomas has coached some of the area's greatest basketball stars over the years under the banner of the Evansville Basketball Club. His primary purpose has been to give the athletes the exposure they need to attract college and pro scouts, but in the process, he and others like George Smith, Chuck Frye, Aaron Thompson and Jeff Anderson have put together some pretty incredible teams.

Over the last fifteen years, Mike's teams have compiled an 874-260 record (78%) playing in AAU and independent tournaments across the country. Through his efforts, Thomas, who is a sales consultant in addition to owning a photography business, has seen 75% of his players compete at the college level and has earned the respect of such local standouts as Calbert Cheaney, Walter McCarty and Andy Elkins, to name a few.

One of the club's strongest teams is shown in the photo. This 1992 Mike Thomas Photography team won several tournaments, including the prestigious White River Park State Games.

In the '93 tournament, another of Mike's teams knocked off one of the favorites, the Northwest All-Stars, 120-104 in the semi-finals. The Northwest Stars featured Ohio State standout and Indiana's Mr. Basketball, Charles Macon, but Macon and his teammates were no match for the local boys. Thomas' massive front line of 7'1 Sascha Hupmann (U of E), 6'10 Walter McCarty (Harrison, University of Kentucky) and 6'10 Chris Bowles (USI) dominated the paint, and seven of the local stars scored in double figures: Hupmann (20); McCarty (18); Stan Gouard from USI (18); Jeff Anderson, Memorial and Kent State (18); Chris Lowery from Harrison and Southern Illinois University (14); Bowles (12); and Brent Kell from Harrison and U of E (12).

In the championship game, Mike Thomas Photography conquered the pre-tourney favorite, Columbus, 104-100. Columbus was led by Indiana star Damon Bailey and Purdue players Matt Waddell, Ian Stanback and Matt Painter (now Purdue's head coach). In the title game, the same seven players scored in double figures again, led by Walter McCarty's 22 points

he 1992 Mike Thomas Photography College All-Stars. Front Row (L-R): Mike Thomas, Brent Kell (Harrison, SIU), Travis Trice (Princeton, Purdue/Butler), Chris Lowery (Harrison, SIU), Parrish Casebier (South Spencer, U of E). Back row (L-R): Robert Fraser, Calbert Cheaney (Harrison, IU), Andy Elkins (Bosse, U of E), Chris Bowles (Madisonville, USI), Walter McCarty (Harrison, UK), Jeff Anderson (Memorial, Kent State), Brad Fraser. (Photo courtesy of Mike Thomas Photography.)

MEMORIAL GIRL'S TENNIS: A LEGACY OF LOVE

In the last thirty years, the Memorial Lady Tigers are the only local boys or girls team to win a State team tennis title, and they've done it an amazing five times. How does a small Catholic school program achieve such success when much larger schools have failed? A succession of talented young ladies became friends, then overcame a devastating tragedy, then worked hard to keep a legacy alive. That's how.

Although this success story took place in the 1990s, the tale really began in 1976. The year before (1975), tennis had been sanctioned as a sport by the IHSAA for the first time, and the Memorial program was under the guidance of Chris Payne. When Ms. Payne decided to leave the next year, the school had to look for a replacement, and when officials approached Brenda Walling, a teacher at Memorial, she was only lukewarm on the idea.

"If I didn't do it, the program could have been dropped, "said Walling. "Girls sports had come too far to let it go, so I took it."

While a student at Mater Dei, Walling had experienced the frustration of being a female athlete having no high school sports to play, so she accepted the tennis position and got to work. In her very first year as Memorial's coach, the school advanced players to the State Finals. In those days, under a format different from today's, teams sent a #1 singles player and a #1 doubles team that was usually made up of the team's #2 and #3 singles players. The old system resulted in schools sending its best players but wasn't fair to those who had played doubles all season.

Memorial fared well at the '76 tournament, with Susan Groeger finishing fourth in singles and Barb Hennesey and Elaine Luebbe earning a controversial runner-up finish in doubles. The result was questionable because the opposition, South Bend St. Joe, did not have a boys program, so a boy was allowed to compete in the girls' tournament. Consequently, the male/female combo withstood boos from the crowd after taking the title from Hennessey and Luebbe.

As years passed, Coach Walling came to the realization that, to be competitive on the state level, her girls would need to focus their attention on tennis. Most of her teams had consisted of girls who played two or three sports during the school year, leaving them at a huge disadvantage when tennis season rolled around in the spring. As the Memorial players and parents bought into the new philosophy, the success rate improved dramatically.

In 1982, the IHSAA changed the State tennis format and held two separate tournaments, hosting the team competition one week and the #1singles and doubles competitions the next. Four years later, Memorial took advantage of the new system and began to separate itself from much of its competition by beginning a run of ten straight appearances at the State Finals team competition before Reitz broke the string in 2005.

With her players working year-round and the parents on board, Coach Walling's program was poised for a breakthrough. History was made in the spring of 1991 when the Lady Tigers claimed the State title, making them the first, and still only, Evansville team to

The 1995 State champion Lady Tigers. First Row (L-R): Loren Ingalls, Natalie Palmenter, Margo Stevenson, Nida Poosuthasee. Back Row (L-R): Tricia Trapp, Angela Sabella, Coach Brenda Walling, Ann Schroeder, Courtney Hague, Sarah Speer. (Photo courtesy of Brenda Walling.)

Sara Jane Stevenson was taken from us far too soon but was an inspiration to everyone. (Photo courtesy of Dr. Peter and Patti Stevenson.)

1995 State singles champion Margo Stevenson. (Photo courtesy of Brenda Walling.)

1995 State champion doubles team Angela Sabella (left) and Tricia Trapp. (Photo courtesy of Brenda Walling.)

win a tennis State championship. Memorial's girls were on top of the world, and their future looked bright with the majority of the players returning.

And then the unthinkable happened.

During spring break of 1992, Sara Jane Stevenson, one of the team's best players, was on vacation on Sanibel Island in Florida with her family. Sara Jane and her mother, Beth, were riding a moped when Beth lost control. Sara Jane's father, Peter, and her younger sister, Margo, were following in a car and were the first on the scene. Peter, an ER physician, worked tirelessly to save them, but both were lost in the accident.

The tragic news spread rapidly through the community as Memorial and especially Sara Jane's teammates mourned the loss of the talented player and her mother, one of the team's biggest supporters. A prayer service and vigil were held at the school, and a tribute to Sara Jane was included in the yearbook. A tree was planted on the school's campus in Sara Jane's memory, and Dr. Stevenson and other contributors established an annual scholarship in her honor that recognizes an athlete each year who demonstrates athleticism and leadership qualities.

Miraculously, the team kept it together well enough to reach the semi-state but eventually fell to Jasper. It is not unreasonable to speculate that, had the team not been mentally and emotionally drained and had Sara Jane been in the lineup, the Lady Tigers probably would have repeated as champions.

The following year, another trying situation presented itself. Margo Stevenson, also an excellent player, was set to become a high school freshman, and there was speculation as to what was best for her. Her father contemplated sending her to Mater Dei to avoid the constant reminders of her sister at Memorial. Margo and Peter opted, however, to return to the warmth of the 'family' they loved. Margo had grown up watching her sister and her friends playing tennis, and the team often hung out together at each other's houses. Her choice was to follow in her sister's footsteps and join her friends as a Lady Tiger.

With Margo stepping up as a freshman, Coach Walling's girls did it again, winning the '93 State title. But they were far from finished. In 1994, the girls came through again, and in '95, they not only won the championship for a fourth time but they did it in record fashion. For the first time in IHSAA history, under the new format, one school captured the team title while also winning the singles and doubles championships. The '94 doubles champs were Angela Gabella and Tricia Trapp, and the singles winner was none other than Sara Jane's little sister, Margo Stevenson. The 'Triple Crown' was a State first and has only been duplicated once since, by Park Tudor in 1998. In addition, ALL SEVEN Memorial girls were named to the All-State team by the Indiana High School Tennis Coaches Association.

With a constant flow of talent and a system that worked to perfection, Memorial finished its streak with another State title in 1996. Brenda Walling takes little credit for the success, calling herself a "sponsor," but the fact remains that she is one of the few coaches in the state who can claim five State championships. Looking back on the run, Walling, who retired from coaching tennis in 1999, takes pride in Memorial's team concept.

"We had great depth, they were all friends, and they worked hard," she stated. "Courtney Hague played #2, and she could have played #1 at almost any other school. She finished (her career) 104-0. It was just a phenomenal group of kids."

Coach Walling also credits the parents' dedication and outside coaches who helped the girls as they prepared for and competed in tournaments around the country in the off-season. "Anna Hazlett (who teaches tennis and is the mother of Heritage Hills State champ Stephanie Hazlett) has been a big influence on youth tennis in this area for many years. She's a great lady and has great instruction technique," Coach Walling noted. Walling also credits other pros who have helped, like Don Martin from the Tri-State Athletic Club and Ross Brown, former U of E coach who now heads up the program at USI.

Several of Memorial's players, using the skills they developed over the years, took their games to the next level, such as Courtney Hague (Marshall), Angela Sabella, (U of E) and Tricia Trapp (Toledo), to name a few. But the one Walling feels would have had the best chance to play big college tennis was Sara Jane Stevenson. Though she was here far too briefly, her name will always be associated with Memorial's first girls State championship.

The Lady Tigers' tennis legacy includes eight appearances in the State Finals in 26 years, and their five titles place them second in the state, tied with Park Tudor and seven behind Indianapolis North Central's twelve. In addition, Memorial finished as the State runner-up three times ('90, '98 and '05), joining Harrison ('79 and '81) and Jasper ('92, '02 and '03) as the only area teams to do so more than once.

As Brenda Walling reflects on her years guiding Memorial's tennis program, she understands how a group can impact future groups and how an unselfish philosophy can propel a team to new heights. "Once you start developing a tradition, the kids start to follow," Walling explained. "Our girls were thrilled to just be playing, and they all just wanted to be part of the team."

With a run of excellent players who overcame the most extreme adversity imaginable, Coach Walling and the Memorial Lady Tigers were the first, and still only, program in the 33-year history of the IHSAA Tournament to capture four consecutive State titles.

USI: FROM UGLY DUCKLING TO SWAN

When officials from Indiana State University-Evansville (now USI) decided to venture into the world of collegiate athletics, thoughts of dominating a tough conference or gaining national recognition were the farthest things from their minds. And when the first men's basketball coach was hired, there was not even an inkling that, 27 years later, the school would not only capture a national basketball championship but would also boast a quality athletic program across the board.

In many ways, the metamorphosis of USI athletics mirrored that of the school itself, as it was born in meager surroundings and transformed over the years. The brainstorm became a reality in 1967 when Byron Wright, who was the school's business manager at the time, approached a young John Deem and asked him if he had ever played basketball. When Deem responded that he had played high school ball, Mr. Wright popped the question and asked Deem if he would be willing to coach. At 23 years old, the small amount of extra income appealed to Deem, and he accepted the challenge, making him the first paid coach in school history.

At that time, the extension campus of Indiana State was located in the old Centennial Grade School building, a structure that had been condemned and abandoned by the Evansville school system. Although the facility was sufficient to hold classes for the 412 commuter students at the new college, Deem had to search elsewhere for a basketball court. The only gym Mr. Deem could find to accommodate the games was Plaza Park Grade School, with games starting at 9 p.m. For practices, he struck an agreement with the local YWCA in downtown Evansville, which allowed the team access from 9 to 11 p.m. Though the hours were not appealing, the practices at the 'Y' would allow for some interesting moments and some reflective smiles when the players would look back years later. "We actually became entertainment for many of the young ladies," John Deem recalled. "Sometimes we had more people at our practices than we had at our games."

With the venues secured, Deem's next task was finding a team. With little to offer but a challenge, flyers were placed around 'campus' to test the waters. Since the decision had been made to abide by NCAA regulations, requiring a 2.0 grade point average and a minimum of 12 hours of classes, only ten of the thirty who tried out were eligible. So when the dust cleared, Deem had his ten-man team.

Virtually every player was from a local background, and many were starters on their high school teams. Amazingly, four of the members of the school's first team in 1968-'69 were products of Evansville North High School's basketball program. Dwayne Zehr and Abe Krause had played for Coach Jim Rausch in the mid '60s, and Dave Senning and Dale Fehd were members of North's 1967 State championship team. The remainder of the ISUE roster consisted of: Bill Joergens, Greg Wezet, Mike Meyer, Byron Sanders, Robbie Kent and Skip Courier.

With the team now in place, Deem went in pursuit of uniforms that he could afford on his miniscule budget. He found the answer a few blocks away from the school when the West Side Nut Club came to the rescue, purchasing shiny blue and gold uniforms from Gus Doerner Sporting Goods, making ISUE's first school colors blue and gold.

Coach Deem and his boys entered some intense competition against teams from industrial leagues and one- and two-year colleges, like Henderson Community College, Brescia, Lockyear Business College and Sam's Technical Institute (now ITT). As the season wore on, John Deem developed the four-corner offense that was made famous by Dean Smith at North Carolina. Deem doesn't insinuate genius on his part, however, saying it was done "out of necessity to preserve energy" for his dedicated but tired boys.

During that historic season in '68-'69, the team played in the school's first out-of-town tournament, in Harrisburg, Illinois, and finished the season a respectable 6-6. The team members, who played for the sheer love of the game, were rewarded with letters after their season and got together in 1994 for a 25-year reunion. John Deem had proved that he was up to the task and had completed his mission ably. After one year, he stepped aside, knowing that the groundwork had been laid and that it was time for him to pass the baton to a more experienced coach.

In the fall of 1969, ISUE was moved from the cramped confines at Centennial to the far west side campus where the school is now. The 'campus' consisted of two buildings, a Science Center and Administration Building, connected by a walkway. The 1,600 commuter students attended classes in both locations, and the change of scenery provided a fresh start for the students and for the school's new basketball coach.

The administration found their new leader right in their own backyard when they hired Jerry Alstadt, who had fashioned several successful seasons at Rex Mundi High School on Evansville's north side. Alstadt had accepted a similar challenge when he was asked to build Rex Mundi's program from the ground up as the new school opened in 1957. Within a few short years, the young coach built the Monarchs into perennial contenders, leading them to a #1 state ranking during the 1962-'63 season before losing to Bosse in the sectional. In addition, the following year, Alstadt led Rex Mundi to the Final Four in the State Tournament, making them the first Indiana Catholic school to make it to 'the Big Dance'.

Alstadt's first team at ISUE played an industrial league schedule similar to Coach Deem's the year before, and in Alstadt's second season, the program was set to play an intercollegiate schedule. Going into the 1970-'71 season, the coach had few resources at his disposal to attract players. In addition, he was competing for local talent with Evansville College (U of E), who had attained lofty status at their home just a few miles down the Lloyd Expressway. In fact, while ISUE was beginning its first season in a collegiate league, Evansville College, led by Don Buse, was launching a season that would give the school its fifth national championship.

USI's first basketball team. Front Row (L-R): Greg Wezet, Mike Meyer, Dwayne Zehr, Bill Joergens and Byron Sanders. Back Row (L-R): Assistant coach Jack Engelke, Dale Fehd, Dave Senning, Robbie Kent, Skip Courier, Statistician Bill Brandsasse and Head coach John Deem. Abe Krause was not present for the picture.

In the early days, USI consisted of just two buildings connected by a walkway. (Photo courtesy of the USI archives.)

Alstadt's 1970-'71 team was predominantly local, with players such as: Ken Wannemueller, John Stocker and Kim Schiff (Mater Dei); Michael Young (Rex Mundi); Dana 'Popcorn' Finn (Reitz); Lee Joe Begle (Ferdinand); Bob Swan and Bob Grannan (Gibson County); Randy Flamion (Spencer County); and Steve Feagley (Warrick Country). Rounding out the team were: Joe Rivers (Vermont); Dave Williamson (Southmont); and Leon Swope (Cairo, Illinois). The team finished a respectable 6-10 playing many of the same teams that USI plays today, such as the University of Wisconsin-Kenosha, the University of Missouri-St. Louis; Southern Illinois-Edwardsville, IUPU-Ft. Wayne and IUPUI.

Alstadt continued to fight the uphill battle that came with the job of developing a new program, and attracting athletes to the fledgling school was not an easy task. "We had very few resources," Alstadt explained. "There was no money to speak of, but we were able to offer half-tuition (scholarships)."

With no home arena to show off or lavish road trips to promise, Alstadt plugged away to lay a foundation on which the program could grow. His early teams practiced at Rex Mundi at 6:00 a.m. (not exactly a great selling point for a potential recruit), and his teams played their games at Roberts Stadium at times that wouldn't conflict with the Aces or other events. Although Roberts Stadium was an impressive place to play, Alstadt admitted that the games created an odd atmosphere, with "maybe 200 fans" in the cavernous arena.

During Alstadt's four years at the controls, his teams competed well under less than ideal circumstances, with records of 6-10, 4-20, 8-15 and 12-14. Although he never got to experience the success he had seen at Rex Mundi, he had done the grunt work it took to put the program on the right track. In his final season, Alstadt finally was able to take his team on the school's first legitimate road trips, when they traveled to the University of Wyoming and Colorado State. In addition, his teams were the first to wear the school's now-familiar red, white and blue colors and to bear the nickname the Screaming Eagles.

Coach Alstadt left ISUE in 1974 and coached at Southridge High School for three years before accepting the position of dean at Vincennes University-Jasper, where he served until his retirement. With the ISUE basketball program up and running, he turned the keys over to Rockport native and popular Evansville Aces alum Wayne Boultinghouse. It was now the Boulder's job to take ISUE to the next level.

Upon his arrival, Boultinghouse found himself facing the same challenges as his predecessors, but changes were on the horizon that would enable him to build a competitive program. With no housing on campus, landing recruits from outside the area was not easy. "Parents were concerned about their kids getting to class on time (from off-campus housing) and that they were going to eat right and be safe," Boultinghouse confided.

The program also had a 'second class' stigma attached to it, and Coach Boultinghouse was very familiar with the reason why. "When I started, we had an NAIA (National Association of Intercollegiate Athletics) affiliation," he pointed out. "Evansville College was College Division (now known as Division II). I knew we weren't going to have the respect as long as we remained NAIA because of the college NCAA Tournament being held in Evansville and Evansville College's success." So with his eye on his goal, Boultinghouse went to work.

A small step that added some stability to the program was finding a gym that the Screaming Eagles could call home. Since they couldn't afford to go 'new', the administration decided on a 'fixer-upper'. Their choice was the historic old Central Gym in downtown Evansville, and despite the occasional problems with a leaky roof, it didn't take long for the team and the fans to fall in love with the character that still existed in the dilapidated structure.

The old Central Gym is deserted here, but it was rocking during ISUE games in the '70s. (Photo courtesy of the USI archives.)

Central Gym had sat dormant since 1971, when the Central High School students and faculty moved to their new school on North First Avenue. But with some TLC and elbow grease, the facility was ready (well, almost) by the start of Boultinghouse's first season. "We opened our home schedule with Franklin College," the Boulder explained. "I remember the paint was not dry on some of the seats and some people got paint on their clothes."

During the first season in the gym, crowds were small, maybe 250 to 400, but at least the team had a place to practice and a 'home gym' for games. After a 6-19 season, Boultinghouse, who was also the school's athletic director, worked hard with school officials to move the program forward. The first step was a new affiliation, and Boultinghouse joined the late Dr. Charles Bertram and others to ensure that the school met the required criteria to move to NCAA Division II status. At the same time, the local contingent helped to form the Great Lakes Valley Conference, and after countless meetings, the GLVC was in place and ISUE basketball was poised for a breakthrough.

As the basketball program was blossoming, the school was also beginning to slowly build a comprehensive athletic program. In 1975, ISUE was also fielding a baseball team and had some impressive success in golf, thanks to Dave Williamson, who also played basketball, and a young Jim Hamilton, the son of late legendary golfer Bob Hamilton and the current golf coach at the University of Evansville. Shortly thereafter, women's programs were initiated under Boultinghouse's guidance.

Along with ISUE, the charter members of the GLVC included Bellarmine, Northern Kentucky, St. Joseph's College, Kentucky Wesleyan and Indiana Central (now the University of Indianapolis). With the conference in place, rivalries began to develop, and the old central Gym was once again a beehive of activity. As interest grew, the old-fashioned atmosphere was re-kindled, and those who were involved learned to appreciate the quirkiness of the nostalgic environment.

"Folks had fallen in love with old Central Gym because it was as much of a 'pit' as you could get," laughed John Deem, who broadcasted ISUE games on WKKR radio and is still with the university today. "What a basketball venue that was! It was old and decrepit ... and wonderful! It was falling apart, and all the seats were, maybe, six feet above the floor, and the fans just ascended upward. It was just one of those great gymnasiums of old where you could stomp the wooden floors and just raise a ruckus."

With a new 'home', a new conference and a new affiliation, Coach Boultinghouse endured one more losing season (11-15 in 1975-'76) before catapulting the program to prominence. As rivalries heated up, games against Weslyan, Tennessee State, Western Illinois and others were drawing 4,200+ fans for home games, and the players responded. In 1976-'77, Boultinghouse was told that if his team won their last three games, they would make the NCAA Tournament. But after they did, they were ignored when the selections were made. Though disappointed, the fiery young coach had led the school to a 19-8 record, the school's first winning season, and the team would enter the following season with something to prove.

Boultinghouse and his boys followed the '76-'77 season with another banner year, finishing at 19-9 and making the program's first appearance in the NCAA Tourney. The Boulder followed with three more winning seasons before stepping down from his position, and he is quick to recognize some of the players whose efforts helped the program develop into a legitimate contender.

Wayne mentioned DeJuan 'Spider' Rowser, who was actually recruited by Boultinghouse's predecessor Jerry Alstadt. Rowser was arguably the school's first legitimate superstar, having been enticed by Alstadt to come to ISUE from Detroit. As a result of DeJuan's success, his brother Emanuel also came to town to play for Coach Boultinghouse.

Boultinghouse also mentioned Lawrence Knight, who only played for the Eagles as a freshman before leading the nation in rebounding in junior college and becoming a first round draft pick of the NBA's Utah Jazz.

Several local players were also instrumental in Wayne's success at ISUE, like Tell City's Paul Werner, who transferred in from the University of Kansas, and John Brown, who played at Washington High School with Indiana's Mr. Basketball Steve Bouchie. Dan Labhart, who starred at Boonville, was another local who was described by Boultinghouse as having "outstanding leadership qualities as a freshman and a maturity that defied his years." The Boulder also mentioned local products Kelly Williams, a 6'8 power player from Poseyville, and 'Big John' Hollinden, who transferred from Oral Roberts University as a 7'6", 212-pound beanpole and left as a 245-pound All-American.

The 1980-'81 season was Wayne's last as the coach at ISUE, and his final team finished 21-8 and was the first group to play in the new arena on the west side campus. Just like John Deem and Jerry Alstadt, Boultinghouse had done what was asked of him and had led the program to new heights.

After his first two seasons, Wayne Boultinghouse never had another losing season, and he finished with a record of 111-79. When asked why he stepped down, Wayne explained that the responsibilities of serving in multiple capacities had simply become too overwhelming. "I was the A.D., the coach, the trainer and I was burning the candle at both ends," he admitted. "My father was very ill, and it just got to me physically."

Wayne stayed at the school as Director of Development (raising funds) from 1981 until 1986. After that, he joined the Kentucky Weslyan staff as associate head coach under Wayne Chapman for four years and then became the Panthers' head coach from 1990 to 1996. In '96, he returned to his roots and served as the head girls basketball coach and assistant principal at South Spencer High School until his retirement in 2002.

Boultinghouse was a tough act to follow at ISUE, but a series of coaches performed admirably over the next eleven years. Boultinghouse assistant, Creighton Burns, kept the transition smooth when he took over the progam in 1981 and finished his three-year term with a 40-43 record. Burns was followed by Mark Coomes, who came over from Wabash Valley College. Coomes was an outstanding coach who stayed only one year before leaving to join Lou Henson, his wife's uncle, as an assistant at the University of Illinois.

Coomes was succeeded by Mark Bial (pronounced Beel), a tireless worker from the state of Illinois. Bial was the first coach to lead the team under the school's new name, the University of Southern Indiana, after the school became independent in 1985. Bial had two strong seasons (19-9 in '85-'86 and 24-6 in '86-'87) before finishing his final season 13-15.

Next in line at USI was Lionel Sinn, a Hoosier native who had coached at Bethel College in Tennessee. Sinn had three winning seasons during his four years at USI before he left in 1992. At that point, ISUE/USI had a 22-year record of 309-272 (53%), but the quiet campus on Evansville's west side was about to be awakened with the arrival of a flamboyant young coach who would turn the USI campus on its ear and launch the Screaming Eagles into the stratosphere.

When Bruce Pearl arrived at the USI campus in 1992, he was inheriting a program that had finished the previous season 10-18 under Lionel Sinn. Although the 32-year-old Pearl had no head coaching experience, he would implement a system at USI that he had helped develop under the watchful eye of Dr. Tom Davis. To say that Davis was Pearl's 'mentor' would not do the term justice, since Bruce Pearl's entire career to that point was as an assistant under the highly successful coach.

Pearl served as Davis' administrative assistant from 1978 to 1982 and learned the inner workings of a basketball program while an undergraduate at Boston College. After graduating cum laude in '82, Pearl followed Davis to Stanford, where he was an associate head coach for three years. Pearl then followed Davis to the University of Iowa and was Dr. Davis' assistant and right-hand man, specializing in full-court pressure defensive tactics and coaching post players for the Hawkeyes. During his six-year stay at Iowa, Pearl helped develop several pro players, including Brad Lohaus, Acie Earl, B.J. Armstrong and Kevin Gamble.

For his efforts, Pearl was recognized as one of the top Division I assistants in the country by *Basketball Weekly* in 1988, and four years later, he was lured to USI. Although the vast majority of local fans had never heard of him, it wouldn't take long for the affable young coach with boundless enthusiasm to pique their curiosity. Little did they know that he was about to take them on the ride of a lifetime.

With his high-octane style of offensive basketball and relentless pressure defense, Pearl led the Eagles to the greatest turnaround in GLVC history in his first season as a head coach. Using mainly players he had inherited, Pearl took the program from 10-18 (4-14 GLVC) to 22-7 (15-4) and a spot in the NCAA Division II Tournament.

Pearl followed his inaugural season with another banner year, leading the Eagles to a 28-4 record and making it to the final game of the NCAA Tourney. After a loss to Cal State-Bakersfield in the finals, the coach whose boyish grin had made him a curiosity two years earlier was now making true believers of the entire community.

As the 1994-'95 season began, Coach Pearl's passion seemed contagious as he worked with his own recruits and encouraged high expectations from the media and fans. The Eagles opened the season with four wins, which included winning the USI/Kenny Kent Toyota Shootout for only the second time in school history. In the first game of the Shootout, USI downed Winona State 92-79 behind 31 points and 11 rebounds by Stan Gouard. The following night, the Eagles won a high-scoring affair (107-101) over top-20 Tampa, with Chad Gilbert leading the way with 30 points.

With the #1 national ranking in hand, the Eagles headed for Southern Illinois-Edwardsville, only to have their bubble burst when they were run out of the gym 124-105. To add insult to injury, USI showed that they were anything but invincible when they dropped a home game against conference foe Northern Kentucky, 96-90. For the first time since his arrival at USI, Bruce Pearl had lost two consecutive games and the Screaming Eagles plummeted out of the top 20. The team had sputtered, but before long, Coach Pearl would have them purring again like a well-oiled machine.

A trip west was the perfect remedy as the Eagles flew to Las Vegas for the High Desert Classic. USI opened with a 96-68 romp over Cameron, followed by a character builder that would challenge their makeup as a team. In the second contest, USI roared back from a 17-point deficit to defeat Washburn, a team that had advanced to the Elite Eight of the previous year's NCAA Tourney. The Eagles overcame a 7-point Washburn lead in the final minute and pulled out a 107-103 victory in overtime. Even more amazing was the fact that, of the eleven players who made the trip, six fouled out, giving the team's bench some valuable experience under pressure.

With the pedal to the metal, the Eagles cruised past their next 14 opponents, including an impressive 117-83 laugher over #8 Kentucky Weslyan. The streak brought USI back up the rankings to the #3 spot before Kentucky Weslyan halted the streak with a 97-90 win to gain revenge over their arch-rival.

As the season wound down, Coach Pearl and his boys were in a battle for the GLVC crown with Weslyan and Northern Kentucky, and when all was said and done, USI had finished third behind Weslyan and conference champion Northern Kentucky. But it wouldn't be long before the Eagles would see the familiar faces again.

The 1995 Great Lakes Regional was one of the most powerful regionals in Division II history, led by the three GLVC rivals. Northern Kentucky, the #1 seed in the tourney, was ranked #9 nationally, while Weslyan entered the tournament as the #2 seed and boasted a #3 national ranking. USI was the tournament's #3 seed and finished the regular season at #5 nationally.

Although the three teams seemed evenly matched and the Eagles trailed both in the GLVC standings, USI captured the regional title in dominating fashion. After eliminating Hillsdale 95-86 in the first round, the Eagles breezed past Weslyan 102-81 and then took care of Northern Kentucky 102-94. The Eagles were led in the regional by the three young men who had carried much of the load during the season, Stan Gouard, Brian Huebner and Chad Gilbert. Gouard averaged 17.7 points and 11 rebounds and was named to the All-Regional team. He was joined by Huebner (17.0

points) and Gilbert, whose 25.5 points and 9.5 rebounds per game earned him the award for the regional's Most Outstanding Player.

The Eagles left Cincinnati with a second straight regional title and were three wins from the ultimate prize. They were now on their way to Louisville to take care of some unfinished business from the year before.

USI opened with a ho-hum 108-93 victory over New Hampshire College and followed that with an 89-81 win over #12 Norfolk State. For the second year in row, they were one of the last two teams standing, but their final challenge would test the team's resolve to the max. With a strong contingent of Screaming Eagles fans amidst the 5,000 onlookers at the Commonwealth Convention Center, the Eagles looked primed and ready, but looks can sometimes be deceiving.

From the opening tip, USI looked lethargic and overmatched as they fell behind by 22 points in the opening 11:30 of the game, and when the horn blew to end the first half, the Eagles were fortunate to trail UC Riverside by only 18 points. USI had managed to hit only 18.8% of their shots (6 of 32) and only 41.2% from the line (7 of 17). The performance was shocking to everyone, prompting Coach Pearl to say later, "I couldn't believe that we were in the biggest game of our lives and that was happening."

As the second half started, the Eagles reflected the fiery attitude of their coach and began to work their way back into the game. Sophomore Marc Hostetter ignited the comeback with eight points in the first five minutes to draw USI to within ten points of Riverside, and the Eagles looked poised and determined. USI tied the game at 62 at the 2:20 mark and took the lead for good 64-63 on a jumper by Cortez Barnes. Although the first twelve minutes of the game had belonged to the Highlanders, the last two minutes were all USI, as the boys outscored Riverside 9-1 to give the school its first national title in any sport.

In only three seasons, Bruce Pearl had led the Screaming Eagles to two national title games and one championship. For his efforts, he was named the 1994-'95 National Coach of the Year, and his team leader, Stan Gouard, was named a first team All-American and was honored as the NABC Division II Player of the Year.

During the championship season, Gouard and Chad Gilbert led the team in scoring in 19 of the 34 games, with strong support from Scott Boyden, Cortez Barnes and Brian Huebner. Gouard also led the team in rebounding in 20 of the 33 games, including a remarkable nine games in a row. The team finished the season 29-4 with records of 14-1 at home, 8-3 away and 7-0 on neutral courts.

In the Elite Eight, the Eagles shot .435 from three-point range, with Hostetter leading the way at .556 (5-9), followed by Huebner at .400 (6-15). Five players averaged between ten and fifteen points in the team's final three games: Huebner and Gilbert (14.7), Hostetter (14.3), Barnes (12.3) and Gouard (10.7). In addition, the team showed excellent depth, both during the tournament and the regular season, with support from Boyden, Larry Eady, Kevin Caldwell, Neil Coyle, Joel Thomas, Shawn Aldridge, Tom Tooley and Ken Troutman.

Bruce Pearl spent six more seasons at USI after the championship season, and although he never won another national title, he did put up some amazing numbers. During his tenure at the school, he finished with a record of 231-46 (83.4%), making him the winningest active coach in America. He won at least 22 games every season, including a school record 29 in 1994-'95. On February 19th, 2000, he became the quickest coach in history to win 200 games, doing so in only 240 games, breaking the record (250) held by Everett Case of North Carolina State from 1947 to 1954.

USI's 1995 national champions. On the floor (L-R): Ken Troutman, Neil Coyle, Stan Gouard (beside trophy), Marc Hostetter, Joel Thomas, Chad Gilbert, Larry Eady. Standing (L-R): Ray Simmons (SID), Scott Boyden, Tim Tooley, Cortez Barnes, Shawn Aldridge, Brian Huebner, Joe Patton (Manager, far back), Bruce Pearl (Head Coach), Steven Pearl (Coach Pearl's son), Kevin Doyle (Manager, far back), Rick Herdes (Asst. Coach), Brad Schmitt (Manager, partially hidden), Craig Martin (Asst. Coach), Jennifer Riggs (Manager), Chris Diaz (Athletic Trainer)

Bruce Pearl (Photo courtesy of the University of Southern Indiana, Athletic Department.)

Coach Pearl guided the Screaming Eagles to the national tournament during all nine seasons he was here, and USI was ranked #1 at some point during each season from 1994 to 1999. With the consistent success Pearl enjoyed at USI, it was no surprise when the ambitious young coach left in 2001 to pilot a floundering program at Division I University of Wisconsin-Milwaukee and then took over at the University of Tennessee in 2005. After his great success here in Evansville, it was highly unlikely that the Boston-born coach would stay put for a long run like U of E's hometown hero Arad McCutchan. After more impressive results at Wisconsin and Tennessee, Pearl has shown that he deserves what he has gotten, and local fans should feel fortunate to have witnessed his talents for the nine seasons he was here.

In 2001, Pearl turned over the reigns at USI to his long-time assistant Rick Herdes, and Herdes has performed admirably. For five years, Coach Herdes recorded 20-win seasons with a fast-paced philosophy similar to Bruce Pearl's. Herdes' only hiccup during his tenure was the 2007-'08 season, where his team was decimated by injuries.

From the first season when John Deem scraped together a makeshift team of local boys in blue and gold uniforms through the evolution of the program guided by Jerry Alstadt, Wayne Boultinghouse and others, the USI basketball program has flourished. In addition, the beautiful campus located on 350 acres of rolling wooded hills on Evansville's west side has expanded its athletic program dramatically. Over the years, the school has produced many fine athletes as new sports were added, and several have placed themselves among the best in the country. John Deem and Jerry Alstadt deserve credit for 'hatching' the Eagles nearly forty years ago, and coaches and athletes since and in the present have stepped up to uphold the tradition. With room to grow and a strong foundation, USI will have every opportunity to continue to develop athletes, like those on these pages, who will strengthen the tradition and keep the Screaming Eagles flying high.

Chris Bowles, from Madisonville, Kentucky, came to USI in 1990 after transferring from Western Kentucky University. The 6'10", 225-pounder averaged 19 points and 10 rebounds during his career and became the first USI player to score over 2,000 points and pull down over 1,000 rebounds. Bowles was USI's leading scorer for four straight seasons (1990-'94), and as of 2008, is still the last player to score over 40 points in a game, with a school record 45 points at Northern Kentucky on Valentine's Day 1991.

(Photo courtesy of the University of Southern Indiana, Athletic Department.)

Stan Gouard was one of the key figures in USI's 1994-'95 run to the Division II national basketball championship. The 6'6", 200-pound guard/forward was named the NABC Division Player of the Year in 1995 and led the Eagles in both scoring (18.9) and rebounding (8.8) during the championship season. The two-time Division II All-American also set a single season record for points scored (623) and still holds the school records for steals in a game (8), season (66) and career (176).

(Photos courtesy of the University of Southern Indiana, Athletic Department.)

Elly Rono, from Rift Valley, Kenya, became USI's first individual national champion when he won the 1997 NCAA Division II Cross Country Nationals in Kenosha, Wisconsin. His time in the 10k race of 31:13.9 was forty seconds faster than the second place finisher.

The 6'3", 148-pound Kenyan was also a four-time All-American in track and won national championships in both the 5,000-meter indoor and 10,000-meter outdoor runs. After leaving USI, Rono continued to compete and finished fourth in the 2003 IMG New York City Marathon.

Catcher Kevin Brown was a first team All-American in 1993 and a third team All-American in 1994 for USI and still holds several single season school records, including highest batting average (.442 in 1993), home runs (14 in '93) and total bases (127 in '93). He also ranks second in career RBIs (145), total bases (320) and home runs (27). In his last two seasons with the Screaming Eagles, Brown gunned down 44 of 76 runners who attempted to steal, an impressive 58%. Kevin was drafted in the second round (56th overall) of the 1994 major league draft by the Texas Rangers and spent seven seasons at various professional levels, which included playing in 85 major league games.

(Photo courtesy of the University of Southern Indiana, Athletic Department.)

LONG-RANGE SNIPERS

The Edward F. Steitz Award has been given each year to the Division I player who leads the nation in three-point field goal percentage. For two straight years, the award went to players from right here in southern Indiana – Jeff Anderson (Memorial, Kent State) in 1993 and Brent Kell (Harrison, U of E) in 1994. By the way, the following year, the award was won by Brian Jackson, who was not an area high school player, but played for U of E.

Left: Jeff Anderson   Right: Brent Kell
(Photos courtesy of Mike Thomas Photography.)

'BIG JOHN' HOLLINDEN: A GIANT OF A MAN

Though John Hollinden was seen as a freak of nature by many, those who knew him saw the gentle giant as a lovable, hard-working young man with maturity beyond his years. With a stature that makes it impossible to blend in, Hollinden took his blessing (or curse) in stride and was appreciated by all who knew him. His character never wavered as he struggled to live up to his potential in his high school and college years and as he dealt with tragedy as a young adult.

When John left Holy Redeemer Grade School in 1972, he already stood 6'9, but his rapid growth had left him awkward and fragile. His parents, Joe and Ann, were both highly intelligent and were excited for John and his sisters to continue their educations at Rex Mundi High School. When word of Rex Mundi's closing was announced, the Hollindens were upset with the local diocese and vowed not to send their children to either Memorial or Mater Dei.

As word of John's situation spread to Central coach John Wessel, he took a keen interest in the lanky teenager and the obvious potential that comes with a boy his size. "He was skinny as a rail," Wessel remarked when asked about his first impressions of Hollinden. "He couldn't run much, and they wouldn't let us put him on weights for a couple years because he was growing so fast."

Although Wessel couldn't pinpoint John's weight while at Central, he determined that Hollinden was well under 200 pounds. Wessel also explained that John's height was not a physical oddity, but that his stature came naturally. Both of John's parents were tall, as were several other relatives, including his uncle, Fred Hollinden, who was 6'8 and served as a coach and principal at Jasper High School.

Wessel and his assistants, Steve Fritz and John Chapman, worked diligently to develop 'Big John' both physically and mentally. In today's lingo, he would be known as a 'project', and the Central coaches felt that he was worth the extra effort. Early in the process, the coaches instructed John to stand on an eight-inch box so that he could touch the hoop. The purpose was to illustrate that if he could just jump eight inches, he would be playing above the rim.

As a JV player at Central, John stood 7'1 and was finally allowed to work with John Hunter, a former Mr. Indiana, to develop his strength. Even as a sophomore, his weak body prevented him from executing routine skills on the court. "If you would throw a ball just a foot outside his body, he couldn't catch it," Coach Wessel pointed out.

As the coaches continued to work with Hollinden, his skills slowly began to catch up with his body, and thanks to the patience of his coaches and teammates, John became a force on the floor. As a senior, Hollinden stood 7'4 and could touch the rim standing flat-footed. Although he only averaged ten to fifteen points a game, his presence in the middle gave opposing offenses fits. Wessel learned later that many coaches were having players hold up tennis rackets in practice to simulate John's long arms as players tried to shoot.

Wessel himself had to make adjustments due to John's extraordinary altitude. "I had to learn how to stand away from him" Wessel joked, "because you could break your neck just looking up at him. So when I called timeout, I had to maintain my distance."

Coach Wessel appreciated John for many reasons, not the least of which was his dignity when confronted by the taunts of opposing fans. Wessel recalled a night during John's junior year when a Terre Haute crowd was merciless toward Hollinden from the opening whistle. "He kept his mouth shut and never reacted," Wessel recalled. "When I asked his father about it, he said, 'John's been taught that you don't win battles by talking to ignorant people.'"

Wessel also appreciated Hollinden off the court, as well. Just like his sisters, John was a straight-A student, and he was also an accomplished musician. Though he was quiet and unassuming, Wessel says that John loved people. "He had a funny side to him," Wessel revealed. "He had a t-shirt he wore that said, 'Yes, I am 7-foot-four!'" Wessel also chuckles about the time he was walking down the hallway behind John as the big man was doing an impersonation of Coach Wessel having an angry moment. When John discovered that his coach was watching, the entire crowd was in stitches as John's face turned red.

Although Hollinden was still somewhat of a curiosity, his size still attracted the attention of college coaches. U of E made a strong bid, but the greatest effort came from Oral Roberts University. ORU's Bobby Watson (who would later take the U of E job and perish in the devastating plane crash in 1977) was a frequent visitor, even bringing Oral Roberts himself with him on one occasion. Although Roberts' arrival on his personal jet was hyped by the local media, John was very low-key and unimpressed.

As Coach Watson pursued John, he learned that dealing with the Hollindens wouldn't be easy. According to John Wessel, Watson once said, "I've never been through such a drilling! His mother wanted to know how many Doctor's degrees we had on staff. She asked questions I'd never been asked before."

With his parents' blessing, John left for Tulsa in 1976 and spent two years at ORU before homesickness got the best of him. Now 7'6 ½ and weighing 235, John came home to ISUE (now USI) to play for Wayne Boultinghouse.

After sitting out a year, Hollinden played the same role he had filled while at Central as a moderate scorer but a demon on defense. John's two years at USI were Coach Boultinghouse's final two seasons, and the two-year record of 41-17 was the best of the coach's seven-year tenure with the Eagles. "Without question, John Hollinden has been a major force in our winning the past two years," Boultinghouse said to the press. "I have never witnessed a more intimidating player."

Opposing coaches were also generous with praise for the ISUE big man. "I played against Kareem Abdul-Jabbar," said Billy Keller, the Indiana Central University coach who had just witnessed a ten-block performance by Big John. "Hollinden brings back memories of Jabbar. You have to totally change your game with him in there."

Hollinden finished his career in 1981 and was named a second team All-American by *Basketball Weekly*. Nearly thirty years later, he still holds school records for blocks in a game (17 against Kentucky Weslyan in 1981), a season (200, '80-'81) and career (365).

With his schooling behind him, John assessed his options in the spring of 1981. He was selected in the ninth round of the NBA draft by the Dallas Mavericks but decided instead to head to Sweden to play pro ball in Europe. On September 25th, the day before he was to leave, he made the rounds to say good-bye to many of his friends. As he traveled from a party to meet up with some fraternity brothers, he hit a patch of gravel on an S-curve on Lower Mt. Vernon Road and crashed his new automobile. As he said in a special series in the *Courier*, "That was when I realized I wasn't going to Sweden."

Those who read the *Courier* series were touched by the big man's words and his strength of character. He spoke of how he knew that he had to remain calm during the long wait for an ambulance to arrive and how "the first real shock of pain" hit him when the paramedics straightened him out.

John's lower thoracic vertebrae had been crushed in the accident, nearly severing the connection between his legs and brain. As he analyzed his status, he tried to gain perspective and appreciate that at least he was still alive.

After he was stabilized, Hollinden underwent surgery at Deaconess Hospital that used the tips of his hipbone to fuse the broken vertebrae. After six weeks, he was taken to the Rehabilitation Hospital of Chicago to begin the arduous process of recovery. During his twenty-week stay, he endured constant frustration as he dealt with the realities of the injuries.

Through it all, he learned to deal with his slow improvement and the improbability of ever walking again. As his series in the paper concluded, John spoke with the same unique insight that he displayed as an awkward teenager at Central, saying "I'm not glad it happened, but I have to admit that some good has come of it. I appreciate life so much more now. One of these days, I'm going to have a 'crash and burn party' and invite some friends over and celebrate being alive."

John Hollinden knew that although he could never again use his legs, he still had something to offer. He went on to become the co-captain of a wheelchair team, the Evansville Rolling Thunder, and was an ambassador for the United Way of Southwestern Indiana campaign.

Eventually, Hollinden's legs had to be amputated because of complications from the accident, and in 1992, he passed away. It's hard to comprehend what it would be like to go through life as a freakishly tall person, but Hollinden's upbringing enabled him to not only survive but to thrive under the constant scrutiny. There's no doubt that he eventually developed into an impressive basketball player, but the story of his abbreviated life was about much more than athletics. Rather than avoiding attention and curiosity, he stood tall and embraced it. He overcame obvious shortcomings as a player and persevered to become exceptional, while also excelling as a student and musician. But above all this, he touched the lives of those who knew him with his grace and sense of humor, and he overcame tragedy with a deep-seeded philosophy that wouldn't let him wallow in self-pity. John Hollinden's life was much too short, but the impression he left on others while he was here was as monumental as Big John himself.

(Photo courtesy of the University of Southern Indiana, Athletic Department.)

LEANN FREELAND: A SMALL TOWN GIRL WITH BIG DREAMS

LeAnn Freeland didn't have the advantage of playing for a large high school with lots of exposure. What she did have, however, was a load of natural talent and a desire to excel. All she wanted was a chance, and she found that chance at the University of Southern Indiana, where she became the most decorated athlete, male or female, in the school's history.

LeAnn was born on June 23rd, 1975, the same year USI started its women's basketball program. The youngest of three children, Freeman grew up in the tiny town of Fairfield, Illinois and was raised by her father, Carroll, a farmer, and her mother, Donna, a village treasurer. Although neither of her siblings was particularly sports-minded, LeAnn inherited her athletic genes from her father, who had given up sports to work the family farm. As her father coached her in the family's backyard, LeAnn's body and her passion for competition grew.

"I was always big for my age," LeAnn said from her office in Indianapolis, "and I was ultra-competitive. Anytime I played anything with anybody, I always wanted to win. That's one thing that helped me excel."

Freeland was six-feet tall as an eighth grader, and although she only grew another inch, her size enabled her to stand out in her rural community. Because of the small population, she and a few other girls found themselves competing with boys, which proved to be a blessing in disguise for the ambitious youngster.

Freeland earned 13 letters at Wayne City High School, four each in basketball, softball and track, and one in volleyball. An example of her athleticism could be seen each spring as she competed in both softball and track. Being the only member of the 'girls' track team, she would practice softball and would only appear for track on the day of the meets. Often, her first jumps and throws of the year were at the first meet. Despite her lack of practice, she did attain a respectable height of 5'3" in the high jump.

In basketball, LeAnn averaged 27 points a game as a sophomore and in the mid-20s her next two seasons, despite being double-teamed. Although she was named to the Class A (small school) All-State first team as a senior, Freeland did not attract a lot of attention from colleges. She did draw some interest from NAIA schools and junior colleges, but the school that seemed to be the best fit was the University of Southern Indiana.

Thankfully, USI coach Chancellor Dugan had looked beyond the small-town backdrop to find a young lady who could help the program reach heights never before achieved, and when Dugan approached Freeland, the coach made a believer out of her.

"Coach Dugan was a great recruiter," Freeland explained. "One thing that sold me on the university was she said that if I went to USI, by my senior year, we'd be playing for national championships. And that was a bold statement considering the best they had done previously was 15-15.

"I really bought into what she was telling me, and my senior year, there we were playing for the national championship. We set a goal, and we got there together."

As a freshman at USI, LeAnn was an occasional starter and was second on the team and tenth in the GLVC in rebounding, averaging 7.5. She was also the team's third leading scorer for the season at 11.6, but she averaged nearly 18 points in her last ten games, with a high of 27 against Ashland. Perhaps her greatest stat during her inaugural season was the team's record. The Screaming Eagles finished at 12-6, which was incredible considering the program's record the six years prior was 42-127.

Freeland's sophomore season, 1994-'95, was her coming out party, as she averaged 24.4 points and 9.1 rebounds per game and led her team to a 22-5 record, the best by far in school history. She also led the Eagles to the school's first ever GLVC title and their first berth in the NCAA Division II Tournament.

LeAnn long before she became the #1 Division II player in the country. (Photo courtesy of the Freeland family.)

As an individual, Freeland set the school single game record for points in a game (50 against IUPU-Ft. Wayne) and the school's single season record for blocks with 69. She also set a single game record for USI and the GLVC with ten blocks against the University of Indianapolis. In addition, she set USI's single season scoring record with 658 points, making her the first USI player, male or female, to score over 600 points in a season. For her efforts, LeAnn was named the GLVC Player of the Year and received national recognition when she was honored as a Kodak/WBCA All-American and the NCAA Division II National Player of the Year by *College Sports* magazine.

In her junior year, Freeland led USI to its second straight NCAA Division II Tournament appearance and became the first USI player to score 600 or more points in consecutive seasons. Earning All-American honors once again while leading the team to a 22-7 season, she also took over the school's career scoring lead halfway through the season. The greatest female player in USI history had fashioned an impressive career, but there was one goal that had yet to be reached.

With the program in full swing, Coach Dugan and her star were poised to make a run as the 1996-'97 season began. In the second game of the year, USI lost to Michigan Tech 84-73 and then reeled off 25 straight victories to finish the regular season 26-1. For the third consecutive year, LeAnn had led her team to the NCAA Tourney.

Ironically, the Screaming Eagles opened the tournament against the last team to beat them, Michigan Tech. After avenging the loss with a 66-48 win, USI knocked off Northern Michigan (78-67), Delta State (70-55) and California Davis (70-62) to reach the Division II Finals. Although USI fell to North Dakota State in the final game, LeAnn and Coach Dugan had turned what seemed like a pipedream four years earlier into a reality.

Freeland is quick to share credit with her USI teammates, especially Eileen Weber, who was a year younger. "She was a great player, and she was an All-American also," LeAnn said. "She was quite a talent, and she was a genius, as well. She had a 4.0 GPA (majoring in Chemistry). She was attending USI on a Presidential Scholarship, and she was quite a catch for the University of Southern Indiana."

With talented teammates like Weber, Freeland finished her college career as one of the most successful athletes in school history. She became the first USI women's player to score over 2000 points (2,269), and she became the GLVC's all-time leading scorer (1,524 points) and rebounder (629). In addition, she was named the GLVC Player of the Year for the second time and was honored as an All-American for the third consecutive season.

Freeland scored at least 20 points in 60 of the 115 games she played at USI. She also topped 30 points eleven times, 40 points twice and scored 50 once. When she left USI, she held sixteen school records, including the career record for steals (167). But Freeland's most impressive numbers relate to her consistency and leadership. In her final three seasons, she averaged 24.4, 21.6, and 21.1 points and 9.3, 9.5, and 7.4 rebounds per game. Most astonishing, though, was the fact that, after four seasons where USI had won only 25% of their games, Freeland's USI teams compiled a four-year record of 91-24 (79%). LeAnn had helped Chancellor Dugan complete her mission by turning the USI women's basketball program into a winner.

After graduation, LeAnn tried out unsuccessfully for the Charlotte Sting of the WNBA before pursuing her dream of becoming a coach. For a year, she taught Social Studies at Castle Junior High before receiving a call from Rick Stein, who had assisted Chancellor Dugan at USI and had taken over the program when Dugan left for Florida Atlantic.

LeAnn served as Stein's assistant until she landed a top assistant position at Florida Gulf Coast in Ft. Myers. After four years there, Freeland was offered the head coaching position at the University of Indianapolis, and in her first year there, had the Greyhounds fighting for a GLVC crown.

In 2004, Freeland was inducted into the GLVC Hall of Fame, and USI selected her to be honored in its Hall in 2008. Coming from a high school with only 47 students in the senior class, it's not clear where this small-town girl learned to think so big, but somehow she learned how to believe and what it took to achieve. "The most important thing is to believe in yourself," LeAnn responded when asked the secret to success. "You have to believe that, at any point and time, you're the best player on the floor, even if sometimes that's not the case. Work ethic is where you build your confidence. When everyone else is taking a day off, you're working to try to get better."

LeAnn Freeland is a true success story. She led her college team into uncharted waters and transformed herself into one of the best players in Division II basketball. In the process, she rewrote the USI record books, and now she's using her skills and competitive nature to distinguish herself as one of the best young college coaches in America.

(Photo courtesy of the University of Southern Indiana, Athletic Department.)

MIKE PEGRAM: THE MAN WITH THE GOLDEN TOUCH

Mike Pegram would be the first to tell you that he has been blessed, not only financially but also in terms of the friendships he has enjoyed over the years. From a financial standpoint, one might say that the odds were in Mike's favor when he drew his first breath in a hospital in Fort Knox, Kentucky, the depository where over 4,000 tons of America's gold is kept. It is also no coincidence that he would become an excellent athlete and eventually fall in love with the horse racing business, where he would rise from humble roots to become one of the most successful thoroughbred owners of his generation.

When Mike's father, James, had completed his service in the Army in 1955, he and his wife, Golda Mae, left Fort Knox to return home to Princeton with three-year-old Mike and his six-year-old brother Jim in tow. The family would eventually grow to six when younger brothers Demont and Gil were born. While in Princeton, James Pegram owned the Palace Pool Hall and spent his leisure time working with his sons on their athletic skills and taking family outings to Ellis Park to watch the ponies.

James was a talented athlete himself and grew up playing ball with Brooklyn Dodgers legend Gil Hodges (for whom his youngest son was named) on the fields of southwestern Indiana. As a reliable catcher who could hit, the elder Pegram was good enough that he signed a contract with the St. Louis Browns out of high school and played minor league ball for six years.

Jim Jr. and Mike were also exceptional athletes during their years in Princeton, and both played basketball and baseball in high school. Jim recalls watching the strong Princeton American Legion teams, coached by his father, during the period when Bob Griese was pitching for Funkhauser. In high school, Jim was an "average" basketball player as a 6-foot guard, but was an outstanding catcher and first baseman on the Princeton Legion team that captured the state championship in 1964. In 1967, Princeton won the sectional in the first year of the IHSAA State Tournament, with Jim hitting over .400. After high school, Jim headed south to Edison Junior College for a year before spending a year at IU and two years in the U.S. Navy.

During Jim's senior year at Princeton, Mike Pegram was already starting to show his athletic promise as an athlete by becoming the ace of the Tigers' pitching staff during the sectional championship season. As he grew into his solid 6'2", 190-pound frame, Mike became a star in both sports. Pitching for his father in Legion ball, he once struck out 23 hitters in a game, and he led the high school basketball team in scoring as a sophomore with a 20-point average. Princeton also won a basketball sectional during Mike's high school days. Playing alongside teammates like Dale Lovelace and Bill Smith, Princeton battled Wood Memorial to the wire before Mike nailed a 40-footer at the buzzer for the win.

After Mike's senior year, James Pegram decided to pull up roots and drive west to invest in McDonald's franchises in Sacramento, California. For one year, Mike came back to play baseball at IU, but then realized the potential with McDonald's and joined his father back in California. It was during the early years of building his ultra-successful business that the allure of the horse racing world became too much for Mike to resist.

In the late '70s, Mike and his father co-owned a couple of thoroughbreds in Kentucky, and Mike scored his first win at Ellis Park with a horse named Storm Strike. It was also during this time that he developed a relationship with an up-and-coming trainer named Bob Baffert. After three years of success, primarily with quarter horses, Mike decided to take a deeper plunge into the world of thoroughbred racing, and with Baffert by his side, Mike quickly made an impression in the Sport of Kings.

Although Pegram and Baffert had produced many winners before, their first major thoroughbred champion was Thirty Slews, the son of Slewpy. 'Slews' was purchased at the Keeneland auction for $30,000 as a yearling, and under the watchful eye of Baffert, won multiple stakes races, including the million dollar Breeders' Cup Sprint.

Perhaps the pinnacle of Mike Pegram's career in racing came in 1998, when he and Baffert produced two Eclipse Award winners. Silverbulletday, a descendant of Northern Dancer, was

Mike Pegram (right) and Bob Baffert have been friends and successful business partners for many years

purchased at auction for $155,000 and went on to capture the Eclipse Award in the two-year-old filly category. She also won the Kentucky Oaks and was the three-year-old filly champion the following year, producing over $3 million in earnings before she was through.

Mike's second special horse of 1998 was a knock-kneed bay colt that would provide Pegram and Baffert with thrills beyond belief, as well as a heartbreak that would last a lifetime. Because of his homely appearance, Real Quiet was available for only $17,000 at auction, but over time, the scrawny colt would blossom into a bargain basement beauty that would eventually bring Pegram and Baffert to the brink of immortality.

Real Quiet, nicknamed 'the Fish' by Baffert because of his narrow frame, lived up to his meager billing early in his career, going winless in his first six races. As the Kentucky Derby hype began to crescendo in the spring of 1998, Real Quiet was little more than a whisper among the sport's pundits. But after a half-length victory in the Derby and a two-length win in the Preakness (both over runner-up Victory Gallop), the horse that nobody wanted was creating Triple Crown buzz around the globe.

On Belmont day, Mike Pegram was surrounded by friends as he contemplated the historic moment. It had been twenty years (Affirmed in 1978) since a horse had been able to win the sport's Big Three in a five-week period, and several had come close but fallen short. Experts questioned if Real Quiet had the strength for the 1½-mile distance and the fortitude to compete down the track's expansive home stretch. As the race played out, Real Quiet quashed any doubts about his courage as he barreled for home with Kent Desormeaux aboard. He was three on top as he hit the 16th pole with his crooked knees driving like pistons, but lurking behind was jockey Gary Stevens atop Victory Gallop. As the two neared the finish, Pegram's horse gave every ounce he had to give as the crowd held its collective breath. When the results were announced that Victory Gallop had prevailed by a nostril, Pegram and his cronies felt the cruel sting of defeat after one of the closest losses in Triple Crown history.

Throughout the Triple Crown experience, Mike's brother Jim was at his side, and both felt the emotional extremes of the five-week roller coaster ride. Jim, who had also owned horses in the past and now makes a living as a jockey agent, appreciates the unique opportunity he and his brother had in 1998.

"The emotion when Mike won the Kentucky Derby was incredible," Mike recalled. "We were down by the rail where a lot of the grooms were watching the race. Then you see those colors on the jockey's silks (McDonalds red and gold) when they're turning for home. When he went by us, he was about three (lengths) on top and we were just holding our breath and saying, 'Hang on, baby! Hang on!' And then, when he hit the wire, it was just pure emotion. We all got in a circle and were hugging with tears coming down all our faces. And our father had passed away (in 1987), so we were thinking of him."

Jim also recalled the Belmont and the classy way his brother conducted himself after the devastating loss. "It was a huge blow to get that close to winning the Triple Crown," Jim explained, "and there was a $5 million Visa bonus for winning all three. There were 100,000 people screaming, and we were walking back and there were reporters converging from all directions looking for a story. But all Mike could say was, 'I hope they got the beer iced down at the barn.'

"Mike had flown a lot of people in," Jim continued, "and he had a huge party planned at the Garden City Hotel near the track. We were worried it would be like a morgue (because of the loss), but it was just the opposite. Everybody showed up and had a great time. Mike had just suffered one of the toughest losses anybody's ever suffered in a horse race, but for somebody who just got beat in the Triple Crown, he was a hell of a host."

Real Quiet, the horse no one wanted, was named the 1998 three-year-old male Eclipse Award winner and finished his racing career with over $3 million in earnings. Mike Pegram continued his hot streak the following year with Silverbulletday and has since saddled numerous stakes winners as an owner. In 2001, a horse named Captain Steve, purchased for $70,000, captured the $6 million Dubai World Cup and went on to earn nearly $7 million with wins in several other major stakes races.

Today, Pegram keeps a stable of 20 horses at Santa Anita in California to train under Baffert and his staff. In 2007, the team produced yet another Breeders' Cup champion when Midnight Lute (named for Mike's good friend Lute Olsen) captured the sprint. In addition, Pegram is looking to the future with his own breeding stock, including several broodmares, led by their super-starlet Silverbulletday.

Throughout his successful rise in the business world and despite his fame and fortune in horse racing, Mike Pegram has remained loyal to those who knew him as a youngster. "We had a lot of guys from Princeton at the Derby," Jim Pegram recalled, "and getting to the winner's circle was a zoo. You had to cross over the track to get there, and security stopped a lot of Princeton people. Mike told them, 'If you don't let these people in, there's not going to be a picture,' With the TV people in panic mode because they were coming back from commercial, Mike stood firm and his life-long buddies were permitted in to share the moment with their friend.

Jim Pegram strongly believes that Mike's popularity and the respect he has earned are by-products of the upbringing he experienced while in Princeton. "Mike is a very smart businessman," Jim said, "and he's in tune with what the little guy wants. Growing up in southern Indiana, it was so competitive then and sports were tremendous. At the time, you don't realize how much that's getting you ready for what's ahead, and Mike learned his lessons well. He learned how to lose, and he learned how to win and how to handle himself. You know, there's an old saying that, 'when you get to the winner's circle, act like you've been there before.' Mike's very competitive, but he's smart enough that, in horse racing, he lets Baffert do the training. He's smart enough to know that, as an owner, your job is to hire the right trainer and then get out of the way. And that's why he's been so successful."

Throughout his thirty years in the horse business, Mike has developed relationships with some of the biggest names in the world of sports, including close friendships with basketball coach Rick Pitino and NFL coach Mike Tice. But from his first win at Ellis Park with a horse named Storm Streak to the winner's circle of the sport's grandest event, he has kept his life in perspective. He knows that he has led a charmed life, and it is only appropriate that he makes his home in a place called Paradise Valley.

With his wife Mary Ellen and his children, Amy, Tiffany and Tim, Mike Pegram has lived the American dream. But despite all the honors and financial rewards, he has never forgotten where he came from.

BOONVILLE SOFTBALL: HE BUILT IT, AND THEY CAME

In 1985, the IHSAA sanctioned the first State Tournament for girls fast pitch softball, and since that year, the winningest coach in the state resides right here in southwestern Indiana. Mike Wilson built his Boonville softball program the same way he built the beautiful field that his players call home – one step at a time.

Wilson moved to Boonville in 1966 and played baseball and football at Boonville High School before graduating in 1976. Under football coach Bill Harrawood, he played offensive tackle and was the long snapper on the only Boonville team to reach the State Finals. As a pitcher on the baseball team, Mike won all three sectional games his senior year, a rare feat that was aided by rain delays.

Mike accepted a baseball scholarship to USI but never played because of a broken arm suffered in an auto accident coming home from a practice. He then transferred to and graduated from Indiana State before coming home to start his teaching and coaching career.

Wilson began as a freshman basketball and assistant baseball coach and then became the school's varsity baseball coach in 1984 and '85. The following year, some parents petitioned the school board to initiate a softball program for girls, as schools up north had done the previous year. "Three girls, Deanna Bacon, Tammy Lohr and Krystal Green were good enough to play baseball up to the high school level," Mike explained. "Deanna actually came out for the (high school baseball) team and was going to make it."

The school board agreed to approve the program on a trial basis and turned to Mike to head up the effort. "I had coached women's softball (slow pitch) in college and had enjoyed it," he noted. The board offered Mike $1,000 for the job, $1,600 less than the school's baseball coach, but Mike accepted anyway and went right to work.

"I had a core group: a pitcher, a catcher and a shortstop," Wilson pointed out, "and then the girls found some other kids to play. The first year, our record was 1-5. There weren't many teams in the area playing – Cannelton, New Harmony and maybe one more school."

Boonville played their home games on a nearby league field. "It had no dugouts," Wilson recalled, "but it had a backstop, and I think we had a fence." The uniforms the girls wore that first season were the same ones they would wear for the next six years.

The Lady Pioneers ended that season as one of eight regional champs statewide to go to Indianapolis and compete for the State title. They lost their first game at State 7-6 to Center Grove after leading 6-1 going into the sixth inning. Six of the Boonville players on the field at the end of the game were freshmen, which laid the groundwork for the program's future.

Although Wilson's girls were successful in the early years, 1991 was the real beginning of a process that would not only thrust the program to unparalleled success but would inspire Mike Wilson to construct a facility that would become a source of pride for the entire community. When a new softball diamond was built next to Boonville's baseball field, the layout was basic, with dugouts, chain-link fence and backstop. Although Wilson appreciated his new digs, he had much bigger aspirations, and his background as a shop teacher would pay huge dividends over the next few years.

With the help of dedicated parents, both financially and physically, Wilson set out to create not just a ballpark, but an environment that would provide a nostalgic atmosphere where fans could spend a couple hours watching some quality softball.

"Do you remember when you were a kid and built a tree house?" Mike asked. "Well, this is my tree house. We put covered grandstands on both sides, and we moved both dugouts farther from home plate, because the game is played mostly on the infield. I put our (Home) dugout into the ground to increase visibility (for the fans). I borrowed a backhoe and laid the block, and then I hit a sewer line. So (while we were at it), we decided to put a bathroom in our dugout."

With youthful enthusiasm, Mike then explained how his recollections of days gone by inspired him to add some features that make the facility unique from any other. "Right after the movie *A League of Their Own* came out, I liked the wooden fence," he said, "so I got a guy to give me a barn. I tore it down and cut all the pieces to six-foot and wrapped my outfield fence in the barn wood. We also built a wooden scoreboard that scorekeepers walk on and hang the numbers (reminiscent of the good old days at Bosse Field and other parks). I used street lights to illuminate balls, strikes and outs."

Even more creative thinking resulted in some ideas that added unique perspective

Boonville High School's 2006 State champs. Front Row (L-R): Mallory Trice, Dana Martin, Ashley Snodgrass, Courtney Seiler, Allyson Bryant, Kelli Ritchison, Lynn Fletcher, Lauren Inman, Laura Cabrillas, Kala Seiler, Kaitlyn Kroeger (mgr.). Middle Row (L-R): Meagan Collins, Anne Broadhead, Erika Taylor, Ellee Houston, Abby Schnur, Sarah Bruner, Kyla Lutz, Allie Hoover, Ashlee Winstead, Jaimie Stutsman. Back Row (L-R): Lee Houston (asst.), Mitch Wilson (mgr.), Roger Anderson (asst.), Coach Mike Wilson, De Bacon (asst.) Ron Bacon (asst.) and Mike Metzger (asst.). (Photo courtesy of Mike Wilson.)

Mike Wilson's 'Field of Dreams'. Notice the chairback seats Wilson purchased from Atlanta's Fulton County Stadium. (Photo courtesy of Mike Wilson.)

and tradition at the park. A small section of seating came from some upper-deck chairback seats from Fulton County Stadium in Atlanta. Mike bought them for $28 apiece, and now they're pre-sold to season ticket holders for $50 for a 10-game pass. These seats are passed on when seniors graduate, and the freshmen then have a chance to buy them. Another charming feature is found under a large shade tree out near the scoreboard. Mike came up with the idea to elevate some porch swings above the fence so that fans could sit in the shade in a swing and watch the game from the outfield.

The Boonville softball mentality is to make the experience more than a softball game; they want to make it an *event*. A message screen over the scoreboard displays the name, number and batting average of each hitter, and the deck over the concession stand allows for even more panoramic views for bystanders. Wilson also believes that another reason the games attract 200-300 spectators on average is the excellent food served by the volunteers. "We cook a lot of pork chops, cheeseburgers and taters," he said with pride. "Nothing compares to it, because it's like an old ballpark."

Although Boonville's facility is one of the best, and certainly most unique, in the state and perhaps even the country, it also doesn't hurt that the girls at BHS consistently put a good athletic product on the field for fans to watch. When asked the key to the program's success, Coach Wilson responded quickly with the words "sound defense." Each season, the girls spend about 70% of their practice time on defensive skills and situations, while the coaches expect them to do most of their hitting work on their own. The program's defensive prowess is reflected in the fact that Boonville holds team state records in most shutouts in a season (27 in 2006), fewest errors in a season (15 in 2006) and the best two seasons with the most errorless games (22 in 2006 and 21 in 2004).

Wilson also recognizes that he has been fortunate to have had excellent pitching, an absolute must in the world of fast pitch softball. Over the years, Boonville has been blessed with strong hurlers who could dominate opponents. Wendy Wood ('92-'95) was a four-time first team All-Stater who is the school record holder in wins for both a season (23 in 1992) and career (67). Sisters Shannon and Rachel Emmons combined for 88 wins during their careers from 1997-2000. Wood and Mindi Wilson are first and second in career no-hitters at Boonville with 10 and 8, respectively.

Over the last twenty years, Coach Wilson has witnessed the development of many fine players and has experienced some sweet victories and bitter defeats. When asked to pinpoint his most memorable players and games, he first acknowledged that Shannon Emmons was probably his best all-around player. Emmons was an outstanding pitcher and also holds several school career offensive records (hits-167, home runs-13, and RBIs-132).

When it comes to memorable games, Wilson cites a loss to Castle in 2001 as perhaps his most painful. Boonville had a senior-laden team, and Castle went on to win the State championship, leaving Mike and his team to wonder what might have been. He also remembers a big win in 1994 against Turkey Run, the defending State champs, when Boonville's Lisa Winchester made a diving catch to save the day.

But, without doubt, Wilson's greatest memory was when the 2006 season resulted in the school's first State title and showcased Wilson's choice as the best pitcher in Boonville history. After six previous appearances at the State Finals and no championships to show for it, Wilson decided to take a different approach. "We called 2006 our 'no frills tour', Wilson explained. "It used to be, when we would win the regional and advance to State, everybody wanted to have a party every night. We were worn out and not prepared.

"I said, 'Alright, we're not taking a charter bus', and we had only one night where we had ice cream after practice. We cut out all the excess. You know, when you've been there several times and not got it done, maybe it's time to try something else. It seemed to work."

The 2006 season also featured the emergence of junior pitcher Erika Taylor. As a sophomore, Wilson says that Erika was just another hard-throwing pitcher. "Then we asked her to develop a rise ball," Wilson recalled. "That's the difference between a good pitcher and a great one who can strike out just about anybody in the lineup."

Taylor followed her coach's advice and perfected her rise ball, as well as a changeup. As a junior, she shared the pitching load with another excellent hurler, Kyla Lutz. Over the course of the year, Erika's fast ball had reached the 63 miles per hour level, which Wilson thought was significant. "When you hit 60 (mph)," Wilson explained, "you can see the strikeout totals go up. And adding a rise ball, the strikeouts go up another level."

Although Taylor's win-loss record was 19-2, compared to Lutz's 12-0, Coach Wilson decided to go with Erika in the State Tournament. His hunch proved to be right when she not only showed her talent on the mound but also her courage as a competitor.

In the morning game of the regional, Taylor injured an abdominal muscle. With Boonville leading 6-0, she left the game

and watched as Lutz finished strong to seal the win and then pitched a solid game to win the title that evening. The Lady Pioneers were on their way to State, but the status of their pitching ace was up in the air.

Playing through the pain, Taylor tossed a no-hitter in the semi-final against Northridge and followed that effort with a gutsy two-hit victory over New Prairie for the State title. After the adrenaline wore off, Erika's pain was so severe that she couldn't throw for five weeks following the victory.

The next year, Taylor returned to a team that had graduated ten seniors from the year before. She navigated the season undefeated and didn't lose until the finals of the State Tournament. She walked away from her career at Boonville with virtually every school record, some of which will last a long time.

Taylor finished with a career ERA of 0.28 while holding her opponents to an .084 batting average. Strikeouts were her specialty, as she set school marks for a season (284) and a career (747). She also owns the top five spots for strikeouts in a game (23, 20, 19, 17 and 16). In 62 games, Erika allowed only twelve earned runs and set school records for no-hitters in a season (8) and a career (15), including four perfect games.

Erika Taylor is just one in a long line of stars who have progressed through the Boonville softball ranks. In his 22 years as Boonville's softball coach, Mike Wilson has worked his way to the top of his profession, winning more games than any high school coach in Indiana history. He finished the 2007 season with a career record of 465-91-2 (83.6%), and Boonville has won the Big 8 Conference every year since the conference was founded in 1994. The Lady Pioneers have won a state record 17 sectionals and 10 regionals (#3 in the state) and have made eight State Finals appearances (also #3). With a State runner-up finish in 2007 in addition to the 2006 championship, Mike Wilson and his girls have developed one of the best softball programs in Indiana, and Boonville's fans know they are part of something special. His vision of what the program could be and his efforts to build his field of dreams have provided an atmosphere of winning for the Boonville faithful to enjoy year after year. Brick by brick and board by board, Mike Wilson built it, and the people came.

Background photo: Boonville's Erika Taylor rewrote the school's record books and led the Lady Pioneers to the 2006 State championship.

Bottom Left: Wendy Wood holds the Boonville record for career no-hitters with ten.

Bottom Right: Shannon Emmons was dubbed Coach Mike Wilson's "best all-around player." She and her sister Rachel combined for 88 career wins as pitchers for the Lady Pioneers.

(Photos courtesy of Mike Wilson)

IHSAA STATE CHAMPIONS:
SOFTBALL

School	Year	Record	Coach
Castle (3A)	2000-2001	29-6	Pat Lockyear
Memorial (2A)	2001-2002	25-10-1	Bob McFall
Gibson Southern (2A)	2002-2003	29-4	Jason Blackard
Gibson Southern (2A)	2004-2005	28-3-1	Jason Blackard
Boonville (3A)	2005-2006	32-2	Mike Wilson

HERITAGE HILLS FOOTBALL: PIPELINE TO THE PROS

Santa Claus, Indiana is a small eclectic community that melds an upscale citizenry who enjoy the amenities of beautiful Christmas Lake Village with the grass roots natives who have worked the land and manned the area's businesses for generations. Amidst the cozy community sits beautiful Heritage Hills High School, and firmly entrenched in the school is the tradition-rich Patriot football program. For 36 years, the success of the football program has been unparalleled in the area, and with an enrollment of less than 750, it is remarkable that five Patriot players have used their Heritage Hills experiences as a springboard to professional football.

The Heritage Hills football program was only six years old when the North Spencer School Board brought in a young coach named Bob Clayton. Prior to Clayton's hiring, Heritage Hills had experienced moderate success under the school's first coaches, Roger Snow (26-33 in five seasons) and Bob Ashworth (8-2), who left for Evansville Reitz after only one season. Clayton hit the ground running when he arrived in 1978 and gave the school its first undefeated season three years later. As the program developed, the coaches noticed that although the Patriots were competitive, they weren't where they needed to be to compete against the elite programs.

"In the early years, we'd play Tell City and get beat. The same with Memorial," said Tom Goldsberry, who assisted Clayton for sixteen years and had two sons go through the program. After analyzing the situation, the conclusion was that the other teams were simply bigger and stronger.

"We started a summer conditioning program," Goldsberry continued. "One group would be in the weight room while the other was outside running. When they didn't make (a designated) time, they ran until they did. The year we started the program was the first year we beat Memorial."

As the boys got stronger, Coach Clayton's wide open offense and tenacious 5-2 swarming defense looked even more imposing, and the young coach made plans to develop a winning program that was top-notch in every phase.

Clayton used the lessons he learned as an athlete at Mater Dei to instill a sense of pride in players and fans alike, and he laid a foundation by working from the ground up to fulfill the vision he had for the program. First, he visited the VFW and other local organizations to rally their support, and with the help of some key backers, the Quarterback Club grew into a dynamic booster club.

With the help of assistants like Goldsberry, Bob Hawkins, Stan Jochim, Chris Sigler, Aaron Mundy, Gary Hoke and others, Clayton started and then supported a flag youth program that blossomed into a tackle league where the high school coaches had to work as referees to keep the league viable. But most importantly, he used his no-nonsense approach and almost obsessive attention to detail to convince the players that second best was not an option. Each year, the tradition grew stronger and Patriot players developed a swagger that only comes with success.

Though Clayton's passion was the catalyst for the transformation, the coach believes that the basics for a winning program were there when he arrived. "I think the keystone for our success out here is the work ethic in this community," Clayton explained.

"All these kids who get involved in this program, if they don't have a work ethic, we're going to teach them real fast. Fortunately for us, most of them do. There's no excuse for a kid in this school not to have a job sometime. There are too many opportunities, and most of the players have jobs. Now (after years of success), people know the work ethic is part of the program."

Heritage Hills players also know that Clayton is a relentless taskmaster who has driven away more than a few who couldn't stand the verbal barrages for which he is famous. His scathing tirades are also tempered with a sarcastic wit, as he shouts out such proclamations as, "It's a beautiful day, gentlemen, and you get to spend it with *me*!" But those players who stick it out and buy into his philosophy believe that they are better people because of Coach Clayton.

"You'd better show up at practice," noted Jon Goldsberry, a star running back in the late '90s. "As a coach, he's ruthless! He knows how to motivate kids, and he has a great football mind. You'd better be ready to go full speed, and you'd better know where you're supposed to be on the field, or he'll let you know about it.

"Until my senior year, I was scared to death of him, but then I realized that this guy really knows what he's talking about. There are kids every year who can't handle the screaming and the workouts. There's so much character and discipline in these Heritage Hills kids, and that carries on to life in general and being successful. But he's also been a good friend and mentor."

When Clayton is asked about the demands he places on his players, he is candid about his approach. "People talk about mental toughness all the time," he began, "and I decided to do a little research and to quit throwing terms around like I knew what I was talking about. The first place I thought about was the military, so I read some books about the Navy SEALS and people like that. Almost every book said that you teach mental discipline through very, very hard physical discipline. If you can get someone to achieve something they didn't think they could do, they find out something about themselves. It really helps them grow."

Coach Clayton is a stickler for detail, and a goof at practice is tantamount to pulling the pin from a grenade. When he was asked about his disciplinary tactics, Clayton was more than willing to explain, using his typical 'colorful' style of speaking. "When there's a mistake made in practice, a bomb goes off. If that ball hits the ground, man, the (stuff) hits the fan. You can't stop during a game; there's no time or place for that on game night. But in practice, you do address those things. We convince these kids that if they make less mistakes than our opponents, we'll win most of our games. We will not tolerate mistakes of any kind, and they get addressed severely in practice."

After 31 years with Clayton at the controls, parents and players get few surprises. They know what they're in for, and they know the odds are very good that they will be part of a winning football team. They also know that Coach Clayton won't forget them when the final second ticks off the clock at the end of a season. The program has seen over 50 of its players move on to play college ball, and Clayton and his staff are often heavily involved in the process. When Tom Goldsberry was an assistant, he and the other coaches decided to devise a system to help those players who wanted to play at the next level. "We had so many good athletes that nobody knew about," Goldsberry said. "So many kids were slipping through the cracks. I got on the internet and looked at these recruiting agencies, and they had these profile sheets, so I printed one out and started making them myself."

Bernice King, the mother of Bruce King, who starred for the Patriots in the early '80s, is very aware of how Clayton sees to it that any player who aspires to play in college gets the opportunity. "When he saw something in a kid," Ms. King explained, "he worked to get recruiters down here to look at the boy. He didn't just let it happen; he worked at it."

In addition to the many Heritage Hills players who have played college ball, it is even more amazing that the small school in rural Spencer County has also seen five of its alumni play professionally. Two of them, Ken Dilger (an '89 grad) and Jay Cutler ('01) reached star status in the NFL, and three others had varying degrees of professional success.

Chris Sigler, who now is on Coach Clayton's staff and serves as the team's 'eye in the sky' in the press box, was an All-State quarterback who also played defensive back for Clayton in the early '80s. Sigler led the Patriots to an undefeated season in 1980 and was selected to the South All-Stars. He was recruited vigorously by the University of Michigan and IU, and he chose the Hoosiers because they arranged for him to play both football and baseball.

After a great career at IU, Sigler had a short career with the Ottawa Rough Riders of the Canadian Football League, and in his very first game tied a CFL record with three interceptions.

Jon Goldsberry had a dynamic combination of size and speed that made him a dominant force for the Patriots in the late '90s and 2000. At 215 pounds, he was an 11-flat sprinter on the track team and a State runner-up in wrestling. On the football field, Jon was a physical linebacker and a punishing runner who played on the Heritage Hills team that was led by quarterback Jay Cutler and won the 2000 State championship.

Goldsberry was also an excellent punter, averaging well over 40 yards and setting the school record for the longest with a 66-yard bomb. He finished his career with school records for the longest run from scrimmage (94 yards) and most rushing yards in a game (205), while scoring 85 TDs and rushing for 3,498 career yards at 9.2 yards per carry.

Jon was recruited by many schools as a punter, but in his mind, "kicking was for sissies." As he became older and wiser, he looked at things differently, saying "Five years later, after five surgeries and getting beat up, I'm thinking, 'I wish I would have been a punter!'"

The injuries he mentioned were tears in his knee (ACL, MCL, and meniscus) during his freshman year at Purdue. No longer the fastest and strongest player on the field, as he was in high school, Goldsberry realized that he'd have to do things he'd never done and work harder than anyone else if he was going to help Coach Joe Tiller and quarterback Drew Brees win football games. Limited in his mobility, the 6'3, 235-pound Goldsberry became a star on special teams and as a lead blocker at fullback, and that experience gave him a shot at the NFL.

Jon fought nagging injuries during a brief NFL career on practice squads and pre-season stints with Buffalo, Tampa Bay and Chicago before limping away to pursue a career in computer graphics and programming. He truly believes that, with a little better luck with injuries, he could have contributed in the NFL. But he is also realistic and appreciates that at least he is one of the small percentage of college players who got to cash an NFL check.

Bruce King was a four-sport athlete for Heritage Hills, earning eleven varsity letters in football, basketball, baseball and track. As a power runner for the Patriots, he teamed with Chris Sigler to produce some of the program's finest years. While at Purdue, Bruce played against Sigler and his Hoosiers and was actually tackled in the open field by his high school buddy. After the tackle, the two good friends laughed and rolled around on the ground, prompting the officials to step in and break up the 'fight'. In Bruce's senior year, the Boilermakers, behind quarterback Jim Everett, accomplished the rare feat of defeating Michigan, Ohio State and Notre Dame in the same season.

After being drafted in the sixth round (126th overall) by the Kansas City Chiefs, King spent a year and a half with K.C. and Buffalo before beginning a career in corporate promotions sales.

When asked if he saw pro potential in any of his five eventual pro players, Bob Clayton was prepared to answer. "You know, I get asked that a lot about these kids, and I can't believe there's a high school coach in the nation who can look at a high school kid and say, 'That boy's going to be an NFL player.' We don't worry about that. My job is to get them to the next level (college), and then what they do from that point on is up to them."

With superb athletes like the five future pros and touchdown machine Cole Seifrig, who holds several school records, such as points scored in a game (42), points in a season (308 in '02) and career points (656), the Patriot program has been a football juggernaut for over thirty years. In the 1980s, Heritage Hills won 70% of their games, and then they won 83% in the '90s and 93% in the 2000s. The Patriots have captured the conference

Bob Clayton has led Heritage Hills to unparalleled success. (Photo courtesy of the Evansville Courier.)

championship 21 times, including a stretch of eleven in a row that started in 1997 and was still going after the 2007 season.

Bob Clayton's Patriots have reached the sectional championship game 18 out of 24 years and have won the Class 3A sectional nine times. They have also captured eight regional titles, two semi-states and one State championship. Clayton's playoff record, as of 2007, is 58-22 (72.5%), and his overall coaching record is 284-62 (83.5%). Perhaps most remarkable is the fact that, in Clayton's 31 years in Santa Claus, the Patriots have suffered a losing season only once, going 4-6 in 1989.

Like a well-oiled machine, the Heritage Hills Patriots keeps pumping out winning seasons year after year as each team develops the persona of its spirited coach. Bob Clayton's philosophy is simple, and it works. Just be who you are, never waver and, last but not least, work your butt off. Clayton is humble enough to not take himself too seriously and cocky enough to believe whole-heartedly that what he is doing is right. With a tireless work ethic, a great staff and the support of dedicated parents and fans, Clayton has conjured up a sure-fire recipe for success.

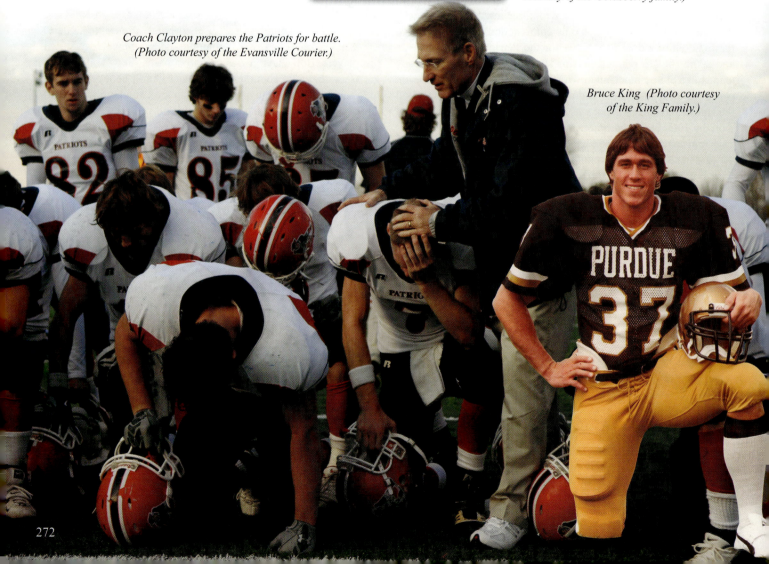

Chris Sigler (Photo courtesy of Indiana University, Media Relations.)

Purdue's Jon Goldsberry holds the Old Oaken Bucket. (Photo courtesy of the Goldsberry family.)

Coach Clayton prepares the Patriots for battle. (Photo courtesy of the Evansville Courier.)

Bruce King (Photo courtesy of the King Family.)

JAY CUTLER: GOD-GIVEN TALENT

By all accounts, Jay Cutler was a natural when it came to athletics, and he made the transition from one sport to another look easy. As his young body developed, his confidence grew as well, and by the time he entered Heritage Hills High School, Patriot fans were expecting great things. And Cutler didn't let them down.

As a high schooler, Cutler was a phenomenal all-around athlete, earning first team All-State honors in both football and basketball and honorable mention as a shortstop in baseball, hitting over .400 as a junior and senior. He was a three-year starter for Coach Bob Clayton at both quarterback and safety, and his teams amassed an amazing 37-2 record with him in the lineup. His junior season, in 2000, was probably the greatest year in Patriot football history, as Heritage Hills outscored opponents 746-85 (roughly 50-6 per game), including a school record 90-0 shellacking of Pike Central. Cutler finished off the dream season in style as he lateraled the ball to Cole Seifrig then caught a pass from Seifrig in the end zone on a crucial play that helped clinch a 27-24 3A State championship win over Zionsville.

As a senior, Cutler broke several school records, including completions for a season (122) and career (248) and yards passing for a season (2,252). As a safety, he intercepted nine passes, ranking him 12th in the state. Jay's all-around athleticism and intelligence enabled him to secure a scholarship to one of the finest academic institutions in the country, and his leadership would help make Vanderbilt University a force in the tough Southeastern Conference.

Cutler started 45 games at Vanderbilt, the most starts by a quarterback in school history, and never missed a game due to injury. In 2002, his freshman season, he set school records for touchdowns (19) and rushing yards by a freshman (393) and rushed for more yards than any other SEC quarterback that year. As a sophomore, his numbers improved, as he completed 187 of 327 passes (57.2%) for 2,347 yards and 18 touchdowns. In his third season, Cutler's efficiency ratings were remarkable with a 61% completion percentage (147 out of 241) for 1,844 yards with ten TDs against only five interceptions. His efficiency rating at the end of the season was an excellent 134.8, the highest of his college career. Although his numbers for his career had been good, they were nothing compared to those he would put up during his senior season in 2005.

Cutler's real emergence occurred during his final season, and NFL pundits jumped on the Cutler bandwagon. Against tough competition, the Santa Claus native scorched opponents for 3,072 yards on 273 of 462 passing (59%) with 21 TDs and only nine INTs. Cutler became the second Commodore to pass for more than 3,000 yards in a season and the first to win the SEC Offensive Player of the Year award since end Bob Goodridge in 1967.

Vanderbilt knocked off solid programs like Arkansas, Ole Miss and Tennessee in 2005 and rang up Florida for 42 points in a double overtime loss to the #13 Gators. When the Commodores ended their season at Tennessee with a 28-24 win, it was Vanderbilt's first over the Vols since 1982, the year before Jay Cutler was born. Jay threw for 315 yards against Tennessee, making him the first QB in school history to pass for 300+ yards in four straight games.

In 2005, Cutler was a first team All-SEC selection, and he finished his tenure at Vanderbilt with several school records, including total offense (9,953 yards), TD passes (59), passing yards (8,697), completions (710) and touchdowns (76). The remarkable thing, however, is that he did it at a school known more for its brains than its brawn, prompting Denver Broncos safety John Lynch to reflect back and tell the press, "If this guy can take a bunch of future doctors and lawyers and have them competing against the Florida Gators, this guy is a stud!"

Jay Cutler had ignited a fire in Commodore fans that they hadn't felt in years, and he also stoked the imaginations of professional scouts and coaches who were now looking at Vanderbilt as an unlikely source for a man who might possibly become a star quarterback in the NFL.

At 6'3 and 230 pounds, Jay certainly had the size of a pro signal caller, and many experts had him ranked third behind QBs Matt Leinert of USC and Vince Young of Texas. Other experts rated him #2 behind Young, and still others, including ESPN's Ron Jaworski and Chris Mortensen, thought Jay's arm strength made him the best quarterback in the draft. Some compared his style to future hall of famer Brett Favre, and Cutler increased his stock value when he bench pressed 225 pounds 23 times and ran a 4.77 40-yard sprint at the NFL scouting combine.

Several teams expressed interest in Cutler, but the Denver Broncos surprised everyone when they traded their 15th and 68th picks to move into position to select Jay with the eleventh

(Photo courtesy of Vanderbilt University, Media Relations.)

pick in the 2006 NFL draft, just behind Young (third) and Leinert (tenth).

Cutler was quickly promoted from Denver's third quarterback to the second spot, ahead of Brad Van Pelt, after his impressive performance at training camp. After a solid preseason, Broncos coach Mike Shanahan announced that he was handing the offense over to Cutler to give the team, in his words, "the best chance to win now."

In his debut after replacing Jake Plummer, Cutler was 10 for 21 for 143 yards with two TDs and two interceptions in a 23-20 loss to the Seattle Seahawks. His second touchdown, to Brandon Marshall, was a 71-yarder that was one of the longest TD passes in a debut in league history.

On December 10th, Jay completed two TD passes to tight end Tony Scheffler in a span of 48 seconds, tying the mark of Charlie Conerly and Bill Swiacki of the New York Giants in 1948 as the fastest in NFL history by two rookies.

Jay won his first NFL game the next week as he earned the best efficiency rating for a Broncos rookie since John Elway's 117.4 during his first season in 1983. Cutler completed 21 of 31 for 261 yards and two touchdowns against one INT for a rating of 101.7 in a 37-20 victory over Arizona.

When Cutler delivered two scoring passes in a 24-23 win over Cincinnati, he set another standard when he became the first rookie QB in NFL history (second overall) to throw for at least two TD passes in his first four games as a pro.

Cutler's first season was inspiring, and he finished the year with a hard-fought overtime loss to the 49ers that left the Broncos one win shy of a playoff spot at 9-7. He finished his first campaign with the third-highest TD to interception ratio (1.8) since 1970 among NFL rookies with at least 125 attempts.

Jay's second season, 2007, was his first full season as the Bronco's starter. He opened the year by passing for 304 yards in a come-from-behind win and directing a 42-yard drive that resulted in a Jason Elam field goal as time ran out. Later in the season, Jay scored his first rushing touchdown against the Colts in the same stadium where he had led the Heritage Hills Patriots to a State title seven years earlier.

Cutler also bested Vince Young's Tennessee Titans in a Monday night game, going 16-21 for 200 yards and two TDs and a passer rating of 137.0. A few games later, he scored an even higher rating in a 41-7 blowout over Kansas City, throwing for a career high four TDs and a rating of 141.0.

Although the Broncos missed the playoffs again at 7-9, Cutler started every game and put up good numbers. He completed 63.6% of his passes (297-467) for 3,497 yards. He also tossed for 20 touchdowns with only 14 interceptions. His passing yardage and completion percentage ranked as the seventh- and third-best, respectively, in franchise history.

Jay Cutler led Vanderbilt into uncharted waters. (Photo courtesy of Vanderbilt University, Media Relations.)

Cutler has always been the kind of athlete who never backed down from a challenge, and in 2008, during the off-season, he was faced with one that caught him completely by surprise. In May, he announced that he had developed Type I diabetes and cited weight loss at the end of the 2007 season as an early indicator. Although he will be insulin-dependent, experts have stated that the disease is very treatable and that it should not preclude him from continuing his NFL career. Just as many others have done, including baseball stars Jackie Robinson and the Cubs' Ron Santo, Jay's competitive fire will help in his fight to overcome the disease.

From the time Jay Cutler was young, he has had a desire to excel and a knack for defying the odds. With support from fans back home, it is a good bet that Jay will use the same God-given talents that made him a multi-sport star at Heritage hills to continue his career as one of the best young quarterbacks in the NFL.

KEN DILGER: SUPER BOWL CHAMPION

Heritage Hills High School has an amazing record for developing pro football players, and the most successful of them all was a player who was not highly recruited and had to adjust to a position he'd never played before. With his small town upbringing as a foundation, Ken Dilger carved out an impressive career as a professional by becoming a mainstay for the Indianapolis Colts and a go-to-guy for the Super Bowl champion Tampa Bay Buccaneers.

Dilger was raised in the small town of Mariah Hill by his parents, Dennis and Jane. Ken and his two older brothers, Kevin and Keith, were all blessed with good size, and they learned the virtues of hard work by watching their father as he put in long hours as a mechanic in the family business. Ken spent his summers baling hay and doing carpentry work, which helped develop his physique and prepared him for what lay ahead as an athlete.

When he entered Heritage Hills in 1985, Dilger was 6'1 and was part of the early success that eventually evolved into perennial football dominance by the Patriots and made them one of the most respected programs in the state. The 1980 team, which starred Chris Sigler and Bruce King, had finished undefeated, and Dilger's teams continued the success, winning 24 of 30 games his last three seasons there.

(Photo courtesy of the University of Illinois, Sports Information.)

During his high school career, Dilger was a three-sport athlete, earning All-Conference honors as a frontline player in basketball and as a pitcher/outfielder in baseball. In football, the 6'5, 215-pounder stood out in more ways than one as a quarterback and strong safety. "He was a big kid," said head coach Bob Clayton. "He was the biggest kid on the team. He was bigger than all our linemen. He could run a quarterback sneak for five yards, and we threw the ball a lot and put him in the Shotgun (Formation)."

After earning a spot on the South All-Stars, Ken began the process of finding a college. As a quarterback from a small school, he hadn't gotten the publicity to attract interest from many larger schools, so he looked hard at teams like Ball State, Indiana State and Toledo. Very late in the process, the University of Illinois entered the picture. With just one week left before the signing deadline, Coach Clayton received a call that gave Dilger an option that seemed all but impossible the day before.

"Randy Rogers, who had coached at the University of Evansville, had gone to the University of Illinois as an assistant coach," Coach Clayton explained. "He called about Ken and said, 'Can we get him to come over? It's the last weekend for a visit.' So he did, and the Sunday night before Ken got back, Randy called me and put (Illini head coach) John Mackovick on the phone. He said, 'This is the kid we love; we want him.'

"He said all their scholarships were gone and Ken would have to come in January (and they would get him a scholarship). They couldn't put it in writing because it's illegal."

According to Clayton, the process known as 'gray-shirting' is common and is based on the athlete taking the coach at his word.

"I talked to Kenny's parents," Clayton added, "and they decided to go with it because Randy Rogers, who I felt was an ethical man, assured me that Mackovick was ethical, too. And it worked out for Ken because that year, he went in and winter-weightlifted and participated in spring ball. Then the next year, he red-shirted and got bigger, stronger and learned the system."

With a stronger body and a year's exposure at Illinois, Ken began to work to earn a spot with the Illini, but circumstances developed that would create yet another option for Ken as a player.

With six quarterbacks on the roster, Ken didn't get much practice time during the first two weeks. The offensive coordinator explained the situation as a logjam at the QB position and informed Ken that, at the tight end position, there were only two seniors and two redshirt freshmen. Dilger thought the solution was obvious and made the transition.

Ken admits that it took awhile to get used to the physicality, but he felt that he was a natural for the position as he learned it. It also helped that he bulked up to 255 pounds.

In 1993, Dilger's senior year, the Illini finished 8-4 and beat East Carolina in the Memphis Liberty Bowl, and during the telecast, the announcer spoke of the young tight end's NFL potential. Although he had a solid season, Ken was overshadowed by three outstanding linebackers at Illinois who were media darlings: Dana Howard, everybody's All-American; Simeon Rice, the #1 pick in the NFL draft; and Evansville's own Kevin Hardy, a #2 NFL draft pick.

Dilger was selected as a second-team All-Big Ten tight end and began to work NFL combines in February to hopefully sell the scouts and coaches on his potential as a pro. After completing the physical drills and interviews used by teams to evaluate a player's mental makeup, Dilger was selected by the Indianapolis Colts in the second round (#48 overall) of the 1995 NFL draft. After a Big Ten career that almost didn't happen and a position change that Ken never would have imagined, he was returning to Indiana as a professional football player.

As the Colts experienced several ups and downs, Dilger's contributions were major during his stay in Indy. As a rookie, he caught 42 passes, most of which were delivered by Jim Harbaugh. The Colts had a great season, falling one game short of the Super Bowl, losing a 20-16 heartbreaker to Pittsburgh when Colt receiver Aaron Bailey dropped a pass in the end zone in the closing seconds.

In '96, Marvin Harrison was chosen in the first round by the Colts and Indy finished 9-7 during an injury-filled season in Lindy Infante's first year after replacing Ted Marchibroda as the Colts' head coach. Dilger was steady once again, with 51 catches in what would prove to be the most productive season of his career.

The Colts suffered a miserable year in '97, losing the first ten games before finishing 3-13. The Colts were plagued once again by injuries and also lost team owner Bob Irsay, whose death enabled son Jim to take over and clean house. Again, Dilger was productive with 43 catches.

In 1998, the Colts welcomed new president Bill Polian, new coach Jim Mora and #1 draft pick Peyton Manning. Ken snared 31 passes during a 3-13 season that featured flashes of brilliance from the talented QB out of the University of Tennessee. When asked if he saw the potential in Manning, Ken says that it was easy to see that great things were ahead for the young quarterback. "You could tell he came from a great background of football knowledge," Dilger replied. "He came in right away and took control of the huddle. By the way he played the game, you could tell he would be one of the all-time greats."

The Colts surprised everyone when they selected Miami running back Edgerin James over the highly-touted Ricky Williams of Texas in the '99 draft. Dilger grabbed 40 passes as Manning and Marvin Harrison started to gel and James was a force on the ground. The Colts set an NFL record for the largest turnaround when they totally reversed their '98 season with a 13-3 record. Talk of a Super Bowl came to a sudden halt, however, when the Colts' porous defense was exposed in a first round playoff loss to the Tennessee Titans.

Dilger continued his steady play for the next two years, with 47 and 32 catches, respectively, and earned Pro Bowl honors in 2001. As plans were made for the 2002 season and new head coach Tony Dungy was brought in, Ken received the biggest shock of his career. Out of the blue, he was notified that he would be saying good-bye to the team that he considered family and the city that he called home.

As Dilger prepared for a trip to his first Pro Bowl, he received a note via Federal Express. It seems the Colts management was concerned with the limited mobility that resulted from cartilage damage in his left knee. They were also concerned about Ken's scheduled $1.64 million salary for 2002. Although their reasons may have had merit, what broke Dilger's heart the most was the cowardly method used to deliver the news.

"We didn't know it was coming. My agent didn't even know," Dilger said from his home in Indianapolis. "You know, you spend seven years with a team and become a fixture in the community, and all of a sudden they release you with no warning. It kind of shocked everybody."

Dilger never really understood the Colts' reasoning and has said that he would have gladly taken a pay cut to remain a Colt. The hurt was obvious when he spoke to a reporter from the *St. Petersburg Times* in 2002. "Yeah, it hurt," Dilger confessed. "I only missed three games and played through every injury you could imagine. I never really got a reason, an answer. Bill Polian never called me to let me know why. He just didn't want me around there anymore, I guess."

Fortunately for Ken, there was a team who appreciated his abilities. Jon Gruden, head coach of the Tampa Bay Buccaneers, felt that Dilger could provide something the Bucs were lacking. One of their tight ends, Dave Moore, was a much better receiver than a blocker, and their other tight end, Todd Yoder, was just the opposite. With Dilger, they found a man who could play in any situation, as an excellent receiver and a man who could block the huge and athletic defensive ends in the NFL.

At 31 and aching from knee pain, Dilger considered retirement, but Gruden's persistence convinced him to re-think his plans. With Ken anchored at tight end, he was part of something that his teams in Indy had never accomplished. In his very first year with Tampa Bay, Dilger was part of the ultimate NFL experience. He and his Buc teammates did something the Colts could not do. They walked out of Qualcomm Stadium in San Diego on January 26th, 2003 as the Super Bowl champions after knocking off Gruden's former team, the Oakland Raiders, 48-21.

After two more seasons in Tampa Bay, Ken's physical aches and pains began to take their toll, and the big man evaluated his situation. "I had had four knee surgeries during my college and pro career," Ken said. "I was still playing 90% of the plays, and it was taking a toll on my body." With the prospect of more pounding for another season and the fact that his daughter was going to start kindergarten, Ken and his wife, Heidi, decided it was time to start phase two of their life together. With no regrets, they packed up and returned to a place they'd always thought of as home, Indianapolis.

Over ten seasons of NFL ball, Ken had caught 356 passes for 4,099 yards and 24 touchdowns. He had also appeared in one Pro Bowl and secured a Super Bowl ring, not a bad resumé for a kid from Mariah Hill, Indiana. In his final game in the NFL, Dilger displayed his versatility and value as a team player when he played tight end and also became the team's long snapper because of an injury to a teammate.

Dilger wasn't the first Bob Clayton protégé to make it as a pro, but he was by far the most successful. No matter how long Heritage Hills continues to produce professional football players, one thing will never change: history will always show that Ken Dilger was the first to make it big and the first to earn a Super Bowl ring.

JASPER'S MATT MAUCK: NATURAL TALENT, NATURAL LEADER

From his days as a multi-sport athlete at Jasper High School to his unusual journey to an NCAA national championship, Matt Mauck stayed grounded and kept his priorities in order. His athletic career was not marked by gaudy statistics or highlight reel performances but was best exemplified by his leadership and his ability to raise the level of his game when the stakes were highest.

Although Mauck was born in Evansville, his family moved to Jasper when Matt was only two weeks old. Roger Mauck, Matt's father, played football at Evansville College, and he and his wife Kathy supported all three of their children in their athletic activities while they were growing up. Older brother Geoff competed in football, wrestling and track at Jasper and now serves as the offensive coordinator for Jasper's football team. Younger sister Libby was a pitcher on her high school softball team and was a setter on the volleyball team at Tusculum College in Tennessee.

As a youngster, Matt was not the type to veg on the couch. "From the time I was able to walk, I always had a ball in my hand," Matt said. "My next door neighbor was Phil Buehler, and we both loved sports and were outside all the time. We had the original Nintendo and that was the only thing I've ever had, and I didn't even play that. So I think the big difference for me from kids you see now is that we were outside all the time, especially in the summer."

As Matt grew, he paid his dues and developed toughness by serving as a tackling dummy for his brother and Geoff's good friend Scott Rolen. As Matt grew and matured, he was the star running back for the junior high teams, but the coaches approached him with other plans. "They tried to convince me to play quarterback," he explained, "but I had no interest because, at Jasper, the quarterback is not a glamorous position."

As Mauck entered the high school program, the team's personnel presented the first opportunity for him to demonstrate his leadership qualities and his team-first mentality. "My freshman year, we had Kevin Cartwright, who was a pretty good running back a year ahead of me," Matt recalled, "so it looked like it would be good for the program if we could get both of us in the game. Pat True was my freshman coach and convinced me to give quarterback a try. I always threw the ball well, but at Jasper you just don't grow up dreaming of being the quarterback."

Matt Mauck gains ground for the Jasper Wildcats. (Photo courtesy of Jasper High School.)

Matt slowly fell in love with the position and earned the starting quarterback spot as a sophomore, leading the team to the State semi-finals before losing to Indianapolis Roncalli. In his junior year, Cartwright's senior year, Jasper advanced one game farther but lost in the final game of the 1997 State Tournament to South Bend St. Joe. As a result of the team's success, Mauck began to receive letters of interest from colleges, but his all-around athletic abilities would open up another option before his high school career was over.

In addition to his talents on the gridiron, Matt also stood out on the basketball court and especially on the baseball diamond. For years, he traveled with a baseball team called the Indiana Bulls that was made up of some of the best players in the state and traveled the country. Matt knew the experience was beneficial, but with the hectic schedule, he knew that something had to go. The decision was a no-brainer, and he opted to forgo his senior season of basketball, even though it was his favorite sport. "I never had a time to enjoy myself," Matt explained. "I wanted a break, and it looked like I was going to get drafted (in baseball), so I felt like I should concentrate on baseball."

Mauck's evaluation was spot on, and his focus on football and baseball produced excellent results, creating a dilemma that was both invigorating and gut-wrenching. As a senior quarterback, Matt guided the Wildcats to a 7-2 record, passing for 940 yards and rushing for 567. Although his potential was stymied because of Coach Jerry Brewer's ground-oriented style, Mauck's intelligence and leadership still created interest from college coaches, especially Coach Lou Saban from Michigan State.

In baseball, Matt was even more amazing, and he impressed Jasper baseball coach Terry Gobert with more than just his skills. Gobert had seen Mauck's physical potential early on, but he was also sold on Matt as an individual, as well. "He was a man-child," Gobert said. "When he was a freshman, he looked like he was 22 years old.

"Here's a guy who played third base for three years (Mauck joined the program as Jasper great Scott Rolen left), and his senior year, I moved him to center field for the team's sake. And he also pitched a lot more."

As Gobert reflected on Mauck's senior season, his respect for the young man was obvious. His greatest memory was of the 1997 State Tournament and how Matt rose to the occasion to help Jasper earn its second straight title and the state's last under the one-class system. "He beat Richmond (as a pitcher), who was ranked #1, in the semi-state," Gobert pointed out. "We had to take him to the hospital the night before because he was dehydrated. Normally, he threw the ball in the mid-80s, but he was over 90 miles per hour that day and pitched the game of his life. We won the State, and he won the Mental Attitude Award."

Matt finished his senior season a perfect 10-0 on the mound and 20-4 for his career, and as a result of his performance both on the mound and as a position player, the 6'3, 210-pounder was named Indiana's Mr. Baseball. As he looked back on his senior year, Mauck knew that a tough decision would have to be made very soon.

"I really wanted to play both (football and basketball) in college," Matt pointed out. After being told that Coach Saban would allow him to do both, Mauck pondered his situation. As a straight-A student, he wanted to further his education by studying Pre-Med, but he was also intrigued with the possibility of major league baseball.

"Scott Rolen kind of opened the doors for a lot of guys (by bringing in major league scouts)," Mauck explained. "Phil Kendall (from Jasper) was drafted the year before me by the Brewers. A lot of scouts would come around during the off-season to look at me. For me, it was always my dream to play a sport professionally. It all happened so fast that, to me, it just made sense to give it a try."

Mauck was selected by the Chicago Cubs in the sixth round of the 1997 major league draft, and after breaking the news to Coach Saban, he headed to Mesa, Arizona for Rookie Ball. At Mesa, Matt was given the option of pitching or playing in the field, and he started his career well, hitting .285 as a third baseman.

In his second year, Terry Kennedy, a long-time big league catcher, thought that Mauck reminded him of himself and suggested that Matt try catching. Mauck had never worn catching gear before, and when he did put it on, it appeared that fate stepped in. "It was funny," Mauck noted, "just after I switched to catcher, the Cubs drafted Jeff Goldbach (from Princeton, Indiana), so he and I were competing against each other."

As the second season wore on, Matt was becoming disillusioned and felt that something was missing. "When you play minor league baseball, you have to LOVE baseball. For me, I missed the camaraderie of football and team sports," Matt explained, "Baseball is said to be a team sport, but it's very individualized. So, for me, it just didn't match up with my personality."

Matt found himself playing A-Ball with the Lansing Lugnuts in Michigan for his third season. Coincidentally, Lansing is the home of Michigan State University. On one of his days off, Mauck scheduled a sit-down with Lou Saban and expressed his feelings in hopes of finding an answer to a lingering question. "You know, I like baseball, but I don't know if it's something I can do for a long time," he told Saban. "Is it still an option for me to come here and play football?"

Saban's response: "We've got a scholarship waiting for you if you want it. Just let me know."

Matt had a great second half of his third season, hitting over .300, but he had an epiphany midway through his fourth season: "If you're not passionate about something, you shouldn't do it," he realized.

It was time to move on, and Mauck enjoys joking with people today saying, "I retired from baseball at age 21."

By this time, Coach Saban had left the Spartans for LSU, but when Mauck called, the "welcome, Matt" was still out. Matt was excited about the decision, and it quickly became obvious that he was not the typical college player. "I got along with everybody, but what helped me was that I hadn't gone to school for three years and I looked forward to going to class and learning," Matt said. "A lot of guys dreaded going to class because they had come straight from high school."

In July of 2000, Mauck went to work on strengthening his arm, because he hadn't picked up a football in a long time. Though he was a bit rusty, his maturity and leadership skills were evident to everyone. In an article for *Sports Illustrated*, Coach Saban spoke of Mauck's work ethic, citing how Matt would stay late to take extra snaps. In the same article, a teammate called Mauck "the hardest worker on the team."

Entering his second year, Matt was still a backup, and when the time came, he admitted that "it felt good to just get hit again" because the contact was something he hadn't felt in five years. At the end of the season, the Tigers had made it to the SEC championship game against #2-ranked Tennessee, and Matt's parents, Roger and Kathy, took their seats at the south end of the Georgia Dome to watch the game. Little did they know that they were about to witness a turning point in their son's career.

After starting QB Rohan Davey left the game with a broken rib, Matt's parents were shocked when their son jogged onto the field. Their fears subsided, however, when Matt proceeded to lead the Tigers to scores on six of seven drives. With his 4.5 speed (in the 40-yard dash), Mauck rushed for two touchdowns in a 31-20 upset and helped LSU earn a berth in the Sugar Bowl, their first major bowl bid in fourteen years. In the process, Mauck was also named the game's MVP.

In '02, Matt won the starting job over Marcus Randall and Rick Clausen and led LSU to a 5-1 record before tearing ligaments in his right foot, ending his season. As he rehabbed the injury, he began to see the misfortune as a blessing in disguise. "The rehab probably helped me more than anything," he admitted. "Before that, I was more of a running quarterback. Because of my foot, I couldn't do that anymore, so I spent the whole time working on my drop back passing and really improved as a thrower."

Matt earned back his starting position as the 2003 season began, but the 25-year- old had no idea that he was heading for an experience that seemed next to impossible a few short years earlier. After an 11-1 regular season, losing only to Florida, LSU topped

Matt Mauck delivers a pass against Tennessee. (Photo courtesy of Louisiana State University, Sports Information.)

Georgia in the conference championship game. After much controversy, Southern Cal, who was #1-ranked in both polls but #3 in the BCS ranking, was the odd man out, leaving the Tigers to battle Oklahoma for the national championship.

On January 4th, 2004, Mauck led his 6-point underdog Tigers to victory over powerful Oklahoma. In front of a national audience, he methodically led his offense while the defense dominated the Sooners in a 21-14 win. Mauck overcame several sacks and finished the game with 13 completions in 22 attempts for 126 yards to enable LSU to share the national title with USC.

Although Matt still had a year of eligibility left at LSU, he decided that, at 25 years old and with his stock as a quarterback at an all-time high, it was time to enter the 2004 NFL draft. He was selected in the seventh round by the Denver Broncos but was cut after his first season and then picked up by the Tennessee Titans. He spent the whole 2005 season on the active roster at Tennessee and started the final game against the Jacksonville Jaguars, but it soon became obvious that his future with the team was in jeopardy.

Entering the 2006 season, Mauck became expendable to the Titans and was cut when they drafted Vince Young and signed Kerry Collins as a free agent. After week two, he was re-signed to the Titans' practice squad. With three games to go in the season, Matt herniated a disc in his spine that cut off contact with a nerve in his calf. The damage killed the nerve, and Matt is hoping, even today, that the nerve will regenerate.

Although Matt Mauck's NFL career was cut short, it doesn't diminish what he accomplished during his playing days. From the time he was young, he has been successful wherever he's been, and although athletics played a major role in his life, it never defined who he was. While pursuing his sports dreams, Matt was always aware of the importance of academics. He knew that if his body ever let him down, his mind would be there to pick him up. Today, he is hoping to either play again or head to dental school while he and his wife Jill start a family. Regardless of how things work out, if his past is any indication, it's a safe bet that, whatever the future holds for Matt Mauck, he will be a winner.

MICHAEL LEWIS

Michael Lewis was one of the most prolific scorers in Indiana high school history, and the 1996 grad set a standard at Jasper High School that may last for many years to come. The southpaw took to the game naturally as the son of Dennis Lewis, the current athletic director at Jasper, and the grandson of the popular ex-commissioner of the IHSAA Gene Cato. Michael currently holds seven of the fourteen top spots on Jasper's all-time list for points in a game, ranging from 41 to 46 points, and is the school's career scoring leader with 2,138 points. He is also the school's single-season leader with 852 points and holds Jasper's top two spots for season scoring average with 31.6 ('95-'96) and 27.1 ('94-'95).

As a senior, Michael led the state in scoring, was a first team All-Stater and was named to the Indiana All-Stars. His scoring ability and all-around game earned the 6'2 fireball a scholarship to play for Bob Knight at IU. During his years with the Hoosiers, Lewis' respect for 'the General' grew, but his hard-nosed competitive nature occasionally led to confrontations with the equally-stubborn Knight.

Over the years, the volatile relationship helped Lewis develop into a player that Knight grew to respect. Playing with All-American A.J. Guyton for four years required Lewis to change his mindset, and his versatility and unselfish attitude enabled him to make the adjustments. Amazingly, the scoring machine from southern Indiana finished his career in 2000 as IU's all-time career assist leader with 545, including a remarkable 15 in one game. Instead of challenging Calbert Cheaney's scoring record, he placed his name at the top of the assist list above such players as Quinn Buckner, Isiah Thomas and Damon Bailey. He also finished tenth on the all-time career list in steals, and holds the second spot for steals in a game with eight.

Ironically, during his senior year, Lewis played for Knight in the first game ever played in the new arena at Texas Tech. No one could have known at the time that Knight's tumultuous career at IU would end after Lewis' senior season and that Knight would soon return to Lubbock as the coach of the Red Raiders with Michael Lewis as his graduate assistant. After two years at Texas Tech, Lewis left to join the staff at Eastern Illinois with the intention of using his talents and competitive nature to build a coaching career of his own.

(Photos courtesy of Jasper High School.)

SUPER FAN!

Jasper super fan Frank Ebenkamp has bled black and gold for over eighty years. To illustrate his dedication and loyalty, when he started his stopwatch at Jasper's first track meet in 2008, it marked his 63rd consecutive year working as a timer for the Wildcats.

Frank Ebenkamp
(Photo courtesy of Jasper High School.)

IHSAA STATE CHAMPIONS:
BOYS TENNIS

Team	Year	Coach
Jasper	1999 - 2000	Ed Yarbrough

Individual	School	Year
James Sublett	North	1973-1974
Brian Ritz	Day School	1986-1987

STEPHANIE HAZLETT: A COMPETITOR AT EVERY LEVEL

Stephanie Christine Hazlett wasn't born with a tennis racquet in her hand, but it didn't take long for her mother to realize that it might be a good idea to give it a try. "At about age two, she was always batting something," recalled Anna Hazlett, Stephanie's mother. "She'd use a broom or whatever to knock anything that would roll on the ground. She would hit balls and break windows. And she had this competitive drive in her, even when we would play Candyland or Chutes & Ladders, she'd get mad when she didn't win."

In the early years, Anna was careful to give her daughter the exposure and guidance she needed without crossing the line that could have led to frustration or burnout. And it may very well have been those decisions made in Stephanie's formative years that allowed her to become a champion in high school, on the junior circuit, in college, and as a professional.

Although she came from a golfing family, Stephanie's mother became an accomplished tennis player herself after she was discovered by the tennis coach while playing recreationally at Florida State. Her athleticism enabled her make the school's tennis team and then move on to compete on the Virginia Slims Tour, the forerunner of today's WTA. A few years later, she would use those experiences to guide her daughter through the challenges of competitive tennis.

When asked when she first saw Stephanie's true potential as a player, Anna thought briefly and then answered, "I could see it probably at around ten that she had a lot of athletic ability. But it also helped that we lived out in the country, because it did not allow her to get on the court every day, something some overzealous parents might have insisted upon."

Both Stephanie and Anna agreed that another wise decision was finding someone else to coach the talented youngster. "When we were on court, we butted heads, just mother and daughter stuff," Stephanie admitted. "Having my mom out there telling me what to do that wasn't mother-daughter related, I just didn't like it."

Mom was quick to agree. "If you're going head-to-head every day on the court and also head-to-head at home," Anna explained, "well, too much of a good thing wasn't a good thing. When we traveled (on the junior circuit), it worked out well because we couldn't always afford to send a coach with her, so since we had that separation during the actual training, we worked together well when we traveled."

Both Anna and Stephanie's father, Steve, shared the responsibilities of trying to maintain a normal life while being immersed in the grind that is junior tennis. Until she was twelve, Stephanie played other sports also. "I played soccer and softball," she pointed out, "and then when I was twelve, I qualified for the 14 & under (tennis) Nationals. I was also on the select soccer team and the all-star softball team, all at the same time, and it was just too much. And that's kind of when I had to make a decision about what I wanted to do."

During her junior tennis career, Stephanie won countless titles. Among them were the Midwest Open Championships (with participants from six states) in 12 & under, 14s, 16s and 18s; the Gateway in St. Louis (back-to-back) in the 18 & under; and the National Clay Court Championship in doubles.

One sacrifice Stephanie made was missing out on some of her high school experiences during her years at Heritage Hills. In addition to missing several social events, her travels even limited her availability to play on the school's tennis team. As a freshman, she was undefeated until the State Finals, when she was beaten by Bonnie Bleecker of Indianapolis, who, ironically, would later become a college teammate.

Stephanie was also undefeated her sophomore year but did not play in the State Tournament because she had won the highly prestigious Easter Bowl tournament and was invited by the USTA to represent her country in Europe.

Her junior season at Heritage Hills culminated in Stephanie's only State championship, following another undefeated season. She wasn't able to compete her senior year because she graduated a semester early to move to Tampa, Florida's Palmer Tennis Academy. From there, she stayed in Australia for a few weeks to play some professional tournaments (as an amateur) before returning home to graduate with her class.

Throughout her years at Heritage Hills, she won a State title and was one of the most sought-after high school players in the country by college tennis coaches. After careful consideration,

(Photo courtesy of the Hazlett family.)

Stephanie decided to play for a consistent national contender, the University of Florida Gators.

As a freshman at Florida, Stephanie was a member of the Gators' NCAA championship team. Playing Duke for the title at Notre Dame, it was Stephanie's victory over Kathy Sell at #5 singles that clinched the win and launched the celebration. Sell, from New Jersey, was a familiar opponent to Stephanie because they had met several times on the junior circuit.

Although Florida did not win another national title, they did finish in the top three in the country for the rest of Stephanie's college career, and Stephanie was twice named an All-American.

After discussing her options with her parents, Stephanie decided that, after graduation, she would test her skills at the professional level. It didn't take long for Stephanie and Anna to realize that, unlike the WTA's (Women's Tennis Association's) top tier, where players live like royalty and travel with entourages, the lower level tours can take a heavy toll in more ways than one.

First of all, the tour is not cheap, and Stephanie was aware of the sacrifices her family was making to help her with expenses. She started at the $10,000-level tournaments (like the one she won here in Evansville) and then eventually moved up to the $25,000 and, eventually, the $75,000 level. After a while, she was paying her expenses with her winnings and was competing against players who ranked in the top 100 in the world. But after two and a half years, the challenges of the tour were more than Stephanie could bear.

"When I finished playing on the tour, I was #260 in the world, so I didn't quit playing because I wasn't successful," Stephanie explained. "I quit because I wasn't happy; I wasn't enjoying the lifestyle. I was traveling all over the world by myself from tournament to tournament, bag to bag, hotel to hotel. Making all the travel arrangements, trying to play at a high level, going to countries where I didn't know the language, it just wore on me. I called my mom and said, 'I'm lonely, and I'm not happy.'

"As a pro, I went to Australia, Mexico, Hawaii. I was scheduled to go to Japan when I came home because I ended up in the hospital. I had full body cramps from dehydration after playing in the jungle in Mexico. After a three-set match, they had to take me off the court on a gurney. It was April of '04, and I felt like someone had beaten me with a bat."

Stephanie returned home and, after she recuperated, joined her mother running the high performance program at Advantage Court & Fitness in downtown Evansville. She is now sharing her passion with students who range in age from ten to eighteen. Some of her protegés (in 2007) included Harrison's Whitney Wilson, who earned a full ride to Michigan State; Memorial's Maria Casaletto, who was on her way to West Point on a full ride; and Ben Carroll from Memorial.

As a teacher, Stephanie knows that physical fundamentals are important, but she quickly points out that it was the mental side that made her a standout. "I thrived under pressure," she said with conviction. "I loved it. The closer the match, the better I played. I'm on court six to eight hours a day teaching, and I'm not physically in shape to play. And, I'm telling you, as competitive as I am, if I'd go out and try to compete, I'd probably hurt myself. I'm hitting all the time (with students), but it's nowhere near the level I'm used to competing at."

It's easy to see why Stephanie Hazlett was so successful as her jaw tightens and her eyes focus while she talks about why she loves to compete. There is no doubt that she is one of the finest tennis talents to come out of this area, and her records over the years are proof of her success. Perhaps the person who best put her talents in perspective is Ross Brown, the former tennis coach at U of E and current coach at USI. He once told Anna that he didn't realize until several years after Stephanie was in college how rare it is, and that someone with her ability just doesn't come along very often.

Stephanie stretches to return a shot while playing doubles at Florida. (Photo courtesy of the Hazlett family.)

Even at age seven, Stephanie had excellent concentration. (Photo courtesy of the Evansville Courier)

MATER DEI WRESTLING: DECADES OF DOMINANCE

When it comes to the sport of wrestling, no school in the state of Indiana has shown more consistency over the years than Evansville Mater Dei. Under the leadership of two outstanding coaches, each with their own special talents, the Wildcats' wrestling program has served as a (red and) gold standard in one of the most grueling and mentally challenging sports known to mankind.

Wrestling is a sport that exposes an athlete in ways no other sport does. When he's on the mat, a wrestler has no place to hide, as every flaw and every emotion is exposed. There are no teammates to blame and no excuse about the opponent having a size advantage. As the young man squares off with the enemy, the anguish, the anxiety and the pain are out there for the world to see.

The sport is also physically taxing, not only on the days of matches but on the practice mats as well. The discipline it takes to make weight is also unique, as the young men shun simple temptations to which every other teenager can succumb without consequence. For several months out of the year, a candy bar, a donut or even a juicy steak are as much an obstacle as the opponents the wrestler faces. The sport requires absolute dedication and mental toughness, and it would not be an exaggeration to say that no wrestlers reflect the values of their coach as those who have toiled under the tutelage of Mater Dei's Mike Goebel (pronounced GAY-bul).

Mike Goebel was born and raised in Evansville, the middle child of a family of 17 children. Along with his eight brothers and eight sisters (all born within a 26-year span), Mike worked the truck farm owned by his parents, John and Rita Goebel.

Andy Goebel was the first son to play sports at Mater Dei and set the example for the others to follow, including Mike. After graduating from St. Phillips Elementary School, Mike was a two-year starter in both wrestling and football at Mater Dei before his graduation in 1970.

Amazingly, Goebel graduated from USI in just 3½ years while working the night shift at the Evansville Association for the Blind, a sheltered factory workshop. He graduated in December of 1973 with a degree in Social Studies and taught for a semester at Christ the King before taking a job at Mater Dei. For three years, he assisted in both football and wrestling before being lured away to become the head wrestling coach at Castle High School. In 1978, Mike returned to his alma mater to head up the wrestling program and coach the JV football team. For 18 years, he called the offensive plays for Coach Frank Will until he was named the head football coach upon Will's retirement in 1996.

When Goebel accepted the football position, it was unusual for a person to hold the head coaching position in two unrelated sports, and Mike quickly learned the challenges involved. "It takes a lot of time, and you have to have great assistant coaches and a lot of good support," Goebel confessed. "It's pretty consuming organizing wrestling camps and summer workouts. You have football camps and fund-raisers and on-site camps for freshmen through varsity and youth football, and we have a collegiate wrestling camp here in June (2007)."

Although he is known far and wide for his wrestling program, Goebel has also built an impressive resumé in football, and he's very aware of the obstacles his program faces as a small Catholic school. "We learned a long time ago with the (lack of) size of our kids, you can't go toe-to-toe," Goebel revealed. "So we try to do things to neutralize or equalize. The first guy I sat down with was U of E coach Randy Rogers, and I got a lot of great ideas from him. I like the wide open offense, and we've been fortunate to have some very good quarterbacks.

"Defensively, I've had great luck with Darin Knight and my brother Gary Goebel as defensive coordinators. They shoo me away during games, and I have every confidence in them." The system seems to work, as the Wildcats are perennial contenders despite competing against much larger SIAC schools, and when the season's over and the class system kicks in, Mater Dei is usually battle-tested and ready to make a tournament run. The run-and-gun style has served them well over the years, with a 2A State title in 2000 and a runner-up finish in '01.

Goebel realized that in a small school atmosphere, athletes are expected to spread their talents over multiple sports out of necessity, and he has opted to look at the situation as a positive one for both his sports. "We encourage our kids to play other sports," Goebel pointed out. "In my mind, wrestling and football go so well together. I can pick out a wrestler on a football field any day, and most of them are on defense. On our defense this past year ('07), nine of our eleven starters were wrestlers. In order to compete in wrestling, you have to be skilled in defending yourself – hand control, balance, one-on-one situations. A lot of the techniques used in wrestling are the same you use in tackling."

Although Goebel is one of the most respected football coaches in the area, it is his wrestling program that sets him apart from mere mortals. In a sport he hadn't even heard of until he was a freshman in high school, he has developed a system that has become the benchmark in the state and has produced records that may never be equaled again in the world of Indiana high school wrestling.

Every year, he and long-time sidekick Randy Helfrich evaluated 50 to 60 wrestlers and transformed an elite few into a powerhouse that dominated its competition year in and year out. The mystique that toyed with the psyches of opponents seemed almost supernatural, but Goebel believes the explanation of Mater Dei's success is really very basic and that it started from the time his wrestlers were very young.

"Almost all of them wrestled in our feeder program," Goebel said. "We had grade school coaches at each school, and we had our own meets. Some kids started in kindergarten. Our coaches are great, and they're all volunteers. It's pretty exciting around here on a Sunday afternoon when our grade school wrestling's going on, because this gym is packed. All the schools wrestle at once."

Goebel is also quick to respond when asked about past accusations that the Catholic schools recruit to get the best athletes. "We have zero kids come here from public schools," he disclosed. "Every football player and every wrestler started out here. The bonds are strong here. I passed out bios at the State wrestling finals and every wrestler on our varsity this year ('07) had at least one parent who graduated from here, and every one of our wrestlers went to one of our Catholic feeder schools."

The "bond" that Goebel mentioned is also a key ingredient in the formula for Mater Dei's unparalleled success. "We have fan support that I think is second to none," Goebel noted. "We wrestled Mishawaka and we had them outnumbered three, maybe four (fans) to one. For our athletes, it's a privilege to wrestle in front of a crowd like that because they get the energy from the crowd."

Mike's sister, Joyce Rhoades, has been a loyal fan for nearly fifty years and is well aware of the difference the crowd makes. "Mike says that the fans are the adrenaline that keeps the wrestlers going," Joyce said. "I've been around since 1959, and I've seen great-grandparents there and grandparents and uncles and cousins. It's just continuous."

Family loyalty is one reason the Mater Dei roster has featured names like Weinzapfel, Mayer, Boots and Zenthoefer over several generations.

Those who have witnessed a Mater Dei wrestling crowd know that their presence is much more than just numbers. The red and gold-clad mob are also more than willing to express their opinions during the course of the event, which doesn't always endear them to opposing fans. Wildcat fans also know that, as a known powerhouse, the target is always on their backs.

"Just putting on a Mater Dei singlet doesn't mean you're automatically going to go out and win," said Janice Schuble, another of Mike's sisters. "You have to be prepared every time you step out there, because everybody's out to get you. There were some people who just didn't like Mater Dei. We lost the SIAC in 1994 (a rare occurrence), and the whole crowd just went crazy. They always root against us, but, you know, you expect it. If it were the opposite, we would be doing that too."

Hair Today, Hair Tomorrow
Mike Goebel sports his famous afro as he raises his hand in victory as a wrestler at Mater Dei. (Photo courtesy of the Goebel clan.)

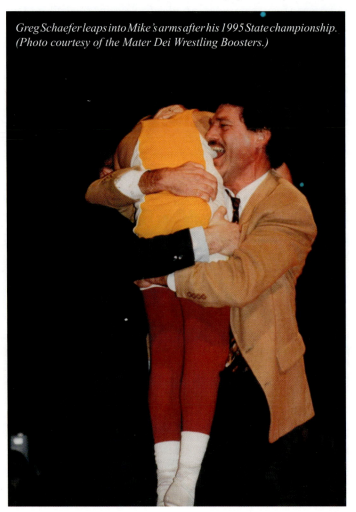

Greg Schaefer leaps into Mike's arms after his 1995 State championship. (Photo courtesy of the Mater Dei Wrestling Boosters.)

While it seems to some that the Mater Dei freight train is on automatic pilot every year, no one realizes more than Mike Goebel that success is anything but automatic. Goebel learned a long time ago that to be the best, you have to wrestle the best, and he has made a concerted effort to do just that. "We try to wrestle the best competition we can," he explained, "and I do want to say that the competition around here is outstanding. Everyone goes in cycles, as we do, but it's not been an easy task. That's one thing that I stress every day (to my wrestlers) is that there are no givens."

While Goebel appreciates the battles he's had with programs such as Jerry Latham's Reitz Panthers, Grodie Crick's Central Bears and Bob Harmon's Castle Knights, he also is adamant about seeking out other competition from the Midwest. Mike remembers being motivated to find the toughest competition when a friend passed along a comment he had heard. Early in Mike's career, the head coach at Delta, a school that had won five straight State titles, saw Mater Dei's potential and said, "I hope they never branch out and wrestle other people, because they don't know how good they can be."

The remark made Goebel take stock in his program, and although their travel distance was limited by IHSAA regulations, they sought out elite tournaments within the designated area and brought in the best teams they could find for their annual Mater Dei Holiday Classic. The result was a battle-hardened team that always seemed to be ready to perform at its best during tournament time, with wrestlers who seemed to reach deep inside themselves when things got tough.

"We may not always have the best individuals," Mike Goebel concluded, "but if you put our team out there, there's something to be said for the work ethic those guys have. Our kids are fighters!"

To put it more succinctly, Mike's sister, Janice Schuble, feels that "our parents raised a bunch of overachievers."

Loyal Mater Dei fans have been treated to numerous big matches over the years, and some of them played out with the drama of a best-selling novel. Mike remembers coaching his brother Chris, who wrestled heavyweight at only 184 pounds. "There was no weight limit then, and he was wrestling this monster named Calvin Bird," Mike joked. "At one point, the only part of Chris's body I could see was his right shoe!"

Goebel also recalled a regional when the Wildcats were down 17 points to Central. Central had nine guys in the finals and Mater Dei had only seven, which meant the Wildcats had no realistic chance to win. In dramatic fashion, all seven wrestlers won to steal the regional title from the Bears by a point and a half.

Steve Ford, a sportswriter who has covered local wrestling for nearly twenty years, remembered a dramatic match in the late '90s. "Mike Bishop was wrestling Carmel," he recalled. "Bishop had a brace on his leg as big as a house. He hadn't been able to wrestle in the individual tournament because he got hurt, but he trained and came back in the team competition in one of the most inspiring matches you'll ever see. It was a match Mater Dei should not have won."

Ford also mentioned another huge win by David Hisch. Hisch was one of the last three wrestlers in a match, all of whom had to win for Mater Dei to beat Hobart for the State title. Once again, all three came through to pull out the victory.

Mike Goebel also points out memories that stand out in the program's history as defining moments, like the school's first State champion, heavyweight Bill Trainer in 1953 under Coach Joe Gossman. Goebel has fond memories, as well, of his first

Blake Maurer is one of a select few to win an Indiana State title four times. (Photo courtesy of the Mater Dei Wrestling Boosters.)

State champ as a coach, Tim Boots, a 177-pounder in 1980. Mike also cherishes a rare feat accomplished only once at Mater Dei and only seven times in the history of Indiana high school wrestling – father and son State champions. Goebel coached Chris Wildeman when he won the 145-pound division in 1981 and Chris's son, Sam, when he won in 2003.

Sam Wildeman made history twice, in fact, during the '03 State meet. He was also part of a magnificent run that Wildcat fans will never forget. Craig Weinzapfel, who finished the year 41-0, started things off when he captured a title. Then, the raucous Mater Dei crowd sat and watched as the next three matches went to Dustin Nosko (152), Sam Wildeman (160) and Blake Maurer (171). In an age when it is rare to even have four wrestlers make it *into* the finals, Mater Dei pulled off a feat that will almost certainly never happen again, four individual State championships in a row!

Blake Maurer, part of the champion quartet of '03, was also one of only seven Indiana wrestlers to capture four State titles in the sport's 84 seasons of IHSAA competition. His first three titles were all won in exciting fashion, and his match in '03 is considered one of the best in Indiana history. After a battle with Alex Jolly of Mishawaka for three periods and a 'sudden death' overtime, the two were still deadlocked. The final tie-breaker was a 'rideout', where one wrestler starts in the 'up' position and the other 'down'.

Maurer chose 'up', an unusual choice, and had to maintain control of Jolly for thirty seconds to win. If Jolly escaped, he would get to raise his hand in victory. The match almost ended quickly when Jolly put Maurer on his back. But Maurer maintained control, bridged with his legs and got off his back. Late in the period, Jolly got to his feet with Maurer holding his leg. Jolly did a flip, and there was a mad scramble as the seconds ticked off. When the buzzer sounded, Maurer had control practically by a shoelace as the Conseco Field House crowd erupted.

"It was the match everybody wanted to see," recalled Randy Helfrich. "They were both undefeated and had huge credentials. When it went to overtime, the joint was rocking with a deafening noise."

Another athlete who distinguished himself among other great wrestlers to wear the red and gold singlet is Matt Coughlin, who was a State runner-up as a freshman and sophomore and the 153-pound champion in 2004 and 2005, finishing 87-0 his last two years. Coughlin became the school's first national high school champion and Evansville's first ever NCAA Division I All-American, when he finished sixth as a 149-pounder at IU in 2008.

Coughlin and Maurer are but two of the hundreds of Mater Dei wrestlers who are part of the legacy left by Mike Goebel's leadership, and when asked about the secrets to such success, Goebel is quick to divert praise away from himself and onto others. In addition to the strong support of parents, fans and the Mater Dei Wrestling Club, who support the program through donations and fund-raisers, Goebel praises the efforts of coaching volunteers who are prevalent at every level from the feeder schools to the varsity. He also realizes that much of the program's success belongs to a man who was at his side every step of the way, assistant coach Randy Helfrich.

Mater Dei wrestling fans are all in agreement when it comes to the roles played by the program's terrific twosome. The short and stocky Helfrich is considered the "technician" and Goebel the "motivator." Even Coach Goebel uses these descriptions when asked about the program's operation, and he is abundant with praise of his trusted assistant and friend, saying, "Randy Helfrich is the most knowledgeable high school wrestling coach I know."

Goebel and Helfrich have known each other since Randy was in the seventh grade, and the two have traded many a barb through the years. At his retirement banquet in early '08, Mike reflected back on the beginning of their coaching association in 1978 and the 'growth' the two have experienced since. "Randy was a cross between an anti-war protester and Rambo," Goebel joked, to the delight of the crowd. "He had real long hair and six pack abs. As you can see, he got his hair cut and he traded his six pack for a half-barrel."

Helfrich enjoyed some retaliation, however, when he alluded to an astounding feat that he accomplished as a coach in his own right. Over his career, Randy won a staggering 450 consecutive dual meets as a junior varsity coach, a national record for any sport at any level, and one that may stand until the end of time. Not to be outdone, Randy spoke of the days when he and Mike were assistants under Joe Gossman and made fun of Mike's afro by saying he resembled "a pale Dr. J." Randy also couldn't resist the urge to make reference to his own dual meet record, saying, "It is my pleasure to introduce the man who compiled a dual meet record of 533-14-2." (long pause) "It would be almost impossible to imagine *anyone* who could have a better record than that!"

For Helfrich and the hundreds of others who said farewell to Mike Goebel on that special night in January of 2008, it won't seem the same without Mike Goebel wrenching his body as he sat mat-side while a Mater Dei wrestler struggled for a pin. They'll miss his soft-spoken, humble style while away from the sport as well as his familiar fierce intensity as he stared daggers at an official. Although those individual memories are strong, the thing

Randy Helfrich (left) and Mike Goebel at work. (Photo courtesy of the Mater Dei Wrestling Boosters.)

they'll miss most is the effect he's had on athletes and fans over the span of his 29-year career.

Perhaps nothing could sum up his impact better than a handwritten letter from a mother who wanted to express her appreciation to Goebel. She said, in part: "I know when Tim won State, when anyone asked him how he did it, he would always tell them, 'I had to do it for Mike.' ... I'm as proud of you as if you were my own son. I know your mom is." (Dorothy Boots).

Steve Ford, who has witnessed and written about Mike's success for many years, revealed what he believes is the true secret behind the program's dominance. "People ask me, 'What is the difference at Mater Dei?', and I say, 'When Mike Goebel tells kids they can win, they believe it.' It's everything Mike Goebel stands for and his program stands for: passion, commitment, winning and winning right."

Not surprisingly, in the past, Goebel received offers to head up programs with better facilities and a more lucrative financial package, but that just isn't his style. "Yeah, it's happened," Goebel confessed, "but my family's here. I've had numerous opportunities, but I've always looked at my friends and the support level here."

Because of that support and the love he has shared with the wrestling family at Mater Dei, Mike admits that the 29 years went by "like the blink of an eye," and he wasn't going to step down until he was sure he could walk away with a clear conscience. He felt 2007 was right for him and for the program. "I'm not getting any younger," he said after his final season, "but I want to make sure the program continues. Wrestling is a grueling season. We practice New Year's Eve, New Year's Day, Christmas Eve. It's been 29 years. What I gave was the best that I could, for the most part."

More than anything, Goebel will miss his wrestlers. "It doesn't come easy, and whether the guys were champions or they didn't wrestle at all, everyone in that wrestling room contributed," Goebel stated. "I've called on just about every wrestler at some point, and any record is a shared record."

As is only fitting, Goebel is passing the torch to a member of the 'family', Greg Schaefer, a wrestler who created a true Kodak Moment himself when he hurled himself into Goebel's arms, with cameras flashing, after he won his first of two State titles as a 101-pound freshman in 1995. Though the transition won't be easy for Goebel, he's confident that the program is in the right hands. "I miss wrestling. I'm not going to deny that", Goebel confided,

Mike and his one-year-old daughter MacKenzie. (Photo courtesy of the Mater Dei Wrestling Boosters.)

"but I'm completely at peace with it because I know we've got the right man to carry on the tradition."

For over thirty years, wrestling has been Mike Goebel's life, and he realizes the toll it can take on a man. Fortunately, he has been able to share it with his children. His son Zach, known as 'Bo' to those close to him, was a wrestler on Mike's final State championship team in 2007, and his daughter MacKenzie was only 11 days old when Mike held her in his arms after his first State title in 1986. With 'Mac' finishing school at IU soon and Zach starting a football career at Murray, Mike will now have time to share more of their lives as they start families of their own.

With his wrestling career behind him, Goebel's accomplishments can now be placed among the very best in the sport's history. On a state level, he has no peers, and on a national level, he is among the greatest ever. A career can be looked at from several perspectives, and if numbers are your thing, then get ready to be amazed, because when it comes down to stats, Goebel's record speaks for itself.

After examining the numbers relating to Mike Goebel's 29-year career at Mater Dei, it is no mystery why he was named the Indiana Coach of the Year eight times, the national Coach of the Year twice and is a member of the Indiana Wrestling Hall of Fame. But even more impressive than his numbers are the ways in which he has touched people's lives.

Randy Helfrich ended his humorous roast of Goebel on a serious note saying, "He demanded and would expect only the best, and that's what makes Mike Goebel the greatest coach in Indiana wrestling history. You are and always will be my hero."

But perhaps the words that best summarized the sentiments of those who love Mike Goebel were spoken by Jeremy Goebel, Mike's nephew and a former Mater Dei wrestler, who paid an emotional tribute to his uncle at the January banquet saying, "I admire so much what Coach Goebel has done. How he instills greatness in his wrestlers and somehow gets every single wrestler he's ever had to step outside himself and wrestle better than he ever thought he could. If I'm half the man, half the coach, half the father that Mike Goebel is, then I'd consider that a successful life."

BY THE NUMBERS
MIKE GOEBEL'S 29-YEAR CAREER

- State Record
- † National Record

- 360.5 points scored in a sectional ('03)
- 283.5 points scored in a regional ('03)
- 262 individual sectional champions
- 231.5 points scored in a semi-state ('03)

- 198 individual SIAC champions
- 160 individual regional champions
- 158 points scored at State meet
  135 consecutive dual meet victories (Jan.'91-Jan.'98)
  117 consecutive dual meet victories (Jan.'98-Jan.'03)
- † 97.4% dual meet winning percentage (533-14-2)
- 72 individual semi-state champions
  29 consecutive City team championships
- 29 consecutive sectional championships
- 29 consecutive regional championships
  27 SIAC championships
  24 Indiana State records
- 23 semi-state championships
  22 Individual State champions
- 18 Consecutive semi-state championships
  14 All 14 wrestlers advanced to regional ('02,'07)
  14 All 14 wrestlers advanced to semi-state ('96)
- 13 individual sectional champions one year ('83, '02, '03)
- 12 regional dual meet championships
- 12 semi-state dual meet championships
- 12 IHSAA team State championships
- 11 regional champions one year ('03)
- 11 State finalists one year ('96,'07)
- 10 IHSAA dual meet State championships ('96-'03, '06,'07)
- 9 Consecutive team State championships ('95-'03)
- 4 back-to-back-to-back-to-back State champions ('03)
  1 team State runnerup ('87)

IHSAA STATE CHAMPIONS:
WRESTLING

Individual	School	Year	Weight Class	Record
Bill Trainer	Mater Dei	1952-'53	Hwt	
Fred Happe	Mater Dei	1963-'64	145	
Sammy Lamb	Bosse	1972-'73	132	
John Jeske	North	1976-'77	126	31-0
Tim Boots	Mater Dei	1979-'80	177	33-2
Jeffrey Harp	Reitz	1980-'81	105	33-0
Chris Wildeman	Mater Dei	1980-'81	145	31-0
Steve Noriega	Central	1981-'82	98	34-1
Darren Grimwood	Harrison	1982-'83	132	32-0
Chip Elderkin	Mater Dei	1985-'86	112	36-0
Buzz Mieras	Mater Dei	1985-'86	138	30-4
Martin Salters	Princeton	1985-'86	Hwt	34-4
Bret Schnur	Mater Dei	1986-'87	145	37-0
Gabe Zirklebach	Mater Dei	1987-'88	103	39-0-1
Stan Gress	Southridge	1987-'88	189	38-1
Greg Matheis	Jasper	1987-'88	Hwt	36-0
Jason Greer	Princeton	1988-'89	189	40-2
Jason Greer	Princeton	1990-'91	189	38-1
Matt Armentano	Mater Dei	1992-'93	152	39-1
Andy Schneider	Mt. Vernon	1992-'93	Hwt	47-1
Matt Deters	Castle	1993-'94	103	39-0
Chase Akers	North Posey	1993-'94	160	38-2
Andy Schneider	Mt. Vernon	1993-'94	Hwt	45-0
Greg Schaefer	Mater Dei	1994-'95	100	33-2
Thad Oldham	Castle	1994-'95	142	40-0
Darren Happe	Central	1994-'95	185	45-0
Pat Mayes	Castle	1994-'95	215	39-0
Thad Oldham	Castle	1995-'96	145	40-0
Nick Mayer	Mater Dei	1995-'96	160	40-0
James Brimm	Central	1995-'96	189	39-1
Josh Hardy	Princeton	1996-'97	171	40-3
Greg Schaefer	Mater Dei	1997-'98	119	45-0
Josh Hardy	Princeton	1997-'98	171	43-0
D.J. Radnovich	Gibson Southern	1997-'98	215	47-0
Craig Weinzapfel	Mater Dei	2000-'01	112	39-3
Blake Maurer	Mater Dei	2000-'01	130	42-0
Allen Weinzapfel	Mater Dei	2000-'01	160	35-3
Blake Maurer	Mater Dei	2001-'02	145	43-1
Craig Weinzapfel	Mater Dei	2002-'03	145	43-1
Dustin Nosko	Mater Dei	2002-'03	152	23-2
Sam Wildeman	Mater Dei	2002-'03	160	37-1
Blake Maurer	Mater Dei	2002-'03	171	43-1
Matt Coughlin	Mater Dei	2003-'04	152	45-0
Blake Maurer	Mater Dei	2003-'04	171	45-0
Chad Ruggeri	Mt. Vernon	2003-'04	275	37-0
Anthony Williams	Central	2004-'05	119	46-2
Matt Coughlin	Mater Dei	2004-'05	152	42-0
Taylor Vieck	Vincennes Lincoln	2005-'06	189	38-0
Caleb Schmitt	Castle	2006-'07	135	47-1
Matt Powless	Memorial	2006-'07	171	51-0

School	Year	Coach
Mater Dei	1985-'86	Mike Goebel
Mater Dei	1994-'95	Mike Goebel
Mater Dei	1995-'96	Mike Goebel
Mater Dei	1996-'97	Mike Goebel
Mater Dei	1997-'98	Mike Goebel
Mater Dei	1998-'99	Mike Goebel
Mater Dei	1999-'00	Mike Goebel
Mater Dei	2000-'01	Mike Goebel
Mater Dei	2001-'02	Mike Goebel
Mater Dei	2002-'03	Mike Goebel
Mater Dei	2005-'06	Mike Goebel
Mater Dei	2006-'07	Mike Goebel

JAMEY CARROLL: LITTLE MAN WITH A BIG HEART

A sign hung by Larry Carroll's front door reads, "A baseball fan and his old bat live here." Less than two years after the passing of his wife Patty, the humorous placard remained as a tribute to the woman who shared Larry's dedication to raising three sons who loved to play ball. For years, the couple sacrificed so that sons Jason, Jamey and Wes could chase their dreams. Middle son Jamey defied all odds on his road to success, and his only regret is that his mom wasn't in the stands as he stepped to the plate in the 2007 World Series.

Larry Carroll loved sports as a youngster but admits that he didn't play in high school because he was too busy chasing girls. The girl he finally caught was Patty Schoonover, a pretty girl from Harrison who ran track in the late '60s. According to Larry, Jamey looks very much like his mother and also inherited her footspeed. Realizing his own mistakes as a teenager, Larry was clear about his expectations of his sons when he told them, "Leave the girls alone and stay in sports, and Dad will take care of you."

And Larry was true to his word. For 28 years, he worked the midnight shift at Alcoa, and he used 18 of those years to coach the boys. "It's not that I knew more (about baseball) than anyone else," he explained. "It's just all the extra time I put in with them, throwing extra batting practice, hitting extra ground balls. I'd work the midnight shift during the summer and I'd get off and then we'd go to the ballpark. We would spend all day there, and we enjoyed it."

Jamey Carroll is very aware of the impact his parents had on the boys' success. Fresh off his World Series experience, his first words were validation that he wouldn't be where he is today without them. "I was blessed having a family that allowed us kids to play sports," he said. "Our parents were running three kids to three different fields, and we played baseball, basketball and football. Without them giving us the opportunity to see what we were good at, none of this would have been possible. That's where it all started."

All three of the Carroll sons were excellent athletes with great potential. Jason, the oldest, was always an all-star baseball player growing up, but his first love was football. As a senior baseball player at Castle, he led all of southwestern Indiana in batting average (.538), home runs (8) and RBIs (44). "He was a big kid," Larry pointed out. "He was 6'3, 265 pounds (as a senior). He got all the size in the family. When he was twelve years old, we always had to show his birth certificate at the tournaments."

Jason's size and talent on the football field earned him a scholarship to IU as a center. After two years of battling huge defensive linemen, his knees were shot and he transferred to USI, where he earned a teaching degree. After three years of teaching, he entered the business world and now owns his own insurance company.

Wes Carroll, the youngest of the boys, had the advantage of growing up with two older brothers and possessed the most pure athletic ability, according to his father. "The first time I saw him play I said, 'He'll be in the big leagues some day,'" Larry recalled. "He was tremendous in little league. It seemed like every game he would go five for five with two home runs. When he was eight, he hit a home run over the center field light pole at East Little League field."

As a high schooler, Wes excelled at both baseball and football, and head football coach John Lidy talked to him about playing quarterback. Larry pulled his son aside and suggested he pick a sport. His choice was baseball, but had he chosen football, he would have been a part of Castle's 1994 State championship team. Wes went on to a great career at Castle and was selected the Metro Player of the Year after his senior season.

After high school, Wes signed with U of E, where he started at second base as a freshman and at shortstop the next thee years. In his first year, Wes became U of E's first freshman All-American when he hit .288 with 18 doubles. Like his brother Jamey, who had played at Evansville years earlier, he played in every inning of every game during his career with the Aces. Wes had followed in Jamey's footsteps at Castle and at U of E, and soon he would follow him into professional baseball.

In the 2001 major league draft, Wes was selected in the 37th round by the Philadelphia Phillies and was a roommate his first season with current superstar Ryan Howard while they were with the Class A Clearwater Phillies. After two years in the Phillies organization, the club had an abundance of infielders, so Wes was traded to the Montreal Expos, the same organization where Jamey had worked his way up to the parent club.

(Photo courtesy of the University of Evansville, Sports Information.)

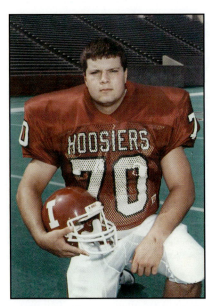

Jason Carroll was the biggest of the boys and played football for the Indiana Hoosiers. (Photo courtesy of Larry Carroll.)

One of the highlights of Wes's minor league career took place when he was called up to 'the bigs' to play a spring training game in Miami. For the first time ever, the Carroll boys were on the field together. Because the call-up happened so quickly, Dad didn't get to see Wes (at second base) and Jamey (at shortstop) turn a double play.

After five years of playing the minor league numbers game, Wes faced a decision that is all too common at that level. With his lack of footspeed hindering his progression, he watched as others who were highly paid passed him by. He reported to spring training in 2006 but decided to hang up his spikes after a week or so and moved home to become an assistant coach at U of E. Two years later, in July of 2008, the university was searching for a replacement for departed head baseball coach Dave Seifert and found their man right in their backyard. Wes received the school's vote of confidence and began another chapter of his life as the new head coach of the Aces.

When Wes came home in 2006, Jamey was entering his tenth season of professional baseball, but his journey from the small fields in southwestern Indiana to the scenic parks of the major leagues was one that would demand everything he had, both physically and mentally.

Although Jamey Blake Carroll was the biggest of the boys at birth (9 pounds), he was always the runt of the litter as he competed. But his lack of size only served as motivation for the spunky athlete. His father could see the fire burning at a young age, and he proudly observed as Jamey proved all the doubters wrong. "My best year in sports was when Jason was a senior (at Castle) and Jamey was a sophomore," Larry said. "Jamey started at shortstop and hit .468.

"Jamey will tell you any day of the week that he has the least ability of the three boys, but it was his work ethic and desire and heart that made him successful."

Larry went on to cite an example of Jamey's resolve to make it as a player. "In his junior year at Castle, he had Division I scouts from all over the country looking at him," Larry recalled. "But two weeks before the season started, he broke his right arm (playing basketball with friends). He had compound fractures (through the skin) and had to go through 4 ½ hours of surgery at IUPUI. Still to this day, he has four stainless steel plates and thirty-something screws in there. They didn't know if he would ever throw a baseball again, but he would go to Castle's practices and stand there and catch and swing the bat with one hand."

In 1992, after an outstanding senior year at Castle, Jamey headed to John A. Logan College with the intent of moving up to a Division I program. That goal was soon accomplished when U of E coach Jim Brownlee offered him a scholarship to play for the Aces.

Despite his size, only 5'10 and 170 pounds, Jamey's quickness and consistency began to attract attention from major league scouts during his junior year. He recalls very well the attitudes and comments that for so many years had become commonplace. "They'd (pro scouts) shake my hand and say, 'Hey, you did a good job today, but, man, you've got small hands,'" Jamey recalled. "I just didn't understand. I mean, the bat's not that big; the ball's not that big; why do my hands have to be big?"

Jamey and his family had become accustomed to the criticism, but Patty, Jamey's mother, was not afraid to speak her mind. "My mom had the best response," Jamey said proudly. "She would tell them that the best thing I do is field the ground ball, and being short just makes me closer to the ground. I thought, 'Hey! That's a good one!'"

After a sterling career with the Aces, Jamey was cautiously optimistic about his future. He had played hard every minute he was on the field and hoped that someone had noticed. "Jamey always said, 'You play hard all the time because you never know who's watching you,'" said his father. "In high school, you never know what college coach is there, or in college, what pro scouts are watching, or in the minors, if the managers or owners are there watching you.'"

Jamey's words proved prophetic when he was selected in the 14th round of the 1996 draft by the Montreal Expos. After he was drafted, the scout who was responsible explained why he suggested Jamey. According to Larry Carroll, the scout told Jamey: "Do you know why I drafted you? When you were playing in Omaha (when U of E played Creighton), I was there with a stopwatch on you. You hit a ball to the shortstop in the first inning and I timed you to first. In your last at bat in the eighth inning, you hit one back to the pitcher and I timed you to first in exactly the same time (as the first at bat). You were still running the ball out on a ball to the pitcher in the eighth as you were on a ball to short in the first."

Jamey looks back on the day he was drafted and says that he was thrilled but amazed when he got the call. Realistically, he was hoping to be picked up as a free agent after the draft was over. In fact, he was working out with the Evansville Otters to stay in shape and to possibly play with them if the phone never rang.

On the first day of the draft, he was contemplating whether to go to an evening workout with the Otters, but he decided he wanted to be home just in case a miracle happened. He left a message with the Otters' office and then hunkered down for the evening. Twenty minutes later, the phone rang, and he was certain it was the Otters returning his call. Instead, it was the call that every ballplayer prays for. Jamey wouldn't have to try to catch on as a post-draft free agent; he had been selected by the Montreal

Jamey, 13, and Wes, 8, are ready to play ball. (Photo courtesy of Larry Carroll.)

Jamey, age 7, in his T-Ball uniform. (Photo courtesy of Larry Carroll.)

Expos on the FIRST DAY of the draft.

Like a kid at Christmas, Jamey still gets a kick out of describing the scene when his childhood dream came true. "My older brother (Jason) was there, and I jumped up in his arms and he swung me around and I banged my knee on a post in the house," Jamey revealed. "It knocked us both to the ground, and it wasn't until later that I realized, 'Hey! That hurt pretty bad!'"

In two weeks, Jamey was on his way to start his career at a mini-camp in Vermont. Playing A-Ball in the short-season New York-Penn League, his team won the title and Jamey received a championship ring.

The next season, he played for the West Palm Beach Expos in the High-A Florida State League as a utility player. His coach there, Doug Sisson, loved players who worked hard and became an advocate for Jamey at meetings where decisions were being made.

In his third season, in 1998, Jamey started spring training again in High-A Ball in Jupiter, Florida, but at the all-star break, he was called up to Double A. In Harrisburg (PA), his team won the Eastern League championship, giving Jamey his second ring and prompting him to think, "This minor league stuff is pretty cool!"

In '99, he started in Double A again and had his best minor league season, hitting .292 and making the all-star team. Once again, his team won the title, and they did it in dramatic fashion. In the final game, Jamey was on deck in the bottom of the ninth. With his team down by three and the bases loaded with two outs, future major league star Milton Bradley blasted a grand slam for the win.

Jamey started the 2000 season just one step below 'the bigs' at Triple A Ottawa. After a slow start, he was sent back to Double A for a month, where he regained his confidence and earned a promotion back to Triple A. His season at Ottawa was also nice for his family because it gave his parents a chance to watch him when the team played nearby in Louisville and Indianapolis. Jamey had a good season, hitting .280, and realized that he could compete at that level.

In 2001, after playing second for years, the club asked Jamey to become a utility player. As he struggled with his reduced playing time, he began to wonder, "I'm not getting any younger. What else can I do?"

After several trades, Jamey became the odd man out in 2002, with no place for the team to put him, and he began the year on the 'phantom DL'. Three weeks into the season, he was asked if he would be willing to return to Double A. His answer: "I just want to play!" Three days later, a player on the parent team, Jose Macias, was injured, and when a Triple A player was called up, Jamey was asked to return to Triple A to take his spot. When he returned, the only spot open was third base, and the coach suggested that if Jamey was going to be a true utility player, he should learn the position. Jamey accepted the challenge, and the coach motivated him by saying, "I'm going to play you until you prove that I shouldn't." Jamey responded with one of his best seasons, and even hit a few home runs.

As the Triple A season wound down, Jamey was mentally prepared to test the market as a six-year free agent. One week after returning home to Indiana, he received a call saying that the parent club wanted to know where he was. Jamey was confused but thought the call might be an indication that he was being called up to the majors for the end of the season. "I woke up my dad," Jamey recalled, "and I said, 'I'm not sure what's going on, but I may be going to the big leagues.' I woke up my brother and told him that we needed to go over to U of E and hit. As soon as I got there, I got a call, and the guy says, 'Congratulations, when can you get to Chicago?' I told him, 'There's a plane leaving every hour.' I just said that; I didn't even know."

After celebrating briefly with his family, Jamey headed out to meet up with the Expos for a doubleheader in Chicago, but he arrived too late to hit with the team and wasn't activated for the first game. Although he was eligible to play the next day, he was not able to take batting practice because it was the first anniversary of the 9/11 disaster and pre-game ceremonies were held in honor of the tragedy. With his family in the stands, he checked the lineup card and discovered that he was starting at third base and hitting second. He hadn't hit or even taken a ground ball for several days, and he was about to step to the plate at historic Wrigley Field.

Jamey played every day for the last two and a half weeks of the Expos' season and became a favorite of manager Frank Robinson. Robinson became a supporter and would work hard to see that the utility player would get his shot, but Jamey was starting to wonder if he was fighting a losing battle. The world of professional baseball is a complicated maze, and the path to the brass ring can take many unexpected turns. In professional football and basketball, players on the bubble usually know in a year or two if they have a legitimate shot. But minor league baseball is a different animal. During any given season, there are hundreds, perhaps thousands, of players of varying ages and levels of experience trying to catch a break and move up through the hierarchy of the system. An injury here or a trade there can impact a player's career forever, and it's difficult to play while constantly looking over your shoulder. Those like Jamey, who aren't 'bonus babies' with millions of dollars invested in them, can only hope and pray that the pieces fall in place to give them a small window of opportunity to prove their worth. The process is long and arduous, and as time passes, it takes its toll on even the most passionate player.

After six years in the minors, Jamey began to wonder if it was time to move on. He had been offered a job as the dean of students at a school in Tampa making much more money than he had made in the minors, and he weighed that opportunity against the $9,000 he would probably make if he returned to baseball as a minor leaguer. He reflected on the years he supplemented his income by stacking newspapers in West Palm Beach or sold vacuum cleaners door-to-door just to get by. He thought about the hours of overtime his father worked at Alcoa so that he would have the money to help his son if he needed it.

Jamey was at a crossroads. He had just come off one of his worst seasons and he was 28 years old, but his will wouldn't let him give up. Perhaps he remembered the words once spoken by legendary Dodgers star Maury Wills, who had worked with him while he was in the minors. "Jamey, don't you ever give up," Wills told him. "There's still room in the game for the little guy." Jamey decided to get back to work, and his efforts would eventually pay huge dividends.

In 2003, Jamey spent his first full season in the majors, hitting .260 and starting 53 games for the Expos – 46 at third base, five at second and two at short. 2004 was a little better, as Jamey made 50 starts at four different positions – second base (35), third base (8), shortstop (6) and left field (1). He finished at .289 for the season and hit .320 as a pinch-hitter. But although his life as a journeyman minor leaguer was over, Jamey was still searching for a comfort level.

Also in 2003, Jamey's father suffered a severe back injury while coming home from work one morning. Immediately after the collision, his first thoughts were of baseball. "When they cut me out of my vehicle," he recalled, "I said, 'Somebody up there has a lot more baseball for me to watch.'"

2005 was a challenging year for Jamey, both professionally and personally. Baseball history was made when the Expos moved the franchise to Washington D.C., bringing major league baseball back to the nation's capital for the first time in 34 years. The new Washington Nationals front office also had fresh ideas about Jamey's role, making him a starter at third base. Once again, Carroll had to adapt by changing his mental approach to the game. As a utility player the past several years, he would play maybe two days in a row and then sit for ten days. He could place his focus solely on one at-bat as a pinch-hitter or on one or two innings as a defensive replacement. But as a starter, he would have to maintain that focus every inning, day in and day out.

Although his production at the plate was adequate, he excelled in the field, with zero errors in 118 chances, the most without an error in the majors. After a solid season, he left for home, not knowing that one of the biggest challenges of his life awaited him.

Following the '05 season, the Carroll family was struck by a sudden tragedy that would leave them all devastated. In December, Patty Carroll died as a result of complications from pneumonia at the age of 54. "It was a big shock to all of us," Larry recalled. "It was like she walked out here in the street and got killed. It happened that fast."

Still reeling from his loss, Jamey returned for spring training for the 2006 season, and both he and his father believe that the events that soon followed were more than just happenstance. Shortly after his arrival, Jamey was informed that he had been traded to the Colorado Rockies. Oddly, one of the first things Jamey thought of was his mother. It was widely known that Patty's favorite color was purple, and Jamey saw it as a sign that he was going to a team who used purple as their predominant color. But the trade to the Rockies turned out to be much more than just a color coincidence. The team philosophy and the compassionate personnel were a godsend for the Carrolls.

"It was like fresh air, a fresh opportunity," Jamey admitted. "Their arms were wide open. It floored me how different the atmosphere was (from the Expos/Nationals), how family-oriented they were. And that's when I needed it more than ever."

Jamey went on to tell how well his father was treated, also. Larry was going through tough times as well, and his spirits were buoyed when the Rockies allowed him in the dugout for batting practice and in the clubhouse before and after games, a rarity in major league baseball.

Jamey holds Cole Patrick and Mackenzie Joyce shortly after their birth on March 28th, 2008. (Photo courtesy of Jamey and Kim Carroll.)

"The Rockies had the understanding that this isn't going to last forever," Jamey said. "Clint Hurdle, our manager, always said he wishes that, when he played, he would have had his dad around."

With a new lease on life, Jamey had the best season of his career in 2006. He led all National League second basemen with a .995 fielding percentage, finishing second in the majors to Oakland's Mark Ellis' .997. Jamey only made three errors all season, and two of them occurred when he was playing in shallow right field on a shift for slugger Barry Bonds.

At the plate, Jamey hit .300 with five home runs from the lead-off spot to go with 36 RBIs, 23 doubles and 5 triples. He also led the team with 22 infield hits and averaged 4.15 pitches per plate appearance, fifth in the league. He started 102 games at second base, seven at short and one at third and had the highest assist per nine innings ratio among all second baseman in the majors, 3.99, easily a club record. His first home run of the season was the first he had hit in 663 at bats, and he had consecutive four-hit games on June 6th and 7th.

Anyone who follows major league baseball knows that .300 is a magic number, of sorts, when it comes to batting average. The fact that Jamey ended 2006 hitting exactly .300 can be attributed in part to the wisdom of Rockies manager Clint Hurdle. Paul Gries, an ex-player and successful coach at Central High School, was told about the situation by Jamey's father. "Jamey's dad told us that in the next to last game, Jamey got two hits to put his average at .300," Gries explained, "and then Hurdle took Jamey out. The last game, he didn't play Jamey at all. Jamey didn't understand, and he didn't realize until somebody told him later, 'Jamey, Coach did that for a reason; he didn't want to take the chance that you would drop to .297 or .298. You'll have the rest of your life to say you hit .300 in the major leagues one year.'"

Jamey Carroll had found a home, and following the season, the club rewarded him with a two-year, multi-million dollar contract. After 800+ games over seven minor league seasons and some frustrating experiences in the majors, his dedication and perseverance had paid off. Although Jamey probably felt that his dream had come true, there were even more dreams to be realized in 2007.

In spring training for the '07 season, the team added second baseman Kaz Matsui to the roster, resulting in yet another

Jamey Carroll always loved to draw. After getting some tips from outstanding local artist Jon Siau, Jamey came up with a unique idea of gathering keepsakes from his days as a player. Instead of having players he admires just sign a ball or bat, he draws a caricature of them from an online photo and then asks if they would sign it. If they agree, he sends a clubhouse worker over to have it signed. Among his collection are signed pictures of Ryan Howard, Matt Holliday, Todd Helton and John Smoltz.

adjustment for Jamey. Although he was upset at first, Jamey finally put his emotions aside and accepted the fact that he would have to re-learn the utility role. With his contributions defensively and as a role player, the Rockies made one of the greatest late-season runs in major league history.

The team won 13 of the last 14 games to force a play-in game with San Diego for the last spot in the playoffs. The one-game playoff had all the drama a fan could want, including a controversial ending. With the score tied at 6-6 in the top of the 13th inning, San Diego's Scott Hairston put the Padres up with a two-run homer. In the bottom of the inning, Padres closer Trevor Hoffman gave up back-to-back doubles to Kaz Matsui and Troy Tulowitzki to make it a one-run game. Matt Holliday followed with a triple, tying the score. With nobody out, Jamey Carroll stepped to the plate and smacked a line drive to the outfield. Holliday tagged up and slid into home head first, and the crowd waited for the call. Though many question if he touched home plate, Holliday was called safe, meaning Jamey's sacrifice drove in the winning run, sending Colorado into the playoffs.

The Rockies continued their streak by sweeping Philadelphia and then Arizona to win the National League pennant. Colorado had won 20 of their last 21 games and, miraculously, were going to the World Series.

Before the Series began, there was much debate about how the sweep of the Diamondbacks could prove to be a negative for the Rockies, and whether it was the eight-day layoff or just a dominant performance by Boston, the Rockies were swept by the Red Sox. In Jamey's lone appearance in the Series, he brought local fans to their feet with a blast that nearly cleared the fence and would have kept his team alive in the eighth inning of the final game.

Although the Rockies lost the Series, in a few short weeks, the Rockies rode an emotional high that few teams get to experience. After every playoff series, the boys in purple celebrated like children, and Jamey will never forget the feeling because, thanks to the Rockies' philosophy, his dad was right there in the locker room with him getting showered with champagne and beer.

After the 2007 season, Jamey was traded to the Cleveland Indians, and he viewed the move with the perspective of a man who understands and appreciates the world of professional sports. Though the transaction would close the door on a remarkable chapter of his life, he understood that a new window of opportunity was opening. "The Rockies gave me an opportunity to see if I could play every day in the big leagues. I am thankful for my time there and to be able to share a tremendous year in '07," he said. "To have a chance to be a part of history, winning 21 of 22 games and to be in the World Series, are parts of my career that I can now share with my family and friends. I am excited for my time in Cleveland, a new challenge being in a new league with a team that has tons of history. I couldn't ask for a better situation. Who knows where the rest of my career will play out, but I do know that I will keep playing and working hard to give my team the best chance to win."

With his move to Cleveland in 2008, Jamey was embarking on yet another leg of his storybook journey through the world of professional baseball, but '08 would also present another special moment and yet another role to play for the little man with the big heart. On February 28th, Jamey and his wife Kim welcomed twins Cole Patrick and Mackenzie Joyce into the world, and their arrival offered every bit of the excitement he felt during the fall of '07. Those who know Jamey have no doubt that he will be a wonderful father because of the values he learned from his own parents. Their example enabled him to beat the odds and to build a life playing the game he loved.

From the ecstasy of the improbable hot streak that took the Rockies to the World Series to the disappointment felt after being swept by the Red Sox, Jamey had lived his dream. His only regret was that Patty Carroll wasn't there to share the experience. Even today, he can't talk about his mother without choking up.

When asked what his mother meant to him, Jamey's voice trembled and the emotions flowed freely. "She was one of the hardest working ladies I've ever known," he said through his tears. "She made me realize that, if you want anything, you have to work hard at it. Nobody's going to give it to you. She was a prime example of that.

"It was a blessing to grow up in the home where I grew up because I wouldn't be who I am if it weren't for her and my dad. They were just blue collar people trying to make their way. Mom gave everything to everybody, and it's a shame she couldn't be here to see the dream come true. To get traded to the Rockies, who wore purple, and to have this success, I can't help but think she's up there in Heaven pulling some strings. Not a day goes by that I'm not thankful for who she was."

Jamey Carroll is a class act, and he is generous in giving credit to teammates, coaches and especially his parents, Larry and Patty. Larry is the typical proud father who can talk endlessly about all three boys and can rattle off stats and memories as he flips through countless pages from the stacks of scrapbooks in his home. After two years, Jamey still feels the pain from his mother's passing, and there's no doubt that he believes she's still looking over him even today. For all who knew her, it's nice to think that when they look at the sky and see a glistening purple hue, it's Patty Carroll's way of telling each of her boys, "I'm proud of you, son."

Jamey Carroll had often thought about drawing a portrait of his mother, Patty, who passed away in 2005. Jamey agreed to create this portrait to memorialize Patty in the pages of this book.

The subjects in the preceding pages represent a cross-section of the very best athletes, teams, and venues that have been a part of our history over the last century. They and many more like them have provided memorable moments that have made southwestern Indiana a great place for true sports fans to live. As the years go by, it is important that mothers and fathers pass along these stories so that young area athletes are aware of their heritage. With their help, the legends will live on.

In the current sports world, the class system in some sports has muddied the water somewhat as far as determining the best of the best, but as always, somehow the cream always comes to the top. As a final tribute, we will honor the future by recognizing a few of the athletes whose feats haven't yet withstood the test of time but whose accomplishments might be recognized someday on the same level as those from the past. These young athletes have all distinguished themselves in their chosen sports, and many of their greatest stories have yet to be written. So as we say good-bye to our past and look ahead to our future, we make a final tribute to just a few of our…

LEGENDS IN THE MAKING.

Curtis Painter (Vincennes Lincoln/Purdue) (Photo courtesy of the *Evansville Courier*.)

FahKara Malone (Memorial/Purdue) (Photo courtesy of the *Evansville Courier*.)

Luke Zeller (Washington/Notre Dame).
(Photo courtesy of the *Evansville Courier.*)

Tyler Zeller (Washington/University of North Carolina)
(Photo courtesy of the *Evansville Courier.*)

IHSAA STATE CHAMPIONS:

BOYS GOLF

Team	Year	Score	Coach
North	1999-2000	608	Larry Tindle

Individual	School	Year	Score
Bob Hamilton	Reitz	1933-1934	72
Jerry McRae	Mater Dei	1958-1959	72
Chris Dayton	Washington Catholic	1988-1989	146

GIRLS GOLF

Individual	School	Year	Score
Suzanne Noblett	Castle	1982-1983	76+
Suzanne Noblett	Castle	1984-1985	74

David Erdy (Castle)
(Photo courtesy of the *Evansville Courier*.)

Paul McIntosh (Reitz/ Southern Illinois University,)

Bryce Brown (Harrison/South Plains College) (Photo courtesy of the *Evansville Courier*.)

Natalie Schmett (North) (Photo courtesy of the *Evansville Courier*.)

AND…

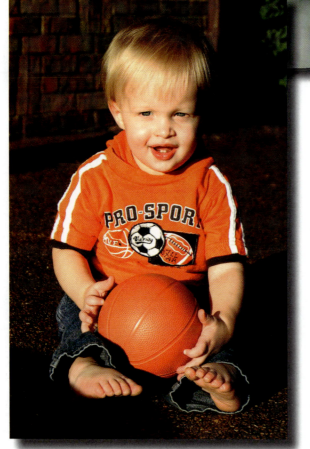

Parker, my grandson (You never know!)

ACKNOWLEDGMENTS

This book could never have been written without the help and support of the following people:

The River City Round Table
    Ed Cole
    Casey Eaton
    Bruce Lomax
    Rick Pittman
    Dave Sandefur
    Jack Weatherholt
    Ben Willis
    Joe Willis
    Steve Willis
Shelly and Steve Adlard
Hugh and Carol Ahlering
Jerry Alstadt
Bill and Mary Altmeyer
Marty Amsler
Brett Bardwell
Gary Barnett
Bob Beck
Marvin Beglin
Dave Bell
Andy and Jennifer Benes
Cyril Birge
Wayne Boultinghouse
Ron and Barb Brand
Jerry Brewer
Buster and Beth Briley
Karen (Mattingly) Brucken
Don Buse
Mark Buse
Bruce Byers
George Byers
Jim and Carol Byers
Phil and Joan Byers
Bill and Fran Calkin
Dale Campbell
Jerry and Bernice Canterbury
Jamey Carroll
Larry Carroll
Calbert Cheaney
Gwen Cheaney
Bob Clayton
Jerry Clayton
Steve and Patti Clutter
Jim Crawford
Cheryl (Dowell) Crowell
Jeff Crowley
Dr. Susan Dellinger
Dennis and Jane Dilger
Derrick Dowell
John Drof
Barb Dykstra
Charlotte Eaton
Chase Eaton
Kelly Eaton

Shanyn Engler
Bob Ewin
Pete Fisher
Marlon Flemming
Bob Ford
Steve Ford
LeAnn Freeland
Marty Garafalo
Joe Gengelbach
Gary Gilles
Grant Glackman
Mike Goebel
Larry Goffinet
Jon Goldsberry
Tom and Janice Goldsberry
Glenn Grampp
Paul and Mary Gries
Bill Griese
Bob Griese
Jim Hamilton
John Hamilton
Don and Sandy Hansen
Ken Hansen
Kevin Hardy
Bob Hargrave
Haley Harris
Larry Harris
Randy Harris
Bill Hazelip
Anna Hazlett
Stephanie Hazlett
Randy Helfrich
Wayne Henning
Don Hess
Mike Hodgen
Greg Hofmann
Larry Humes
Jim Hummel
Doug Hurt
Broc Jerrel
Dave Johnson
Jerry Jones
Roger and Beverly Kaiser
Dave King
Bruce King
Duane and Bernice King
Morris Klipsch
Keith Kohlmeyer
Kendall Kreinhagen
Mary Mason Kron
Alan Lander
Cassandra Lander
Vicki Lander
Richard Lankford

Bob Lochmueller
Steve Lochmueller
Chris Lowery
Mike Madriaga
Harold Malicoat
Wayne and Charlotte Malotte
Mitch Marsch
Don Mattingly
Randy and Melissa Mattingly
Virginia Mattingly
Kathy Mauck
Matt Mauck
Norma Maurer
Rob Maurer
Walter McCarty
Norm McCool
Allen McCutchan
Jerry and Joyce Memering
Quentin Merkel
Zora Miller
Mike Minton
Scott Mitchell
Gene Morgan
John Morrow
Joe and Judy Mullan
Rich Nau
Russ Neathery
Don Niemeier
Andy Owen
Chris Owen
Louise Owen
Mike and Susan Owen
Jim Pegram
Mike Pegram
Bobby Plump
Duane Poole
Jerry Purdie
Jim Rausch
Pat Rayburn
Steve Reed
Bob and Jane Reinhart
Lanae Renschler
Connie and Larry Renschler
Gene Ress
Morris Riley
Joyce Roades
Carolyn Roberts
P.M. and Sara Sanders
Willie and Irene Saucer
Hugh Schaefer
Dave Schellhase
Fred Schmalz
Brian and Ann Schmett

Janice Schuble
Les Shively
Pat Shoulders
Jerry Scott
Charlie Siesky
Chris Sievers
Gordon Slade
Tom Slade
Michelle Slayton
Jerry Sloan
Bryan Speer
Larry Stallings
Dr. Bill Stedman
Dr. Peter and Patti Stevenson
Rick Stippler
Allen Stremming
Jim and Barbara Studwell
Scott and Jenny Studwell
Mary Lou Taylor
Father Ted Tempel
Bill and Norma Thomas
Mike Thomas
Mike Thompson
Judy Turner
Tom and Brenda Turner
Talmadge Vick
Bill and Mary Vieth
Bill Vieth Jr.
Gary Virgin
Dean Volkman
Eileen Volkman
Mike Volkman
Ron Volkman
Lee Walden
Bob Walker
James and Woodie (Sublett) Walker
Brenda Walling
Ron Wannemueller
Dayle Wedeking
Pat Welch
Steve Welmer
Ed Wessel
John Wessel
Rick Wheeler
Jerry Whitsell
Bob Winchell
Mike and Tracye Wilson
Chuck Winters
George Wright
Will Wyman
Mort Zachter
Ed Zausch
Brenda and Larry Zoller

ACKNOWLEDGMENTS (CONT.)

Arizona State University
  Steve Rodriguez
Boonville High School
  Bernie Meyer
Bosse High School
  Bob Adams
  Larry Cochren
Castle High School
  John Evers
Central High School
  Alicia Gooch
  Ira Harris
  Paul Neidig
Collegiate Images
  Tim Williams
The Dubois County Bombers
The Dubois County Museum
  Mary Ann Hayes
  Marilyn Kress
The Evansville African-American Museum
  William Miller
Ellis Park
  Bob Jackson
The Evansville-Vanderburgh School Corporation
  LeKita Hart
Forest Park High School
  Lee Begle
  Doug Louden
Georgia Tech University
  Dean Bruchan
Harrison High School
  Jay Burch
  Dennis Bays
  Pat Malone
Heritage Hills High School
  Josh Heldt
The IHSAA
  Blake Ress
The Indiana Basketball Hall of Fame
  Don Chambers
  Ruth Coffey
  Roger Dickinson

The Indiana Football Hall of Fame
  J.D. Morris
Indiana University-Media Relations
  Theresa Perkins
Indianapolis Brebeuf Jesuit High School
  Andy Fagan
  Mike Marshall
Jacksonville University
  Josh Ellis
Jasper High School
  Tony Ahrens
  Terry Gobert
  Dennis Lewis
Kentucky Wesleyan College
  Roy Pickerill
Long Beach State University
  Roger Kirk
Louisiana State University
  Michael Bonnette
Madison High School
  Ken Brunner
  Harold Lakeman
Mater Dei High School
  Joe Herrmann
  Sara Wagner
Memorial High School
  Bruce Dockery
  Patty Vann
McCleansboro High School
Mt. Vernon High School
  Gary Redman
  Clint Winemiller
North High School
  Brenda Weber
  Bob Cuprison
Oakland City University
  Dave Terrell
Princeton High School
  Andy Elkins
Purdue University
  Tom Schott

Reitz High School
  Beth Hagen
Tecumseh High School
  Bill Fritz
Tell City High School
  Maurice Harpenau
University of Evansville
  Bob Boxell
  Daryl Buente
  Tom Benson
University of Illinois
University of Kentucky
  Meredith Melson
University of Missouri
  Kate Lakin
University of Nevada - Las Vegas
  Mark Wasik
University of Southern California
  Tim Tessalone
University of Southern Indiana
  John Deem
  Barb Goodwin
  Jennifer Greene
  Dan McDonald
  Ray Simmons
Vincennes Lincoln High School
  David Hill
Vincennes University
  Dave Hunter
  Paula Kirk
Washington High School
  Gene Miiller
Wood Memorial High School
  Steve Killian
Willard Library
  Lyn Martin
  Peggy Newton
  Pat Sides

INDEX

A

Aaron, Hank 63, 64, Henry 62
Abbott, Jim 190
Adams 14, Bob 84, 86, 300, John 13, 14, 38
Adlard, Andy 224, Shelly 224, 229, 230, 299, Steve 224, 299, Susie 224
Adler, Donnie 76
Agee, Jeff 211, 212, Tommy 64
Ahlering 106, 114, Carol 116, 299, George 24, Hugh 5, 25, 55, 105, 111, 112, 113, 116, 117, 299
Ahrens, Tony 142, 143, 300
Akers, Byrle 76, Chase 288
Albin, Lonnie 219
Alcindor, Lew 40
Aldridge, Shawn 257
Alexander 185, Grover Cleveland 17, John 2, 12, 65, 185
Alford, Sam 4, 33, Steve 4, 30
Allee, Slim 18
Allen, George 135, Phog 10, Sam 41, Wayne 144
Alstadt 254, Jerry 173, 253, 255, 258, 299
Alston, Walter 61, 62, Warren 131, 132
Altmeyer 82, Bill 81, 83, 299, Mary 81, 299
Alvey, George 11
Ambrose, John 67, 68, Scott 185
Amsler 51, Jeannie 51, Marty 5, 50, 51, 299
Anderson, Charles 59, 92, Jeff 250, 260, Marc 228, Randy 179, Roger 267
Andres, Ernie 52
Andretti, Mario 231
Andrews, Jim 154
Antonelli, Johnny 61
Arcaro, Eddie 21
Archer, Mike 94
Armentano, Matt 288
Armstrong, B.J. 256
Arnold 164, Brenda 169, John 163
Ary, 'Rip' 106
Ashby, Donald 185
Ashworth, Bob 8, 200, 270
Atkinson, Stan 206
Attles, Al 105
Atwater, Terry 109
Austin, Tracy 180, 181

B

Bacon, Darrell 185, De 267, Deanna 267, Kevin 149, Mary 93, Ron 267
Baffert 266, Bob 92, 265
Bailey, Aaron 276, Damon 215, 250, 280
Ballard, Gene 166
Ballenger, Mike 94
Ballou, Richard 185
Bancroft, Rob 202
Banks, Ernie 63
Bardwell, Brett 299
Bargo, Ken 80
Barnes, Cortez 257
Barnett, Bob 106, Gary 9, 299, George 48, Jim 9, 57, 106, 110, 159, 168, 169, John 166
Barnhill, John 49, 216
Barnum, P.T. 114
Barrato, Johnny 86
Barr, Terry 10
Barry, Rick 49, 80, 89
Barton, Paul 210
Basham, Red 97
Bass, Mike 135
Bates, Edie 107, Marv 82, 107, 113, 131, 132, 169, 231
Bath, Mildred 238
Bayh, Birch 131
Bays, Dennis 163, 234, 300
Beach, Tom 38
Beadles, Virgil 29
Beasley, Mo 94
Beck, Bob 113, 299, Paul 10, 50, 75, 113
Becker, Ralph 8, 9
Begle, Lee 254, 300
Beglin, Marvin 299
Behrman, Chet 231
Belden 202, Jim 202
Bell, Dave 299, Doug 172, 197, 198, Sam 213, 233, Spike 172
Bellew, Bob 194
Bench, Johnny 88, 99
Benes, Adam 190, Alan 190, 191, Andy 5, 6, 99, 147, 148, 189, 191, 299, Bailey 191, Brynn 191, Chuck 191, Drew 191, Jennifer 190, 299, Karen 191, Shane 191
Benner, Bill 213
Benson, Roger 158, 160, 162, 211, Tom 300
Berger, Anthony 40, Mike 143
Berg, John 41, 42
Bernhardt, Don 159, 201
Berra 62, Yogi 59, 178
Bertram, Charles 255
Beverly, Phil 9
Bial, Mark 256
Billips, Chauncey 241
Bing, Dave 89
Bingham, Billy 215
Bird, Calvin 285, Larry 55, 88, 94, 100, 128, 232
Birge, Cyril 5, 23, 39, 40, 41, 299, Jerry 108, 169
Bishop, J.R. 154, Mike 285
Bitter, Larry 67
Black 221
Blackard, Jason 269
Black, Denic 55, 219, 220, 221
Blackford, Craig 174
Blake, Jen 231, Mike 5, 231
Blanchard, Doc 26
Bledsoe, Drew 226
Bleecker, Bonnie 281
Blemker, Don 22
Block, John 199
Bocksthaler, Bill 52
Boehman, Bob 94
Boger, Carl 30
Boggs, Wade 17, 178
Bohnert, Jeff 132
Bohwert 41
Bolen, Freddie 49, 55
Bolla, Sheila 218
Bonds, Barry 292
Bonham, Ron 118, 215
Bonnette, Michael 300
Boots 284, Dorothy 286, Tim 285, 286, 288
Bootz, Harold 20
Bosse, Benjamin 98, 99
Boswell, Ken 63
Bouchie, Bryan 32, 33, Steve 32, 33, 255, Tom 33
Boultinghouse 255, 256, 261, Wayne 4, 108, 109, 118, 127, 254, 255, 258, 299
Bowles, Chris 250, 258
Bowling, Lindsey 218
Bowman, Randy 158
Boxell, Bob 300
Boyd, Bob 175
Boyden, Scott 257
Boyd, Phil 80
Bradfield, Allen 148
Bradley, Milton 291
Bradshaw, Terry 187
Brady, Tom 36
Bragan, Bobby 59
Brahm, Terry 141, 213
Brand, Barb 2, 221, 223, 230, 299, Mike 223, Ron 2, 120, 176, 221, 223, 230, 299, Shelly (Adlard) 2, 55, 219, 220, 221, 222, 224, 229
Brandon, Ken 158
Brandsasse, Bill 254
Bratt, Jim 219
Brauser 146, Charlie 145
Brawn, Peggy 220
Brees, Drew 271
Bretz, Glen 46
Brewer, Jerry 5, 6, 142, 143, 144, 278, 299, Jorene 143, Mel 88
Briley, Beth 119, 299, Buster 5, 79, 108, 109, 114, 118, 119, 120, 123, 299, Della 118, Harold Eugene 118, Junior 118, Wanda 118, William 118
Brimm, James 288
Broadhead, Anne 267
Brodie, John 51
Bronson, Tom 48
Brooks, Scotty 241
Brosmer 200, Chris 200, 201, 202, 203, Dave 200, 201, 202, 203
Brouillette, Edward G. 29
Brown, Bryce 297, Jim 69, John 33, 255, Kenny 200, 201, 203, Kevin 260, Larry 124, Mordecai 'Three Fingers' 15, Otis 131, Roger 55, 126, 171, Ross 252, 282, Victor 184
Browning, Jerry 216, Tyrone 6, 184
Brownlee, Jim 189, 290, Ryan 67, Tim 67
Broyles, Charlie 80
Bruchan, Dean 300
Brucken, Karen 299
Bruin, Lisa 55, 217

Brundige, Bill 135
Brunell, Mark 226
Bruner, Sarah 267
Brunner, Ken 300
Bryant, Allyson 267, Hallie 57, Jim 69, Kobe 149
Buck, Al 84, 85, Jack 215
Buckner, Quinn 280
Buehler, Phil 277
Buente 167, 168, Daryl 111, 112, 165, 167, 169, 300, Gerard 88
Bullard, Paul 108, 109, 110, 118
Buntin, Bill 89, Bull 108
Buoniconti, Nick 135
Burch, Jay 200, 202, 300
Burdette, Lew 62
Burleson, om 171
Burns, Creighton 256, Judy 220
Burris, Roy 29, 30
Burrows, Pembrook 82, 125
Buse, Andrew 126, Andrew Jr. 125, 126, Bev 233, Brad 233, Don 6, 55, 94, 111, 112, 114, 5, 121, 125, 126, 127, 129, 145, 171, 223, 253, 299, Edwin 233, Fay 126, Junior 125, Mark 5, 141, 185, 233, 299, Mary 126, Mary Lou 233, Nina 126, Opal 125, 126, Rex 125, 126, Scott 233, Sue 126
Bush, Felicia 217
Bussing, Bill 2, 103
Butkus, Dick 50, 74, 80, 187, 226
Butler, Brenda Sue 219, 220, Carl 48
Butterfield, Bill 36, 180
Butterworth, Jack 110
Buzea, Craig 249
Byers 5, Bruce 299, Carol 299, George 9, 10, 11, 299, Herman 4, 7, 8, 9, 10, 11, 13, 24, 69, 70, 71, 72, 73, 74, 76, 144, 151, 190, Isabel 9, 10, Jean 190, Jim 9, 10, 11, 72, 76, 77, 174, 186, 207, 299, Joan 299, Phil 9, 10, 27, 56, 57, 190, 191, 299
Byrd, Bill 41
Byrne, Doc 36, Tommy 62

C

Cabrillas, Laura 267
Cagle, Conrad 231
Caldwell, Jim 202, Kevin 257
Calhoun, Robert 198
Calkin, Bill 299, Fran 299
Campagna, Bruce 2
Campanella, Roy 59, 62
Campbell, Dale 299, Earl 187, Jim 81, 82
Cannon, Roger 211, Scott 208, 209, 210
Canterbury 157, 217, Bernice 57, 86, 156, 299, Jerry 11, 12, 57, 84, 85, 86, 152, 155, 156, 157, 204, 216, 218, 299
Carew, Rod 17
Carl, Jon 2, 8, 96
Carnes, William 40
Carp, Barb 227
Carr, Austin 120
Carroll, Ben 282, Cole Patrick 292, 293, Jamey 2, 5, 148, 289, 290, 291, 292, 293, 299, Jason 289, 290, 291, Kim 292, 293, Larry 289, 290, 292, 293, 299, Mackenzie Joyce 292, 293, Patty 289, 290, 292, 293, Wes 289, 290
Carter, Don 193, Richard 185
Cartwright, Kevin 143, 277
Carty, Rico 64
Casalena, Mike 172
Casalena, Pat 172
Casaletto, Maria 282
Casebier, Parrish 225, 250
Case, Everett 257
Cato, Gene 23, 138, 280
Caudell 35, 37, 38, Norris 34, 35, 37
Celania, Joe 79, 194
Cepeda, Orlando 64
Chamberlain, Wilt 89, 100, 123
Chambers, Don 300, Jeff 33
Chapman, John 261, Neil 200, 201, Ralph 165, 169, Wayne 256
Chase, Hal 16, Irving 95
Chavis, Vaughn 77
Cheaney, Calbert 4, 5, 171, 224, 225, 231, 232, 234, 235, 236, 240, 250, 280, 299, Camille 234, 236, Deatris 183, Elizabeth 234, 236, Gwen 234, 235, 236, 299, Julian 236, Sydney 236, Yvette 236

Cheeks, Tom 48
Chester, Deon 200, 201, 202, 203
Chestnut, Jeff 197, 198
Childers, Bud 146
Chinn, Delisa 229
Chitwood, Jimmy 33
Christian, Myron 197, 198, 199, 218, Myron Jr. 199
Cicotte, Eddie 17, 18
Clapp, Elissa Kim 239, Geoff 239
Clark, George Rogers 211, Johnny 249, Mark 49, 110
Clausen, Rick 278
Claybourne, Ken 197, 198
Claycomb, Brent 211
Clayton 10, 94, 154, Bob 6, 111, 112, 144, 213, 270, 271, 272, 273, 275, 276, 299, Jerry 55, 106, 112, 117, 138, 171, 299
Clendenon, Donn 63, 64
Clutter, Patti 299, Steve 184, 299
Coates, Nathaniel 48
Cobb, Steve 185, Ty 15, 16, 17, 18
Cochrane, Joe 76
Cochren, Larry 300
Coffee, J.C. 27
Coffey, Rick 55, 111, 112, 125, Ruth 300
Cohan, George M. 16
Cokes, Hubert 'Daddy Warbucks' 181
Cole, Bob 156, Chad 210, Ed 72, 81, 299
Coleman, Bob 19, 99, Charlie 175, Kelly 55, 105, 107, Prince 185
Colescott, Dave 155, Jack 155
Collins, Clifton 48, Don 81, 82, Kerry 279, Meagan 267
Comandella, Ray 131, 132
Combs 212, Dan 212, John 33, Keith 49, Randy 211, 212
Comiskey, Charles 15, 18
Conerly, Charlie 274
Conley, Larry 164
Conner, Jimmy Dan 154, Sonny 163
Conrad, Jerry 94
Cook, Malcolm 12, 184
Coomes, Mark 256
Coon, Carol 230

Coontz, Jane 242
Cooper, Cynthia 218, Deke 247, Jerry 76
Copeland, Jerry 194
Couch, John 125
Coudret, Ken 72, 134
Coughlin, Matt 286, 288
Courier, Skip 253, 254
Cousy, Bob 35, 154
Cox 106, Clyde 138, Harold 105, 106, 116
Coyle, Neil 257
Crandall, Del 99
Crane, Forrest 30
Crawford, Jim 169, 299
Crawley, Gwen 234, Marion 30, 31, 32, 38, 169
Crews, Jim 104, 189
Crick, Grodie 285
Cronkite, Walter 131
Crook 212, Doug 211, 212
Crosby, Bing 21
Crosley, David 79
Crowe, Cecilia 244, Ed 165, 169, Mandy 242, 244, 245, Ray 57, Robert 244
Crowell, Cheryl (Dowell) 205, 299
Crowley, Jeff 192, 194, 195, 299
Crum, Denny 105, 154
Csonka, Larry 74
Cuellar, Mike 64
Culver, George 48
Cummings, Joyce 196
Cuprison, Andy 247, 248, Bob 300
Cutler, Jay 5, 73, 271, 273, 274
Cutsinger, Larry 55
Czonka 187
Czonka, Larry 135

D

Dampier, Louie 164
Daniels, Mel 55, 126, Tim 165, 169
Davey, Rohan 278
David, Jerry 10, 11
Davies, Jane 144
Davis, Geena 2, 229, 230, Glen 26, Lyman 103, Mike 200, 201, 202, 203, Tom 256
Dawson, Anita 45, Len 134
Day, Mitch 210
Dayton, Chris 296
Deal, Walt 105, 106, 215
Dean, Dizzy 19, 99, 231, Paul 99
Decker, Joe 76, Willie 49

DeCorrevont, Bill 26
Deem, John 253, 254, 255, 258, 300
DeJernett 30, 31, 32, Dave 29, 30, 31, John 'Deacon' 30
Delker, John 24
Dellinger, Susan 2, 15, 299
Demaret, Jimmy 21
DeMoss, Bob 134, 135
Dennis, Leanne 150
Denton, Larry 110
Derrington, Mike 166
Deters, Matt 288
Devine, Dan 51
Dewey, Darrell 192
Diaz, Chris 257
Dickinson, Roger 300
Diedrich, Doug 211
Dilger, Dennis 275, 299, Heidi 276, Jane 275, 299, Ken 4, 5, 271, 275, 276
DiMaggio, Joe 59, 178
DiMuro, Lou 64
Dischinger, Terry 89
Dixon, Al 215
Dockery, Bruce 231, 300
Dodd, Bobby 53
Doerner, Gus 5, 6, 55, 105, 108, 112, 115, 121, 126, Scott 131
Donaldson, Bob 'Jug' 30
Donovan 212
Donovan, Karl 211, 212
Douglas, Camille Cheaney 234, E. 197
Dowell, Cheryl 5, 156, 204, 218, 299, Derrick 197, 198, 199, 204, 218, 299, Dwight 204, Lamont 204, Macon 204, Mamie 204, Pam 199
Downey, Robert 185
Downing 160, 168, Steve 160
Doyle, Kevin 257
Dressen, Charlie 61
Dress, William 25
Drof, John 58, 64, 299
Drone, Beth 219
Drysdale, Don 62, 69, 82
Duckwall 185
Dudley, Chris 241
Duffey, Jim 138, 139
Duff, Mike 131, 132
Dugan, Chancellor 263, 264
Dungy, Tony 276
Durocher, Leo 58, 59
Dykstra, Alan 222, Barb 55, 219, 220, 221, 222, 223, 299,
Dorothy 222, Stanley 222

E

Eady, Larry 257
Earl, Acie 256
Eato, Casey 299
Eaton, Casey 3, Charlotte 299, Chase 3, 299, Kelly 3, 299, Ron 2, 3, 165, 169, Suzy 2, 3
Ebenkamp, Frank 280
Eck, Angie 211
Eddy, Ray 31, 89
Edison, Thomas 114
Edmonds, Jim 191
Edwards, Bruce 59
Eggleston, Robert 185
Elam, Jason 274
Elderkin, Chip 288
Elkins, Andy 55, 250, 300, Bryant 247
Elkins-Reed, Andy 232
Eller, Carl 74, Hod 18
Ellington, Duke 92
Elliott, Pete 80
Ellis, James C. 92, Josh 300, Mark 292
Elmendorf, Sarah 169
Elmer, Jeff 247, 250
Elway, John 226, 274
Emerson, Gary 25
Emmert, Roger 215
Emmons, Rachel 268, 269, Shannon 268, 269
Engelhart 30, Ed 'Jingles' 29
Engelke, Jack 254
Engler, Shanyn 299
Erdy, David 296
Ernst, Tom 162, 211
Ervin, Toni 219, 221
Erwin, Larry 105, 106, 107, 108, 116, Todd 197
Evans, Brian 235, Charlie 103
Everett, Jim 271
Evers, John 300, Johnny 200, 203, 248, 249
Evert, Chris 181
Ewin, Bob 138, 139, 299
Ewing, Patrick 241

F

Fagan, Andy 300
Farley, Dick 23, 41, 42, 43
Farmer, Charlie 159, Chotsani 238
Farrand, Cindy 183
Fats, Minnesota 181
Faulkner, Jerry 160
Fausch, Franklin 19
Favre, Brett 273
Fawcett, Farrah 228
Feagley, Steve 254
Feeble, Stanley 58
Fehd, Dale 165, 169, 253, 254
Fendrich, Gary 70, Jerry 70, 72
Fenner, Greg 140, 166, 182, Lane 80
Fentress, Krista 183
Ferguson, Virgil 215
Fichter, Brad 215
Fidrich, Mark 'the Bird' 99
Fine, Charley 32
Finn, Dana 'Popcorn' 254
Fintress, Randy 197
Fisher, Charlie 10, 11, 12, Pete 12, 299
Fitzgerald, Jim 79
Fitzsimmons, Cotton 126
Flake, Jerry 33
Flamion, Randy 254
Fleck, Clarence 40
Flemming, Marlene 188, Marlon 185, 188, 299, William 188
Fletcher, Lynn 267, Tim 159
Flick, George 185
Fluty, Bill 113, 127
Flynn, Mike 154
Ford, Ace Whitey 62, Andrew 171, Bob 4, 89, 128, 145, 158, 159, 5, 165, 167, 168, 169, 170, 171, 299, Cliff 79, Gerald 100, Kara 171, Lucille 170, Polly 171, Rob 171, Robert Alan 170, Steve 285, 286, 299, Whitey 178
Fox, Beverly 19, Don 19, Elizabeth 19, Ervin 'Pete' 19, Helen 19, Jimmy 19, Pete 5, 6, 69, 99
Foxx, Jimmie 19
Foy, Eddie 16
Foyt, A.J. 92
Francis, Chet 23
Franklin, David 242, 244
Frank, Rick 67
Franzman, Dan 56
Fraser, Brad 250, Robert 250
Frazier, Walt 100, 110
Frederick, Jay 210
Freeland, Carroll 263, Donna 263, LeAnn 2, 5, 6, 55, 263, 264, 299
Freels, Mark 197, 198
Friddle 30, Burl 29, 30, 31, 38
Fritz, Bill 300, Mike 79, Steve 147, 261
Fromholz, Jake 99
Frye, Chuck 250
Fulkerson, A.O. 31
Fuller, Tony 148
Fulton, Brenda 243
Funderburke, Lawrence 235
Funkhauser 265
Funk-Niemeier, Michelle 229
Fuquay, Helen 196

G

Gabella, Angela 252
Gabriel, Roman 51
Gaddis, Bob 8, 96, 248
Galloway, Gus 115, Lowell 115
Gamble, Kevin 256
Garafalo, Marty 299
Gardner, Carl 47
Gardner, Joyce 38, Willie 57
Garland, Bud 33
Garnett, Connie 81
Garrett, Bob 79, Cornell 184, Wayne 63
Garshnek, Sonya 228
Gaudin, Bob 206, 207
Gearlds, Katie 157
Gee, Junior 55, 109
Gehrig, Lou 61, 178
Geiser, Angela 219
Geisler, Erin 239
Gengelbach, Joe 299
Gentry, Gary 64
George, Eddie 226, Jeff 248
Giannini, Jim 81, 82, 83, 166
Gibson, Kirk 99
Gibson, Randy 201
Giesler, David 'Jody' 106
Gilbert, Chad 256, 257, George 76
Gilham, Bob 56
Gilles, Gary 201, 299
Gill, Jenae 242, Pete 94
Gilmore, Artis 82, 100, 123, 125, 140, 182, Eugene 30
Given, Charlie 84, 86
Glackman, Grant 184, 185, 299
Glaser, Chris 189
Gleason 18, William 'Kid' 17
Goad, Charles 132
Gobert, Terry 77, 143, 278, 300

303

Goebel, Andy 283, Chris 285, Gary 283, Jeremy 287, John 38, 283, MacKenzie 287, Mike 6, 283, 284, 285, 286, 287, 288, 299, Rita 283, Zach 287
Goedde, Julie 204
Goffinet, Larry 299
Goldbach, Jeff 278
Goldsberry, Janice 299, Jon 270, 271, 272, 299, Tom 270, 299
Gonzalez, Tony 64
Gooch, Alicia 300, Geoff 221, Mike 94
Goodman, Chris 138, Mildred 45
Goodwin, Barb 300
Gorsage, Wesley 31
Gosman, Marty 40
Gossman, Joe 285, 286
Gouard, Stan 250, 256, 257, 259
Gourley, Harold 206
Grafton, Tad 183, 185
Graham, Buddy 94, Greg 235, Jim 79, 156, 206, Otto 26, Pat 235
Grampp, Glenn 151, 299
Grannan, Bob 254
Grant, Chet 27
Gray, Marvin 124, Ryan 197
Grayson, Nancy 246
Greenberg, Hank 98, 99
Green, Bill 121, 128, Bob 62, Dave 109, Krystal 267, Rickey 148, Ricky 148, Steve 154
Greenburg, Hank 19
Greene, Jennifer 300
Greer, Jason 288
Greif, Abby 239
Grele, Roy 27
Gress, Stan 288
Grevey, Kevin 154
Grieger 84, 85, Gary 84, 85, 86, 89, 120, Russ 55, 108, 109, 110
Gries, Aaron 67, Mary 299, Paul 5, 49, 78, 147, 148, 189, 190, 292, 299
Griese 187, Bill 133, 134, 299, Bob 2, 4, 23, 51, 73, 74, 75, 76, 85, 88, 89, 133, 134, 135, 136, 147, 173, 174, 203, 216, 265, 5, Brian 135, 136, Ida 133, Joyce 133, Judi 136, Sylverius 133, 134
Griffin, Roger 69

Grimwood, Darren 288
Groeger, Susan 251
Groh, Heinie 16, 17, 18
Grote, Jerry 63
Grove 30, 32
Grove, Art 30, 31, 36
Gruden, Jon 276
Grundhoefer, Danny 52
Guenther, Bob 84, 86
Guest, Valerie 219
Gustafson, Gerald 69
Guyton, A.J. 280
Gwynn, Tony 17

H

Haag, Charlie 37
Hacker, Brenda 228
Haffner, Scott 129
Hagemeyer, Opal 125
Hagen, Beth 300
Hague, Courtney 251, 252
Haight, Mark 141, 145
Hairston, Scott 293
Halas, George 19, 50
Halbrook, Hal 105, 107
Hale 184, Bruce 'Slick' 80
Hall, Bob 61, Jason 249, Joe B. 154, 164
Haller, Ed 24
Hamilton 2, Bob 2, 5, 6, 20, 21, 255, 296, Charles 54, Jim 20, 21, 255, 299, John 20, 21, 299, June 20, Lee 5, 6, 23, 46, 106, 152, 155
Hanebutt, Elmer 106
Haniford, Earl 248, 250
Hanks, Tom 2, 229
Hansen 72, Chad 74, Don 5, 10, 51, 70, 72, 73, 74, 75, 76, 80, 299, Ken 70, 71, 73, 74, 75, 299, Melody 74, Sandy 74, 299, Wendy 74
Hape, Bill 8
Happe, Darren 288, Fred 288, Susan 150
Harbaugh, Jim 276
Harbert, Chick 21
Hardaway, Penny 128
Harden, Catherine Grace 227, Curry 228, Lanae Renschler 227, 228, Madeline 227
Har, Doug 72
Hardy, Brian 225, Camden 226, Carol 225, Herbert 224, Imelda 224, Josh 288, Kevin 4, 5, 73, 224, 225, 226, 232, 235, 240, 242, 275, 299, Langston

226, Terrie 226
Hargrave, Bob 24, 25, 27, 28, 299
Harker, Martha 150
Harmon 32, Bill 30, Bob 215, 285, Charles 30, 31, 32, John 103
Harp, Doug 70, Earl 38
Harpenau, Maurice 300
Harper, Lloyd 114
Harp, Jeffrey 288
Harrawood, Bill 170, 267, John 55, 94, 105, 106, 107, 117, 138
Harrelson, Ken 63
Harrington 208, Trey 207
Harris, Cynthia 145, Franco 187, Haley 5, 6, 145, 146, 299, Herbert 29, Ira 300, Larry 5, 6, 55, 76, 145, 146, 168, 215, 299, Linda 58, Randy 59, 65, 299
Harrison, Dutch 21, Gus 27, Marvin 276
Harte, Oscar 24
Hartford, Bill 132
Hart, John 6, 7, 8, LeKita 300
Hartman, Jill 204
Hartwick 112
Haskins, Don 164
Hassler, Erik 2
Hauck, John 24
Havlicek, John 40, 52, 108
Hawkins, Bob 270
Hayes, Mary Ann 300, Woody 151
Hayhurst, Lowell 154
Hazelip, Bill 116, 117, 122, 299
Hazlett, Anna 252, 281, 299, Stephanie 5, 239, 252, 281, 282, 299, Steve 281
Head, Pat 217
Hebert, Terry 245
Heckendorn, Kraig 131, 132
Hedde, Elizabeth 239
Hedge 185
Heffernan, John 185
Heinrich, Jim 151
Heldt, Carl 71, 225, Josh 300
Helfrich, Randy 284, 286, 287, 299
Helm, John 33, Julie 32
Helton, Todd 293
Henderson, Herb 19
Henke, Emerson 104
Hennenberger, Larry 154
Hennesey, Barb 251
Henning, Dan 67, Mike 67,

148, Wayne 299
Henry, Don 9, 56, 57, Walt 109
Henson, Lou 256
Herber, Paula 92
Herdes, Rick 257, 258
Hermann, Garry 17, 18
Herrenbruck, Kenny 56
Herrmann, Joe 300
Hert, Mickey 211
Hess, Don 299, Walter 24
Hester, Carrie 217, Donita 234
Heuring 184
Hevron, Beverly 52, 53
Hickrod, 'Sugar' (Shug) 76
Hicks, Ron 56
Higgs, Edmund 219
Hildebrandt, Jim 165, 166, 169
Hill 128, David 211, 212, 300, Robert 211, Vep 215
Hillenbrand, Billy 5, 24, 25, 26, 27, Inge 27, Joe 24, 25
Hillman, Darnell 55
Hinga, Jim 109
Hinkle, James 'Bud' 24
Hinton, Rovella 45
Hirsch, Duane 67, Elroy 27
Hisch, David 285
Hitler, Adolf 23
Hoagland, Dick 166, 169
Hobson, Randy 189
Hodges, Barbara 62, Bob 116, Bobby 58, Charlie 58, 62, Cynthia 62, Gil 2, 5, 6, 23, 58, 59, 61, 62, 63, 64, 65, 69, 116, 153, 265, Gil Jr. 61, 62, Irene 58, 62, Joan 61, 62, 64, 153, Marjorie 58, Mike 299, Russ 61
Hoek, Sean 210
Hoffman, Bob 23, Greg 172, Paul 23, 43, Trevor 293
Hofmann, Catherine 239, Greg 299
Hogan, Ben 21, Snake 76
Hoke, Gary 270
Holder, Larry 55, 215
Holland, Hollis 29, Steve 145, 165, 166, 169
Hollen 158
Hollen, Roger 158
Holliday, Matt 293
Hollinden 5, Ann 261, Fred 261, Joe 261, John 255, 261, 262
Holman, Bill 34
Holmgren, Mike 157

Holocek, Jon 225
Holstein, Jim 109, 127
Holt, Brian 67
Holton, Charles 103
Hooker, Earl 103
Hoover 167, Allie 267, Jerry 75, 100, John 151, 166, 175, Wayne 175
Hope, Bob 21
Horn, Alan 72
Hornbostel, Charles 6, 23
Hornsby 17, Rogers 16, 17, 62, 64
Hornung, Paul 74, 97
Hostetter, Marc 257
Hough, Jim 187
Hougland, Richard 165
Housman, Ed 69
Houston, Ellee 267, Lee 267
Howard, Dan 47, 71, Dana 225, 226, 275, Elston 62, Ryan 289, 293
Howell, Don 202
Hudson, Bob 76, 105, 107, 113, 122, 131, 132, Charlie 24
Huebner, Brian 256, 257
Huff, Don 163, Joe 200, 201, 203
Huffman, Harold 52
Humes 109, 110, 111, 114, Cecele 120, Eddie 120, Elizabeth 120, Frank 120, Frank Jr. 120, Howard 120, Junior 120, Larry 6, 38, 79, 85, 86, 89, 108, 109, 110, 112, 114, 117, 119, 120, 121, 123, 126, 147, 173, 5, Louise 120, Willie 120
Hummel, Jim 100, 115, 299
Humm, Shawn 248, 250
Hunt, Bryce 242, Franklin 22, 23
Hunter, Catfish 178, Dave 300, Harry 29, John 261
Hupfer, Clarence 110
Hupmann, Sascha 250
Hurdle, Clint 292
Hurley 128
Hurt, Doug 250, 299
Hussane, Yussif 99
Hutchison, Richard 211
Hyder, John 52, 53

I

Imel, Bob 56, 57
Infante, Lindy 276
Ingalls, Loren 251
Ingraham, Hoyt 185
Inman, Lauren 267
Irsay, Bob 276, Jim 276
Issel, Dan 171
Itskin, Claude 29
Iverson, Allen 241
Ivy, Marcus 185

J

Jabbar, Kareem Abdul 40, 61, 124, 149, 261
Jackson, Bo 68, Bob 300, Brian 260, Charles 48, David 248, Joe 17, 18, Keith 136, Ontario 248, Reggie 64, Ron 215
Jacobs, Mack 184, 185, Mark 6
James, Edgerin 276
Jaracz, Thad 164
Jaworski, Ron 273
Jeffries, Mike 166
Jenkins, Ferguson 63
Jensen, Adele 192, Just 207
Jerrel 35, 36, 37, 38, Bryan 'Broc' 23, 34, 35, 36, 37, 38, 171, 299, Rush 35, 37, 38
Jeske, John 288
Jesop, Ron 165, 169
Jochem, Larry 67
Jochim, Stan 270
Joergens, Bill 253, 254
Johann, Bob 71
John, Curt 111, 125, 126, 127, 129, 159, 166
Johnson, Chris 198, Da Shay 247, Dave 2, 60, 64, 77, 100, 124, 299, Jeremy 250, Kevin 241, Larry 241, Leroy 193, Lyndon 120, Magic 149, Ron 109, 156, 204, 220
Joiner, Michael 132
Jolly 286, Alex 285
Jone, Dontae 241
Jones 63, Carson 5, 6, 54, 55, 230, Cleon 63, 64, Danny 70, David 165, 169, Jerry 54, 299, Jim 215, John K. 103, K.C. 160, Norman 185, R.A. 'Cowboy' 92, Reese 13, 14, Robbie 197, Ron 6, 141, 185
Jordan, Leroy 225, Michael 124, 126, 128, 138, 241
Joyner, Mike 131
Julian, Cory 144

K

Kahle, Ron 77
Kaiser, Beverly 52, 53, 299, Jim 160, 184, Roger 5, 51, 52, 53, 89
Kaufman, Rich 181
Keener, Joe 106
Keep, James 48
Keily, Louise 45
Kell, Brent 232, 250, 260
Keller 37, 38, Billy 121, 261, Herman 34, 37, 38, 79, 84, 113, 156
Kelso, Katie 152
Kendall, Phil 278
Kendrick, David 197
Kennedy, John 100, Robert 63, Terry 278
Kent, Kenny 193, Robbie 253, 254
Kerr, Red 123
Kidwell, Larry 77, 215
Kiefer, Alena 2
Kiick, Jim 135
Killebrew, Harmon 63, Ken 67, 68
Killian, Steve 300
Kilpatrick, Arnold 37, Orvel 34
Kimani, Joseph 246
Kim, Chong 237, Elissa 2, 5, 237, 238, 239, Eugene 237, Jane 237, Jin 237, 238, Soo Jin 237
Kimmell, Mike 211
Kiner, Ralph 62
King, Bernice 271, 299, Billie Jean 181, Bob 58, Bruce 271, 272, 275, 299, Cory 201, Dave 193, 299, Duane 299, Edith 75, George 89, 154, Harry 22, 34, 37, Jeff 67, Larry 175, Maury 132, Monty 197, 198
King Edward VII 21
Kingston, Kevin 131, 132, Rick 109
King, Whalen 185
Kirby, Leslie 48
Kirkpatrick, Mark 132
Kirk, Paula 300, Roger 300
Klecko, Joe 187
Klier, Leo 31
Klipsch, Morris 58, 299
Klusmeier, Jimmy 248, Karl 71
Knapp, Gene 79
Kneis, Cade 143
Kniese, Mark 132
Knight 154, 162, 240, Bob 4, 40, 52, 108, 128, 160, 231, 235, 280, Darin 77, 283, Lawrence 255
Knipping, Greg 132
Knott, Bob 52, David 52, Larry 52
Koch, Natlie 242
Koehl, Bob 141
Koester, Chris 247
Koewler, Susan 219
Kohlmeyer, Bob 36, 55, 106, Keith 299
Koonce, Cal 64
Koosman 64, Jerry 63
Koressel, Richard 138, 139
Koufax, Sandy 62, 69
Kramer, Brenda 243, Ron 10
Kranepool, Ed 63
Kratzer, Lucy 194
Krause, Abe 81, 82, 83, 253, 254
Kreinhagen, Kaiden 157, Kendall 155, 156, 157, 299, Kevin 157
Kress, Clara 194, Dennis 163, Marilyn 300
Krieg, Lisa 55, 220
Krodel, Dave 41
Kroeger, Kaitlyn 267
Kron, Dick 163, Mary 163, Mary Mason 299, Max 163, Tom 2, 5, 6, 79, 84, 154, 161, 163, 164, Tommy 89, 120
Kuehn, Harvey 82

L

Labbe, Ed 134
Labhart, Dan 255
Lackey, John 211
Laettner 128
LaGrange, Ron 233
Lakeman, Harold 300
Lakin, Kate 300
Lamar, Chuck 106, Dwight 'Bo' 112
Lambeau, Earl 'Curly' 19
Lambert 82, Steve 81, 82, 83, Ward 'Piggy' 37
Lamb, Sammy 288
Lancaster, Ron 174
Lander 5, Alan 216, 299, Cassandra 6, 141, 156, 183, 216, 217, 218, 299, Keith 247, Matt 216, Ted 49, 55, 216, 218, Tim 197, Vicki 6, 156, 216, 218, 299, Zora 216
Landrey, Lisa 211
Landry 158, Larry 158, Tom 50

Lanier, Bob 171
Lankford, Jeff 214, 215, M.R. 214, Ray Jay 214, 215, Richard 5, 76, 77, 214, 215, 299, Steve 215, Stuart 214, 215
Larsen, Don 61
Larson, Gary 74
La Sell, Ashley 244
Latham 36, Gene 36, Jerry 285
Latshaw, Leigh Ann 55
Lattner, Joe 211
Laughery, Kevin 54
Lawrence, Charlie 88, 89
Lawson, Bruce 49, Chris 235
Layden, Elmer 27, Frank 124
Leaf, Brad 55, Ryan 136
Leaman, Jack 110
Lear, Pinky 97
Leary, Todd 235
Lease, Kemper 206
Ledgerwood, Norma 38
Lee, Clyde 89, Jimmy 154
Leinert 274, Matt 273
Leland, Jim 99
Lemmons, Abe 140
Lendl, Ivan 181
Leonard, Bobby 10, 126
Lewellen, Norm 12
Lewis, Barney 131, 132, Brian 143, Dennis 280, 300, Marvin 226, Michael 4, 6, 94, 280
Lidy 249, Allen 250, John 6, 144, 200, 201, 202, 247, 250, 289, Vince 247, 248, 249, 250
Lindauer, Derek 147, 212, Dirk 147, 148
Lindenschmidt, Larry 75
Liquori, Marty 213
Litchfield, Bill 41, 42
Little, Larry 135
Lloyd, Russell Sr. 131
Lochmueller 5, Bob 23, 55, 89, 153, 215, 299, Christi 155, Liz 154, Nancy 153, 154, Steve 153, 154, 299
Lockyear 85, Gene 84, 85, 86, 88, 141, 185, Pat 201, 202, 269
Loge, Joe 77
Logel, Gene 47, 67, 134, 231
Lohaus, Brad 256
Lohr, Tammy 267
Lomax, Bruce 35, 114, 115, 117, 122, 299
Lombardi, Joan 61, Vince 97
Long, Paul 218, Willie 169
Lord, Holyn 237, 238
Louden, Doug 300
Louis, Joe 21
Lovelace, Dale 265
Lovelette, Clyde 46
Lowery, Chris 5, 137, 225, 232, 235, 240, 242, 250, 299
Lucas, Jerry 40, 52, 89
Luebbe, Elaine 251
Luegers, Bub 108
Lukas, D. Wayne 92
Lurker 106, Mel 55, 105, 107, 108, 116
Luttrell, Joe 215
Lutz, Kyla 267, 268, 269
Lynch, Justin 77
Lyon, Mick 207
Lytle, Howard 103

M

Macias, Jose 291
Mack, Connie 15
Mackovick, John 275
Macon, Charles 250
Madden, Jerry 56
Madison, George 185
Madonna 2, 229
Madriaga, Edith 75, Mike 5, 50, 75, 76, 79, 88, 136, 229, 299
Magee, Lee 16
Malicoat, Harold 105, 197, 299
Mallory, Bill 225, 247
Malone, FahKara 294, Karl 124, 236, Pat 300
Malotte, Charlotte 299, Wayne 299
Manchette, Tammie 219
Mangin, Leroy 30, 31
Manning, Peyton 276
Mantilla, Felix 62
Mantle, Mickey 21, 61, 62, 63, 178
Maples, C.V. 8, 9
Marchibroda, Ted 276
Marcy, Lawson 103
Maree, Sydney 213
Marginet, Sherrill 215
Marion, Shawn 148
Marsch 187, Mitch 186, 224, 225, 299, Scott 225
Marshall, Brandon 274, Jim 74, Mike 300, Penny 2, 46, 91, 229, 230
Martin, 79, Billy 62, Calvin 49, 184, Craig 257, Dana 267, Dean 21, Don 252
Martinez, Tino 190
Martin, Gregg 111, 112, Jim 211, Leon 6, 185, Lisa 219, 220, Lyn 300, Mickey 69, 75, 78, 79, 88, 134, Tom 141, 185
Martzolf, Katie 228
Marvel, Jerry 56, 57
Marx, Gary 82
Mashburn, Jamal 155, 241
Mason, Bob 69, Mark 165, 169, Marshall 197, Mary 163, Randy 172, Rick 172, Ronnie 172, Rusty 172, Steve 67
Matheis, Greg 288
Mathews, Jack 34
Mathewson, Christy 16, 17
Matsui, Kaz 292, 293
Matthews 35, 36, 37, Eddie 62, Jack 34
Mattingly 5, Bill 172, 'D' 176, Don 2, 4, 67, 68, 88, 99, 148, 5, 173, 176, 178, 179, 190, 191, 231, 299, George 185, Jerry 55, 76, 78, 88, 110, 134, 147, 172, 173, 174, 176, 177, 179, Jill 173, Jordan 179, Judy 172, Karen 173, 299, Mary 172, 176, Melissa 172, 175, 177, 179, 299, Michael 174, Michelle 173, 174, Mike 172, 176, Preston 179, Randy 172, 173, 174, 175, 176, 177, 178, 179, 186, 299, Taylor 179, Ted 80, 88, Virginia 45, 46, 299
Mauck, Geoff 143, 277, Jill 279, Kathy 277, 278, 299, Libby 277, Matt 5, 143, 277, 278, 279, 299, Roger 277, 278
Maurer 286, Blake 285, 288, Norma 299, Rob 190, 299
Mautz, Lynn 109
May, Jeff 247, Scott 128
Mayer 284, Nick 288
Mayes 250, Patrick 249, 250, 288
Mayo, Harold 13, 14
Mays, Willie 63, 216
McAdoo, Bob 6, 148, 149
McBride, Gator 225
McCain, John 57
McCardell, Keenan 226
McCarty, Joy 240, Walter 4, 5, 171, 231, 232, 235, 240, 242, 250, 299
McClary, Charlie 155
McCool 35, 36, 37, Maxey 37, Norm 34, 35, 36, 37, 206, 299
McCormick, Mac 158
McCoy, Bill 33
McCracken, Branch 10, 52
McCullough, Steve 166
McCutchan 104, 105, 106, 108, 109, 110, 111, 121, 128, Allen 113, 114, 115, 299, Arad 23, 34, 80, 84, 104, 105, 106, 112, 113, 114, 115, 116, 117, 118, 119, 122, 123, 125, 127, 130, 156, 173, 5, Bernice 113, Jeannie 45, Owen 113, Virginia 113, 114
McDaniel, Paul 69, Wayne 69
McDonald, Ben 190, Dan 300, Frank Jr. 210
McDowell, Matt 200, 201, 202
McEnroe, John 181
McFall, Bob 269
McGannon, Tommy 24
McGee, Leola Rogers 188, Pam 218, Paula 218, Tony 235
McGill, Bill 108
McGinness, Clem 103
McGinnis 160, 168, George 126, 160, 215
McGlothin, Lowell 42
McGothlin, Kern 23
McGowan, Dick 76, Maxey 37, 38
McGrady, Tracy 149
McGraw 64, John 15, 17, Tim 63, Tug 63
McGuire 107, 185, Al 40, 105, 107
McHugh, Dan 207
McIntosh, Paul 8, 297
McKay, John 135
McLain, Denny 231
McLean, Jack 231
McLendon, John 49
McMahon, John 243
McMillan, Ruth 45
McMillin, Bo 26
McMinnis, Lawrence 103
McNair, Steve 226
McNally, Dave 64, Ryan 242, 244
McNeil, George 110
McRae, Jerry 296

Meadows, Adrian 169, A.L. 165
Mehringer, Justin 143
Meier, Bob 215
Melson, Meredith 300
Memering, Carolyn 158, Jerry 2, 54, 158, 159, 160, 162, 166, 171, 299, Joyce 299
Menke, Bill 22, 23, Bob 22, 23
Mercer, Leah 55, Ron 155, 241
Merfeld, Steve 104
Merkel 177, 178, Greg 67, 68, Quentin 5, 67, 68, 77, 177, 299, Shawn 68
Merriweather, Porter 49, 171, Graham 208
Merten, Nancy 153
Metzger, Mike 267
Meyer, Bernie 300, Mike 253, 254, Ray 105, Steve 94
Meyers, Jim 76
Mieras, Buzz 288
Miiller, Gene 38, 300
Mikan, George 154
Mikes, Mike 207
Miles, Bob 33, Brian 48, 197, 199, Walter 48, 79, 199, 216, 218
Miller 41, Andy 248, Bud 155, Cheryl 204, 217, 218, Claude 40, Harlan 103, Jane 52, John 81, Johnny 81, Reggie 204, 241, Roger 110, Ryan 68, Steve 33, 131, 132, Todd 67, William 300, Zora 299
Mills, John 189, Mike 203, Scotty 241
Minton, Mike 72, 134, 173, 299
Mitchell, Jack 210, Scott 299
Mollenkopf, Jack 79, 134
Mominee, John 75, 79
Monroe, Dee 42, Earl 100
Mooney, Jennifer 220
Moon, John 151, Keith 131, 132
Moore, Dave 189, 276
Mora, Jim 276
Moran, Pat 17
Morgan, Gene 94, 299, Joe 18, 99, Kenny 168, Ray 81, 82
Morrall, Earl 135
Morrell, Sandy 230
Morris, Jack 99, J.D. 300, Jim 81, 83, Jim Jr. 83, Mercury 135

Morrow 221, John 299, Missy 219, 220, 221, 222
Mortensen, Chris 273
Moss, Paul 194
Mott, Bill 92
Mount, Rick 171, 215
Mueller, Brad 67
Mueth, Warner 192
Mulherin, Tommy 105
Mullan 197, 198, Jeff 197, Joe 79, 80, 88, 197, 199, 299, Judy 299
Mullin, Chris 241
Mundy, Aaron 270
Murphy, George 8, Grady 67
Musgrave, Shawn 67
Musial, Stan 17
Musselman, Bill 111
Myers 85, 86, Jim 34, 38, 84, 86, 98, 110, 156, 162, 164, Steve 69

N

Naismith, James 49
Namath, Joe 50
Nash, Cotton 99, 118, Steve 241
Nass, Al 94
Nater, Swen 160
Nau, Rich 9, 11, 71, 72, 73, 299
Navratilova, Martina 180, 181
Neal, Craig 33
Neathery, Russ 192, 193, 195, 299
Neel, George 125
Neidly, Paul 300
Neighbors, Kareem 247
Nelson, Byron 20, 21, Don 124, Greg 82, 125, 140, 166, 167, 182, Willie 100
Netolicky, Bob 55
Nettles, Jim 99
Newcomb, Jim 79
Newman, Russ 137
Newsome, Jerry 128
Newton, C.M. 241, 242, Peggy 19, 98, 300
Ngugi, John 213
Nicholson, Kimberly 242
Nickro, Phil 64
Niehaus, Marty 108
Niemeier, Don 299, 'Big' Tom 6, 85, 88, 109, 173
Niles, Ned 47
Noblett, Suzanne 296
Noblitt, Andy 241
Noriega, Steve 288

Norris, Woody 31
Northerner, Bob 106
Northington, Greg 168
Norton, Andrew 207
Nosko, Dustin 285, 288
Nossett, Jim 105, 106
Nowell, Mel 108
Nunes, John 207

O

Oakley, Charles 241
Oberstar, Lia 244
O'Daniel, Joe 193
Ogg, Charlie 11
Oldham, Thad 288
Oliver, Jerry 160
Olsen, Lute 266
Omer, Dave 33, 38
O'Neal, Shaquille 61, 128, 241
O'Neill 42, Leo 'Cabby' 23, 38, 41, 42, 43
Oosterbaan, Bennie 10
Orth 72, Charlie 70
Ortiz, David 249
Osborne, Davey 110
Overton, Jeff 156, Ron 156
Owen 5, 220, Andy 150, 151, 247, 248, 299, Archie 11, 72, 75, 76, 136, 150, 151, 152, 216, 231, Chris 150, 151, 299, Leanne 150, 152, Louise 2, 6, 45, 144, 150, 151, 152, 156, 2, 216, 219, 220, 221, 222, 224, 299, Martha 150, Mike 150, 151, 152, 248, 299, Sarah 150, Susan 150, 152, 299
Owens, Jesse 2, 23, Rodney 165, 169
Oxley, Cathy 219, 220, Kevin 38

P

Pace, Frank 140
Padgett, Bob 6, 7, 8, 29, 78, 188, Robert E. Jr. 2
Padilla, Doug 213
Page, Alan 74
Painter, Curtis 294, Matt 232, 250
Palmenter, Natalie 251
Palmer, Jim 64
Papariella, Dave 67
Parkman, Bob 166
Parrish, Lance 99, Steve 81, 82, 166
Paterson, Rob 207
Patton, Joe 257
Payne, Chris 251

Payton, Walter 187
Pearl, Bruce 137, 151, 256, 257, 258, Steven 257
Peerman, Donna 45
Pegram, Amy 266, Demont 265, Gil 265, Golda Mae 265, James 265, Jim 265, 266, 299, Mary Ellen 266, Mike 5, 265, 266, 299, Tiffany 266, Tim 266
Perez, Tony 99
Perkins, Brittany 239, Theresa 300
Peters, Jay 158
Pettit, Margaux 238
Petty, Lori 229, 230
Pfender, Gary 80
Pfoff, Brandon 77
Phillips 16, 157, Bill 15
Pickerill, Roy 300
Piersall, Jimmy 63
Ping, Don 24, 25, 26, 27, 113, 151
Piniella, Lou 178
Pippin, Scottie 241
Pirnat, Bob 24
Pitino, Rick 92, 137, 240, 241, 242, 266
Pittman, James 211, Rick 101, 299
Plain, T.L. 107, 158, 162
Pletcher, Todd 92
Plummer, Jake 274
Plum, Milt 51
Plump, Bobby 39, 40, 41, 105, 138, 299
Podres, Johnny 61, 62
Polian, Bill 276
Polley, Jerry 84, 86
Poole, Duane 196, 299, Justin 196
Poosuthasee, Nida 251
Popp, Edwin 40
Porter, Darrell 99
Powell, Boog 64
Powless, Matt 288
Pratt, Howard 111
Prefontaine, Steve 213
Presley, Elvis 100
Prevo, Sammie 196
Prim, Lazel 48
Pritchett, Bob 77, 215
Prout, Kim 211
Pruett, Marv 109
Prullage, Ed 13
Pujols, Albert 191
Purdie, Jerry 299

Q

Qualls, Jimmy 64

Quattrotchi, Amanda 157
Query, Eonnis 211

R

Radnovich, D.J. 288
Rake, Frederick 55
Rakow 85, Ken 84, 86
Randall, Marcus 278
Raney, Garland 30
Rath, Morrie 17
Rausch 80, 166, 167, 168, 169, Jim 23, 38, 79, 88, 110, 165, 166, 167, 169, 170, 253, 299, Mary Ann 169
Rawlings, John 46
Rayburn, Charlie 34, 192, Pat 299
Rayl, Jimmy 164, 215
Raymond, Alisa 141, 183
Reagan, Ronald 100
Reasor 72, Tom 70
Rea, Tom 31, 39, 40
Redd, Jeremy 247
Redman, Gary 300
Reeder, Duce 248
Reed, Merle 56, 57, Neil 4, Steve 299, Terry 6
Rees, Don 'Butch' 106
Reese, Pee Wee 59, 62, 65
Reeves, Dan 226
Reichert, Manson 36
Reid, Elizabeth 183
Reinhart, Bob 5, 51, 52, 53, 54, 299, Jane 52, 299
Reisinger, Bob 105
Reising, Ken 106, 107, 108
Remmert, Dave 206
Renfro, Adam 184, Carl 53
Renschler, Connie 227, 299, Lanae 5, 6, 150, 227, 228, 239, 299, Larry 227, 299, Todd 227
Ress, Blake 300, Gene 299
Rettenmund, Marv 127
Reynolds, Chris 235, Jerry 126, 148, 160
Rhoades, Joyce 2, 284
Rice, Andy 67, David 81, 82, Simeon 225, 226, 275
Richardson, Bill 2, 29, 76
Richeson, Bill 215
Ricketts, Shane 248
Rickey, Branch 17, 58
Riffert, Ronald 185
Riffey 30, 32, James 31, Jim 30, 31
Riggs, Clarence 12, 23, 56, 165, Dave 84, 110, David 86, Jennifer 257, Walter 23, 46, 110
Riley 80, Morris 11, 47, 75, 79, 80, 136, 151, 169, 231, 299, Pat 124, 149, 164, Scott 69
Ritchie, Steve 215
Ritchison, Kelli 267
Ritter 35, 36, 37, 38, Julius 'Bud' 34, 35, 36, 37, 38, 85, 86, 118, 119, 120, 121, John 160
Rittman, Marilyn Jean 194
Ritz, Brian 280
Rivers, Joe 254
Rizzuto, Phil 62, 178
Roades, Joyce 299
Robbie, Joe 135
Roberts, Carolyn 299, Gerald 143, Henry O. 'Hank' 100
Robertson, Bailey 57, Oscar 40, 43, 52, 57, 89, 100, 123, 126, 215
Robinson, Brooks 64, David 241, Frank 64, 291, Glen 241, Jackie 59, 62, 274, 'Truck' 160, Virginia 113
Rodgers, Bill 246
Rodriguez, Steve 300
Roesner, Ray 55, 94
Rogers, Buddy 215, Mike 197, Randy 225, 275, 283, Scott 202
Rohleder, Joe 143
Rolen, Ed 79, Scott 79, 94, 190, 191, 241, 277, 278
Rolley, Houston 74
Rollman, Barry 81, 82, 165, 169
Rommel, Bill 184
Rono, Elly 259
Roseboro, Johnny 69
Rose, Pete 99
Ross, Larry 175
Rothstein, Arnold 17
Rottet, Ed 39, 40
Roush, Edd 2, 5, 15, 16, 18, 91, 92, 99, Essie 16, 17, Fred 15, 18, Laura 15, 17, Will 15, 16, 17
Rowe, Curtis 171
Rowser, DeJuan 'Spider' 255
Roy, Jumbo 61
Rubsam, Brad 67
Rueger, Thomas 242, 244
Ruether, Dutch 18
Ruggeri, Chad 288
Ruiz, Gaston 132
Rumbach, Paul 41
Rupp, Adolph 31, 54, 115, 118, 140, 160, 163, 164, Pete 81
Russell, Bill 89, 100, 123, Cazzie 89, Rodney 201, 202
Russler, Bill 79
Ruth, Babe 178
Ruthenburg, Phyllis 246
Ryan, Buddy 92, Nolan 63, 64

S

Saban, Lou 278
Sabella, Angela 239, 251, 252
Sakel, Bob 55
Sallee, Slim 18
Salpietra, Tony 248, 249, 250
Salters, Martin 288
Sandefur, Dave 299
Sanders, Barry 187, Byron 253, 254, P.M. 55, 105, 106, 108, 117, 299, Sanford 215, Sara 299
Sandleben, Lance 165, 169
Sandy, Mark 131
Santo, Ron 274
Sartore, John 67
Saucer, Irene 47, 299, Willie 47, 216, 299
Sayers, Gayle 50, 51, 74
Scales, Chris 201
Schaefer 212, Barry 81, 82, Greg 284, 286, 288, Hugh 212, 299, Jack 11, 97
Schayes, Dolph 153
Scheffler, Tony 274
Scheitlin, Bob 200
Scheller, Bobby 223
Schellhase, Al 'Shelley' 89, Cheryl 230, Dave 4, 23, 49, 69, 76, 78, 80, 5, 85, 88, 89, 109, 120, 134, 147, 171, 299, Dave Sr. 88, 89, Doug 89, Elizabeth 89, Julie 89, Marge 88, Mike 88
Scheu, Leo 24
Schiff, Kim 254
Schitter, Dana 239
Schlimmer, Ron 69
Schlundt, Don 10
Schmalz 207, Fred 207, 208, 210, 299, Linda 207
Schmett, Ann 299, Brian 299, Natalie 298
Schmidt 35, 37, 38, Ben 143, Chris 143, Gene 34, 36, 37, Harv 145, Jerry 143, Luke 143, Mike 64
Schmitt, Brad 257, Caleb 288, John 242
Schneider, Andy 288, Earl 6, Jack 162
Schnur, Abby 267, Bret 288
Schnurr, G.B. 103
Schoenbachler, Earl 'Chief' 24
Scholz, Erwin 'Podjo' 34, 35, 37
Schoonover, Patty 289
Schott, Tom 300
Schreiber, Mary 230
Schroeder, Ann 251
Schroer, Steve 69, 75, 79, 88, 134
Schuble, Janice 284, 285, 299
Schuetz, June 20
Schulteis, Ed 94
Schultz 184, Jeff 67, 68
Schulz, Pat 67, 68
Schutz, Tom 41, 42, Urban 40
Schwartz, Chad 184, Craig 183
Schwitz, Frank 10, 75, 106, 147, 152, 156, 166, 236, Joe 46
Schwoeppe, Ann 141
Schwomeyer, Herb 23
Scism, Dan 21, 42, 47, 113
Scott, David 77, Debbie 77, J.D. Jr. 77, Jerry 5, 76, 77, 299, Jim 56, 57, Larry 76, Roy 76
Seaver 64, Tom 63
Seifert, Dave 290
Scifrig, Cole 271, 273
Seiler, Courtney 267, Kala 267, Larry 192
Seisky, Charlie 225
Sellers, Don 141, 185
Sell, Kathy 282
Senning, Dave 165, 169, 253, 254
Senzell, Irv 193
Shanahan, Mike 274
Shepherd, Billy 55, 171
Shike, Charles 132
Shirk, Tony 203
Shively, Les 119, 299
Shoulders, Andy 246, Lisa 246, Pat 5, 245, 246, 299, Samantha 246
Shucker, Paul 194
Shula, Don 135, 231
Shymanski 206
Siau, Jon 2, 101, 140, 151, 183, 237, 238, 239, 293, Palmer 2
Siderwicz, Bill 201

Sides, Pat 300
Siegel, Ed 23, Mark 131, 132
Siegfried, Larry 52, 108
Sierra, Ruben 191
Siesky, Charlie 141, 156, 166, 182, 299
Sievers, Chris 299
Sigler, Chris 270, 271, 272, 275
Simmons, Marty 104, Ray 257, 300
Simpson, Ernie 131, Julienne 217, O.J. 74, Wallis 21
Sinatra, Frank 100
Singer, Cyrinus 40
Sinn, Lionel 256
Sisler, George 17
Sisson, Doug 291
Sitzman, Chris 200
Skelton, Larry 154
Skiles, Scott 198
Slade 82, Gordon 81, 82, 83, 151, 299, Tom 299
Slayton, Michelle 299
Slifer, Sandy 74
Sloan 109, 110, 111, 121, Bobbye 120, Brian 123, Gerald Eugene 122, Jane 122, Jerry 5, 54, 55, 80, 100, 104, 108, 109, 110, 111, 112, 115, 119, 120, 121, 122, 123, 124, 126, 147, 173, 236, 299 Ralph 122
Slyker 104, Bill 103, 113, 115, W.V. 8, 9
Smallins, James 49, 138, Jim 107, 117
Smallwood, Ed 5, 105, 106, 107, 108, 110, 112, 116, 117, 137
Smith, Bill 265, Clyde 12, Corey 109, Curtis 184, Dan 142, Dane 145, Dean 149, 253, George 250, Greg 131, 132, Jan 230, Jim 108, 109, Jimmy 226, Justin 33, Kathryn 183, Nan 238, Pam 132, Preston 165, 168, 169, 172, Rick 111, 125, 145, 168, Ron 69, Ronnie 185, Tracy 184, 185
Smoltz, John 293
Snead, Sam 21
Snider, Duke 62, 63
Snodgrass, Ashley 267, Ronnie 185
Snow, Roger 270
Snyder, Bob 50

Sobers, Ricky 126
Son, Jim 69
Soutar, Dave 195
Southwood 85, Gene 46, 170, Jerry 84, 86, 109, 170
Southworth, Andy 249
Spahn, Warren 61, 62, 99
Sparks, Dan 148, Otis 76
Speaker, Tris 15
Speer, Bryan 225, 232, 235, 240, 299, Sarah 251
Spicer, Lloyd 201
Splittorf, Paul 24
Spradling, Brian 211
Sprague, Ed 190
Spurlock, Leroy 52
Spurrier 249, 250
Spurrier, Steve 6
Stallings, Larry 5, 51, 299
Stanback, Ian 250
Stanchin, Sara 238, 239
Standish, Jess 9
Starks, John 241
Starr, Bart 51, 97
Stavely, Jerry 69
Stayton, Johnny 156
Stearman 128, Bill 127
Stebbins, Monte 111
Stedman, Bill 2, 13, 14, 158, 159, 162, 299
Steffen, John 40
Steinbrenner, George 49
Stein, Rick 264
Stenftenagel, Ed 41, Jerome 'Dimp' 41, 42
Stenftenagel, Mick 143
Stengel, Casey 63
Stephenson, Bob 223, Larry 166, Stafford 131
Stevens, Gary 266
Stevenson, Beth 252, Margo 239, 251, 252, Patti 252, 299, Peter 252, 299
Stevenson, Sara Jane 238, 252
Stewart, Ben 250, James 132, Jay 225
Stieler, Matt 67
Stiers, Chante 221
Stippler, Rick 299
Stirsman, Milt 197
Stockdale-Woodley, Rebecca 246
Stocker, John 254
Stock, Francis 24
Stockton, John 124, 236
Stoll, Roy 215
Stone, Bill 215, Norb 25
Stram, Hank 89
Stremming, Allen 299

Stryzinski, Ron 211, 212
Stucke, Mike 70
Studer, Pete 176
Studwell, Andy 186, Barbara 186, 187, 299, Bill 186, Jenny 187, 299, Jim 186, 187, 299, John Scott 186, Sally 186, Scott 5, 187, 299
Stutsman, Jaimie 267
Sublett, James 280
Sugar, Melissa 242
Suggs, Patricia 219, Tricia 219
Sullivan, Eric 84
Summitt, Pat 204, 217
Surles, Dirk 55, 232
Sursa, Steve 82
Susott, Jeanine 144
Sutton, Natasha 183
Swallow, Essie Mae 15
Swan, Bob 254
Swiacki, Bill 274
Swoboda, Ron 63, 64
Swope, Leon 254
Swords, Robert 185

T

Talbert, Jerry 193
Talbott, Robin 211, 212
Talley, Joe 154, 163
Tapp, Kevin 225
Tarkenton, Fran 50
Tasa, Eric 248
Taylor, Bill 45, Bryan 131, 132, Erika 267, 268, 269, Fred 226, Mary Lou 45, 46, 152, 299, Robert 211
Tempel, Ted 133, 134, 299
Tenbarge, Jeff 68
Tepper, Lou 225
Terrell, Dave 300
Tessalone, Tim 300
Tharp, Mary Edith 45
Theus, Reggie 123
Thomas, Anthony 185, Bill 299, Calvin 30, Danny 135, Isiah 280, Jim 80, 185, Joel 241, 257, Kelly 220, Kenny 80, Mike 129, 240, 241, 250, 299, Norma 299, Otha 185
Thompkins, James 48
Thompson, Aaron 250, Bill 69, 'Ho-Ho' 192, 193, Jim 215, Mike 173, 299, Price 103, Sam 99, Susan 55, 220
Thomson, Bobby 61
Thorpe, Jim 16

Tice, Mike 266
Tiller, Joe 271
Tilley, Don 34
Tindle, Larry 296, Roger 69
Tinker, Joe 15
Tinner, Charlene 218
Tinson, 'Hack' 25
Tittle, Y.A. 27
Todd, Marvin 40
Tolbert, Kris 211
Tooley, Tim 257, Tom 257
Toon, Bill 24
Topping, Dan 21
Torre, Joe 64, 179
Torstrick, Edward 192
Townsend, John 200
Trainer, Bill 285, 288, Tom 73
Tramill, Eugene 185
Trapp, Tricia 239, 251, 252
Traylor, Bill 113, Mike 210
Trgovich, Pete 160
Trice, Mallory 267, Travis 215, 250
Troutman, Ken 257
Tucker, Kayla 183
Tulowitzki, Troy 293
Turner 158, Brenda 299, Judy 299, Mike 168, Tom 54, 158, 159, 160, 162, 299
Turpen, Bud 194
Twilley, Howard 135
Tyler, Tyrone 175

U

Uecker, Bob 99
Unfried, Adam 67
Unitas, Johnny 51
Utley, James 166, Paul 79, 109

V

Van Arsdale 89, 162, 215, Dick 163, Tom 163
Van Brocklin, Norm 74
Vance, Charlie 49
Vanderplough, Jeff 203
Vander Meer, Johnny 58
Vandeveer, Mike 231
Vandeventer, Jerrill 232
Van Gundy, Jeff 241
Vann, Patty 300
Van Pelt, Brad 274
Van Pham, Ty 132
Van Winkle, Leslie 242
Vaughn, Harold 184, Jim 192, 193, 195
Ventura, Robin 190
Vernon, Mickey 63
Vick, Inez 48, Talmadge 47,

48, 299
Vieck, Taylor 288
Vieke, Tim 211, 212
Vieth, Bill 206, 207, 208, 210, 211, 299, Bill Jr. 2, 206, 207, 208, 209, 210, 299, Mary 206, 299, Tim 209, 210
Virgin, Debbie 156, Gary 156, 299, Kendall 155, 156
Vogel 165
Volkman, Dean 69, 78, 79, 80, 88, 299, Ed 5, 78, 79, 80, Eileen 5, 78, 79, 80, 299, Mike 49, 75, 78, 79, 80, 88, 147, 299, Ron 73, 78, 79, 88, 107, 216, 299
Vote, Libby 238

W

Waddell, Evie 197, 198, Matt 250
Wade, Butch 110
Wagner, Honus 17, 18, Sara 300
Wainman, John 244, Jonathon 242
Walden, Lee 137, 138, 299, Vickie 137
Walker 167, Antoine 241, Bob 49, 138, 139, 156, 166, 167, 169, 170, 299, Chris 6, 185, Clarence 'Foots' 54, 148, 160, James 299, Jimmy 89, Kent 167, Robert 165, Wendel 31, Woodie Sublett 5, 152, 180, 181, 299
Walkey, Kim 238
Wallace, John 241
Waller, Fred 192
Walling, Brenda 239, 251, 252, 299
Walters 104, Dick 104, 197, John 159
Walton, Bill 160
Wambach, Linda 222, 223
Wampler 184
Wannemueller, Ken 254, Ron 100, 299
Ward, Amy 183
Warren, Mike 110
Washington, John Ed 131, 132
Wasik, Mark 300

Watkins 110, 111, Sam 108, 109, 111, 119, 173
Watson 131, Bobby 130, 131, 132, 231, 261, Don 47, 75, 136, 156, 200, 231, Jenny 211
Wayne, John 37
Weatherford, Larry 128, 166, 171
Weatherholt, Jack 139, 299
Weber 220, 221, 264, Bill 200, Brenda 300, Bruce 232, Dick 193, Eileen 263, Elmer 7, 8, 9, George 9, Joe 219, 221
Webster, Mike 187
Wedeking 82, 166, Dayle 140, 299, Vaughn 5, 81, 82, 125, 140, 141, 166, 167, 182, 184
Wedgewood, Terry 81, 82, 166, 182
Weeks, Dave 111
Weidenbenner, Brenda 183
Weinzapfel 284, Allen 288, Craig 285, 288
Weir, David 208
Weis, Al 64
Welch, 299
Wellemeyer, John 111, 112, 125
Weller, Mark 52
Wellman, Nick 249
Wells, John 8, Lauretta 183
Welmer, David 127, Gary 127, Steve 5, 55, 112, 114, 125, 127, 128, 129, 299, Susan 127
Welsh, Pat 134, 176, Stan 201
Welu, Billy 193
Werne, Earl 194, Mona 194
Werner, Paul 255
Wessel, Bob 138, Ed 10, 11, 69, 88, 97, 136, 156, 299, John 147, 261, 299
Westergaarde, Jess 99
Westfall, Stacy 211, 242
West, Jerry 52, 89, 100, 123
Westrum, Wes 63
Wey, Charlie 86, Chuck 84
Wezet, Greg 253, 254
Wheat, Zack 17
Wheeler, Rick 299
Whetstone, Harry 122

White, Bob 41, 42, Bootsie 160, Eddie 187
Whitehead 35, 37, Gene 34, 35
Whitsell, Jerry 10, 55, 56, 57, 299
Wicks, Sydney 171
Widmeyer, Jimmy 17, 18
Wiechner, Louis 41
Wildeman, Chris 285, 288, Sam 285, 288
Wilder, Betty 45, Don 45, 152, Lois 45
Wilhelmus, Gil 86
Wilhite, Kathy 169
Wilke, Edward 103
Wilkerson, Bobby 128, Greg 215
Wilkes, Keith 'Silk' 160
Wilkins, Lenny 124
Wilkinson, Randy 170
Will, Bob 24, Frank 200, 283, Hermie 25
Williams 111, Anthony 288, Bob 35, David 183, 184, Dee 23, Eric 148, Herb 109, 110, 111, 121, 122, 173, 241, Howard 168, Jason 249, Kathy 169, Kelly 255, Lamont 200, Lefty 18, Levron 247, 248, Lynnie 183, Perry 135, Ricky 276, Robin 231, Tim 300
Williamson, Dave 254, 255
Willis, Ben 299, Joe 138, 139, 299, Steve 138, 299
Wills 292, Lauretta 183, Maury 291
Wilson 85, Del 194, George 135, George Jr. 135, Jean 194, Jeanne 169, John 84, 86, 106, Marcus 6, 117, Mike 6, 267, 268, 269, 299, Mindi 268, Mitch 267, Tracye 299, Whitney 282, Wood 268
Wimsatt, Bill 24
Winburn, Marion 'Tony' 131, 132
Winchell, Bob 5, 166, 182, 183, 185, 299, Cara 183
Winchester, Lisa 268
Windham, Rhonda 218
Winemiller, Clint 300
Winfield, Dave 178
Winfrey, Oprah 48

Wingfield, Delores 38
Wininger, Brett 143, Pete 30
Winstead, Ashlee 267
Winternheimer, Steve 81, 82, 141
Winters, Chuck 299
Wise, Dale 55, 105, 106, 107, 108, 116
Witte 212, Courtney 148, 211, 212
Wolfe, Johnny 13
Wooden, John 40, 54, 55, 89, 105, 115, 118, 140, 160
Wood, Ralph 9, Wendy 269
Woods, Dick 180, Jackie 76, Jim 180, Phyllis 180
Woolfolk, Jermaine 247
Woolridge, Charles 48
Worthy, James 149
Wright, Byron 253, George 181, 192, 299
Wuchner 41
Wyman 158, 159, 160, 212, Ann 161, Orlando 'Gunner' 5, 23, 38, 84, 119, 158, 160, 161, 162, 163, 211, 212, 215, Katherine 161, Molly 161, Sally 161, Will 161, 162, 299

Y

Yager, John 106
Yarbrough, Ed 280
Yeagley, Jerry 206
Yepremian, Garo 135
Yestingsmeyer, Earl 56
Yetsko, Mark 203
Yoder, Steve 127, Todd 276
Young 274, Leonard 65, Michael 175, 254, Stan 215, Vince 273, 274, 279

Z

Zachter, Mort 65, 299
Zaharias, Babe Didrickson 21, George 21
Zausch 119, Ed 108, 109, 110, 114, 118, 299
Zehr, Dwayne 253, 254
Zeller, Luke 29, 33, 295, Tyler 33, 215, 295
Zenthoefer 284
Zirklebach, Gabe 288
Zoller, Brenda 243, 299, Larry 243, 244, 299

AUTOGRAPHS

AUTOGRAPHS